THE
THEATRE

*Three Thousand Years
of
Drama, Acting
and Stagecraft*

William Shakespeare. The most pleasing likeness of the theatre's supreme poet-dramatist. [From an engraving by William Holl, based on the so-called "Droeshout original" portrait in the Shakespeare Memorial gallery at Stratford-on-Avon.]

THE
THEATRE

Three Thousand Years of
Drama, Acting and Stagecraft

by SHELDON CHENEY

REVISED AND RESET
ILLUSTRATED EDITION

With a New Bibliography

DAVID McKAY COMPANY, INC.

NEW YORK

First Edition October 1929
Reprinted
October 1930, January 1935
October 1936, January 1942
July 1943, October 1945
June 1947, May 1949

Revised and enlarged edition, 1952
Reprinted
February 1953, November 1953
October 1955, August 1958
February 1960, June 1961
March 1963, January 1966
December 1967

Revised and reset edition, 1972

Designed by C. R. Bloodgood

Library of Congress Catalogue Card Number: 74-155254
Printed in the United States of America

Contents

v

Preface to the Fourth Revised Edition

I N WRITING the Preface for this edition, marking the third major enlargement of *The Theatre,* I need add only a few words to explain my objectives and those of the publishers. The most important feature is the addition of about sixty illustrations. There are innumerable amendments and patches in the text of the older chapters, and at the end, fifty pages of new text. As of 1970–71, the subject has grown, and we now present this enlarged edition.

My original purpose was to write a concise history of the institution and the art of the theatre: a history broader in scope than any then available, in that I was including, along with materials about the drama, a record of actors and acting, and of changes in the physical theatre— stage, decorative background, costuming—and in types of audience. Broadening my canvas still further, I was trying to show the theatre of each period as emerging from a certain sort of social background, primitive or civilized, spiritual or worldly, courtly or democratic.

The intention was to present all this readably and a bit dramatically. If I must err—and what writer does not?—it should be on the side of picturesqueness, impulsive devotion to theatre people, and, toward the end, enthusiasm. After all, I said to myself, I have been simmering along for years in the picturesque theatrical stew that is Broadway. I'll pick my materials for dramatic vividness, and gauge my language as a man of the common theatre, on occasion downright theatrically. Fresh from five years' experience on Broadway, five hectic, heartbreaking, pleasurable years, I thus set out to write the "story" of the world theatre, Broadway-wise.

The result, as judged by the critical reception, was not bad. Practically no reviewers, aside from the British, resented the manner of the writing. Many commended the plan of a continuous history in which drama, acting and stagecraft were described as coordinate parts of one over-all art of the theatre. As for myself, I liked the book; certainly it was better than several others I had written. I confess that I was proud of the set of illustrations. It still seems to me the most *explaining* series of pictures in any historical book about the theatre: showing "how it was" in the playhouse of this time or that, filling out gaps in the text account, graphically presenting playhouse forms, typical scenes, costumes, actor-personalities. In any case, the book had its success, one printing following another down to 1967.

In facing up to the necessity of rewriting, in 1970, I became aware, as never before, that the original book had been written toward the end of a Golden Age, in a glow of optimism. I had failed (as most men had failed, and not only writers) to foresee the Great Depression of the thirties. In the United States, at least, the professional stage then entered upon a decline which has been only slightly arrested, in a season here or there, in all the years since. Hitler's dictatorship, Stalin's bureaucracy, the devastation of World War II, austerity in Britain, chaos in the Orient, increasing commercialism in the arts—these all affected segments of theatre history, and in general signaled a decline of the stage art in places where it had significantly flourished. Now I have taken into account these generally tragic changes. I have tried not to lose the sense of joyousness that is of the very fabric of the theatre art. But even a long-range optimist can hardly disguise that in America the professional theatre is sadly down as we reach 1970, both quantitatively and qualitatively. In New York—unfortunately the country's yardstick—the count of fullsize theatres fell from a total of about eighty legitimate houses in 1930 to fewer than thirty in 1970, with the yearly total of new productions dropping from about two hundred to seventy. Deterioration in the quality of the plays offered has been equally disheartening.

Nevertheless, it would be a very pessimistic historian who would prophesy that the institution is headed for extinction, or even for a permanently lesser place in men's affections. In writing of the years of decline I have tried to present facts, then to emphasize the innovations that promise renewed life.

Now, as to credentials. If any reader asks, did I see the many productions I have described as historic, I intend to refuse an answer, taking refuge in the traditional historian's justification. Was Gibbon there during the Decline and Fall? Did Prescott see with his own eyes the Conquest of Peru? As a matter of fact, my credentials might be regarded as good concerning theatre productions and personalities within my own lifetime. I first saw that type figure Sarah Bernhardt when she played *Phèdre* in the Greek Theatre at Berkeley; again, several times when she staged those oft-repeated "farewell tours," it might be in New York or Ann Arbor; and years later I hurried from Amsterdam to Brussels one day after hearing that she was opening in a new play, in an attempted final "comeback." (Tragic it was in a way, for we all knew that she was a saddened old woman, physically crippled, with only one leg—but there was magic in her performance, divinity if you will.) I saw practically all of the Divine Sarah's contemporaries, French, English, American. As Hamlet there were John Gielgud, Walter Hampden and John Barrymore (in that order, please) and others. A few of the great creative figures were friends offstage: Laurette and Isadora, Edith Wynne Matthison, and Ethel Barrymore. I used to climb those imposing stairs in the *Théâtre des Champs Elysées* in Paris to pass the time of day with Louis Jouvet, and even oftener I climbed the steeper stairs at the end of a trolley line near Genoa to spend an hour or an afternoon with Gordon Craig. I was at Salzburg when Max Reinhardt first staged his famous *Everyman* on the cathedral steps there, and I enjoyed his historic production of *Danton* at the *Grosses Schauspielhaus* in Berlin (perhaps the theatre, a "circus theatre" and "theatre of the five thousand," was historic, rather than the play). Farther afield I attended the Passion Plays at Thiersee and Erl and Oberammergau; and modern-classic productions in the Roman Theatre at Orange and in the Roman Amphitheatre at Verona. Curiously enough I met up with a company from the Moscow Art Theatre first in Vienna, but later saw their inimitable productions in New York, and finally in Moscow. The memories crowd in: the overwhelming production of Toller's *Masse-Mensch* at the old *Volksbühne* in Berlin, and, as a contrast, the first production of the gently charming *Our Town*, in New York (enjoyed also in five varied revivals, at summer theatres, festivals, etc.—in one I sat through the rehearsals).

Thus I may say that theatrically I have been around. And so, if some contemporary eventful productions have escaped me (as yet), say, the tribal love-rock musical *Hair* and some of the Absurdist way-out offerings, I still can plead at least an average historian's preparation. Truly I had a wonderful time.

A preface properly comes to an end with acknowledgements. Reversing the customary order, I will name first the friends who have helped with this revision, reverting later to the debts incurred during the writing of the original edition. (I am reminded of the stagehand who started the revolving stage in the wrong direction.)

The largest debt, outweighing all others, is to Professor Henry Goodman of the Department of Theatre Arts, University of California at Los Angeles. Years ago most of the prints and photographs from which the book's illustrations had been reproduced went into the collections of that department. Henry Goodman and the members of his staff traced down sixty of these prints and made them available for rephotographing, a service for which I am deeply grateful.

A special debt is owing to the Walter Hampden Memorial Library at the Players in New York City, and to its librarian, Louis A. Rachow; and to the William Seymour Theatre Collection at the Princeton University Library, where Mary Ann Jensen, its curator, extended friendly and helpful aid in tracing fugitive materials. At the museum of the City of New York I received invaluable aid from Samuel Pearce and Melvin Parks. From the Hoblitzelle Theatre Arts Library at the University of Texas, and Frederick J. Hunter, came photographs I had sought in vain elsewhere. To the several other libraries and museums that responded to my requests with a single print or two, I can only express general gratitude. (We have printed a credit line under each reproduction.)

A few individuals must be mentioned for special contributions to this revision: Dr. Arthur B. Hopper, who wrote an entirely new bibliography for the book; Paul Meyers of the New York Public Library Theatre Collection, a famous center for theatre study; and James Hamilton, a practical theatre worker who is not above conducting classes at New York University. I must thank also, for courtesies in connection with added illustrations, the New American Library (Mentor Books) and the Yale University Press.

For the rest, here are parts of the "Author's Acknowledgment" from the original edition:

I have incurred indebtedness to most of the scholars and "authorities" who have published standard studies of the drama in the time-periods traditionally observed, Greek, Roman, Mediæval, etc.—for mine is not a book based upon original research, but rather a compressed survey, a conspectus of the flow of the art through all periods. The specialists and their books are named in the Bibliography. I can only acknowledge my obligation to them with a general "thank you!" I must add, however, that I owe special thanks, for manifold courtesies, to the librarians of the American Library in Paris, the New York Public Library, and the Library of American Studies in Italy, at Rome, and to the Keeper of Printed Books of the British Museum in London. To

Robert Edmond Jones, to Gordon Craig and to Professor Gilbert Murray I am more particularly obligated for quotations in the text.

In regard to the illustrations, my debt to publishers is large. I have to thank Edith J. R. Isaacs of *Theatre Arts Monthly* for unfailing encouragement and assistance; and the following firms have courteously granted permission to reproduce pictures over which they exercise copyright control: The Macmillan Company, New York, and Macmillan and Company Ltd., London; J. M. Dent and Sons, London; George G. Harrap and Company Ltd., London; D. C. Heath and Company, Boston; The John Day Company, New York; The Eclipse Press, London; The Century Company, New York; T. Werner Laurie Ltd., London; "The Stage," London; W. W. Norton and Company, New York; Michael Joseph, Ltd., London; and Theatre Arts Books, New York. The Directors of the New York Historical Society, of the Smithsonian Institution, of the Victoria and Albert Museum in London, and of the National Gallery in London have given permission for reproduction of drawings or paintings owned by their respective institutions; and other prints have been supplied by Dr. Joseph Gregor, Gordon Craig, Arthur Edwin Krows, Kenneth Macgowan, Culver Service, the Bettmann Archive and the Kean Archives.

Where so many illustrations are gathered together, including many by artists long since dead, and others from books published by firms long since disappeared, it is difficult to establish a standard of procedure in regard to acknowledgments. I have noted the artist's name if it could in any way be traced; but as for tracking down the publishers in order to request formal permission, I have done this uniformly only in regard to books published since 1900—that being in line, I believe, with the intent of the copyright law and with the usages of courtesy between publishers. I must add, however, that the originals of some illustrations, particularly older ones, came into my possession as fugitive prints, perhaps unduly separated from parent volumes, by purchase at the bookstalls on the quays of the Seine and other places where the niceties of literary etiquette are not uniformly observed.

As regards the text, I think I have exerted all due human caution to safeguard the accuracy of dates, spellings, etc. But the book has been written "on the road," and missed the painstaking processes of verification that would have preceded its publication had I worked patiently in a book-lined study at home. Truly, I am the man who wore out public-library dictionaries and encyclopædias in half the capital cities of Europe, verifying dates and names; but I am sensible that errors may have crept in—that one or two may have persisted into later editions. My hope is that there may be a counter-advantage in this: that the "story" I have told has gained in vividness and pictorial interest through the circumstance that I was traveling, that I was in Rome when the Roman chapter was written, in Florence for the Renaissance, and successively in London, Berlin, Paris, New York, and many another centre of theatre activity.

Certainly the writing of the book afforded a welcome excuse for making the tour of ancient theatres from Orange and Arles to Taormina and Syracuse; for excursions to measure the stage, it might be at Versailles, or Potsdam or Vicenza; for darting off to catch a unique performance at Salzburg or Monte Carlo, at Stuttgart or Pasadena or Brussels. From this pilgrimage I gained two overwhelming impressions: of the vast variety of the theatre art, and of the oneness, the unfailingness, of its magic. Wherever theatre is, the audience participant comes to magic, perhaps to sustained magic. It may last hardly longer than that pregnant moment between the fading down of the house lights and the rise of the curtain, that moment when the conscious mind is stilled and the way opened for some deeper faculty of understanding, of soul-enjoyment. The great play may prolong the fullness of satisfaction through the two hours of performance, and in memory through a lifetime. I have tried in my history to convey just a little of this magic to the reader, over and above dates and names of plays and stages. My wish is that I may have increased for you, dear reader, this essential "feel for the theatre": that, after reading the pages that follow, your experience of the show may be a little fuller and richer for contact, in the book, with the stages and actors, the plays and the audiences, of ages past.

And so, Dionysus be with you!

DIONYSUS

DIONYSUS came down from the wild mountains of Thrace into Hellas, worshipped as a god of the groves and the fields and of fertility; and with the very special power of lifting mortals to a share in divine ecstasy. The people of Greece took him for their own, the common people. They were filled with his spirit and honored him (and themselves) in joyous festival and ritual and wild revels; until he was so celebrated that he could no longer be excluded from the company of true Olympians. And so, with elements of the earth and of wildness clinging to him, and trailing an uncommon sympathy with humankind, he became the youngest of the Greek gods.

As was the way in those times, the guardians of orthodox religion made a myth to account for his coming. The All-father Zeus had loved the beautiful princess Semele, daughter of Cadmus. Misled by the jealous Juno, this mortal asked that her Heavenly lover appear before her once in all his glory. In the flaming splendor of his presence Semele was utterly and ecstatically consumed. But her child Dionysus, delivered before his time, was saved from the flames by the great God, his father, who sewed up the babe in his own flesh. Hidden thus from the prying eyes of Juno, Dionysus came to maturity, and in a second birth was miraculously delivered into the world, a true god, son of Zeus, mystic wanderer.

But to the people he remained first of all the god of nature and of wild things, and of all human-divine wild impulses. It was seen that earlier deities of the earth and the fields, of the groves and the vineyards, had simply awaited his coming; and he was known now as Dionysus and Bacchus, as Bromius and Nysæus.

At once god of the joy-giving vine and of mystical inspiration, he brought to his celebrants a spiritual intoxication. He entered into their being, they became gods in his name: Bacchants and Bacchantes. Theirs was the Dionysian experience. He exacted neither adoration nor worship from them; rather he accorded them a share in his ecstasy, they celebrated, god-like, joyed in "doing," danced, marched, sang.

Bacchus, a Faun and a Bacchante. Antique sculptured relief in the National Museum, Naples. [Alinari photograph.]

Drama grew directly out of the Dionysian celebrations, out of the rites, the dances, the songs that were sung, the parades with cymbals and torches and masks, in honor of Dionysus; and the consecrated place of the revels was called a "theatre." Some of the celebrants became priests, and these later were called "actors"; and others, who had led in the singing, who could even invent new songs, became poets, and by a final extension of grace, dramatists; and still others became the audience, those who asked no more than participation in the spirit, the emotional exaltation of Dionysian celebration.

And what has been finest in the theatre, down through the ages, is the Dionysian intoxication, the exaltation out of emotional-spiritual participation, the transcending dramatic experience. No other god has so discovered divinity to the god in-man; no other art has so contacted the mystic creativeness of its artists with the receptiveness in the spectator's soul, has so immersed its audiences in the glow of the spirit.

Dionysus has lived twenty-five hundred years. Today a world that had almost learned to scorn him turns back, with the old hunger of the soul, the old impulse toward divine living, with not a little of the old wildness. For we later mortals, as we view about us the decay of moralistic religions, the chaos of conquest-mad civilizations and the spiritual bankruptcy of the prosperous-scientific life, we seek again the roads to emotional-spiritual inundation, to ecstasy, to the experience of God.

We turn confidently back. For Dionysus is immortal and the theatre lives alway.

THE
THEATRE

Three Thousand Years
of
Drama, Acting
and Stagecraft

CHAPTER

1

The Theatre,
Human and Divine

W HEREVER and whenever humans have progressed beyond the mere struggle for physical existence, to gods and recreation and self-expression, there has been theatre in some sense: a place for acting, dancing, dialogue, drama, in the ordered scheme of life.

The resultant world drama, the collective theatre, from primitive dance to modern journalistic play, from divine ritual to profane representation, from Greek tragedy to "the pictures," escapes, in its confusingly various aspects, all recorded definitions of "theatre" and of "drama." If one could spread out a picture of the world's stages, if the entire pageant of their activities could be momentarily fixed on a magic canvas, the spectator would know at once that no definition ever can be broad enough, elastic enough, to snare in words the elements and the modes of the art, the facets and the directions of theatric-dramatic life.

The diversity and the confusion arise no less from the mixed form and the composite method—this being the art where all arts meet—than from the dual nature of the impulse underlying dramatic expression; call it divine and human, or religious and social, or spiritual and convivial. There are other significant parallels and contrasts; for gaiety and glow are of the very essence of theatre, while "dramatic" suggests the event that cuts directly and vividly into life, having to do with the deepest currents of man's being, with personal crises and the intensest

1

Forgetting the nineteenth century "picture" scene, the reader should visualize the actor in continually changing relationship to his background. This is a simple platform stage for classic revivals, of the early Renaissance. [From a drawing by Warren D. Cheney, after a model based on old prints.]

moments of experience. But most notably, theatre is the art where spiritual light illumines human living.

In the absence of definitions, each man will form his own mental one—first of all from what he has seen in theatres, but filling out the impression, the outline, from such parts of the world-picture as may have come to his notice.

Let us suppose for a moment that such a picture, of the theatre in all ages and all places, in all its varieties, is spread before us, on a gigantic and crowded canvas. Immediately one beholder sees "the drama" as the main motive, and is off tracing its development; another sees the actor as all-important, and the story of acting as the key to the composition; and still another sees the form of the stage and the elements of stagecraft, the ways and means of bringing drama to the audience, as a predominant interest. But the man who wishes to bring the whole picture into focus, who hopes to have the view complete, finds it necessary to see beyond all these to a deeper design that binds the picture together, to a thing that is "theatre" in the largest sense.

It is one of the pleasant facts about theatre-study today, that in regarding a single play performance the student or artist has learned that no one element constitutes the chief or essential matter; recognizes, rather, that the several "means" of the production contribute to a total effect that is the all-important thing, a complete theatrical action accomplished. Actors, lights, movement, dialogue, noises, silences, color, scenery, stage, he marks for what they are, the resources of the art made expressive when combined in a procession or flow. Over and above the seen-and-heard elements, he is attentive to a rhythmic wave that registers beyond the conscious minds of the spectators, like a tide to the soul.

Just so, in regarding the larger composition of the world theatre, the student or interested playgoer—or reader—must vision a similar binding force, a theatrical unity, an all-encompassing aura; for it is this that lends design to the actor in relation to the drama, the physical theatre and the craft of staging. And it is this that I shall try to keep forward throughout my story of "the theatre art." The sensuous glow and the deep emotion arise alike out of elements deeper than colored lights and enchanting setting, beyond the actors' performances, beyond drama.

If, however, one holds in mind this broader effectiveness, one may profitably disengage the drama or the actor briefly from the larger design; and as introduction to the history that begins in the next chapter, I wish to pause with the reader for the briefest "over-look" at the

The theatre a part of the temple group. A reconstruction by A. von Gerkan of the Greek-Roman theatre at Priene. (This is the interior of the upper theatre shown at the top of the following page.)

Ancient and recent European theatres contrasted. Above, a reconstruction of the theatre at Priene, as seen from the outside, showing the large open auditorium and the small stage building. Below, a sectional view of the Paris Opera House, illustrating the immensity and the elaboration of the stage, with eight floors of machinery above and below, and the extensiveness of the social rooms, as compared with the "place for seeing" which is the first essential in any theatre. [The drawing above from A. von Gerkan's *Das Theater von Priene*. The section by Karl Fichot and Henri Meyer, from a reproduction in *Illustrirte Zeitung*.]

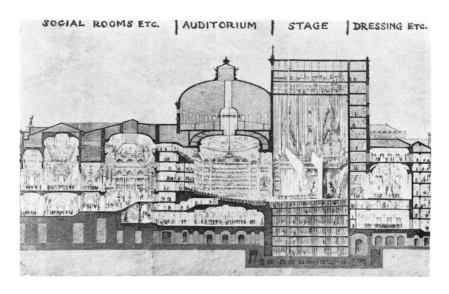

three component elements—hoping that this may help us to orientate ourselves, to find the best beginning point for a trip through the mazes of the world-picture.

The actor, the human medium by which the drama speaks to us— it is he who lends vividness, intensity, and humanity to the art beyond any possible in mere paint, stone, or sound—the actor has a history that spans the whole gulf between priesthood and bawdry. Actors have been the servants of gods, and mentors of manners, but again they have been panderers to men's grossest appetites. In Greece long after the Dionysian rites and revels gave way to composed plays, they were privileged and honored members of society; but in Rome they fell to sad depths of disgrace. Thereafter they were honored by governments and entertained by kings and queens—nay, commanded and pled with to attach themselves to courts; and other governments branded them as vagabonds, and other kings banished them and persecuted them as undesirables, rogues, and idlers. The Church called them into its service, but again excommunicated them, and through many centuries refused them Christian burial. Today kings knight them, but within our own lifetimes we have heard bishops crying out that no good ever has come from the theatre, or ever will come, because for a person to go on the stage is in itself a besmirchment of character. (Yet announce that a well-known actor will be at Mrs. Smyth's at tea on Tuesday, and your invitations won't half go round those who want to come.)

The story of what these actors do, of acting in the narrower sense, illustrates in little a truth pertinent to the whole theatre art: that from Greek times to twentieth century, there has been a wider and wider deviation from *conventional* methods toward *naturalism*. (This is a thread we shall follow, from earliest chapter almost to latest.) In Greece a fine stateliness of gesture and movement, together with beauty of diction, constituted the art of acting; the very conditions of the actor's appearance made for slow and broad declamation: the immense bowl-like theatre, the mask hiding facial display, the stuffed-out costumes and cothurnus-boots. In each succeeding age thereafter, in Rome, in Renaissance Italy, in France, England, Germany, down to "the era of great acting" in the eighteenth century, there is the recurrent report: "acting now became more human, more real, more life-like than ever before." Finally, with the coming of electric lights, characterization arrived at a perfection of outward naturalism. From being a convention, it had progressed through all the stages of part-artificial-part-imitational portrayal until it arrived at photographic representation of familiar men and women.

The path is not so straight along which we may trace the changes in the physical playhouse; but the difference at the two extremes is no less marked. Barring a few very modern houses, the theatre has run down from openness and nobility to a form that is cramped and trivially fussed-up. From the dancing-circle as stage, perhaps in some sacred grove, at the foot of a hillside hollow, through the beautifully proportioned wooden, then marble playhouses of the Greeks, and on to the magnificently showy theatres of the Romans, was logical progress. Thereafter the forms change, waver. But through it all the theatre building follows the curve of so-called civilization: rises as a reflection of aspirations, spiritual flowerings and service to gods: stands beside temples and cathedral altars when man is most spiritual, has its appointed place in palaces when courts are most royal, most magnificent; but again falls to rude makeshift in dark centuries, or becomes a tawdrily ornamented show-box in materialistic ones—and so to the pinched peep-hole proscenium-frame affair of the realistic era of the early twentieth century.

And so too, the story of the drama. There is the same gulf between the Greek play, with its inexhaustible depths of emotion and its beautiful poetry, and our contemporary, pinched, realistic, peep-hole plays. Again the progression has not been direct: rather the history of dramatic literature has been dotted with glorious periods. Shakespeare came twenty centuries after Sophocles. As recently as the early nineteenth century Goethe and Schiller worked something of the same splendid magic. Since then the poetry (as well as the ecstasy and the fervor) has weakened, almost disappeared.

There are those—count me not among them—who say that the curve has been downward only in obedience to the law of *audiences:* that spectators, from being splendid-minded and spiritual, have become sentimental, trivial, and prying, and that the theatre inevitably comes down to please them. But it is probable that there are good audiences everywhere, if the political, economic, and spiritual conditions are ripe for good drama, good theatres, and acting and staging. And indeed there are some hopeful ones—count me among *them*—who refuse to be long depressed by the obvious cheapness of most of the dramatic output of today, by the trivially over-ornamented playhouses, the journalistic plays, the uncreative acting. For we see in a mighty activity—the *livest* stages of all time—the beginnings of a new upward curve: a physical theatre going back to a new simplicity (not primitive, but simple as the automobile is simple: why not a theatre as clean-walled, sheer of line, tranquilly comfortable as your car, and equally bright, warm, pleasurable?); drama that escapes the photographic-reportorial mold, that weds a new daring to a new human intensity of life; acting that is less imitation than revealment.

But most of all we see a new spirit emerging in the Western theatre.

And really it is the intangible spirit of an institution or a race or a nation that carries it triumphantly down the ages. Certainly it is the flaming eternal spirit of the stage that has driven the course of dramatic art through the great and the decadent, the glorious and the terrible periods of mankind's history. It has sustained the theatre when the foundations of living and of liberty seemed breaking up, and it has persisted through the wrecking of empires and the waging of devastating wars and the proliferation of science.

We may indeed have our pessimistic days, when we gain a perspective on the immediate theatre of today, down in the market-place, its activities pursued as energetically as those of food-selling, baseball, or stock-brokering. In spite of seeing that an extraordinary amount of

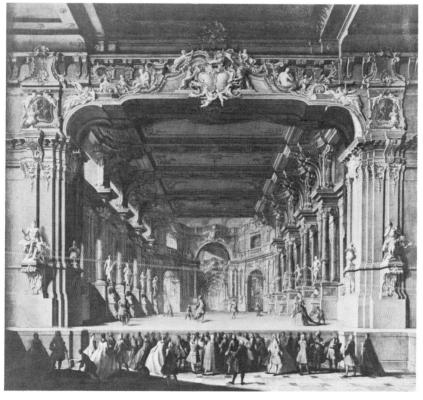

A Renaissance stage, with a typical "picture" scene behind a proscenium frame. In contrast with the theatre designed to emphasize the actor, this is an example of the theatre of emphasized scenic display—and the beginning point of the courtly staging that persisted from about 1600 to 1900. [From a painting ascribed to Ferdinando Bibbiena, in the National Gallery, London.]

material wealth is flowing into the playhouses, that an amazing number of shows will be seen in our town this year, that the institution is simply bursting with hustle, enthusiasm, effort—in spite of this typically tumultuous outpouring of effort, we recognize a separation from the deeper springs of life. Perhaps never, we think, has the stage been further from the divinity with which it was marked in other eras. It has dug down into human experience not in a way that uncovers di-

A performance at Shakespeare's Globe Theatre in London, about 1600. This drawing by Maurice Percival, after a reconstruction by John Cranford Adams, emphasizes (in comparison with other illustrations in the chapter) the variety of used stages, the changing ideas about "setting," and the shifting status of the actor as a dominant or passive figure. The "thrust stage," as shown here and in the following illustration, foreshadows stages in many experimental theatres of the mid-twentieth century.

vinity, but in a way that shows humanity its weaker face, that lays bare deformities and perversities and flea-bites. It has become a narrow, prying, gossipy-minded theatre, with the bigness and the fineness gone out of it. Only once in a hundred visits do we glimpse rapture or high nobility or sheer purging beauty.

An eighteenth century French theatre that retained the picture setting but made the actor predominant by bringing him down into the midst of the audience. Note the aristocratic boxes combined with a large pit for standees. The theatre is believed by some authorities to be the famous *Hôtel de Bourgogne* in Paris; it is of a type known as "tennis-court theatres." [Redrawing by the author after contemporary sketches by P. A. Wille.]

And yet each one of us, in his collective experience, has known that other divine theatre. In the playhouses of our time we have been stirred by the old expectant excitement, have revelled in being part of a gay responsive crowd, have felt our nearness to the gods in the hushed auditorium, when everything on the stage and in the world fell into a unison, stilling the conscious mind; have been miraculously purged by tragedy, have been healed with the tonic of laughter at comedy, have felt pleasantly sinful, have been revolted, have been lifted again to the realm of beauty, wisdom, and perfect understanding.

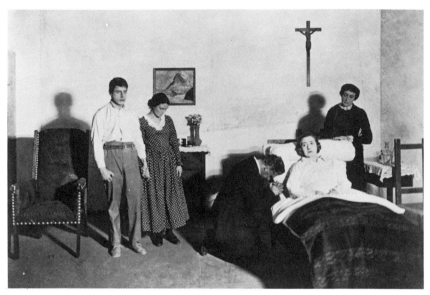

A scene in Bjornson's *Beyond Our Power* at the *Volksbühne* in Berlin, about 1920. The actors include Friedrich Kayssler, kneeling, and Helene Fehdmer, in the bed. An example of the most familiar type of staging in the first half of the twentieth century, in realistic "box-set" interiors, simplified for increased emphasis on the actors. [Photograph by August Scherl.]

This is how it is—on that hundredth attendance:

Here we are in the mercifully darkened auditorium, whole banks of us facing the glow of the stage. We are a little too hot this summer night. For an hour we have watched people acting in and out of a perfectly ordinary plot, with flashes of humor here and there, a pretty intrigue posed, youth drawing toward beauty. But we have not quite been able to forget the heat. The appealing story, the facile acting, the color and light manipulated now with such virtuosity: everything is *pleasant*—that is just the word. But the actors are obviously working, this show of color and light and designed movement remains an accompaniment, the story is a diversion not too moving to be seen dispassionately, from the outside, from the hot auditorium.

Then in a sentence one of the actors makes us catch our breath. The story, the accompaniment, the night are forgotten. Everything drops into place, quietly, the house becomes doubly hushed, a thousand souls strain forward toward one little group there on the dais in the centre. Our bodies are motionless, our throats contracted, strange emotions press in, we feel the hot tears welled behind our eyes. A "moment" has come. Before the silence proves unbearable, this actress, this woman standing there before us, must speak, must move. We wait, suspended. In this hush the slightest thing she does or says may precipitate the thousand watchers into tears and grief, into perfect understanding, into gentle laughter. The sudden quivering of her lips—what is that to make a thousand men and women draw their breath in a stifled sob? Her half-articulated "yes" tears us like a knife plunged into our own flesh.

For a few moments we have known a cessation of the outward life of the world. We have known an intensification of the life of the spirit. Everything has been so clarified that a gesture, a poetically right phrase, a sob, seemed to resolve all that has puzzled us in living, seemed to lift us up, to glorify us.

This is the moment toward which all drama tends. This is the inundation of the spirit, in beauty and clarity, toward which the art of the theatre gropes. And this, in a world from which divinity and mystery have been unsparingly shorn, this is as near as we are likely to come to the divine and the spiritual. It is the Dionysian experience, our ecstatic participation in the divine life. Unless you have known that moment, you have not really penetrated into the theatre. It is, of course, the thing that escapes all definitions of theatre or drama.

And whatever may be the direction of the next great change in the stage art—and epoch-making changes are pending—we may be sure that the artists of the theatre will be working around somehow to this revealing moment, this transcending of surface life, will aim to afford us, the spectators, that clarity, that absolute of spiritual participation.

For we are humans, and during some moments the actors have made us gods.

CHAPTER 2

Where the Theatre Came From, and When

M AN DANCES. After the activities that secure to primitive peoples the material necessities, food and shelter, the dance comes first. It is the earliest outlet for emotion, and the beginning of the arts. Civilized man of today, despite ingrained inhibitions and cultivated reserve, instinctively expresses emotional joy by action; primitive man, poor in means of expression, with only the rudimentary beginnings of spoken language, universally expressed his deeper feelings through measured movement. Nature about him moved rhythmically, in the wave motion of the waters and in the wind-blown fields; the sun and moon rose and fell; his own heart-beats were rhythmic. It was natural, then, that he should create rhythmic movement to externalize any felt joy.

He danced for pleasure and as ritual. He spoke in dance to his gods, he prayed in dance and gave thanks in dance. By no means all this activity was dramatic or theatric; but in his designed movement was the germ of drama and of theatre. The dance exists even today, separately, for all the purposes to which primitive peoples put it; but somewhere in its history it gave rise to this other more inclusive art. In Cambodia the very name for theatre means "dance-house." Records of the dancing figure, in painting, sculpture, and written account, go back almost as far as the existence of those arts. In addition to these historic records there is the analogy of scores of "backward" peoples still living in the darker spots of the world today: the African jungles, the South Sea Islands, the United States, etc. Wherever "primitive" peoples are found and their customs studied, there is ritual and usually dramatic dance.

Not only did drama as such—the art in which *action* is a pivotal material—arise out of primitive dance; in its later development it took to itself another element born of dance-gesture: poetry. The modern European drama traces its ancestry to Greece, and the common as-

African masks for primitive dramatic dances. At left, a Basonge mask, from Nigeria: at right, a Bakuba mask, from the Congo. [These and the masks on page 20 are from drawings by Warren D. Cheney.]

sumption is that it became important as an art-form when the ritual dances were combined with elements out of dithyrambic poetry. But recited poetry had been a second child of the dance, in this manner: the noises man made, as he rhythmically moved, took on the measure of the swaying body and the tapping feet, gradually became war-song or prayer, developed into traditional tribal chant, ultimately led to conscious poetry. (It is no chance that the unit-measure of verse is called the "foot," or that the words "ballad" and "ballet" are so alike.) Music, too, which can hardly be dissociated from the theatre's beginnings, traces its ancestry to the sounds made to accentuate the primitive dance rhythm, the stamping of feet and clapping of hands, the shaking of rattles, the beating of drums and sticks.

Dance, then, is the great mother of the arts. It is impossible to say when or where it developed first. It came to mankind in a thousand places and at a thousand times, wherever an isolated group came to

We cannot know what comedy-dances the prehistoric tribes may have had (though gorillas are said to have a lively sense of humor); but the type is not wholly unknown among primitive peoples studied in modern times. Hunting or battle scenes may be burlesqued, and quite often there is the clown character: the man who hits hard but always misses or strikes somebody or something other than the object intended. Imitations of the motions of animals or birds may also be made richly humorous.

Most of the examples, when examined, however, will be found to come within the range of religious or initiatory dance. The love-pantomimes range from idyllic duets to what seems in the European mind obscene representation. The action usually concerns itself with that still favorite theme, the man who admires, desires, parades, sues, and the woman who is coy, teases, holds back, finally yields. But even in many of these amatory examples the significance is religious: related to fertility rites or phallic symbolism.

The savage's world is almost universally peopled with all-powerful gods or spirits. These are associated with the forces controlling nature, with "causes," or perhaps with the souls of dead ancestors, or with fabulous animals or trees or stars. At any rate, man's welfare depends upon the spirits being on his side. He must do what will be pleasing to them, he must indicate to them what he wants, he must never omit to show them his appreciation of favors. The primitive seldom worships in our later sense. The Amerindian of our arid West does not vaguely pray for rain; he does something: he dances a Rain Dance to his gods. Other tribes do Sun Dances. A tribe facing starvation does an Antelope Dance.

Dance is so essentially the primitive method of showing attention and devotion to the spirits that almost everywhere the place for dancing precedes the temple. Here the chief representative of the gods, medicine man or priest or witch doctor, devises dances for such different purposes as appeasing a spirit who has withheld the rain or the sunshine, or driving out the evil spirit in the body of a sick member of the tribe, or securing luck to the new wine.

Three of the religious dances mentioned may be considered as of a special sort known as food ceremonies. The tribe wants rain to make the crops grow, in order to have more food. Its first recourse is to the gods who can send all blessings. They must be shown rain, and so the Rain Dance is performed: clouds gathering, lightning flashing, thunder roaring, finally rain falling—tableau, happiness. With some of the Southwestern Amerinds, the priest or medicine man is first of all "Rain-maker," for the heavens can provide no other gift so precious as water.

This sort of ceremony, for the increase of plant food, developed, as the importance of agriculture grew, until finally there emerged those seasonal festivals, particularly of the Springtime and the Harvest, which persist over practically all the world today, not seldom with mimetic and symbolic dance. The planting, the harvesting, the first tasting of the new wine—these all suggest special forms of ceremonial and revel. Earth-gods and wine-gods here entered into man's pantheon.

A religious-dramatic ceremony of the Amerinds: the Bull Dance of the Mandan tribe, as depicted by an eye witness, George Catlin. [By courtesy of the Smithsonian Institution.]

Even before the plant ceremonies, probably, there were the animal-food dances. In that stage of savagery where hunting was the chief occupation in life, threatened starvation must be met by direct measures to replenish the game supply. The Mandan Indians of northern Missouri used to stage a "Buffalo Come" dance when meat became scarce. And if the gods were slow in answering, the dancers continued the ceremony in relays for days; indeed, until scouts sent in word from the country round that herds of buffaloes had been sighted. In New Britain a love dance of the birds is held, to suggest that the game-birds might well have greater fertility, and consequently the natives a more abundant food supply.

The known initiation ceremonies are chiefly rituals performed when a boy comes to puberty, when he is to be initiated into man's estate in the tribe; and this is often an initiation into a secret society at the same time, so that complete evidence of the nature of the dances has seldom been recorded. The boy's education, beyond such elementals as hunting and fishing, may have been entirely neglected up to this time. Now he must know the tribal history and the tribal rules and customs. So the maturer tribesmen act out for him the myths and legends of the

The Buffalo Dance of the Mandan Indians. [By courtesy of the Smithsonian Institution.]

totem, graphically, through pantomimic dance. Many of the most interesting known animal dances originate from this totemic teaching, and hero-ancestors are common figures. There are some tribes that shape the initiation ceremony primarily to place the boys and young men in fear of the elders of the tribe, so that the latter may keep control of communal affairs; and here the dances strive toward awe and terror—which explains the fearsome aspect of many primitive masks.

War dances occur among practically all primitive tribes. They seem at first to have two objects: to get the gods on the side of the performer in the fight to come, and to stir the warriors themselves to a "concert pitch" of bravery and daring. The building up of war-frenzy by dance is an instance of those types of performance in which the elements of drama, religion, and practical purpose are inextricably mixed. Loomis Havemeyer describes a war dance of the Naga tribes of Northeast India as follows:

> It commences with a review of the warriors who later advance and retreat, parrying blows, and throwing spears as though in a real fight. They creep along in battle array, keeping as near the ground as possible so that nothing shows but a line of shields. When they are near enough to the imaginary enemy they spring up and attack. After they have killed the opposing party they grab tufts of grass, which represent the heads, and these they sever with their battle axes. Returning home they carry the clods over their shoulders as they would the heads of real men. At the village they are met by the women who join in a triumphant song and dance.

Another war ceremony may serve to carry us over from a review of general primitive dance to the field where drama is recognizably emerging as a separate and complete entity. Henry Ling Roth reports a Dyak native play as follows:

> One warrior is engaged in picking a thorn out of his foot, but is ever on the alert for the lurking enemy, with his arms ready at hand. This enemy is at length suddenly discovered, and after some rapid attack and defence, a sudden lunge is made at him and he is dead upon the ground. The taking of his head follows in pantomime . . . The story then concludes with the startling discovery that the slain man is not an enemy at all but the brother of the warrior who has slain him. At this point the dance gives way to what was perhaps the least pleasing part of the performance—a man in a fit, writhing in frightful convulsions, being charmed into life and sanity by a necromantic physician.[1]

A surprise element of a different sort is found in a play reported by Professor Ernst Grosse, with a "plot" akin to a legend found in the folklore of many peoples. An Aleut pursues a bird, and finally brings it down with an arrow. The hunter then laments, and the dead bird rises up and turns to a beautiful woman, who falls into his arms. Here, and in the Dyak example, are elements of a consciously compositional sort. The discovery of the slain man's identity as brother, and the metamorphosis of the bird-woman, are clearly steps beyond mere narrative war and hunt dances, adding emotional complication and dramatic complexity.

How this added dramatic element is strengthened, until finally drama

---

[1] Quoted from *The Natives of Sarawak and British North Borneo*, by Henry Ling Roth (London, 1896).

becomes more important than dance, perhaps stripping off all dance elements, is particularly illustrated in the religious rituals. Gradually a priesthood evolves: ordinary man cannot take too much time from his hunting and warfare to keep in touch with the gods. The priests, once appointed and looked up to, strive constantly to make stronger their position. They must prove that they are in touch with the spirits, that they even sway the decisions of the gods. Rituals become more complex, everything that increases the element of mystery is played up. A clan of priest-actors emerges. It is especially trained for dance and pantomime. Ultimately a body of dramatic works, not incomparable to the later Christian "Mystery Plays," comes into being. At this time, of course, there is no written dramatic literature.

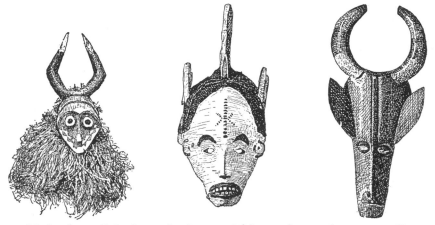

Masks for religio-dramatic dances. African, nineteenth century. From, left and center, Bapende and Ibo tribes; right, an undetermined tribe.

The fraternity of the Areoi in Polynesia, originally a secret society with religious duties and privileges, exhibits the whole range from ritual dance to comparatively complex play, in the "repertoire" which its members take to the tribes on different islands of the Polynesian group. The strictly religious dances and pantomimes, we are told, are there followed by lengthy historical sketches, amorous pantomimes, and comedy-pieces. The Duk-Duk Society of New Pomerania, also descended from a religious priesthood, takes its expanded plays from village to village.

Now obviously I have not been writing *history* here; though in this chapter I am beginning my account of the historic theatre. I have taken evidence from modern primitives, from sources as widely separated as the South Sea Islands and the American plainland, as the Aleutian Islands and Australia, as Borneo and Central Africa. It has seemed to anthropologists that modern man might justly infer from the occurrence of dramatic dance in these separated localities an almost universal dance activity, and that this is safely comparable to the pre-Greeks and others from whom the known European and Asiatic theatres inherited. In short, knowing how the undeveloped, even savage, races of today dance, we may picture our hairier ancestors as similarly dancing, on the occasions of births, deaths, matings, hunts, wars, seasonal changes, initiations, sacrifices to the gods, etc. Knowing how their ritual dance became dramatic, we may picture an almost world-wide theatre activity that existed before (and long after) what is usually regarded as the birth of Western drama in Greece in the sixth century B.C. We shall do better not to try to detail the picture too exactly: there must have been a multitude of types of dance. And often the elements of rhythmic movement, lyric and narrative, are mixed; and æsthetic impulse is by no means to be disentangled from religious impulse and practical purpose. But now we are sure that just as there were long ages of "prehistoric man," there were almost equally long ages of prehistoric dance and rudimentary drama.

Of the theatres we know next to nothing, and can infer but little. There is one outward dance custom, however, that is notably widespread, and it can be ascribed to ancient as well as modern primitives with the greater certainty because it emerged at the earliest dawn of historic drama: the use of the mask. In the great ethnographic museums there is no object more outstanding than the colorful ritual masks, none on which primitive artists everywhere have expended more care and more devotion. We need not inquire here whether the purpose of the mask was wholly characterization and heightening of dramatic effect. We know that with tribe after tribe the mask was worn in dance and dramatic sketch. Sometimes it is recognizably a "disguise," a known animal or type of man or perhaps the spirit of a departed ancestor. More often it is a conventionalization, a symbol, or itself the god. Occasionally it seems to be that thing so sought after by a few contemporary mask-makers, an abstraction of an emotion, fear or grief or jealousy. If it is sometimes explained as the outward sign of membership in a secret society or cult, we may remember that these societies were little more than groups of actor-priests. They knew well that the wearer took on mysteriously and mystically the spirit of the totemic animal or god or ancestor to whom the mask was, so to speak, erected.

We shall come to masks again, and here we need note only the prevalence of this aid to dramatic effect, among primitive peoples, and the elaborateness, picturesqueness, and jewel-like intricacy—not to say beauty—of many examples. The animal which gave the mask its reason

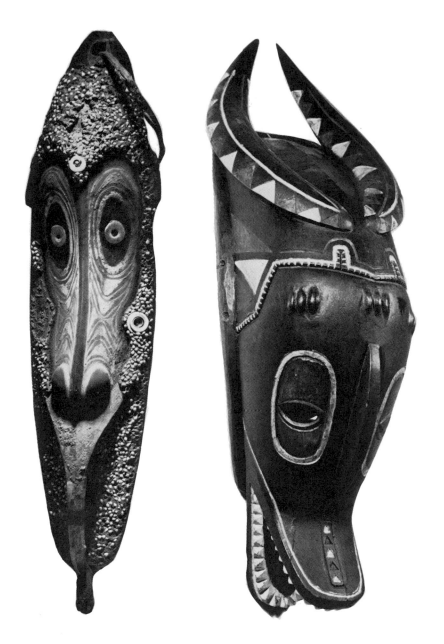

Some of the finest primitive sculptural art went into the making of masks. At left, a mask of the Iatmul people of New Guinea, carved in wood, decorated with shells, seeds, etc., and painted. At right, Antelope mask of the Guro tribe of the African Ivory Coast, of wood, painted. [By courtesy of the Lowie Museum of Anthropology, University of California, Berkeley.]

for being was a common bear or buffalo, or perhaps a hawk or a horn-bill. But the mask itself is a work of art, precious, expressively molded, enriched, worthy of a god. The simpler forms are made of light carved wood, painted or stained. But there are more elaborate ones incorporating almost every material light enough to be worn: stiffened cloth, hides, shell, precious metals, beads, feathers, cork. Some ancient examples are formed over the front portions of human skulls. The awe-inspiring masks are a special and particularly interesting class. I have tried in choosing my illustrations to show the range graphically, in subject matter, in degree of elaboration, and territorially. The least "artistic" of the masks are the real animal heads, like those worn in the "Buffalo Come" dance of the Mandans, described a few pages back; the more elaborate ones may be as different as the abstract or awesome or humorous examples shown here and on adjacent pages.

A finely sculptured wooden mask of the Tsimshian tribe of Amerindians, British Columbia. [By courtesy of the Museum of the American Indian, Heye Foundation, New York.]

While Greek, Hindu, Japanese, and other early racial theatres can be traced back to known dance origins, it would be dangerous to presume that drama never emerged as mimetic action, unaccompanied by rhythmic movement. There are authorities who believe that the hunting dance, based on an actual episode or exploit, grew out of the retelling of the story around a camp-fire. Robert Edmond Jones has given a hypothetical account of such a spontaneous emergence of drama-story, with so much of understanding of the theatrical impulse, and with such vividness, that I reprint it here. From it the reader may feel a more direct sense of the inevitableness of drama than from all that has been said about dance and ritual; and it will serve to emphasize—or perhaps bring back into proportionate importance—that other main-root of the stage art, the sheer impulse to reproduce, to image, to retell the heroic episode in vivid action.

Let us imagine ourselves back in the Stone Age, in the days of the cave man and the mammoth and the Altamira frescoes. It is night. We are all sitting together around a fire—Ook and Pow and Pung and Glup and little Zowie and all the rest of us. Over on that side of the fire the leaders of the tribe are sitting together—the strongest men, the men who can run fastest and fight hardest and endure longest. They have killed a lion today. We are excited about this thrilling event. We are all talking about it. . .

The lion's skin lies close by, near the fire. Suddenly the leader jumps to his feet. "I killed the lion! I did it! I followed him! He sprang at me! I struck him with my spear! He fell down! He lay still!" He is telling us. We listen. But all at once an idea comes to his dim brain. "I know a better way to tell you. See! It was like this! *Let me show you!*"

In that instant drama is born.

The leader goes on. "Sit around me in a circle—you, and you, and you—right here, where I can reach out and touch you all. . .

"You, Ook, over there—you stand up and be the lion. Here is the lion's skin. You put it on and be the lion and I'll kill you and we'll show them how it was." Ook gets up. He hangs the skin over his shoulders. He drops on his hands and knees and growls. How terrible he is! Of course he isn't the real lion. We know that. The real lion is dead. We killed him today. Of course Ook isn't a lion. Of course not. He doesn't even look like a lion. "You needn't try to scare us, Ook. We know you. We aren't afraid of you!"

And yet in some mysterious way, Ook *is* the lion. He isn't like the rest of us any longer. He is Ook all right, but he is a lion too.

And now these two men—the world's first actors—begin to show us what the hunt was like. They do not tell us. They *show* us. They *act* it for us. The hunter lies in ambush. The lion growls. The hunter poises his spear. The lion leaps. We all join in with yells and howls of excitement and terror—the first community chorus! The spear is thrown. The lion falls and lies still.

The drama is finished.[2]

If mimicry, growing out of the imitating, reproductive impulse, came first, before dance and the other elements of composite theatre, we may well say, "that, then, was the way it was." In any case, noting how much of human nature and of theatre understanding there is here, we may be sure that this is one way in which drama occurred in many places and at many times—before the known birth of the theatre in

---

[2] From a lecture delivered at the University of California, at Berkeley, as printed in *Theatre Arts Monthly*, September 1927.

Greece. We may say still that it is very rudimentary drama: two characters; a story with only a bare beginning of plot, as compared with later design and complexity; produced spontaneously, without rehearsal. But when the actor has thus repeated his story often, it crystallizes, takes on design, becomes perhaps a ritual-drama of all hunting instead of the recounting of one actual hunt—leads inevitably to a story-music-dance theatre as the race advances culturally.

In closing this brief survey of the beginnings of drama among primitive peoples, I must add that I don't take a great deal of stock in talk about "backward" peoples in this connection. Certainly their drama

A highly conventionalized mask, with more than one face.

meant more to the tribesmen than theatre does to "civilized" mankind in the twentieth century. According to our material and scientific standards, their civilization was crude; but dramatically and religiously they felt more deeply, expressed more intensively, lived their productions more emotionally than the "advanced" peoples of today.

In dances lasting hours, even days, with constantly varying steps and figures, a mis-step was considered a crime against the tribe and an offense to the gods. In some cases among primitives today, if the slightest mistake is made the dance is stopped, and the whole ceremony must be repeated. Among the Maoris if even a single word is dropped or incorrectly spoken in certain rituals, the mistake is believed to presage the death of the performer. In other cases a mistake is actually punishable by death. (A note of this might profitably be posted on the call-boards of our opera houses and little theatres!) Nor does this precision pertain only where solo or small-group dancing is practised. Among the Australians several tribes would sometimes join together for the *corroborry* dances—four hundred participants have been counted at once—and yet the accounts agree that a remarkable precision obtained. Incidentally an official director of the dance was leader and called the directions, another step toward complex theatre.

AS THE curtain of obscurity lifts, then, historic man emerges already possessed of a certain degree of culture and civilized custom. As he first comes into the light, he brings dance and dramatic ritual with him. There are such gaps in our knowledge, however, that we need pause over only two later ancient nations before the Greeks. Let us inquire what were the dramatic features of the famous Egyptian religious ceremonials, and what were the dramatic elements in Hebrew literature and life. Of the other pre-Greek civilizations we have practically no theatre knowledge. We know very little about the forms of ancient Egyptian dance, so far as that goes: little beyond the fact of its existence and wide prevalence. But there is contemporary evidence about one form of religious play and certain types of celebrative pageant.

Osiris, the chief Egyptian god, legendary king-divinity, was the central figure of a "Passion Play" bearing notable resemblances to those still performed in the twentieth century. In a document estimated to date from 2000 B.C., we have an outline description of the ceremony and drama as then executed. The purpose was exactly that of the famous Oberammergau and Tyrolean Passion Plays of today, and of the Persian Passion Play of Hussein; that is, they all served or serve to keep vivid in the memories of the faithful the sufferings and triumph of a god. The historical background of the Egyptian play is this: Osiris after ruling wisely was treacherously murdered, and his body was cut in pieces which were scattered to a great distance. But his wife Isis and her son avenged the murder, gathered the pieces for pilgrimage relics, won back the throne, and established the cult of Osiris-worship. The Passion Play, recounting the sufferings of Osiris, and culminating in his resurrection, became an annual event.

The evidence that is available outlines only the ceremony at Abydos, but other Passion Plays were performed yearly at Busiris, Heliopolis, and elsewhere. Very little is included about the "theatre" or surroundings. The incidents, indeed, are described as progressive, moving from place to place, and very different in kind, ranging from pure mimetic drama to processionals and even sham battles. (Drama is here still very much entangled with practical life, for those who were taken prisoners in the "sham" battles are supposed then to have acted the least desirable rôles in a ceremony of human sacrifice.)

What we know is that King Usertsen III sent a man named I-kher-nefert to Abydos to build a new shrine to Osiris; he regulated the ceremonies and festivals for the gods, and built certain of the "properties" used in the Passion Play, such as the sacred boat duplicating that in which Osiris had set forth on his expedition against his enemies. This is recorded on a stele[3] now preserved in a Berlin museum; from this "document" we learn that I-kher-nefert himself played important parts in the drama that year:

"I performed the coming forth of Ap-uat when he set out to defend his father . . . I drove back the enemy from the Neshmet Boat, I overthrew the enemies of Osiris . . . I performed the 'Great Coming-forth,' I followed the god in his footsteps . . . I made the boat of the god to move. . . ." And so on to the great climax: "I caused him [Osiris] to set out in the Boat, which bore his Beauty. I made the hearts of the dwellers in the East to expand with joy, and I caused gladness to be in the dwellers in the West, when they saw the Beauty as it landed at Abydos, bringing Osiris Khenti-Amenti, the Lord of Abydos, to his palace." From which we may visualize the Passion Play as something *like* this (relying on the learned Egyptologists for certain collateral bits of evidence):

A great pageant-procession of priests, attendants, and worshippers, including warriors, sets out from the "palace," our actor-recorder going first, personifying Ap-uat. A float representing the sacred boat of Osiris is the central feature of the procession, and is guarded by groups of attendants as it moves. At a given point on the line of march, actors representing the enemies of Osiris attack the boat. The forces of Ap-uat drive them off. The procession then continues to the temple. At this point a purely dramatic scene is enacted, in the "Coming Forth" of Osiris from the temple. It ends with the departure of his body for the tomb, to the accompaniment of sacramental ceremonies and mass-laments. Along the procession route again there is a battle, and here, we are told—by later Greek historians—many actor-warriors died of their wounds. After this there seems to have been a recess for the audi-

---

[3] Known as the Stele of I-kher-nefert. The date is of the XIIth Dynasty, about 2000 B.C. My excerpts are taken from the chapter on "Shrines, Miracle Play and Mysteries" in E. A. Wallis Budge's *Osiris and the Egyptian Resurrection* (London and New York, 1911).

ence; for the "following of the god in his footsteps" is interpreted to mean that the actors searched for the lost body of Osiris—for three days, it is said (this is primarily a devotional play, remember); and on each day another sham battle is fought.

When the body has been found the procession forms again, the body is placed in state on the rich float, and the whole company resumes the interrupted march to the tomb—actually a mile and a half from the Temple of Osiris. Another great battle is fought, probably at dawn, and Ap-uat's forces win a decisive and final victory, symbolizing the defeat of the murderers of Osiris and the rout of his enemies at the hands of his avengers. The procession returns to the palace whence it originally started; and there is staged the final glorious scene in which Osiris reappears as a living God, in the sacred Neshmet Boat, bringing joy to the people as a symbol of their coming resurrection. And so the pageant and drama blend again into worship and ritual.

Naturally I-kher-nefert mentions only the parts he played, for at that time it would be taken for granted that everyone would know all the details about the drama itself; and this leaves us with only a scrappy conception of the play, four thousand years later. But his stele affords the world's oldest report of a dramatic production.

There are references, mostly on tomb walls, to many other resurrection plays. The "Pyramid Texts" indicate the existence of Passion plays even earlier than 3000 B.C. And pageant-like plays were a customary feature of Coronation festivals through a thousand years or more. A curious variation or outgrowth of the Osiris Passion Play has been termed by Egyptologists a "medical play"; in this the affliction of the hero-god is not a dismemberment but a sickness, and his way to resurrection a cure. It is supposed that pilgrim-spectators so identified themselves with the central character that they experienced renewal, and "cures" both physical and moral. But all these other plays are unrecorded except in meager passages and drawings on tomb walls. They probably involved dialogue and sustained impersonation; but as yet I-kher-nefert's report of an actual presentation is unique.

The Greek historian Herodotus, traveling in Egypt in 449 B.C., a millennium and a half after I-kher-nefert's time, recorded that he saw two survivals of the Passion plays; but he reported that they were too holy to be described. He noted them as having influenced the mysteries from which early Greek drama had emerged.

THE BIBLE contains many references to the dance, ranging from Miriam and the Hebrew women going out "with timbrels and with dances" after the drowning of Pharaoh, and the exhortation in the Psalms to "praise his name in the dance," to the performance of Salome before

Herod—often re-enacted and often abused. But it would be hazardous to try to reconstruct on this evidence any certain picture of a type of dancing. That the dance persisted in later Christian worship, re-enforced with non-Hebrew elements, is certain: a decree of the year 744 was necessary to abolish "dancing-places" in and about the churches, and there was another in the twelfth century.

As a matter of fact, a group of boys called *Seises*—because originally six in number—still dance in costume, to music, before the high altar in the Cathedral of Seville, at several church festivals each year. There is a legend to the effect that when a Pope some centuries ago again determined to ban all dances in churches, he was asked particularly to exempt the *Seises*. His bull stipulated that they could continue until such time as their costumes were worn out. The authorities therefore never provided new costumes without sewing on patches off the old, by which they technically conform to the decree, and so still enjoy the indulgence of His Holiness. Other isolated examples of Christian ritual dance can still be found in Catholic countries.

But for us it will be more fruitful to inquire into the *literary*-dramatic parts of the Bible. The *Book of Job* and the *Song of Solomon* are actually cast in dialogue form. Both may be described as long dramatic poems rather than as poetic drama; and since we know nothing of any ancient performances of them with action, we shall do better to consider them for their dramatic-poetic merit rather than as stage pieces (not forgetting, however, that both have been "adapted" in modern times for occasional production).

The Song of Songs is an idyll in dramatic form. The action, insofar as it is indicated or implied, seems processional rather than designed for a set stage. It may be that the composition is made up of grouped chants or songs, thus possibly allying it with the older rituals and progressive dance-dramas; or it may have been designed for recitative purposes rather than for combined speaking-and-acting. Its sheer artistic value as poetic dialogue is such, however, that one cannot omit it from consideration: in the accepted English translation it stands forth as one of the most beautiful things in dramatic literature.

Professor Richard G. Moulton, in the *Modern Reader's Bible*, has arranged the various books in the forms they originally had. Since there is still some controversy over the matter, the following lines may be quoted as indicating definitely the dialogue origin; the words "among the daughters" and "among the sons" seeming final proof of *two* speakers. (The early texts of the Bible are written without separation even of the words, like this: IAMAROSEOFSHARONALILYOFTHEVALLEYS.)

THE BRIDE

I am a rose of Sharon,
  A lily of the valleys.

THE BRIDEGROOM

As a lily among thorns,
  So is my beloved among the daughters.

THE BRIDE

As the apple tree among the trees of the wood,
  So is my beloved among the sons.

The entire scene wherein this passage occurs is exquisite poetic dialogue. But as an example of the more sustained lyrical-emotional
speeches, one cannot do better than quote:

THE BRIDE

The voice of my beloved! Behold, he cometh,
  Leaping upon the mountains,
  Skipping upon the hills.
My beloved is like a roe or a young hart:
  Behold, he standeth behind our wall,
He looketh in at the windows,
He showeth himself through the lattice.
  My beloved spake and said unto me:
"Rise up, my love, my fair one,
  And come away.

"For lo, the winter is past,
  The rain is over and gone;
The flowers appear on the earth;
  The time of the singing of birds is come,
  And the voice of the turtle is heard in our land . . .
Arise, my love, my fair one,
  And come away."

We shall go far before we come again to poetic dialogue so finely
lyrical as this. If as drama it is as slow-moving, as "reminiscent," as the
pre-Æschylean dithyrambs, it has, nonetheless, a continuous action of
thought, even movement toward a foreshadowed end. We wonder
whether the ancient world knew other works by the unnamed Hebrew
author. If a theatre, a place for productions of which this is the only
remaining, the literary part, existed in those times, we may mark it as
rich even in comparison with those of Fifth Century Greece or of
Elizabeth's time in England.

Job, chosen more often than any other book out of the Bible group
as a world masterpiece of literature, is more definitely dramatic in

structure than is *Solomon's Song*. Job is presented, a main actor going through a series of events, in a drama that may seem in our energetic times to lack direct theatric action; but which has a well-stressed action of spiritual thought, even of emotion.

After the short explanatory prologue, it begins with (shall we say, the curtain goes up on?) Job's soliloquy:

Let the day perish wherein I was born;
And the night which said, There is a man child conceived!
  Let that day be darkness;
  Let not God regard it from above,
  Neither let the light shine upon it!
  Let darkness and the shadow of death claim it for their own . . .
Because it shut not up the doors of my mother's womb,
Nor hid trouble from mine eyes!

From this beginning it passes through five distinct acts in dialogue, until Job's final summarizing words to the Lord:

I had heard of thee by the hearing of the ear;
But now my eyes see-eth thee:
Wherefor I abhor myself, and repent
In dust and ashes.

The drama of Job's soul is over. The Bible author adds the conventional happy ending in a brief few paragraphs of narrative at the end, as epilogue. In the body of the work he has written what remains in translation one of the finest literary dramas of all time.

YET—much as I may enjoy these beautiful things, there is something lacking out of my fullness of satisfaction at this point: precisely because I cannot talk definitely about theatre as well as drama, about stages and actors and movement as well as about texts. Gathering together all the fragments treated in this chapter, these texts and these Passion Play outlines and these reconstructions of primitive dance, we may return to the solid fact that the first complete theatre that we know about, the first surviving drama coupled with a constructed theatre and a method of presentation, is the Greek. We have discovered where the theatre came from fragmentarily—and approximately when; but we have yet to get any full view of it as a rounded-out living human institution.

CHAPTER
3

Tragedy:
The Noble Greeks

IN GREECE, in the sixth and fifth centuries before Christ, there was a flowering of beautiful living and of the arts such as mankind never had known before; and Tragedy then was born. In the progress of humankind in the Western world during twenty-four centuries since, there has been no rival to Greek civilization. No other state has ever reached the standard set by the Hellenes in those accomplishments esteemed by men to be most high, most desirable, most beautiful. Other races and other countries, even single cities, have had their brief periods of creativeness, have carried conquest farther, have won miraculous victories over material obstacles to progress. But the proudest boast a nation can make is that of being successor to the ancient Greeks. In short, there is world recognition that for a considerable period the people of Hellas solved better than any other the problem how to live their lives reasonably and finely.

Not only in those too stressed accomplishments of winning wars with courage and daring, thus protecting and expanding their civilization, and in feats of strength and physical perfection, but more especially in the fields of artistic and intellectual accomplishment, they came to a surpassing achievement. Perhaps most important, they adjusted art and life to a perfect balance; philosophy and living sustained each other. They made their buildings lovely, they learned to adorn beautifully rather than lavishly, they were wise in their pleasures, cultivating those of the emotions, the mind, and the æsthetic senses, those that may be enjoyed with least danger of satiation, headache, or bore-

dom. Even today, their architecture, their poetry, their sculpture—
and their drama—spread before us glories almost unmatched.

Such has been the estimate of Greek civilization in numberless histories; the Classicists ruled for centuries in Western universities and in
common schools. Greece was the criterion by which the institutions
and the heroes of later nations were universally judged. The Greek
ideal was all but unassailable.

Nevertheless in the twentieth century there came—within a period
of revolutionary change in the visual arts, and of wide examination of
traditional institutions—a lessening of reliance upon Greek standards.
A new interest in the arts of the Orient and of primitive peoples ac-

Masked performers of the Old Comedy period, on a rudimentary platform stage with stairs to the orchestra. [After a vase painting.]

companied new explorations of the values inherent in the Christian
medieval civilization in Europe. The devotion to Greek studies remained, just as the classics of Greek dramatic literature held their place
in the highest category of tragedy-writing. But the view of other
ancient cultural achievements broadened.

In studying the Hellenic theatre, we cannot avoid some consideration of *religion* as an element in Greek life, and as a thing comparatively lacking in the life of today. The drama in Greece was inextricably bound up with religious feeling and religious observance. A lived

and companionable religion, inspirational but seldom rule-making, was at the base of Greek life. It was a religion not of conformance but of celebration. It left man free to create, himself god-like. Exercise of the artist's creativeness, in architecture and sculpture, in the service of the gods; dramatic ritual, dancing and full theatre production; games and processions: all these arose from spiritual and devotional sources in the hearts of the people. The drama from its beginnings to the day of late comedy was intertwined with religion, a part of sacred ceremonial.

In thus enlarging upon the part that religion played, it is necessary to make a distinction between the Mystery religions of which Greek tragedy was an expression, and the pantheistic Olympian religion that claimed wide popular allegiance. It was the latter, because it was less god-given than human—with the failures and the caprices of men attributed to fickle gods—that eventually failed the Greeks and permitted their civilization to end in catastrophe. The tragic theatre was close to that other, diminishing religion that found its deepest significance and its highest devotion in the Eleusinian Mysteries. It was there that philosophy led men to a consciousness of the divine; and it was there that communal ecstasy led into dramatic celebration. In the rituals of the Orphic, Dionysian and Eleusinian cults, as in those of the Pythagorean fraternity, there were elements inherited from the Egyptian Mystery "plays," and others from Asiatic sources. These passed on into the earliest drama of the Athenians. The chorus, so typical of all later Greek drama, is especially a survival from the mystery cults.

Bands of Greek revellers met to celebrate when the time of vintage had come. They went swinging through the town streets and the country groves in processions, or danced and sang in improvised "dancing rings." They drank wine, as was doubly appropriate when the new grapes were in, and they sang of, and to, Dionysus, the wine-god. They had begun by making sacrifice to him, by pledging their allegiance, their devotion. But as his spirit entered into them, it transformed them, too, into gods. The glow of man-made revels, of marching shoulder to shoulder, of shouting and singing and laughing, changed to a divine ecstasy. The god-in-man became alive, radiant, social, inspired.

In such a time only the arts could satisfy: the dance and poetry and music. Not that the many listened silently and reverently, in those early days, while a few recited or danced or played sweet melodies. Where every youth or maid was in some measure a god, all joined in—though the most god-like might improvise the poems for chanting, or lead a special band of dancers. Still it was all very mixed, very boisterous—and perhaps it ended very wildly. For this god Dionysus, who symbolized the fields and the harvest and the red wine, who had the special power of entering into the soul of a man or a woman, had been first of all a god of all wild things, and of a magic fertility; and the ecstasy that he brought might be of many sorts. It was divine and exalting and exquisite, but there was nothing to keep it from being "loose."

There are, indeed, elements in Greek religion, and particularly in the wild god Dionysus, that are shocking to many upright and kindly people, beyond the sheer superstition that was the foundation for all deification. For one thing, the Greek was fully aware of the beauty of the human body, counted its creativeness as part of the great creative divinity governing life, associated its beauty and its reproductive functions with the richness and fruitfulness of the earth—seed-planting, germination, vintage, harvest—and celebrated one with the other. The phallus, fashioned in symbolic or realistic likeness to the male generative organ, was an ordinary property of vintage processionals and

Masked performers in a Greek Comus. [From a vase drawing reproduced in *The Greek Drama* by Lionel D. Barnett.]

earth-god ceremonials. That these occasions, in those days when true drama was germinating in devotional festivals, sometimes were marked by freedoms and excesses warranting the name "orgies," can hardly be questioned. But to read such an extreme meaning into any great part of Dionysian celebration, or to understand drunkenness for that "intoxication" which the Greeks valued so highly, would be unwarranted and evil. The early Greeks gave due place to sex as a determining element of spiritual life, their festivals included devotions to the gods of fruitfulness, and phallic celebrations had much to do with the rise of the dramatic art. But a sense of divine cause informed all these things.

Dionysus, out of one attribute or another, is father of full-fledged tragedy and comedy as well as the more directly appropriate Satyr-play. We may consider him as the successor of those gods of fertilization and of harvest-time fullness whom we met in connection with primitive dance and ritual. But he is more. In his identification with the human, with the source of the highest ecstasy within one, he seems miraculously born to father the divine-popular art. Those earlier names of his, Bacchus and Iacchus, carried some connotation of a god who is hailed with loud cries; and what band of celebrants could utter loud cries—Iacchus! Iacchus!—without movement, dance? And that ecstasy within, would it let one go away after a sacrifice without getting up a pageant-procession? And in a procession should one merely march and sing and throw jests? No; sooner or later, one who is a god must *act* the god. Divine inspiration demanded no less than first the act of acting, then the art of acting. How did it come about?

Aristotle, the first great authority on matters dramatic, writing two centuries later, chronicles the birth of tragedy and comedy in this manner: "Both tragedy and comedy originated in a rude and unpremeditated manner, the former from the leaders of the dithyramb, the latter from those who led off the phallic songs." There is one significant emphasis here: on the *leaders* of the dance and song. From it we infer organization, and that those who led the singers and dancers became the first identifiable actors. For the essential change from mere group-dancing or processional came when one performer *separated himself* from the group of Dionysian worshippers and assumed another character than his own, impersonated.

There are various conjectural accounts of how the separation came about, how it led to responses from "chorus" to "leader," how the action grew from chance repartee to incident, to story in dialogue. But we may be content if we have a clear picture of the band of revellers, ivy-crowned and with faces masked or streaked with wine-dregs, marching, dancing, singing, joshing; celebrating Dionysus, carrying grape garlands and phallic emblems, drinking the wine, working up that ecstasy which is the realest devotion to this god; and when the band is organized, for dance or for procession or for choral singing—we know not just what—we see one participant step out (most likely the poet), see him take a part different from the others.

Long before this time the Greeks had been accustomed to enjoy melic poetry. Poems had long been sung with musical accompaniment, and sometimes to the accompaniment of dance. From this source and from the great store of epic story-poem and lyric, from Homer and from his fellow-poets, the literary elements for tragedy were drawn. Joined with the mimetic elements out of the dance-revels, they served to form the dual foundation for the majestic edifice of Greek tragic drama.

The "dithyramb" mentioned by Aristotle was a special form of poetry sung by the revellers at the festivals of Dionysus, recounting the story of the god, or at least honoring him. Confusingly, the dithyramb was itself later expanded and crystallized into a truly dramatic form, was composed specifically for chorus and leader. It was this that came to be called "goat-song," and therefore this form that gave tragedy its name. For the word seems to come from τράγος, goat, and ὠδή, song—but whether in reference to the sacrifice of a goat during the ritual, or because a goat was given to the poet as prize, or on account of the goatskins worn by the chorus as followers of Dionysus, is not certainly known (there are a dozen other guesses almost as plausible).

In these beginnings of tragedy there is an influence, too, an influence not to be measured or traced, out of straight recited poetry, poetry put over by a reciter up on a platform or in a cleared space before an audience, as distinguished from the choral dithyramb and the other song-dances. Minstrels had long ago made their recitations popular, and their materials were those out of epic poetry that later went into tragic drama. How close the declaiming minstrels may have approached to acting, no one may hazard.

Up to this time the lines of development, the streams leading into true drama, have been not only vague but scattered: from Ionian, Doric, and other sources as well as Attic. But from the first recorded acting,

Greek vase with a painting of masked actors on a platform stage, of a period before the emergence of the Classic theatre, possibly of the sixth century B.C.

the story may be told by the record of the Theatre of Dionysus in Athens. This is truly the most important single theatre in all history.

Let us say that we are now in the middle period of the sixth century B.C. The Dionysian Festivals used to be held over on the north side of the Acropolis, where there were a dancing circle and some rude seats. But under Pisistratus, just after mid-century, perhaps, this potential "theatre" has been moved to the location where one may still see the half-ruined Theatre of Dionysus today, twenty-five hundred years later, in the sacred precinct of Dionysus Eleutherius on the southeastern slope of the Acropolis. Close to the god's temple a dancing-circle, the ὀρχήστρα, has been tamped hard, and some wooden seats set up against the hillside hollow. (There is no stage.) Under Pisistratus, too,

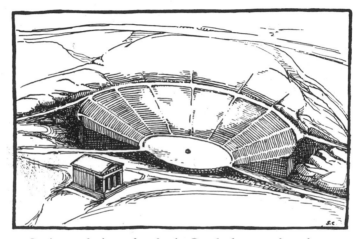

Conjectural view of a classic Greek theatre when the stage was still only a tamped circular space for actor-dancers: auditorium shaped in a natural hillside hollow, orchestra, and a nearby temple—without any built stage.

the Athentian festival known as the Great or City Dionysia has been expanded, a new Temple of Dionysus has been built, and dramatic "contests" have been inaugurated.

The first decisive record of acted drama dates from this time, and the earliest name in the annals of acting. In the year 535 B.C., Thespis of Icaria was winner in the first tragedy contest. He achieved immortality more especially, however, because he is supposed to have introduced the actor as such, *in addition to* the leader of the chorus. These two henceforward are to engage in dialogue, and the actor is to impersonate various characters, with different masks and changes of costume. Thus the tragic drama is safely set on its two-fold foundation:

mimetic-dramatic art and literary-dramatic art are indissolubly joined. The play text may still be very crude—hardly more than a series of poems spoken alternately by chorus leader and actor. No "plays" by Thespis have survived, though he is chronicled as both poet and actor. But the period of mere improvisation, of mere chant-and-response, is past.

The "cart of Thespis," for some reason become a world-symbol of the wandering actor, is probably wholly a thing of myth. Nor is there more than conjecture as basis for the often-repeated statement that while the chorus grouped themselves around an altar in the centre of the orchestra, Thespis mounted a table from which he addressed their leader. (This table, perhaps that on which the goat was sacrificed, was long supposed to have been the first step toward a stage, although there is no real proof of the existence of any platform stage, elevated above the orchestra-area, until centuries later.)

It was only ten years after Thespis' epoch-making innovation that Æschylus was born. He was destined not only to become one of the world-masters of tragic drama—the greatest, some people still believe— but to be remembered as an innovator almost as notable as Thespis. He introduced a second actor. Sophocles, who lived his life wholly within the fifth century B.C., added the third actor. In the slowness with which the actor took on importance, during this period of developing tragedy, one may read a truth too often forgotten: choral dance was the essential feature, the very heart of drama. The chorus was still the pivotal element in Thespis' time: the *acted* portions of the play were considered as the interludes, the dance-chants as the main design. The connected episodes only gradually took on significance as plot. Æschylus cut down the predominance of the chorus, but only with Sophocles did compact acted-spoken drama take first place.

Thespis is credited with "making up" to the extent of wholly disguising his face with paints; and then with the invention of the mask. There is conflict here with the theory that the mask was a survival from primitive ritual-dance. But there can be no doubt that from Thespis' time masks continued as an aid to impersonation through the whole story of the Greek theatre.

The two annual occasions particularly distinguished by performances of drama were religious festivals in honor of Dionysus. One, the Lenæa, in honor of Dionysus Lenæus, held in winter, incorporated more of comedy than of tragedy into its early revelry and into its later programmes; though contests in tragedy are known definitely to have been included. The other, the Dionysia, in celebration of Dionysus Eleutherius, held in the spring in the sacred precinct containing temple and theatre, may be considered the real cradle and home of tragedy. From

A Greek dancer. Terra cotta figure from Tanagra, in the *Bibliothèque Nationale*, Paris. [Giraudon photograph.]

535 B.C., when Thespis received the first given prize, to the decadence long after Æschylus, Sophocles, and Euripides, performances of tragedy regularly graced the City Dionysia. Very truly it may be said that on its dedicated ground Greek drama budded, flowered, and died.

The festival included, in the epochal fifth century, processions, rites, concerts, games, contests in poetry and chorus singing, and performances of tragedies, comedies, and satyr-plays. For five or six days the people of Athens took holiday from their accustomed occupations, to enjoy feasting, revelling, music, and theatre productions. The dramatic events filled the last three days. On each of these occasions, five plays were presented, probably three tragedies, a satyr-play, and a comedy (it seems that at some periods more comedies were included, perhaps on earlier days). In any case, the tragic contest consisted of three consecutive days' productions, each poet being assigned one day's programme, to which he must contribute three full tragedies and a satyr-drama as an after-piece. The Greek plays were very much shorter than is the modern full-evening entertainment; but four or five dramas must have constituted a formidable single programme. Let us remember, however, that the people of Athens were keenly devoted to literary and artistic activities of all sorts, and the contests for the prizes in tragedy and comedy roused wide public interest aside from the intrinsic theatrical values of the individual plays, and beyond the religious significance of the events. Victory in any of the games, music contests, or literary competitions brought honor and glory not only to the winning individuals but to all their relatives and to their cities or districts.

At first each tragic poet composed his plays as a trilogy, connected in subject, perhaps making them all deal with the adventures of one protagonist. Later the dramatists might present a group of unrelated compositions. During the fifth century B.C. only one performance of each play was given in Athens, except that by special decree, after the poet's death, the tragedies of Æschylus could be revived in subsequent years. It is well to remember, however, in these days of playwrights with an eye to a possible "long run," that in those earliest decades of the theatre's existence, when some of the immortal dramas were being written, they were literally designed for a day only. In a moment we shall inquire what are their special qualities, as drama, that have made them live through twenty-four centuries. First let us try to reconstruct a picture of the conditions under which they were presented.

The Greek theatre is an extraordinarily simple, but an extraordinarily pleasing place. From the tamped circle for dancing, with surrounding benches, it has now grown into an architectural bowl, graceful in outline, symmetrical, but not yet in any way ornate. About the full round orchestra, tiers of seats rise up, two-thirds of the way round, nestled into the Acropolis slope, divided by aisles into wedge-like sections. At the far side of the dancing circle an unpretentious stage-building, the *skene*, has been erected. It probably has a portico along the front, between two wings that come forward protectingly toward the auditorium. There still is no raised stage (one must repeat it, because from our knowledge of later theatres we always look first for a platform); there is no "scenery," and there are very few properties. Close-by, ever a reminder that this is a sacred precinct, is the lovely little Temple of Dionysus. Not that any of the fifteen thousand spectators is likely to forget the religious significance of the occasion, of the plays to come, even of the theatre itself.

The theatre at Epidauros as partially restored in the late nineteenth century. The best example of the early classic theatre, with full orchestra circle.

For did we not three days ago assemble with them, in the nearby Odeon, to witness the "parade" of the dramatists, actors, and chorus, all dressed up gorgeously for this ceremonial? There we heard the announcements, the names of the poet-playwrights, of the *choregi* (the patrons or "backers" of the poets, in modern parlance), and of the plays. No doubt about the seriousness, the dignity, and the significance of all this: these performers, producers, and dramatists are specially honored members of Athenian society. What they are to present during the coming holidays is to be no mere amusement to while away idle hours, but rather a sacrament—though imbedded in a festival of revelry and games. Even in this preliminary ceremony they are wearing crowns; and we are told that at the end of the contest one of the tragic poets and his *choregus* will be crowned with that more prized emblem, the ivy.

At the opening of the festival, too, we have been witnesses at a stirring ritual and procession. The citizens of Athens have gone forth in all their holiday finery to escort the statue of Dionysus back to its home.

At break of day they have begun to assemble at the shrine, till all the city seems gathered here in the precinct of Dionysus, by the theatre: the *Archon*, the priests, and the city fathers, the chosen ones who are to carry the statue and those who bear the sacrifices, the guards of honor, the choruses, the actors, the groups of contesting singers, the poets, those who later will be the audiences but who now are taking personal part in the ceremony, men, women, children, aristocrat, noble, and freedman.

Swift hands disengage the statue from its pedestal when the chief priest gives the word; the appointed carriers bear it aloft, through the city, out to a park-like place in the country near the Academy, while the procession reverently follows. Now the god's image is placed on a pedestal under the olive trees, and the sacrificial rites are held. The rest of the day is a "let-down" time, given over to games, feasting, and lighter forms of amusement. Then at night the crowd gathers again at the statue, the procession back to the city starts: the crux of the celebration, annual symbol of the first bringing of the image to Athens from Eleutheræ. Here is something out of the pre-drama days, the joyous worshippers marching by torchlight back along the road to the Acropolis, bearing the statue aloft, carrying the jars of wine and the garlands and symbolic crowns, dancing, improvising, singing. Here indeed, in the revelry and the spirited bandying, are survivals of the elements and the impulses from which the seeds of theatre sprang. Then the statue is placed in the theatre, which the celebrants now rededicate with suitable rites for the musical and dramatic events of the morrow.

The next day, and perhaps another, are given up to the dithyrambic contests; five hundred men and boys, come to Athens from all parts of Greece, sing in competition for the choral prizes. Ten groups in all offer their songs before the holiday audiences, not without dancing: a parallel to that other source of tragic drama, the old-time sung poetry. But it is the morning of the following day that we await.

There is still the darkness before dawn as we make our way toward the theatre. Just the first faint streaks of light have made beautiful the eastern sky, but already all Athens seems awake, excited, hurrying toward the enclosure of Dionysus.

We are soon glad that we came thus early, for we are jostled by the crowds, and it is clear that not all these ticket-holders can squeeze into the auditorium. There is room for the overflow up there on the heights above the shaped bowl, but in the dim chill light, that seems far, far away from the dancing-orchestra where the action will pass. We gaze down curiously at this consecrated circle, with the altar of Dionysus at the very centre; and beyond to the low *skene*, the background building with its pillared lower story that might be a palace front or a temple, with its three doorways facing us from the main wall, and its two "wings" or *paraskenia* thrust forward at each end—as if to enclose the acting-dancing space, so that no part of the "drama," the doings, may escape.

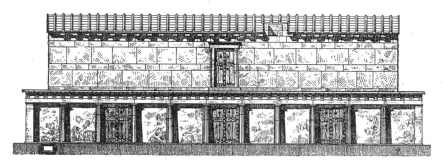

A conjectural reconstruction of the stage building or *skene* in the theatre at Priene, before addition of the raised stage for acting. [From a drawing by A. von Gerkan.]

Light, and still more light, till the theatre seems bathed in the dim freshness, the pale clarity, the loveliest moment of the day. Ah, what a moment for a drama to begin! And indeed, everything is in readiness now. The priests of Dionysus are in their chairs of honor—their thrones —down on the very edge of the orchestra; and the bowl above them is like a teeming beehive, so alive is it with human beings.

A herald! Yes, now he is calling forth Sophocles, first of this year's contestants for the tragedy prize. And the play is on. For there, around the altar of the dancing-circle, a crowd of "supers" has gathered, Theban citizens, miserable, suppliant. And one stands a little apart, a priest. Forth to them comes an actor, majestically, masked and in kingly robes. His voice breaks into the morning silence with startling resonance, with the measured stately beauty of words severely chosen, richly intoned.

My children, fruit of Cadmus' ancient tree
New springing, wherefore thus with bended knee
Press ye upon us, laden all with wreaths

And suppliant branches? And the city breathes
Heavy with incense, heavy with dim prayer
And shrieks to affright the Slayer.
                                . . . Seeing 'tis I ye call,
'Tis I am come, world-honored Œdipus.

This then will be the story of Œdipus the King, most tragic, most
terrible. This actor and the priest now are telling us what we already
know (our minds flash back to the old legend), how Œdipus, having
slain the Sphinx and delivered Thebes, married the widowed Queen
Jocasta, ruled happily twelve years, then found a pestilence destroying
his city. We know more, too horrible almost for words: that this pestilence has come from the gods, because all unwittingly Œdipus has
killed his own father, the former king, and now is married to his own
mother. But these characters in the play, this proud Œdipus, and the
Queen whom Sophocles will make so noble, so touching, do not know.
Like the gods themselves, this day we shall watch the fearful truth unfold to them.

Œdipus and the Priest have told us now the misery of the Theban
people; and the King—oh, irony!—pledges to seek out the cause of the
sorrow, to cast it out at whatever cost. But now the Suppliants crowd
toward the gateway beyond the orchestra, where Creon is entering.
He, the brother of Jocasta, comes from Delphi with messages from the
Oracle: there is an unclean one in the land, he who slew Laïus, the
former king, and he is to be punished before the blight can be lifted.
We watch as Œdipus and Creon build in dialogue toward the first
climax: to that moment when the King goes back through the palace
door—yes, that simple proscenium has become to us a palace now—
vowing to search out the slayer of Laïus.

The Suppliants give way to the Chorus of Theban Elders. Half-
chanting they come, half-dancing, with slow stateliness, threading their
way over the dance-circle, taking up position as prayers to Apollo:
"A voice, a voice, that is borne on the Holy Way" . . . Here is the
old religious dancing-procession, here the old devotional pattern showing through the design of the new human drama. They chant, they
repeat the story of the pestilence, they implore the mercy of the gods,
they call on Apollo, Athena, Artemis, Zeus, Dionysus.

Œdipus is coming again forward from the palace. He speaks, he
ponders, he calls on the guilty slayer of Laïus to come forth and be
banished. He sends for the blind prophet Tiresius. We listen to these
two, the King ruthlessly tracking down clue after clue, the old prophet
holding back the knowledge—till spurred beyond control:

Thou art thyself the unclean thing!

We see the deluge of Œdipus' wrath at this incredible accusation, until the patient Tiresius pours forth his whole prophecy, foreshadows the tragedy to its end:

> Thou dost seek
> With threats and loud proclaim the man whose hand
> Slew Laïus. Lo, I tell thee, he doth stand
> Here. . .
> His staff groping before him, he shall crawl
> O'er unknown earth, and voices round him call:
> "Behold the brother-father of his own
> Children, the seed, the sower and the sown,
> Shame to his mother's blood, and to his sire
> Son, murderer, incest-worker."

Like a relief from storm the Chorus comes, bringing a lyrical interlude, chanting, commenting upon the ways of gods and men, affirming faith in Œdipus—and relieving the tension with the sheer visual beauty of the dance-design.

But Creon returns, eager to defend himself against Œdipus' charge that he has instigated the accusation against the King; and as these two come near to an encounter with swords, Jocasta enters before us:

> Vain men, what would ye with this angry swell
> Of words heart-blinded? Is there in your eyes
> No pity, thus, when all our city lies
> Bleeding, to ply your privy hates? . . .

And it is she who brings to her King the first gleam of self-doubt. We see him now, losing his assurance, a dread beginning to creep in. He tells how once he killed a noble in a chariot, where three roads crossed. He was fleeing from Corinth; a prophecy had said he would kill his father and marry his mother—and so he had fled the court. And meeting this old man on the way, he had killed him and his guards. But Jocasta, stirred now by a deeper dread, sends for a herdsman, since banished to the hills, who saw Laïus murdered.

We of the audience settle back, and let the strain fall a little from us as Œdipus and Jocasta go in; we note the strophes and antistrophes of the Chorus rather idly—we have come to a human suspense that lyrics and dance cannot beguile us from. Now here is Jocasta again before us saying,

> So dire a storm
> Doth shake the king, sin, dread and every form
> Of grief. . .

But, as she prays to Apollo, a Stranger arrives by the gateway, hailing the Chorus, asking for the King. For a moment we are inclined to find relief, with Jocasta, in the news he brings. The King of Corinth, Œdipus' reputed father, is dead, and the old prophecy of patricide seems disproved. But suddenly a new dread is aroused. The Stranger discloses that Œdipus was not Corinthian at all, but was a Theban babe rescued from a wild mountainside where he had been left to die.

Ah, mark you, while this unfolds between Œdipus and the Stranger, how Jocasta turns aside, a sickness growing in her mind! Will no one there notice her as she totters?—now her head goes down into her hands. She knows! This King, her husband, is her own babe. No need to wait the coming of the herdsman. A quick effort to restrain Œdipus from seeking confirmation; then she goes, in horror, hardly daring a farewell. For us in the audience *her* tragedy is already complete. The Chorus this time interrupts only for a moment. All eyes watch for the herdsman's coming.

How crisply Œdipus questions him! On the brink of disastrous knowledge, he searches out the reluctant truth with uncanny directness, without mercy. This is an inevitable structure. We see circumstance after circumstance nailed in; till suddenly Œdipus shines out— we know it is like this in his own mind—with all the guilty knowledge on him: himself son of Laïus, murderer of his own father, incestuous husband to his own mother, brother to his own children! As he rushes into the palace, this time, we have need of the let-down of the choral interlude. Still we have little heart for the lyrical comment—for we know that at this very moment, offstage, the physical climax of the play is taking place. We know that a Messenger, as is the wont, will come and recount to us the more horrible happenings, which perchance we could never have faced in the actual acting-out, under this pitiless morning sunshine. Now the Messenger is before us speaking:

Like one entranced with passion, through the gate
She passed, the white hands flashing o'er her head,
Like blades that tear, and fled, unswerving fled,
Toward her old bridal room, and disappeared
And the doors crashed behind her. But we heard
Her voice within, crying to him of old,
Her Laïus, long dead . . .
And, after that, I know not how her death
Found her. For sudden, with a roar of wrath,
Burst Œdipus upon us. . .
He dashed him on the chamber door. The straight
Door-bar of oak, it bent beneath his weight,
Shook from its sockets free, and in he burst
To the dark chamber.

> There we saw her first,
> Hanged, swinging from a noose, like a dead bird.
> He fell back when he saw her. Then we heard
> A miserable groan, and straight he found
> And loosed the strangling knot, and on the ground
> Laid her.—Ah, then the sight of horror came!
> The pin of gold, broad-beaten like a flame,
> He tore from off her breast, and, left and right,
> Down on the shuddering orbits of his sight
> Dashed it: "Out! Out! Ye never more shall see
> Me nor the anguish nor the sins of me . . ."
>   . . . Like a song
> His voice rose, and again, again, the strong
> And stabbing hand fell, and the massacred
> And bleeding eyeballs streamed upon his beard,
> Wild rain, and gouts of hail amid the rain.
>   . . . All that eye or ear
> Hath ever dreamed of misery is here.

And then Œdipus is led in before us, blinded and bleeding. The old men of the Chorus turn away to escape the sight. But in a sort of sick horror we face this broken King, this abased human being. He gropes his way forward, calling on the gods, glorying that he has made himself a dungeon, "dark, without sound . . . self-prisoned from a world of pain," cursing the shepherd who saved him as a babe.

> O flesh, horror of flesh! . . .
>   In God's name,
> Take me somewhere far off and cover me
> From sight, or slay, or cast me to the sea
> Where never eye may see me any more.

But now he has one thought more: his children, his two little daughters. There they are, Creon is bringing them before us and him.

> Children! Where are ye? Hither; come to these
> Arms of your—brother, whose wild offices
> Have brought much darkness on the once bright eyes
> Of him who grew your garden; who, nowise
> Seeing nor understanding, digged a ground
> The world shall shudder at . . .
>
>   Creon, thou alone art left
> Their father now, since both of us are gone
> Who cared for them. Oh, leave them not alone.
>   . . . So young they are, so desolate—
> Of all save thee. True man, give me thine hand,
> And promise . . .

For a moment only he weakens, and clings to the children. But we see them dragged from him. Creon says, "Seek not to be master more." And as Œdipus is led away, the Chorus chants again. As it too disappears, we are warned:

> Therefore, O Man, beware, and look toward the end of things that be,
> The last of sights, the last of days; and no man's life account as gain
> Ere the full tale be finished and the darkness find him without pain.

At the end of this utterly moving, purging, terrible drama, we spectators wake gradually to the world about us. There is something absurdly trivial about the things we do when the Chorus has finally disappeared: we stand and stretch, and perhaps turn a little away from the sun—and titter because a man is sobbing near us. Our feelings are very close to the surface, and we have a tendency to lose sight of the audience around us in recurring fits of "star-gazing." We are shaken—and yet there is a glow of beauty in our souls, a brooding, a healing ecstasy. We have been through high grief, have descended into terror and sorrow, so terrible that all the pettinesses of life have been stripped away. Now we seem to have come out on the other side, cleansed. Somehow the soul seems to stand up and take the light, naked and glorious.

Twice more we are to suffer through tragedies of Sophocles this day. But we shall welcome them. We await, content.

WHAT is it that puts this mood of high suffering into tragedy? What is the secret of the majesty of these Greek dramas, that brings their audiences close to the gods, that purges human life of its weaknesses, bitterness, and shallowness, that inundates the spectator in exaltation and a god-like pity? The theme and story have not been pretty. We have been conducted through a tale of incest, suicide, murder—a very welter of revolting crime (we shudder to think what any playwright of our more "natural" time would make of the material). But we have not shuddered at Sophocles' telling, nor have we been revolted; somehow our suffering and grief have been kept on some loftier plane.

In the first place the combination that is *theatre* has come right, the majestic poetry matched by nobly dramatic story, the whole set forth in stately acting and in the chanting and rhythmic movement of the Chorus. The vast and nobly proportioned playhouse has some fitting appropriateness too. This is sustained theatre, without let-down to mere anecdote-telling or picturing or individual impersonation. The tragedy has passed with sweep, with unbroken passion, majestically, with a splendid inevitability. It is the art that in its completeness goes beyond dramatic literature or acting or setting or dancing.

And yet if we would know more of the secret of its effectiveness, we must ask about those elements of the art separately. Of the sheer poetic values, there is already evidence enough in the excerpts quoted. Even in translation (always a weakening process) there is obvious tragic beauty in line after line. In the original Greek there was perhaps even more of majesty than becomes evident here. In the modern "Greek Theatre" at Berkeley, I have found myself strangely moved by the beauty of the spoken Greek verse—declaimed nobly, it seemed to me, with an echo of that bigness, that solemn serenity and slowness, that must have characterized performances in the ancient theatres. It is a quality unmatched in the prettier liquid Italian as I have heard it in the

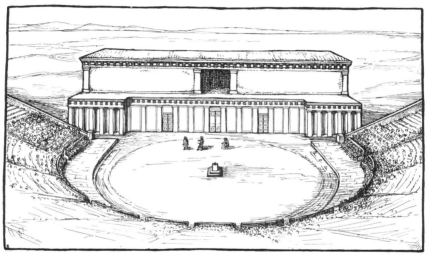

Conjectural drawing of the early stage building of the Theatre of Dionysus at Athens, based on research by James Turney Allen, about 1925.

old Roman theatre at Taormina, or in the more nasal French and heavier German and English, as listened to divers times, indoors and out. Let us grant, then, that each language has its special excellencies, that may or may not be capitalized for theatric uses; and that there seems to have been a perfection of adjustment in Greek tragedy, language values contributing nobly to poetic expressiveness and poetic sweep. And yet, despite the loss of those values, we may read, in Gilbert Murray's translations (from which all my quotations from the Greek tragedians are taken), Greek dramatic works as stirring, as packed with poetic beauty as any to be found on the world's library shelves—with the one exception of Will Shakespeare's plays.

The theatre artist or craftsman, either seeing a Greek masterpiece in production or reading a text, never fails to marvel at the sheer technique of *play structure* exhibited in these works. The Greeks set up models for tragedy that have been seldom deviated from in any later age: a play form that induces in the spectator interest, emotional intensity, suspense and a sort of completion of sorrow, a final radiantly sad contentment. The great simplicity of the fifth century drama, as compared with later developments, the directness of action when the descriptive dithyrambs had first been transformed into dialogue and action, lends a monumental impressiveness to the play. There is something almost fragmentary about these texts, a magnificent isolation from fussing-up ornament, or pretty sentiment or rhetorical flourish. They are like sculptures chiselled out of sheer rock, massive and noble, before modelling and anecdotal subject-matter and "charm" were thought of.

But these qualities arose out of a purely theatrical genius. The conception was thoroughly dramatic, the method born of stage cunning. (The poets, remember, were leading actors.) In later ages a whole literature on the subject of "dramaturgy" has grown up, and the Greek play structure has been pulled to pieces, analyzed, made the basis for rules and "laws." These analyses are bloodless things, little useful to any later dramatist—but the fine directness and the effective action-articulation of the individual plays remain a source of inspiration and a profitable field of study for the general reader. There is in them a well-marked progression from introduction and exposition to opening movement, growth, climax, fall, or return, and finally to denouement or catastrophe. It is a structure calculated to induce the maximum of attentiveness and of emotional response. We shall come again to this subject of play-building and play-writing formulas, along with consideration of the "unities" and other "laws," when we arrive at the days of the French Classicists and their codifying of legitimate dramatic usage. At present let us only mark the Greeks as master technicians.

The subject-matter of Greek tragedy was definitely limited by the conception of the theatre as a religious institution. It simply never would occur to the dramatists to go outside the field of gods and legendary heroes for their plots or stories. The stirring deeds, the crimes, the hereditary sins, the expiations—these were the subject material, usually with a conflict of will between gods and hero or between lesser and greater gods. Every spectator knew at the beginning of the play what the outcome would be—just as we today can foresee every incident in any Christian Passion Play; but the dramatic tension and suspense were none the less sustained and powerful. And the high subject-matter, the revered gods and heroes and kings, and the piteously courageous struggles and the crushing dooms, lent a magnitude of emotion to the plays which perhaps cannot be encompassed in mere domestic tragedies and human love-dramas.

The so-called "unities" were conventions observed in the shaping of the plot-action, and are supposed by some commentators to account for the qualities of grandeur and solemnity that characterized Greek serious drama.

Of the three unities, of Action, of Time, and of Place, only the first seems now to have any universal validity. It is obvious enough that the action of a play must have a unity of flow, must be of a piece, must hold together: as much might be claimed in regard to the characteristic material of any art, of the color in painting, the mass in sculpture, the flow of sound and idea in poetry. Without unity of action the stage-production fails of holding the attention, of precipitating emotion and mood, of creating sustained *theatre*.

The rules to the effect that the dramatists must compress the time of the action into one day, and show its every scene passing in one place, seem to us today to be wholly arbitrary limitations. In certain periods the superstitious reverence for these "laws" hampered playwrights and caused some of the bitterest critical battles in the history of the theatre. The Greek dramatists, so close to what had been a narrative-devotional exercise, pushed out slowly from under the limitations seemingly imposed by the conditions of dithyrambic choral performances and of the very simple form of the dance-theatre. Usually they took a single episode from a myth, dealing with an event in the life of a hero, and this they treated as if it happened in a single day; and as there was then no conception of "setting" the drama (witness the total lack of "scenery"), the action occurred in one place. But later commentators elevated these circumstances into rules to be respected by all serious dramatists. One may believe that the observance of the unities *helped* to further the monumental simplicity and impressiveness of Greek drama, without insisting that similar observance be exacted from later playwrights when theatre conditions have completely changed—any more than one should insist that gods and heroes remain the only protagonists or that a Chorus continue to comment upon or sum up the action at intervals. Aristotle in his *Poetics* codified the usages of Greek writers in a way that has been very useful and at times illuminating to the Renaissance and modern worlds, but he also embalmed some ideas in phrases that have created mischief down the ages.

Æschylus, first of the great tragedy writers, retained in his dramas more of the simplicity and literary conception out of the old dithyrambs, than did Sophocles and Euripides; certainly always a less involved plot than is illustrated in *Œdipus the King*. He was more epic in two senses: the true epic greatness, the monumental fragmentary method, with little effort to polish down to a smooth articulated dramatic flow of events, was characteristic of all his powerful and magnificent plays; and the subject-matter of the epic poets, the mythology and the legendary-historic stories, with their vast religious implications, was dearer to him than were the more human legends that Sophocles and Euripides were to weave into touching dramas.

Æschylus came when the impulse of the dramatic poets had run out along the old lines; he turned to the budding drama, but he brought his gift into the service of Dionysus on the austerer side, came sombrely, holding himself aloof from the more humanly intimate aspects of Dionysian celebration.

From the few known facts about his life, we may learn much—and presume more—about the reasons for his becoming the first great dramatist of the world. He knew intimately the rituals and mysteries from which the drama developed; for his birthplace was Eleusis, and he doubtless dreamed over the impressive ceremonies there. He had been born of a noble family, in 525, and by 499 he is known to have competed in a dramatic contest. As a soldier he distinguished himself at Marathon and at Salamis, digging down into the depths of life as is the way of poet-philosophers gone to war. He was a traveller, too, and

The Theatre of Dionysus in Athens. One of the most famous in all history. The ruins as they survive are from a reconstruction during the Roman era, with raised stage and an orchestra cut down from the original full dancing circle.

several of his trips to far-away Sicily (where he produced some of his plays) are chronicled in contemporary records. For forty years his life was bound up intimately with the dramatic contests at the Great Dionysia in Athens and with the Theatre of Dionysus. Between 499 and 458, when the *Oresteia* was produced, he is supposed to have written ninety plays. Seven complete texts of his tragedies exist today. He won the tragic prize twelve times.

Those who have called Æschylus "the father of tragedy" had in mind not only his transcending poetic genius, by which he elevated the drama far above the level touched by his predecessors, but also his innovation in introducing a second actor. When there had been only a Chorus leader and one actor, conflict and dramatic structure had been possible within only a limited range. When Æschylus provided two actors (each capable of taking several parts successively, with change of mask and costume), he opened the way to elaboration of plot and characterization, and made the dialogue less a means of telling what had happened than a revelation of direct conflict.

Still, the earliest of his plays extant, *The Suppliants* (also the oldest Greek play that has been preserved), escapes but awkwardly out of the old limitations. It is compounded of a great deal of lyric poetry and a little dramatic action. More than half the lines are given to the Chorus, and in general the characters tell *about* what is done instead of doing it. The whole forms but a single episode rather than a chain of events with cause and effect and inevitability. The Suppliants are the fifty daughters of Danaus, King of Egypt, who have escaped into Argos, fleeing the fifty cousins who seek them in marriage. These Suppliant Maidens are the Chorus. Their leader and Danaus recount their flight and implore the gods for a favorable outcome. The King of Argos hears their petition for protection, hesitates, from fear of offending the gods or his people, goes out to consultations. Word is brought that decrees have been passed welcoming the fugitives. The ship of the pursuers is sighted and the Egyptian Herald comes to try to drive the Maidens back to the shore. But the King of Argos has arranged to take them within the city walls, and they file out of the orchestra, jubilant, going to the sought-for safety and protection. There is indeed action here in a small way—but what simplicity and slowness, what lack of suspense as compared with *Œdipus the King!* The values are largely in the lyric portions.

In the later plays of Æschylus there is growing dramatic elaboration, increase of conflict, greater theatricality. One of the finest of the tragedies, to be sure, *Prometheus Bound*, is very static: Prometheus is chained to a rock, in the first scene, as punishment for giving fire to mortals, and the rest of the play consists of his dialogue with the

Chorus and successive characters; till at the end he "vanishes." But conflict is implicit in the situation of a minor god who has defied Zeus. We may read here, indeed, a drama not without parallels to *Job*. And while the almost actionless play is a complete drama, the reader should remember that in the time of Æschylus each play was part of a related trilogy or tetralogy, and was presented with the others on a single programme.

But in the *Agamemnon* Æschylus has come to full-plotted and highly theatrical composition. The note of impending doom is sounded in the first speeches, and there is immediate joining of action. Clytemnestra has been unfaithful and now Agamemnon is coming home. As the action develops toward its climax and catastrophe, the speeches are long, the descriptive passages many. But here already is Greek tragic drama developed into its characteristic largeness, majesty, and inevitability. Nor is the poetry as such less telling; Clytemnestra is speaking, before her returned King, Agamemnon, who has given no sign that he knows her guilt:

> Ye Elders, Councils of the Argive name
> Here present, I will no more hold it shame
> To lay my passion bare before men's eyes.
> There comes a time to a woman when fear dies
> Forever. None hath taught me. None could tell,
> Save me, the weight of years intolerable,
> I lived while this man lay at Ilion.
> That any woman thus could sit alone
> In a half-empty house, with no man near,
> Makes her half-blind with dread! And in her ear
> Always some voice of wrath; now messengers
> Of evil; now not so . . .
>   Aye, many a time my heart broke, and the noose
> Of death had got me; but they cut me loose.
> It was those voices always in mine ear.
>
> . . . .
>
> From all which stress delivered and free-souled
> I greet my lord . . .

Agamemnon is the first of the plays forming the *Oresteia* trilogy; and there are many who hold the opinion that this group not only marks Æschylus' greatest accomplishment but also the supreme achievement in Greek tragic drama. There is an immensity of outline, a sweeping majesty of action, that is hardly to be matched in the later annals of the theatre; and with it a Miltonic greatness in the poetic garment, an austere, aloof beauty of language. But one may still find Sophocles the better craftsman, and Euripides the more sympathetic dramatist of human characters. Æschylus lived in a golden time, reflected perhaps a fineness and a simple dignity that were implicit in Greek life around him. There was a kindly faith then, linked with high purpose and a splendor of soul. Sophocles reflects more the polish of art in a later softer time; and in Euripides there is a restlessness, a questioning, that seems to grow out of the early decadence of Greek life.

Sophocles marked progress toward both stricter dramatic intensity and greater freedom of dialogue. He went on toward a more compact and articulated play structure; and he lost a little of Æschylus' austere beauty of line in favor of a freer, sweeter language. All this change is in perfect keeping with what we know of his life: that he was orderly, that he was universally loved for his good nature and sweetness, that he put great store by the graces of life. A nobility and stateliness of character were his; but he could not be so perfectly the flower of the Periclean Age, were not these attributes attuned more to the love of man and less to an Æschylean magnifying of the gods.

Sophocles was born in 495 B.C. He died in 406 B.C., and during his lifetime had written nearly a hundred plays. Seven remain with us in complete form today. He is reputed to have given up acting at an early age because his voice was weak; but of course he "produced" his plays as well as writing them. It was he who introduced the third actor into Greek tragedy.

As to the qualities of his playwriting, we may be content with *Œdipus the King* as a characteristic example. We have seen how perfectly this built up, in dramatic suspense and intensity, from opening to close; how the order of unfoldment is consummately handled for the holding of the spectator's attention; how each bit is tied in to the main structure, each scene, each thought, each lyric contributing to the stream of living action. Where Æschylus had hewn out gigantic designs—a bit "mad" he was, they say, when he came to the writing of a play—leaving rough edges for the sake of the larger impression, Sophocles was the perfect craftsman, gaining first his proportions, then his finer adjustments, and over all a harmony of expression. Unity, symmetry, convergence, order—these he understood beyond criticism. No one in the whole history of the theatre has surpassed him as theatric technician while still compassing great beauty. (As mere skilled workmen, the "well-made-play" people of the nineteenth century may have gone further in building a perfectly articulated play-frame, but they put little in that frame; and the realistic playwrights build as skilfully for sensation and shock—but there is in them little of serenity or high beauty.)

Œdipus the King is usually considered the masterpiece among Sophocles' works; and the excerpts I have quoted may stand for the quality of his poetic genius—as the outline must stand here for example of his play structure. Still it should be noted that others may prefer his *Antigone* or *Œdipus at Colonus* or *Ajax* or *Electra*. In the end, whichever plays one reads or sees produced, one will be stirred by the spectacle of man sorely tried in the grip of Destiny, man brave in the adventure of life, with a little of the divinity of those gods who make of him a plaything. And one should see always, in the mind's eye, the beauty of the Greek bowl-theatre, of the majestic acting, of the rhythmic Chorus movements; and should hear, in the mind's ear, the sonorities of poetic lines declaimed, chanted, in recitative. For these are theatre works, not just magnificent poetic stories.

He who long ago wrote, "I laud Æschylus, I read Euripides," indicated in a few words a difference that scholars have discussed in hundreds of weighty volumes. Æschylus probably has suffered later from the very splendor of his works; Euripides has gained from the intimacy and simple humanity of his.

Euripides was born in 480 B.C., only fifteen years after Sophocles; but he is invariably tagged as the representative of a different age— has even been called "the first modern." Some put down to temperament his great divergence from the traditional line, poetically, dramatically, as a thinker. Born less nobly than his great predecessors, he was intended first for an athlete, then seems to have tried painting. But he turned out a student and dramatist—he produced his first play at twenty-five—and always he lived apart from civic and social interests. His predilections were for meditation rather than for a part in the life of the times.

If we were to study carefully the history of the period, we should discover many background reasons why he portrayed human beings rather than human symbols in his dramas, why he ascribed malignant as well as divine traits to the gods, why his work ended often with a questioning of life. For just then a new skepticism was creeping over Hellas. The unquestioning prostration of man before fate, the blind glorification of the gods, was no longer demanded. There is ample reason to believe that Euripides had little belief in those gods; still he was forced to include them in his plays, for theatre production and theatre-going were a form of religious exercise. Well—then he would show the gods as they are. And humans too.

Another inference or conjecture is that the audiences he catered to were less cultivated than of old. He must touch them more closely to hold their interest. They no longer listened for the traditional beauties of the chanted word, for the interpolated pæans to gods; they no longer counted beauty of eurhythmic movement a prime ingredient of drama. They must see, hear, and suffer with beings like themselves.

And so Euripides humanized the drama. Perhaps after all he did it out of the pity in his own heart; but there it is, a drama throbbing with human sorrow, with sympathy. It is no part of our present plan to inquire into the æsthetics of the matter: whether the austerity and elevation of earlier tragedy are preferable to that which is character- ized rather by pathos. Euripides has been severely censured by purists —and yet most people, while they praise Æschylus, read Euripides. His works are closer to us.

He introduced some expedients that are easily challenged. His pro- logues seem sometimes like too-easy solutions of the problem of put- ting background facts before audiences. And his *deus ex machina*, brought in arbitrarily to solve the knotty problem of the drama, is clearly illogical, a trick. And there is not here Sophocles' sense of pro- portion and harmony, nor his inevitability.

Still, *popularly*, Euripides was the favorite Athenian dramatist at the end of his life and after. He stirred up more of criticism and opposi- tion, but his questioning of gods and his portrayal of pitiable men were eagerly awaited and hailed. It is easy to see how *The Trojan Women*, picturing terribly the horrors of war, and the sorrows following thereon, would move a Greek audience—as, indeed, it has moved many of us in very recent times. His introduction of love, a terrible illicit love, in *Hippolytus*, would startle the Athenian audience because no such human story had ever been acted out before in a theatre. And his study of *Medea*, the spurned strong woman, her love turned to hate, murdering her own children to have revenge on her lord—there had never been a character portrait like that before.

The stage building at Oropus, as conjecturally restored by E. R. Fiechter. [From Fiechter's *Die Baugeschichtliche Entwicklung des Antiken Theaters*.]

Still, Athens as a whole was not ready for playwrights who publicly criticized war, who showed up the gods as petty and abominable, who fought for the underdog, no matter who was thereby wounded. The judges at the contests awarded him only five prizes—out of ninety-two plays presented. And finally the uneasiness over his unorthodoxy crystallized into a decree of exile. Even the great dramatists were not safe from the fickle censure of the volatile audiences that gathered in the Theatre of Dionysus. Once spectators had thought that Æschylus revealed too much of the secrets of religious mysteries, in a play production, and to save his life he had been forced to take refuge at the altar of Dionysus in the centre of the orchestra, an inviolate sanctuary. (It is said that when he was tried later for the offence, it was his fame as a gallant soldier, not as a dramatist, that won his acquittal.) The earlier tragedian, Phrynichus, in a play called *The Capture of Miletus*, had so stirred bitter recollections in the hearts of the spectators that he was fined a thousand drachmas, while a law was passed forbidding further dramas on the subject. Euripides had seen his plays stormily received more than once. And finally he was driven from Athens altogether. His services to his city were not at an end, for it is recorded that the people were wont to sing his choruses in the street, and that when the Spartans were about to burn Athens they were reminded by a snatch of song that this was Euripides' city and refrained.

His last play—not quite finished, indeed—was written during exile; and to the fact have been attributed certain sentiments in it, and an increased tendency to brood on the problems of life. It is from this drama, *The Bacchæ*, that I shall take those quotations which will, I hope, indicate how Euripides carried on the noble tradition, and how he departed from it to attain to other excellencies. He made his lyric choruses such gem-like insets as no poet had achieved before him:

CHORUS OF MAIDENS

Will they ever come to me, ever again,
  The long long dances,
On through the dark till the dim stars wane?
Shall I feel the dew on my throat, and the stream
Of wind in my hair? Shall our white feet gleam
  In the dim expanses?
Oh, feet of a fawn to the greenwood fled,
  Alone in the grass and the loveliness;
Leap of the hunted, no more in dread,
  Beyond the snares and the deadly press:
Yet a voice still in the distance sounds,
A voice and a fear and a haste of hounds;
O wildly laboring, fiercely fleet,
  Onward yet by river and glen . . .

LEADER

Happy he, on the weary sea
Who hath fled the tempest and won the haven.
Happy who so hath risen, free,
Above his striving. For strangely graven
  Is the orb of life, that one and another
  In gold and power may outpass his brother.
And men in their millions float and flow
And seethe with a million hopes as leaven;
  And they win their Will, or they miss their Will.
And the hopes are dead or are pined for still;
    But whoe'er can know,
    As the long days go,
That to live is happy, hath found his Heaven!

But he was no less master of the line that carried along the action. We
have seen in *Œdipus the King* how the murder, suicide, or other violence too sensational for human eyes is accomplished offstage—an invariable rule in Greek tragedy—and how a messenger recounts the
event (often with the most moving effectiveness). In *The Bacchæ* the
Messenger is telling how the luckless Pentheus intruded on the Bacchantes:

Then came the Voice again. And when they knew
Their God's clear call, old Cadmus' royal brood,
Up, like wild pigeons startled in a wood,
On flying feet they came, his mother blind
Agâvê, and her sisters, and behind
All the wild crowd, more deeply maddened then,
Through the angry rocks and torrent-tossing glen,
Until they spied him in the dark pine-tree.
                    . . . 'Twas his mother stood
O'er him, first priestess of those rites of blood.
He tore the coif, and from his head away
Flung it, that she might know him, and not slay
To her own misery. He touched the wild
Cheek, crying: "Mother, it is I, thy child,
Thy Pentheus, born thee in Echîon's hall!

Have mercy, Mother! Let it not befall
Through sin of mine that thou shouldst slay thy son!"
  But she, with lips a-foam and eyes that run
Like leaping fire, with thoughts that ne'er should be
On earth, possessed by Bacchios utterly,
Stays not nor hears. Round his left arm she put
Both hands, set hard against his side her foot,
Drew . . . and the shoulder severed! . . .

It is fitting perhaps that our brief study of the great Greek dramatists should end with the closing lines of Euripides' last play; for they are spoken by the Chorus, that typically Greek theatric "character," and they show how the religious-fateful spirit had persisted through the golden and silver ages—and they occur in a play which goes back for its subject-matter to the legends of Dionysus, to whose glory the theatre had been created:

CHORUS
There be many shapes of mystery.
And many things God makes to be,
    Past hope or fear.
And the end men looked for cometh not,
And a path is there where no man thought.
    So hath it fallen here.

Or is it better to end finally on the *human* note of Euripides' work, as a foreshadowing of the future? For he rebelliously tinged high art with realism. Mrs. Browning summed up our love of him:

Our Euripides, the human,
    With his droppings of warm tears,
And his touches of things common
    Till they rose to touch the spheres.

WHEN one knows the distinctiveness of Greek tragedy, and has tasted the works of Æschylus, Sophocles, and Euripides—and has met Aristophanes in comedy—one has the essentials of the Greek drama. Reserving, then, all consideration of comedy for another chapter, we have only the lesser facts about the tragic theatre to explore: the changes in the "playhouse" and in methods of production during the later periods and decline of Greek drama.

There were a great many tragic poets, to be sure, besides those three who stand before the world as the Greek masters. Some are known only because their names are chronicled as contestants in the annual festivals, others from chance references or from extracts quoted by later grammarians. But the general reader, even the student of theatre history if he is not specializing on the Greek period, need not burden his memory with further names. He should know merely that the great tragedies were endlessly imitated. For five or six centuries the contests were continued, and new plays were offered as late as the Roman Hadrian's reign in the second century A.D. After the great fifth century B.C., revivals of the early masterpieces became commoner, and in the third century customary. As time went on, the festivals of Dionysus in other cities or towns drew on the treasury of Athenian drama, and the more significant plays were thus shown time and again. As early as 472 B.C., Æschylus presented at Syracuse in Sicily the plays with which he had won the tragedy contest at Athens the year before.

Eventually troupes of players went out to provincial celebrations to present the more "popular" dramas. These "artists of Dionysus" may be considered the first players' guild—or "actors' union." When the Roman theatre had been securely founded, the Greek tragedies were given in Rome, both in the original tongue and in translation; and eventually the plays of the master dramatists were heard through the vast territory of the new Roman Empire as well as in the old Greek colonial cities. In Athens itself productions are recorded as late as the fifth century A.D.

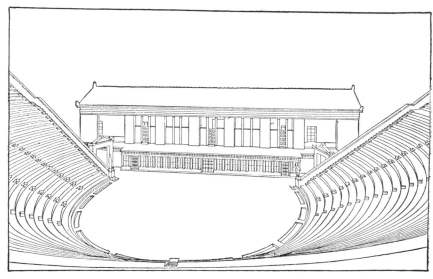

The theatre at Ephesus in Hellenistic times, as reconstructed by Fiechter. Note that the orchestra is still large but that the platform stage is added. A transitional example, between true Greek and Roman types.

Thus within a century of the birth of drama, Athens had claimed a group of dramatists who stand in the small company of stage immortals: Greek life had come to full expression in the religious-artistic compositions of three playwrights, in whose work is the very flowering of Hellenic civilization and genius; whereas the Greek theatre for eight or nine centuries after their era subsisted on dramas wholly inferior or on revivals of the works of these masters.

The Greek physical playhouse, however, continued its development throughout the decadent period of drama, toward that Greek-Roman form which was a direct forerunner of the Renaissance theatre, and unmistakably ancestor of the theatre of today. In the golden age of

Greek playwriting, it had been a comparatively simple arrangement of ringed seats, flat space for choral movement and acting, and a low porticoed *skene* at the back. The auditorium and *skene* were separated by wide entries, and the whole layout had an openness which was never again to be characteristic of theatre building.

Gradually, however, the dancing-space, the orchestra, was contracted, and the stage building brought in closer, enlarged, made more important. Finally the top of the portico became a platform stage, added to the orchestra for acting, and behind it the second story of the *skene* began to be elaborated toward that immense stage wall which is so typical of Greek-Roman and Roman theatres.

There is no example that can be called the typical Greek or the typical Roman playhouse; designing of the buildings was always subject to local conditions and to changing demands of the play-producers. But when the platform stage had been added, the theatre exhibited those features considered fundamental to theatre building in all later eras; features whose arrangement in relation one to another determine the world's general grouping of theatres into named types. The auditorium (*theatron*) or place for seeing; the *orchestra*, at first the place for dancing and acting, then dividing that function with the stage, and ultimately to be contracted and absorbed into the auditorium; the *stage*, at first a mere platform for lifting the actors into view, but in later times to become the floor of a stage-box; and the scene, at first a stage building beside the dancing circle (the word *skene* meant merely hut or tent), then more strictly the wall behind the platform stage, neutrally architectural but increasingly ornamental. (When the stage is finally pushed through an opening in the wall, the term "scene" will be transferred to the picture surrounding the acting space, within the stage-box—but that will be long after classic times.)

There was so little "scenery" in the Greek orchestra, or on the Greek stage, that more than brief mention of the subject would be unwarranted. For a very long time scholars took for granted that the Greeks utilized painted settings. But no contemporary descriptions survive, and most scholars today agree that conjecture and misreading of vague references alone bolstered the idea of elaborate Greek scenery. If painted settings existed, it seems likely that they were merely architectural façades painted in to save the greater expense of building a composition of columns, pilasters, niches, etc. In other words the background remained wholly neutral and conventional. There was no attempt at illusion in setting. The poet's words accomplished any necessary shift in *milieu*.

In the decadent Greek theatre, when the influence of Roman love of spectacle had crept in, the story may have been different. In the same way stage machinery for "effects" doubtless multiplied in Roman times. And there is evidence that at least one machine, a crane for the ascent or descent of the gods or humans, was introduced quite early. This was apparently rigged in such a way that an actor could be lifted from the orchestra or stage-platform to the top of the scene-building. It is supposed that Euripides utilized the device—whence the phrase

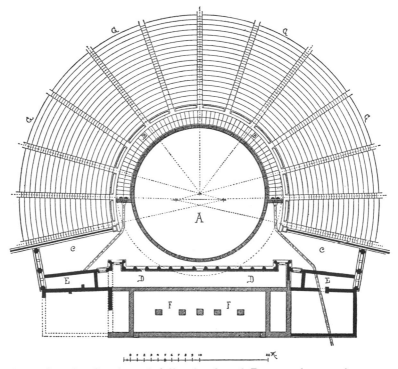

Plans of early Greek and fully developed Roman theatres in contrast. Above, the theatre at Epidauros, sixth-fifth centuries B.C. Opposite, the Theatre of Marcellus in Rome, first century A.D. (From *Das Antike Theater* by Eduard Moritz.)

deus ex machina—but it is in Aristophanes that the chief evidence is found. It is obvious that the comedy-writers would grasp at the opportunities for fun-making in any such crude and mechanical aid to tragic drama; and we are not surprised, in *The Clouds*, to find Socrates suspended in a basket half-way between heaven and earth, reading philosophy.

There is less evidence about a machine called the *eccyclema*, though more need for it, judging by the internal evidence of the plays. It is supposed to have been a revolving platform, designed to be swung out through the central portal of the *skene*, on which actors could be shown in "tableau." In tragic drama the murder scene in Æschylus' *Agamemnon* is usually instanced: the slaying is, of course, committed offstage, and then Clytemnestra is shown standing over the dead bodies of Agamemnon and Cassandra. This group is conjectured to have been wheeled out suddenly by means of the sliding or revolving platform.

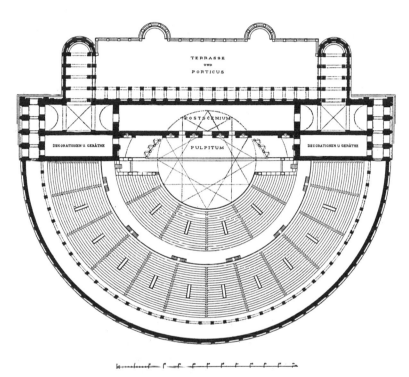

Just as all these matters of playhouse form, scenery, and machines have been subjects for controversy, so the question of the mode of acting in the great fifth century has been debated, cursed about, and endlessly written about in recent years. And here again opinion has radically changed within a generation. For it turns out that evidence about the cothurnus-boot, about extravagantly stuffed-out costumes, and about huge masks, belongs all to a later time. It now seems likely that the human figure was little exaggerated in size in the Æschylus-Euripides period, though it was richly costumed, and that the masks were not then the grotesque and high-built affairs pictured in late Greek and Roman paintings and sculptures. Acting was doubtless artificial and declamatory, but we may best imagine it as stately, free-moving if slow-moving, and not at all incapable of naturally affecting moments. The mask (necessary because an actor often impersonated several characters successively in one play, if for no other more subtle reason) made facial play impossible.

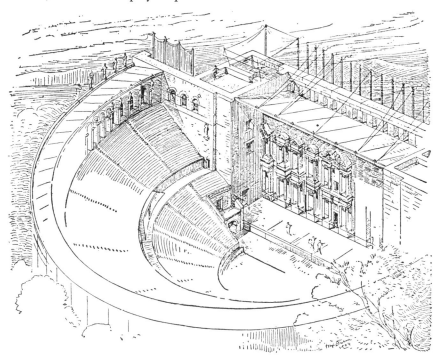

Reconstruction of the Roman theatre at Aspendus, showing the true Roman bowl-like form. Note the contracted orchestra, the large raised stage, and richly decorated stage wall. [From Durm's *Baukunst der Römer*.]

The mask was a convention, a symbol or an abstraction of the emotion chiefly associated with the character. One who has studied masks may feel sure that a certain range of expression is possible, through the turning of the mask to catch the light in different ways, through the movement of the head, etc. But the adoption of the device is a deliberate limitation of intimate human expression in one direction to gain broader, perhaps more god-like values in another. We may vision the Greek actor developing a language of gesture and movement far more expressive than any on the stages of today; and in our imaginative ears we may hear him speaking, chanting, singing, through a range of "recitative" quite beyond the capabilities of modern players. There is evidence enough that acting was an art which exacted lifelong study and devotion, and that shades of expressiveness were diligently sought after.

Acting had become a recognized profession even in the time of Æschylus, and grew in importance through the fifth century. After the decline of playwriting, acting was still further elevated as a separate art, until the contests of actors came to be considered more important than those of the dramatists. The Actors' Guild became a

Greek statuette of a tragic actor. Note the mask and the rich costume. (But the blocks below the feet are not cothurnus-boots, as once believed, but merely the pegs by which the statuette was fixed into a base.) [From *Le Théâtre Grec*, by Octave Navarre.]

powerful economic and social organization, and members enjoyed special privileges, as religious workers.

As the drama declined, the Chorus receded in importance. It had been the connecting link between pre-theatric revels and full literary drama. The interludes of music, poetry, and "dance" that it provided were an enrichment of the dramatic design through the time of Euripides. The tragic tension seemed to demand these let-downs—like our entr'actes, but with an added value. The Chorus moved in procession or mass formation, rhythmically, harmoniously, as a visual re-enforcement of the meaning of the choral odes. The words were chanted or sung. In sense they were a comment on the action to come or a supplication to the gods, or a lyric decoration. Throughout the great period they added to the emotion aroused by the action; or perhaps it is better to say that they deepened the emotion while offering relief from the stormier heights of the action. We have seen how in Æschylus' first play the Chorus claimed attention more than half the time—survival from the period when the drama formed the interludes, and the dancing-singing the main design. We have seen too how Euripides imbedded the most beautiful lyrics in his plays, for the Chorus; but we should note that these were put in more like added decoration than had been the case with Æschylus and Sophocles. And indeed, one infers that Euripides added odes as a matter of custom and tradition,

Mask sculptured on a terra cotta plate. From Myrina. Hellenistic. [By courtesy of the Museum of Fine Arts, Boston.]

without any conviction that they belonged to his dramatic structure which unfolded the fortunes of human beings. From that time the Chorus was unnecessary to drama. The Chorus Leader had been one of the chief actors ever since Thespis added the first player to bandy words with him. But now we shall never meet him again—although in later-day expositors, prologue-speakers, *premières danseuses*, and endmen, we may find certain of his duties performed.

Some pages back mention was made of the Choregus, the financier back of play-production. Athens developed a system under which a wealthy citizen could be called on to produce the play-programme of a certain poet, bearing most of the expense of the performance. If his poet was successful in winning the contest, the Choregus was crowned and shared the honor with his dramatist. He helped the dramatist to pick the actors and chorus members, paid salaries to cast, musicians, trainers, etc., and provided costumes. But as he was thus sharing with the actual theatre-workers in religious service, he seems to have been content.

The touch of the ridiculous that always followed the sublime experience of the tragedy productions in Athens is to be found in the satyr-plays. Each programme on each of the three days dedicated to the tragic contests included three tragedies and a satyr-drama. Thus all the great dramatists were forced to write these burlesque and apparently licentious pieces. Comedy had long ago gone its separate way and had crystallized into a set form. Perhaps neither tragedy nor comedy seemed to the Athenians to carry on directly the traditions of the old Dionysian phallic-revels. At any rate, the satyr-drama survived as a separate entity through the entire fifth century. The invariable central

Masks for satyr-plays. [From *Dissertatio de Larvis Scenicis*, by F. Ficoronius.]

feature was the Chorus of Satyrs, hairy fellows with horns, tails, and phalluses, who could be relied upon to convulse any audience by their antics. For the rest there seems to have been the strangest mixture of heroics and buffoonery. Sometimes the tragedies would be followed by one of these ludicrous burlesques in which the very same protagonists, heroes and kings, would be seen from a comic angle, brought down to the grotesque and often indecent by-play of rough-and-tumble farceurs.

Today the juxtaposition of the two extremes, the noblest tragedy the world has ever known and farces physically licentious, seems inexplicable unless, perchance, we remember that Dionysus had two sides, that if the divine ecstasy that he evoked might well lead over from song, dance, and music to serene drama, the wildness of him might lead away in another direction to loose dance and mimicry. The satyr-drama was the old phallic dance—so appropriate to the god of wine and of fruitfulness—made dramatic but not elevated. The Athenians were loath to leave out of the Dionysia anything so perfectly expressive of that so-beloved god. Besides, the god himself might not like it if his satyrs were discarded.

Roman tragedy was never more than an adulteration of the Greek. The only name that is accounted worth remembering out of the thirty-odd known Latin tragedy-writers is that of Seneca; and his are the only plays preserved. They have achieved world-wide fame less for inherent virtues than for the influence they exerted in later eras as models for successive groups of Neoclassicists.

Seneca lived in a time when simplicity and serene splendor had gone out of the Western world. In the first century of the Christian era, in the reigns of Caligula and Claudius and Nero, a man who was politician, Senator, Consul, lover to empresses, philosopher, and a prolific writer in many fields, would have little chance to compass the high beauty of Æschylus or the brooding human pathos of Euripides. There was brilliancy in the time and a brilliancy in Seneca—but it was wholly a surface quality. He rewrote in drama the old tragic stories of Œdipus and Medea and Agamemnon; but the Greek elevation of feeling is gone, sincerity has fled, poetry is lost in rhetoric. Life has gone out of tragedy; the characters are vehicles to carry moral ideas, the action is violent, the verse is shaped to the uses of exaggerated declamation.

This is florid, even dull art, full of bombast and mannerism; and yet for a period covering centuries it was esteemed as the supreme body of tragedy in the world's dramatic literature, above Æschylus, Sophocles, and Euripides. It is doubtful whether these rhetorical tragedies were ever produced in the "regular," the popular theatres at Rome: those turbulent audiences would hardly relish the long didactic speeches, the overload of ornament and the slow action. But there they are, a curiosity of the world stage, important because Italian and French critics of the Renaissance almost persuaded the whole Western world that tragedy must remain Senecan for all time.

Tragedy was never again to be quite as monumental, as serenely splendid, as soul-cleansing, as it was in the fifth century before Christ. A further extension of *humanity* is to grace it in Shakespeare's time, and gloriously fine poetry; but there are those who will tell you that in turning away from Greek tragedy we are setting our backs upon the finest that the tragic stage has known.

CHAPTER
4

Comedy:
Greece and Rome

I F WE had been in the audience at the Theatre of Dionysus on
that spring day in 423 B.C. when an actor impersonating Socrates was suspended in a basket midway between the earth of the orchestra and the heaven of the proscenium-top, we might have found in the
episode a key to the understanding of a broader truth about Greek
comedy; in short, that this was a drama of action and of situation, not
of character-conflict. If we had heard declaimed those lines in the play
that portrayed the great Socrates as little better than a quack-philoso-
pher and mischief-maker, we might have inferred, quite justly, that
caricature and personalities made up a generous part of what little
"characterization" there was in Old Comedy. (If a none-too-well-
authenticated legend is accurate, we might also have seen the real Socrates—so like a comic actor, with his pot-belly and his jovial satyr-face
—rise up among us and stand for the crowd to look at, to show that
he too enjoyed his caricature.)

That same day we should have witnessed, too, a production of *The
Wine-Flagon* by Cratinus, which won the prize over Aristophanes'
The Clouds: a play doubtless well suited to the Dionysian Festival, in
which the respective virtues of wine-bibbers and water-drinkers were
(none too solemnly) explored. We may imagine how the fun of drunkenness was capitalized there. The following year we could have witnessed at the Lenæa a production of Aristophanes' *The Wasps*, and at
other times *The Birds* and *The Frogs*, each with its Chorus appropriately dressed, and coached to all the comic antics that could be built

71

on the imitation of wasp and bird and frog; from which we might have been convinced that comedy, even after Euripides' death, had not advanced so very far from the old masquerade processionals of vulgar phallic-revellers. In these several plays, moreover, we might have marked in the dialogue not a little of ribald jest and downright dirty allusion; for vomitings and bedbugs and manure-heaps and worse supplied some of the motives now bound up with custard-pies, bladders, and banana-peels, and the mention of mothers-in-law; and the triangle relationship was handled not with delicacy but with Rabelaisian heartiness.

Out of such materials was the comedy of the fifth century compounded, with little continuity, less inevitability, and no serious character-drawing. From which you will judge, dear reader, that the Athenians did not have "high" comedy.

Greek comic actor. Hellenistic terra cotta figure from Myrina. [In the Museum of Fine Arts, Boston.]

If we distinguish "high tragedy" from a less elevated sort, we must grant that the Greeks were masters beyond all others. They lift the reader or spectator, they kindle the imagination, open the gates to a divine pity, light up the soul, exalt the emotions in sorrow—and leave one cleansed. With orderly action and noble poetry they lead us through from a beginning expectancy to a radiant satisfaction. Someone has said that any petty playwright can agitate the soul, but only a master of tragedy can exalt it—and the saying is one to be remembered as we progress from Greek drama to modern realistic play; and exaltation is the key-note of fifth century tragic drama. This was indeed "high" tragedy.

But in comedy, where we are told that the test of the best is "thoughtful laughter," and that seriously important comedy grows out of logical character-development, we can only mark the Greek sort as *low*. It never in all its history rose to unity of feeling, sustained satire, or sympathetic tilting at the foibles of human character. So far as we know it at first hand, in surviving texts and fragments, and in pictures, it retained the more vulgar, violent, and farcical elements out of the fathering comus-revels. During the "great" period of Athens it paralleled modern burlesque and musical comedy closer than modern legitimate comedy.

Remembering the singing, joshing bands of revellers that used to celebrate Dionysus at the seasonal festivals, bantering back and forth, carrying the wine-jars and the phallus, dressed up in outlandish costumes and masks, we may see how these marchers became a "Chorus"; and how, either through a leader stepping out to impersonate or a clown or mime joining the group, comic repartee was born. The

Comedy masks. [From Ficoronius.]

dressed-up revellers were common to many festivals in many places, but somewhere their impromptu celebration—or masquerade—came to be called a "comus"; and when the dramatic element had entered, the name "comedy"—comus-ode or "revel-song"—was passed on to designate amusing drama for all time.

The roots of *Athenian* comedy are obscure; the comus-performances seem to have been brought to Athens in the first half of the sixth century, but it is uncertain which villages or districts gave this or that ingredient or influence. It is only certain that phallic processions were at the source of it, that the more obvious costume elements—disguises as birds, animals, etc.—and the masks persisted in the comedy-choruses, that the celebration found its way from the sacred groves and the town streets into the theatre; and that there the outward form already assumed by tragedy (dialogue with choral and lyric interludes and dances) influenced it toward the structure we find in Aristophanes' plays. The actor, some say, was a Dorian clown; others, that he simply developed out of being the wittiest and loudest shouter among the revellers.

Before Aristophanes, who we may feel was coarse enough, in all conscience, the Dionysian comedy went through some sort of refining process. The Chorus was organized until it had the set number of twenty-four members; a loose continuity was adopted, from prologue to *exodus*, with action-scenes and lyrics alternating between; and a point was established at which a contest or debate was added, and another at which a *parabasis* or author's speech was set in. Plot, or something approaching it, was introduced. As the dramatic scenes gained in relative importance, over mere processional and song, sketches and "turns" like those in our vaudeville were increasingly added, or travesties and comic dialogues like those in our revues. Until, when "contests" in comedy were instituted, with three dramatists each offering a group of three compositions, the thing now known as "Old Comedy" was as much a set form as was composed choral tragedy.

Even before Aristophanes, in the works of Cratinus and Eupolis, comedy came to have purpose. It might be political satire, or travesty on a literary or social figure, or ridicule of a cult—and in this direction the violence of the attack, the intensely personal invective, the wildness of the charges, seem to us to go beyond the bounds of reason. Of course this was understood to be farce and foolery, where truth was stood on its head. The gods themselves were caricatured; and a demi-god like Heracles might afford great fun when brought on drunk. But constantly through the framework of satire and purposeful ridicule obtruded those older buffoon elements, the grotesque parades, the licentious dances, the mere monkey-shines. And—sometimes these obtrusive and little-related elements or snatches of satire were lifted to the realm of stirring poetry or imaginative incident.

It is there that Aristophanes comes in. It is not the "thought" or the incisive parody in his works that is generally important—indeed he shows himself a good deal of a reactionary in his plays, sighing vaguely for the good old days, and damning progressive tendencies along with the precious posing cults. But he was a poet, and his lyrics are often of surpassing charm, and his imagination often carried him out on amazing flights; he had, moreover, a masterly touch at light verse, wherein he seasoned with wit the flowing lines and passing pictures. He by no means escaped the "gigantic indecency of Old Comedy," and his graceful verse turns easily into channels of brutal caricature and heavy buffoonery. But by grace of a poet's gifts he rose above all his fellow dramatists in his own time, and has been a touchstone down the ages. "Aristophanic" is the term we still use for witty and biting comedy clothed in free-flowing verse.

It happens that eleven of Aristophanes' plays are the only complete comedies that have survived to us from Greek literature, out of thousands written by scores of authors. He is credited with more than fifty plays in all. He lived from about 448 to 385 B.C.

Roman comic actors. [From Ficoronius.]

As an example of the structure of Old Comedy, we may take *The Wasps*, which Aristophanes brought out at the Lenæa in 422, probably receiving the first prize for it. The immediate subject-matter is the Athenian jury-system, but the attack is aimed at Cleon, the demagogue to whom the "jurors" were politically bound. Philocleon is an inveterate jury-server; but Bdelycleon is trying to break up his mania by keeping Philocleon imprisoned in his house. The door is guarded by two slaves, but the prisoner almost escapes by one ruse or another, crawling out windows or chimneys or along the roof, or hanging under the belly of a donkey. He is aided by the Chorus, his fellow jury-maniacs, who are symbolically dressed as Wasps. The action is interrupted by the "contest," a debate for and against the dignity and importance of jury-sitting. The Chorus is convinced by Bdelycleon's arguments, but Philocleon is heartbroken at the prospect of giving up his pleasures of the court-room. So Bdeylcleon arranges for him to have a trial at home. A dog is tried for stealing a cheese; and is acquitted by a trick, to the horror of Philocleon. The *parabasis* is now introduced, in which Aristophanes takes the audience to task, reviews his life as playwright and explains points about the present play. The chief characters go off to a feast and drinking party. After a choral interlude Philocleon comes back drunk. He is pursued by other guests who bring charges of abuse against him; and particularly he is threatened with action for carrying away the flute-girl from the feast. But now Philocleon believes no longer in law-courts and juries.

Thirteen terra cotta statuettes of actors, found in a single grave in Athens. Of the period of Greek Old Comedy. [In the Metropolitan Museum of Art, New York.]

PHILOCLEON

Yah! Hah! summon and cite!
The obsolete notion! Don't you know
I'm sick of the names of your suits and claims.
　Faugh! Faugh! Pheugh!
　Here's my delight!
Away with the verdict-box! . . .
　　　　　　　Mount up, my dear.
See now, how cleverly I fetched you off,
A wanton hussy, flirting with the guests.
You owe me, child, some gratitude for that . . .
Be a good girl and don't be disobliging,
And when my son is dead, I'll ransom you,
And make you an honest woman. For indeed
I'm not yet master of my own affairs.

I am so young and kept so very strict.
My son's my guardian, such a cross-grained man,
A cummin-splitting, mustard-scraping fellow . . .

BDELYCLEON

You! there! You there! You old lascivious dotard!
Enamored, eh? Ay, of a fine ripe coffin.
Oh, by Apollo, you shall smart for this!

PHILOCLEON

Dear, dear, how keen to taste a suit in pickle!

BDELYCLEON

No quizzing, sir, when you have filched away
The flute-girl from our party.

PHILOCLEON

Eh? What? flute-girl?
You're out of your mind, or out of your grave, or something.

And so on. One of them claims this is the flute-girl beside them, the other that it's only a torch; they examine the girl to make sure. They set to dancing, and the Chorus ends the action by dancing out of the orchestra after Philocleon, singing:

Come draw we aside, and leave them a wide, a roomy and peaceable
  exercise ground,
That before us therein like tops they may spin, revolving and whirling
  and twirling around . . .
On, on, in mazy circles; hit your stomach with your heel;
Fling legs aloft to heaven, as like spinning tops you wheel . . .
For never yet, I warrant, has an actor till today
Led out a chorus, dancing, at the ending of the play.

There are comedies of Aristophanes that would illustrate better his imaginative reach—*The Birds* and *The Frogs* in particular; and it would be unfair to go on without quoting a few lines of his more felicitous choral lyrics. In *The Peace* there is the understanding eulogy of country life:

Ah, there's nothing half so sweet as when the seed is in the ground,
God a gracious rain is sending, and a neighbor saunters round . . .

Then we'll sit and drink together,
God the while refreshing, blessing
All the labors of our hands.

Oh, to watch the grape of Lemnos
Swelling out its purple skin,
When the merry little warblings
Of the Chirruper begin . . .

One might quote almost endlessly from the pleasant jingles in the eleven plays, and vary the fare acceptably with a serious ode here, a serenade there, or a rollicking song. That would indicate the comic richness—and quite rightly suggest that the richness is patchy. But only the reading of complete plays can convey the variety and spice that kept the festival audiences in gales of laughter. The very freedom of the play form permitted an exuberance and an extravagant fancy seldom again enjoyed in comedy. The slap-stick elements later descended into farce, while the poetic felicity and the satirical elements were carried up and into the dignified realm of thoughtful comedy. It may be added that we have in English a series of exceptionally spirited and understanding translations of Aristophanes' plays, by Benjamin Bickley Rogers (from which the excerpts here are taken).

Of the conditions of representation in the time of Aristophanes, there is scant authentic information. Here, as in tragedy, the actors all were men. Their costumes were extravagantly unreal, fanciful, or grotesque. The vase-paintings indicate a common use of animal disguises in the Choruses. The actor's figure was heavily padded out, on the stomach in front and lower down behind. A phallus was commonly

A musician and a chorus of six masked actors: three horsemen and three horses. Drawing by Mel Klapholz after a painting on a vase in the Berlin State Museum. Attica, about 650 B.C.

worn. Actors and Chorus were masked, and here grotesqueness seems to have been carried to extremes. Where an actor impersonated a well-known person—like Socrates in *The Clouds* or Euripides in *The Frogs* —the mask would be a recognizable caricature. Elsewhere a wild fancy reigned. The wide mouth in certain of the masks indicates the use of a sort of short megaphone, built in to aid the actor in making his voice carry to the uppermost rows of the vast auditoriums. In certain theatres of this or a slightly later time, there was a raised platform stage (perhaps not in Athens, perhaps only in the Italian provinces at first—and perhaps not in the "regular" theatres at all, but only where comedy stages were improvised for fairs or street productions).

So much we know from the small sculptures and the vase-paintings that have been preserved. But there is nowhere a description of the complete theatres, or of stage settings, or of the choral manœuvers. Nor do we know more than the meagrest facts about the music that was so important a feature of early comedy.

There is equally a gap in our first-hand knowledge of the literary form of comedy after Aristophanes, for no complete texts have survived. For more than a half-century a transitional type flourished which has sometimes been termed Middle Comedy. At this time the plays became less topical, less extravagant—and less insulting. While men in the public eye might be butts, and while social or political movements might be parodied, it was rather home life or street life that provided the comic materials; and the type characters that we shall meet down into Renaissance times were introduced: the parasites and the testy fathers and the cunning slaves, the procuress and the country bumpkin. The Chorus was set back into a minor position, as interlude; the debate and the *parabasis* were shorn off the play-frame; and with these changes, of course, vanished the lyric beauty of true Aristophanic comedy. What may be called the ballet-burlesque elements disappeared too. Comedy gained in dramatic continuity, in plot-complexity, in human interest. But the old grotesque farcical masks persisted.

Menander, chief dramatist of the New Comedy, who lived from 342 to 291 B.C., crystallized playwriting into a new mode. He picked up the Middle Comedy where its thirty-nine more or less obscure practitioners had left it, and he gained something also out of Euripidean tragedy. He is the culminating figure in the late Greek theatre.

Euripides, you will remember, had brought tragedy down from the regions of gods and legendary heroes to a preoccupation with human emotion. Comedy was now ready to abandon its old irresponsible gaiety and extravagance, to be curbed with the bridle of unified human story. Menander made plays that obviously dealt with real everyday life; characters might still be types rather than individualized human

The Greek dramatist Menander examining masks. Of the period of the New Comedy. [A marble relief in the Art Museum, Princeton University.]

beings, but types that you might meet just around the corner; plotting became an art; even a certain sentiment and pathos were introduced. In short, here was a long stride toward modern character-comedy.

Though the names of sixty-four writers of the New Comedy are known, not a play-text in the mode has survived. Reports agree that Menander was head-and-shoulders the outstanding practitioner. He achieved a further fame from the imitations or adaptations of his comedies left to us by the Romans Plautus and Terence. From these have been gained most of our knowledge of the New Comedy. Scholars are always hoping that a text of Menander will be turned up out of the sands of Egypt or a Greek tomb.[1] If so, we may find that Aristophanes is not the only superlatively great name to be remembered out of the Greek comic theatre.

---

[1] This near-miracle did happen. Recently—out of the sands of Egypt—a papyrus was recovered, with the complete text of the *Dyskolos*. But the scholars, after assessing the play, have been puzzled because it did little to explain the reputation of Menander as supreme master of Greek New Comedy. Perhaps just a lesser work. . . .

ROMAN comedy, insofar as it took lasting literary form, was hardly more than a reflection or survival of Greek types, with only minor native elements; and it is a question whether the more "serious" comedy ever found its way deeply into the affections of the Roman people. The really popular forms were those that we would term "slap-stick" —without continuity, and with the elemental appeal of knockabout antics, raw jests, and banana-peel episodes. It seems worth while, then, to go back to the several sources of popular farce, before looking for real Roman comedy.

Comic actor seated on altar. Greco-Roman bronze figure, probably portraying a character in a play by Plautus of the third century B.C. [In the Art Museum, Princeton University.]

Although there was little connection between religion and drama at Rome in any known period, the first introduction of actors into the city occurred in 364 B.C. as an attempt to propitiate the gods who just then were inflicting a pestilence upon the people. In nearby Etruria a form of drama already had been developed out of the rituals of an agricultural people honoring rural gods at harvest and vintage time, or celebrating festivals of marriage, birth, etc. The Etruscans had paralleled the Athenian progression from mere processional with singing and dancing to responsive improvisation, and then to separation of actor or actors from the main body of celebrants.

The earlier of two distinctive Etrurian forms, known as the Fescennine Verses, may have been hardly more than a chant at first, but de-

veloped into a sort of counter-play, with ample opportunity for interpolated dialogue, jest, and banter. It was a farcical, half-improvised
amusement form, elaborated casually from group revelry. The word
"Fescennine," according to some, comes from *Fescennium*, the name
of an Etrurian village where the entertainments may have originated,
or according to others, from *Fascinum*, a phallic symbol. If one accepts
the latter view, there is again a remarkable parallel to the dramatic beginnings at Athens. In the opinion of some scholars the Fescennine
Verses were only incidentally a *step* on the way to full-fledged theatrical production; they were more especially a species of entertainment
developed in connection with marriage rites. Weddings, of course,
have afforded more material for comedy, down the ages, than any
other one subject—I say it in all seriousness, referring to comedies on
the stage. And they may well have provoked in Etruria a hilarity that
became organized, found itself set down in verses, was chanted in the
form of responses, and thus contributed to the stream of true dramatic
development. Somewhat later this form was introduced into Rome,
and it became so licentious and abusive that ultimately laws were passed
to suppress it.

But meantime the later Etruscan entertainments known as *saturæ*
had found favor with the Roman people, forming the real bridge to
Roman dramatic beginnings. Based perhaps mainly on the Fescennine
Verses, but with some relationship also to recited comic story, the
saturæ had been the earliest truly dramatic type to develop on Italian
soil. They apparently had little plot; they were acted comic scenes or
sketches, in verse, performed with dancing and music. The form was
still not so far removed from those of the vintage celebrations: the very
name *saturæ* has a connection with one of our synonyms for "full."
The actors were known as *istri*, which through the Latin *istriones* gave
us ultimately our still current word "histrionic."

When the Romans brought a company of Etruscan performers to
their city in 364 B.C., erecting for them in the Circus Maximus the first
Roman stage, it was perhaps only a music-and-dancing entertainment
or perhaps a production of *saturæ* (in an unintelligible tongue) that
was added to the *Ludi Romani* or city games and merged into a genuine Roman popular comedy. The Etruscans, a people of still debated
origin, thus gave to the then uncultured Romans their first dramatic
activities, in addition to such epochal gifts as arch-construction and
contact with Greece and the Orient. The Romans long since, before
Republican days, had known how to borrow profitably from the Etru-
rians: had had Etruscan kings for a century, had ended that line of
kings when Rome was strong enough to stand against all enemies, had

absorbed some knowledge of, if not taste for, the arts, even while distrusting Etruscan luxury and culture.

The entertainments that most clearly stand for a people's comedy in Rome itself, that will persist through both Republican and Imperial periods and lose themselves only in the darkness that finally settles over decadent Rome, are the *mimi* and the *pantomimi*. The *mimus*—for which our word "mime" is hardly a fair equivalent—was a combination form in which the farce-sketch in dialogue was accompanied by dancing and songs, with occasional acrobatic and other trimmings. Its subject-matter seems always to have been taken from low life (the authorities all use that term), there was definite plot, and in time such stock characters as the parasite and the knave appeared. The *mimus* may be considered substantially a native Roman development, although it inherited elements not only from the *saturæ*, but from another imported form called the *Atellanæ*, and doubtless from chance importations of performances from the Greek colonies in Sicily and the extreme South of Italy—places soon to be parts of the Roman Empire.

The rustic Atellan farces, so-called because brought to Rome from Atella in Campania, are among the most distinctly defined types in all the puzzling array of popular comedy, and notable as foreshadowing a Renaissance form. They regularly dealt in brief compass with rural life, and although the plots were of set mold, the actors indulged freely in improvisation. The plays were peopled by stock characters, the stupid husband or father, the glutton, the knave, etc.—here again we meet clear forerunners of the characters in the fifteenth and sixteenth century *Commedia dell'Arte;* and like the players of the *Commedia* the Atellan farceurs wore masks. This type ran its course of popularity in Rome, from the late third century on, sometimes on its own stages, later as afterpieces to the Greek-style dramas; until the similar *mimus*, which had derived generously from it, crowded it out. But before adding my last word about *mimi* and *pantomimi*, let me go back and tell about the more literary comedy, based on Greek models, that ran its course between the early popular farces and the final triumph of *mimus, pantomimus*, and spectacle. The reader should keep in mind, however, that it was at all times the cruder comedy that was a more natural, and probably a more appreciated growth at Rome. Leaving no traces of a dramatic literature, it was still, on its own ground, a more vigorous and a more distinctive development than the still surviving literary drama of Plautus and Terence.

When the Romans conquered the Greek Tarentum, in 272 B.C., they opened the way for the introduction of true Greek drama into their capital city. There were as yet no Roman theatres: the popular farces were being presented on stages temporarily erected. (Another full century was to elapse before the building of the first complete theatre in Rome, auditorium as well as stage, and then only of wood, for temporary use.) There were no "cultivated" audiences; the Romans of the time were hard-headed, materialistic, unimaginative fighters, with the admirable qualities of courage, enterprise, and a sense of integrity and justice (when these did not interfere with patriotism and conquest),

A comedy scene on a platform stage. [After a vase drawing.]

A comedy scene on a platform stage. [After a vase drawing.]

but with no taste for any but practical education, none for the arts, none for personal refinements. But Greek influences began to run in a strong tide, and in 240 B.C. there was added to the festival of the *Ludi Romani* a performance of a tragedy and a comedy in the Greek fashion. Livius Andronicus, come to Rome from his native Tarentum, presented the two plays, in Latin, in adaptations that he had made from the Greek. At Tarentum the Dionysian Festivals had been modelled on those of Athens, and the actor-author was well able to introduce correct Athenian methods. From that time forward theatrical representations were part of holiday festivals, and Roman literary drama was committed to Greek forms.

When the greatest of the Greek plays, now already centuries old, were presented, even in translation or adaptation, their brilliancy and vigor were such that the beginning Roman dramatist might well despair of creating new forms so telling, even with his greater liberty in subject-matter and in conditions of presentation. At any rate, he elected to follow Greece. We have already seen how the tragedy writers of Rome weakened the play, mistaking rhetoric for passion, melodramatizing and debasing the Euripidean type. The comedy writers, picking up the "New Comedy" of Greece as model, came off not quite so badly; but certainly they left little that was brilliant, or startlingly original, or essentially Roman. Out of the score of known names of Roman dramatists, Seneca alone is generally remembered in connection with tragedy, and Plautus and Terence as writers of comedy. A post-Terence type of literary comedy—the *fabulæ togatæ*—although more native in materials, ran its unimportant way to an early death.

So frankly Greek were the characters in the Latin plays of Terence and Plautus that they were regularly interpreted as Greeks, wearing Greek clothes, and the scene was usually Athens. But profiting by the divorce of the theatre from religion, and observing life more independently, Plautus succeeded in adding something of Roman vigor and swiftness of dialogue to the borrowed Greek plots. One might have expected Plautus and Terence to succumb to the popular demand for coarse humor and farce in their adaptations. But there was a very distinct break between the few at the top and the masses below, in Rome, culturally as well as in political-economic-social life. The "literary" dramatists, resisting the pressure of the masses for a wholly gross type of comedy, continued to imitate Greek originals, adding at first nothing cheaply topical or sensational or suggestive. There are freedoms of speech and frank recognition of facts of living that often made their plays distasteful during the polite nineteenth century; but compared to what the *mimi* and *pantomimi* are described to have been they are pure as the drifted snows.

A Roman tragic actor. Note the mask which he has just removed. [From an Alinari photograph of the Roman fresco now in the National Museum, Naples.]

Titus Maccius Plautus was born in 254 B.C., just about the time when the first Roman dramatists were forsaking mere translation and adaptation for a more serious attempt to write Latin plays (but still according to Greek pattern). He soon took rank as first, and at that time the only, Roman comedy-writer of importance. His plays are still extant to the number of twenty, out of a possible one hundred and thirty in all. One or two of them are familiar to every college student who has reached sophomore Latin; and *The Menæchmi* has achieved an even wider fame as the model for Shakespeare's *Comedy of Errors*.

Plautus (the name means "flatfooted") owed to Menander and his

Masked actors on a Roman stage, against a profusely decorated stage wall. [Drawing after a contemporary bas-relief.]

fellow-dramatists a debt that cannot be computed in the absence of the Greek originals. But it is certain that although the Roman playwright retained even the scenes and costumes of the Athenian models, he added much of life by way of local color, of Italian fashions and manners and landmarks.

The Menæchmi is laid in Epidamnium. A stolen twin boy has been brought there in childhood, has grown up, married, inherited wealth. Thither comes unknown his brother, whose name has been changed to that of the lost boy. So the local Menæchmus and his twin are both roaming the same town. The one has a wife with whom he has quarrelled, and he is now going to visit a courtesan, to whom he carries one of his wife's dresses. Into this situation walks the other twin, is welcomed warmly by the courtesan, and dressed down by the wife. The fun arises chiefly out of the position of the local twin when the other has queered him with both courtesan and wife, with the aid of a tattling parasite, a doctor who is called in to pass on his sanity, etc. Complication follows complication till the twins meet and happily recognize each other.

In the reading, this five-act comedy seems bald and obvious; the real values in it can be detected only when one carries along in the mind a picture of skilled, heavy-hitting farce-actors filling in the character outlines and the situations with a wealth of telling action, stage tricks, and "business." That, of course, is just what one would expect in a time when there were no theatre auditoriums, when stages were street platforms, and audiences street idlers or the jostling crowds at "games" or fairs. And yet let us give Plautus his full due: to invent or adapt the framework for such players, and to make the dialogue after a fashion literary, without clogging the action, is a distinct achievement. And the more credit is his because he lived in a time when the Latin language was still, so to speak, in manufacture; he helped, indeed, by his comedies, to crystallize it in its finer form. But perhaps it is more significant to us that he was himself an actor—and in all probability, also "producer" of his plays. From this we may know why Plautus rather than the more refined Terence was the oftener revived on later stages—though less studied in the schools.

A captive brought to Rome about 200 B.C., named Statius Cæcilius, is sometimes named as the next important dramatist; but no texts of his have survived. It is rather Publius Terentius Afer, a native of Carthage, born a few years before Plautus' death (184 B.C.), who is invariably bracketed with Plautus in any review of Roman comedy-writing. Six plays of his making survive, though none is wholly or even substantially original. He went back to Attic comedy and took freely what he needed, particularly from Menander. But he is a link between Greek and modern comedy in that he made the play-form more compact, and added a certain ease of manner. Where Plautus is considered an inferior craftsman to Menander, careless and over-vigorous, though livelier, Terence carried on the refining, character-humanizing process.

Terence was a slave, but was early manumitted. At an early age he won sudden interest among the *literati* of Rome through the reading of his first play, the *Andria*. But his short later career was checkered. Enamored of Greek perfection, in a gross time, and stung by charges of plagiarism, he is supposed to have fled Rome for his idealized Athens, and to have died in Arcadia of heartbreak when his manuscripts were lost.

He is in one sense out of time and place. Local color is notably absent from his comedies. An African by origin, a Roman by circumstance, his whole aim was to revive something fine out of Greece in the new Latin language. Elegance, refinement, style, were his goals. Plautus had taken the Greek New Comedies as ready framework for farce-comedy suited to Roman crowds, Terence reverently preserved all that he could of Menander's virtues in finely literary Latin. His polished metrical texts marked almost the earliest Latin poetic achievement with stylistic beauty. He was literary creator in the technical surface sense without any inner originality. Perhaps his whole accomplishment is more important as preserving Menander indirectly, in some sort of adaptation, than from any typically Roman aspect. And yet who shall say whether the clear-flowing light-footed verse is transmitted from the Greek or added by the Roman adaptor? Even the saws and proverbs that are so common in the six plays—"Fortune favors the brave," "Many men, many minds," "While there's life there's hope," etc., etc.—may be from the one or the other. In any case, as written, Terence's plays were little to the liking of Roman audiences. This fastidious art was too delicate for its era.

As an example of the progress made at this time toward the modern human plot, one might cite *The Eunuch*, best known of all Terence's plays. The comedy was placed (as was usual) at a street-crossing, with a house on either hand; the one belonging to Thaïs, a courtesan "of the better class," the other to the father of her favored lover Phædria. Thaïs is trying to protect a girl whom she has brought up, who was taken away from her and sold as a slave but is now restored as a gift by Thraso, an old soldier and an unwelcome admirer. At the same time Phædria is presenting her with a Eunuch. But Phædria's younger brother, having fallen in love with the girl, takes the Eunuch's place, is set to watch over her, and improves the opportunity to seduce her. All plans now seem wrecked, until Thaïs proves that the girl is not a slave but free-born; so that the seducer marries her, while Phædria scares off Thraso, takes Thaïs under his protection, and only lets the old braggart soldier into the happy circle at the price of paying for much entertainment all round.

This is obviously a fable with more than usual of human relationships wound into it. And there is some little characterization, of a skilful, even tender sort. It is an indication of Terence's aloofness from current coarseness that even the scene of the deflowering of the girl is handled delicately. But the stock characters of parasite, soldier, and interfering father stalk in and out of the action. The boisterousness of Plautan action and vulgar incident is lacking; in spite of the free relationships indicated in the plot, comedy is becoming "refined."

The period during which Latin comedy-writing flourished—the word perhaps implies too much—lasted hardly more than a hundred years, roughly 250–150 B.C. The plays of Plautus and of Terence (who died very young, 159 B.C.) persisted in occasional production until the Augustan era, and exceptionally under the late Emperors. But the sort of comedy that is serious enough in thought, in values, to be perpetuated in written texts, was practically crowded off the stage by farce and spectacle a hundred years after its birth—or introduction.

IN ROMAN-GREEK comedy the Chorus had disappeared. Therefore one may be sure that the theatre was no longer the old Greek structure in which the orchestra, as dancing-place, is the essential feature. The

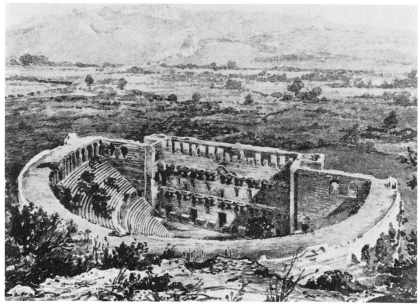

The classic theatre that best survived into the early twentieth century was that at Aspendus. [From Lanckoronski's *Städte Pamphiliens und Pisidiens*.]

exact form of the later Roman playhouse is known, from only partially ruined examples existing today. But there were no permanent theatres in Rome in the days of Terence and Plautus. It was five years after Terence's death, indeed, that construction of the first stone theatre was started; and when half-completed it was torn down by order of the Senate, being considered a menace to the strict self-discipline and flint-like character which the government was attempting to conserve in the Roman citizen. It had even been decreed by law in an earlier time that no auditorium seats should be erected in Rome, lest the spectator at a play find himself too comfortable. Nevertheless, despite old Cato's bitter fight against anything Greek, against anything smelling of self-indulgence, anything new, anything imaginative, the Romans were already slipping toward worse forms of luxury, toward a taste for display, and art of a soft exhibitional sort.

At any rate, the Roman theatre of the period was essentially a stage and a place for seeing, where the Greek had been shaped around a circle for dancing. The Etruscan dancers and actors had had stages, the Atellan farces were acted on platforms, it may even have been an Ital-

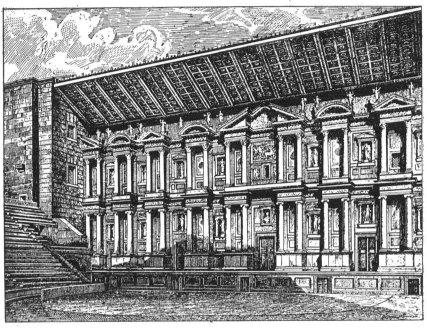

A reconstruction of the decorated stage wall of the Roman theatre at Aspendus. [From a drawing by Niemann in Lanckoronski's *Städte Pamphiliens und Pisidiens.*]

ian influence that led to the introduction of a raised stage into the late Greek playhouses. Certainly it was a platform stage for which Terence and Plautus wrote.

But rather than try to reconstruct in detail the Plautan stage, production, and audience, upon incomplete evidence, let us turn instead to the theatre of the Imperial age. In every sense it is more characteristically Roman. Its plays perhaps still are reminiscent of something in Euripides and Menander, but playwrights have been found to bring the drama down to the taste of the spectacle-loving populace; theatres have been built in keeping with the showy temples and palaces of a magnificent world-capital; and the audiences—well, let us spread out the whole detailed picture:

The population of Rome is no longer that hard-headed, abstemious, practical race of citizen-soldiers, trained first of all to courage, personal integrity, and love of state, which has carried the city by the Tiber well on the way toward world conquest. Long ago the old authority has crumbled, character has weakened, the dikes put up against luxury have been at first undermined, then swept away. The ruthlessness necessary for conquest has turned to cruelty, in government, in amusement, in each man's struggle against all others. Corruption and greed among the rulers are matched by dishonesty and fawning in the great mass of plebeians.

The small group of patrician families of old has been all but decimated by literally centuries of terrible wars; not least destructive, the civil wars within Rome. New patricians have been elevated from the ranks of the lower classes, even freedmen not long since slaves. Adventurers have flocked here from all the vassal cities held by Rome. The old stock, that once held to itself all privileges, all wealth, even while holding to the old virtues and discipline, is gone. The corrupt, the cheap-minded, the sensation-lovers, are as often as not at the very top. Old vices permeate all circles, new vices are welcomed. Religion is a superstitious observance—to be remembered as an excuse for holidays, or, suddenly, as something to be indulged in after a bad dream or a thunder-storm. Anyway, the gods are known to have given in to those very weaknesses and desires which man wishes to indulge. Where in other days, without marriage laws, the Romans had practised monogamy and sexual continence as part of a well-ordered life and the obvious road to happiness, promiscuity is now hardly frowned upon. The theatre, in times of corruption, ever makes infidelity its favorite theme, and panders openly and brazenly to the sexual appetites.

For a time Cæsar Augustus has put an end to anarchy, plundering, and unhindered corruption. He has brought back system, law, and, in a sense, justice. He has ended Republicanism by making himself the State. He has set out to dignify Rome with monuments worthy of the capital of a world empire. He has built or restored innumerable temples, basilicas, public buildings of every sort. These are larger, more massive than any known before, thrown skyward with Roman engineering genius. But the ornament is from Greece, made more elaborate, more showy, more finicky. Colored marbles from all lands, creamy travertine, colored stucco; bronze statues, rich mosaics, gilt traceries; arches of triumph, fountains, pools, parks. Augustus boasts that he himself has rebuilt the magnificent Pompey's Theatre, has erected a stone theatre in honor of his adopted son Marcellus,[2] has encouraged Balbus to build a theatre. And these are supplemented by hippodrome, amphitheatre, circus, and *naumachia*.

Augustus tries to bring back the old character, the old virtues; even while his poet Horace sighs over the lost simple country pleasures. Augustus puts into lasting banishment his own daughter Julia when he finds that she has become little better than a woman of the streets; but he cannot more than frown upon the other noble courtesans, wasters, degenerates—there is indeed some question about his own indulgences. Sudden wealth, that greatest of all tests of a man or a nation, has poured in and overwhelmed the resistance of those in high station in Rome, wealth and the soft luxuries it buys, and the soft vices that come fawning after it. And below is a populace driven by despair, unreligious except when scared into some sort of observance, preferring idleness to any sort of industry—the actual slaves do the hard work —living as far as possible off the bounty of the rich, and expecting those rich to furnish periodic amusement in theatre, arena, or circus. The government distributes grain, its last means of staying in power, and decrees games and theatrical productions, paying out of the public funds to contractors who arrange the shows for the people (quite far are we now from Athens, where the drama was religious, and those presenting it an honored and privileged class!).

Or else private citizens pay for productions free to the public, as part of their show of wealth, or to celebrate triumphs, or even for

---

[2] Fortunately this Marcellus who gave his name to a still outstanding theatre in Rome is not the soldier of the same name who laid siege to Syracuse and destroyed its theatre; dramatic irony goes not so far. But I add a pertinent note from my guidebook to Sicily: "The Romans raised the siege against the city, which had been strengthened by Archimedes, and at last after two years of terrible sufferings, it fell into the hands of Marcellus in 212. The Roman soldiers plundered the city and murdered the inhabitants. Archimedes, engaged in his mathematical studies, was killed. The temples and theatres were destroyed and an enormous booty of valuable works of art taken to Rome. Most of the inhabitants were massacred, the remainder fled across the sea. The parts of the city on mainland [including the sites of theatre and amphitheatre] were deserted and soon the place where magnificent Syracuse, ruler of the Greek world, had stood, became a wilderness." I add the quotation here for the reference to Marcellus, but it illuminates the background against which the Roman theatre developed: the violence and insecurity of life, the frequent destruction of theatre buildings, and the way in which Rome "secured" art. This was the time of Archimedes and Theocritus in Syracuse, about two centuries after the picturesque ruler Dionysius I, himself a tragedy-writer and poet, who had built magnificent buildings and fostered all the arts. The theatre destroyed by Marcellus was presumably of the Greek type; but after this time a magnificent Roman theatre, the largest of all known examples, was constructed on the site. A great part of the auditorium may be seen there today, as well as parts of the stage and the under-stage passage-ways and construction.

funerals. Candidates, too, win favor by supplying a day's entertainment. Of course they all give "what the public wants"—a phrase almost invariably interpreted by "managers" in terms of the worst element in any potential audience. When the Republic had faded into the Empire there were already seventy-six holidays in the year, with fifty-five given up to theatrical productions. This is to grow later into a total of practically six months of holidays in the year, with one hundred and one given up to dramatic performances, ten to gladiatorial contests and sixty-four to chariot-racing.

On one of these holidays, when theatre performances have been announced—let us say at about the time when Jesus of Nazareth is preaching in far-away Palestine, a country not too distant to be under Roman rule—we set out with thousands of other Romans to find our seats in Pompey's Theatre. From someone privileged we have obtained "tickets," little bone tablets stamped with seat and section numbers. Down through the great Forum we go, between rows of porticoed temples, grand basilicas, fountains, arches, with the sun flashing on marble and bronze and gilt—a little proud we are to be a part of all this magnificence and show, proud that our Rome is now the most obviously "artistic" city in all the world. We meet processions: actors going early to the theatre, with their chariots and horses and other "properties," and hundreds of supernumeraries; priests, whole colleges of them, going to celebrate rites and offer sacrifices in the temples of the gods, with their sacred implements borne along by surpliced helpers; a chorus, perhaps, boys and girls of noble birth, chanting votive songs; the procession of the horses, chariots, and charioteers on the way to the Circus Maximus, where tomorrow they will race. And everywhere the people hurrying along, bedecked for the holiday, mixing with the uniformed soldiery, the thousands of police, the picturesque "colonial" officers. Here are patricians carried in gorgeous palanquins by slaves, and one must jump quickly at times to keep out of the way of the heedless private chariots.

Perhaps there are three theatres offering plays this day—it was often so—but it is to Pompey's Theatre that we are going. We remember with a chuckle that Pompey had to employ a shrewd ruse to get this playhouse built at all, only a generation or two earlier. To build it was against the law. But he erected a tiny temple to Venus at the top of his auditorium, which technically made the curving rows of seats merely steps to a shrine—and the whole was dedicated as a temple! But the theatre seats are there, added Pompey, in his invitations . . .

What a magnificent theatre! We note as we take our seats that the shrine is little more than a niche in the stately colonnade that runs around the top of the "bowl"—really a half-bowl, with rows and rows of seats

Two contemporary depictions of Roman theatre scenes. Above, a mosaic panel of masked performers on a Roman stage. Below, a scene with a slave and two women in a New Comedy. [From an Alinari photograph of the mosaic now in the National Museum, Naples; and from a reproduction of the fresco, in *Die Denkmäler zum Theaterwesen im Altertum,* by Margarete Bieber.]

in widening semi-circles, so many that fifteen thousand of us are to find places in it today. Down in the centre, on the flat, like half of the old outgrown Greek "orchestra," chairs of honor have been placed, not for the priests any longer but for the Senators. That, indeed, will add to the show; you know what Senators are, swollen with power and riches, coming in with their slaves and their over-dressed women-folk, lording it around!

The stage has grown from that tiny scaffolding once set up in the Circus Maximus, to this massive stone platform, three hundred feet long, bounded at back and sides with a wall as high as the colonnade about the auditorium, a wall ornamented as richly as a temple or palace façade, story on story of columns, porticoes, niches, with colored marbles, statues, gilded edgings; and above it, a richly decorated stage roof. The auditorium is still open to the sky—this is distinctly an open-air structure—but the Greek separation of "scene" and "cavea" is gone; the theatre is more solidified, massive, integrated. But most noticeably, it is more decorative, more displayful, with a gorgeousness now deemed a proper addition to drama. We are reminded, indeed, that this stone theatre is not the most gorgeous of all: that not long since, in that time when temporary wooden theatres were erected for each new occasion, M. Æmilius Scaurus put up a playhouse in which the wall behind the stage displayed no fewer than three hundred and sixty columns and three thousand statues, together with "relief-plaques of glass"—and the gods only know what additional decorative plunder from his Eastern conquests.[3] Was it Pliny who remarked that in Rome there are as many statues as inhabitants? But after all, this bowl of Pompey's, rich and colorful enough, and just now filled to overflowing with excited and brightly garbed people, is proper setting for our taste of Roman Imperial drama.

A hush, while the announcements are read, of what is to be played or presented, with possibly just a little propaganda for him who spends a fortune to afford the esteemed people a holiday. The announcer adds an appeal to the audience to give their attention quietly and respectfully. One looks at one's fellow-spectators curiously—God! what a mob! Why haven't they gone to the bloody arena contests instead?

What plays are announced? We fill out our picture a bit conjecturally here, for the programmes have not been transmitted to later historians. Let us take it for granted, conveniently, that the morning is given up to a drama, or say two, of the old Greek pattern—but they

---

[3] I am indebted for many figures and descriptions to James Turney Allen's *Stage Antiquities of the Greeks and Romans and Their Influence* (New York, 1927); and for the background of Roman life to Grant Showerman's *Eternal Rome* (New Haven, 1924).

will be debased now so that this audience will stay—and the afternoon
to the popular forms, to *mimi* and *pantomimi*.

What is this opening procession, this parade across the stage, filling
it with pageantry, with movement, color, crowds? The play? Not yet.
The actors? Yes—we know the chief ones by their masks and their
stuffed-out costumes (for this is a vast auditorium for a mere man to
dominate). But these others seem to be not at all acting—men driven,
rather. That's it, of course! The procession of captives from So-and-
so's latest Eastern triumph. Hundreds of them. Here come the horses
too. Perhaps there will be camels, even elephants. Maybe a king in
chains will be led across the stage—many another has.

And the play itself is interrupted by just such pageants at intervals:
sometimes frank unrelated spectacle, gorgeous or sensational, other
times filling out the dramatist's intention. Is a handful of supers a fit
stage mob for a Roman audience? No, bring them on by the hundred.
Shall a score of horses suffice when a hero-protagonist rides out at the
head of his cavalry? A half-thousand crossing the stage will better fill
the eye. So here we have them, to tremendous applause, marching
through a drama that we faintly recognize as descendent from a noble
Greek model. Realistic battles, floods, processions of exotic animals,
interrupt the flow of action.

One wonders a little whether the Roman dramatist seriously wrote
this for tragedy, whether he may not have taken a grand theme in
burlesque spirit. Still, here are noble speeches, delivered with telling
gesticulation and spirited vocal display. Here are passionate appeal,
violent murder, and rhetorical revenge. These players—slaves, freedmen, foreigners—may be little better than outcasts and thieves in real
life, but they know how to tear a passion to tatters. The chief among
them, the fellow with the deep powerful voice, rises to the position of
opera soloist at the most perfervid moments of the play. There is
accompanying music too. Then there is something reminiscent of the
old choruses, and it helps the entr'actes to pass painlessly.

In the following comedy, there is hardly more left of Greek pattern
than in the tragedy. The change this time is not toward spectacle, but
rather in the direction of cheaper horse-play and broader jests. These
later adapters have known how to borrow profitably from the local
mime-makers. The masks too are more caricature-like, more grotesque,
more obvious. Old-favorite characters have become stock figures that
appear in play after play: we look for our favorites, the inevitable
hoodwinked father, the courtesan, the parasite, the pimp, the heiress.
Here they all are, spread out in complication after complication. We
laugh. It is not the "thoughtful laughter" that true comedy is supposed
to inspire. It is hardly a healthy animal laughter. There is something

unworthy, even dirty, about it. The comedy-writers have gone too far.

Then after lunch, returning to the theatre for the performances of the *mimi* and *pantomimi*, we learn that the comedy-writers and the actors of the morning had, comparatively, not gone far at all. Given the low-life theme of the *mimus*, the license of improvisation, and the gross taste of this audience, literally anything goes. No jest is too broad, no situation too suggestive, no gesture too disgusting, to "get by" with these spectators. The actors wear no masks—the obscenities somehow come nearer thus. There is a Chorus which sings appropriate songs and dances appropriate gestures. The whole entertainment is a medley of dialogue-sketch, ballet, and song, strung on a farce idea. For the first time women have come on to the "regular" stage as actors and dancers, and their performance is as like as not a shameful display and an invitation. Along with these things that were to seem to later civilizations so inexplicably degrading in a mass entertainment, there is much that is merely farcically funny, characters and caricatures that evoke spontaneous laughter, old tricks that unfailingly "knock 'em off the seats." Again we laugh. But we know that comedy has kept pace with Roman degeneration and licentiousness.

Now follows a "pantomime"—and one of those miracles so common to the stage. A single masked performer comes before the audience. Behind him a chorus takes its place, and an "orchestra." Alone the actor gesticulates and dances a short mythological play, while the chorus sings the text. With a "clapper" on his foot he emphasizes the cadence of the verse to the rhythm of the music. He develops a surprising theatrical intensity, induces a mood that holds this entire uncouth audience spellbound. Perhaps he has changed mask and costume as he impersonates various characters. At any rate, for a time true drama has reigned again, in a single player's performance. Through sheer virtuosity, an audience has been made attentive, has been swayed, has been deeply satisfied.

It is, indeed, a full tragic drama reduced and intensified into the performance of one actor standing for many actors. Long ago Livius Andronicus, the story goes, finding himself hoarse after too many consecutive performances, gave over the singing of the songs to a boy, and thereby suddenly found himself free to accomplish a much more expressive and effective performance of the meaning through silent acting alone. The boy's part grew to a chorus, the actor's gesticulation became a rounded-out and completely theatrical thing. The Roman pantomime had taken form.

But if this two-century-old sort of drama held the audience on this particular day in Pompey's Theatre, the same actor's next number, bringing the *pantomimus* closer in spirit to the *mimus*, pleased them

better. Why couldn't he stop after that one triumph? Even in the more
serious pantomime the scenario had necessarily taken only the more
effective parts of the legendary story, with a leaning toward the violent
and the amorous portions. But now, in this second piece, with this
vigor turned toward the coarse and suggestive methods of the *mimus*,
with the single actor's added opportunity for physical display, one has
a new sort of sensational display—yes, vulgar beyond words . . .

If we have a real love for our Rome, we walk back through the
Forum with something approaching melancholy in our hearts. We

Stage of the Roman theatre at Orange, as reconstructed by Camille St.-
Saëns. Note the vast scale of the building and decoration in relation to the
actors on the stage.

have felt, in the theatre at first, something of the old glamour of the
stage, of the stilled expectant auditorium. But by late afternoon it is
worn down to a feeling tattered, drab, uncomfortable. Is it only imagination that leads us, here among the temples, shrines, and triumphal
arches of the Forum, to see in the encrusted decoration, gilt, and sculptured stone and colored stucco, to detect in all this magnificence, a
note of pretence, of tawdry and vulgar showiness? How wholesome
is this art of conquering Rome? Is it really noble, fine, soul-stirring,

breeding an ecstasy of the emotions, like the early Greek? Or is it showy, sensational, wearying?

The better theatre, the theatre not too mixed with sensuality, continues in a small way, even in the Rome of the Empire; though small audiences mean curtailment. Plays in the earlier styles are still written; but there is very little of originality, of lasting value in them. The original Greek plays are presented too, in the Greek, for a small group of educated Romans, for the resident Greeks, for other special groups in Rome.

In the one matter of acting, considered as an individual exhibition, the Romans have probably made progress beyond their teachers. The great actors even take students for training in the intricacies of the art. Late in the Republican days, Quintus Roscius has trod the stage, creating a lasting tradition of effective acting. He is said to have appeared one hundred and twenty-five times in a single year. He became a friend of Cicero, was honored by Sulla, and outgrew the stigma attaching to the playing profession in general. Why that profession was dishonored in this particular period of history becomes clear from our study of the mimes and pantomimes, and from our knowledge that most actors were slaves. The actor was denied the rights of a citizen, he was legally *infamis*, socially an outcast. There is reason to believe that before the time of the late Emperors, at least, he deserved his classification with panderers and thieves.

It was at Rome that the first dramatic performances by night took place. Plays were acted by the light of flares; though we may put this down as more a "stunt" for the sake of novelty than as a step toward the artificial-light stage of today. The Romans introduced, too, as a regular thing, that paid claque which has proved a nuisance in more than one later era. When productions were so frequent, it became necessary to hire theatrical "contractors"; at so much per performance, they would undertake to deliver a "show" to the people. Often the contractor was an enterprising young actor, who played leads and hired or owned other actors for support. It meant money to him if his production was properly appreciated and acclaimed. He may even have been paid in accordance with the apparent success achieved with his audience. Therefore bands of paid clappers were organized, whose business it was to whip up enthusiasm and if possible stampede the audience into demonstrations. There are reports of the reverse activity: crying-down of the productions of opposition actor-managers. Riots occurred in this connection. One may be sure that it is a decadent or artificial art to which a claque must be called in; the productions in the degraded Roman theatres show some analogy to the "grand" opera

houses of today, where the claques are often brazen, and disturbing to
any artistic atmosphere.

But the changes instituted in matters of production, in the late Roman theatres, are grouped largely around the growth of spectacle as
an element. Stages had been greatly enlarged, mass effects were common; but beyond this, there was a love for trick effects and surprise.
Rome had for centuries displayed appreciation of tight-rope walkers,
jugglers, and similar entertainers, as evidenced in many a fresco and
mosaic. The machinery of the Greek stage, which had been developed
for a few stock effects, most notably thunder at the entrance of a god,

Architectural decoration of the stage wall in a typical Roman theatre.
A reconstruction by G. von Cube based on contemporary evidence in mural
paintings preserved at Pompeii. Note the standard three doorways, but
with the unusual feature of a stairway before each door.

and the *deus ex machina* appearing to resolve the drama, was now elaborated to include devices for apparitions, trap-door disappearances,
flying figures, thunder and lightning, etc. Vitruvius gives contemporary
evidence about stage conventions, and Pollux, writing in the second
century A.D., listed a great amount of mechanical paraphernalia for
spectacle-making.

No complete accounts of painted stage scenes are extant, but references indicate that at least essays had been made in this direction. In
general, the reader should dismiss the idea of localized background as

an element of staging in ancient times: it simply had not been thought of. The stage was obviously a stage, not a representation of a place. The dramatist told in the dialogue where the actors were supposed to be, or else it was self-evident from the relationships of the characters present; and that was enough for audiences not trained to expect "real" backgrounds. Before Vitruvius' time a device had been introduced for *indicating* change of scene pictorially: three-sided sign-boards on pivoted standards bore on the three faces differing pictured scenes, two architectural (one for tragedy, one for comedy) and the other pastoral. There is very little evidence as to the extent to which these *periacti* were in use. But in his famous *Ten Books on Architecture* Vitruvius wrote of them: "When the play is to be changed, or when gods enter to the accompaniment of sudden claps of thunder, these may be revolved and present a face differently decorated." We shall hear of Vitruvius and his descriptions of the scenes again, in the era when artists of the Renaissance apply his directions specifically to the designing of full-stage settings. But the whole matter is too involved, the authorities too contradicting, to permit us to infer changing painted settings in Roman times.[4]

One can only conjecture how far the Romans went in developing spectacle as a separate complete stage art, independent of other elements. Most of the contemporary references involve it on the one hand with the presentation of debased literary drama, or on the other with such events as triumphal entries and funeral celebrations. Protests against the intrusion of unrelated spectacle into plays were frequent and sometimes bitter. Cicero exclaims, "What pleasure is there in seeing six hundred mules in the *Clytemnestra*, or three thousand bowls in *The Trojan Horse*, or infantry and cavalry engaging in battle in gay-colored armor?"—and this on the occasion of the opening of Pompey's Theatre, as early as 55 B.C. Horace uttered scathing criticisms of the audiences of his day, because they preferred spectacle and sensational exhibition to poetic and literary drama. In the Epistles he wrote: "For

---

[4] I disagree with many other writers on this subject, in that I see in several references to painted stage scenes only an indication that the usual *neutral* architectural background occasionally was frescoed on the stage wall, instead of built out in relief. In many old churches in Italy one may see a chapel with a painting surrounded by elaborate architectural stonework, topped by sculpture in the round. The adjoining chapel, however, may have the central religious painting, but around it only a *painted semblance* of columns, pediments, and sculpture— the means to add the decoration in actual stonework having failed. It seems to me wholly likely that the mentioned "painted scenes" in theatres of Roman or late Greek times were entirely or mainly of this sort: a flat wall with a conventional architectural and sculptural composition frescoed in, without reference to realistic *placing* of the play. This is not scene painting or play setting in the later accepted sense.

four hours or more the curtain is kept down while squadrons of horse and bodies of foot are seen flying; presently there passes the spectacle of unfortunate kings dragged with hands behind their backs; chariots of every kind and shape hurry along."

The reference to "the curtain kept down" is indication that certain of the Roman theatres had front curtains, raised from slots along the edge of the stage, which were let down when the play started and raised when the action was done. In the larger theatre at Pompeii and at Arles one may still see the slots into which the curtain-rollers fitted.

The Roman arena at Nimes, France. [ND photograph, by courtesy of French Cultural Services, New York.]

Every play producer knows that when it comes to the question of "effects," one may astonish more by the sudden disclosure of great masses of actors, or a fight in full swing, than by showing actors coming in or the fight just commencing. Thus the curtained stage may fairly be considered an outgrowth of the Roman love for sensational intensive incident.

At any rate pageantry, interspersed with thrilling effects, flourished in Rome as we know it to have flourished only once in later history, in the melodramas of the *Boulevard du Crime* in Paris, and the closely connected spectacles of the London stages of the nineteenth century. But the Romans had an advantage for the audiences of a bloodthirsty epoch: they could mix a realism into their stage battles, murders, seductions, etc., that later civilizations forbade. The conqueror returning home, ordering a show for the people, was able to supply thousands of real soldiers, horses, chariots, thousands of captives in strange garb, thousands of slaves bearing trophies, real gold, statues, costly stuffs.

Against this background their theatrical managers might sacrifice lives in real battles to the death, and no one to object—or employ slave girls for who knows what exhibited iniquities. (One might a worse tale unfold!)

Now spectacle may be a legitimate enough form of theatre art. We must recognize that there are many forms of "theatre," and that each may be right in its place—so long as it is true to stage materials. But the Roman mind, we feel, was too realistic, too sensation-seeking, and the theatres too large, perhaps, for any sort of subtle spectacle. For that era of violence, conquest, and decadent living, the sensational episode, the cruel personal strife, the astonishing piled-up magnificence were right. The theatre shaped itself to the violence, the license, that was Rome. At first the producers had taken the regular drama and interpolated unwarranted spectacular incidents; then they mixed in the thrills of *real* battle, real crises, with theatre elements. So real were the dangers of the "drama" toward the end, indeed, that the Romans, in making over the Greek theatres, erected barriers between orchestra and auditorium, lest spectators be injured or killed by error.

That the theatres designed for drama were later utilized for out-and-out gladiatorial contests is amply proved by the evidence of late Roman writers and by traced changes in still existing stages. The arenas were not enough for the bloody spectacles; the theatres must be taken over. There is even reason to believe that the lower portion of the Theatre of Dionysus in Athens, most glorious of all ancient playhouses, was reconstructed under a Roman Emperor to be rendered water-tight, so that mimic naval battles might be staged there. Already Rome had several amphitheatres specially designed for such sea fights.

In these *naumachiæ*—really auditorium bowls with lake centres—two fleets of triremes of equal "tonnage" were manned by warriors and set against each other. A friendly parade of the vessels (and they were truly decorative) preceded the main event; and it is recorded that the participants were instructed to win the battle with as little damage as possible to ships and combatants. But in a country where slaves and captives were regularly set to fighting against each other to the death, or against wild beasts, in vast amphitheatres for the edification of the public, the sea battle was sure to be bloody enough. One commentator adds the illuminating note that when the lake was emptied after a production the bodies of the *naumachiarii*, the actors, were dragged away without ceremony to the animals' dens. The form of amusement here is not to be considered too seriously as a type of drama; but one may pause with real admiration for the logical buildings developed for the mimic battles. The *naumachia* of Julius Cæsar is reputed to have been nearly two thousand feet long and two hundred wide, with an en-

circled lake on which a battle with fifty triremes might be staged.
The little picture of a *naumachia* here is cut down for the better
showing-out of the detail, and is perhaps conjectural in many ways.
But what a pretty and logical "theatre" for its special purpose! The
Colosseum at Rome has aqueducts which archæologists say were used
to flood the arena for sea fights, and at the amphitheatre at Pozzuoli
one may trace out today just how the arena was filled, how large the
lake was, and how emptied.

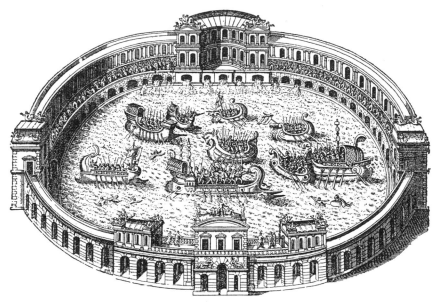

A Naumachia or theatre for mimic sea-fights. [From *La Machinerie au
Théâtre*, by E. M. Laumann.]

The pictures of the Colosseum and of the Circus Maximus show the
more usual activities of man-and-beast fights and chariot-racing. There
we may safely leave the subject of Roman spectacle. Stage tragedy had
ended in plain butchery—itself indeed had been "butcher'd to make a
Roman holiday."

Comedy, as we have seen, had come to knock-about and often indecent farce and dance. Insofar as the truly gorgeous theatres of Rome
were used under the late emperors, their stages saw only spectacle,
vulgar antic, and suggestive jest. Over most of the lands conquered
by Rome those magnificent playhouses were built, in Italy and Sicily,
in Greece and Asia Minor and Syria, in Northern Africa and in France
and Spain. Today one goes to the half-ruined theatre at Orange and

tries to reconstruct the picture of the original audience assembled there, and the plays on the stage. The auditorium and the scene are modelled after the grandest and most lavish of the ornate theatres at Rome. But the date of its opening was in the second century A.D., many years after the decadence of Roman taste, when spectacle and farce were all that remained in place of dramatic art at the capital. Did these palatial colonial playhouses, then, see nothing else? One hopes that some day evidence will be uncovered to the contrary. In the cities that were first Greek, then Roman, like Taormina and Syracuse in Sicily, the whole

Two exciting substitutes for the dramatic theatre in Roman times. Above, a painting by C. Ademollo of a chariot race in the Circus Maximus. Below, a painting of a man-and-beast spectacle in an amphitheatre. The reader should recognize the vast circuses and other amphitheatres as historical theatre buildings; in later centuries, even up to the twentieth, acting companies frequently set up their stages facing the ancient tiers of seats. (See, for instance, illustration at page 251).

pageant of Greek drama at its height, changing Greek-Roman plays, and finally degraded Roman production, naturally would be seen.

A new protagonist comes into the story of the last days and eclipse of Roman drama. The record of the increasingly obscene mimes and pantomimes is spotted with reports of attempted official censorship; but the censors had neither nobility of character nor conviction behind them. Then came the Christian Church, with conviction, moral courage, militant antagonism to sin and personal indulgence. As the darkness of decay falls over Rome, the drama is seen fleeing before the righteous wrath of the Church fathers. Actors become wandering vagabonds—though their tribe and their art never quite disappear. The Greek and Roman theatres fall into decay, are made over into fortresses, are built full of huts, are torn down stone by stone for the sake of the rich building materials in them—until in the nineteenth and twentieth centuries a few are cleared out, reclaimed, rededicated with Greek tragedy and comedy, or modern drama and opera. The play texts of the Greeks, and of Plautus and Terence, are forgotten, except as they afford study to monk-grammarians—until a nun of Saxony writes ecclesiastical plays after their pattern in the tenth century. Indeed, it is the Church that drives the drama into outer darkness, deservedly anathematized and despised, before Rome's story is wholly done, and it is the Church that will bring back drama as a preceptor of righteousness, an aid at the altar, when centuries have passed in penance.

CHAPTER
5

Sensuous and
Intellectual Theatres:
The Orient

IN LIFE there are pleasures that we call sensual and sensuous, pleasures of the senses, varying from wholly animal satisfactions to something bordering on the æsthetic and ecstatic. This range of pleasures cannot easily be set off from those deeper sorts that we term spiritual and intellectual; though the Puritans tried to mark out limits to legitimate enjoyment, barring as guilty all the sensuous as well as the animal-sensual sorts: pleasure in rich color, dancing, imagery, erotic excitement, brilliant design, gay music, etc. In recent centuries, particularly, our rigid Anglo-Saxon Protestant civilization tried to taboo the sense-activities; it brought about a colorless epoch culminating in the drab nineteenth century.

Now it is a fact that this civilization did not result in a real prohibition or suppression of the baser sensual pleasures: there are signs enough in German, British, and American life of coarseness, of realism, and materialism. But it did largely kill out the more admirable sensuous enjoyments in life and in art. And so, since our discovery of the harm wrought by a too-rigid Protestantism, of the evils of moral hypocrisy, ethical formalism, and thin sentimental or ponderously didactic art, we have been reassimilating color, brilliance, tactile values, melodious movement, fantasy, and music. While trying to avoid what seem like refinements of sensuality in Oriental life, the European-American has been consciously studying those elements that afford the sensuous glow and fulness to Eastern art. For we had obviously gone too far the other way, toward a dark and stark coded life, had denied the senses too intolerantly, had made our arts too rigid, realistic, and pale.

Personally I feel that life may be enriched for us by an indulgence of our instinct toward color, light, dreamy music, imagery, and form-enjoyment. Our theatre might gain—I believe is gaining—much from the reintroduction of the discarded sensuous elements. And indeed, Western art would have been a darker and more meagre affair without the colorful influences from the East that came with a succession of "calamitous" invasions through a long period of history. I feel that the greater ease of communication today may help us, not to import— God forbid!—some of the elements of Oriental art into our own, but to awaken again our æsthetic sensibilities, to absorb the feel for imagery and color, and to express ourselves more fully in the richer overtones of dramatic performance. Nor do I see in such a change anything incompatible with our Western idea of drama, as an activity touching on spiritual crisis and purgation of the emotions. All the depth, the emotion, the high beauty, the poetry of the finest European plays might remain and yet the lighter elements be woven into the pattern of the action. I imagine, indeed, that the plays of Æschylus and Euripides as performed in the Dionysian tradition at Athens were characterized by an abounding life and colorfulness not at all in keeping with the nineteenth century conception of a white classicism; with a gloss of music, measured rhythm of movement, and conscious voice-play; and that the productions of the Elizabethan theatre were rich and full and glowing far beyond the comprehension of the nineteenth century scholar-producers.

The Oriental theatre and drama, doubtless, hold elements which will never be wholly understood by the spectator out of the West. It is difficult to understand the reaction of the audiences to the Chinese twelve-hour plays or to the brief Japanese *No*, in all the facets of their enjoyment. The Orientals, in avoiding almost entirely the range of tragic emotion, as it is expressed in a compact, ascending-descending action-structure by our most skilful dramatists, may build into their productions some other central effectiveness which we miss. But there can be no doubt of the superiority in the two ranges lying on either side of ours: the sensuous, decorative, image-making field and that at the other extreme, of formalized intellectual art, where the effectiveness lies in traditional precisions, a widely understood symbolism and a meticulous fastidiousness—the field of a skilfully thought-out and embroidered art rather than a spontaneous expression.

Our survey of Oriental drama here, then, may well begin with the reservation that there are some depths that our minds may not reach, and with the understanding that we shall only flounder futilely if we try to judge its excellencies by the standard of our own essentially and starkly emotional theatre; and further, that there are sensuous qualities that we may learn about with advantage to our own civilization. Even the only half-Oriental Hindu theatre has been so often written about unsympathetically, from the set viewpoint of what the European theatre *is*, that a caution against closed-mindedness seems necessary.

The origins of the theatre in India are lost in a haze of myth and speculation. If we set aside the legend of divine and deliberate creation of the drama, and the conjectures about the emergence of dramatic story from dance-and-song, we find that we cannot go back of the second or first century B.C. with any certainty; and it is only with the emergence of Bhasa's and Kalidasa's plays that we learn about theatrical activity in any detail. In other words, we find ourselves immediately

Two masks for actors in Japanese *No* plays. [In the Victoria and Albert Museum, London. Drawings by Warren D. Cheney.]

in the golden period of Sanskrit dramatic composition, without knowing more than stray facts about the preceding birth and rise of the art. Nor is it possible to declare certainly, within a century or so, when Kalidasa lived. The Hindu people are careless about recording such details: it is characteristic that a mere fact of this sort, so prized by the Western mind, escapes the East in favor of the spirit, the enjoyment of the work. But roughly we may say that Indian drama flourished from the fourth century A.D. (which is probably just before Kalidasa's time) to the tenth century. It was probably a growth independent of Greece, Persia, or other countries with which India had commerce in the formative period in the several centuries on either side of Christ's birth, although there is definite proof of Greek influence on some of the other arts. The Indian drama is characterized most notably by great poetic-idyllic beauty, is preoccupied with the loves of men and women or with heroism, always ends happily, avoids unseemly or violent emotion or incident, and is innocent of the unities of time and place, and of that inevitability and dramatic drive which is so typically Greek.

But let us go back to the legend of divine and miraculous origin. During the Golden Age there could be no need for drama, because the sadness that is a part of every dramatic story could mean nothing where sorrow and pain are unknown. But in the following Silver Age, the gods asked the All-father to create a new art which would give pleasure to the eye and the ear alike. So Brahma took from the four existing Vedas the elements of recitation, song, mimetic art, and "sentiment" or "passion," and combined them in a new art-form.

The other gods contributed further elements—Shiva, sometimes identified as the Indian Dionysus, gave the dance—and Brahma caused the divine architect to build a playhouse where the sage Bharata would set forth the new-born drama in production. "Bharata" became, indeed, one of the names for "actor."

If we refuse to accept this account as gospel truth—*our* gospel—we may yet let it serve as indication of a religious origin of Hindu theatric art. There are dramatic elements in the sacred books, and we may again conjecture that dance-ritual (the gods themselves are conceived of as dancing) and dialogue-hymns had to do with the beginnings of drama. But as in Greece it was probably the element out of recited epic that ultimately resolved the form of the new art. A typically religious touch long survived in a brief ceremony or benediction before the beginning of the play proper, and scraps of "Mystery" plays survived down the centuries even to our times. At any rate drama emerged, after dance, song, ritual, recited poem and epic. And if you prefer to consider this the real story of the birth of the Indian theatre, you can see how the native impulse to ascribe everything to a divine creator might have taken the word for actor as the beginning point of a legend, and from that imagined a sage named Bharata who received the art from heaven, and who became the tutelary deity of the Hindu drama. As a matter of fact the work on dramaturgy which is associated with Bharata's name became as a bible to all later Sanskrit dramatists. No body of drama has been more rigidly held within a set of rules.

The language in which the earlier dramas were cast was perhaps the Prakrit, a popular form, as distinguished from the Sanskrit, a language then reserved for the use of the Brahmins and for learned works. It is not clear when Sanskrit became the language of literature; though we know that after its introduction plays were translated out into the vernacular tongues. For a long time Sanskrit and Prakrit were mixed in the same play, according to the superiority or inferiority of the characters speaking: Gods, kings, nobles, Brahmins, and the like spoke in Sanskrit, women, thieves, policemen, etc., spoke in Prakrit. Even in later times there were characters who spoke appropriate dialects. But when we come to the first plays that we can label complete literary dramas, Sanskrit is predominantly in use. The text was ordinarily composed in prose with a great deal of verse inset, the verse varying widely in form even in a single play.

The first great name in Sanskrit drama is Bhasa, a dramatist to whom thirteen recently discovered plays are attributed. But because a controversy still rages about this attribution, and because two later plays are generally considered the masterpieces of the Indian theatre, we may turn directly to Kalidasa, the author of *Shakuntala*, and then to *The Little Clay Cart*, which is attributed to a legendary king-dramatist named Shudraka.

According to the Indian scholars, Kalidasa was the brightest of the "nine gems of genius" who adorned the court of King Vidramaditya, in the first century B.C., but unromantic English and German scholars have apparently destroyed this pretty legend and have placed the dramatist in the fourth, fifth, or sixth century A.D., with the latest evidence inclining the casual reader to say "400 A.D. is close enough." His first play, called *Malavikagnimitra*, which has mercifully been translated into *Malavika and Agnimitra*, contains references to Kalidasa's illustrious predecessors, Bhasa, Saumilla and Kaviputra, indicating a large body of highly esteemed earlier dramatic works, now mostly lost. The prologue contains two lines that have perhaps been too seldom quoted:

> Wise men approve the good, or new or old;
> The foolish critic follows where he's told.

The play is a conventional comedy, with fairly good characterizations, and pretty love passages. The second of Kalidasa's plays is variously called in translation *The Hero and the Nymph* and *The Tale of Urvashi Won by Valor*, and is said by those who have read it in the original to contain one act of surpassing idyllic loveliness; though Kalidasa seems to have debased a legendary story of great tragic beauty to the estate of a pleasant love-comedy.

Shakuntala, however, is the masterpiece not only among Kalidasa's works but perhaps of all Oriental drama that has been translated out into European tongues. It exhibits many essential characteristics of the Hindu drama: in its long prose passages embroidered with the prettiest of poetry, its idyllic setting, its pleasing imagery, its story of love and misunderstanding and languishment, its decorous avoidance of violence, its happy ending so obviously devised to leave everyone in the best possible humor after the last lines.

Malwa dancing girls entertaining Akbar in 1560: a painting by the artists Kisu and Dharm das. Most of the pictures of Hindu and Persian "theatres" center upon the throne of the royal spectator rather than upon a stage and shaped auditorium; and we may infer that the average theatre was an informal arrangement of platform, throne, and surrounding space for less important spectators, in a palace court or hall, instead of the rigid bowl-facing-a-stage of the Western nations. [From a painting in the Victoria and Albert Museum, London, by courtesy of the Directors.]

The rather slight story opens with a woodland scene. King Dushyanta and his Charioteer have pursued a spotted deer into an idyllic grove. Just as the King is about to bring the deer down with an arrow, a voice calls on him to spare it, for this is the sacred precinct of a hermitage. While resting, the King is smitten with sudden love of Shakuntala, a maiden of surpassing loveliness, ward and supposed daughter of Kanva, the pious hermit-father; and without revealing his true identity, he finds occasion to serve Shakuntala, establishes that she is of divine not lowly birth, and exits feeling that

> She would not show her love for modesty,
> Yet did not try so very hard to hide it.

In Act II there is hardly more action than a summons to the court, which Dushyanta evades by sending back his Clown, and his decision to remain at the sanctuary grove in order to be near Shakuntala. The rest is lyric retelling of the meeting, and praise of the hermit-girl. A third act shows the King invading the hermitage garden, overhearing the sweet confidences of Shakuntala and her girl-companions; and then his declaration of love—ending in a notably delicate and poetic scene of dalliance. In the following act the audience discovers that Shakuntala gave herself to the King in "voluntary marriage," and that he went back to his court; and now there seems some doubt whether he will keep his promise to recognize her publicly. She is with child, and after pious offerings are made, she sets out with attendants for the distant capital, to claim her right as wife and queen.

But the King's memory has failed him. He renounces her; and she is unable to bring proofs because she has lost in the sacred river the signet ring he had given her. Just after she leaves the King's presence in misery she is reported as miraculously snatched away to Heaven. The King is left uneasy in his conscience.

In the next act a fisherman who has found the ring brings it to the palace; whereat the King's memory is restored, and thenceforward he spends his time sorrowing, languishing for his lost love, and brooding over her beauties and virtue. All this is seen by a heavenly nymph sent to find out for Shakuntala whether the King has repented. His repentance has indeed been so sincere that the Heavenly Charioteer appears to convey Dushyanta to the celestial regions. The last act shows the King come to Indra's realm and welcomed by the gods. He is touchingly united with his son, now a manly little boy; and then with the forgiving Shakuntala. It is discovered that the loss of the ring and the renunciation grew out of a curse, and that the King is not to be blamed for his apparently ungallant behavior. The reunited

King and Queen set out with their boy to rule over their land with
Indra's blessing.

Here is a tale that might be out of a child's fairy-book. But in the
tenderness of the sentiment revealed in the telling, in the poetic garments in which it is clothed, and in the noble characterizations, there
are notable virtues and many of the devices that are typical of the
Hindu theatre.

At the very beginning, before the play proper, is the blessing to the
audience, the invocation to Shiva. And immediately one is transported
into an idyllic region (called up by the poet's words and not provided by scene-painters with muddy canvases). The characters who
tread through these pious groves and sanctuary gardens and royal
courts are more than humanly beautiful, the King quite wonderfully
handsome, good, and gracious, a resplendent knight and yet a chival-
rous protector of his humblest subject; while Shakuntala runs the
entire range of feminine loveliness, from a flowerlike maiden-shyness
to womanly fortitude and nobility. Even the child in the briefest of
scenes is nobly sketched. And by contrast there is that usual figure,
the Clown, confidant of the King, not too obtrusively humorous here,
but serving as foil and as dramatic tool: the half-insolent servant-
companion who in effect says, Hurry up and sit down, King, because
"I can't sit down till you do," and who half-mocks while showing
out to the audience the King's nobility and his sentiments.

Here too are the usual opportunities for telling "asides"; two parties
on the stage unknown to each other. Almost at the opening the King
hides in the forest to watch Shakuntala and her friends at their girlish
amusements, discovering and retelling to the audience in poetic
descriptions the loveliness and nobility of this hermitage child. Again
in the garden scene Dushyanta is concealed, and tells the audience
first of his fears, then of what the girls on the bench are doing, then
of his joy when Shakuntala confesses to the other girls her love of the
King. This byplay, this poetic retelling, is one of the most typical devices employed for more richly embroidering the action with lyric
beauty. In the first act, too, is an opportunity set in for pretty bits of
individual acting, when Shakuntala is troubled by a bee and has
opportunity for graceful pantomime, while the King comments on it
in an eighteen-line lyric. There is also one notably humorous scene,
by way of comic relief, when the fisherman is brought in by abusive
policemen, who switch suddenly to considerate friendliness when they
see the King's rich reward for the return of the lost ring.

The most notable quality of the play, however, is the high level
of the verse—and this is very difficult to indicate briefly, because part

of the charm is in the pervasiveness of the sentiment, re-enforced by continual felicitous allusion to the beauties of nature, by imagery, and by literary music cues. In the garden, Shakuntala has pretended to go away, hiding in an amaranth hedge—she will see how long the King's love lasts. He lifts reverently the lotus-chain she has dropped.

KING

The perfumed lotus-chain
  That once was worn by her
Fetters and keeps my heart
  A hopeless prisoner.

SHAKUNTALA (looking at her arm)

Why was I so weak and ill that when the lotus-bracelet fell off, I did not even notice it?

KING (laying the lotus-bracelet on his heart)

Once, dear, on your sweet arm it lay
And on my heart shall ever stay;
Though you disdain to give me joy,
I find it in a lifeless toy.

SHAKUNTALA

I cannot hold back after that. I will use the bracelet as an excuse for my coming. . .

So she returns to him. But he makes conditions before he will return the bracelet.

SHAKUNTALA (feeling his touch)

Hasten, my dear, hasten.

KING (joyfully, to himself)

Now I am content. She speaks as a wife to her husband. (Aloud) Beautiful Shakuntala, the clasp of the bracelet is not very firm. May I fasten it in another way?

SHAKUNTALA (smiling)

If you like.

KING (artfully delaying)

See, my beautiful girl!
  The lotus-chain is dazzling white
  As is the slender moon at night.
  Perhaps it was the moon on high
  That joined her horns and left the sky,
  Believing that your lovely arm
  Would, more than heaven, enhance her charm.

SHAKUNTALA

I cannot see it. The pollen from the lotus over my ear has blown into my eye.

KING

Will you permit me to blow it away? . . . (*Shakuntala darts a glance at him, then looks down. The King raises her face. Aside*)
> Her sweetly trembling lip
> With virgin invitation
> Provokes my soul to sip . . .

And so on. This lyric lightness lies over the play like a rosy glow. Even Shakuntala, denied verse utterance, clothes her prose occasionally in poetic form and meaning. When the lovers have been interrupted, and Shakuntala is being led away by her guardian, she turns to the hedge concealing the King: "O bower that took away my pain, I bid you farewell until another blissful hour."

The "theatres" in which such plays were presented in the time of Kalidasa can be reconstructed only half conjecturally. So far as known, there were no permanent playhouses in India before the nineteenth century. But the many royal palaces afforded perfect facilities for producing plays before select audiences—and drama was distinctly a caste development, for the educated few. Usually a great hall or the central outdoor court was chosen. The king or prince, his retinue and his guests were grouped at one side, perhaps around a throne or royal box; a space would then be appropriated to the actors, dancers, and musicians.

No special background was erected, except for one curtain (behind which were actors' quarters, from which came offstage noises, Voices, etc.). The rest would be the naturally pleasing architecture and decoration usual to the palace: rich, neutral, perfectly fitted to the sensuous-sentimental lyric-drama to be presented. Doubtless the arrangement varied in numberless minor ways at different times and in different places, but the stage seems always to have been simple, open, and perhaps not even raised above the level of floor or pavement. One might argue a platform stage from the fact that the word used to designate the chief-actor or director originally meant "architect" or "carpenter." But such impermanent stages were bound to be simple.

Not only was there no attempt at illusive scenery, but the play-text was such as to forbid "settings" even in revivals where "stage decoration" is usual. *Shakuntala* opens with the coming of the King and his Charioteer into a wood; but neither they nor the surroundings remain stationary. The King is pursuing a deer. "Pursue as I may," he exclaims, "I can hardly keep him in sight." To which the Charioteer replies: "Your Majesty, I have been holding the horses back because the ground was rough. Now we are on level ground, and you will easily overtake him." A moment later he adds:

> The lines hang loose; the steeds unreined
> Dart forward with a will.

Apparently they gain on the animal; then a Voice tells them the deer must not be killed. The chariot stops. The King and a hermit hold converse. Then again they drive on; till finally they come to that part of the pious grove where the main part of the act is played.

It would be my judgment that even the chariot here is imagined, along with the settings; and that a very little physical movement would be employed to suggest the journey. But there are many guesses as to that.[1] If the *acting* must carry the whole burden of narrative and picturing, it must be notably skilful in both gesture and voice-expression. And we know that these branches of the art were diligently studied. Like every other subject in the realm of the arts and philosophy, acting was analysed, its excellencies and vices pigeon-holed, and elaborate structures of rules erected for the guidance of those who practised it. The actors wore no masks, and women played the female characters. As in Greece, the actors in the literary theatre were an honored group in society, at least at one time; though through the ages there was also an obscure street theatre in which performed a class of actors and tricksters little better than vagabonds and thieves.

Whether Shudraka was only a mythical king or a real one, whether he wrote *The Little Clay Cart* or had a court poet write it, whether the play is mainly a recasting of an earlier work by Bhasa: these are questions for the Sanskrit scholar to puzzle over. We may better enjoy the drama on its merits. It is somewhat less typical than *Shakuntala*: it deserts the usual kings and high-born maidens for less exalted pro-tagonists, a ruined, if noble, merchant and a comparatively virtuous courtesan; it comes nearer to violence than any other well-esteemed play (but the "murder" proves not to have been successful); it com-bines the love plot with a story of political change; it is less idyllic than usual, nearer to the domestic-drama type; it employs less of verbal decoration and imagery. By these very tokens, it escapes a certain mo-notonous harmony and laziness that sometimes pall on the Western

---

[1] A romantic picture of the first production of *Shakuntala*, conceived of as played in operatic settings, is to be found in *The Indian Theatre*, by E. P. Horr-witz (London, 1912); but the whole book seems half-fanciful. The most accessible and probably the best translation of *Shakuntala* is in *Kalidasa: Translations of Shakuntala and Other Works*, by Arthur W. Ryder (London & New York, Everyman's Library). The excerpts here are from Prof. Ryder's text.

reader or spectator; is livelier, more inventive, more varied, more vigorous.

The noble-minded courtesan, Vasantasena, is driven to seek protection in the house of the virtuous Brahman-merchant Charudatta, to escape the unwelcome attentions of Sansthanaka, brother-in-law of the perfidious King Palaka; and at nightfall she leaves her jewels in Charudatta's keeping. They are stolen, and Charudatta honorably gives his wife's necklace to Vasantasena by way of restitution; but the stolen jewels are also returned to her through her maid, who has taken them from the thief. Meantime a virtuous young herdsman has been imprisoned by the wicked King, but escapes. Vasantasena goes to Charudatta's house and while there she generously gives to his small son gems with which to buy a new gold cart, because he doesn't like his one of clay. In leaving, Vasantasena steps into the carriage of the hated Sansthanaka, mistaking it for that of Charudatta—which, indeed, is immediately occupied by the escaped herdsman. Vasantasena is dishonorably wooed by Sansthanaka, virtuously repulses him and apparently is murdered by him. Sansthanaka then denounces Charudatta as the murderer, and the latter is condemned by the King to death. The headsmen are about to do their duty by the unfortunate, when the revived Vasantasena appears, thus proving Charudatta's innocence. Immediately news is brought that the herdsman has killed the King, has proved his own right to the throne, and has granted a principality to Charudatta. Vasantasena is legally raised out of the estate of courtesan, and is therefore free to marry Charudatta.

Within the ten-act plot, of which this is a bald outline, there are minor intrigues, comic scenes, elaborated social incidents, whatnot. One of the most amusing scenes, though an interruption of the story, is that in which a burglar, at his working, sets forth the principles of robbing as a fine art, quoting freely from the revered treatises on robbery. It would be possible to quote lyric bits as sweet as those from *Shakuntala*—though it is said that we who do not know Sanskrit at first hand, not realizing the difficulties of translation from the infinitely rich variations of the language, can only guess at the lyric beauty of the originals.

But even in translation it is evident that the brooding gentleness of Kalidasa, his pervasive felicity, cannot hang over a varied and intimate tale like this. *The Little Clay Cart* is, indeed, an isolated phenomenon, an achievement in a type of play unfamiliar to the place and the time out of which it was born.

With their passion for intellectual order, the Indian theorists divided the field of the drama into a number of types based on the use of the different legitimate elements of composition, the caste of the protagonists, supernatural elements, the employment of legendary or real-life plots, the intensity of the erotic emotion, etc., etc. At first there were ten divisions of the "higher drama," and eighteen of the "lower." But even the names of these types are confusing, and we need note them only as an indication of formalization in playwriting—a sort of caste test in dramaturgy. Such coded rules doubtless had much to do with making the Hindu drama the limited though lyrically beautiful thing that it is.

Nor need we pause over the later dramatists—except Bhavabhuti. This writer, of the eighth century, composed three plays that have survived to us. They are not characterized by that sweet harmony and that smooth-flowing action so notable in earlier drama. The poetry in which the action is clothed rises to more stirring moments: there is more vitality in the emotional scenes and more grandeur in the descriptions of nature. Bhavabhuti is, too, closer to the realities of life than Kalidasa, has deeper insight, more forceful imagination; he even escapes from the old prohibitions in regard to violence. But the pretty fancy, the meticulous workmanship, the lyric delicacy are gone. Gone, too, its literary simplicity, for in the descriptive passages are elaborations and exaggerations that foreshadow the decline of Hindu drama into the grandiose and the artificial. Native commentators have called Kalidasa "the grace of poetry," and Bhavabhuti "the master of eloquence."

And indeed, the period from the ninth to the fourteenth century is one of decay; and after the fourteenth, India is to contribute practically nothing to the history of the world theatre. The confusion of changing languages, the rigidities of the caste system in social life, the codification of rules of practice for the artist—these are circumstances hostile to the art that above all others is social in its implications, direct in appeal, and more emotional than intellectual. The drama got lost in refinements and verbal ornament, went away into strange regions of florid rhetoric and literary jugglery.

The Indian theatre, indeed, may owe its worst as well as its best features to the fact that it was a *class* institution. The director of a play asks, "What are those qualities which the virtuous, the wise, the venerable, the learned and the Brahmans require in drama?" and is answered: "Profound exposition of the various passions, pleasing interchange of mutual affection, loftiness of character, delicate expression of desire, a surprising story and elegant language."

The description indicates at once the slightness or shallowness of Hindu drama, and the delicacy, elegance, and harmony attained by its greatest practitioners. In accepting the injunction to please only the most learned and the most fastidious minds in the land, the dramatists cut themselves off from all that is deeply stirring, that moves the soul and cleanses the spirit—the very thing that we of the Western world consider essentially dramatic. Instead they please us graciously, dreamily, sentimentally, and sensuously. They are masters in that little bit of the dramatic field that lies over against lyric poetry and decorative painting. We may find the perfect analogy in Indian and Persian painting: in the child-like fancy, the transparent coloring, the delightful freshness, the dew-drenched sweetness; but having experienced this slight and utterly disarming lyric beauty, we may on occasion want to get back to our own Michelangelos and El Grecos, to our Æschylus and Euripides and Shakespeare. For Indian drama is gentle and lulling but never splendid.

Those who are its unreserved apologists point out that it attains to the peace of the East and avoids the restlessness of the West. We others, finding that peace pleasurable, yet doubt its profundity. We see in drama and in theatre at their highest some implication of peace attained only after gripping struggle, the more radiant calm of serenity after storm. Perhaps a racial difference will always prevent us from judging eye-to-eye with the Hindus.

THE Chinese theatre offers even greater difficulties to the Western mind. Chinese drama has no literary values for us, and the conventions of presentation are so different that almost insuperable barriers to understanding are set up. It is significant that the only so-called Chinese play that has made a considerable success in the West is a pieced-out romance with only vague relationship to any existing Chinese drama, with certain naïve customs of staging played up for prettiness or for humor. Memories of *The Yellow Jacket*, indeed, may well serve as guide to what will prove of interest to the Western student in approaching the Chinese stage: not plot or dramatic intensity or spoken poetry, surely, but a child-like fairy-tale freshness, surface glamour, patches of theatric-poetic invention, and a naïveté that to us is too often humorous.

It is the stage conventions, then, rather than the drama, that may give us pause even in a brief survey of the important theatres of the world. We may sit six or seven hours at a stretch in a Chinese playhouse and suffer fearful periods of boredom between pleasant periods of wonder and delight—but afterwards we shall always hold in memory the *way* in which poetry was occasionally conjured up for us, and the theatric brightness of the stage.

The playhouse itself is typically a platform for acting and a place for seeing. The stage is open, without concealing curtains, uniformly lighted throughout the show and wholly innocent of wings, scenery, or machinery. This is a place for acting, undisguised, but pleasantly designed. The wall at back has two doorways, one for the actors to enter from, the other for their return to the green-room (the actors' common room). There are fairly elaborate playhouses in the larger cities, but the greater number of Chinese theatres are temporary or movable structures which can be set up in street or field. Always, however, for audiences made comfortable in boxes or for those standing in the street, the simple projecting stage with two doorways at back is standard. Indoors or out, this stage has a roof, usually ornamental like that of a temple.

It is in the temple, of course, that we may seek the origins of the Oriental theatre. The Chinese have always been lovers of ritual and ceremony. Dance and music in religious exercises go back beyond historical evidence, into legend and myth. Certainly near-dramatic dancing was common here in temple and palace long before the era of Thespis and Æschylus. One need only remember that the Golden Age in China is supposed to have been at the time we would designate the seventeenth and sixteenth centuries B.C. Nearer to historical certainty, perhaps, is the report that the Emperor Ming Huang, of the eighth century A.D., after a trip to the Moon where he saw skilled actors, formed the first dramatic company and erected a stage in his pear orchard; whence the name still assumed by many players, "Members of the College of the Pear Garden," or "Youths of the Pear Garden."

Truly literary drama, however, seems to have come into its own only in the late Middle Ages. At least the types of play still predominating today on Chinese stages appeared in great number, and apparently without earlier imperfect or transitional forms, during the Yuan Dynasty, 1280–1368. It happened at just the time when a conqueror had thrown out all the old court literary men and scholars. Suddenly the theatre, theretofore held inferior to poetry and other intellectual arts, blossomed. It might be better to say that the theatre came up part way to meet literature, and that high literature (then in the learned classic language) stooped part way to meet the vernacular stage.

Truth to tell, dramatic literature in China never reached the importance a Sophocles or a Shakespeare endowed it with in the West. The Chinese themselves make no claims for it; and even allowing for the lack of language-embroidery values possibly lost in translation, the Western reader may agree that Chinese plays are little more than melodrama or hack journalistic plays—or grand opera *libretti*. The situations are pretty well standardized, the characters run to obvious types, the "effects" are neither deeply dramatic nor cumulatively emotional. All that the Western mind craves in tragedy is overlooked or dissipated: taut dramatic structure, suspense, psychologic truth. The casual nature of the plot, indeed, explains that apparently shattering confusion in the auditorium, the constant coming and going of spectators, the tea-drinking, the conversations and eating and even

A Chinese actor in typical gorgeous costume. [From a drawing by Kenyon Cox, in *Century Magazine*.]

games while the actors are getting through a particularly unimportant passage. There is no continuity of mood, no built-up tension. The performance probably lasts from late afternoon till after midnight; but the programme includes several plays. As the actors from one go out the exit door, the players of the next enter by the other, so that action is continuous. And so is the music that sounds so squeaky and clangy to Western ears. (The extremely long plays, we are told, running to thirty-two and forty-eight acts, are reading rather than acting versions.)

Watching the Chinese audience at times, one knows that the spectators are enjoying values largely lost to the outsider. One guesses that
these are of two sorts: first, the *acting*—the Chinese theatre, from projecting bare stage to conventions of playing, is designed to give first
prominence to acting as an art; and second, a sort of operatic effectiveness induced by the music and the chanting delivery combined
with the more truly histrionic virtues. In addition there is the sensuous richness of costumes, properties, and imaginatively evoked *milieu*.
The instrumental music, of course, adds value only for the initiated.
To those trained in appreciation of the European scale and to harmony and melody, it seems monotonous, harsh, and shrill. The musicians sit at the back centre of the stage, always in sight of the
audience. The dialogue is at times spoken, but mostly chanted. The
delivery is absolutely unreal, and a world of convention exists in the
gestures, posturing, intonation, and shadings of artificial expression.

In the subject matter of the plays there is a range almost as broad
as in the West. No arbitrary line is drawn between tragedy and
comedy. In the one direction, deep tragedy in our sense is lacking,
though pathetic situation and sob-scenes may be witnessed. But
heroic deeds, most often built around filial piety, or historical-military
exploits, are commonest in serious drama. And in the other direction
there is every sort of humor, from a tender sort to slap-stick. "Broad"
jests go well; but it is common knowledge that the playwright who
takes to indecency to hold his audiences is tormented by evil spirits
so long as his play holds the boards.

Chinese plays are sometimes classified as either "historical" or
"civil," with farces as perhaps an extra and unimportant sort. Military and patriotic plays, and heroic legendary ones, are, of course,
historical. The civil group is largely domestic drama, wherein virtue
triumphs. "Criminal" drama forms a considerable subdivision. But
sometimes there are plays of satirical purpose, often with the priests
or old superstitions as target. When all is said about the literary side
of Chinese drama, however, the fact remains that there is no serious
effort to match great action with great poetry, to re-enforce the
dramatic emotion by the revealing word. The actor, moreover, takes
what liberties he likes with the written text, cutting and improvising
freely.

The characters tend to standardization: Emperors and generals and
heroes in the historical genre, together with demons and spirits; the
honest wife, the jealous husband, the light woman, the villain, etc.,
in the civil plays. The poor student who ultimately overcomes all
difficulties and rises to high office is a favorite. The military hero
performing marvels of valor is another. Traditional make-up and

costuming, known to every theatre-goer, characterize many figures in
dramatic literature—almost as definitely as in the Italian *Commedia
dell'Arte*, though with less of caricature. An understood convention is
the coloring in face-painting (the faces are often made-up until they
are to all practical purposes masks): a whitened face denotes a wicked
person, a red face is honest, a gold face heavenly, a streaked face belongs to a robber,[2] and so on. A bride wears a red veil, deceased
ancestors wear black veils or else strips of paper hanging from their
right ears, a sick person wears an opaque yellow veil. Corrupt officials
wear round hats.

Despite these elementary aids to understanding, much more is left
to the spectator's imagination than in the theatres of Europe—even
more than was left before Realism brought in detailed scene and
photographic fidelity to "life." Out of a stage with a few rich hang-
ings, a rug underfoot, and a half dozen properties, the Chinese actor
and a Property Man will suddenly conjure up a cherry orchard in
blossom or an idyllic lake with boats on it or Heaven. And you see
these places believably, far more believably than in the elaborate
painted settings of the "illusive" scene designer—in the shape and colors
of your own ideal vision of the places. A handful of bits of paper
fluttering down, after the Property Man has tossed them up, evokes
the whole "feel" of a snowstorm; when once you know that a banner
carried behind a general denotes a thousand soldiers in his army, you
subconsciously count the banners and know that to all intents and
purposes one, two, or three thousand men are following him into
battle; when a character paddles the air rhythmically with an oar, the
whole pretty scene of placid water and boating flashes into the mind.
Sometimes the means are more concrete: the Property Man sets up
two poles, a cross-bar and a silken hanging—and lo! the stage has
become a throne room; or he sets up a little piece of wall, and the
General acts out elaborately the convention of taking a city.

This Property Man is, indeed, the very symbol of the noble artificiality of the Chinese stage. He is dressed in black or blue, and
therefore is, symbolically, invisible to the audience. He is always on
the stage, and may even have assistants; but the audience never thinks
of him as entering into the play. He is the wizard who sets down a
ball of red cloth to show that the actor's head has been cut off, he
may help the General off with his priceless coat before a piece of
business that might soil it, he touches off the fireworks to indicate
that this latest entrant is a ghost from Heaven, he places the chair

---

[2] I have followed here the account of A. E. Zucker in *The Chinese Theatre*
(Boston, 1925); other authorities give different though no less exact rules.

which becomes a mountain over which the hero laboriously climbs. But never does he interfere with the illusion of the scene.

If suggestion and convention thus work wonders in evoking something more subtly theatrical than picture scenery, the actor does his part in creating atmosphere and belief. A ritualistic stage fight shows not one blow struck, but all the activity and excitement of battle; and no one doubts which is victor, when vanquished sneaks off and the hero proudly follows. This actor will climb stairs by merely lifting one foot high off the floor after the other, or else go all the way from Peking to Thibet by walking a few times around the stage rug (though he may then announce where he has arrived). Then, too, he can leap off the table in such a way that you know he has jumped down the well, a suicide. He mounts and gets down from horses, or

Two masked actors in *No* plays. [From old Japanese wood prints.]

gallops on them, and washes his hands in imaginary pools, and backs up to a bamboo pole and throws his head back to show he has been hanged. But it is the drummer who tells you the time of night by beating out the hours the while all other instruments are still.

The one unfailing physical richness of the production is in the costumes. The wardrobe of a Chinese troupe is costly even when judged by Western "revue" standards. Minor characters dress magnificently, literally beggars in silks, and chief characters are no less than gorgeous and resplendent. Thus in one detail there is material basis for the imaginative splendor, the glamour, of the Oriental stage. But it is from the imagination of the spectator that the larger richness and the more poetic achievement come.

The actors for such a theatre must be long and carefully trained, and many years are spent by the young player in specialized education. It is obvious that something more than the casual European training is necessary when an actor must be able not only to die gracefully on the stage but then to get up and exit with exactly the stoop that will tell the audience his body is being carried off by four bearers. Incidentally many young men must be trained to the simulation of feminine charms—even to dainty walking in cramped shoes; for the women's parts until very recently have been taken by men—at least since the eighteenth century when women were banished from the stage by royal decree, after an Emperor took an actress to wife. (One is puzzled a bit to know whether actresses were then considered too good for the theatre, or if the measure was a precaution against possible repetition of a misalliance.) The most famous player in China in recent times, Mei Lan-Fang, is remembered chiefly for his masterly playing in feminine rôles. He was possibly the greatest living actor of his era.[3]

As a matter of fact, Chinese plays are not so exclusively non-realistic and imaginative as I have perhaps suggested. The means is always imaginative and conventional, as compared with staging in the Occident. But sometimes grossly realistic incident is included in a play—and of a sort very distasteful to Western spectators. But perhaps that is a matter of "taste": our own tragic heroines, suffering from too much love, though emotionally moving to us, would be distressing if not ridiculous to the Chinese.

---

[3] Since these lines were written Mei has died. Before the end he enjoyed an enormous success outside China. Actors and critics in Russia, Germany and America extraordinarily praised his exquisite and revelatory portrayals. It should be added that in 1950–1951 the Chinese workers' theatres came to the fore, in the image of the Russian propaganda stage, with *Agitprop* brigades, Blue Blouses, and all. Again in the 1960s, during the revolution headed by Mao Tse-tung, student and labor groups staged great numbers of propagandist playlets.

Since Western influences have flowed strongly in the Orient, the customs of the theatre have changed. Actresses now appear, there are companies that adopt more and more of Realism in staging, there are even "little theatre" groups devoted to Western "ideals." But China is too big a country, and too sluggish, to swallow alien art at one gulp. And it is more than possible that the old stage, with its childish fairy-tale quality, its rich glamour, its way of making poetic incident and imaginative beauty appear out of acting and a platform and a few properties, has virtues unknown to the theatre farther west—and essentially theatrical virtues.

IN Japan caste determined a sharp division between aristocratic and popular theatres. For the nobles there came into being a drama highly intellectualized, rigidly formalized; for the people there was a freer drama. Over both sorts was the sensuous richness, the calculated decorativeness, that is of the very spirit of Japan.

The noble drama, the *No*-play, is today the most important survival in the world from the ritualistic theatre of elder times, from the days when ceremonial beauty was more important than plot or emotional content. The *No*—the word corresponds to our "drama" in the larger sense—has at once an austerity inherited out of the religious rites at the temples, and a formal delicacy and a colorful richness added out of the feeling for æsthetic expressiveness. Drama never eschewed more completely Realism in all its aspects: surface truth to appearances, imitative mimicry, and transcription of human emotion. As soon as it developed out of ritual dance into a form compounded of music, dance, incident, and words, the *No* took on rigid conventions.

The single *No*-play is brief, shorter than the average Western "one-act" drama; and in the reading it is often so slight that it seems merely a reminiscent bit, of great lyric charm but undramatic and even bald. The secret is that the text is only a framework hung with poetic allusion and pretty words. What we would call the dramatic element, the tension-and-clash, is either non-existent (as in many examples) or comes from some traditional and racial reaction to a given situation or deed. The values that the educated Japanese expects in a *No*-drama are utterly different from those that we rate highest in our theatre: they depend for their effectiveness both upon a recondite knowledge and upon appreciation of ceremonial excellencies.

Several plays are produced on one programme, and it is typical that the arrangement, the order, of the plays is considered of greater importance than the individual content. A programme is as carefully constructed, balanced, as a religious ritual. It presents, indeed, a "service." The several parts are chosen and placed with a view to total harmony, to decorative pattern, to a sequence of feeling as subtly estimated as is the arrangement of movements in a complex musical work. There is here something approximating the Western formula of preparation-rise-climax-and-fall; but the emotional sequence is the smaller consideration: the greater importance is in the adjustment of the poetic, imaginative, and decorative details.

One may find a hint of the care taken in these matters and of the delicacy of enjoyment, by recalling that in Japan flower-arrangement is a highly developed art, and that the nobles used to have a ceremonial game known as "listening to incense," wherein blended perfumes were distinguished and brief allusive titles written to fix the poetic thought evoked by each sort.

In explanation of the insubstantial character of the *utai*, or *No*-play text, it might be said that the object is to present an image rather than to lay out an action; and those who have got at the purpose of the "Imagist" poets will understand more exactly the creative intent of the dramatist. The play was written for the few, for discriminating art-lovers, for select audiences traditionally trained to subtleties and to a set of conventions.

A legend tells that the dance from which the *No* evolved was invented by the gods: when one of their number, the all-important Sun-goddess, hid away for a long time in the rock-cave of Heaven, causing universal darkness, the others invented a dance which one of them performed on the top of an inverted tub; and the Sun-goddess came out to see what was the hollow noise made by the dancer's feet. (The sound of the dancer's stamping on the wooden floor is still a characteristic touch in the *No*-play.) But later the other elements were added to the pantomimic dance, and it is probable that Buddhist priests were the first "playwrights." In the fourteenth century Kwanami Kiyotsugu crystallized the form of the *No*, and it was due to him that it was taken under court protection. Thereafter specially honored poets and specially dedicated companies of actors created that store of *No*-plays and *No*-rules that has been the treasury of the aristocratic players for five hundred years since. Always the limitations and the finenesses of noble origin—of the association with gods, priests, emperors, lords—have persisted.

It is said that almost every word in a *No*-play means far more than the word alone says: there are traditional associations through centuries-old use by poets; overtones, double meanings, and vague indications. The values are heightened by the delivery, in a sort of chant. The movements of the actors and dancers are no less rich in symbolism, allusion, and suggestion. Music (the musicians here again are placed on the stage) binds the whole performance together. The usual instruments are a flute and three types of drum.

The stage is as unvarying as the methods of delivery: a rectangular platform with a temple roof. At the back is a conventional representation of a pine-tree. A bridge or trestle runs off at one side to a green-room. The auditorium is on three sides of the projecting platform. The wooden stage floor is specially constructed to afford a drum-like resonance to the dancer's stamping. The entire stage is ornamental

A *No* stage with actors. [Drawing from *Plays of Old Japan: The No*, by Marie C. Stopes.]

but without any illusive scenery or machinery. Properties are but sparingly used. The fan, according to an accepted symbolism, may stand for many things: the spectator transforms it into this or that object called for by the action, just as he constructs his own imaginative setting in accordance with the poet's words.

The actors are supplemented by a Chorus of six men or more who squat on the stage throughout the play, chanting at intervals. In the design of the drama the Chorus serves practically the same function as in the Greek theatre, as re-enforcement or commentary or to instruct the audience. The main actors, all men, are two, three, or four in number. They enter with ceremonial slowness, and every gesture for every feeling or thought is prescribed by rule. All characters except young men are represented by masks, the impersonality of the acting being thus increased by suppression of facial play. The masks are beautifully carved, and are wholly formalized; but within non-realistic limits they have a considerable range of expressiveness. The gestures and posturing of the actors are equally unreal, symbolic, and according

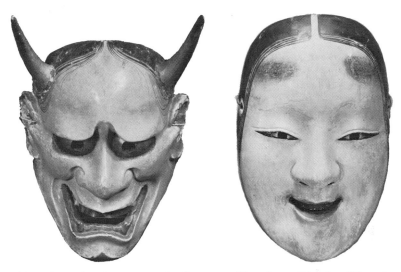

Carved masks for actors in Japanese *No* plays. [In the Victoria and Albert Museum, London.]

to an understood formula. The danced portions of the action are wholly unlike the freer dancing of the West—call it "Greek" if you like—and yet wholly unlike the artificial gyrations of the European ballet. Again it is the ritualistic, ceremonial element that predominates. The actors' costumes are of sumptuous richness; and the magnificence of the costumed figures has full effect on the simple stages, quietly decorative and a perfect background. It may be added that in olden days the audience likewise came in full ceremonial dress, as they would if the *No* were still only a ritual dance at a temple on a holy-day.

It is difficult for the Western mind to recognize such acted-danced art as essentially drama. We of the Occident demand the free play of emotion for full appreciation of acted drama; and here the intellect seems always to control. But after all, "drama" merely means something done, an act; and assuredly there is no authority to say that the ritualistic, formalized action is less noble than the imitative-emotional sort. We shall do better to grant that here is a sort of dramatic art different from ours, finely decorative to all eyes, and affording even to unaccustomed spectators sudden glimpses of a different beauty, intellectual, fanciful, subtle, poetic. At one side a sort of sensuous harmony, of color, music, and movement, lulls one; at the other, there is the constant play of pretty meaning, of description, metaphor, philosophical thought, which we may understand when our wits have been sharpened by long training—the whole rendered clearer by being lifted above human emotion to a region of impersonality.

The *No* has existed six hundred years or more as the privileged art of an aristocratic class. Today it is played by descendants of the actors of Kiyotsugu's time. But with the almost chaotic changes in social life in Japan during the last half-century, lines between classes have been broken, and no one may foresee the future of such a very special type of art. Perhaps there will be an aristocracy of the spirit—or of the intellect—to keep it alive. Meantime certain of its elements, its utter precision, its decorative richness-in-restraint, its stylization, its poetic intensity, have been well studied by certain Western artists who have guessed that the mastery of Realism is not the whole battle of the theatre.

In one sense the *No* exists like a curiosity out of the past. The hereditary guardians let no changes be made after the sixteenth century. The old methods, the old subjects, the old costumes and masks, are preserved, so that one views a *No*-play as one views a survival of medieval art—but Chartres Cathedral or the Sainte Chappelle is none the less beautiful for not being modernized.

There is, however, a popular theatre in Japan which has changed with the times. The *Kabuki* was scorned by the nobles and the intellectuals through all the earlier centuries. This more vulgar theatre, less intellectual, less bound by aristocratic code and traditional methodism, compromised with popular taste, with sensationalism, with Realism. Even so, it is characterized by formalities in presentation that place it worlds apart from European drama; but it is less distinctively different—and for that very reason less interesting to the spectator out of the West.

The *Kabuki* theatre is supposed to have originated out of the performances of a woman dancer, O-Kuni, about 1600; to her dancing—perhaps religious at first—were added elements out of the *No*-plays and out of the exhibitions of popular entertainers. It is chronicled "that O-Kuni was beautiful, that she was skilled in calligraphy, that she had a sympathetic nature, loved flowers and the moon, and that a snowy evening or a maple scene in the autumn inspired her to poetry." We may take the description as warrant that, as the *Kabuki* developed, it did not swing *very* far toward the unrelieved Realism of the West. Indeed much was taken over bodily from the *No* theatre:

the playhouse was but slightly changed, the conventions of staging were made less rigid, even while a similar ceremonial beauty was exacted, music continued to make the play almost operatic, and plots began to touch on common life as well as legendary deeds. Just after O-Kuni's time the women performers predominated; but their alarming popularity, and perhaps some moral laxness, led the government to forbid all but male players. By the mid-seventeenth century men's companies were firmly established, and thenceforth the *Kabuki* was the accepted entertainment of the common people.

The few changes in the playhouse, from the *No* model, indicate the direction of change in the performance. (There was, incidentally, a strong influence from the Chinese theatre too.) The stage was still the rectangular platform with audience on three sides; and for long the ornamental roof persisted in actuality—though later a painted representation or symbol of it sufficed. But in addition to the bridge from the green-room, one or oftener two bridges were built forward from the stage through the auditorium, for more effective entrances: the "flower paths" which have recently come in for wide discussion after adoption into European and American "revue" theatres. Thus pageant-like and spectacular effects were facilitated. Trap-doors in the stage floor added opportunity for tricks and surprises. To the stately acting and the old measured posturing out of ritual were added extraneous effects quite like those known to Western melodrama and opera. The form of the auditorium is sufficiently shown in the illustrations, except that it should be added that the audience squats in the many boxes: there are no seats. Mats and cushions provide "comfort," and small stoves are sometimes utilized by more fortunate spectators. Since the performance lasts from early morning (originally from dawn) to late afternoon, there is inevitably considerable coming and going, not to mention eating and drinking.

The properties for such a stage naturally became more elaborate, and the settings grew from mere suggestions to fairly explicit indications of reality. The drift toward illusive setting became so strong, indeed, that the Japanese invented the revolving stage (originally for the doll-plays), for swift change of background, long before the idea was developed in European theatres. But the search for novelty and for natural effects on the *Kabuki* stage went on even while the producers adhered to the Chinese convention of the "invisible" Property Man. He still comes and goes in a way that would shatter the illusion in any Western playhouse.

With the austere example of *No*-acting before him, and yet in a theatre where novelty and sensation counted, the *Kabuki* player necessarily found himself pulled in the two directions of a high conventionalization in acting and of naturalism. So it is no matter for surprise that two schools grew up, distinguished by their devotion to the one or the other ideal. And yet all Japanese acting (up to the experiments in imitation of the Occident in the twentieth century) must be visualized as unreal and at times ritualistic. An actor may

Two Kabuki theatres. Above, a seventeenth century theatre, with a stage roof of the old temple type. Note the realistic properties. Below, a theatre in 1798, when the roof had become a symbol only. Here the floor boxes for spectators are clearly seen. [The print below is by Utagawa Toyokuni, reproduced in *Kabuki: The Popular Stage of Japan*, by Zoe Kincaid.]

play a death scene with a dragging-out of the agony very distressing
to the uninitiated—twenty minutes of dying in the midst of his gore—
but the naturalism of it is not that photographic sort affected by
Western actors today. The measure of progress away from the high
stylization of the *No* is indicated by the abandonment of the rigid
mask in favor of a conventional painted make-up: faces are painted in
traditional ways to symbolize traditional characters. The *Kabuki* actor
must be a dancer and a pantomimist as accomplished as the players of
the *No*, though his posturing is less tightly restricted by code.

The plays are not of great poetic value, and are considered rather
as "vehicles." Still at least one dramatist whose works are popular on
the *Kabuki* stage, Chikamatsu, who lived from 1660 to 1724, has been
called by recent commentators "the Shakespeare of Japan"—though
one awaits better translations than are now available before endorsing
the title. The range of plays is from heroic tragedy to melodrama, and
from satire to farce. Farcical interludes, one might add, are played in
Japan even between the most serious numbers on a *No* programme.
The most famous play in the *Kabuki* repertory is one dealing with the
legend of the Forty-seven Ronin.

Perhaps one detail will serve to fix the *Kabuki* drama in our minds
—as conventionalized theatre making concessions to Realism—better
than any other. Among the common properties is a velvet horse.
You will remember how the Chinese actor mounted his wholly
imaginary steed and galloped away. But for the Japanese audiences
this make-believe was not enough. So the *Kabuki* horse is constructed
and walks around on the four legs of two minor actors; their bodies
and heads are completely hidden within the body of a quite realistic
animal, that knows every trick of kicking, plunging, trotting, etc.
There are even actors who specialize in being horses' legs. This velvet-
covered living property, common to all *Kabuki* stages, is the very
indicator of the degree of their Realism. *Kabuki* lies half-way between
Chinese imaginative theatre and Western photographic theatre.

In Japan a third theatre is important, but too "special" to demand
more than a paragraph here. The "Doll Theatre" or puppet theatre
has held its place for centuries. Chikamatsu and other important playwrights wrote more plays for the dolls than for the *Kabuki* companies
(though their puppet-plays were soon absorbed into the other theatre); and there has been constant give-and-take between the marion-
ette-stage and that of the *Kabuki* players. It is said that historically,
dancing dolls preceded the doll-play. But music, acting figures, and
recited story were brought together in one entertainment, about 1600,
and marionette shows have been popular ever since. In Japan far more
of talent was expended in making the puppet performance sensuously

beautiful and the lines poetically engrossing than ever was the case in Europe. Without making the mistake of judging by the Punch and Judy shows or other degraded descendants of the old Italian (originally Greek and Roman) puppets, we may feel sure that the West never knew a doll theatre quite so elaborate, quite so definitely patterned to æsthetic considerations, as the Japanese. The traditional fine craftsmanship, the perfection of decorative adjustment, the love of impersonal art, the delight in miniature loveliness of any sort—all these elements went into the making of the world's most skilful, and most esteemed, puppet theatre. But it is a far cry to that very specialized stage, from the emotionally intensified drama, and the human actor, at the heart of our present story.

Javanese puppets. [From *Javanische Schattenspiele,* by Otto Höver.]

In Java there exists a national dramatic activity almost wholly shaped by puppet-invention. Side by side are a theatre of shadow-figures (old beyond history), a theatre of manipulated puppets, and a theatre of dancing human-actors whose movements are conventionalized out of the mechanical doll-gestures. Thus at least one country gained its mimetic art not from humans imitating nature or dancing instinctively, but from a ritual-toy originally made in a formal-decorative likeness to man. This curious round-about development, from convention to convention, may well leave to us, as our last—and most memorable—thought about the Oriental stage, an impression of purposeful unreality, of formalized theatric beauty.

CHAPTER
6

The Theatre
in the Church

THE THEATRE is especially the shrine of Venus. In fact it was in this manner that this sort of performance came up in the world. For the censors were often wont to destroy, in this very birth, the theatres more than any other thing, consulting for the morals of the people, as foreseeing a great peril accruing to them from licentiousness. Pompey the Great, less only than his own theatre, when he had built up that stronghold of every vice, fearing that the censors might one day cast reflections on his memory, placed over it a temple of Venus, "under which," said he, "we have put rows of seats for the shows." Thus did he cloak this damned and damnable work under the name of a temple, and by the aid of superstition eluded the rule. . . Whatever there be peculiar and proper to the stage, with respect to the dissoluteness and postures of the body, they consecrate to the soft nature of Venus and of Bacchus, the one dissolute through her sex, the other through his wantonness; while such things as are done by the voice, by music, by wind and stringed instruments, have for their patrons Apollos and Muses and Minervas and Mercuries. Thou must hate, Christian, those things, the inventors whereof thou canst not but hate . . .

In like manner also we are commanded to love no immodesty. By this means therefore we are cut off from the theatre likewise, which is the private council-chamber of immodesty, wherein nothing is approved save that which elsewhere is disapproved. . . . The very harlots also, the victims of the public lust, are brought forward on the stage, more wretched in the presence of women, from whom alone they are wont to conceal themselves . . . Blush the Senate! Blush all ranks! let the very women, the destroyers of their own modesty, shudder at their doings before the light and the public, and blush this once within the year . . .

Nay, in all the show, no offence will more meet us, than that very overcareful adorning of the men and women. The very community of feeling, their very agreement or disagreement in party-spirit, doth, by their intercourse, fan the sparks of carnal lust. Finally, no one in entering the show, thinketh of any thing more than to see and to be seen . . . What manner of thing is it to go from the Church of God into the Church of the Devil? from the sky (as they say) to the stye? . . .

Why may not such men be in danger of devils entering into them? for the case hath happened, the Lord is witness, of that woman who went to the theatre, and returned thence with a devil. Wherefore when the unclean spirit, in the exorcism, was hard pressed because he had dared to attack a believer, he boldly said, "and most righteously I did it, for I found her in mine own place." It is well known also that there was shown to another in her sleep, on the night of the day in which she had heard a tragedian, a linen cloth upbraiding her with that tragedian by name, and that this woman at the end of five days was no longer in the world. . .

What wilt thou do, when discovered in this estuary of impious voices? . . . think what becometh of thee in heaven. Doubtest thou that in this crisis, in which the Devil is raging against the Church, all the Angels are looking down from Heaven, and marking every man, whosoever hath spoken blasphemy, whosoever hath listened to it, whosoever hath ministered with his tongue, or with his ears, to the Devil against God? Wilt thou not then flee from these chairs of the enemies of Christ, this seat of pestilences . . . ?

The quotation is from Tertullian, from the *De Spectaculis*, or treatise *Of Public Shows*, as the translator, the Rev. C. Dodgson, phrases it. This pious work was written about A.D. 198, just after the author's conversion to Christianity, when there was, indeed, evil enough to grow indignant about in the Roman theatres. But the descriptive portions, though they may conveniently remind us of the degradation of the classic stage, have even more value here for the light they throw on the temper of the Christian fathers, and the relationship of the theatre to the fear of devils and of the angel-spies of God. If the quotation seem over-long for such a brief book as this, let us reflect that these few paragraphs contain, by implication, practically the whole history of the theatre in Europe over a period of centuries—nay, for nearly a millennium.

Tertullian has, indeed, set forth graphically not only the iniquities of the Roman stage of his time, but also the means by which the Christian Church was to strangle theatric art and prevent its rebirth for eight hundred years to come. Note well the righteous zeal, the true Christian priest's burning indignation with the works of the Devil, growing at once out of love for the souls of men and out of intolerance. Note well the distrust of the pleasures of life, even of such apparently innocent ones as dressing-up and of congregating socially. But note chiefly the way in which the reader is warned about one who died after being seen in a theatre, and of another who was possessed by a Devil out of the playhouse. For fear is to be the great weapon of the Church in the age to come, the weapon with which drama is to be killed. The terror of Devils and of a Hell after death for those who disregard the priests—this is to outweigh love of show and of the arts.

There are, of course, other contributive causes for the long lapse before another theatre is born; in the social conditions of the times, and in the break-up of the Roman Empire under the repeated invasions by barbarous Northern tribes. (They were not so barbarous as the Romans in many ways, but uneducated to drama and the arts.) It was Christianity, nevertheless, that was most hostile, most militant, that deliberately set to work to stamp out the art sacred to the pagan Dionysus.

If you read Tertullian's treatise to the end, you may detect in his closing picture, of the Christian world as a show, a prophecy of what the theatre is to be when next the mimetic spirit in man emerges.

> Dost thou breathe me a sigh for goals and theatres? . . . Behold uncleanness thrown down by chastity, perfidiousness slain by faithfulness, cruelty beaten by mercy, wantonness overlaid by modesty . . . But what sort of show is that near at hand? the coming of the Lord, now confessed, now glorious, now triumphant. What is that joy of the Angels? what the glory of the rising saints? . . . There remain other shows: that last and eternal day of judgment . . . the persecutors of the Name of the Lord, melting amid insulting fires more raging than those wherewith themselves raged against the Christians; those wise philosophers, moreover, reddening before their own disciples, now burning together with them . . .

Prophetic, because the favorite scene in the next great drama of the world is to be the realistic casting of the damned into Hell; and along with it will be the whole acted story of the coming of the Lord and the glorification of the Saints; and after that the Morality plays in which "perfidiousness slain by faithfulness" will be the end and motive. Tertullian wrote methaphorically of this Christian "spectacle"; but a thousand years later the priests of his Church will be acting out on stages the very scenes he so graphically sketches in words.

As a last reminder of the Roman stage, one may note that a later famous Churchman, Arius, of the fourth century, outlined a plan for a Christian theatre to combat the lewd ones of the pagans; but nothing tangible resulted—perhaps because Arius was excommunicated for his heretical doctrinal views. The Roman theatre (which then was the amusement not only of the old capital and colonies, but of Constantinople and the Eastern Empire) persisted through the fifth and into the sixth century after Christ's birth, then died in the bitter conflict with

The altar area of a mediæval church as an ideal stage. The Romanesque church at Solignac, Limousin, about A.D. 1100.

the increasingly powerful Church. Some of the later Fathers even went so far as to trace the fall of the Roman people to the influence of the depraved theatres. The last contemporary reference to the Roman stage is in a letter dated 533.

After that we may picture the wandering actors as producing scraps of their old plays at courts, at private festivities, even occasionally at a crossroads or in a city street, surreptitiously. But they are no longer true comedians, presenting complete "dramas"; with their sketches they mix jugglery, knife-throwing, tumbling, tight-rope walking—or they lead along a trained bear to provide the "feature" act.

No one can say just how far acting declined, how close drama approached toward total extinction. But before the old tradition died entirely, a new element entered into entertainment, the element of recited poetic story. It came not only from the South but from the North, from the Teutonic gleemen. Without being truly dramatic in itself—without becoming *acted* story with impersonating performers—it kept alive the *personal telling* of dramatic incident. At its best it became an accepted art—minstrelsy—which in turn gave rise to a literature that is the most important survival of the early Middle Ages, the *Chansons de geste*, the *Romans* and the *Contes;* at its worst, it afforded the miserable jugglers and "mimes" an additional item for a very degraded repertory of "turns," an item that at least preserved a vague relationship of miming to literature.

The history of the true strolling player is lost, roughly from the sixth to the twelfth century. But the history of the singer or reciter is picked up even before the Church finally succeeds in suppressing the theatre with a stage and actors; and there are records of the German *scop* almost from the time when he separated himself from communal folk-singing to his emergence as honored court-minstrel. In France, England, and Germany, the activities of the popular singer-reciter can be traced, no less in the annals of courts and feudal castles than in the prohibitions of a Church that still made no distinctions between the better and the worse sorts of entertainer.

It would be easy to read too much theatric importance into the singing of the *troubadours* and *joculatores*, of the gleemen and the minstrels—the subject is a fascinating one. But these entertainers are a link and little more. Occasionally, doubtless, an impassioned reciter impersonated a character in true dramatic fashion, and there are passages in the romances that run into dialogue; but such are exceptions to the rule. We may rather consider the minstrels as an interesting *substitute for* the theatre in the darker centuries. They sang, or chanted, the things that have been the material of drama in other times: of heroic deeds, and legendary braveries, of men and women in love, and of funny happenings. A verse in *Cursor Mundi*, a fourteenth century poem, sums up their repertory:

Men lykyn jestis for to here,
And romans rede in diuers manere . . .
How kyng Charlis and Rowlond fawght
With Sarzyns nold they be cawght,
Of Tristrem and of Ysoude the swete
How they with love first gan mete,
Of kyng John and of Isombras,

Of Ydoyne and of Amadas,
Stories of diuerce thynggis,
Many songgis of diuers ryme,
As english, frensh, and latyne.

As yet there were no ballroom stages, and we may picture the glee-man and his harpist arriving unannounced before the castle gates, singing and playing a merry lay; invited in; entertaining lightly at dinner and afterward taking place at one end of the great hall, while the lord or prince (who could not read, or but painfully) and his ladies and guests would group themselves close, to hear a chanted tale of Charlemagne, or a metrical romance, perhaps the *Roman de la Rose*. This was the typical performer and the typical audience of the times.

The very flowering of minstrelsy came in the eleventh, twelfth, and thirteenth centuries, when real theatre had hardly emerged out of church service.

One other development during the centuries when the European theatre was, so to speak, "dark," demands passing notice here—in order that we may avoid violating chronology too ruthlessly: the growth of a body of more or less Christian folk-custom and folk-play bordering on the dramatic. The Church could not kill out the festival spirit in the peoples whom it gradually won to itself, partially by conversion, partly by conquest, when Christian overcame non-Chris-tian nation. Wisely the Church compromised, and took to itself a cer-tain number of the less ungodly and less ribald ceremonial customs. For the rest, it waged an unsuccessful fight against survival of the old tribal dancing, the joyous processionals, and even the pagan supersti-tions as to what rites would make the new wine ferment or render the old field fertile. Through ten centuries, from the establishment of Christianity as the recognized religion of civilized Europe to the Renais-sance, there are records of the outcroppings of the folk-drama instinct.

These are not enough related to afford basis for argument about a typical seventh or ninth or eleventh century dramatic phenomenon; but the examples are by no means isolated. Rather is there evidence that in many places and almost continuously people were reverting to rituals and dances that the Church had forbidden as heathenish. Perhaps the most notable feature about the known festivals is that they group themselves naturally around seasonal changes and the divisions of the agricultural year. As always in "primitive" folk-expression, the dance is at the heart of the matter. The new wine is to be tasted, perhaps; then a special day or night must be named for celebration. Two sorts of dance became common, a group-dance around a fire or a Maypole, or whatever else stands for the Dionysian altar of other days; and a processional dance through the fields and the village streets. The marchers may be costumed, and of course assuming masks adds to the fun; in some cases, chant and response between leader and chorus are the rule. Here indeed is the perfect parallel to the fertility rites in Greece at that moment when Thespis stepped forward and added the first actor-impersonator, to be followed soon after by Æschylus and Sophocles. We may almost infer, from twelfth and thirteenth century folk-custom, that if the drama were not then being reborn in the Church, a full-fledged secular drama would have developed independently quite soon. The amorous note of modern romantic comedy was already crossing with the dramatic dance— where the folk festival and minstrelsy came together. After the medieval Mystery and Miracle dramas, the people's Sword-dances and Mummers' Plays—both growing out of folk festivals, derived in turn from pre-Christian ritual—will lead on in a direct line to later fully theatrical, non-religious drama. One may add, too, that the Christmas Plays that grew up in the Church are characterized by elements attracted from other seasonal occasions, not entirely unmixed with pagan custom. But let us turn to the orthodox beginning of Christian drama.

A woodcut of the Mass, indicating dramatic elements. [From a book illustration dated 1499.]

In the tenth century, or perhaps the ninth, priests in a Catholic church conceived the idea of inserting into the Mass a song with the words apportioned to two or more singers or chanters. With the strictly orthodox aim of "fortifying the unlearned people in their faith," they planned to picture an incident to their congregations by the vivid means of living impersonators; instead of letting one stationary singer tell *about* the incident in Latin words that not one out of a thousand of the faithful understood.

The custom spread. No such aid to understanding had been introduced into the Church in ages. Soon the Mass—itself a dramatic-symbolic representation of the Last Supper, in the broader view—is divided into the read parts, the sung parts, and the acted parts. On special occasions, a whole acted episode is introduced.

At first the "scene" is very simple. A priest, specially vested, sits by "the sepulchre," while three others approach as if seeking something.

> "*Quem quæritis in sepulchro, Christicolæ?*" chants the one.
> "*Jesum Nazarenum crucifixum, o cælicolæ,*" chant the three.
> "*Non est hic, surrexit sicut prædixerat.*
> *Ite, nuntiate quia surrexit a mortuis.*"

The seekers turn to the choir, saying "*Alleluia! resurrexit Dominus.*" The guardian of the sepulchre says, "*Venite et videte locum,*" and lifts a curtain to show that the "tomb" is empty. There follows the anthem, *Surrexit Dominus de sepulchro;* and then the hymn *Te Deum laudamus,* while "all the bells chime out together."

Thus the congregation has seen pictured out the incident of the Three Marys and the Angel at the tomb of Jesus. There are several varying texts of this particular "trope" (or addition to the service) dating from the tenth century, and one from Winchester Cathedral has full "stage directions" as above outlined.

The Church service has had, of course, almost immemorially, many of the contributive elements that go to make up ritual drama: ceremonial movement, colorfulness of setting, musical accompaniment, even an approach toward dialogue, in antiphonal singing, in the two halves of the choir answering each other in song. But it is the introduction of dialogue between priests representing "characters" that marks the true birth of "the theatre in the church." Scholars call the incidents inserted into the Mass "liturgical drama," that is, part of the liturgy or service. They are the first steps toward the Mystery Play, or complete drama on a Scriptural subject.

From the tenth to the thirteenth century there are many texts, marked by growing elaboration, both in wording and in directions for acting and setting. The language changes from Latin to a mixture of Latin and vernacular, and finally to French or German or other popular tongue. Singing or chanting gives way to speech. The single incident grows into a series, until the Easter group provides all the materials for a real Passion, the Christmas group for a Nativity, and the Ascension group for a Resurrection Play. The "stories," of course, are taken as directly as possible from the Bible—it will be some time yet before the profane have their way in regard to "popular" concessions and additions. The natural progression, when the first acted incident was successful, would be to the episode next following in the legendary story: the *quem quæritis* sketch, bound around the showing-out of the

Painting by Hieronymus Bosch: *Christ Brought before the People.* The Flemish artist, a master of character drawing, was close to the popular theatre and probably painted this spirited scene after witnessing a religious drama of the time.

empty tomb, would be followed by a scene in which the Three Marys hold up to view the cast-off burial-clothes as token of Jesus' resurrection. And so on until a completed story is enacted. There is, of course, no more dramatic or theatric legend in history than that of the Christ, none more profoundly moving.

Just when or where the grouped liturgical dramatic "inserts" may be said to have become independent religious "plays," no one may venture to say. Before the first "Passion" or other Mystery Play was acted, however, there had been attempts at literary playwriting by Church people. In the tenth century a nun of the Gandersheim Abbey in Saxony, Hrosvitha by name, had written six comedies after the model of Terence, on religious themes, hoping to inculcate in her readers greater faith or love of chastity or Christian heroism. Terence had been—for reasons a bit difficult to fathom—a favorite author with the Christian scribes and scholars; and it may have been that the good nun wished to combat the dangers of the original unchaste plays with others of an opposite moral tendency. But her writing was flat, her dramatic sense defective; and it is even questioned whether her comedies ever came to amateur production even in her own prescribed orbit. Equally limited in influence was the famous Χριστοῦ Πάσγων, or *Passion of Christ*, written about the same time; which is of value chiefly because it incorporates bodily several hundred lines out of Euripides' plays, including passages nowhere else preserved. These isolated survivals may indicate a considerable monastic activity in imitating classic drama; but it was almost entirely a literary exercise and unrelated to the drama that was growing out of the tropes. Indeed, there are few phenomena in the history of the theatre more striking than the utter independence of the mediæval religious drama from classic influence—after a great dramatic tradition had once existed, and while the half-ruined classic playhouses still dotted the European world.

The Mystery Play would find in the cathedral, of course, an appropriate and truly beautiful "setting." The providing of a manger here, of a throne for Herod there, and a suggestion of the road to Egypt to one side: these simple arrangements would prepare the altar and choir area for a whole group of incidents: the Birth of Jesus, the Adoration of the Shepherds, the Three Wise Men, Herod and the Slaughter of the Innocents, and the Flight into Egypt. In a thirteenth century Orleans manuscript, there are preserved six Mysteries designed to be given in this simple way, besides four that are more properly to be termed "Miracles," that is, incidents in the lives of the Saints instead of dramatized episodes out of the Bible story. All are written very briefly, in verse and prose, and with the obvious intention that hymns and anthems be sung at appropriate intervals. The priests are the actors (the choir boys joining in when needed, as in *The Slaughter of the Innocents*).

It is useless to inquire seriously into the degree to which the acting was realistic or ritualistic at this time; but as *picturing* to illiterate people was the first aim of the religious drama, we may infer, in passing, that excursions toward realism occurred quite early. We shall see shortly the most curious mixture of naïve and realistic effects, when the play has been transferred to the secular guilds. At present, we may remember the impulse toward, perhaps the need for, a sense of actuality in

Scenes in the choir area of a church. [Part of an engraving by Hans Holbein.]

the representation; but that in the (usually) raised altar area of the church there was an ideal "formal" stage, needing no further decoration, but already suited to the placing of a throne, a manger, or a rich sepulchre, or to serve with slightest change as a palace or Heaven or Paradise. This was the stage of the "Collective Mystery" as it was performed in the cathedral (though not to push the analogy of physical theatre and church too far, it should be added that on occasion the action and the stations were carried out into the nave or side-aisles).

The next step is the building of a simple stage outside the church, or perhaps the arranging of the "stations" on the church porch: again an ideal setting for drama, with opportunity still for church music, with the doors handy for entrances and exits. The clergy are here still the actors.

As an example of the play in the transition period, when the drama

is midway between liturgical trope and guild-play, one may read the
Adam which is accounted the oldest drama in the French language.
It is supposed by some authorities to have been written in England,
where French was then in use alongside the scholarly Latin and the
vulgar English. (Incidentally the first play in English is said to be the
Jacob and Esau of the Wakefield Mysteries.) Where the early tropes
had been hardly more than paraphrases of a few lines of Bible text
(in Latin), one finds in the *Adam*, though incomplete, an elaborated
story, with sharply characterized protagonists, written out with considerable theatric ingenuity if without great literary merit. It is designed obviously to be played before a church, as indicated in one of
the stage directions noting that God goes into and out of the church;
and the absence of any large number of enumerated scenes would make
it an ideal piece for representation on the porch.

How far drama had now travelled from mere pictured incident (not
unlike a living replica of those sweetly colored wood or wax tableaux
that one sees in Catholic churches at festive times even today) toward
a "professional" completeness and skill in the representation, is illustrated in the *Adam* stage directions. I quote the following from E. K.
Chambers' translation, with his connecting paragraphs:

"A Paradise is to be made in a raised spot, with curtains and cloths
of silk hung round it at such a height that persons in the Paradise may
be visible from the shoulders upwards. Fragrant flowers and leaves are
to be set round about, and divers trees put therein with hanging fruit,
so as to give the likeness of a most delicate spot. Then must come the
Saviour clothed in a dalmatic, and Adam and Eve be brought before
him. Adam is to wear a red tunic and Eve a woman's robe of white,
with a white silk cloak; and they are both to stand before the Figure,
Adam the nearer with composed countenance, while Eve appears somewhat more modest. And the Adam must be well trained when to reply
and to be neither too quick nor too slow in his replies. And not only he,
but all the personages must be trained to speak composedly, and to fit
convenient gesture to the matter of their speech. Nor must they foist
in a syllable or clip one of the verse, but must enounce firmly and repeat what is set down for them in due order. Whosoever names Paradise is to look and point toward it."

After a *lectio* and a chant by the choir, the dialogue begins. The
Figure instructs Adam and Eve as to their duties and inducts them into
Paradise.

"Then the Figure must depart to the church and Adam and Eve walk
about Paradise in honest delight. Meanwhile the demons are to run
about the stage, with suitable gestures, approaching the Paradise from
time to time and pointing out the forbidden fruit to Eve, as though per-
suading her to eat it. Then the Devil is to come and address Adam.

"Then, sadly and with downcast countenance, he shall leave Adam, and go to the doors of Hell, and hold council with the other demons. Thereafter he shall make a sally amongst the people, and then approach Paradise on Eve's side, addressing her with joyful countenance and insinuating (*blandiens*) manner."

Now the last scene is at hand.

"Then shall come the Devil and three or four devils with him, carrying in their hands chains and iron fetters, which they shall put on the necks of Adam and Eve. And some shall push and others pull them to Hell; and hard by Hell shall be other devils ready to meet them, who shall hold high revel at their fall. And certain other devils shall point them out as they come, and shall snatch them up and carry them into Hell; and there shall they make a great smoke arise, and call aloud to each other with glee in their Hell, and clash their pots and kettles, that they may be heard without. And after a little delay the devils shall come out and run about the stage; but some shall remain in Hell."

Thus have we come to the dramatic stage representation of that Hell which Tertullian, one thousand years before, had sketched in his word-picture of "the Christian world as a show"—while damning out all theatre shows as works of the Devil. Here is the Church utilizing the art of drama, not as an appendage to the service, but as a complete and separate thing, pre-written by priest-dramatists, rehearsed, acted by specially trained clergy-players—educated not to "foist in a syllable or clip one of the verse," and to "enounce firmly." Others are trained even to produce the proper offstage noises, clashing the pots and kettles of Hell.

In noting this singular incorporation of the theatre into a so-long-hostile Church, we should not overlook that the Church has brought to drama theatric virtues of its own kind, of a sort not to be duplicated in later history. The pageantry of the Catholic service, the stirring sacred music, the impressive architectural background, the sincerity and conviction in delivery—many a later theatre, though more literary and more professional, fail of importance for lack of these.

Imagine the porch of Rheims Cathedral arranged for a play like *Adam*. The Paradise is a simple booth built up on the top step, within the central recessed portal; it is richly curtained, and stands out as a colorful note against the sculptures and traceries of the monumental façade. The other simple "stations" are placed close by; lowest of all, the yawning Hell-mouth. The costumes make the processionals a lovely interplay of movement and color. The music drifting out from the cathedral is doubly impressive as one looks up at the great Rose Window; where else could a heavenly choir be so appropriately concealed? And whence could come the thundering voice of God so convincingly, so nobly? The actors too—these are no mere mummers, coming from and returning to some empty space behind canvas flats; these are the servants of God, appearing from and returning to his House. And do they not speak his Word? How then doubt that this is one of the noblest theatres the world has known?

But even the cathedral-theatre can be desecrated. This time it is the Church itself that turns wild and matches the impressive use of drama at the altar, with ribald revelry and profane mockery at other moments. When the common people carried on their folk-customs in

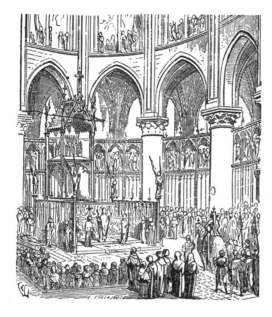

Sketch after Viollet-le-Duc's reconstruction of an eighteenth-century dramatic ceremony in the Cathedral of Notre Dame, Paris.

spite of prohibitions and occasional suppressions, making heathenish glee at New Year's and May Day and Christmas, the lower clergy claimed their right to celebrate too. The scores of minor churchmen who would be attached to a great cathedral did not always look up reverently to their superiors as the true and infallible representatives of God. In fact there was often resentment or jealousy, even hatred, between the minor and the major Fathers. And the New Year's celebration of the lower clergy became a recognized dramatic burlesque of the regular church service, with bitter and licentious caricature of high priests and bishops.

The New Year's "doings" of the church underlings were variously known as the Feast of Fools, the Feast of Asses, etc.—sufficient indication of the irreverence involved. From the end of the twelfth century on, the festival spread from France over most of the Continental Catholic countries, and it had its counterpart in the later Feast of Boys and the brief rule of the "Boy Bishop," a custom that came to flower more particularly in England. At first the participants were the "subdeacons," but these were joined by other classes of the humbler church workers; and the occasion was in the beginning the Church celebration of the Circumcision. Election of a presiding officer by the guild of vicars was at one time a feature of the occasion, and other serious purposes were often involved. But chiefly the Feast of Fools was the annual revel of the lower clergy, in which their human feelings and their cussedness broke loose— "an ebullition of the natural lout beneath the cassock," as Chambers puts it—culminating in their burlesque of sacred services with one of their own number acting the bishop or archbishop.

There were feasting (not excluding drinking) in the church, dice-playing at the altar, singing of ribald songs to Church tunes, mock sermons, etc. Rubber was burnt instead of incense, and the "Alleluia" was brayed. A parody of the Flight into Egypt is known to have been played, with a real ass brought to the altar rail. Each part of the mass then ended with a bray, and the people of the congregation responded with a "hee-haw"—oh, yes, you may be sure the townsmen came quite gladly to these sacrilegious services.

Some later writers are inclined to trace the whole Feast of Fools phenomenon to the first entry of a donkey into the church, as a natural property in the solemn Biblical plays. Anyway, the ass became a symbol of the affair, and the cowl worn by the mock high-church-man soon had donkey-ears as the distinguishing feature. There are some writers again who say that the festival can be traced back to the ninth century, when a fool at the court of Michael the Drunkard, at Constantinople, was allowed to desecrate a church, playing through a mock service in the Patriarch's robes; and that he then rode out on an ass with his revellers to meet the real Patriarch, and utterly upset the solemn procession which that dignitary was heading. This might, indeed, account for the prominence of the ass in the later feasts, and for the substitution of the chief actor for the Church head; the legend has, moreover, the advantage of lifting the guilt from Church people to a secular fool.

There exists a thirteenth century manuscript of the *Festa Asinaria* of the Beauvais Cathedral. When the ass was welcomed into the cathedral doors, and toasted with wine, the celebrants sang a nine-stanza chant, ending (in Gayley's translation):

Say Amen, most reverend Ass, (*they kneel*)
Now your belly's full of grass:
Bray Amen, again, and bray;
Spurn old customs down the way.
  Hez va! hez va! hez va! hez!
  Open your beautiful mouth and bray;
  A bottle o' hay, and the devil to pay.
  And oats a-plenty for you today.

To this feature was added the service as worked out in the Feast of Fools more strictly considered. As known particularly from the records of Sens Cathedral, it would begin with the jangling of the bells

The Fools ill received. Note the cowls with asses' ears. [From a book illustration by Albrecht Dürer, 1497.]

on New Year's Eve. Then at a certain point in the service, where occur the words "He hath put down the mighty from their seat, and hath exalted the humble and the meek," the sub-deacons would repeat the verses over and over, working them up into a hilarious refrain, finally ousting their superiors and carrying on the service as a burlesque. Masks would be brought out, bottles opened, and the Feast was on. Then followed a procession through the town, aping the usual solemn religious "progression," with dancing, serenading, and ceremonial visits at important houses—and the taking up of a collection. The *Dominus Festi* was variously known as the Bishop of Fools, Archbishop of Fools, *roi des fous, abbas stultus,* etc.—even the titles of Cardinal and Pope were daringly invoked.

It is only too obvious how this framework would be seized upon by the more rowdy elements in the Church, and among the townsmen for that matter, for the development of drunken and licentious scenes in the cathedral, of bitter parody of religious offices, of staging mock Mysteries, of corrupting such traditional ceremonials as the choir boys' processions. Indeed there seems no possible excess to which the Fools did not stoop during the next four centuries. The Church Fathers kept up a running fire of prohibitions, indictments, condemnations. In the thirteenth century the Bishop of Lincoln twice prohibited the *festum stultorum,* as "an execrable custom permitted in certain churches, by which the feast of the Circumcision is defiled," and as "a vain and filthy recreation hateful to God and dear to devils." In 1445 the Archbishop of Sens wrote that "all observers should tremble and blush at the enormity of the sacrilege by which a decorous and pleasant festival graced by the name of our Lord has been turned into an obscenity."

In the same year the Theological Faculty at the University of Paris issued a letter[1] to the bishops (the real ones) which summed up the abuses:

> Priests and clerks may be seen wearing masks and monstrous visages at the hours of office. They dance in the choir dressed as women, panders, or minstrels. They sing wanton songs. They eat black puddings at the horn of the altar while the celebrant is saying mass. They play at dice there. They cense with stinking smoke from the soles of old shoes. They run and leap through the church, without a blush at their own shame. Finally they drive about the town and its theatres in shabby traps and carts; and rouse the laughter of their fellows and the bystanders in infamous performances, with indecent gestures and verses scurrilous and unchaste.

As the zealous Fathers once spent three centuries scourging the actors from the stages of Rome, they now spend three centuries ridding

---

[1] Translated by Chambers. The quotations in this and the next chapter are from three excellent books. Always to be ranked first is that scholarly, heavily annotated, almost monumental work by E. K. Chambers, entitled *The Mediæval Stage* (Oxford, 1903). Far less exhaustive, but easily readable, is *Plays of Our Forefathers,* by Charles Mills Gayley (New York, 1907). A very good introductory account appears with the more important play texts in *English Miracle Plays, Moralities and Interludes,* by Alfred W. Pollard (Oxford, 8th revised edition, 1927).

their own House of a semi-theatric desecration. They are betrayed often within their own walls, they make a prohibition effective here only to see the abuses flower more licentiously there; they disagree among themselves. A few, wiser than their fellows, try to divert the comedy and burlesque of the Feast of Fools into the channel of the now secularized Mystery and Miracle Plays.

The serious religious drama that grew out of the solemn trope of the Mass, and out of the Mystery at the altar and on the cathedral

What happened to the classic theatres during the Dark Ages. The Roman theatre at Ephesus in the early twentieth century—the only theatre mentioned in the Bible.

porch, has now absorbed more popular elements, by way of realistic incident and farcical episode and spectacle. It already is being pushed away even from the church porch, by a clergy grown suspicious of its popularity and afraid of its vividness and its humor. The theatre is going out of the Church possibly for all time. (Though an occasional drama or ceremonial pageant may be acted there at special festival times.)

In Perugia, in 1425, the great preacher St. Bernardino of Siena listed among his statutes of reform—which went far to redeem one of the most disorderly and vice-ridden communities in Europe—a prohibition of the scandalous performances staged in churches on certain feast-days; and there are recorded prohibitions of even later date. But in general the Ass and the Fools have now been pushed out of the churches. They will turn up again, along with God and the Saints and the Devil, in the outdoor plays on the stages of guilds and fraternities. When all is said and done, regarding the theatre in the Christian church, it should remain in our minds that the true Mystery productions were among the most reverent, moving and engaging in the history of drama.

CHAPTER
7

The Medieval Spirit
and the Stage

THE little drawing shown on page 157 may serve as a "text" for a brief disquisition upon the spirit of the Middle Ages, in relation to some curiously contradictory aspects of the popular theatre. It is redrawn after a miniature in an illuminated play manuscript, and it shows a stage as arranged for the Valenciennes Passion Play.

It is one of the oldest records extant of a stage with illusive settings. As such it throws light on the audiences of the later religious theatre: they are simple-minded folk who demand "picturing" of the play backgrounds. Above all, they want graphic representations of the two places that are most in their minds: Heaven and Hell. If anything, they are the more interested in Hell. Indeed, long before this time (the Valenciennes production was in 1547) Hell-mouth has become the most prominent "station" of the several that are built on a long platform to serve the actors in Mystery and Miracle Plays. And the medieval audience demands particularly that the imps out of Hell shall be very active in hustling sinners into the belching smoke and flame, that the damned be shown in torture, and that the best of all comic actors play the part of the Devil. This Devil is the favorite of all the religious characters in the medieval theatre.

We have come now to a period when an old form of human civilization is breaking up. Politically, the feudal era is past. The society under which a lord ruled over each section of the country, when practically all the people dwelling therein were economically

and legally dependent upon that sovereign—little better than slaves—
is giving way to a society in which the third estate is to be powerful.
Manufacturing has taken on a new importance, trade is developing,
money is now in the hands of bankers instead of in the treasuries of
the sovereigns (as like as not they ruined themselves by going on the
crusades). A new "middle" class is claiming a place in the sun.

Just as ninety-nine out of a hundred men, in the centuries just past,
had been politically subject to the feudal lord, so they had been
mentally and spiritually subject to the Church. Even now they were
forbidden to think any thoughts not approved by the Church Fathers; they were taught that all intelligence began and ended with
those specially appointed by God to look after men's souls; they were

The stage of the Valenciennes Passion Play of 1547. An exact contemporary record of the mediæval stage that spread out simultaneously
several Biblical localities, from Heaven through earth to Hell. [Redrawing
by the author after the original miniature by Hubert Cailleau.]

encouraged to believe that this life is merely a brief passage, through
a vale of tears, during which one must prepare for the all-important
Life-after-Death. One might seek to make this earthly visit pleasurable
only at risk of spending the remaining lifetimes roasting in Hell, instead of basking in a Heaven of sweet-toned harps and golden pave-
ments. The Churchmen, moreover, pointed out that the emissaries of
the Devil in Hell and of God in Heaven are always at one's elbow,
the demons trying to pluck one away into paths that lead to perdition,
the Angels of God trying somewhat feebly to hold one in the ways
of righteousness. The demons are the more active, and they seem to
be everywhere, even in one's own being—it is they, not qualities in
the man's own make-up, that tempt to lust, to anger, to impiety. Only
by staying close to the Church, by obeying implicitly, by taking no
chances of thinking new thoughts, can a man be sure of salvation.

Of course a demon gets him once in a while; but then there is the Confessional, and Absolution. The Church, too, has magic relics that scare away demons. And there are Saints with special powers of protection. Christ has become too awesome a figure to serve as a personal idol. These Saints are nearer to the penitent or supplicant human being; and there is the Virgin Mary, who long ago has been elevated to first place among those who intercede at the Throne for poor mortal sinners, who long since became the favorite idol of millions of men and women who obediently gave up their old tangible gods but still feel the need of praying to a seeable deity.

So there is, at this time in the history of Christianity, in these later Middle Ages, a structure of superstition, of demons and idols and magic, hardly less crude than that which impelled the savage to his ritual dancing a few chapters back. We may mark the liturgical drama as a development by which the Church hoped to bring closer to its people the reality of its multitudinous saviours (the One who is at the heart of Christianity was almost obscured in those days). Tertullian, who had argued, in the second century, that the theatre was sinful because idolatrous, might now have found a new truth in the charge. The characters at the altar were largely idols shown—as is the way with drama—in the life.

Which brings us back to the audience and the Valenciennes stage. These spectators were just escaping from the estate of unthinking and fearful idolators. Whenever the Virgin Mary comes on to this platform stage, they will be reverent, thrilled, worshipful. They will cross themselves piously at this or that incident or allusion. They will accept solemnly the crudest sorts of stage "effects" for the sake of a vivid retelling of a beloved Bible-incident. But there is in them a new spirit too; the prominence of Hell-mouth on the pictured stage is the measure of it. Just as the people have escaped from under the heel of a feudal lord, they are claiming a certain freedom from Church domination. The priests, finding the comic element in the Biblical plays increasing, out of all proportion to the religious teaching, have finally thrown the drama out of many of the cathedrals and churches, with expressions of disapproval. The people take up the religious drama, disregard clerical warnings, make the productions semi-civic affairs, and turn the Devil into a comic character. They will still go to Mass on occasion, and say their prayers and make the sign of the cross at the proper times; but they will defy all attempts to interfere with what they now consider their legitimate pleasure.

We may recall, too, that this is the time when they begin putting into great secular buildings the energy, the money, and the art that hitherto have been poured into the cathedrals. The modern idea of

An ancient sketch of Christ in Limbo, indicating the popular interest in Hell-mouth as a "locality" in the multiple settings of the times. [Reproduction of a woodcut by M. Burg, in William Hone's *Ancient Mysteries Described*, 1833.]

A second example of the "simultaneous scene," as recorded during a production at Cologne in 1581. Note that the temporary stage is supported on barrels. [From *Das Bühnenbild*, by Carl Niessen.]

"the state" is emerging. Man is finding scope for a certain degree of independent thought, is escaping from mental subjugation. Neither reverence nor superstition is wholly erased. The best physicians—those who have royal warrants and have prevailed upon the kings to burn their rivals as impostors—prescribe dung-beetles and crickets boiled in oil for the cure of "stones," and wrappings of red flannel to drive away the smallpox.

It is only by recognizing such contradictions, of credulity and a new will to learning, of superstition and independence, of naïveté and elaboration, of piety and grossness, in the life of the times, that we shall understand the Miracle Play and the *Sottie*, the Morality and the Interlude. If we had time, indeed, it would be illuminating to trace in detail the changes in religious thought in Europe during the next three hundred years, especially the steps toward the Reformation; and to study the racial, lingual, and political developments which later were to culminate in the Renaissance. All these had influence upon the stage. But in the multiplicity of forms of religious drama, in the gradual change from the Latin of the Priests to half a dozen vernaculars, in the progressive shifting of emphasis away from didactic elements to amusing and literary ones, we shall be sadly lost if we do not concentrate our attention on the three or four play types that stand out most clearly, considering them somewhat apart from their sources and their relationship to the seething currents of political, social, and cultural life.

For the rest, we need remember only that the theatre is in a state of flux, that the Passion as given in Italy will be different from that at Paris, or Basel, or Augsburg, or Ghent, different in language in the later days, in methods of staging, in extent of secular escape from Church domination. And yet from Florence to Aberdeen, from Seville to Riga, the European world is alive with dramatic endeavor growing out of the one source in the trope. It is not even accurate to say that in one place the liturgical drama gives way to Miracle Play at such-and-such a time, or religious play to farce; they are being acted concurrently, with countless variations shading off into ritual processions, tableaux, spectacles, etc. Even the ecclesiastic authorities are divided again and again upon the question of total exclusion of the drama from the Church. One can only note that *roughly speaking*, the fourteenth century witnessed the change from cathedral-altar or porch to market-place stage, from priest-domination to secular control.

One of the few contemporary pictures of a Miracle stage was made by Jean Fouquet, a miniaturist who lived from 1415 to 1483. From the redrawing shown here, the reader may see that the fifteenth century stage was less elaborate than that used for the Valenciennes

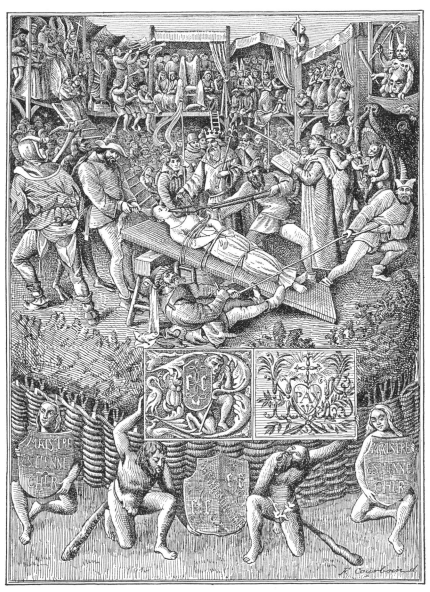

A contemporary illustration of a mediæval Miracle Play. A scene in the drama depicting the martyrdom of Saint Apollonia. Note the booth stage in the background, as yet with little pictorial localization. [From a drawing by F. Courboin after the miniature by Jean Fouquet, in Paul Albert's *La Littérature Française*.]

Passion Play a century later. Hell-mouth is the only pictured (or sculptured) setting. For the rest there is a row of raised booths in which certain of the episodes are to be played, ranged round an open stage on which an incident is now being acted out. The story is that of Saint Apollonia, the scene a typically vivid one of torture. Apollonia was an early martyr who had preached Christian salvation in Alexandria, suffering therefor a violent death by burning, at the hands of the tyrant governor—her own father, some accounts say. The legend is typical of those hundreds upon which the Miracle Plays were based:

> As the maiden grew up and flourished as a flower in grace and beauty, her mother ceased not to relate to her the wonderful circumstances of her birth; and thus she became a true Christian at heart. . . So he baptised her; and suddenly there appeared an angel holding a garment of dazzling white, which he threw over the maiden, saying, "This is Apollonia, the servant of Jesus! Go now to Alexandria, and preach the faith of Christ." She, hearing the divine voice, obeyed, and preached to the people with wondrous eloquence. Many were converted; others ran to complain. . . The governor commanded her instantly to fall down and worship the idol set up in the city. Then St. Apollonia, being brought before the idol, made the sign of the cross, and commanded the demon who dwelt within to depart; and the demon, uttering a loud cry, broke the statue, and fled, shrieking out, "The Holy Virgin Apollonia drives me forth!" The tyrant seeing this, ordered her to be bound to the column; and all her beautiful teeth were pulled out, one by one, with a pair of pincers; then a fire was kindled, and as she persisted in the faith, she was flung into it, and gave up her soul to God, being carried into Heaven by His angels."

In such a legend the opportunities for effective dramatic portrayal are enormous. The story would be known; the audience would look forward to each succeeding incident with the anticipation one feels in going back to a familiar place (*surprise*, by the way, is no valued element in drama). The characters are vivid: the beautiful virgin, the tyrant, and above all, the dazzling angels and the demons. God himself will appear to receive the martyr at the end. And, as we see in Fouquet's miniature, the torture scene can be made (in modern stage parlance) a knockout. Here are the torturers and their pincers; here is the old sure-fire dramatic incident of the innocent maiden unjustly abused. For this audience the abuse is realistically, grossly shown; but the spectators will be as deeply moved when angels out of that curtained booth-Heaven above come down to take vengeance and to carry the martyred maiden up to glory, and when the demons,

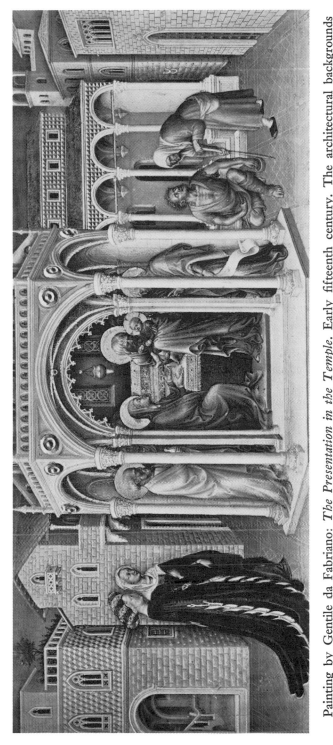

Painting by Gentile da Fabriano: *The Presentation in the Temple.* Early fifteenth century. The architectural backgrounds in the paintings of the time are often exactly those of the acted plays. [In the Louvre, Paris. *Archives Photographiques.*]

after a realistic struggle, march the torturers over to Hell and cast them down into flaming perdition. Look sharp and you will see one of the imps behind the torturer at Apollonia's head; they were constantly roaming about, prodding people, exhibiting their antics at every opportunity; even making sallies off the stage and out into the audience on occasion.

Who wrote the texts of these dramas? It is a question with many answers—and not so very important, because the written-out dialogue seldom has great literary value, or theatric values beyond a melodramatic effectiveness. Originally the text was written by a priest or a monk; there may be a dozen versions, used in this and other towns, each with its variations, each with accretions that have gathered as the play progressed farther from the Church, as new groups of secular producers and actors added bits to make the performances more popular. We may find an analogy today in the Passion Plays of the Tyrol and the Bavarian Alps. One town or village presents a play that was written by a local priest, another has a text immemorially old that has been readapted every ten years by successive producers; but over at Selzach in Switzerland, where they had no one with a flair for literary composition, they use a text borrowed with permission from the Ober-Ammergau players. Some such explanation can doubtless be made to cover the phenomenon of the mediæval religious drama of which these modern Passion Plays are survivals or revivals. Certainly some of the old English Miracles were close adaptations of French texts.

Still, there are a few names of authors known to us today, such as the French Jean Bodel, who elaborated a Miracle story, with St. Nicholas as the pivotal figure, until it contained a battle of Crusaders and Saracens, a court scene, tavern revels, a robbery, and the usual pious conversations, miracles, and final glorifications; and Ruteboeuf, who dramatized the story of the Priest who sold his soul to the Devil, repented, and was saved by the intercession of the Virgin Mary; and Hilarius, who may have been English rather than French, and who wrote (in Latin occasionally mixed with French) three plays that have survived, a *Miracle of St. Nicholas*, *The Raising of Lazarus*, and *Daniel*.

Of the French Biblical plays, Mysteries rather than Miracles, there are three groups or cycles that particularly demand mention. Those dealing with Old Testament history are known as *Le Mystère du Vieux Testament*. As collected and printed in 1500, with 44,325 verses, this work is supposed to represent a compilation from many authors. Of the collective *Nouveau Testament* Mysteries, there are several versions, that of Arnoul Greban being best known. It is in 34,574

Episode in the Life of St. Cecelia, by an unknown Tuscan painter, four-teenth century. The likeness to stage setting is notable. [In the Uffizi Gallery, Florence, Italy. Alinari photograph.]

verses, and was written in the mid-fifteenth century. The third group is known as the *Actes des Apôtres*, and the 61,968-line manuscript contains so many added Miracles that it is said to have played through all the Sundays for seven months in Paris in 1545.

Returning now to that theatre for the Valenciennes Passion Play with which we opened the chapter, we may inquire more particularly about the way in which a "cycle" is there presented. Here on the stage at one time are (more or less literally) a temple, a palace, city gates, pavilions, towers, a dungeon, a fenced field, a sea with a ship, etc., flanked by Heaven and Hell. It is obvious what a range of drama can be played, illusively, with such a "layout." By only a slight extension of the imagination, the main neutral playing space, the "downstage centre," becomes identified with one or another "station" as entrances are made from there or as actors are disposed to lead up to that station as centre of interest. In the picture, which the artist Hubert Cailleau designed for a manuscript of the play, only two of the "places" are occupied by actors: Hell with its demons and victims, and Heaven with God the Father supported by the Four Virtues. (See page 157.)

Not all the stations were called into use in a single day. The Passion here was presented in twenty-five installments, the usual performance including two or three incidents or acts, but occasionally only one, or again four. Thus the first day saw the acting of the story of Mary's parents; the fourth day, the birth of Jesus, the Adoration of the Shepherds, and the Coming of the Three Wise Men; the tenth, the Conversion of Mary Magdalen, and the Sermon on the Mount; the eighteenth, the Last Supper, and the Orchard scene; and so on.

One with a sense of theatrical values will note that, in the division into episodes, there is little attempt to follow the emphasis of the gospel-writers: the material now is reshaped with an eye to human and spectacular values. The story of the Magdalen is generously developed, a half *journée* is given to the *Décollation de Saint Jean*, presumably the Salome story, and a full performance is devoted to *Apparitions de Jésus Ressuscité*. And again we may note the prominence of Hell-mouth on the stage as indication of apocryphal tendencies; for where in the passion proper is there such emphasis on the Devil's doings? This is borrowing from the Miracles, where the enemies of the Saints invariably and visibly went to Hell.

The text of the Valenciennes play is apparently unlike any other, and yet is a free borrower from earlier versions, particularly that of Greban. A special prologue and epilogue have been added at the beginning and end of each of the twenty-five divisions. The opening lines (as a sample of the workaday verse) are:

Seigneurs, si vous prestez silence
Ce jour venant demonstrerons
La naissance de precellence
De Marie, qu' onnorerons. . .

A contemporary report and the contracts and financial accounts of the production tell much about the performers and the methods of staging. At first thirteen "superintendents and conductors" were appointed to have charge, and the preliminary tasks were parcelled out: three undertook to arrange the text and distribute the rôles, one to construct the stage, another to arrange the *mise-en-scène*, another to see to music, another to devise the machinery and effects. Besides those among the "superintendents" there were thirty-eight important actors, each appearing in many of the twenty-five performances and often in multiple rôles; besides a great many minor players including little children "*qui étaient anges.*" The actors' contracts indicate a strict discipline: lateness to rehearsals laid one open to a fine, drinking more than one's authorized portion during a performance was forbidden—and so was talking-back at the directors. Financially, the actors could elect to win or lose with the organizers, or be content with the thanks of all concerned. (As a matter of fact there was a profit of 1230 *livres*.) The actors worked hard and even underwent danger. It is chronicled that at Metz in 1437 both the crucified Christ and the hanged Judas were cut down just in time to escape death.

Seats were provided for a certain number of the audience at Valenciennes, in temporary pavilions—but it is to be doubted whether at this time the ordinary spectator demanded more than an opportunity to stand where he could see the stage. E. Grasset has made a conjectural reconstruction of the "theatre" and performance as seen from a box in the pavilion erected for the socially important spectators. You will note that he has elaborated a little the stage and its stations as depicted by Cailleau.

At the time, what impressed the populace of Valenciennes most were the mechanical wonders that were introduced. In our next chapter we shall see how stage tricks are already, in the sixteenth century, being glorified in the masques of the Italian courts; but here we meet for the first time contemporary descriptions of mechanical spectacular effects. An account by Henry d'Outreman (quoted in Petit de Julleville's valuable *Histoire du Théâtre en France: Les Mystères*) includes mention of "strange and wondrous things" seen each day, "the secrets of Heaven and Hell being so altogether mystifying that the populace could take them as miracles." People appeared and disappeared magically; "Lucifer rose out of Hell, no one seeing

The Valenciennes Passion Play of 1547 in progress. A recent reconstruction of the scene, by E. Grasset, based on the contemporary sketch by Cailleau, showing use of the "stage of the simultaneous scene."

how, borne on a dragon"; water was changed to wine in a way passing belief, so that "more than a hundred spectators wished to taste this wine," and five loaves of bread and two fish were apparently multiplied so that a thousand people partook thereof; the Devil changed his form; the thunder and the sundering of the rocks were like miracles anew. In connection with Hell and Purgatory, there were flames, a caldron of boiling oil, cannon, and turning wheels to which sinners were lashed (all to be seen in the sketch). In many other cases the Hell-mouth was so constructed that the frightful jaws opened and closed realistically, and we may infer as much on this Valenciennes stage.

Hubert Cailleau decorated the text manuscript with twenty-six other sketches, of scenes in the play. But he has given rein to his fancy; the backgrounds and groupings, no doubt, reflect at least the intentions of the producers, but there are figures seen in distant landscapes, and other features, impossible of accomplishment on a stage. These "painter's conceptions" may serve to remind us that mediæval graphic art is full of representations of those places and those incidents that were commonest on the Passion stages; so much so that one often is tempted to think that this or that picture must have been designed directly from a dramatic representation. Indeed, the books on the mediæval theatre are full of such might-be illustrations. It was even a favorite device of painters and sculptors to execute multiple works, with a dozen scenes shown side by side within one frame— a perfect parallel to the station stage. But it is only prudent to conclude that the influence is just as likely to have occurred the other way around, the stage people learning from the artists rather than the artists depicting the stage production. Incidentally, you will find Hell-mouth as a graphic representation of the entry to the Devil's domains in contemporary paintings, sculptures, woodcuts, tapestries, frescoes, embroideries, etc.

Now it is obvious that in the later Passions something of the old nobility has gone out of religious drama, that some cheap features have crept in. The wondrous "effects" have little to do with essential soul-cleansing inspired theatre. They are overstressed; they doubtless obscure some of the better elements that remain from the days of the simpler Mysteries. Drama has come again to a transitional period. Within a century Corneille's tragedies will be given in the regal court-protected theatres of Paris. Already Passions in the capital city are licensed only to the *Confrérie de la Passion*, an association of tradesmen-actors, forerunner of professional companies.

There are, too, a great number of secular organizations in scattered towns, producing more especially plays glorifying the Virgin Mary.

An example of painting with multiple scenes, representing various localities, at the time of simultaneous stage scenes. Pisan School. [In the Campo Santo, Pisa, Italy. Brogi photograph.]

Christ in Limbo: Detail of painting by Duccio. Hell-mouth was a popular "Feature" in the backgrounds of paintings, as it was on the stages of the religious plays. [In the Museum of the Duomo, Siena. Alinari photograph.]

Unconnected with the Church, these groups of amateur actors—
"literary fraternities" perhaps better describes them—carry on that
Mariolatry which Catholicism had so long officially fostered, sometimes dramatically. But the secular variations of the Mary stories ran
into unadulterated romance. The Virgin came to be adored as more
than an inaccessible Mother of God; rather as most lovable of mortals,
as queen of beauty, as goddess-musician. On the stages of the time, she
was a veritable *dea ex machina;* and often she pulled a reprehensible
sinner out of the fire, as well as a worthy believer, if only he called
on her in sufficiently adoring verse. The cycle of *Miracles de Nostre
Dame* is as important in the body of Middle Ages' dramatic literature
as the three Mystery cycles already mentioned.

In Paris and in other large cities there were also organizations carrying on *farce* from the point where the Feasts of Fools had relinquished
it (if indeed they did not directly give over the impetus toward satire
and comedy). Some of the *confréries,* of law-clerks and other secular
groups—known at times as *sociétés joyeuses*—produced farces with no
other object than amusement and satire. Sometimes this satire was
aimed bitterly at the Church; but it also scourged those given to pretension or folly in any walk of life. It was the early gross form of later
French satirical comedy—that was to bloom so finely when French
vulgar comedy and Italian *Commedia dell'Arte* together fertilized the
genius of Molière.

What has been, indeed, in the hands of the Fools and the Asses, mere
fooling—the name *sottie* persists—is in the fifteenth century shaped,
under literary influences, into something approaching true comedy. It
is as early as 1470 that *Maistre Pierre Pathelin*, the masterpiece of mediæval farce-comedy, appears. It is an engaging presentation of the
trusty theme of the shrewd lawyer outdone, of the swindler swindled.
Pathelin, in order to outwit his draper, undertakes to defend a shepherd
whom the draper accuses of stealing sheep. He tells the thief to answer
"Bah" to every question asked him in court, and the draper is thus so
confounded that he bungles the case and is sent away reprimanded,
and the shepherd is acquitted as a nit-wit; but when Pathelin asks for
his stipulated fee, the shepherd still answers only "Bah"!—and successfully sticks to it. It is to the court scene here and the draper's confusion
that we owe the admonition, "stick to your muttons."

One might trace a fairly certain line in the development of French
comedy from the first known author, Adam de la Halle, of the thirteenth century, through the early *sotties,* through the unknown author
of *Pierre Pathelin,* to Gringoire, the famous writer of political farce-
satires in the early sixteenth century. He wrote a play called *The
Prince of Fools* in which he presented the Church (as *Mère Sotte*),

the Pope, the King, and the Common People—really an attack on the Pope. But the treatment of these belongs rather to another chapter, when the literary play and the permanent playhouse are again solidly established in society. It is more to the point that we know here that farces—often grossly indecent ones—were acted in conjunction with the Mysteries, sacred and profane all on one platform, equally enjoyable to the medieval mind.

In the British Isles the early history of the religious drama was very like that in France, from liturgical beginning to Mystery and Miracle. But the later cycles of plays presented by the trades-guilds were "staged" in ways that have special interest. There was, of course, a gradual change from the Latin of the Church service to the vernacular, and from domination by priests to independent production under the care of the guilds. From the fourteenth to the sixteenth century the

A scene on a wagon stage in an English perambulatory Miracle Play. [From an early nineteenth century engraving by David Jee, in Thomas Sharp's *A Dissertation on the Pageants or Dramatic Mysteries Anciently Performed at Coventry*.]

plays were widespread; records of them exist in more than a hundred towns. In the later period the performances are no longer in or even near the churches—and out of the search for a suitable "theatre" grew the perambulatory system of presentation that is so distinctively Medieval English: the productions on wagon-stages. It is a system that well preserves the picturing method, without the necessity of building "simultaneous" settings on an over-long stage. Larger audiences could see the plays, moreover, as each stage-wagon, with its incident, appeared at several places in the town successively, before different groups of spectators—always, doubtless, before the windows of him who gave most liberally to the pageant fund. But let a contemporary attendant at the Chester Plays, one Archbishop Rogers, writing in 1594 or 1595, describe the system for us (but in modernized spelling):

> Every company had its pageant, or part, which pageant [wagon] was a high scaffold with two rooms, a higher and a lower, upon four wheels. In the lower they apparelled themselves, and in the higher room they played, being all open on the top, that all beholders might hear and see them. The place where they played them was in every street. They began first at the abbey gates, and when the first pageant was played it was wheeled to the high cross before the mayor, and so to every street; and so every street had a pageant before them at one time, till all the pageants for the day appointed were played; and when one pageant was near ended word was brought from street to street, that so they might come in place thereof exceeding orderly, and all the streets have their pageants afore them all at one time playing together; to see which plays was great resort, and also scaffolds and stages made in the streets in those places where they determined to play their pageants.

In some productions there are scenes requiring two of the pageant-wagons to appear together, and at times the actors apparently descended from the cars—"Herod shall rage on the pagond and also in the streete." Horsemen took their parts beside, not on, the wagons. For the rest, the reader will best round out his mental picture of the production by studying the reproduction of David Jee's engraving herewith (though it was made several centuries later).

Each trade-guild that was charged with the production of an act or incident owned its own pageant-car; and we may read into the circumstance an explanation of the splendor of costuming and the elaboration of stage effects. For each guild would be vying with all the others to make its act the most impressive and most magnificent. The costuming ran into regal display at times; and there are certain notable conventions, such as the Saracenic dress of Herod, the animal-headed demons, the Divinities with gilt hair and beards, winged angels, etc. The wagons and costumes were kept from year to year, and doubtless were elaborated between one Corpus Christi production and the next. The expenses were met by an assessment upon the guild members for "pageant-silver," and citizens' contributions. Productions sometimes began as early as five o'clock in the morning, in order to permit the necessary playing time—reminder of the Greek performances that started at dawn.

The extant manuscripts of the guild-plays, of which there are four fairly complete—of the Chester, York, Wakefield (Towneley) and Coventry Cycles—indicate considerable borrowing from town to town,

A woodcut by Lucas Cranach, showing the episode of the *Mocking of Christ*. Note the stage and part of the audience in a balcony.

and not a little adaptation from French originals. It is known, too, that in each town there might be text changes from year to year, sometimes two incidents being joined together, at other times an act being subdivided to afford opportunity for additional guilds to take part. The English cycles were more extensive than the French, commonly covering the entire distance from Creation to Day of Judgment. Careful thought was given, apparently, to the distribution of the acts among the guilds: the shipwrights had the incident of the building of the ark, the barbers the baptism of Jesus, the vintners the incident of the water turning to wine, the bakers the Last Supper, and so on. It was impossible that there should be such appropriateness through all the list of incidents: among the forty-eight scenes as arranged in the York production of 1415, one may note, as sample assignments, that the tanners were to present "God the Father Almighty creating and forming the heavens, angels, and archangels, Lucifer and the angels that fell with him to Hell"; the hosiers to do "Moses lifting up the serpent in the wilderness; King Pharaoh; eight Jews wondering and expecting"; the plumbers and patternmakers offering "Jesus, two Apostles, the woman taken in adultery, four Jews accusing her"; and the saddlers and glaziers combining to present "Jesus despoiling Hell, twelve spirits, six good and six bad."

In the acting of the guild members we may infer a real spontaneity and an effective sincerity. Shakespeare made high fun out of the ama-

Performance on a church porch. An etching by Jacques Callot, of the early seventeenth century.

teur acting of rustics in *A Midsummer Night's Dream*. But instead of visualizing the ineptitude and crudity of the playing there, we may better judge for ourselves from the performances of peasant-actors today, in Passion Play and folk-drama. The Oberammergau productions are world famous; but there is an even closer analogy in the performances at remote villages such as Thiersee and Erl—where peasants, woodsmen, and small tradesmen act the Passion with an absolute lack of self-consciousness, with conviction and often with grace. Simplicity, sincerity, and naturalness in amateur acting, where the performance is lived spiritually by the player, ofttimes bring him to that region trod by the professional actor only after a life-time of training and experience.

All was not sincerity and reverence, however, in the Miracle productions (in England the term "Miracle" is commonly used to designate both plays dealing with legends of the Saints, and the "Mysteries" of the Bible story). Gross farcical scenes, humorous, and sometimes not too careful about the kind of humor, are intruded by way of comic relief. In choosing two representative excerpts from the Miracles, it seems well to include one with a touch of comedy. In the *Noah's Flood* incident of the Chester Plays, Noah is completing the ark and invites his wife to come aboard:

Wyffe, in this vessel we shall be kepte:
My children and thou, I woulde in ye lepte.

NOYES WIFFE
In faythe, Noye, I had as leffe thou slepte!
  For all thy frynishe fare,
I will not do after thy reade.

NOYE
Good wyffe, doe nowe as I thee bydde.

NOYES WIFFE
Be Christe! not or I see more neede,
Though thou stande all the daye and stare.

NOYE
Lorde, that wemen be crabbed aye,
And non are meke, I dare well saye,
This is well seene by me to daye,
  In witness of you ichone.
Good wyffe, lett be all this beare,
That thou maiste in this place heare;
For all the wene that thou are maistre,
  And so thou arte, by Sainte John!

(They work for a time to finish the ark, and all go in except the Wife. She refuses to budge unless she can take her gossips along.)

NOYES WIFFE
The loven me full well, by Christe!
But thou lett them into thy cheiste,
Elle rowe nowe wher thou leiste,
  And get thee a newe wiffe.

NOYE
Seme, sonne, loe! thy mother is wrawe:
Forsooth, such another I doe not knowe.

SEM

Father, I shall fetch her in, I trowe,
  Withouten anye fayle. . .

JEFFATTE

Mother, we pray you all together,
For we are heare, youer owne childer,
Come into the shippe for feare of the weither,
  For his love that you boughte!

NOYES WIFFE

That will not I, for all youer call,
  But I have my gossipes all.

SEM

In faith, mother, yett you shalle,
  Whither thou wylte or (nought).

NOYE

Welcome, wiffe, into this botte.

NOYES WIFFE

Have thou that for thy note!

NOYE

Ha, ha! marye this is hotte!

For example of the more serious parts of the cycles, outside the
Passion proper which follows closely the Bible original, one may best
read the *Abraham and Isaac* play in the Brome manuscript, or the similar *Sacrifice of Isaac* in the Chester group. In an excerpt from the latter, one feels the breath of human tragedy entering again into drama
writing, not without human delicate pathos. Abraham has been commanded by God to go out on the hill and sacrifice Isaac.

ISAAKE

Father, tell me or I goe
Wheither I shal be harmede or noe.

ABRAHAM

Ah! deare God! that me is woe!
  That breakes my harte in sunder.

ISAAKE

Father, tell me of this case,
Why you your sorde drawne hase,
And beares yt nacked in this place,
  Theirof I have great wonder.

ABRAHAM

Isaake, sonne, peace, I praie thee,
Thou breakes my harte even in three.

ISAAKE

I praye you, father, leane nothinge from me,
  But tell me what you thinke.

ABRAHAM

Ah! Isaake, Isaake, I must thee kille!

ISAAKE

Alas! father, is that your will,
Your owine childe for to spill
Upon this hilles brinke?
Yf I have treasspasede in anye degree,
With a yarde maye beate me;
Put up your sorde, yf your wil be,
  For I am but a childe.

ABRAHAM

O, my deare sonne, I am sorye
To doe to thee this grete anoye:
Godes commaundment doe must I,
  His workes are ever full mylde.

ISAAKE

Woulde God my mother were here with me!
Shee woulde kneele downe upon her knee,
Prainge you, father, if yt may be,
  For to save my liffe.

ABRAHAM

O! comelye creature, but I thee kille,
I greve my God, and that full ylle;
I maye not worke against his will. . .
  . . . .

ABRAHAM

Lorde, I woulde fayne worke thy will,
This yonge innocente that lieth so still
Full loth were me hym to kille,
  By anye maner a waye.

ISAAKE

A! mercye, father, why tarye you soe?
Smyte of my head, and let me goe.
I pray you rydd me of my woe,
 For nowe I take my leve.

ABRAHAM

Ah, sonne! my harte will breake in three,
To heare thee speake such wordes to me.
Jesu! on me thou have pittye,
 That I have moste in mynde.

ISAAKE

Nowe father, I see that I shall dye:
Almightie God in magistie!
My soule I offer unto thee;
Lord, to yt be kinde.

 (*Here let Abraham take and bynde his sonne Isaake upon the alter;
let hym make a signe as though he woulde cut of his head with his
sorde; then let the angell come and take the sworde by the end and
staie it. . .*)

While this human note was creeping into the Miracles—like a foreshadowing of the Elizabethan playwrights—a radically different sort
of play was developing in the "Morality." The form came to blossom
most. fully in England, and one of the best examples is dated as early
as 1405: the *Castell of Perseverance*. In the field of drama the Morality
corresponds to the Allegory in poetic literature. The characters are
personifications, and the central theme or struggle—seldom very dramatic—is between the good and the evil in man, or between Good and
Evil for Man. The extant examples, with one exception, interest us less
than the Miracles, for they are likely to be endlessly dull. Were it not
indeed for the presence of two characters out of the older drama, the
Devil and Vice, we should find the moralities well-nigh intolerable.

 These two, like a vaudeville team introduced into a modern revue,
Vice incessantly badgering the Devil, lighten up the slow-moving action, and take the curse off the greyness of the abstractions that serve
as *dramatis personæ*. Of course, our ethical nature applauds when Virtue triumphs, when Wisdom, Sobriety, Charity, Obedience, draw Humankind to their side; and we equally rejoice when Folly, Gluttony,
Pride, Voluptuousness, and Avarice suffer a fall. The characters are
not all quite so abstract: there are Bad Habits, Imagination, Mankind,
Good Counsel, Bad Luck, Bad-end, Colic, Dropsy, Pill, even Dinner,
Supper, and Banquet. Indeed there are shadings that carry us beyond
the Idea to the human character standing for Hypocrisy or Snob-

bishness or Gossip—true beginnings of satirical comedy or character comedy.

Everyman is the exception that makes all readers pause when they are about to give over Morality Plays as nothing more than a curiosity of species. For here the moralizing and didacticism are balanced by very human conceptions of Fellowship, Good-Deeds, Death, and similar characters; and one feels a real dramatic pull in the struggle for Everyman's soul. The play was evidently a favorite of its kind, too, in the sixteenth century, for there were several early printed editions;

A French farce of the late Middle Ages. [From an old print as reproduced in Paul Albert's *La Littérature Française*.]

and there exists a translation in Dutch (or, as some believe, the Dutch original from which the English version was made). The play has achieved new fame in our times, through some excellent English and German revivals; and at Salzburg the *Jedermann* performance before the cathedral was the central attraction of the annual dramatic festivals —though Max Reinhardt used a somewhat rococo version, and lost some of the medieval naïveté while recapturing much of the effectiveness of cathedral background, church music, and simple outdoor staging.

As in France, it is impossible to disentangle the beginnings of English secular drama from the manifestations of late religious drama. The French Feast of Fools had a later counterpart in the revels of the English choir boys: characterized by feasting, burlesque of the Church service, processions, and a *dominus festi*, who here became known as the Boy Bishop. A line may be traced down from the boy-revels to secular dramatic activity. Other lines come down from the court entertainments, not without relationship to the minstrels, and from the folk customs—particularly those that culminated in the Sword Dances and the Mummers' Plays.

When the festival of the renewal of life in the earth, the turn of the year, had grown into set form, with certain recognized dances, and with named participants (the Doctor who restored life was a regular character), it came to the estate of drama; and this drama was carried out widely, by its folk performers, into the houses of nobles and into the courts—where, indeed, the minstrel beginnings, the "mummings" and new-fangled Renaissance masque-importations from Italy became inextricably mixed. Even the court masque had had local antecedents, in the "ridings," the royal "entries," and civic pageantry.

The word "interlude" that is commonly used to denominate, roughly, the drama that came after the Moralities and before the true English comedy, is almost hopelessly vague—and almost lost in the haze of scholars' disputes over its origin and application. It has been employed to describe the early court entertainments—as a dramatic and musical interlude, or perhaps ballet, at a banquet—and a certain sort of Morality, and the earliest farce sketches that came after the Miracle Plays. In the last signification, it is seen as a main transitional agent between, say, the humorous incident of Noah trying to get his wife aboard the ark, and the comedies of the immediate predecessors of Shakespeare. John Heywood's "farces" are called interludes. They are the first group of wholly secular plays in English; they escape from the moralizing purpose and from any connection with Bible history or the legends of the Saints. They are not notable for either characterization or dramatic vividness; but with Heywood the drama has returned to a preoccupation with human people and with undisguised entertainment values. The way is prepared for the entry of the Renaissance spirit into the English theatre.

Religious drama does not die immediately, of course. The Miracle cycles are to be presented as late as Elizabeth's reign. But already in the Moralities, historical characters are appearing—prophetic hints of the coming Chronicle plays. And there are school stages whereon even classic revivals are known. But in ending our mediæval chapter it is more profitable to glance at the countries we have not found time to explore. The German-speaking nations particularly, while offering a parallel to France and England in the pervasiveness of the Mysteries and Miracles, provide at least one striking variation in methods of "staging." In addition to the pageant-wagon system that we have noted as more especially typical of the English guild productions, and the simultaneous scene on one long stage as recorded from Valenciennes and other French towns, there is here a method of transforming a whole city square or plaza into a theatre, with processional action from station to station.

Thus at Lucerne in 1583 the Easter Play was given in the Market Square, with Heaven built at one end (like a fortified and turreted castle), the Temple, the Synagogue, the tree for Judas' hanging and

A religious play with scenes acted at separated station stages in a square in Copenhagen in 1634. Here again Hell-mouth is a prominent feature. [Drawing by Warren D. Cheney after an old print.]

other stations ranged down the two sides, and Hell-mouth at a far corner beside other "localities." The diagrams for performances on two successive days leave us doubtful whether the crowd followed the actors from station to station, without any spectators ever being seated, or if there were balconies or other points of vantage from which the entire "theatre" could be seen. And by the way, for many years everyone believed that there was another sort of fixed stage for Mysteries, upon which the stations were built up in three-decker fashion, so that three episodes might be played successively in booths on (so to speak) the first, middle, and top floors. In some cases the lowest deck is marked as Hell, Purgatory, etc., the middle one as the World, the top one as Heaven and Paradise; but there is also mention somewhere of a nine-deck stage. The mistake probably arose from the fact that Heaven was commonly placed higher than the other stations in a simultaneous scene, and sometimes Hell lower; and from the confusion of a description of the *spectators'* boxes or benches with the booth stage. At any rate, the "authorities" now frown upon any mention of superimposed stages. In Italy and in Spain the pageant-cars became very popular, but usually with one movable wagon-stage serving for a whole drama. And in those countries today there are festivals in which the plays on wagons are a central feature.

Most important of all survivals of the medieval theatre, however, is the decennial Passion Play at Oberammergau in the Bavarian Alps. In this twentieth century, the rude wooden theatre in that out-of-the-way town is better known than any other playhouse in the world, is more sought out by pilgrims, is more praised for its performances by all classes of theatre-goers. The stage is an interesting—perhaps unfortunate—compromise of traditional religious-play architectural scene and modern box-stage for changing painted settings: the permanent stations for the medieval stage appear at each side of a proscenium-arched, curtained inner stage, with nineteenth century scene-shifting paraphernalia. But the actors retain their old faith, their sincerity, their reverent devotion in acting. In the course of the years since 1633, when the first performance was given, there have been many modifications in text, in music, in methods of presentation; but the spirit of medievalism has persisted—on its better side. Some of the crudity of those times, and much of the naïveté, have been rubbed away. We may resent the intrusion of the almost-as-crude painted settings that are now introduced; but one cannot see the production, or talk with the actors, without knowing that here is some spirit of service, a conviction, a devotion—something very beautiful, something typically medieval—that is lost out of the rest of the theatres of our times.

CHAPTER 8

The Glorious Renaissance —with Reservations

I N THAT "Renaissance" period which is the chief glory of
Italian history, the story of the theatre is not marked by the
emergence of a drama in any way comparable to the amazing contemporary achievements in the realms of intellectual research, painting,
sculpture, and architecture. In those other fields the Renaissance was
both a rebirth of a forgotten spirit and a flowering of creative activity: first the Revival of Learning which sometimes gives the period its
name, then prodigious individual feats of scholarship, startling advance
in freedom of thought, the creation of the masterpieces of Giotto,
Brunelleschi, Michelangelo, Titian, and Leonardo da Vinci, and others
whom the world still counts among the great artists of all time.

Yet the theatre in this period, however magnificent its advance in
the outward trappings of drama, however colorful its accompaniment
to the opulent social life of the time, failed to bring into existence a
single play of lasting world-importance. We go to Florence today to
see Giotto's paintings or his lovely Campanile, and Brunelleschi's cathedral dome, or Michelangelo's sculptures; and we may, as we wander
through the palaces, the piazzas, the gardens, reconstruct a picture of
the lavish court productions, and a picture of the robust vulgar popular
comedy; but nowhere on the bookshelves shall we find a play text
comparable to the poems, the stories, and the histories that came out
of the half-fabulous Italy of the fourteenth to the sixteenth centuries.

The Italian Renaissance, none the less, marks the birth of the modern
stage. If the recreating process, in regard to drama, was less complete

A diagrammatic view of a theatre for revival of the Roman classics, fifteenth century. Note the special balcony for the *aediles*—charged with keeping order—and the single musician at a corner of the stage. The form of the stage is better seen in the next following illustrations. The fanciful designer has here set the theatre over a bordello. [From the Trechsel edition of Terence's plays, Lyons, 1493.]

185

here than in the other arts, the revival, the return to ancient forms, was no less epochal. Medieval art had sprung largely from alien, unclassical origins; the theatre of the Middle Ages particularly had come from a new source, wholly Christian, a separate thing, little connected with the tradition of Greece and Rome.

The Italian Renaissance accomplished the transition from the mediæval to the modern theatre by wholly cutting off the religious drama and its type of stage; by returning the course of dramatic development to the old channel of classic times. The revived models of play forms, though failing to inspire any Italian Shakespeare, marked out the way for Spain, for England, for France—and for what followed, even down to the Realism of today. In another direction, the change was even more immediate; in Italy a new type of theatre building was developed, and the transition was accomplished from mere acting on platforms or in areas to acting in painted settings. In summary, the Italian Renaissance gave the world a new place for play-producing, and a new method of dressing the drama; and indirectly it fathered Shakespeare, Jonson, Corneille, Racine—and the rest.

"Humanism" is sometimes offered as the key word to unlock the mystery of the sudden rebirth, the flaming passion that was the Renaissance. For centuries all thought, all research, all "culture" had been dominated by the Church; the individual man could not be considered, conceived of, judged, as a being apart from his religion, from the rules of Christian conduct, from theological law and organization. Almost suddenly the time became ripe in Italy for man to turn the light of reason on himself, to dignify himself, to become creative (and incidentally, to commit all those excesses that go with sudden freedom from over-restraint). From being afraid to walk except in fixed paths, suspicious of or apathetic to beauty, accepting ignorance as a good pleasing to God and the Church, striving, if imperfectly, to be prepared for the all-determining judgment after death, the individual man emerged into a world where reason told him it was possible to live happily, to exercise the intellect, to create beauty, to determine his own destiny. With exuberant spirits, with enthusiasm, with animal vigor, he set out to triumph. From the uncovering of Greek and Roman texts, sculptures, and buildings, he gained new conceptions of life, of art, of reasonable pleasure. He threw himself into new efforts at creation, imitatively at first, then with superb independence and originality. He indulged a very passion for all that was antique, collected and recopied manuscripts, uncovered monuments, wrote detailed essays on the ancients, picked up the lost impulses to poetic composition, scientific investigation, and philosophic speculation.

He even questoned the Church—leading not so indirectly to the later

Reformation. His self-assertiveness was soon to lead to a new era of discovery, to the epochal development of the printing-press, to the invention of mechanisms destined to revolutionize war, exploration, and living. All these things followed on what was essentially a rediscovery of the freedom and the power of the human spirit.

Stage of the theatre shown on page 185. Curtained receptacles for the entrances and exits of characters in Terence's *Andria* are shown. [From the Trechsel edition.]

The Renaissance was Europe-wide; but Italy emerged first from the condition of insecurity, superstition, and widespread ignorance that had cloaked the continent so long. By a conjunction of political, commercial, and racial circumstances, which we need not explore here, the Italian peoples first felt the breath of intellectual curiosity, were stirred by the new ideal of human freedom. This was no united Italy in the present-day sense: the communes or cities or minor states were still waging continual warfare with one another, the forces of the Papacy and the Empire were at each other's throats, foreign rulers held large parts of the Peninsula under Spanish or French or Germanic rule. Party strife among the nobles often made a city-state the seat of civil wars and anarchy. But amid the reign of violence, terror, cruelty, and political perfidy, the flower of learning and art somehow sprang up, grew straight and beautiful, enriched the world for all time.

Perhaps only the sword in the hands of nobles with passionate imagination could wrest from those violent times the wealth, the margin of leisure and the magnificence which made possible the creative activities of the artist, under protection and generous patronage. Certainly, it was at the courts of men we would call "tyrants" that learning flourished, that scholars from abroad were entertained, that "circles" were established for the discussion and comparison of ideas and the dissemination of knowledge; that theatres were established. Here the bridge was

Scenes from early Renaissance revivals of plays by Terence on platform stages with curtained backgrounds. [From the Trechsel edition.]

formed that led from the world of Greece and Rome to the world of the future; here was the new valuation of human achievement apart from Church or State. From the courts—and the popes, too, were great princes, as well as ecclesiastics, in those days—the enthusiasm spread, from nobles and artists and scholars to adventurers and tradesmen and idlers. The foundation was securely and widely laid for modern intellectual and artistic activity.

We may say that Dante, if you like, embodied the final expression of the spirit of the Middle Ages—his mysticism, his faith, his self-negation and his prophetic and exhortatory method all warrant the statement—even while he foreshadowed the intellectual freedom to come. It was rather Petrarch who opened the door full to the new spirit. He was the first great figure among those who gave humanism and liberalism to Italy, at once creator and inspirer of other men. Boccaccio was more clearly the literary artist. It would be futile to speculate why these writers and half a dozen lesser poets and novelists failed to write importantly for the stage. In a later time the material of some of the world's treasury of plays was drawn from their translated works. But it is pertinent to remember that they opened the way for the drama to

THEATRVM

A fifteenth century revival of a play by Terence. In order to have the actors face the reader, the artist has placed the auditorium behind them: two full balconies and a base with three boxes, designed into a fantastic structure that reverts to the Gothic style. [From the Grüninger edition of Terence, Strassburg, 1496.]

189

treat hitherto forbidden subjects and emotions. The Church had judged the classics vicious on several scores; it had condemned literature as extolling alien gods, as impelling loose living, as failing to prepare the spectator for the life-after-death, as making attractive a human concept without theological authority. However the Italian dramatists of the Renaissance may fail to put life or effective drama into their plays, an all-important freedom had been won by these earliest writers. Human life—not merely Bible legends—would thenceforth provide the raw material for serious drama.

To understand why those who did turn to the theatre, the earliest Renaissance playwrights, wasted their substance in crassly imitational works, it is necessary to hold in mind the all-pervading passion for a rediscovered antiquity. Academies were formed for the study of every detail of Latin and Greek manuscripts and monuments. The texts of Plautus, Terence, and Seneca were brought to light, subjected to scholarly commentary, gravely and devotedly brought to the stage—probably with as complete loss of the *spirit* of the plays as is usual in "school" revivals today. In their aim of making the theatre of the new era the most perfect imitation of that of the ancients, certain of the academies built what they deemed to be classic playhouses (an activity that profoundly affected the course of theatre-building in later times, as we shall see). In the academy theatres and on the stages temporarily erected in court ballrooms, the Latin plays were soon being given widely—and not without spectators genuinely interested, in a scholarly way. (But Perrens in his *History of Florence* shrewdly says: "the spectacle being free, nobody had the right to find fault.")

In following out first the development of literary drama—setting aside momentarily the more colorful pageant-making, spectacle, and farce-comedy—we need not linger long over those writers who slavishly copied the old play models even while attempting new subject-matter. Earlier than the true period of the Renaissance there had been isolated examples of plays written in the Roman manner; Hrosvitha had composed her not-too-Terentian comedies, and there had been other monastic attempts to reconcile churchly and pagan literary ideals. There had been considerable activity, too, at the universities and schools in various parts of Europe, in the revival of Plautus and Terence; a general vagueness covers the subject, but there is evidence of widespread Jesuit productions, and indications that a special type of stage, entirely separate from the mediæval and possibly not unconnected with the classic, had been developed for such revivals.

But the rebirth of classic drama is generally ascribed to the fourteenth century; its full effect was felt in the mid-fifteenth, when the Roman Academy under Pomponius Lætus was producing both Roman drama and imitations in Latin, while groups at Ferrara, Florence, Siena, Venice, Naples, and elsewhere were either staging similar performances or soon to follow suit; and the first truly original works in the vernacular belong to the sixteenth century.

Stage setting for a play dealing with the life of St. Margarita of Corona. [From a German woodcut, 1488.]

By stretching our definition of drama a bit, we may trace Renaissance tragedy back to 1314 or thereabouts, when Albertino Mussato produced his *Eccerinis,* a very short tragedy on an Italian subject, and his *Achilleis,* on a classical theme, both written in Latin in imitation of Seneca. Likewise, literary comedy may be traced back to a lost play by Petrarch, after the Terentian model, also of the first half of the fourteenth century. By 1450 the imitation of the ancient dramatists was in full swing. Latin long remained the preferred dramatic language; and the classic theme was favorite over local or modern story—it was part of the reaction against too much Church that Greek and Roman gods, heroes, and legends, should be given as wide currency as possible. At a time when scholarship was so revered, the study of the ancient languages so general in the upper circles of society, dialogue in Latin would find both court and Academy audiences understanding and responsive. Necessarily, however, the plays of the period are hopelessly inferior to the classic models; not a playwright's name need be remembered from the period. A curious sidelight is thrown on the limitations of the scholar-writers of this Latinized century when one reflects that even Dante and Petrarch then suffered neglect from being in the "vulgar" tongue.

With the early sixteenth century, composition of plays *in Italian* began in earnest. Gian Giorgio Trissino is generally credited as the first "regular" Italian tragedy-writer. His best-known play, *Sofonisba*, was composed in 1515, several times printed and finally staged in 1562. In his life and in his writing this author affords a key to an understanding of the times and of the failure of Italy to produce a great dramatist during the Renaissance. Trissino was, according to Symonds,[1]

Pithias   Thais   Cherea

A revival of the *Eunuchus* of Terence, staged presumably in Germany, in the architectural settings that had then become popular in Italy. [From the German edition of Dinckmut, Ulm, 1486.]

"a man of immense erudition and laborious intellect, who devoted himself to questions of grammatical and literary accuracy, studying the critics of antiquity with indefatigable diligence, and seeking to establish canons for the regulation of correct Italian compositon. . . . He set himself to supply the deficiencies of Italian literature by producing an

---

[1] *A Short History of the Renaissance in Italy*, taken from the work of John Addington Symonds by Lieutenant-Colonel Alfred Pearson (London, 1893). This is a useful abridgment of Symonds' standard *Renaissance in Italy*, still, I think, the most readable book on the subject.

epic in the heroic style, and a tragedy that should compare with those of Athens. The *Italia Liberata* and the *Sofonisba*, meritorious but life-less exercises which lacked nothing but the genius for poetry, were the result of these ambitious theories."

In short, Trissino wrote a correct, imitative, dramatically dead trag-edy. In following the ancients he made the further mistake of taking Seneca rather than the Greeks for model. Most of the Italian tragedy of the time reeks of Senecan violence and horror, and of Senecan rhet-oric, without the clarity, inevitableness, and poetry of the Greek.

After Trissino one may mention, as similar practitioners, important in their own time, Rucellai, Aretino, whom we shall hear about in con-nection with comedy, Cinthio, who first invented his own plots (whose *l'Orbecche* "is accounted the best and the bloodiest"), Dolce, and that Tasso who is to appear again when we study the pastoral drama. Through all this time, from 1502 till the eighteenth century, when the circle of development will have been completed through Italy to Paris and back again to Italy in the influence of French classic tragedy, there is a gain from mere narrated event toward acted drama, a gain in free-dom of subject-matter, a gain in variety of metric forms. But until Alfieri, Italian tragedy hardly achieves a text of world significance.

The transition from productions in Latin to productions in Italian came slightly earlier in comedy than in tragedy. The close of the fifteenth century was already seeing comedies produced in the ver-nacular, both translated works and imitative plays by Italian authors. Almost immediately the most important playwright of the Renaissance makes his appearance: that Lodovico Ariosto whose epic *Orlando Furi-oso* is so much finer than any of his dramas, though of the latter sev-eral survive and are highly esteemed in Italy to this day. Ariosto lived from 1474 to 1533, in the very heart of the Renaissance, and his mate-rials reflect the bigness, the audacity, and the moral looseness of his time. His *Lena* is especially esteemed as a picture of society at Ferrara, beyond its values as comedy. He is a main link between ancient and modern drama.

Of those whose names are offered as precursors of Ariosto, in the invention of native comedy, there is Boiardo, whose play of 1494 or earlier seems, however, to have been more adaptation than original. There is Dovizio, later to be Cardinal Bibbiena, whose "disreputable but entertaining" farce-comedy *Calandra* was based on Plautus' *Me-næchmi*, but "enhanced the comic effect at the expense of morality." It was produced at Urbino about 1509, passed triumphantly through all the courts of Italy, and later so pleased Pope Leo X that he had it repeated often for his entourage and guests in Rome. And there is Ricchi, who is set aside by most commentators because his "first Italian comedy in verse" is an adaptation of the Morality Play rather than in classic tradition.

Beside Ariosto stand Niccolo Machiavelli and Pietro Aretino—as picturesque a pair of libertines as ever graced the theatre. In a time when men lived and loved wildly, passionately, cruelly, dissolutely, when the shrewd fighter who cared least for personal or public honor was most likely to become ruler and to amass riches, when violence and perfidy and insolence were as ready weapons as physical courage, these two authors wrenched comedy finally free from classic limitations and used it to amuse and to portray the society about them. They chased the pedants out of the field: the men who always worked at second hand, taking other people's opinions and bowing before classic precedent. They were the first to forget Plautus and Terence.

"I show men as they are, not as they should be," exclaimed Aretino; and he might have been speaking for Machiavelli as well. They both had the directness, the incisiveness, the spontaneous surface truth implied in that statement. Their plays were indubitably powerful, lively, vivid in scene or incident, absorbing for their unabashed view of sensational living, often witty in dialogue; yet they lack the final unifying, cementing, dramatic quality that might have made them comparable to Molière's portraits of a later age, or Sheridan's spirited satire.

It has been said that Aretino typified the dissolution of the genius of the Italian Renaissance, that he embodied the fault that lay at the heart of Italy's failure to develop a national drama: his inherent coarseness made impossible any eternal fineness in his plays; that his baseness and grossness, mental as well as outward, stand for the degeneration of Italy's culture as they do for the shallowness of the man's talent, and its instability. Aretino, in a magnificent gesture, struck the shackles of pedantry off drama; but his self-confidence, his malice, and his sensuality betrayed him as artist. There are those who say that he was most notable as ushering in the methods and the era of the modern press—publicity, blackmailing, reporting, *realism*, sensationalism, the newspaper drama.

One might outline the plot of Machiavelli's *Mandragola*, and quote a few passages, by way of better showing out the state of comedy in this time—we have sampled the drama of other periods in that way. But taste and custom have so changed that the play seems simply not to belong to the theatre or any body of theatre-goers today; is not important in the wider (or is it the narrower?) view. Suffice it to say that the theme is that one most beloved by the Latin races, the way in which a married woman takes a lover, this time made piquant by the husband who connives at his own betrayal—the whole set forth with unexampled cynicism.

That we should so immediately come upon two such sinister figures, so soon after Ariosto, is, indeed, an index to the life of the "scholarly" theatre of the time. Largely, the literary drama had exhausted itself in lifeless imitation. The first writers who bring vigor and originality to it are these almost incredible libertines: that Aretino "whose very name

Scenes with masked actors in plays by Terence, of the late mediaeval period. [From a Latin manuscript in the *Bibliothèque Nationale*, Paris.]

should be written in asterisks," and the Machiavelli who is permanently memorialized in our language by two equally suggestive phrases, "Machiavellian" and (as some say) "the old Nick." Scores of other playwrights' names and a list of known comedies that runs into the thousands, bear witness to a prolific period during and after the lifetimes of Aretino and Machiavelli; but literary comedy in Italy practically died with them.

THERE is, however, a brighter side to the story of the Italian Renaissance theatre. As soon as we get away from the lasting play-

Illustration of masks for a play by Terence. [In the Latin manuscript at the *Bibliothèque Nationale*, Paris.]

text as a criterion, away from consideration of literary drama, we find evidences of extraordinary theatrical activity. The popular street comedy, the improvised drama of the *Commedia dell'Arte*, developing almost without any written dialogue, is spirited, sheerly theatrical, admirably original; without escaping the coarseness and licentiousness of the times, it is, in the early Renaissance, vulgar without cynicism, expressive, and endlessly amusing. And in the court theatres, *production* as an art is developing a new elaboration, a new magnificence, in keeping with the abounding life and lavish display of the rival noble families. The stage is playing its brilliant part in the reckless and colorful advance of human freedom.

Florence, as it was the cradle of the Renaissance, also is the home of its most opulent achievements in the arts. The Florentine courts, rivalled as they are by memories of the Gonzagas in Mantua, of the Court of Ferrara under the Estes, and of others no less brilliant, still stand out in greater, in epochal magnificence. The Medici rulers are the very type of Renaissance soldier-politician, merchant-prince, and ruler-patron. The Medici popes, though less sensationally unreligious, less spectacularly permissive, than some others, and less bloody, did most to turn the papal court at Rome into a gorgeous and majestic replica of the glittering secular courts that their forefathers had established in the city on the Arno.

These nobles and their courtiers, their rivals who have bowed to them or who watch for a chance to assassinate and usurp, even while contributing to the pageant of social display and art endeavor, their favorite ladies and their kept poets, all these enter into a colorful show of courtly extravagance seldom equalled in other eras. Florence at one time has thirty palaces within its walls. Only a bit lower down is a population cultivated, vitally alive, mentally independent, art-loving. If below that there are circles touching on poverty, wretchedness, and crime almost incredible—never, we are told, was mere human life held at lower valuation—we may shrug our shoulders because they have nothing to do with the regal productions at the courts.

Cosimo de' Medici, corrupt tyrant, egotist, cynic, unprincipled fighter, is yet the great patron of the arts, bringing scholars from afar to his court, giving enormously generous commissions to architects, painters, sculptors, for the embellishment of Florence, meeting poets on their own ground as understanding critic, collecting works of art and manuscripts, and keeping copyists busy, making his palace the centre for literary, philosophical, and artistic societies and coteries, founding the Platonic Academy—in short, while earning politically the title *pater patriæ*, putting into his debt by wise munificence art lovers down the ages.

Then Lorenzo the Magnificent: his very name, as put down in a dedication by Machiavelli and perpetuated by all later historians, is a spur to our imagination in picturing his theatre. Lorenzo was the very incarnation of the free spirit of the Renaissance, himself a poet and scholar of no mean ability, writer of lyrics for the carnivals, the patron who did most to unite the two currents of antique revival and Italian effort, no less enthusiastic and spirited in intellectual pursuits and art patronage than in the adventures of love, tilting, and political intrigue. It is this sort of prince that we may visualize as decreeing that on a certain night a play of Terence shall be performed, exactly in the ancient manner, on the ballroom stage; on another night the newest tragedy (after Seneca) of his latest poet-protégé; or on another evening a masque, with so-and-so's dancers and perhaps those diverting "settings" which the artists have been bringing indoors piecemeal from the entries and pageants.

The *drama* that the princely theatres of these tyrants fostered, as we have seen, failed to come to world importance. What is it, then, that lends such lustre to the Renaissance stage? Chiefly the magnificence of the outward trappings; and then the perfect fitness of theatre activity to the life of the times. Rediscovery of old elements of theatrical art—in playhouse forms, in setting, in machinery—and new opulence of visual display: these are gains perfectly in the spirit of the day. The regally decorated palace ballroom becomes a theatre; its stage takes on an appropriately wasteful decorative richness.

We catch the spirit of the occasion best by seeing through contemporary eyes. (We may forget for the moment that the accounts deal with another court than the Medicean, and that the date is a year after the great Lorenzo's death: the Venetian court is equally typical.) Thus Beatrice d'Este, writing from Venice in May, 1493, to her husband, the Regent of Milan:

> After dinner and a little rest, a large company of gentlemen came to conduct us to the *festa* at the palace. We travelled in barges, and, when we reached the palace, were conducted into the Great Hall. There a grand tribunal was erected at one end of the hall, in two divisions running the whole length of the walls, and in the centre of the hall a square stage was placed for dancing and theatrical representations. We ascended the tribunal, where we found a number of noble Venetian ladies, one hundred and thirty-two in all, richly adorned with jewels. . . During the dancing, I left the hall and retired to rest in another room for an hour. When I returned it was already dark. A hundred lighted torches hung from the ceiling, and a representation was given on the stage, in which two big animals with large horns appeared, ridden by two figures, bearing golden balls and cups wreathed with verdure.

A theatrical production in a Florentine ballroom theatre. A print by Jacques Callot of a court masque in 1616, in the great hall of the (now) Uffizi Palace. Note the performers on the dancing floor as well as on the raised stage; and the non-architectural scenery. It is said that this etching in which Callot fixed the natural ring-line of the standing spectators helped to determine the form of the later "horseshoe" auditoriums. [From *The Theatre of Tomorrow*, by Kenneth Macgowan.]

These two were followed by a triumphal chariot, in which Justice sat enthroned, holding a drawn sword in her hand inscribed with the motto *Concordia*, and wreathed with palms and olive. In the same car was an ox with his feet resting on a figure of St. Mark and the adder. This, as your Highness will readily understand, was meant to signify the League, and as in all their discourses to me the Prince and these gentlemen speak of your Highness as the author of the peace and tranquillity of Italy, so in this representation they placed your head on the triumphal arch above the others. Behind the chariot came two serpents, ridden by two other youths, dressed like the first riders. All these figures mounted the tribunal in the centre of the hall, and danced round Justice, and after dancing for awhile, their balls exploded, and out of the flames, an ox, a lion, an adder, and a Moor's head suddenly appeared, and all of these danced together round the figure of Justice. Then the banquet followed, and the different dishes and *confetti* were carried in to the sound of trumpets, accompanied by an infinite number of torches. . . When the banquet was finished, we had another representation, in which two youths on serpents played the chief part. A messenger arrived, riding on a triumphal car in a boat . . . and a little while afterwards the triumphal car of the League appeared again, followed by four giants. The first one carried a horn of foliage and fruit, the two next bore two clubs with gold and silver balls, or catapults, while the last carried a cornucopia, similar to that borne by the first giant in his hand. Then came four animals in the shape of Chimeras ridden by four naked Moors, sounding tambourines and cymbals or clapping their hands. They were followed by four triumphal cars, bearing figures of Diana, Death, the Mother of Meleager, and several armed men—four or five persons in each chariot, the whole intended to represent the story of Meleager, which was fully set forth from his birth to his death, with interludes of dances . . . The Bishop of Como was sitting by me all the evening, and his infinite weariness at the length of the performance and his dislike of the great heat in that crowded hall made me laugh as I never laughed before. And in order to tease him and have more fun I kept on telling him that there was still more to come and that the acting would go on till tomorrow morning. . . When at length we reached home, I supped frugally and then went to bed, as it was already three o'clock. The gown that I wore after dinner was a crimson and gold watered silk, with my jewelled cap on my head, and the rope of pearls with the Marone as a pendant. I commend myself to your Highness. Your Excellency's most affectionate wife,

BEATRICE SFORZA VISCOMTIS

Here indeed is drama subordinated to the new elements out of pageantry and decorated dance-ballet. Here are monsters, giants, serpents, chimeras, chariots, allegorical figures, mythological story, and interludes of dances, in place of unified dramatic action; and the whole is mixed with feasting, richly adorned and bejewelled ladies, bishops, lords, and such—not wholly unconnected too, with political purpose.

The Latin comedies were still being presented, and Italian ones; a few years later Beatrice's sister, Isabella d'Este, writing after performances at the Court of Ferrara, remarks: "These plays are certainly full of vain words, and are not without doubtful passages to which some persons might take objection. All the same, they are amusing, and excite much laughter, chiefly owing to the frequent changes of voice and excellent performance of these actors." And in the same year Isabella sees at Mantua productions with the new emphasis on grandeur of staging:

> On Friday *Philonico* was given, on Saturday *Il Penulo* of Plautus, on Sunday the *Ippolita* of Seneca, on Monday the *Adelphi* of Terence. All of these were admirably recited by skilled actors, and received the greatest applause from the spectators. . . I should fail in my duty if I did not write to tell you what, indeed, requires a better scribe than I am—all the magnificence, grandeur, and excellence of the said representations, the beauty of which I will try to describe as briefly as possible. . .

The narrator then goes on to describe a luxuriantly decorated stage and hall, with paintings by Mantegna, a grotto, arcades, foliage, banners, and "the blue vault of heaven, studded over with the constellations of our hemisphere." Certainly Plautus and Terence and Seneca have come to a new magnificence of setting here.

Still another report by Isabella herself begins with a comment on the sumptuous costumes for five comedies, which were so many that "those which were worn in one comedy would not have to be used again," though there were one hundred and ten actors, men and women. And in 1508 Bernardino Prosperi writes from the Court of Ferrara a letter[2] that sums up the whole drift of dramatic performance away from mere play and acting toward glorified scenery, dance, and regal pageantry:

> On Monday evening the Cardinal had a comedy performed, which was composed by Messer Lodovico Ariosto, his familiar, and rendered in the form of a farce or merry jape, the which from beginning to end

---

[2] The quotation here and one at the end of the chapter are from *The King of Court Poets: A Study of the Work, Life and Times of Lodovico Ariosto,* by Edmund G. Gardner (London, 1906).

was as elegant and delightful as any other that I have ever seen played, and it was much commended on every side. The subject was a most beautiful one of two youths enamored of two harlots who had been brought to Taranto by a pander, and in it there were so many intrigues and novel incidents and so many fine moralities and various things that in those of Terence there are not half of them; for the parts were cast to honorable and good actors, all from without, with most beautiful costumes and sweet melodies for interludes, and with a morris-dance of cooks heated with wine, with earthen pots tied in front of them, who beat time with their wooden sticks to the sound of the Cardinal's music. But what has been best in all these festivities and representations has been the scenery in which they have been played, which Maestro Peregrino, the Duke's painter, has made. It has been a view in perspec-

The scene for satyr-plays as devised by Serlio.

tive of a town with houses, churches, belfreys and gardens, such that one could never tire of looking at it, because of the different things that are there all most cleverly designed and executed. . .

What is this new "scenery" that so many of the Renaissance chroniclers wonder at and joy in? What, we may ask, is its place in the theatre art? Where did it come from? In Greek days, we are fairly certain, there was no attempt at placing a play in illusive settings. In Roman times the architectural stage wall was elaborated into a richly decorated background; but painted picture settings were either unknown or so rare that they escaped all historians. Just about this time the producers of Miracle Plays and Mysteries were developing the simultaneous scene with grouped picture-bits; but that is an activity not likely to have influenced greatly the Renaissance architects and play producers.

The architectural scene for comedy as prescribed by Sebastiano Serlio, in a book issued in 1545. [From reproductions in *Theatre Arts Monthly* of the originals in Serlio's *Architettura*.]

The impulse toward the illusive setting and pictorial "effects" probably rose from the same source in the two cases: the priests began to picture out the Mystery incidents because they were dealing with naïve audiences with child-like minds, and gradually the picturing method spread to the backgrounds; and in Renaissance Italy the producers set out a comedy in "a view in perspective, such that one could never tire of looking at it, because of the different things that are there," for the same reason, to raise delight by clever portrayal of place and with surprising trappings. And it always seems to me that the best explanation of the strange things that happened in the name of stage decoration, then and in later centuries, is that the producers adopted the principle of putting in a lot of things to please the children. It is a question, indeed, whether the coming of perspective-picture settings has not been more of a curse than a blessing to adult drama (though I believe in color, lighting, and the visual element in general as a major contributing element in production). Anyway, it was at this time that "scenery" flowered; and until the early twentieth century the painted-perspective setting will claim its showy place on all the stages of Europe.

The origins of the picture scene are badly entangled. Our writer from Ferrara in 1509, Prosperi, praises "a view in perspective of a town with houses, churches, belfries and gardens"; the designer of it, the Maestro Peregrino, may have been carrying on a tradition of the outdoor *Commedia dell'Arte* stage, whereon a rudely indicated street between two rows of houses was standard; an idiom that may possibly be traced back into Roman times. In any case we may be sure that Peregrino also was claiming classical precedent for his "view in perspective." You will remember that Vitruvius had written of the *periacti*, devices by which change of scene was indicated (it didn't take place) in Roman times. He described three scenes as they appeared on the three faces of a turning prism, two as architectural views with buildings, for tragedy and comedy, and the third a pastoral view, for satyr-plays. It seems likely that the Renaissance scholars and artists misread the description and set out to apply the principle to full-stage scenes, not merely to an indicating device. The rediscovered treatise by Vitruvius, *De Architectura*, had been published as early as 1486.

What the artists after that made of the Vitruvian scenes is best illustrated from plates in a volume of Serlio's famous *Architettura*, first published in 1545 and then reprinted and translated in the chief countries of Europe. I reproduce the three scenes according to Serlio herewith; because no other pictures of real or supposititious settings ever had so extraordinary an influence upon methods of staging. In a sense the series went far to establish the perspective setting, architectural and landscape, as the approved thing for the theatres of Europe. Of course Serlio had had opportunity to see many perspective scenes worked out on Italian ballroom stages—perhaps saw this very one in Ferrara in 1508.

The architectural scene for tragedy. Note the severer architecture here as compared with that of the comedy scene shown on page 203.

At any rate the "street perspective" became the common *play* background (the masques, interludes, etc., had another novelty in a less austere, pageantry scene, as we shall see in a moment). Another example is pictured to illustrate the point. And to make a long story very short, the architectural perspectives throve and throve, until in the next century operas and sometimes even plays were being exhibited in those gorgeously elaborate architectural compositions that are associated with the illustrious name of the Bibbienas, who, even to four generations, dwarfed the actor with the towering magnificence of arches, columns, cartouches, and wreaths. You will find their works illustrated in the next chapter—because they are so essentially operatic.

Aside from a misconception of Roman scenery, the architects of the Renaissance gained from Vitruvius a knowledge of the architectural

A typical perspective scene, with built architectural units before a painted backdrop. Setting for *Il Granchio*, Italy, 1566. [From *Scenes and Machines on the English Stage during the Renaissance*, by Lily B. Campbell.]

The Theatre of the Olympian Academy at Vicenza. This may profitably be compared with the reconstructions of the theatres at Orange and Aspendus, for proof of its relationship to the classic playhouses. It is really a small Roman theatre roofed over. The perspective vistas beyond the doorways were added in 1585, a few years after the building of the theatre.

form of the ancient theatre. When an academy planned to build a "classic" playhouse, the designers could read Vitruvius, perhaps explore some ruins, and construct a fairly close approximation to a Roman auditorium and stage. One such theatre survives today, almost exactly as it was constructed in 1580 and the few years following: the Theatre of the Olympian Academy at Vicenza, known also as the Palladian Theatre, after the architect. The photograph opposite shows how like the building is to a small Roman theatre roofed over. After the death of Palladio, the architect Scamozzi added the perspective vistas seen through the doorways in the stage-wall—borrowing and intruding a feature already well developed on the free-standing ballroom stages.

And thereby hangs the tale of the coming of the proscenium arch that is the distinguishing structural feature of theatres for three centuries to follow. For there is a theory to the effect that the proscenium arch of the modern theatre is the direct lineal descendent of the central doorway of the Vicenza stage. It occurred like this: Scamozzi put five perspectives behind the doorways, making a stage plan like A over-leaf; other architects and Scamozzi himself wanted to preserve the useful stage-wall and yet open up the perspective to afford more acting space, and Scamozzi developed B as a stage-plan for the theatre at Sabionetta, while the visiting Inigo Jones made the plan C as a further modification. From this it was but a step to push the entire playing space through the portal, arriving at a curtained stage, D, with the decoration of the old Roman stage-wall now persisting only as adornment of the frame to the acting stage.

What we arrive at is that playhouse in Parma which is known as "the first modern theatre"—because it has the first known proscenium-framed stage. Here indeed is an acting space with new potentialities and new limitations. Acting is to be within a space surrounded by walls or "scenery," not out on an open platform. It will be quite a different thing after two hundred years of blanketing by painted settings. And now that those settings can be shown suddenly, by the drawing of curtains—and yes! even changed between acts—the scene-painter is going to be a mighty important man in the theatre.

Before going on to his story, however, let us note that the classic form of auditorium, modified by the influence of the ballroom theatres, determined the form of the seventeenth to the nineteenth century playhouses. The Farnese Theatre at Parma has the new proscenium-framed stage combined with the ballroom floor and "arena" seating of the informal palace playhouses. That arrangement was necessary as long as pageants and social dancing were mixed up with drama (see the picture of a Florentine fête some pages back). The next step is the compromise auditorium in horseshoe shape; it gives a larger number of people a view into the scene behind the frame, by cutting off the ends of the old Roman semicircular auditorium, as illustrated on page 212.

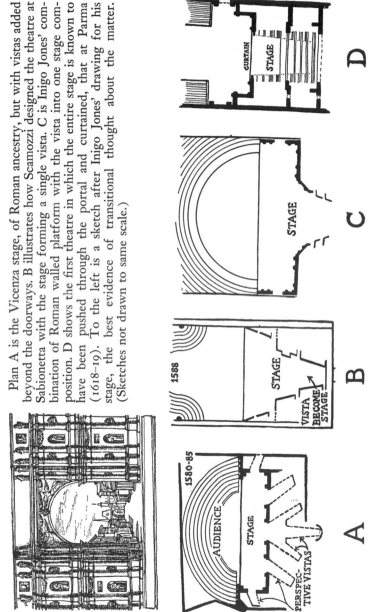

Plan A is the Vicenza stage, of Roman ancestry, but with vistas added beyond the doorways. B illustrates how Scamozzi designed the theatre at Sabionetta with the stage forming a single vista. C is Inigo Jones' combination of Roman walled platform with the vista into one stage composition. D shows the first theatre in which the entire stage is known to have been pushed through the portal and curtained, that at Parma (1618–19). To the left is a sketch after Inigo Jones' drawing for his stage, the best evidence of transitional thought about the matter. (Sketches not drawn to same scale.)

The evolution of the picture scene: showing how the decorated stage-wall of the classic theatre moved forward to become the proscenium frame of the modern theatre, while the vista once seen through the central stage doorway became the full-stage scene, curtained and changeable between plays or between acts.

The "scene" of the Olympian Academy Theatre photographed to show the nature of the vistas added by Vincenzo Scamozzi in 1585.

The stage and proscenium of the Farnese Theatre at Parma, as seen from the "arena" floor. Built in 1618-1619, this is known as "the first modern theatre," by reason of the proscenium-framed and curtained stage—though the auditorium is still of the ballroom type. [From a drawing by J. M. Olbrich in Streit's *Das Theater*.]

It is necessary to go back and inquire where the scene-painter came from (we have discovered the sources of the curtained stage to which he will bring his flats and back-cloth, and we have learned about the architect's built-up scene; but this is a third, independent development). A hint has been dropped about a possible influence from the Miracle and Mystery Plays—which in Italy were presented at times on ballroom stages. But the safer conjecture is that painty, though not exactly painted, settings grew out of the pageant-cars and tableau-stages that had long been a feature of the royal entry, the outdoor *festa*, and the *carrousel* (yes, in France, too). In the open-air fête, the increasingly extravagant pageantry called for increasingly extravagant and in-genious moving or stationary stages, as backgrounds for grouped

Scamozzi's perspective vistas schematized into one "scene." [From Riccoboni's *Histoire des Théâtres Italiens*.]

nobles in sumptuous costumes, or for posed tableaux of amateur actors. The car etched so prettily by Jacques Callot and reproduced on this page is typical; and so is the street "decoration" shown on page 216.

A pageant car, as etched by Jacques Callot.

The Death of Ananias: Tapestry after a design by Raphael. Probably a free redrawing after a stage production of the time. [In the Vatican Museum.]

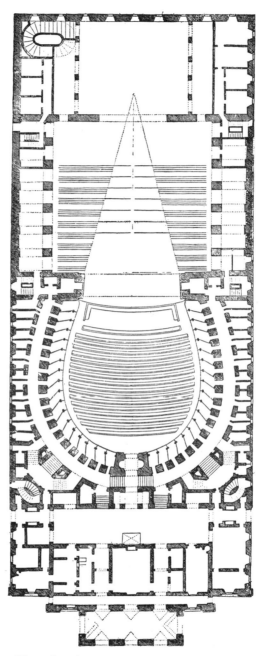

How the vista stage and the horseshoe auditorium crystallized in a theatre form that was standard for the eighteenth and nineteenth centuries. Note the parallel grooves for wing settings on the stage. La Scala Opera House in Milan.

The next step is the introduction of these features into the ballroom as background for masques, for the sort of ballet-entertainment so clearly described by Beatrice d'Este; and from France we have a picture perfectly illustrating the intermediate arrangement of fragmentary tableau "scenery" brought on to the dancing floor (in the *Ballet de la Royne* engraving over-page). From this it is obviously a short step to the full-stage setting on the platform at the end of the ballroom theatre, as illustrated in the picture by Callot of the Florentine masque, earlier in the chapter. The scene here is typically painty; that is, it could not be built up in stucco, and is unarchitectural.

Serlio had given instructions that the buildings in his Vitruvian tragedy and comedy scenes were to be built out in relief, not painted on canvas (and the perspectives at Vicenza are properly thus constructed); but he allowed that the tiny bits at the end of the vista might be painted in perspective to carry on the lines of the carefully built, diminishing rows of buildings on his "street." We may visualize the scene painter enlarging that backdrop year after year, usurping more and more of the space given (so expensively) to the architect's constructions; until finally the painter, providing even architectural scenes so much more cheaply than architect and carpenter, and able to bring landscape effects into the theatre as well, pushes his rivals out the stage-door. The painted perspective setting, thus established in Italy in the early sixteenth century, and spreading northward in the seventeenth, is to rule on the stages of Europe until the twentieth century, when the latest Modernists will suddenly discover that too much picture scenery has been hindering drama and nullifying the better sorts of visual-theatrical effectiveness.

In opera and spectacle, as we shall see, the glorified background will have triumphs of its own. But we may profitably note that it came into the theatre when drama as such was weak. Regarding the theatre art as a thing architectonic, we may say that the gains during the Renaissance were decorative, not structural: ornamental, not organic. As a last thought about the matter, let us remember that Italy at this time had gained something of sumptuousness out of the Orient.

IN CLOSING the chapter, which treats of the period immediately following those medieval centuries when Church had killed theatre, then reared and disowned a separate "religious drama," we may glance at Renaissance theatrical entertainment as it flowered finally in Holy Rome. While the more strict sub-Fathers were fastidiously drawing their skirts away from the now-too-liberal, half-secularized Miracles and Mysteries, Pope Leo X was building himself a private ballroom theatre at the Vatican. I find two accounts of a production there,

A ballroom theatre as arranged for the *Ballet Comique de Royne*, performed in 1581 before Henry III of France and his court. Note the fragmentary settings on the dancing floor, and the full pictorial setting on the rudimentary stage. [From a re-engraving in Pougin's *Dictionnaire* of the print published soon after the performance.]

214

which when pieced together seem to tie up the threads out of the story of the Renaissance theatre: half-original plays, half-classic; emerging painted scenery and opulent trappings; reckless social life as background. John Addington Symonds writes:

Leo had an insatiable appetite for scenic shows. Comedies of the new Latinizing style were his favorite recreation. But he also invited the Sienese company of the Rozzi, who played only farces, every year to Rome; nor was he averse to even less artistic buffoonery, as may be gathered from many of the stories told about him. In 1513 Leo opened a theatre upon the Capital, and here in 1519, surrounded with two thousand spectators, he witnessed an exhibition of Ariosto's *Suppositi*.

Here we may let Edmund G. Gardner take up the account:

His Holiness himself stood at the door to superintend the admission of his guests, letting in with his benediction those whom he thought proper—about two thousand in all. On the curtain was painted the Pope's Dominican jester or buffoon, Fra Mariano, sporting with devils, with the inscription: "These are the Japeries of Fra Mariano." Then, to the music of the pipers, the curtain fell, and revealed a beautiful scene of a city in perspective, representing the Ferrara of the play, painted by Raphael himself, which the Pope peered at through his eyeglass and greatly admired. The stage was lit by candelabra supporting torches forming letters, each letter made by five torches, and spelling *Leo Decimus Pontifex Maximus*. At the obscene equivoques of the prologue, the Pope laughed heartily but the foreigners were scandalized. The comedy was played in the usual style of the epoch, with singing and music between the acts, and at the end there was a *moresca* representing the Fable of the Gorgon. . .

And again Symonds sums up the matter and carries the thought forward:

When Leo was made Pope he said to Giuliano, Duke of Nemours, "Let us enjoy the Papacy since God has given it to us." It was in this spirit that he administered the Holy See. The key-note which he struck dominated the whole society of Rome. Masques and balls, comedies and carnival processions, filled the streets and palaces of the Eternal City with a mimicry of pagan festivals, while Art went hand in hand with Luxury. . . Meanwhile, amid crowds of cardinals in hunting dress, dances of half-naked girls, and masques of Carnival Bacchantes moved pilgrims from the north with wide, astonished, woeful eyes—disciples of Luther, in whose soul, as in a scabbard, lay sheathed the sword of the Spirit, ready to flash forth and smite.

An arch built for the entry of Charles IX into Paris in 1572, designed by Bernard de Palissy. Typical of one of the sources of the "painty" setting. [From Edouard Drumont's *Les Fêtes Nationales à Paris*.]

Nothing could better illustrate the perilous position of the theatre in human society: its transitions from the estate of sublime art to the estate of plaything of the reckless and the vicious. When we meet those scandalized "disciples of Luther" again, they will be suppressing another licentious theatre—which has just given birth to the comedies and tragedies of Shakespeare. And here is the stage of the glorious Renaissance degraded to amuse those prelates and priests who had been divinely appointed, as many believe, to guard the morals and save the souls of their fellow men. The Church, as the Catholic historians are the first to admit, had failed to rise fully out of that incredible state of disorganization, and of shameful licentiousness among many classes of the clergy, which had culminated in the divided papacy of the beginning of the fifteenth century. When betterment came, through the Reformation and the Counter-Reformation, the theatre was destined to suffer at the hands of both parties, the Puritans of the one outlawing it as ungodly and intemperate—and unfairly as papist—and many Catholics condemning it as worldly and impious. But the very freedom of thought and enterprise engendered by the Italian Renaissance was to foster, to the northward, theatres glorious beyond those created or dreamed by the Italians.

Masked actors in a revival of a play by Terence, during the late medieval period. [From a Latin manuscript in the *Bibliothèque Nationale*, Paris.]

CHAPTER
9

A Pretty Interlude—
Pastoral and Operatic

IN ONE minor department of drama the poets of the Italian Renaissance developed a new form and left play-texts of lasting value. Before their era, there had been pastoral poetry but never a memorable pastoral drama. As a by-product of—perhaps an attempted refuge from—the violent and ostentatious life of the times, there came into existence a considerable body of idylls and pastoral plays. A court dramatist could serve his prince never so well else as when he turned his fancy to a dream age, created heroes and heroines who walked amid Arcadian pleasures, and brought pictures of rustic simplicity and pastoral beauty before the un-simple and surfeited ballroom audiences. Perhaps this playwright's manuscript was little more than a framework for a series of pictures, dances, recited idylls; or perhaps as important as a serviceable masque text; but in the end it was somewhat important as a full-fledged example of literary drama.

There was a special rightness, of course, in the appearance of pastoral drama just when the stage for the first time could be set with groves or villa gardens or orchards; the form does seem to need the re-enforcement of pictures—unless it is to be presented in garden or woodland playhouse. The Italian hedge theatre, however, was a second by-product of the amorous-rustic literature, and quite as pretty a novelty among theatre "buildings" as pastoral drama was among play-texts.

Idyllic poetry had beguiled the Romans even when they were at the heyday of their so unidyllic conquering and blood-shedding. But the Greek-Sicilian Theocritus remains to this day the master of the form,

having given the world such lovely lyrics and dialogues of the fabled
sylvan hills and valleys of Sicily that no later poet ever quite touches
our emotions with the same magic. In the Renaissance as in ancient
Rome, we may read some alien spirit, an insincerity, a weak romanticism, into the interest in rustic things: there seems, indeed, here, as later
at Louis XVI's Versailles court, an elaborate affectation. But we may
be sure, too, that there is, between violent intrigues and artificial social
functions, a genuine feeling for country life, a real longing for sweeter,
simpler pleasures. The villas and vineyards of Italy bespeak it, Boccaccio breathed it (his amorous tales, lingering in memory, seem always
to carry something of the fragrance of their garden setting); even
Lorenzo the Magnificent is best remembered (as a poet) for his rural
idylls and mythological sketches. Partly in imitation of Virgil and the
other ancients, partly as an echo from the Italian countryside, pastoral
literature and praise of pastoral life are here ushered in, to become a
lasting pursuit in court circles through Italy, Spain, France, and England for two centuries or more. If Sannazzaro had not written his
Arcadia, it is doubtful whether Sir Philip Sidney would have written
his. And we know how Shakespeare browsed through the transplanted
Italian tales of this time, taking as he willed for a palace-and-garden
comedy to be called *Twelfth Night* or a courtly-rustic piece to be
entitled *The Winter's Tale*.

It was inevitable that the Italian drama, newly emancipated, in the
sixteenth century, from the old classic forms (though not from classic
characters) should absorb this pastoral impulse. As a headline for the
plays of all those dramatists who led up to Tasso, we may write:
Time, the Golden Age; *Place*, myrtle groves and rustic farms, the hills
and woods of mythological countries; *Characters*, Pan and his fauns
and nymphs, Polyphemus, Echo, the Cyprian, and always the shepherds
and the shepherdesses with their crooked sticks—figures embodying
that simple ideal for which every heart in the audience yearned.

The stories are of love, the idyllic love of old-time places and times,
before life became complicated or dull or feverish. Ah, there is a
charming felicity in these legends! Then the Gods had made the world
for lovers alone. The time of day is eternally twilight or the clear
freshness that comes just after dawn. There are no rooms, no streets;
only river banks and pools for bathing and cool grottoes. Arcadia on
the stage.

Torquato Tasso carried the form to its perfection in *Aminta*, enriching the pastoral idyll with exquisite poetry, genuine feeling, and
not a little affecting (if artificially contrived) drama. Battista Guarini
in his *Pastor Fido* added strength and body to the *metier*. These two
breathe the very air of those mythological fields and that Golden Age

which all the true pastoral poets so delicately sighed to recapture.

The *Aminta*, first played at Ferrara in 1573, partly presents and partly tells the charming story of the love of the shepherd, Aminta, for the beautiful virgin, Sylvia, once his playmate but now a follower of the huntress-goddess Diana and cold to the call of love. The play opens, characteristically, with a prologue spoken by *Love, Disguised as a Shepherd*. In two scenes, the situation is set out, Daphne vainly reproaching Sylvia for her insensibility to the pleasures of love, inci-

Parnassus, a painting by Mantegna. Considered by some authorities the most typical expression of the spirit that gave rise to the masques and plays staged at Italian courts in the fifteenth century.

dentally painting a pretty picture of her own finding of delight; and Aminta recounting to his friend Thyrsis the story of his passion for the unfeeling Sylvia.

AMINTA

While yet a boy, scarce tall enough to gather
The lowest hanging fruit, I became intimate
With the most lovely and beloved girl,
That ever gave to the wind her locks of gold. . .

There grew by little and little in my heart,
I know not from what root,
But just as the grass grows that sows itself,
An unknown something, which continually
Made me feel anxious to be with her; and then
I drank strange sweetness from her eyes, which left
A taste, I know not how, of bitterness.
Often I sighed, nor knew the reason why;
And thus before I knew what loving was,
Was I a lover. . .

After these expository and descriptive scenes, a chorus—survival of classic drama—appears and sings of the Golden Age: in this time a chorus of Shepherds, of course. An uncouth Satyr opens the second act with a monologue about love, and goes in search of Sylvia at her bathing-place. Daphne and Thyrsis conspire to bring Aminta and Sylvia together, and Thyrsis tricks the lovelorn shepherd into believing that Sylvia expects him at the pool. The next act opens with the recounting by Thyrsis of the scene at the bathing-place: he and Aminta had found Sylvia bound to a tree, by the Satyr. The monster had fled at their approach; but Sylvia, instead of rewarding her rescuers, had run away like a frightened fawn.

Aminta appears, fresh from an attempt at suicide which Daphne has frustrated; and now comes a nymph—typical "messenger"—bearing word of Sylvia's death during a wolf-hunt. Aminta immediately rushes out to throw himself over a cliff. Sylvia, however, reappears, telling of her narrow escape from the wolf. She is stirred to remorse by Daphne's account of Aminta's grief, and when a messenger brings news of the shepherd's leap from the cliff, she vows she will join him in death, and pauses on earth only long enough to give burial to his supposed cold and mangled corpse. The final act opens with a soliloquy upon the strange ways of Providence—and, indeed, quite miraculously has Aminta escaped injury in his fall. And less miraculously Sylvia and Daphne, searching for his body, came upon him:

ELPINO
. . . But when Sylvia recognized
Amyntas, and beheld his beautiful cheeks
So lovelily discolored, that no violet
Could pale more sweetly, it so smote on her,
That she seemed ready to breathe out her soul.
And then like a wild Bacchante, crying out
And smiting her fair bosom, she fell down
Right on the prostrate body, face to face,
And mouth to mouth.

CHORUS
Did then no shame restrain
Her who had been so hard and so denying?

ELPINO
It is a feeble love that shame restrains;
A powerful one breaks through so weak a bridle.
Her eyes appeared a fountain of sweet waters,
With which she bathed his cold cheeks, moaningly,
Waters so sweet, that he came back to life,
And opening his dim eyes, sent from his soul
A dolorous Ah me! . . .

And Elpino sets off in search of Sylvia's father, who, he tells us, has long wanted grandchildren.

A typical stage scene in the Italian style of the sixteenth century, with settings of architectural units and a backdrop.

Of course this drama skims perilously close to sentimentality, and only the richness and delicacy of Tasso's imagery and verse (quoted here in Leigh Hunt's translation) keep the story from cloying. Everything is maintained on a fanciful plane; there is no reality in these suicides and dangers, no real suspense, no fear that Aminta will not melt the ice that encases Sylvia's heart. But somehow—in our mellower

moods—we are touched by the incidents; and we flow along in a sort
of sensuous delight at the richness of the outward form of the play.
There is not the magic of Theocritus here—Daphne tells us why:

> The world, methinks grows old,
> And growing old, grows sad. . .

The spirit of the Renaissance has added an artificial note to pastoral
poetry. The poets are sighing for, rather than delighting in, a simple
age. But here is an idyllic love sung with lyrical exuberance, a simple
rustic legend decorated most delicately, most appealingly; with the
glow of the Golden Days spread over an imagined world.

For the original audience there was the additional delight of symbolism and local allusion. For Tasso imbedded a long description of
the ideal court, in compliment to his patron; and every character can
be identified with some one of the nobles or ladies of Ferrara society.

Aminta had enormous influence outside of Italy in succeeding years.
It was endlessly imitated; but so seldom equalled that it may rest here
as the one example outlined to serve as sample of the pastoral form,
the typical rustic play. There were over two hundred editions printed
in Italian, twenty translations into French, nine into English, and scores
of scattered ones in all the European languages and even in minor dialects.

The Pastor Fido or *Faithful Shepherd* alone enjoyed similar fame.
It is a more ambitious work, three times as long as the over-brief
Aminta, substituting a complicated plot for the simple fable of Sylvia.
The speeches are similarly long, and most of the action occurs offstage,
to be recounted charmingly by lovers, messengers, and chorus. The
same sincere love of pastoral life floods the speeches, however:

AMARILLIS

> Dear, happy groves!
> And thou all silent, solitary gloom,
> True residence of peace and of repose!
> How willingly, how willingly my steps
> To you return; and oh! if but my stars
> Benignly had decreed
> My Life for Solitude . . .
> No, not th' Elysian Fields,
> Those happy gardens of the Demi-Gods,
> Would I exchange for your enchanting shades! . . .
> The rural maid how blest,
> Who though but scantly drest,
> In homely gown, and plain,
> Unsullied with a stain;
> Rich in herself alone . . .

The idyllic theatre at Villa Gori, near Siena. A typical Italian garden theatre, with clipped cypress hedges replacing the "wings" of the indoor stages.

And as final words from the pastoral drama, we may note the closing lines spoken by Amarillis, in which she touches upon the reason for the combined eternal charm and ephemeral prettiness that grace these compositions. After all, they were composed for noble ladies and gallants who were seeking no more than an afternoon's beguilement from the realities of life.

> . . . And if thou'rt inclined
> To share our bliss, come freely and partake
> Of this our sweet Festivity!

Yes, it was the bliss of festivity that somehow shaped the pastoral drama. It is a drama of refuge, not of living. And in that connection it may be illuminating to add that these two poets who dramatized so

A garden theatre at Villa Marlia, near Lucca, Italy. [From a drawing by Henry Vincent Hubbard, by courtesy of the artist.]

sweetly the legends of "the golden haze out yonder," were both disillusioned and embittered courtiers: Tasso so nonsensically the idealist that he plunged over the verge into actual and imprisoned madness; Guarini withdrawing into a pedant seclusion. Plays echoing theirs will parallel all the types of drama that we explore down to the coming of the democratic spirit; but not in Spain nor in France shall we find the same sensuous exuberance. In England the spirit entered rather into lyrical poetry, into Spenser who breathed it richly and sweetly, and into that Marlowe who could sum up the impulse in

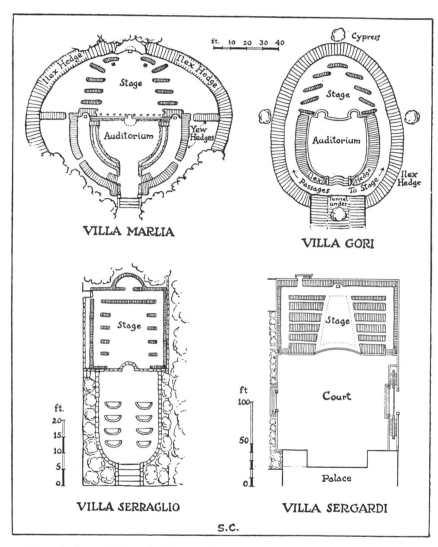

Ground plans of four Italian garden theatres, showing various types, and indicating the toy-like nature of the smaller examples. The stage wings were usually of clipped cypress or ilex hedge, and the stage floor of turf. [From Cheney's *The Open-air Theatre.*]

226

Come live with me and be my love,
And we will all the pleasures prove
That hills and vallies, dales and fields,
Woods or steepy mountain yields—

and into a Shakespeare who cast the pretty glow of it over works stronger, fresher, and more diverting than any that ever came out of Italy—but not so simple.

In adding here pictures and plans of Italian garden theatres, so perfectly fitted for the presentation of the pastoral plays, I must note that these are later in date (so far as we know); that the pastoral drama was staged in the then new and much-appreciated pageant-settings. It is recorded that Tasso, in his mad way, journeyed all the way to Florence to thank the great Buontalenti for his part in setting *Aminta* properly, and gave point to his homage by omitting to pay respects to the Grand Duke. But if the architects and painters were having their way just then on the stages of Italy, at some time later the open-air playhouses came into vogue; and villa theatres in Italian style, with wings and back-drop of gratefully green and neutral hedge, were copied in many a northern palace garden. One is pictured here from the Schloss Mirabell gardens in Salzburg, and you may see the theatre itself there today if you wish. Nor has the vogue entirely passed: in this twentieth century you will find as many garden theatres in California as in all of Italy—and, I dare say, more used.

A production at the garden theatre of Mirabell Castle, Salzburg, Austria.

IN THE house, or the palace, of Giovanni Bardi, Conte di Vernio, in Florence, in the final years of the sixteenth century, a group of *dilettanti* poets and musicians were accustomed to meet, to talk about the arts, to recite and play for one another. These amateurs were stirred by the same passion for art and learning that had impelled their more professional brethren to form academies, to study the achievements of the ancients, and to formulate rules as to what constituted "classic" practice in drama-writing, in music, in versification, etc. Happily the members of the Count Bardi's "circle" were not too bound by the rules of the pedant-academicians—or by exact knowledge of their subject—to venture upon impossibly new and unorthodox experiments. Among them were Vincenzo Galilei, father of the famous Galileo, and two younger musicians named Jacopo Peri and Giulio Caccini.

One day the talk ran upon the method of verse-declamation in the old Greek theatres. It was known that the delivery of the lines had been declamatory if not strictly musical, and that music had accompanied the chanting of the choruses. Why not restore this method in the Florentine ballroom theatres? But the music of the Greeks had wholly disappeared; nor was there any treatise to tell what it had

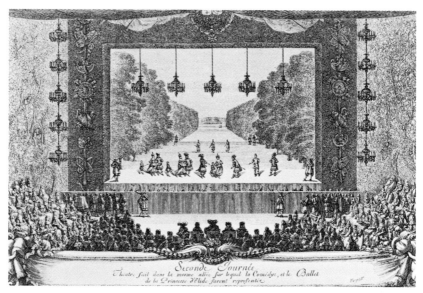

A theatre at Versailles, in which the setting simulated the famous garden *allée* of the palace grounds, with trees as "wings," before a painted backdrop. A performance of a ballet, *La Princesse d'Elide*, in a six-day Court Festival of Moliere's plays, 1664. King Louis XIV is the central figure in the court audience. [From a print after a drawing by Jean Lepautre.]

been. And so the amateurs set out to recreate the Greek drama-with-music. They had a definite object in view, and they were beautifully unhampered by any facts.

What they arrived at was something which none of them had foreseen. (The professional musicians pointed out that they were proceeding blindly, ignorantly.) They came to a new—if hybrid—art form, *Opera*. They failed to recreate, or even to throw any light upon, the

The Royal Theatre, Naples. About 1750. Late enough to be baroque in spirit, the auditorium nevertheless is of the ballroom type. Note the extravagant scenery and the cloud-riding actors.

Greek method of delivery. But they founded a sort of music-drama that has been much with the world ever since; that has, indeed, preempted its biggest and showiest theatres for three hundred years. For while no one admits that opera can ever be a "pure" art-form, and though none of us has ever seen—or heard—a perfect opera, the operatic stage holds its important place in all sophisticated communities, through criticism, calumny, and repeated proofs of its unimportance. The word "opera," by the way, means nothing: merely "work," shortened probably from "work in music." We may adopt such definitions as "a musical form of stage play," or "a drama set to music." The point is that music is no longer merely incidental; it is intended to be of the structure of the piece.

It is possible, of course, to go back and discover some forerunners of opera: particularly in church music as adapted for the Mystery and Miracle Plays, in the court productions of masque and pastoral, wherein music played a generous part (the *Orfeo* of Poliziano should perhaps be specially noted), and in the sung madrigals. But the production that is usually chronicled as "the first opera" is that of Peri's *Dafne*, with Rinuccini's libretto, performed at the Palazzo Corsi in 1597. This rather elementary piece aroused such intense interest that Peri and Caccini's *Euridice*, composed for the festivities in honor of the wedding of Maria de' Medici to Henry IV of France, in 1600, was awaited with excited anticipation by the intellectuals, amateur and professional alike, and by musicians far outside the confines of Florence. This was, incidentally, the first opera produced for "the public"—though one must note that this is not yet the playhouse whither one goes with money to buy a ticket of admission. It was a court-arranged production. *Euridice* became at once the model for imitation and the starting-point for experiment on the part of numberless composers. Opera was an accepted and established form.

In 1607, at the Court of Mantua, the Duke's *maestro di cappella*, Claudio Monteverdi, wrote the music for two libretti by Rinuccini, a *Dafne* and an *Arianna*. These were presented at the celebration in honor of the marriage of a Gonzaga Prince to Margherita, Infanta of Savoy. (I am repeating the point about court-festivity background, so that the reader may recall the richness of the physical investiture of palace productions—we are to see not only the ballet trimmings but the interludes as a whole swallowed by opera.) Monteverdi enlarged the scope of music as an aid to the dramatic story, added boldly to the orchestra, and wrote with so much of originality and imagination that he is credited with being the first of the real masters of the opera. His success with *Arianna* led to an immediate commission to compose another work, and in the following year *Orfeo* was performed. In this the composer dared to use an orchestra of nearly forty pieces. He also introduced bits of melody.

True to its beginnings in supposed imitation of Greek drama, opera had not yet branched out into that sort of melodic display that seems today so essentially the operatic thing; *recitative* was considered the key to the difficult union of drama and music. But once the melodic element was given a bit of play, opera drew farther and farther away from drama presented musically, and closer and closer to a musical exercise with a dramatic legend as its excuse. Of course the whole history of the art in the centuries since has been punctuated by controversies and explosions over this distinction—as is to be expected where a form straddles two distinct arts—and so recently as the late nineteenth century there was an epochal swing back toward "music-drama" as against the over-florid ornamental thing. But the history from Monteverdi, through Cavalli, Cesti, and Scarlatti, and on to the later Italian and French schools of composers, was a record of growing melody, of increasingly interpolated aria, of lessened dramatic directness. It is interesting that the Florentine inventors of opera, who had defied the professional musicians in order to experiment in a musical-dramatic form, were scandalized at Cavalli's innovations in rhythmic melody; they had now become the conservatives, and they were worried that their child, though born of the wayward impulse, should wander out into fields so dangerously uncharted!

But when Cavalli was through it was certain that opera would never go back to the monotony of unrelieved recitative. It was, however, Scarlatti who determined the way for the development of Italian opera —which even to this day emphasizes vocal melody more than does French or German. That in Italy the music became over-ornamental almost immediately, that there was toadying to the singers who were more interested in display-pieces than in furthering the dramatic expression, there can be no doubt. Within forty years the newcomer in the theatre field had grown from timid experimental performance to "grand-opera."

The first public opera-theatre was opened in Venice in 1637: the *Teatro di San Cassiano*. It was so much a success that rival houses sprang up almost at once; and before the end of the century there were eleven theatres in Venice alone. No other Italian city had so many, though this was the period when the serious drama and the opera became professionalized, and were disentangled somewhat from the social life of the courts. In time, Venice, Naples, and Bologna became the noted centres of opera production. In France and England the influence of Italian opera was to be immense, not only in the direct instigation to musical-dramatic composition, but in its effect upon methods of staging and upon the form of the playhouse. The "Italian style" theatre that dominates throughout Europe till the late nineteenth century is really an opera house and not a theatre designed for "legitimate" production.

From the titles of the operas so far mentioned, *Dafne, Euridice, Arianna, Orfeo*, it is clear that the new art was carrying on the tradition of the pastoral drama. The *Teatro di San Cassiano* was opened with the Ferrari-Manelli *Andromeda;* and it was a long time before the librettists escaped out of the classic-story limitation. But Scarlatti (1659–1725) fixed a form for opera as distinguished from ordinary play-writing. He brought in *design*. This characteristic design was broad enough, however, to take in much that in the sixteenth century

Two paintings by Gabriele Bella of seventeenth-century theatres in Venice. Above, the *Teatro S. Samuele*, dating from 1656. Below, a view of a theatre during a festival.

Scene design by Filippo Juvarra, of the seventeenth-eighteenth centuries in Italy. The tiny sketches at bottom seem to indicate that the high archway remained through all the acts of the play, like a second proscenium, the space beyond being transformed by changes of wings and backcloths, between the acts.

Grand architectural settings by the Bibbienas. Above, a drawing by Giovanni Maria Galli-Bibbiena, for an exterior setting. Below, an interior by Giuseppe Galli-Bibbiena, as realized for a dramatic festival at the Court of Bavaria, 1740. [The drawing reproduced from a Brogi photo of the original in the Uffizi Gallery, Florence; the other from an original print.]

had belonged to masque and interlude. The settings, the ballets, the wondrous machine-effects, were soon claiming place between the impassioned arias of the opera singers. Perhaps the mythological libretti were doubly useful because they brought all sorts of opportunity for showy landscape and palatial scenery, and for magical transformations, disappearances, etc.

At any rate, the emergence of opera is accompanied by a continuation of that effort toward ever-more-elaborate scenery that was noted in the last chapter. On the curtained stages the settings could be changed several times in the course of a performance. The perspective setting, grown now from that little symmetrical street scene of Serlio to grand portrayals of the local "square" or many-arched ideal-interiors, was glorified by the Bibbienas into the vast halls and the expansive street vistas that you see in the illustrations here. Magnificent, yes! but he who is interested in drama and acting may well ask, "what has become of the actor now?" Just see if you can find him in these gorgeous palace scenes.

And stage machinery was so developed that no cloud-riding scene, no celestial apparition, no magic appearance or disappearance, no moving sun or moon, was too difficult to attempt. As early as 1486 the Mantuans had seen a court production of the *Menæchmi* of Plautus, out-of-doors, in which a boat with sails and oars, with ten persons aboard, moved across the stage. After that the ballroom stages saw many and marvellous machine-made effects, during plays, masques, and ballets. But the producers of opera made these things a regular adjunct to performance, and they outdid their predecessors in boldness and elaboration. The opera-house stage grew in dimensions and in complexity, not because music or drama or the two in combination needed so much room, but because the public wanted to gape at new miracles of piled-up scenery and of tricked magic effects.

It was these effects as much as the novelty of the musical-dramatic form that led French kings and cardinals to clamor for opera before the seventeenth century was half gone. We shall see how, after isolated importations, the French Court invites an ambitious young Italian page, Lulli by name, to direct a tentatively established official French opera house. With his elevation into authority—with, so to speak, Italian opera under his arm—a new era in staging and theatre-building is in prospect for non-Italian Europe. After some periods of high creation in Spain, England, and France, before the influence has been greatly felt, there will follow a long period during which an operatic incubus is on the theatre.

CHAPTER
10

The Vulgar
Popular Comedy

THERE is a figure that stands for many playgoers today as a symbol of the theatre in its softer, more romantic aspect. Pierrot, in many guises, but always delicate, gently smiling, or charmingly melancholy, is the very antithesis of that crude, violent, and prying figure that can be visioned as the symbol of the realistic stage. Pierrot the moonstruck, Pierrot the pretty, Pierrot the eternal misunderstood lover, Pierrot with a rose in his hand and a fluffy ruff at his throat—this figure represents the other half of the theatre, variously thought of as the poetic, or the soulful, the glamorous or the beautiful half.

Now to me there is something very disturbing about the identifying of the non-realistic, the "ideal" theatre, with any such milky symbolfigure. My readers already know that I put small store by the other, larger, more immediate half, the realistic theatre; but to let Pierrot represent the rest is a typical nineteenth century missing of the essence of the art—typical of dividing the theatre into a half that portrays life "truthfully" and a half that affords *escape*. There is something vaguely unhealthy about this powdered Pierrot, too gentle in an aboundingly vital world, too sentimental, too perpetually sad, too dependent upon sympathy.

The ancestors of Pierrot, curiously enough, are among the most vigorous, the most gorgeously adventurous, the most theatrical—and at times the most robustly wicked—figures in the whole pageant of the stage. Only on the theory of a very devil of a father and a beautiful

236

adventuress of a mother begetting, by contrast, a timid and soulful offspring, can the ancestry of the modern Pierrot be explained. For those who begat him were the actors of the *Commedia dell'Arte*, playing the brilliant, vigorous, audacious, and gay buffoon-comedies that delighted the reckless Latin peoples of the Cinquecento and the Seicento.

If you had wandered into Venice on a *festa* day in, say, 1550—the name Venezia even today will give you something of the feel of the holiday atmosphere, the sensuous color, the liveliness of the place— you might have seen some of these actors of the *Commedia dell'Arte* playing on a platform in the Square of St. Mark's. The crowd about

Commedia dell'Arte players on a stage with curtains, as etched by Jacques Callot. [From *La Comédie Italienne*, by Pierre Louis Duchartre.]

would be, as we say, picturesque; the *magnificoes*, nobly dressed, swelling around; the shrewd tradespeople and shopkeepers and country folk like enough in festival costume—or perhaps just the dress of the country was like that; gondoliers; masqueraders; the beggars and cripples that have crawled out of the incredible poverty and dirt of Venice's "back streets"; all these are mixed in the crowds that surge through the square. Everywhere are vendors, fakers, sellers of sweets, crying their wares and their shows: medicine sellers with patter men, no doubt, jugglers, clowns, acrobats, singers, tightrope walkers, dancers. And above it all the pealing bells, and the color of St. Mark's. Here are a dozen theatres, a dozen noisy performances. But one is the favorite, the embodiment of the festival spirit, the very centre of hilarity in all this field of laughter and noise. For the *Commedia dell'Arte* players are up to their old tricks, improvising a farce with all their mingled vigor, art, and vulgarity. And if you watch the audience, you will see just those qualities reflected, rudely or more delicately, in each face. In a booth, at a fair, the players are perfectly at home.

Let us not try to distinguish the comedians too exactly from those conjurers, clowns, and quack "come-on" men close by; they have not, in this mid-sixteenth century, brought their art to a set form; they are still shaping the *Commedia dell'Arte*—partly by watching shrewdly how the holiday throng shrieks at this new gag or merely titters at that old spitting episode. Out of the very tricks of the swindlers and fakers, as out of an intrigue here stolen from Terence and a page of comic dialogue there out of Plautus, they are manufacturing the "Professional Comedy." As yet only the *characters* are set, vigorous sketches of the stock figures that are to win courts and market-places alike to their praise a century later: Pantalone, from this same Venice; the Doctor from Bologna; the boastful, lying, and timorous-at-heart Spanish Captain—once Italian, out of ancient Rome, but then changed to Spanish because the Spaniards were the swaggerers of Europe, the detested, overbearing overlords of Naples; the mercurial Arlecchino and the knavish Brighella; the maid-servants, and the rest.

The *Commedia dell'Arte* is a thing that must be considered as *theatre* or not at all. It simply does not exist, and never did, as drama or as spectacle; it is a platform, actors, action. Its story used to be left out of the histories—until very recently there wasn't even a fairly full account of it in the English language, because it obviously couldn't qualify as dramatic literature. What else about it, the scholars asked, could be permanently important. Well, for one thing, the glorious spirit of it; and for another, the triumph of the actor as sheer creator.

Its name as commonly translated—the Professional Comedy, or the Comedy of Improvisation—affords a clue to this essential theatric quality. It is the professional's theatre, the work of the members of a craft; not only must the player be a professional in today's sense, but he must be so experienced as actor-producer that he can improvise his part with nothing more than an outline of the scenes in mind. There literally was no text of the play for the actors of the Professional Comedy: merely a scenario tacked up back-stage. The player must supply the rest out of his own inventiveness, wit, and bag of tricks.

The actor today is given words to speak. He expends his talent in "interpretation" of the part. He is half reciter and half creative artist. The comedian of Sixteenth Century Italy made up his part as he went along. He stepped into the scene knowing the end and aim of the action, but not what his fellow actors were going to say; he and his fellows improvised that, partly no doubt from traditional snatches of dialogue, from his own speeches grown effective from long trial, from gags and bits of standard buffoonery, covered by stereotyped "business"; but never in two performances exactly alike, and therefore in a continually changing ensemble, where wits clashed, openings must be jumped at, eccentricities and topical ideas capitalized. Facial display counted for nothing; the actor wore a mask. The mask and costume represented a traditional figure to the crowd. The player must get his

Two *Commedia* players. [Etching by Jacques Callot.]

fun within the character, building it out, caricaturing it, making it witty in its repartee and an object of mirth in its runnings-away, fallings-down, its mistakes, its blindness, its perverse misunderstandings, its impertinences.

(Is it any wonder that a sort of production that called for so much invention, theatrical deftness, and spirit seemed to certain revolutionaries of the early twentieth century the very sum and summit of theatrical art? Brooding on the realistic acting of the time, particularly on the growing tendency toward *personal* acting—the player always acting a variation of himself—those insurgent leaders, delightedly digging up forgotten facts about the *Commedia dell'Arte*, held it up as a sort of rediscovered touchstone of the art. Some such development must arise out of the ashes of the literary-realistic theatre—for only thus could the actor be brought out of slavery to the playwright. There is, however —we may opine—no chance that anything like the Professional Comedy will rise out of the present theatre, or from its ashes if they could be accomplished. The *Commedia dell'Arte*, growing through centuries, before it came to flower, was an answer to a call of the times, is most interesting when studied in relation to the abounding, violent life of those times.)

If Pierrot had ancestors among the characters of the *Commedia dell'Arte*, the latter in turn could trace their lineage to Roman, even Greek forebears. Some elements were everywhere local, the characters changed continually under the impact of public approval and disapproval. Creative actors built out shadowy types to well-delineated figures. But it is possible to identify several Roman prototypes, and no

The *Capitano* on an improvised roadside stage. An etching by Karel du Jardin, entitled *The Charlatans*. Note the monkey seated at a curtain-top, and the open box from which remedies were sold.

one has been able wholly to disentangle the elements of Roman vulgar entertainment from survivals of the Greek satyr-drama or Greek-colonial developments.

The Capitano had a clear likeness to the *Miles Gloriosus* of the Roman literary drama. But it is to the popular *Atellanae* that the *Commedia dell'Arte* is easiest traced, or likened: those short native plays on local topics, wherein the characters were stock figures, played with masks. The "mimes" too, entertainments that included farcical scenes and spectacular elements along with song and dance, utilized characters of strongly marked types, the scheming servants, the swaggerers, and other old favorites that are now reappearing.

No one knows to what extent the fugitive strolling player had persisted or disappeared through the dark ages. We do know that if his companies were broken up, there were at least clowns, dancers, conjurers, pantomimists who bridged the great gap. Perhaps the mimes who had gone from Rome to Byzantium, capital of the Eastern Empire, persisted in Turkish theatrical entertainment, and now were coming back to their native Italy. At any rate, when we pick up the story again, during the earliest years of the Renaissance, the companies are acting at crossroads, in piazzas, at the fairs. They are roaming about, setting up their roadside stages wherever a large enough audience can be mustered. The public is their god, their only mentor, their means of living.

The Church, of course, is against them. When the religious drama, fostered in cathedrals and chapels, had become too secular, too concerned with having a good time, and too little zealous to extend the faith, it had been pushed out-of-doors, and soon the blessing and sanction of the Church fathers were withdrawn entirely. By the time the *Commedia dell'Arte* is taking definite shape we may think of the village priest and the district bishop as distinctly hostile. (Later, to be sure, cardinals are openly amused at the performances of *I Gelosi*—though there is more on the opposite side of the ledger, petitions for suppression, forbiddance of Christian burial to actors, downright persecution.)

No more sympathetic are the courts and the academies—at first. The great princes and dukes are still the patrons of the literary drama, giving encouragement and means to the scholars who vainly imitate the classic dramatists. Along with the neo-classic plays the courts are fostering the masque, a pretty, queenly form of drama that is to revolutionize "staging" throughout the Western world. It is the exact opposite to the *Commedia dell'Arte* in its lavishness, in its other-worldliness, in its gentility. The staging of the street comedy is bare: a platform with curtains, hardly more than a booth, perhaps, or again a convenient roadside embankment; its lavishness is all in the acting. It is of this world, earthy; the populace love it and its only thought of gentility is to show up high pretension and gentle villainy for the enjoyment of the crowd. It has just those virtues that the cultured literary theatre of the time lacks: robustness, genuineness, theatrical zest, originality.

Somewhere during the formative years, before the courts had tired of the literary playwrights, before they invited the *Commedia dell'Arte* companies to come off the streets and into the palace theatres, certain conventions took shape. The comedy setting, developing perhaps from the tradition of the Roman comedy that so often was set "before so-and-so's house," became typically the "street scene." If the booth or platform stage was backed with curtains, these (we know in

Two comedy characters, with a typical *Commedia* theatre in the background, as etched by Jacques Callot. [From the reproduction in Mantzius' *A History of Theatrical Art.*]

certain cases) bore a rude painted representation of houses with a space between. Garzoni speaks of "the scenes scrawled with charcoal." Later, when the wing setting came in, on the indoor stages, houses were represented by the front flats, with others indicated further back, in an arrangement that left the actors unhampered in the central space and down front, while affording them the widest use of doorways for hidings and escapes, windows for serenades, etc. But this vignette of an outdoor stage, where all "scenery" is painted or drawn on a curtain behind the acting space, is typical of the street-theatre days. In later years each character had his own point of entrance, and there was an orthodox method of coming to the front of the stage, bowing welcome to the audience, for the "Parade" or inspection of the actors, etc.

But if the setting became "set" in the years of gradual establishment of the Improvised Comedy as an institution, it was the characters who were crystallizing most definitely and most interestingly. Next to the fact of improvisation, the most distinctive feature of the *Commedia dell'Arte* is the limitation to a dozen or so traditional type theatric figures, each played with a mask and a costume different from the others, each with conventional characteristics and limitations. Even the character's carriage, gestures, and grimaces became known; and a further identification was possible in the dialect he spoke—since the Dottore came from Bologna, Pantalone from Venice, and so on.

An actor assuming a part, incidentally, devoted his life to it, and ordinarily played no other character during his career. One well-known actor is said to have played the Lover at seventy. This concentration on one impersonation, of course, had much to do with the player's adeptness at improvisation.

So closely were the actors identified with their parts that often their personal life was all but lost in the theatrical character. Occasionally an actor was strong enough to bring a new character into the restricted popular pantheon; developing a new line of business, or adding variations in an accepted characteristic, he made two figures grow where only one had been accepted before; or, very rarely, created a niche and a name almost wholly out of his own genius—as was the case with Scaramuccia. Exceptionally a player might give his own name to an older part: as "Flavio" was the name of the Lover for a time, from Flaminio Scala. Isabella Andreini played an "Isabella" part throughout her lifetime, after which the character disappeared. But mostly it was a long process of experiment, experience, and adjustment by which a figure came into being, by public impact; and the types are as common, as easy to comprehend, as the Katzenjammer Kids or Blondie.

In what period the main characters became wholly identifiable—became themselves, so to speak—it is difficult to say. There is a very reasonable air to the argument that the two *zanni* were re-creations of the Roman *sanniones*—certainly their positions as servants and their cunning-stupid ways warrant the inference. The lineage of others is less easily traced or guessed. But in the time we are now considering, before the acceptance of the popular comedy into court circles, there were already a number of set types; and certainly those four central characters, the Dottore, or Doctor of Bologna; Pantalone, the wheezy merchant, from Venice—these two being old men; and the two servants, or *zanni* (our Zany), Arlecchino and Brighella, knaves of opposite temper; and the Capitano. These "masks" appear in many variations later, and under varied names.

Pantalone is the deceived father or husband, the easily-duped old man, of Roman popular comedy—by inheritance or by grace of the undying comic potentialities of senility and cupidity. Often enough he is the cuckold, the old husband of a merry young wife, hoodwinked and deceived—and, as such, perhaps the favorite comic character for Italian audiences. In this Renaissance Italy he is also the Venetian merchant, grasping, overreaching; and at the same time credulous and talkative. He is amorous in an ineffective way, outwitted in his love suits by his son, his servant, or any other. He is the typical old-fool. He wears, of course, the long trousers that bear his name to this day.

The Dottore is the boon companion of Pantalone, the second old man. He is the comic man-of-learning, the pedant, hailing from Bologna, the university town. Many of his comic effects arise from his readiness to spout Latin and his cleverness at presenting facts wrongly. He may be any learned type, physician, lawyer, astrologer, professor; but he is as much a butt as Pantalone in his love affairs and his tricks to save a ducat. If he is a father to one of the girl lovers he is easily outwitted.

The servants or *zanni* are commonly known as Arlecchino and Brighella. Through the course of three centuries Harlequin changed much in character. But in the great days of the Improvised Comedy he was the scheming and cunning valet, the shrewd-but-dull servant to one of the foolish old men, ever aiding the young lovers in their designs and ever cheating Pantalone and the Dottore. (For instance, he tells Pantalone that a noble lady is in love with him, and that a rendezvous can be arranged, but that to spare the lady's reputation Pantalone must dress as a woman. He then goes to the Dottore with the same story. He thus brings the two disguised old men together, each believing the other an amorous but coy lady—in a situation which, as any one can see, lends itself to hearty if not too delicate humor.) Arlecchino is at other times definitely the blundering or foolish servant. He seems always to have been acrobatically alive, bounding on and off stage, appearing at unexpected moments, escaping through impossible openings. His checkered suit was assumed at a rather late date, perhaps along with some of his less buffoon-like traits. In the seventeenth century Dominique lifted the character to the estate of a witty and wise commentator, at the Italian theatre in Paris.

Brighella is the second valet. He is more definitely a caricature, often a cruel one: the dishonest servant, unscrupulous and sensual. He descends to the estate of panderer or thief on occasion. Scapino is either another guise for him, or perhaps his cousin. We might say that these servants are all members of the Rascal family; and we then can add another name to the list: Pulchinella. This is the ancestor of the famous

Punch of the puppet shows. Even in those days he was hook-nosed, old, and energetic. His pugnaciousness was a later accretion. He hailed from Naples.

The Capitano was the Renaissance embodiment of the swaggering officer, the soldier who puts up a bold front but is quaking inside. He tells tales of astounding deeds of valor, but dodges if another but sneezes. He blusters, threatens, parades, but runs away if a servant but

Tommasino (Thomassin) of the *Théâtre Italien* in Paris, with the Harlequin mask. [After an etching by T. Bertrand from La Tour's pastel.]

puts a hand on a wooden sword. He wears fierce moustaches and carries a wicked-looking sword, and he may create terror for a moment; but always at the end he is in flight, his cowardice revealed, his pretensions pricked. Or else Harlequin thrashes him. He appeared first as an Italian officer, but the type was early changed to picture the Spanish overlords. Like most of the *Commedia* characters, the Captain appeared in a dozen variations.

The other types, as they are less caricatured, are less interesting in memory. It is necessary only to record that the elegant young lovers were indispensable to the usual plot, that the valets were regularly matched by the tricky maid-servants (Colombina was the most famous, and lived on in another guise), and that *ballerinas* carried on the dancing.

The scenario which was provided by the head of the company—he was probably the "author" too—for the actors' guidance in the larger outlines of the performance, included not a line of dialogue: only directions for the movements, and lists of the "situations." As the body of scenarios grew, certain "irresistible situations" appeared again and again and again. Naturally the intrigue was a staple basis; and there were certain clustered jokes, bits of buffoonery and gags around each incident. One account says that the actors, moreover, filled in with *lazzi* the empty spots in the scenario, *lazzi* in this sense meaning not only the jests but the tricks, turns and bits of business that the player had learned were "sure-fire" with the average audience. Out of his own repertory, so to speak, the actor provided entertainment that carried over from one planned dramatic peak to the next. He had his own line of conceits and tried speeches that were "in character"; the scenarist thus might call for his "lover's outburst" or his "soliloquy with metaphors" or his tirade in Latin.

In the latter decades of the Improvised Comedy in France, the literary element was somewhat intruded, and the skeletons are largely filled out with lines. There are, however, several extant collections of the unadorned scenario. One is the "Theatre for Fifty Days" collection, with fifty works of Flaminio Scala (Flavio), these being part of the repertory of the famous company known as *I Gelosi;* another is the Corsini Library Manuscript in Rome, which is adorned with interesting sketches of stage settings.

The scope of the drama played by the popular comedians—although most commentators describe it all as farce or buffoon-comedy—is put down by the players themselves, in petitions, etc., as very broad; for instance, an actor of *I Gelosi*, about the end of the sixteenth century, spoke of his company as "setting an example for future actors as to how to compose and interpret comedies, tragicomedies, tragedies, pastorals, interludes . . ." The plot outlines were stolen freely from old plays, from novels, from any source whatsoever; or invented on the basis of remembered incidents, fables, or the latest scandal. The knowledge that so-and-so was in the audience might change the whole drift of scene after scene and afford material for allusion and mimicry. An actor's indigestion and grumpiness might be capitalized, if not by himself, then by his fellow actors. In days when the chamber-pot was a common "prop" on the farce stage, illness as a subject must have yielded more comic values than it does in our times.

The latitude allowed on the stage, of course, was simply a reflection of the latitude allowed in life; and the energy of the actors part of the energy of the Italian peoples. We have seen how the prince-patrons lived, how even the cardinals and bishops accepted life fully as it came, falling in with the lax morality of the time; how court poets made a stupendous joke of infidelity, playing up the lascivious priest along with the noble rotter, the easy-going wife along with the unscrupulous

A roadside stage with Pierrot and Scapin. [A painting by Martin Drolling. French, eighteenth century.]

serving-maid—anything so long as the incidents moved swiftly, so long as the interest never lagged. The same humor was used in the street comedy; and the audiences were, at their own level, as zestfully interested as the nobles, in a hundred activities that had been unknown or forbidden to their fathers. "They found the door of a theatre as irresistible as a café," one writer tells us—and unless you have lived in a Latin country you can't imagine how wholly irresistible that is, to entire populaces.

Of the spirit, the materials, and the speed that went into the productions of the *Commedia dell'Arte*, Philippe Monnier has written, in a passage that seems to have caught in its own accents the breathlessness and swing of the stage performance.[1] He is speaking of the players:

They were all as chock-full of malice as of wit. Mimes, acrobats, dancers, musicians, comedians, all at once, they were also poets, and composed their own piece. They strained their fancy to the utmost in inventing it, and improvised it on the spot as their turn came and the inspiration took them. They were not willing, like silly school-boys, to recite only what they had learnt from a master, nor to be mere echoes, unable to speak for themselves without another having spoken before them. They did not draw themselves up in a line before the footlights, five or six in a row, like figures in a bas-relief, and wait their turn to present their tricks. Rather they were full of impatience, imagination, devilry. They were the great artists of Laughter, the sowers of the golden grain of Gaiety, the servants of the Unseen, the kings of Inspiration. They had only to receive a scenario, which someone had scribbled on his knee, to meet their stage manager in the morning to arrange the outlines of the plot, and to hang the paper within easy reach of the wings; the rest they could invent themselves. Familiarity with the stage and their profession and their art had taught them a whole bundle of tricks and quips. They had a store of proverbs, sallies, charades, riddles, recitations, cock-and-bull stories, and songs jumbled together in their heads. They knew all sorts of metaphors, similes, repetitions, antitheses, cacophonies, hyperboles, tropes, and pleasant figures; and besides they had volumes of tirades, which they had learnt by heart, of soliloquies, exclamations of despair, sallies, conceits of happy love, or jealousy, or prayer, or contempt, or friendship, or admiration, always on the tips of their tongues, ready to utter when they were out of breath. They raised their scaffolding high into the air, and then gave themselves up to their own fertile genius and their amazing caprice. They obeyed all the intemperance and extravagance of their humours. They became nothing but retorts, sallies, conceits, paradoxes, witticisms, mental somersaults. They seized opportunity by the forelock and turned the least accident to profit. They drew inspiration from the time, the place, the color of the sky, or the topic of the day, and established a current between their audience and themselves out of which the mad farce arose, the joint product of them all. It varied at each representation, seemed different every evening, with all the spirit and warmth and alertness of spontaneous creation, a brilliant ephemeral creature born of the moment and for the moment.

The pieces went with the speed of lightning and the noise of Pandemonium. The house was consumed with shrieks of laughter, like the

---

[1] Quoted by permission from *The Mask* of January 1911.

tumult of a whirlwind. It was all lover's intrigue, complicated by disguises, kidnappings, unexpected returns, impersonations and supposititious infants. Retorts, misunderstandings, character-sketches, jests, caricatures, blows, and kicks were their stock in trade. They groped about in the dark and ran into one another and fell down. They mutilated words. They put out their tongues, rolled their eyes, made grimaces. They boxed their ears with their feet. They sang songs and recited, and poured forth proverbs, quotations, precedents. There were scenes of tumult and uproar and inexpressible confusion, in which they were knocked down and got up again, supporting themselves as they could, tripped each other up, got in each other's way, and ran off in the midst of the clatter.

They passed the word round, for instance, to make Pantaloon believe that his breath smelt. Pantaloon blows his horn from the window to proclaim the opening of the chase. Gratiano appears holding a cock, Burattino with a monkey on a chain, and a child on the back of a bear is leading a lion. Harlequin, armed with a blacksmith's tools, draws four of Pantaloon's soundest teeth. He waits on Don Juan at table and wipes the plates on the seat of his breeches before he hands them, or produces his cap, full of cherries, from the same place, and cracks the stones with his teeth and pretends to spit them on the ground. He keeps hissing some tune through his lips or pursues a fly in the air and catches it. He counts his coat-buttons, saying, "She loves me, she loves me not, she loves me." There is only one plate of macaroni between three of them, and they eat it in floods of tears. . . Dreams were grafted on mistakes, marvels on absurdities. Pirouettes, repartees, music, dances, jests, acrobatic feats, grimaces and dumb-show, pantomime and drama, peals of laughter and peals of thunder followed in quick succession. They ran, jumped, turned somersaults, and kicked up their heels, and the piece went like lightning . . . crackled, and sparkled, and glowed, and blazed, and then died away and disappeared. Their whole bodies moved at once. Their hands and fingers, their gestures, almost seemed to speak. Their extravagant fancy broke loose before an audience and burst into fire and soared into the sky, a marvel of balance. Explosions of wild laughter followed, and wild confusion, and a medley of caricatures, dreams, buffooneries, scurrility, poetry, and love.

It was inevitable that a form of art so vital, so genuine—even if so vulgar—should ultimately displace the hothouse pageantry and the pedantic neo-classic drama in the affections of the princes and their courtiers. There are passages out of the diaries and correspondence of the fine ladies of the time, in which they rue the boring hours spent at classic and contemporary plays—relishing only the spirited dance interludes and the machine-made wonders of "the new staging," and sighing for more comedy. There are sad plaints from the local playwright-scholars who suddenly find themselves thrust out of the security of the duke's patronage, and displaced on the palace stage by "popular" travelling companies.

By 1575, certainly, the courts had tired of the imitations of the ancient plays and the dramatically thin effusions of their poet masque-writers. From then on, for a century and a half, the Italian companies of professional comedians were the favorites of all courts, the most-sought-after acting groups of all time. Wars might drive them from one locality for a time, Church pressure might bar them from this kingdom or that for a decade, plagues and hard times might thin their ranks, but throughout the next two hundred years their story weaves in and out of court and social history in a half dozen states of Western Europe.

It was the magnificent courts of the Italian princes that first welcomed them indoors, of course. The Dukes of Mantua and of Ferrara were celebrated patrons of the stage, and the magnificence of the productions in their palaces has been a tradition of all later ages. Without knowing when the actors of the *Commedia dell'Arte* were first accepted at these courts, we find that the later records delightedly chronicle their appearances again and again; and it was a Gonzaga, Prince Vincenzo of Mantua, who in 1586 honored the famous Isabella of the *Gelosi* company by acting as godfather at the christening of her child. But even richer are the records of the triumphs of the comedians at the courts of Venice and Florence, at Milan and Verona and Naples.

Travelling courtiers and prelates and scholars saw the performances and reported glowingly to the stay-at-homes of France, Spain, Austria, Bavaria; and an English ambassador even made them the subject of an official report to Queen Elizabeth. The first important performance by Italian comedians in France was at Lyons in 1548, although it is not clear that this was strictly a *Commedia dell'Arte* company. But by 1571 we find a troupe specifically summoned to Paris on the occasion of the marriage of Charles IX, and taking the French capital by storm. All, we are told, were captivated by the gorgeous fun of the plays, the unexampled spirit of the acting, and the charm of the actors—all, that is, except the officials of the Church. They made representations or something, looking to the fining and banishment of the players; but the appreciation and protection of the king served to quiet that storm. For two hundred years after, despite ups and downs, the troupes of Italian comedians were favorites of the French monarchs, were summoned to celebrate "entries," marriages, and victories, were granted exclusive licenses for certain types of production, were honored not only as artists but as individuals. From them the French actors learned; and it was out of the unliterary Italian *Commedia dell'Arte* that the genius of Molière flowered: out of an alien

A temporary theatre built on the arena floor of the Roman amphitheatre at Verona, Italy. A *Commedia* company, with masked actors, is
acting out a familiar scene; but seemingly no member of the audience looks
toward the stage. [A late eighteenth-century painting by Marco Marcola,
by courtesy of the Art Institute of Chicago.]

popular amusement an actor-playwright took elements that he shaped into the body of dramatic literature which is considered in France the supreme expression of comedy in all time.

Meantime the *Commedia dell'Arte* had been carried into Spain, where apparently the boastful Spanish Captain amused more than he offended, for there are reports of the pleasure of the court of Philip II, and of a lasting influence on native playwriting and acting. Even earlier, in 1568, a company had travelled in Austria and had enchanted the court at Vienna—where Tabarino, indeed, became "Comedian to

A version of the Capitano, as depicted by Abraham Bosse.

his Majesty." In Bavaria the Italian comedy was already known; and a Mantuan company even invaded the distant, and perhaps less appreciative, England. The dialogue, of course, was mainly Italian, wherever the comedians played; but this proved no bar to the enjoyment of performances in which action, buffoonery, intrigue and cartoon-characters entered so largely. We may be sure, too, that the farceurs made rich fun out of their own struggles with the alien language of their audience, mixing words and phrases ludicrously—such an opportunity for mispronunciations and comic misunderstandings was not to be missed.

While there seems much of vulgar clatter, speed, and boisterousness in the Improvised Comedy performances, as generally described, there is a finer side to both the productions and the players. Indeed, in the best period of the *Commedia dell'Arte* the actors included in their number some of the most illustrious people the stage has known, true artists with broad human and social interests. There were, no doubt, whole companies hardly above the estate of those vagabond strolling players who in three or four periods of history caused actors to be classed with rogues, thieves, and other public nuisances. These wandering troupes went back and forth over Southern Europe, setting up their scaffolds at each town on the way, luckily striking a Fair week here, or a feast-day there; but in general taking their luck with a public always eager but seldom too generous; hazardously travelling the roads over treacherous mountains or sun-beaten plains, in storm or fair weather, with their terribly slow canvas-covered ox-carts; taking the

Arlecchino, as played by the actor Martinelli in the sixteenth century. [From *La Comédie Italienne*.]

luck of the country, cheap inn or open field or smelly stable. They were not far removed from vagabonds if fortune failed to favor them for a period; and—well, yes, they did harbor in their companies petty thieves and prostitutes.

But beside these are to be placed the recognized troupes, under dignified leadership, made up of players to whom the queens and princes delighted to do honor. It is recorded that a king after a performance that pleased him called for Scaramuccia and presented his own coach and six to the actor. Kings, dukes, and cardinals gave banquets for the visiting players. There is a record that Tasso wrote most gallantly of the actress Vittoria, at whose side he sat at a banquet given in her honor by Cardinal Aldobrandini, "to which were also invited six other cardinals"—but the records fail to state whether they all came. A few of the actors were made nobles; others held court positions—one was even keeper of the privy purse, on what theory one is puzzled to decide. Tournaments were arranged in their honor, the city bells pealed when they arrived, they doubtless had a weighty collection of those symbols of royal welcome, "the keys to the city." Even these better companies, however, were not free from the hazards of the road. *I Gelosi* were captured by the Huguenots in 1577, and were ransomed by the king barely in time to give their scheduled performance before the court in the State-Hall at Blois.

The company known as *I Gelosi* was the most famous, and probably the most accomplished, through a period following 1570, and it became the favorite at a dozen courts; kings and dukes disputed over its dates and itineraries. But there were other troupes hardly less esteemed. Every member of the *Gelosi* group is said to have been an accomplished artist, such as would have stood out as "star" in many lesser companies. Its leader was Francesco Andreini, who had a rich heritage out of living, culture, and the arts, on which to base his acting. Having started out as a soldier he fell into slavery to the Turks, from which it took him eight years to escape. He was a singer, played many musical instruments, knew five languages, and wrote freely in verse and prose. As an actor he was not content with the usual single type part; he tried his hand at creating new figures, played a dozen variations of the Spanish Captain, and was cast also as the Lover.

But if this Andreini was esteemed, it was his wife, Isabella, who was most sung by the bards, the critics, and the gallants of the times. It is recorded that she wrote well in three languages, played sweetly on musical instruments, and knew much of philosophy—and all that besides being "beautiful in name, beautiful in body, and most beautiful in spirit . . . queen of beautiful and virtuous women." Tommaso Garzoni wrote of her as "an adornment of the scene, an ornament of the theatre, a superb spectacle of virtue no less than of beauty. . . While the world lasts, while the centuries endure, while times and seasons continue, every voice, every tongue, every cry will repeat the celebrated name of Isabella."

It was in 1604 that the company was travelling from Paris toward Italy, when at Lyons Isabella, newly honored by Queen Marie, fell ill and died. And in her death is one of those strange contrasts that dot the history of the stage. This woman "of supreme modesty and perfect innocency of morals," was refused burial in consecrated ground by law of the Church. But the parish priest had the grace to record: "She is deceased with the universal reputation of being one of the most rare women in the world for learning as well as for speaking in many

languages." And the officials of Lyons somewhat made up for the
Church's churlishness by according her all honors, including torch
bearers, mace bearers, and banners accompanying her body to the
grave. And from that day her husband, the celebrated Andreini, never
acted again.

The story of the *Commedia dell'Arte* is rich in figures hardly less
beautiful, less noble, and certainly no less outstanding. There was that
Vittoria, the "Divina Vittoria," who was celebrated as "having proportioned gestures, harmonious and becoming movements, majestic

The later softened types of *Commedia* characters, in France. Above,
Pierrot, Mezzetin, the Captain, and Harlequin; below, Pantalon, Polichi-
nelle, Scapin, and Narcissin. [After engravings in a work by Riccoboni,
reproduced in *l'Ancienne France: Le Théâtre et la Musique*.]

and graceful action, words sweet and affable, sighs delicate and subtle, laughter agreeable and charming, comportment lofty and noble, and showing in her whole person a perfect decorum such as belongs to, and is becoming to, a perfect actress. . . Beautiful magician of love who wins the hearts of a thousand lovers with her words." There was, too, that Florinda who at the court of Mantua, when death by small-pox had snatched a famous singer and left doubtful a command performance, stepped into the rôle and played it so movingly—"drawing from a thousand hearts a thousand sighs"—that from that day she was a favorite and honored player.

Among the men, too, was Giulio Pasquati, whom Henry of Poland termed, in a summons, the "Magnifique," known later by his stage name of Graziano, and called the "Magnifico Pantalone." There was Flaminio Scala, actor, director, and author of fifty still-extant scenarios. And that Lelio, son of the famous Andreini and Isabella, who is reputed to have written literally hundreds of works in drama, verse, "visions," dialogues, etc., etc. These and scores of other vivid figures are lost except in the dusty tomes and manuscripts in Italian libraries; and least of all are they known to English readers.

Half a dozen figures of the period have become legendary, more or less by the caprice of fate. Scaramuccia of the seventeenth century has outlasted all his companions. He who is historically identified with the name, Tiberio Fiorillo, did not even invent the Scaramouche name —another had used it not wholly obscurely before. Nor did he create the character: it was no more than a variation of the Spanish Captain. But his playing was so vivid, his all-black costume so much a trademark, and his influence (particularly on French acting and Molière) so great, that he entered into the gallery of immortals. The character, as distinct from the actor, was, of course, carried on into later Improvised Comedy and French pantomime. It is recorded that without really moving and without saying a word Scaramuccia could keep an audience in roars of laughter for fifteen minutes, by "his varied manifestations of terror of the unseen Pasquariel behind his chair."

The virtuous and the vicious among the Italian comedians, both picturesque in their heyday, and spirited, went separate ways to separate sad fates toward the end of the eighteenth century. A few of the better companies, under a "reform" impulse, absorbed literary elements into their productions and compromised with refined taste. They compromised, too, with the Church and the censors, as evidenced in an address of the actors to the French Court, when Riccoboni's company became the licensed Italian troupe in Paris. After petitions that all other Italian companies and all playing of the stock comedy characters be prohibited, and that no member of the Costantini company be added to the troupe—"through whom all know that the Italian actors who preceded them fell into disgrace at the Court"—they end: "The actors entreat your Highness to make urgent representations at the Court that they may be permitted, as in Italy, the free use of the Holy Sacrament; the more so as they will never recite anything scandalous; and Riccoboni undertakes to submit the scenarios of the plays for examination by the Minister and also by an Ecclesiastic, for their approval." That was pretty near the end of the *Commedia dell-Arte* in France. Out of it grew new glories—but not of the same burgeoning sort.

Pierrot, the French version of the Italian *Commedia* character Pedrolino. [A drawing by Maurice Sand, from his *Masques et Bouffons, 1859.*]

Its end in Italy was more miserable and more deplorable. In the eighteenth century fresh invention ceased, the spirit waned, the Professional Comedy sank back toward those crude, violent, and often licentious types out of which it had flowered. Licentiousness particularly brought about the final eclipse. English travellers naturally enough, when they returned home, reported on the incredible license and disgusting dissoluteness of the shows they had seen in Italy; although this was in the time of the smutty English Restoration playwrights, when London's own stage was the scene for plays that were barred for centuries after. But the tired comedians were salting their now-stale intrigue-plots and stereotyped buffooneries with the very limit of sensational incident and suggestive gesture. Even women in childbirth and mock circumcisions were material for farcical treatment, and the chamber-pot a favorite "prop." Thus went out in a twilight of scurrility, crudeness, suggestiveness, of official suppression and popular apathy, a thing that in its day had been unique, robustly expressive, gloriously alive.

The actor when he had respected his liberty—when he had utilized his freedom from the restraint of the playwright to create richly, from the materials of his times and of the theatre, vulgarly, perhaps, but not licentiously—had made himself master of the theatre to a degree unknown in the annals of playing before or after. He had created one of the most vivid chapters in stage history. But his less talented, less conscientious, and tired followers closed it with a melancholy descent and with something very close to a bad smell.

CHAPTER
11

The Chivalrous Theatre
of Spain

T HE Spanish Captain strutting across the stages of the Italian *Commedia dell'Arte*, boasting, parading, recounting his conquests among fighters and among fair ladies, but starting and trembling if another so much as speaks sharply, and running away precipitately if a sword is drawn or a gun fired—this *Capitano* may well serve to carry us over from Italy to the theatre of Spain. For despite the obvious caricature elements, and allowing for Italian bitterness toward the conquering Spaniard, and the Latin tendency to spit at the stronger man the moment his back is turned, one still may find in the prototype of this stage figure much that is characteristic of the drama and stage of Spain. Indeed, none but a vainglorious figure, a lover and a fighter, a braggart and a bully, could symbolize the sixteenth and seventeenth century Spanish stage. The drama of the period is amazingly varied, but in its most characteristic manifestations it is heroic, extravagant, a bit absurdly romantic, full of physical action; but one suspects that a mere rattling of the critical sword might prove its heroism, its wisdom, and its emotion almost as hollow as the Captain's valor.

The Capitano may have been one of the cruellest caricatures in the whole history of stage portraiture. His lies about his prowess, his oaths, his insolent parading, his fingering of his moustaches, his pride, were gorgeous; but they were contrived so only to get the more fun by contrast, when he took to trembling because the leaves rustled, or paled and ran immediately someone hissed or struck a menacing attitude. But there can be no doubt that under the caricature was the real Spaniard, who entered into Don Quixote and Don Juan. That Spaniard in his nobler embodiment appears thousands of times as the protagonist of Spanish drama. His code of honor, his love-making and his fighting are the very breath of it. Chivalry not only supplied the material for the dramatists but determined the forms of the plays. Valor in battle, a punctilious personal honor, unquestioning obedience to King and Church, romantic love—these were the ideals of the people, which must be reflected back to them out of any drama that was to flourish.

When their national theatre emerged, the Spaniards were racially conscious more than any other people of Europe. They had fought the centuries-long fight against the Moor and had saved Europe to Christianity. They were the great imperialists of the time, with the entire overseas world of America as vassal. They were the chosen of God, the upholders of Catholicism. The flame of patriotism burned fiercely. The theatre must do its bit to keep this flame bright and clear.

There are those who feel that Spain has declined steadily since those brilliant days, and one may hear talk of the debased Spaniard of today. Certainly within the first hundred years of the Spanish theatre, the nation receded from its position as political and military leader in Europe to the rank of a secondary power; the chivalry and glory in the plays was the reflection of a venerated past rather than a mirror of the sixteenth and seventeenth century present. But it may be that in the abounding national success of fifteenth century Spain there were determining elements far less admirable than those to be found in the less vaunting Spain of today; and that in these elements we may find at once the causes of the decline of political power and the reasons for the secondary place now taken by the drama of Spain, despite its one-time brilliant staging and its amazing extent (Lope de Vega alone composed 1800 dramatic works).

In the first place, although the Renaissance had its effect everywhere in Western Europe, it failed to turn the Spaniards from Mediævalism wholly back to the study of the classics as in Italy and France. The Spain of the time of the Inquisition was too fiercely Catholic to welcome that new freedom of thought which was mankind's most precious gain out of the Renaissance. The country preferred mysticism and a conception of life on earth as an interlude between birth and an all-important after-life. There was no questioning of the Faith as in Italy, no new intellectual curiosity, certainly no breaking away toward pagan freedoms in human enjoyments. Curiously enough the national art had gained much of color and richness from the Moors whom the Spaniards had finally expelled, and a certain richness of life might be put on like a cloak by the individual; but the national ideal was rigid with the unbending allegiance demanded by the Church, and with the system of caste that began with the protection of the divine right of kings. These things being the mainsprings of human action, an organized religion and an artificial code of honor ruling all men's actions, drama and literature failed to take on that warm glow of humanism so notable elsewhere. The stage was set to unending duels, intrigues, imbroglios, assignations, revenges, patriotic flatteries, heroics, relieved by farcical under-plots and comic interludes. There was little place here for the thoughtful laughter of Molière, little for the so-human sentiment of Shakespeare; too much of parade and clash for the serener elements of drama to enter.

The Spanish dramatists escaped, indeed, the too-close imitation of classic models which nullified the efforts of the Italian Renaissance playwrights; but they failed to gain the compactness, the theatric directness that a study of Greek plays might have given them. A mediæval looseness characterizes the bulk of Spanish plays, and they exhibit not a little of the monotonous repetition and episodic method of the religious plays designed for credulous and unthinking mob-audiences. Their virtues lie in a vigor of action, a romantic colorful-ness and a rhetorical display seldom matched elsewhere; and not at all in compact, jewel-like workmanship or delicacy of emotion. Their vigor and freedom dramatically link them with the Elizabethan; but they go not so deep humanly, are less imaginative.

Just as the Spanish Captain represented first the swaggering overlord, flaunting the pride of the Vice-regal power through the streets of Naples, but at the same time derived out of the *Miles Gloriosus* of Roman comedy, just so the Spanish drama, though more *national* than any other in Europe, inherited elements out of both the im-mediately preceding Miracle theatres common to all Western Europe, and out of the obscure survivals of Roman dramatic forms. When the Spanish theatre begins to emerge as an institution, shortly after 1500, the incipient drama is close to balladry, and the travelling minstrels or troubadours are already popular. The other and perhaps the stronger root of the new plant is in the Church and religious sketches. Miracles, Mysteries, and Moralities are here played, inside and outside the Church buildings, quite as freely as in France, Germany, and England, but with closer ecclesiastic supervision. Nor will the Church lose its authority over drama for a long time after.

He who is known as "the father of Spanish drama" is Juan del Enzina, who was born in 1468 or 1469; but his sketches for the stage were hardly more than dialogue bits, of pastoral or religious sort. We may pass him over as not intrinsically important and as not deter-mining the course of the Spanish theatre; as also Bartolomé de Torres

Naharro, a Spaniard who wrote in Italy a number of comedies tinged with such grossness and disrespect that the Church Fathers forbade their representation.

It is rather with Lope de Rueda, who flourished in the mid-years of that century that any brief study of the Spanish drama should begin.

The Spanish Captain, as depicted by Abraham Bosse.

He was perhaps only one of a score of similar actor-directors of strolling acting-companies, but he is representative, and of him we have authentic records. It was the great Cervantes who wrote:

> In the time of this celebrated Spaniard all the properties of a theatrical manager were contained in a sack, and consisted of four white pelices trimmed with gilded leather, and four beards and wigs, with four staffs, more or less. The plays were colloquies or eclogues between two or three shepherds and a shepherdess. They were set off

by two or three *entremeses*, either that of the *Negress*, the *Ruffian*, the *Fool*, or the *Biscayan*, for these four characters and many others the said Lope acted with the greatest skill and propriety that one can imagine. At that time there were no *tramoyas* [stage machinery] nor challenges of Moors or Christians either afoot or on horse. There were no figures which arose or seemed to arise from the centre of the earth through the hollow of the stage, which at that time consisted of four benches arranged in a square, with four or five boards upon them, raised about four spans from the ground, nor did clouds with angels or souls descend from the skies. The furnishings of the stage were an old woolen blanket drawn by two cords from one side to the other, which formed what is called a dressing-room, behind which were the musicians, singing some old ballad without the accompaniment of a guitar.

Cervantes then goes on to describe the betterment achieved by Pedro Navarro:

He improved somewhat the setting of the *comedia*, and instead of a bag for the costumes used chests and trunks. He brought the musicians from behind the curtain, where they formerly sang, out upon the stage, removed the beards of the players, for up to that time no actor appeared upon the stage without a false beard . . . except those who represented old men or other characters which required a facial disguise. He invented stage machinery, thunder and lightning, challenges and battles, but these never reached the excellence which we see now. . .[1]

From this description we may easily picture a roadside or marketplace theatre very similar to that which we have already met in connection with the less pretentious Italian *Commedia dell'Arte* companies, and which we shall meet again when we glance at the beginnings of the French theatre. Here the platform is a bit barer, the company of actors smaller, the drama very primitive indeed. The texts of some of Lope de Rueda's pieces—he was playwright as well as director and chief actor—have survived. One is called *The Olives*. A peasant and his wife discuss an olive tree he has planted this very day. The wife's imagination soars till she sees whole groves of fine trees multiplied out of this one plant, and she opines that some day their daughter will be able to sell great quantities of olives at a fancy price, say two *reals* a peck. This strikes the peasant as too high a price to ask. The mother turns to the daughter and orders her to charge two *reals*.

---

[1] Quoted from *The Spanish Stage in the Time of Lope de Vega*, by Hugo Albert Rennert (New York, 1909).

The father counterorders. Each begins to threaten the daughter if she follows the command of the other; then they begin actually to beat her if she will or won't charge two *reals*. Her cries bring a neighbor who inquires what the trouble's about, and the parents have to admit that it is all over olives that are not planted yet.

Such a simple fable is quite in keeping with the simplicity of the plank stage and the lack of settings and special costumes; for there was absolutely nothing by way of "scenery" and apparently no change of costume from play to play. Always plenty of ballad-singing was thrown in. It is hardly necessary to dwell on the likeness of such a "play" to the ballads, in its directness, homeliness, and simple characterization. It demanded scarcely more than did a ballad in the way of stage equipment.

The company was made up of Lope de Rueda, originally a mechanic of Seville, his book-seller friend Timoneda, who likewise wrote plays and acted, and two others who are said also to have been "authors." Their plays were not always so close to the Spanish soil as *The Olives*. There are classical traces in some, others are definitely Italian, and at least one seems to have been lifted from Plautus. But this is really the first essentially and healthily Spanish popular theatre about which there is historically sound information.

At this time the court was toying with adaptations of the Italian pastoral play-form and with other importations: all artificial and negligible. By the beginning of the fourth quarter of the sixteenth century, tragedies in classic form on native historical themes were being attempted. In 1574, too, an Italian *Commedia dell'Arte* company, one of the best, under Alberto Ganassa, came to Spain and performed its comedies at the court, and later in a "corral" or yard theatre, for larger audiences, to great applause we are told, and not without affecting the course of native theatrical endeavor. Lope de Vega, then a boy, remembered these spirited scenes—and characters—well, when he became Spain's greatest playwright. For while the classic revival brought in a literary play-form too rigid for the Spanish genius, and a humanism too free for the anti-libertarian ruling Churchmen, the Italian popular comedy brought elements easily grafted on to such meagre but popular sketches as those of Lope de Rueda.

The next great figure, however, is more literary than theatrical, in his approach and in his achievement. Cervantes, immortal for his creation of *Don Quixote*, and indubitably Spain's greatest writer, failed to write brilliantly for the stage or to turn the course of its development, although he was author of a considerable number of plays. Though he described appreciatively, as we have seen, Lope de Rueda's honest theatre, Cervantes failed to recognize that the qualities of directness, simplicity, and theatricality which he praised in his predecessor were exactly those which he should have built upon in his own work. Cervantes' early dramas, judged in the light of Lope de Rueda's crude but playable pieces, were weak, slow, and untheatric. One can only feel that he remained always the typical literary man, drawn by the glow of the theatre, but seeing it only as a method of making literature more pervasive and palatable, never as an art in its own right, less of words than of action. Moreover, he was under the orthodox Senecan influence.

For a long period he gave up writing for the stage, and in that time Lope de Vega determined the course Spanish drama was to take. But Cervantes, coming back to the attempt late in life, with the new play-forms before him, still wrote comparatively lifeless dramas, declamatory and diffused. His novels later served many playwrights as a rich ground for picking and stealing. But his own dramatic compositions not only are not to be mentioned with his great romance, but are inferior to the plays of his obviously less talented followers.

Perhaps Cervantes had too much knowledge of what the literary theatre was becoming in Italy and other countries, and failed to square this with the stage he saw in Spain. Although Madrid in his time was to see its first permanent theatres built, the stage of his earlier years would be a sad-looking place for dreaming romantic and decorative plays, for elegant and literary performances. The popular theatre was a few bare boards without decoration, with groundling audiences and daylight performances of rude episodes. The "corral" theatres were less crude, but the stages simple. Perhaps Cervantes had tasted in Italy the fare of the new ballroom theatres that were being decked out with pageantry and rich costuming and machine-made trick effects. At any rate, he failed to connect effectively with the existing stage of his own country.

There was another, however, who lived in Cervantes' time, destined to pick up the inheritance from Lope de Rueda and his fellow strollers, and to shape the Spanish theatre to his own genius. Lope de Vega not only paid no false homage to revived classic-literary forms; he almost leaned backward in his eagerness not to bow before them. He once wrote: "When I set out to write a play I lock up all the rules under ten keys, and banish Plautus and Terence from my study, lest they should cry out against me, as truth is accustomed to do even from dumb books. For I write in the style of those who seek the applause of the public, whom it is but just to humor in their folly, since it is they who pay for it."

Thus Lope de Vega aligned himself with those in every age who, usually dangerously, start writing with the primary aim of "pleasing the public." His success went far beyond that of most adherents to the doctrine: he not only established an immediate contact with the popular stage, and wrote for it steadily through a lifetime, but lifted that stage to finer heights and richer accomplishments. But still—and certainly his purveying to a mass-public that demanded sensation, and asked constantly for racial flattery, had something to do with it—he failed to write any drama that has lived through the years with the best out of the Greek, English, French, and German theatres. Incidentally he fractured many of the laws of probability, geography,

Lope de Vega, Spain's greatest dramatist, and probably the most prolific writer of plays in theatre history. About five hundred have survived of eighteen hundred plays he composed. [From an engraving, eighteenth century.]

mythology, and history—and occasionally of morality. He theoretically and openly adhered to the classic unities; but out of his first four hundred and eighty-six plays he observed them in only six.

Lope de Vega, however, *was* the theatre of an age and a country as no other dramatist ever has been. Not that he had no talented and fertile contemporaries: the Spain of the seventeenth century abounded with theatrical life. But in his versatility he practised every form of playwriting, and originated most of those practised by his contemporaries. He took the stage as he found it, handicapped by no literary theories; but he shaped, then dominated, Spanish drama because he instinctively brought literary form and enrichment to it. He began by doing things hardly different from Lope de Rueda's dialogues, with dramatized ballads and interludes, eclogues and religious sketches.

But he went on to pastorals and allegories and chronicle plays, to comedy, farce, cloak-and-sword mystery plays, and heroic tragedy. He is the very mirror of the Spanish stage, and it would have a considerable dramatic literature if no other playwright had ever graced it —for he wrote 1500 works classed as plays, besides more than three hundred works put down as dramatic sketches, religious processionals, etc.

He could not have been so perfectly the protagonist of the Spanish theatre if he had not been also thoroughly the Spanish gentleman, adventurer, and court hanger-on. He tasted early the sweets and the bitterness of love and of fighting; suffered exile; sailed with the Armada; lived scandalously; became intensely Catholic, was honored by the Pope and made titular official of the Church; took his place as a noble, and lived full of rather stormy honors, and as arbiter of the contemporary theatre. If he began by making the form of his dramas pleasing to the popular taste, certainly he had every opportunity to weave into their substance those sentiments and those passions dearest to an idolizing and proud-hearted people. From this we may be sure (without reading all the surviving 450 works) that his plays are filled with action and surprise, with inventive plot and swift movement, with flattery and romantic description, with playings-up to royalty and religion, with farcical interlude and relief characters, with fascinating heroes and seductive heroines. They are, too, deft, clever, fast flowing, with the most skilful mechanical articulation yet known to the world stage.

Their faults lie, of course, in the lack of those serener and deeper qualities that too seldom go with such vigor of action and dramatic facility. The last acts are often feeble. There is little depth in the characterizations, too little of sustained poetic effect without rhetoric, seldom the inevitable moment, the soul-stirring scene at the end of a carefully designed emotional ascent.

We may here again go back to the life of the times for a reason. Violence was as commonplace as in Renaissance Italy. In Spain murder might be committed in the name of Church or King rather than for the material gain of a prince or gentleman, but human life was rated almost as cheaply. And callousness to the value of human life is almost always an accompaniment of art that is showy but fails to go deep. Violence begets a drama rich in conflict and clamor but poor in serenity and spiritual overtones. It may be added that the serious Spanish theatre was kept fairly free of those obscenities that were just then abounding on the Italian stage, even in the court theatres. A natural delicacy seems to have determined a true propriety in both dramatist and actor. There are matters connected with the physical passion of love, and with the sewage problems of the individual, which the Italian parades on occasion with coarse enjoyment, and along which the Frenchman skims with a cynical fascination; but there were no chamber-pots or bridal beds on the "higher" Spanish stages of the time. The street theatres might tell another story, what with the vaudeville sketches and the dancers—and Lope de Vega sometimes wrote for them too.

Among the contemporaries of Lope there were many dramatists both prolific and able, but none who is not overshadowed by his achievement. Ruiz de Alarcon (really a Mexican), Guillen de Castro, who wrote the plays upon which Corneille was to base his epochal *Cid*, Perez de Montalvan, and Tirso de Molina, who is generally credited with creation of the now universal Don Juan character: these are the chief figures among many practitioners. They might warrant closer study had they not lived just at the time of Lope de Vega and just before Calderon. The titles of some of their plays indicate how closely they were following the models set up by their great contemporary: *The Deceiver of Seville, Don Gil in the Green Breeches, The Youthful Adventures of the Cid, Mismatches in Valencia, The Lovers of Teruel, Mercy and Justice, A Bashful Man at Court,* and *Double Vengeance.*

The special conventions of the Spanish theatre at this time include an almost absolute disregard of change of physical setting. Lope de Vega even inveighed against the invading "scenery." The dialogue might carry an indication of change of scene; or the spectator might become aware where the action was taking place simply from the characters present. In the popular or public theatre scenery was practically unknown. The language of the plays lent an enrichment, there being an unusual prettiness for the ear in spoken Spanish; though the lyric loveliness often ran into rhetorical extravagance. The loosely constructed plays might alternate highly flowery passages with the prosiest of commonplace scenes; the play was, indeed, one situation after another, of one sort and another, rather than the carefully articulated, carefully unified and sustained thing that the Greeks had once made it, and that the Elizabethans and the French were to make it again. (With Lope de Vega's mature works, we are well into Queen Elizabeth's time.) Even the verse in a single play might be in a variety of metres, at the same time admitting prose.

The acting on the Spanish stage was well suited to carry on the swift-moving plots, to register the florid speeches, and to cover over successfully the shallow characterizations. For no such vivid acting was known in all the rest of Europe, nothing so spirited, so all-compelling. Even the Italians praised it as vivid and stirring beyond comparison.

The favorite and perhaps the most representative type of play was the "cloak-and-sword" drama, so named from the class of characters chosen for the main plot. No matter how serious or tragic this plot might be, there would be a comic underplot, played by "relief" characters. The most distinctively Spanish figure in theatre history, indeed, is the comic-relief *gracioso*, servant, clown, and chorus, adding fun to the action, sharpening his master's sayings and doings by contrast, keeping up a running fire of comment, not seldom philosophical, being to the leading characters and to the play what Sancho Panza is to Don Quixote. Perhaps the favorite "device"—by which the dramatic knot is untied—is the king-in-disguise.

Performance of an *auto sacramental.* [Drawing by Warren D. Cheney after a painting by J. Comba.]

If Lope de Vega and his fellows could train their muse to the demands of the crowd, in secular drama, they no less easily turned to pleasing the Church on occasion. About four hundred of Lope's dramatic compositions are *autos sacramentales*, a sort of masque combining prologue, farce and religious allegory, designed for acting on the pageant-cars during the Corpus-Christi processionals, and dealing presumably with the Eucharist. In his time the "religious plays" had become very elastic, very mixed, with plenty of features introduced to please the mob; but there is no doubt that the Church sanctioned them, and could have suppressed them.

The *auto* proper was preceded by a decorative procession, probably with monsters, giants, etc., followed by choirs, dancing choruses, priests bearing the Host under a canopy, the king and his courtiers, and finally cars full of actors. At an open-air stage the procession stopped, the crowd knelt, the religious devotions were gotten out of the way, and the acting began. First would be an acted prologue: perhaps a peasant is represented as having come to town for the shows, has lost his wife in this very crowd, decides it is no use to hunt her further and is about to console himself with another when she turns up; then she begins telling him all about the wondrous procession she has seen—which is, of course, the very one the audience has just witnessed. Next comes a farcical sketch: one of Lope de Vega's tells a story not unlike that of *Pierre Pathelin*, of a peasant who outwits a shrewd lawyer, and escapes in the disguise of a blind ballad-singer—giving the audience, of course, a sample of his art.

The *auto* itself is a nominally religious sketch. To take an example from Lope de Vega's works again, we may visualize the actors as presenting *The Bridge of the World*. The Prince of Darkness places Leviathan ("Hell-mouth" is none other than the Biblical Leviathan—or at least his jaws) across the bridge of the world. None can pass without admitting the supremacy of the Prince. Adam and Eve, "dressed very gallantly after the French fashion," agree and pass on. Others of the familiar Bible characters—Moses, David, Solomon—weakly submit. But then comes the Knight of the Cross, who routs the Dark Prince and opens the passage of the world to the Soul of Man. A dance or songs follow.

Lope de Vega also wrote innumerable other religious sketches and plays, including a group of Miracles based on the lives of the Saints and some more strictly Biblical dramas—these latter having occupied his attention during the two years of the ban laid by the dying Philip II in 1598 on all but religious theatrical activity. But whatever the materials and the forms of the drama it remained always close to the people, always popular, and somehow always Spanish. Even during the years of the prohibition, it was a case of making the religious plays popularly appealing, rather than a case of actual suppression of the glamorous and profane elements in drama. The terrible perversion of the Inquisition is nowhere more apparent than in the evasions it permitted in theatre and in literature.

There is only one Spanish name that transcends Lope de Vega's in any department of dramatic mastery. Calderon—more properly Pedro Calderon de la Barca—is usually cited as the greater poet. Less spontaneous and less inventive, and certainly less fecund (he wrote only a hundred plays), Calderon is more imaginative and the richer writer. Spanish to the core—he too is soldier, nobleman, and ardent and narrow Churchman—he exhibits all the brilliant and romantic character-

A conjectural restoration of a corral theatre in Madrid in 1660. There is here a notable likeness to the Elizabethan inn-yard playhouses, in the balconies and windows utilized for the spectators of quality, the mob audience on the ground, and the half-projecting, half-curtained stage. Note also the awning over the audience. Below is the notorious gallery for women, sometimes known as "the stews," which was for long a feature of the Spanish popular theatre. [From *Ten Spanish Farces*, edited by George Tyler Northup.]

istics to be found in the theatre of his predecessors; but in his tragedies he cuts a little deeper into life and decorates the dramatic skeleton more richly. To know Spanish poetic tragedy or near-tragedy in its highest flights, we must read *The Constant Prince* (*Don Ferdinand of Portugal*), *Life Is a Dream*, *The Mayor of Zalamea*, *Love Survives Life*, or *The Physician of His Own Honor*.

The story of this last illustrates that "point of honor," the over-punctiliousness that excuses even murder, which is so favorite a theme in Spanish drama and romance. Don Gutierre de Solis has married a noblewoman, who is true to him in thought and deed. The King's brother, who had admired her before her marriage, finds his passion rearoused through a chance meeting; and it so happens that the husband's suspicions are stirred, and the wife's efforts to cut off any further misunderstanding only lead to Don Gutierre's certainty of her infidelity. He gives her two hours to live; during which she lays herself out for a holy death, with candles and crucifix over her. Don Gutierre brings, blindfolded, a surgeon who bleeds away the wife's lifeblood. But this surgeon, in order to know the house again, imprints his bloody hand upon the door, and straightway reports to the King, who comes to the house. Don Gutierre, from desire to protect his own honor, explains his wife's death as accidental; the King requires him to marry one Leonore, to whom he is already somewhat bound, and who is present. The only delay is over Don Gutierre's desire to leave no doubt that he would defend his honor if a case like that not yet explained to the King, but understood, should arise. The ending is thus translated by Ticknor:

KING

There is a remedy for every wrong.

DON GUTIERRE

A remedy for such a wrong as this?

KING

Yes, Gutierre.

DON GUTIERRE

My lord! What is it?

KING

'Tis of your own invention, sir!

DON GUTIERRE

But what?

KING

'Tis blood.

DON GUTIERRE

What mean your royal words, my lord?

KING

No more but this; cleanse straight your doors.
A bloody hand is on them.

DON GUTIERRE

My lord, when men
In any business and its duties deal,
They place their arms escutcheoned on their doors.
I deal, my lord, in *honor*, and so place
A bloody hand upon my door to mark
My honor is my blood made good.

KING

Then give thy hand to Leonore.
I know her virtue hath long deserved it.

DON GUTIERRE

I give it, sire. But mark me, Leonore,
It comes all bathed in blood.

LEONORE

I heed it not;
And neither fear nor wonder at the sight.

DON GUTIERRE

And mark me, too, that, if already once
Unto mine honor I have proved a leech,
I do not mean to lose my skill.

LEONORE

Nay, rather,
If *my* life prove tainted, use that same skill
To heal it.

DON GUTIERRE

I give my hand; but give it
On these terms alone.

Perhaps nothing could better illustrate the fault that lies under the
great mass of serious Spanish drama: a falsity that seems often to
vitiate the atmosphere of great deeds and heroic sacrifices. The human
element suffers eclipse in the upholding of a code.

Another fragment may serve to illuminate the point, a bit with the best and the worst of Spanish drama in it—the famous soliloquy of Isabel in the last act of *The Mayor of Zalamea*. Edward Fitzgerald despaired of catching the fulness of the original in English verse, and transposed it into prose thus:

ISABEL

Oh, never, never might the light of day arise and show me to myself in my shame! Oh, fleeting morning star, mightest thou never yield to the dawn that even now presses on thy azure skirts! And thou, great Orb of all, do thou stay down in the cold ocean foam; let night for once advance her trembling empire into thine! For once assert by voluntary power to hear and pity human misery and prayer, nor hasten up to proclaim the vilest deed that Heaven, in revenge on man, has written on his guilty annals! Alas! even as I speak, thou liftest thy bright, inexorable face above the hills! Oh, horror! What shall I do? whither turn my tottering feet? Back to my own home? and to my aged father, whose only joy it was to see his own spotless honor spotlessly reflected in mine, which now— And yet if I return not, I leave calumny to make my innocence accomplice in my own shame! Oh that I had stayed to be slain by Juan over my slaughtered honor! But I dared not meet his eyes even to die by his hand. Alas!— Hark! What is that noise?

CRESPO (*within*)

Oh, in pity slay me at once!

ISABEL

One calling for death like myself?

CRESPO

Whoever thou art—

ISABEL

That voice!

(*Exit*)

In ranking Calderon higher than Lope de Vega as a poet, we should remember that his superiority is notable chiefly in a literary way. Lope is by so much the superior craftsman of the stage, so clearly the creative inventor of theatric forms, that there can be no question which is the greater figure in stage history, which the outstanding representative of the Spanish theatre in the eyes of the world.

The contemporaries of Calderon included that Agustin Moreto who wrote (partially by plagiarizing Lope de Vega) *Disdain against Disdain*, a drama often translated, and as near to the type of *human* play then being composed in England as any ever devised in Spain.

Many others continued the popular-romantic play tradition: a few wrote in styles introduced from other countries, quite hollowly; and opera was imported—even Calderon wrote certain pieces with music in mind. Italian scenery and Italian ballroom theatres came in. But only the very popular forms of drama and those in their cheaper aspects, persisted seriously after Calderon. For the political decline of the nation was rapid, and the old brilliancy faded out of life and letters. The stage of the people was too vigorous to disappear—there were forty theatres in Madrid by 1675, and the country was fairly teeming with dramatic endeavor—but no new Lope appeared to lift it again; rather the playwrights went down to it. In the eighteenth century theorists tried to introduce classic writing according to the French formula, and some tried to reconcile the supposed "Greek" dramaturgy with the Spanish national forms as exemplified in the seventeenth century masters; but futilely. Indeed there is precious little to draw our attention back to the theatres of Spain between the late seventeenth century (Calderon died in 1681) and the early twentieth century.

The Spanish stage had been as vividly alive as any in Europe for two hundred years. In that time it developed a national dramatic literature that is both brilliant and distinctive. And yet, as a body of reading texts and as material for translation and revival, this mass of plays assays rather thin. Spain failed to bequeath to the world works that will stir audiences everywhere by their universality, their humanity, and their inevitableness. The virtues of the Spanish were those that interested, amused, surprised, and flattered its spectators, and those that flamed with sudden bursts of rich fun, tragic feeling, and lyrical exuberance. Serenity and sustained intensity of emotion were not here.

As a tag to one of his own plays Calderon wrote four lines translated by Ticknor as follows:

This is a play of Pedro Calderon,
Upon whose scene you never fail to find
A hidden lover or a lady fair
Most cunningly disguised.

And indeed upon the whole Spanish scene those are the standard ingredients: hidings, fair ladies, lovers, disguise, and cunning structure.

CHAPTER 12

Shakespeare

W HEN Elizabeth came to the throne in 1558, England
had responded but timidly to the freshening breath of
the Renaissance. Already there had been a king with Italian tastes,
but Henry VIII, however he may have encouraged the more precious
arts of music and masque-making, had done little to popularize or to
better dramatic productions or to further intellectual research. He
had been too busy, perhaps, politically—freeing the English Church
from Rome was more a political than a religious matter—too busy to
stir his people to emulation of those Italian accomplishments that he
so admired. When Elizabeth became queen, London had not one
theatre, amateur dramatic performances were still more important
than professional, the age of Miracles and Moralities had not passed.
And yet within fifty years we are to see the flowering of a theatre
surpassed by none in history as regards spirit and accomplishment—
and everlastingly important for the dramatic texts it bequeathed to posterity. We are, indeed, at the threshold of the most vital and (with
that of the Greeks) the noblest theatre the world has known.

The push forward during Elizabeth's reign was integral to a larger
national and economic advance. The Renaissance, in freeing men's
minds from domination, had resulted indirectly in the invention of
printing, and a consequent enormous spread of knowledge; and had
brought an era of exploration and discovery that remade the map of
the world, destroying once and for all the concentration in the
Mediterranean of trade and cultural routes, leaving that sea, indeed, at

the fringe rather than the centre of a new European-American world. In the period of expression and expansion that followed the Renaissance, the torch of progress was passed successively from Italy to Spain, from Spain to England. Amid the comparative peace of Elizabeth's reign, the English were better able than any other people to keep the flame brilliantly alight. In the theatre it burned most gloriously.

If there was no playhouse in London in 1558—nor for eighteen years after—we are not to infer that there was little theatrical activity. The Guilds have not entirely given up their plays, though professional travelling troupes have multiplied greatly; the schools and universities are acting Latin plays, translations of Italian plays, and even native plays; the court has had a taste of Italian masques and native miming, and even an occasional glimpse of imported professional troupes; pageant-like productions are a concern of the civic authorities, particularly on the occasion of a sovereign's visit or a Lord Mayor's induction.

We have already seen how the humorous elements (or humorous intrusions, if you prefer) in the Miracles led on to witty interludes as secular as those of John Heywood. The Moralities, too, were changing toward the form known as *Chronicles*. A transitional type between Morality and Chronicle arose in the plays of political purpose: *Upon Both Marriages of the King*, and *Kyng Johan* (wherein the character Sedition is supposed to represent the Archbishop of Canterbury, Usurped Power the Pope, Imperial Majesty the King, etc.); and, as an example which affords a clue to its purpose in the very title, *The Three Laws of Nature, Moses and Christ, Corrupted by the Sodomites, Pharisees and Papists*. (This last piece, of the early sixteenth century, has the following directions for the costuming of certain characters: "Let Idolatry be decked lyke an olde wytche, Sodomcy lyke a monke of all sectes, Ambycyon lyke a byshop, Covetousnesse lyke a popysh doctour, and Hypocresy lyke a graye fryre.") We might spend chapters tracing out how plays of this type led on, with the aid of the ballad influence, to the purely historical Chronicle plays—and Shakespeare's early dramas were in that genre—and how similarly the Devil of the Miracles became the Vice of the Moralities, and finally turned into the Jester who appears so frequently in Elizabethan secular drama. For England at this time is full of transitional dramatic activity, and a multitude of play types and sub-types have been described by historians and scholars. But for us, in a brief tour of the world's theatres, it is better to mark only the pervasiveness of the spirit of experiment in putting the drama to use, as amusement, as political and religious propaganda. as a decorative adjunct to court and civic functions. The theatre has come alive, even if it has not a playhouse, nor yet a memorable artist.

Queen Elizabeth was a patron of the theatre only in a limited way. She had an insatiable appetite for the pomp and show of pageantry and masque; and a comedy was to her liking. But here was no lavish encouragement to dramatist and "decorator," like that of the Italian princes; no commissioning of playwrights to pen serious dramas, no building of magnificent theatres. Indeed, the Court continued to har-bor some narrow prejudices: Chronicle plays were suspect, as not certain to hold kings up in the most favorable light, and soon all religious plays were banned—for no one could tell how some provincial guild might forward heretical doctrine by an uncensored Miracle or a wrongly political near-Morality.

Still the Court was at least passively favorable to the actors and playwriters; and certain of the titled nobles lent their names and a sort of protection to the acting companies. The number of travelling troupes so increased that restrictions were passed on "common players," as distinguished from those under patronage. The Puritans were already attacking the drama—the beginnings of a fight destined to end with the closing of the theatres and absolute prohibition of plays in 1642; but the Court and nobles resisted the pressure brought by the clergy—thus favoring the dramatist at least to the extent of opportunity if he could please public audiences. And it is the popular public theatre that is to give us Marlowe, Shakespeare, and Jonson. Noting the produc-tions in castle halls and palace ballrooms, like those at the colleges, as a separate and somewhat removed activity, we may say that the typical "playhouse" of the time is the inn-yard. It is for the emerging companies of professional strolling players that the young playwrights, the gentlemen-scholars who find conservative literature too tame in a spirited world, exert their energies.

The dramatists known as "Shakespeare's predecessors" exhibit com-mon characteristics which may be marked as reflections of the national life of the times, and of the conditions of inn-yard and roadside representation. A vigor and a richness that often ran into extravagance, a freedom and a sweep that brought into drama unmatched variety and stirring emotional climaxes, without a great deal of cunning in the finer points of craftsmanship: these are qualities easily explained by reference to contemporary living. And where audiences were such that no woman ever went to a public play unmasked, there was double reason for vigor of writing, grandeur rather than intimacy in story, for sacrifice to "acting effects." The early playwright, indeed, reached straight for the strong and the picturesque: "In three hours runs he through the world: marries, gets children, makes children men, men to conquer kingdoms, murder monsters, and bringeth Gods from Heaven and fetcheth Devils from Hell." The professional dramatists treated Italian Renaissance literature as a first-class raiding ground for story, but they put their stealings into the old mediæval form of loose-knit chronicle, with emphasis on violent actable incident.

The first English tragedy that has survived is *Gorboduc*, by Thomas Sackville and Thomas Norton, acted in 1562, a Senecan play on an English theme, in that "blank verse"—unrhymed iambic pentameter—which is to become so glorious an instrument in the hands of Marlowe and Shakespeare. *Gorboduc* is characterized by rhetoric in place of action, and by the old inserted device of "dumb show," passages of explanatory pantomime without words. The earliest "regular" comedy is *Ralph Roister Doister*, a Plautan imitation by Nicholas Udall, of somewhat earlier date, and this was followed quickly by Bishop Still's *Gammer Gurton's Needle*, a racy farce-comedy. Having established these, so to speak, date-marks, we may turn to the dozen dramatists who more definitely established playwriting as a profession, determined the direction of English dramatic endeavor, and wrote the plays to which Shakespeare was to shape his less mature genius—plays, indeed, touching heights that only Shakespeare afterwards passed.

John Lyly was first, and most independent of the early dramatists, and by that token less a true Elizabethan. Or perhaps because he spent his talent chiefly in writing for the Court, and with the companies of boy-actors in mind, he was merely less of the public theatres, and therefore less aboundingly virile and theatric. His work is romantic and elegantly artificial, dealing with legendary themes and characters—sweetly lyrical at times, but tame. Perhaps Lyly's service to the drama was greatest in his "domestication" of prose in English comedy: he marked out a path to be trod by far greater dramatists during his own lifetime. As a notable contrast to him there is that Thomas Kyd who wrote *The Spanish Tragedy*, a melodramatic play which was the best seller of the years around 1590, and which had influence far outside England. It is a violent but readable and playable piece, the perfect example of the tragedy-of-blood then so in vogue. We may exclaim with its King,

What age hath ever heard such monstrous deeds!

but we cannot help marking the fresh vigor of Kyd's writing, and the dramatic directness of the tragic story. Although the Senecan Ghost appears in *The Spanish Tragedy*, the play exhibits an amazing advance, theatrically, beyond *Gorboduc*, which had substituted narrative and description for action, in interminable speeches. Kyd is the typical professional playwright, hack-writing to the needs of a vigorous popular theatre, where the authors of *Gorboduc* had been courtiers, amateurs, and imitators of classically correct authors.

George Peele was a popular playwright, too, but he wrote at least one Court play that surpassed Lyly on the latter's ground. Where Lyly had delicately flattered Queen Elizabeth in allegory and thinly-veiled legend, Peele stepped in with *The Arraignment of Paris*, wherein one saw Jupiter cancel the award of the golden apple to Venus, in order that Diana might step forth at the end of the masque, kneel before the Queen, and present the prize to that paragon of chastity,

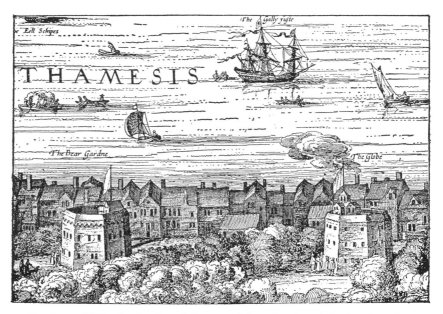

Portion of Visscher's pictorial map of London in 1616, showing the exteriors of two theatres. The flags up mean "performance today." [From a reproduction in *The Stage Year Book*, 1927.]

etc., on earth, the peerless "nymph Eliza." In the public theatre Peele is hardly more than a hack-writer with sound education and a considerable literary gift making progress toward a greater accomplishment.

Robert Greene deserves credit for more than such contributory achievement. If he marred his plays by careless workmanship—just as he marred his life by reckless living, going down to a premature and ugly death—he nevertheless exhibits powers that more than foreshadow those of Shakespeare, in variety, freedom and freshness of invention, that make his own works permanently significant. *Friar*

Bacon and Friar Bungay perhaps best illustrates his humor, tenderness, and freshness.

It has been estimated that of the immense output of the Elizabethan playwrights, not more than one-third has survived in printed form. Plays were quickly written, performed, quickly forgotten. Only the exceptional drama was composed with the thought of book publication; even Shakespeare seems to have considered little the question of preserving the uncorrupted texts of his stage plays. Among the many dramas that have survived, however, those of three other dramatists demand mention. Thomas Lodge only dabbled in playwriting, but did well what he did; and he wrote a non-dramatic *Rosalynde* which has achieved a greater fame as the source of the story which Shakespeare utilized in *As You Like It*. Thomas Nashe likewise was the figure of the versatile Elizabethan writer; and he was dramatist to the extent of being jailed for the too licentious criticism he had written into *The Isle of Dogs*—which may serve to remind us that literary work in this period often involved the author in controversies, forced exiles, imprisonment, and physical encounter.

Last among the predecessors of Shakespeare, and most important—nay, the only true genius among them—is Christopher Marlowe. Had there been no Shakespeare after him, here would have been ample reason for calling the Elizabethan theatre glorious—in four plays composed before Marlowe was killed, at thirty, in a tavern brawl. It is idle perhaps to speculate upon what masterpieces might have been born out of Marlowe's matured genius; and yet one cannot but pause to sorrow over what here was cut off by folly. No other known actual tragedy of theatre life seems quite so grievous, so blighting.

Ben Jonson wrote of "Marlowe's mighty line," and the phrase prepares the reader or spectator for the power and greatness of the dramatist's verse. The qualities are echoed even in the prologue of Marlowe's first play, *Tamurlaine the Great*:

> From jigging veins of rhyming mother wits,
> And such conceits as clownage keeps in pay,
> We'll lead you to the stately tent of war,
> Where you shall hear the Scythian Tamurlaine
> Threatening the world with high astounding terms,
> And scourging kingdoms with his conquering sword . . .

As if to match the sensational excesses of the action, the high astounding terms run off into bombast on occasion; but there is high poetic beauty too—and sometimes human pathos with it. When Zenocrate is dead:

THERIDAMAS

. . . Nothing prevails, for she is dead, my lord.

TAMURLAINE

"For she is dead!" Thy words do pierce my soul!
Ah, sweet Theridamas, say no more;
Though she be dead, yet let me think she lives,
And feed my mind that dies for want of her. . .

Marlowe's second play, *The Tragical History of Doctor Faustus*, if fragmentary as drama, nevertheless treats the Faust legend with magnificent boldness and not seldom in glorious verse. When Helen is conjured up before him, in those last tormented hours, Faust speaks:

Was this the face that launched a thousand ships
And burnt the topless towers of Ilium?
Sweet Helen, make me immortal with a kiss. (*Kisses her.*)
Her lips suck forth my soul; see where it flies!—
Come, Helen, come, give me my soul again.
Here will I dwell, for Heaven is in those lips,
And all is dross that is not Helena.
I will be Paris, and for love of thee,
Instead of Troy shall Wertenberg be sacked:
And I will combat with weak Mcnelaus,
And wear thy colors on my plumèd crest:
Yea, I will wound Achilles in the heel,
And then return to Helen for a kiss.
Oh, thou art fairer than the evening air
Clad in the beauty of a thousand stars;
Brighter art thou than flaming Jupiter
When he appeared to hapless Semele:
More lovely than the monarch of the sky
In wanton Arethusa's azured arms:
And none but thou shalt be my paramour.

And at the end of this play the Chorus speaks those lines so often quoted in regard to the poet himself—murdered while still almost a youth:

Cut is the branch that might have grown full straight,
And burnèd is Apollo's laurel bough. . .

The Jew of Malta and *Edward II* are more mature works, characterized by a dramatic unity that the earlier plays lacked. *The Jew of Malta* is often studied for its likeness and contrast to *The Merchant of Venice;* the central character is equally vivid, but far less human, and the action is more violent than in Shakespeare's carefully balanced, if loosely knit, drama. *Edward II* is usually termed Marlowe's masterpiece, for its superior craftsmanship and characterization. But after all it is the dramatist's poetic richness that entitles him to a place up near Shakespeare. No one before him had written blank verse with such mastery. And, what served equally to endear him to Elizabethan audiences, no one else had packed quite so much of passion into the play form.

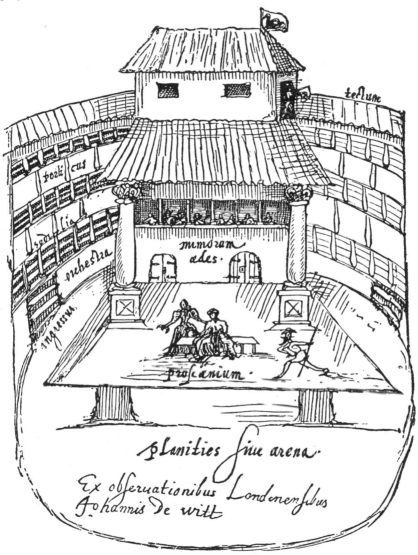

A drawing of the Swan Theatre in London about 1596, by Johann de Witt. One of the few uncontested bits of contemporary evidence regarding the form of the Elizabethan playhouse.

The theatres for which Kyd and Greene and Peele and Marlowe wrote were an outgrowth of the old inn-yard to which the strolling players were wont to resort. In 1576 James Burbage, head of the Earl of Leicester's company of players, opened a playhouse, known as the Theatre, in the suburbs of London, outside the jurisdiction of hostile Lord Mayor and unsympathetic civic authorities. Almost immediately another, known as the Curtain, was built close-by. The houses were constructed on the same open-air model, and it was not until considerably later that a roof was thrown over a building intended exclusively and specifically for dramatic performances. (Don't forget that during all this time the *occasional* performances were going forward at Court, at university, and in the inns of court or halls of the legal societies.)

The public theatres were somewhat like the pictures shown here (I have particularly noted which is contemporary evidence and which later conjectural reconstructions). One may remember that the building as a whole was more or less in doughnut-shape—"a wooden O," as Shakespeare phrased it—and that the tiers of balconies with pit below were an inheritance from the inn-yards, the only play-places the companies had known. The stage naturally varied in the several houses, though its half-roof and its curtained "inner stage" seem to have been fixed features. This is obviously a type of playhouse suited to virtuoso acting, with a platform thrust out into the midst of the audiences. Only a small area is curtained, and there is no opportunity for compelling scenic effects; it is a neutral architectural stage as distinguished from the Italian picture stage.

The changes of scene are accomplished in the imagination of the spectator, stirred by the descriptive verses of the dramatist. In a single act of Kyd's *The Spanish Tragedy*, for instance, there are fifteen scenes played presumably in nine "places." Sometimes, it seems, signboards were put up to tell the audience the scene of the action; but it is likely that ordinarily the lines and the spectator's wit were sufficient guide. Stage "decoration" was not then a consideration. And yet the whole aspect of the theatre, stage, auditorium, actors, and rich costumes, must have been gay, spirited, rich. Nothing else would have served in an era so abounding in life, so adventurous, so self-assertive.

Playgoing was not the orderly activity that it is today. We go to the theatre quietly, to listen attentively to a half-literary exercise. The Elizabethans went to the public theatres boisterously, with little reverence or consideration for dramatist or actor, the dandies anxious to show themselves superior to the entertainment by which they were passing idle hours, aiming at *conspicuous* attendance, and the groundlings in the pit offering vociferous approval or disapproval at every opportunity.

The flag flying over the building to signify "a play is on" brought, indeed, a strange audience: a pit crowd of apprentices playing "hookey," town idlers, a few shameless women, travellers intent on seeing the sights, fighters off duty, seafarers ashore, etc.; and above in the balconies students and poets and a few shrewd burghers or minor Court hangers-on (perhaps with ladies, who dared come only under masculine protection); and on the stage itself the fops and beaux and noblemen,

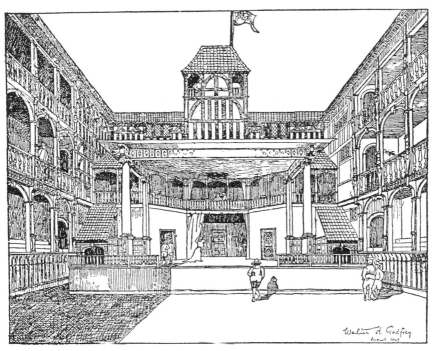

A reconstruction by Walter H. Godfrey of the Fortune Theatre. An Elizabethan playhouse depicted in accordance with the original building contract. [From *Shakespeare's Theatre*, by Ashley H. Thorndike.]

as anxious to be seen as to see, interrupting the action if they willed, smoking and talking and displaying their figures and their finery. To this queer mixture of cultured and uneducated, of lowly and exalted, of those who came for love of drama and those who came to show their superiority, the Elizabethan drama was shaped. No doubt about this vigorous audience enjoying spirited verse or swift action. No doubt about its vociferous reaction if the lines or the action became too slow or too tame. Coarseness went down agreeably, but literary fineness might kill comedy or tragedy. If anything on the stage bored, the audience took to the dice or cards; and always there was much drinking of ale and widespread eating of fruits and sweets.

There are evidences enough, too, that audiences made more direct and violent protest if they really disliked the performance; and it might be a quarrel that had nothing to do with play or actors that ended in disorder and blood-letting. The theatre was part and parcel of the active, feverish, and reckless social life of the time. It has already been noted how Marlowe and Greene went down to deaths attributable to the license and recklessness of the age; many another, playwright and actor and theatre patron, was involved no less in wild adventure, tavern profligacy and violent quarrel. The theatre that knew how to value gentle Will Shakespeare's dramas, was little short of riotous—next of kin to the nearby bear-baiting rings (structurally related, too), and not too far removed from the "stews"—which the nineteenth century more delicately and illuminatingly termed "the disorderly houses."

The actors however were no despised class, as had been their lot in other places and times. At present they were men's companies, with specially trained boys to take the female parts. In Spain, already women had come to the "regular" stage, even in the none too decorous corral theatres; but not in England. To be sure, there had been amateur actresses in the Miracle plays, and Court ladies played in the masques, but the public playhouse was considered no place for them. The guild actors had often been paid—there are records like "6d for God," and "8d for acting Lucifer." But these Elizabethan players are professionals, men studying their art with the double aim of pleasing the groundlings and satisfying that discriminating taste that had somehow grown up vigorous and true.

From Hamlet's famous speech to the actors, we may gather an impression of the playing of the times, from the player who "out-Herod's Herod," the "robustious periwig-pated fellow" tearing "a passion to tatters, to very rags, to split the ears of the groundlings," from him to the actors who "in the very torrent, tempest, and, I might say, the whirlwind of passion . . . acquire and beget a temperance that may give it smoothness"—and who speak the speech "trippingly on the tongue." No doubt Shakespeare suffered from fellow-actors who "have so strutted and bellowed, that I have thought some of nature's journeymen had made men, and not made them well, they imitated humanity so abominably." But while acting then was artificial, stilted, and bombastic if judged by any realistic standard, we may note Hamlet's words about discretion and modesty and temperance as indications of a true interpretative art.

To this vigorous-violent theatre in 1588 or thereabouts came William Shakespeare, from his idyllic home village, Stratford-upon-Avon. One might be wiser to begin, *perhaps* he came to London in 1588 or thereabouts; for a great deal that is commonly put down as fact about Shakespeare's life is inference or based on vague documents and opinions. The story goes that William Shakespeare was born in 1564, son of a butcher who also was a respected town officer, and business-man in several collateral lines; that he attended the local grammar school for a few years, probably gaining a knowledge of Latin; that he worked as apprentice to his father in the butchering business, when the latter was reduced to that trade again by losses in other fields; that he married Ann Hathaway, eight years his senior, when he was a youth midway between eighteen and nineteen; that he was not very happy in family life, and that he ran wild for a time and capped his misdemeanors by poaching on the neighboring estates of Sir Thomas Lucy—and that therefore he ran away from Stratford and eventually found his way to London and the doors of the theatre. There is even less substantiated evidence that he began by holding the horses outside the playhouse (the dandies came from town on horseback); but the tale offers a pleasant starting-point for a dramatic rise-from-the-lowly story. For Shakespeare was soon play-tinker to Burbage's company, and soon an actor.

That he began his serious literary activity by doctoring and adapting old plays, there seems little doubt. It was a common occupation; and there is so much working over even of new manuscripts that some plays seem likely never to be properly ascribed. Peele, Greene, and Lodge have so puzzled later scholars by their collaborative work that no peace is possible where they are studied; and to this day there is only conjecture as to what parts of *Henry VI* came from Shakespeare's pen, and what from Marlowe's or perhaps from those of Greene and Peele, and as to the extent of Shakespeare's service in preparing *Titus Andronicus* for the stage. In that day the manager bought a play outright from an author, for a lump sum; and it was his privilege to have it improved as much as possible before performance.

But Shakespeare became known as an actor before he gained fame as a playwright. He seems to have been a good actor—that about sums up our knowledge of his playing. His name appears in several lists of players, and someone recorded that he "did act exceedingly well." There is almost unanimous praise of him off the stage, however, and we may picture him as amiable, witty, and well-liked, as, indeed, the "sweet master Shakespeare" mentioned in a play of 1601. As to the measure in which he had studied his craft of acting, we have already found indication in the speech of Hamlet to the players. To complete what little we may have here of biography, Shakespeare worked for twenty years on the London stage, as actor and playwright, prospered, bought a part ownership of the producing company that had aided his major triumphs, and retired to Stratford-upon-Avon to spend the last five years of his life in respected ease. He died in 1616.

Shakespeare as dramatist is by so much the greater figure than any other mentioned in these pages, that one despairs even of suggesting the many aspects of his genius. If we are to follow out our plan of glancing at all the theatres of all the nations, we needs must be content with a few words about his mastery in each of the major fields of playwriting, and in each of the forms of theatrical effectiveness, and with a very few quotations to remind us of his "poetry in drama" that so surpasses any other in the language. One's bewilderment arises not so much from the number of plays that may justly be termed masterpieces and immortal—there are hardly a half dozen of the thirty-seven that we would willingly omit from any compilation of the world's best half-hundred dramas; it is rather the infinite variety of them, the richness within each play in its own kind; and perhaps most of all the extraordinary gallery of human portraits formed by the "characters."

For who should say that Hamlet, the most-played figure on the world stage, noble, complex, grievously mad or terribly sane, is more theatrical and more familiar than Falstaff, drunken braggart and beloved sensualist; that tragic Othello or piteous Lear is more immortal than Rosalind or Portia or Viola. What other figures crowd into the mind's eye!—clear, human, bringing dark shadow or smiling reminiscence, as brightly etched as if we had met them but today: Romeo, Juliet, the Nurse, Shylock, Macbeth and Lady Macbeth, the Witches, Bottom, Puck, Iago, Desdemona, Dogberry, Sir Toby, Sir Andrew and Malvolio, Petruchio and Kate, Ophelia, Polonius, Ariel, Prospero, Cæsar, Cassius, Brutus, the Merry Wives. Even then one has not mentioned the gallery of noble historical portraits, in a series of Chronicle Plays that lifted the form to a place beside human-life tragedy. And yet what an amazing variety, what unforgettable characterizations! These figures have gone into everyday currency, are of our daily living as no others save those of the Bible. Every schoolboy knows them, philosophers sustain themselves by rereading their adventures year by year. And, oh, yes! the plays in which they appear are performed quite regularly in those countries where the artistic sensibilities of audiences are keen, and minds eager.

I take it that I should only be insulting my readers by retelling the story of the half-pastoral, half-comedy *As You Like It*, or the part farce-comedy, part tender idyll *Twelfth Night, or What You Will*, or the tragi-comic tale of those so-jumbled characters in *The Merchant of Venice.* One might, indeed, outline a drama in each of those sorts so ably listed by Polonius: "tragedy, comedy, history, pastoral, pastoral-comical, historical-pastoral, tragical-historical, tragical-comical-historical-pastoral, scene individable, or poem unlimited." But you know them all in Shakespeare's originals; and besides, no other plays quite so successfully defy retelling—escape, in their flavor and essence, so completely from the bare recounted structure.

Indeed, there are those who say that Shakespeare's dramas exist too much in characterization and poetry and telling incident and felicitous conceit, that by that token the structure is weak, the play as a whole not truly theatrical. But if one has a perspective on the history of the stage in all times, one may well conclude that it is the theatre of today that is too limited, too restricted, to hold so much of dramatic incident and rich embroidery and far-riding imagination. The box-stage, the picture setting and the proscenium-frame playhouse are inadequate to compass so much that transcends painted picture, realistic situation, and personal acting. Shakespeare is a challenge to any producer; and the man who sticks by the limitations of the still-lingering nineteenth century theatre is impotent in the face of that challenge: and usually he sidesteps by simply saying that Shakespeare is untheatric. But in his own time his plays were supreme upon the stage, were known in performance only—were designed in every feature to *acting.* And they give promise today of becoming supreme again, till some new Shakespeare arises, when the modern stage completes the process of making itself as free, as sheer-for-acting (though not necessarily as bare) as was the Elizabethan. Meantime Shakespeare's texts upon the shelf transcend most other poetry, theatrical and untheatrical; and we do see the plays performed occasionally, well or indifferently.

We may grant, indeed, that the poetic genius, welling up, stretched the dramatic structure awry at times. *A Midsummer Night's Dream* seems mixed and formless and *The Tempest* hardly achieves dramatic unity; but were ever gigantic faults so greatly atoned? For the rest, let us recall, by Shakespeare's own lines, the excellencies of the verse and the perfect fitness of that verse to characters.

Even the "lyrics" are expressions of feeling integral to the character-plot. For what could better sum up the pastoral spirit that freshens *As You Like It* than the song:

Under the greenwood tree
Who loves to lie with me,
And turn his merry note
Unto the sweet bird's throat,
Come hither, come hither, come hither. . .

Or at the very extreme from this, call to mind those lines of Lear that so picture a King basely abused, gone mad, but still a King, in the scene beginning:

LEAR

Ay, every inch a king:
When I do stare, see how the subject quakes . . .

And the change in the next scene:

LEAR

Pray do not mock me:
I am a very foolish fond old man . . .

The opening lines of a play may reveal in their overtones what is to be the "feel" of the drama; as these in *Twelfth Night:*

DUKE

If music be the food of love, play on;
Give me excess of it, that, surfeiting,
The appetite may sicken, and so die.
That strain again! it had a dying fall:
O, it came o'er my ear like the sweet sound
That breathes upon a bank of violets,
Stealing and giving odor! Enough; no more. . .

But when one begins to quote, and starts thinking about these revealing character-passages, so many come that surely one may see there is no more of wonder in the gallery of portaits than in the written verses. Shall it be Portia's "The quality of mercy is not strained," or Othello's "Speak of me as I am," or that scene between Macbeth and Lady Macbeth wherein he fears his hand will "the multitudinous seas incarnadine"; or his cry at her death:

She should have died hereafter;
There would have been a time for such a word.
To-morrow, and to-morrow, and to-morrow,
Creeps in this petty pace from day to day,
To the last syllable of recorded time;
And all our yesterdays have lighted fools
The way to dusty death. Out, out, brief candle!
Life's but a walking shadow, a poor player
That struts and frets his hour upon the stage
And then is heard no more; it is a tale
Told by an idiot, full of sound and fury,
Signifying nothing.

For the rest, let us take one play, the *Hamlet* that is so compact as drama, as theatrical tragedy-of-blood, as character-study, and yet so packed with thoughtful phrases that no other mine yields so much that goes into street usage, that comes with familiar ring to the common ear, that sustains so richly him who rereads a hundredth time. Let us note merely how the thought, the beauty, the human pathos belong theatrically to the stage character speaking, and to those in dramatic impact with him.

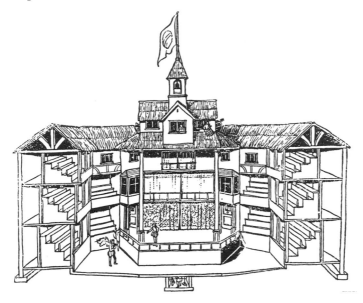

Sectional cut through galleries and view of stage of the Globe Theatre, Shakespeare's "wooden O," in London. [Drawing by Maurice Percival after a reconstruction by John Cranford Adams.]

OPHELIA

O, what a noble mind is here o'erthrown!
The courtier's, soldier's, scholar's, eye, tongue, sword:
The expectancy and rose of the fair state,
The glass of fashion and the mould of form,
The observed of all observers, quite, quite down!
And I, of ladies most deject and wretched,
That sucked the honey of his music vows,
Now see that noble and most sovereign reason,
Like sweet bells jangled, out of tune and harsh;
The unmatch'd form and feature of blown youth
Blasted with ecstasy: O, woe is me,
To have seen what I have seen, see what I see!

And the King characterizes himself in two lines:

> O, my offense is rank, it smells to Heaven;
> It hath the primal eldest curse upon it. . .

But nothing in the language equals, for meat, the soliloquies of Hamlet. I pass over the longer one beginning "O, what a rogue and peasant slave am I," in order to quote another in full, together with its context; this to illustrate finally how Shakespeare wedded poetry to drama, not merely decorating a plot but so binding up character, story, action, and beauty of verse that here is a very summit of the theatric art:

HAMLET

To be, or not to be: that is the question:
Whether 'tis nobler in the mind to suffer
The slings and arrows of outrageous fortune,
Or to take arms against a sea of troubles,
And by opposing end them. To die: to sleep;
No more; and by a sleep to say we end
The heart-ache, and the thousand natural shocks
That flesh is heir to, 'tis a consummation
Devoutly to be wished. To die, to sleep;
To sleep: perchance to dream: aye there's the rub;
For in that sleep of death what dreams may come,
When we have shuffled off this mortal coil,
Must give us pause: there's the respect
That makes calamity of so long life;
For who would bear the whips and scorns of time,
The oppressor's wrong, the proud man's contumely,
The pangs of despised love, the law's delay,
The insolence of office, and the spurns
That patient merit of the unworthy takes,
When he himself might his quietus make
With a bare bodkin? who would fardels bear,
To grunt and sweat under a weary life,
But that the dread of something after death,
The undiscover'd country from whose bourne
No traveller returns, puzzles the will,
And makes us rather bear those ills we have
Than fly to others that we know not of?
Thus conscience does make cowards of us all,
And thus the native hue of resolution
Is sicklied o'er with the pale cast of thought,
And enterprises of great pitch and moment
With this regard their currents turn awry
And lose the name of action. Soft you now!
The fair Ophelia! Nymph, in thy orisons
Be all my sins remembered.

OPHELIA
Good my lord,
How does your honor for this many a day?

HAMLET
I humbly thank you: well, well, well.

OPHELIA
My lord, I have remembrances of yours,
That I have longed to re-deliver;
I pray you, now receive them.

HAMLET
No, not I
I never gave you aught.

OPHELIA
My honor'd lord, you know right well you did;
And with them words of so sweet breath composed
As made the things more rich: their perfume lost,
Take these again; for to the noble mind
Rich gifts wax poor when givers prove unkind.
There, my lord.

In this play, too, one sees prose (which had been brought to the uses of the stage but a few years since) become an instrument flexible, expressive, pat. You may browse through the Polonius and the grave-digging scenes, and find the thoughtful humor in this prose. Nor let us forget, our study being theatre, not mere texts, that the last line of this tragic play of Hamlet is "Go bid the soldiers shoot"—and after, there is the procession bearing the bodies, and a peal of ordnance without.

The dramatists who followed Shakespeare in the Elizabethan age have suffered in history by being directly overshadowed by his fame. It is wholly natural that students should turn first to him who sums up in one group of plays the tendencies of the age, who packs into his dramas every sort of stage excellency of the times. And yet Ben Jonson and John Fletcher and John Webster would be outstanding giants in any other era. When one puts down, also, the names of the additional practising playwrights—George Chapman, Francis Beaumont, Thomas Dekker, Thomas Middleton, John Ford, James Shirley, Philip Massinger, Thomas Heywood, Samuel Rowley—there is such a range of rich achievement as no later age can match. There will be not so many names of notable dramatists to record out of the following three centuries of English theatre history. But again, Shakespeare tops them in every field, tragedy, comedy, chronicle. They are of the same richly active theatre, vigorous, wide-riding, fearing limitation and dullness more than extravagance and violence. As a matter of fact they began to step out of the realm of gorgeous adventure and fun into the field where coarseness and license and melodrama rule. But there was immortal achievement too.

Ben Jonson, more learned than Shakespeare, more a commanding figure among his contemporaries, more a man of the world, was decidedly inferior as a tragedy-writer. Perhaps he knew too much about the classics, and let theory interfere with practice. Thus there is point to the old epigram about Shakespeare being sent from Heaven, Jonson from College (though really he attended neither University). In comedy, on the other hand, he scored a success almost comparable to that of Shakespeare. His plays were less human, less tenderly memorable, less nobly clothed; but in a new field, satirical comedy, they were supreme—and they marked out a path for future dramatists.

The "comedy of humours" which Jonson put forward, no less in practice than in broadcast theory, was a genre in which the sources of action were sought in character rather than situation. Incident grew out of character, was no longer developed for its own sake. Moreover, Jonson maintained, in every man there is a ruling trait, a bias of character—in short, a "humour"—which is the very fountain of comedy. And with *Everyman in His Humour* and *Volpone* and *Poetaster* he proceeded to satirize such weaknesses, leaving to posterity dramas that interest today almost as much as they did in Elizabeth's reign; and *The Alchemist* and *Bartholomew Fair* are hardly less read. It happened that some of Jonson's contemporaries thought they detected in the humours of certain of his characters some of their own less admirable traits, and he soon found himself involved in a bitter stage quarrel, play satirizing rival playwright and rival answering in kind. But Ben Jonson lives for posterity, whereas most of the competing "comedies of humours" remain undisturbed on the shelves, if they got into print at all.

Still Dekker and Marston, the particular antagonists of Jonson in "the War of the Theatres," wrote plays that not only were important in their time but have outlived those of many fellow dramatists. Dekker's *Shoemaker's Holiday,* a realistic comedy, and his *Old Fortunatus,* a romantic comedy, still afford good boisterous fun, and *The Honest Whore* lives by right of sincerity and unusualness. Marston, however, is best remembered for his collaboration with Jonson and George Chapman on the comedy *Eastward Ho.* Chapman approached Jonson in the field of satirical comedy, and put exceptional vigor without very deep characterization into his tragedies—but his name has been repeated of-

A view of actors on a stage of the seventeenth century in England. The characters, the candelabra, the footlights, and the arrangement of stage and curtains prove this to be a post-Shakespearean theatre. [From the frontispiece of Francis Kirkman's *The Wits*, London, 1673.]

tener for his translation of Homer than for his plays. That he occasionally touched heights in his verse may be illustrated briefly in these lines from the comedy *All Fools:*

> How blind is pride! What eagles we are still
> In matters that belong to other men—
> What beetles in our own. . .

Thomas Heywood, dubbed by Lamb "our prose Shakespeare," contributed to the stage a domestic play so direct and human that it is marked as the best of its type in those times, *A Woman Killed with Kindness;* and in comedy Massinger contributed *A New Way to Pay Old Debts,* built around the character of Sir Giles Overreach, which holds its place on the boards today. One other more or less isolated play, Webster's *The Duchess of Malfi,* has stood out in later years; it is a violent but often moving drama, the very play to mark for us how tragedy, which had been ennobled and refined by Marlowe and Shakespeare, now turned back again toward melodramatic and rhetorical ways.

Francis Beaumont and John Fletcher are the most notable team of collaborators among English dramatists. There are those who say that Massinger had more to do with "Beaumont and Fletcher" plays than ever did Beaumont. However the credit be divided, here was joint work that left no mark of the double origin. Nor did the partnership result in drama in a limited field. *The Maid's Tragedy* may be surpassed in fame by the mock-heroic *The Knight of the Burning Pestle* or the tragi-comedy *The Knight of Malta,* or by the straight comedy *Rule a Wife and Have a Wife* (which is more often ascribed to Fletcher alone). But here is the most successful collaboration in the history of the "regular" stage. If there was the late Elizabethan excess of passion in some of the resulting dramas, we may call Beaumont and Fletcher blessed for their burlesque of that very quality in *The Knight.* Still, let us realize that we are well down the other side from the eminence that was the high Elizabethan drama.

In thirty years, roughly from 1590 to 1620, the stage had flowered, had seen Shakespeare triumph and go, had seen almost all the playwrights and plays that have been mentioned. Life in those years had moved swiftly, adventurously, gorgeously. The theatre had risen to be, *par excellence,* the interpreter of the time and its mirror. The great poets were dramatists; often the great dramatists were actors, or resident play-doctors. The stage was at the heart of life. London was still a medieval town of fewer than two hundred thousand inhabitants; but the playwrights brought to its doors Italy and France and Spain, and the fabled lands of the ancients and others unknown to either earlier poets or contemporary geographers. Nor was their offered treasure more notable for these exotic riches than for those mined from a new understanding of the human heart and human foibles. England had had her era of exploration, expansion, richer living. The dramatists had explored and found riches matched in no other field.

During all these years when the public theatres were so prospering, so enriching London life, there were other types of theatre at court and other productions by students, boy companies and amateur groups, as we shall see when we inquire into the masques and plays at court. But the drama of Greene and Marlowe and Shakespeare was written for the wooden-O playhouse, for groundling apprentices and balconied burghers and fops on the stage.

The exceptional new roofed playhouse had come in, and doubtless there were increasing concessions to the demand for richer Italian-style settings—perhaps only more costumes and properties at first, then attempts at suggestive "scenery." But in general the Elizabethan platform-for-acting persisted through the great days. The play was markedly a drama for acting, designed with little thought for scenic dressing or for reading. At this time playwright, actor, producer, and audience were at one in spirit, collaborated together for entertainment, somehow opened the channels from the well-springs of genius—became part of the high, noble, poetic theatre that our minds conjure up at the mention of Shakespeare.

Two contemporary engravings of seventeenth-century curtained stages in England. [From the title-pages of Alabastro's *Roxana* and Richards' *Messalina*, 1632 and 1640.]

CHAPTER 13

The Puritans and the Chapel of Satan

As THAT portion of the kingdom of anti-Christ known as
Theatre-land was further and further explored by the Puritans of sixteenth and seventeenth century England, such iniquities and blasphemies were found seated therein as had scarcely been hinted at by scandalizd Tertullian back in Roman times. And indeed the problem of "the theatre evil" had become more complex. The moralists under the late Emperors, after all, had been fighting against a stage inheriting directly from paganism—if religious in origin, then only by grace of heathenish Gods. But the Elizabethan stage inherited from the Christian Church, was successor to Christian shows, and the Puritans were Christian if anti-Papist. Unlike the decadent Roman stage, too, this one linked up with learned people, with poets, with nobles. But how much more horrible, then, that it should be so lewd, so profane!

The crimes of the theatre, as set forth in Puritan sermons and pamphlets, included these: emptying the churches, perpetuating pagan customs, distorting truth, showing forth profane, seditious, and bawdy stories, teaching knavery and lechery, causing God to visit the plague on London, leading youths into idleness and extravagance, affording meeting-place for harlots and customers, aiding the pope, corrupting maidens and chaste wives, undermining fortitude and seriousness, etc., etc.

The theatre was now thrice damned from the theological standpoint, and even if it had any merits it would be offensive in the sight of God:

298

for had not the Devil invented it, had not he given it to the pagans, had not these pagans bequeathed it to the papists, who allowed it in the House of God? "The ungodly Plays and Interludes so rife in this nation: what are they but a bastard of Babylon, a daughter of error and confusion, a hellish device (the Devil's own recreation to mock at holy things) by him delivered to the Heathen, from them to the Papists, and from them to us? . . . Now they bring religion and holy things upon the stage: no marvel though the worthiest and mightiest men escape not, when God himself is so abused." Thus spoke William Crashaw in a sermon, in 1607—when Shakespeare was acting and writing plays. And as early as 1577 Thomas White had preached as follows:

> Look upon the common plays in London, and see the multitude that flocketh to them and followeth them: behold the sumptuous Theatre houses, a continual monument of London's prodigality and folly. . . Shall I reckon up the monstrous birds that breed in this nest? without doubt I am ashamed, and I should surely offend your chaste ears: but the old world is matched, and Sodom overcome, for more horrible enormities, and swelling sins are set out by those stages, than every man thinks for, or some would believe, if I should paint them out in their colors: without doubt you can scantly name me a sin, that by that sink is not set a-gog: theft and whoredom; pride and prodigality; villainy and blasphemy; these three couples of hellhounds never cease barking there, and bite many, so as they are uncurable ever after. . .

Mentioning the Theatre and the Curtain, then just built, John Northbrooke in 1577 wrote:

> Satan hath not a more speedy way, and fitter school to work and teach his desire, to bring men and women into the snare of concupiscence and filthy lusts of wicked whoredom, than those places, and plays, and theatres are . . . It hath stricken such a blind zeal into the hearts of the people, that they shame not to say, and affirm openly, that plays are as good as sermons, and that they learn as much or more at a play, than they do at God's word preached. . . Many can tarry at a vain play two or three hours, whenas they will not abide scarce one hour at a sermon. . . In their plays you shall learn all things that appertain to craft, mischief, deceits and filthiness, etc. If you will learn how to be false and deceive your husbands, or husbands their wives, how to play the harlot, to obtain one's love, how to ravish, how to beguile, how to betray, to flatter, lie, swear, forswear, how to allure to whoredom, how to murder, how to poison, how to disobey and rebel against princes, to consume treasures prodigally, to move to lusts, to ransack and spoil cities and towns, to be idle, to blaspheme, to sing filthy songs of love, to speak filthily, to be proud, how to mock, scoff and

deride any nation . . . shall you not learn, then, at such interludes how to practise them?

Beside this liberal education offered at the theatre, there were other teachings and effects that seemed to the Puritans conducive to evil—including, one knows not why, the sorrow evoked by tragedy, and laughter.

But let us see the indictment summed up in Philip Stubbes' *The Anatomy of Abuses:*

> Do these mockers and flouters of his Majesty, these dissembling *Hipocrites,* and flattering *Gnatoes,* think to escape unpunished? beware, therefore, you masking players, you painted sepulchres, you double dealing ambodexters, be warned betimes, and like good computists, cast your accounts before, what will be the reward thereof in the end, lest God destroy you in his wrath: abuse God no more, corrupt his people no longer with your dregs, and intermingle not his blessed word with such profane vanities. . . If their plays be of profane matters, then tend they to the dishonor of God, and nourishing of vice, both which are damnable. So that whether they be the one or the other, they are quite contrary to the word of grace, and sucked out of the Devil's teats to nourish us in idolatry, heathenry, and sin. And therefore they, carrying the note, or brand, of God his curse upon their backs which way soever they go, are to be hissed out of all Christian kingdoms, if they will have Christ to dwell amongst them. . . For so often as they go to those houses where players frequent, they go to Venus' palace, and Satan's synagogue, to worship devils, and betray Jesus Christ. . . Do they not draw the people from hearing the word of God, from godly lectures and sermons? for you shall have them flock thither, thick and threefold, when the church of God be bare and empty. Do they not maintain bawdery, infinite foolery, and renew the remembrances of heathen idolatry? Do they not induce whoredom and uncleanness? nay, are they not rather plain devourers of maidenly virginity and chastity? For proof whereof, but mark the flocking and running to Theatres and Curtains, dayly and hourly, night and day, time and tide, to see Plays and Interludes . . .

In answer to these blasts that the terribly sincere and militantly righteous Puritans loosed against the theatres in the years 1550–1620, the dramatists wrote pamphlet after pamphlet;[1] but after all, the best

---

[1] E. K. Chambers in his invaluable *The Elizabethan Stage* (4 vols., Oxford, 1923) prints extracts from sixty-three defences and attacks (from which I have taken my quotations), and adds one hundred and sixty extracts from "documents of control."

answer is in the plays of Marlowe, Shakespeare, Jonson. (Other and more bitter answers were in the caricatures of Puritans in scores of played comedies.)

Here we have come to a time when the line is more sharply drawn than ever before between pious workers and those who live loosely or are complacent about their easy-going neighbors. Just after the English Church had accomplished its divorce from Rome, the reformers had used the drama as a weapon for flaying the Pope and Papists (you remember *Kyng Johan*, written by the Protestant Bishop of Ossory, known as "Bilious Bale"); but now the theatre is definitely down on the side of the anti-Puritans. If it is on the side of the loose-livers, it is also on the side of laughter and high poetry and purging tragedy.

Crashaw in 1610 grouped together "the Devil, Papists, and players." This new alignment may serve to remind us that the Chinese had put special legal restrictions upon actors, barbers, and slaves, while the Romans grouped thieves, panderers, deserters, actors, and reciters in an *infamis* class; while in India, where there was a noble class of players, another group was rated with butchers, fishermen, hangmen, and scavengers, and thus had to live outside the town and pass on the far side of the street from the nobles. In England as early as 1545 "common players" had been officially classed with "ruffians, vagabonds, masterless men, and evil-disposed persons." And almost throughout the glorious time of Elizabethan drama, the civic authorities were with the preachers in the desire and effort to "hiss out of all Christian kingdoms" these "double-dealing ambodexters." What, then, saved them from suppression, exile, and extinction?

The Court of Elizabeth, by tolerance and occasionally by protection, gave the theatres a certain standing, gave the dramatists confidence, permitted gentlemen to go to the play with ease of conscience. This Court was quick enough to strike at a playwright or to punish actors if an unseemly criticism of royalty or any seditious utterance cropped up in a play. But the Queen and the nobles were, in sympathy, on the theatre's side. (Later, of course, the consideration became political: Court against Puritan for control of England.) And in at least one notable case a little later, the governing powers stepped in to punish terribly a heckler of the stages:

In 1632, after seven years' labor on the work, William Prynne, an intolerant moralist and zealot, the very type-figure of the bigot-Puritan, published *Histrio-Mastix*, an eleven-hundred-page blast against the stage and its immoralities. If any sort of crime had ever been committed in or about the theatre or by persons to be connected in name with the stage, Prynne was sure to find the record—and embalm it for all time in this classic of abuse. The material was not new, of course, to the post-Elizabethan readers. But it happened that the luckless author inserted—in reference to a disturbance over one of the earliest appearances of professional women actors in London (*French* ones, of course)—a remark that women players were "notorious whores." At the moment of publication, Queen Henrietta Maria was rehearsing for an amateur performance of a pastoral. Prynne was stood in the pillory, condemned to life imprisonment and a fine, branded S. L. (seditious libeller) on both cheeks—and his ears were cut off.

Aside from the "regular" theatres there was, in the sixteenth and seventeenth centuries, a considerable activity in folk drama and dancing, as instanced here in a scene of "mummers," in a woodcut after Bruegel.

From which one may judge that not all the hatred, intolerance, and militancy existed on one side. And, indeed, one who loves the theatre with more than a passing or a commercial affection, who wants to see the stage unfettered, may still shake a head dubiously over what happened in the Chapels of Satan within the fifty years after Shakespeare's time. For there is little after Ben Jonson and Shirley and Beaumont and Fletcher that has its value today, except those comedies of the Restoration which mix graceful wit and corruption of the spirit more cunningly than any other body of drama in the world.

The bitterness that has existed between theatre-artists and moralists since the period immediately preceding Christ's birth would not have persisted so unremittingly if there had not been well-nigh unbridgeable gulfs between the two parties. For one thing, Christian mankind is temperamentally divided, one half mistrusting the pleasures of the senses, suspicious of laughter, eager to prohibit and suppress the lighter, gayer, more colorful elements of life; the other half clinging to pagan enjoyments, willing to take chances with life, adventurous, valuing sensuous and emotional experience as among the sweetest joys in living. The Puritan, moreover, distrusts frankness; and he knows there is nothing so dangerous as truth. His first impulse is to limit knowledge and experience to a small range, bounded according to a conception of righteous conduct as permitted in the books of a revealed religion.

The artist knows that art, and particularly the theatre, dies of prohibitions and limitation. He fights instinctively against censorship. And yet his battle is made confusing because of betrayals within his own camp. In seventeenth century England, the voluptuaries, the cynics, and the commercialists carried freedom to an extreme that makes many plays of the period unpleasant reading to many readers even in this more permissive time. In our own twentieth century managers and playwrights, with nothing but money in mind, put on the stage sensational pieces, parading violence, nudity, and sexual perversion—and render infinitely harder the way of those who want simple freedom. For us here, the point is that these commercialists carry drama out to a topical or expositional region where subject-matter so intrudes, so absorbs the spectator, that there is no longer any question of the art of the theatre. And if one reads through some of the more successfully suppressed plays of the time of the Stuarts—not only those that by their finer qualities have survived in the Mermaid editions and similar collections—one may feel that then a great many people were using the stage simply for the exhibition of pornographic situation and filth; that the battle of those who wanted only freedom for the flowering of an art was badly complicated by the pushing pack that smelled gold in the exploitation of bawdy tales and suggestive situation.

The temper of the Puritans was such, of course, that a dozen Shakespeares could not have excused the existence of the theatre; but on the other side there seems to have been an unfortunate pouring of all energy into counter-blasts, when a little might so well have been spent in excluding the crowds of harlots from the audiences, and in driving the filth-exploiting producers and actors from the stage. But whatever had been the truth in Shakespeare's time, the theatre was now on the down-track, in many senses. Curiously enough, the plague that periodically swept over London proved the best ally of the Puritans. Several times it accomplished the temporary closing of the playhouses.

In the long history of the contest between those who believe in a free stage and those who favor prohibition or censorship, seventeenth century England provides the most vivid chapter—until the mid-twentieth century. Puritanism never else was either so inexorable or so powerful; the stage was never else so licentious while still sheltering great dramatic art. The struggle ended with the Puritans closing all theatres in 1642; and except for the hang-over to Restoration times, there was never afterwards a period of such bitter battle. We have today our exploiting producers who cloak pornography under "realism." We may wonder at the open and apparently officially arranged soliciting by prostitutes that is customary in some of the larger theatres of Paris; but we shrug our shoulders because the matter touches upon the serious drama hardly at all, is an adjunct to revue-producing.

England alone tried the solution of continued government censorship; and thus denied its theatre-goers much that has given great, and presumably unharmful, pleasure to audiences in other countries—particularly in the case of plays by Ibsen, Shaw, and other thinker-dramatists. The system helped to make the English stage one of the tamest in modern times, with the virtues and the limitations of tameness. But no republican country would permit such arbitrary censorship. As a matter of fact the powers of the censor, the Lord Chamberlain, lasted from Tudor times, when plays were approved or condemned only on political or religious grounds, through three centuries, until the passage of the Theatres Act in 1843, when censorship of obscenity was added. The powers of the Lord Chamberlain, absolute and without appeal, were to be abolished only in the late nineteen-sixties.

With just a word about the "regular" theatres, let us turn to that queen's pastoral that happened to bring a cruel wrath down upon him who called loudest upon God to destroy the players. The public theatres continued without important change in form of playhouse or acting or plays until 1642. Boys still acted women's parts in the men's companies. The troupes made long tours outside London. Playwriting gradually lost the old fire, the old poetry, the high Shakespearean and Jonsonian humor. The swift and tricky Spanish plays particularly afforded materials for adaptation. Violence increased in tragedies, coarseness abounded in comedy. The popular theatres made no effort to escape those evils that linked them too closely to the stews. The war with the Puritans went on, until inevitably there came in 1642 the law suppressing all stage plays—and enforcement, since the Puritans now were in power. At the universities playwriting of an academic sort continued, in both English and Latin. But what overshadows the public theatres in interest, out of the times of James I, is the masque-making, and productions at court. For here there came new elements into English staging, and even a text or two that lasted as literature.

Elizabeth in her time had been fond of masques and of the pageant-like shows that celebrated her comings and goings at the towns away from London. She was an inveterate visitor, and many a noble lived impoverished through succeeding years because he entertained his Queen so lavishly during one of her triumphal pilgrimages. Special pastoral plays were staged in her honor; tableau groups were arranged in the castle garden or woods for her pleasure; masques were presented in the castle ballroom; and sometimes the spectacular elements of Italian staging found their way into these English productions. Ever since the time of Henry VIII there had been a taste at court for French and Italian art, and among the expense accounts of Elizabeth's own Master of Revels there are entries indicating built-perspective settings, trick clouds, painted landscape back-drops, grottoes, and similar features in the approved Renaissance tradition. During the time of Henry VIII, Italian architects and painters had been resident at the English Court.

The pastoral drama, so closely related to the masque in its beginnings, is here again bound up with the court entertainments. In Shakespeare the impulse mixed with others, and his romantic comedies became true dramas with a pastoral freshness and sweetness over them. John Fletcher alone mastered the form in that time; he put more real loveliness into *The Faithful Shepherdess* than went into any other English pastoral play. Even while imitating the Italian *Pastor Fido* directly in some particulars he showed originality and, above all, great poetic felicity. The work is generally spoken of as a poem rather than drama; and indeed its virtues are largely literary. Ben Jonson wrote *The Sad Shepherdess*, an unfinished play, in which he more successfully domesticated the pastoral into an English scene (Sherwood Forest) and to English characters. But with Jonson as with other English dramatists the impulse passed over into the field of masque-writing: if, indeed, we grant that the yearning for unreal prettiness and an artificial simplicity is at the basis of both these sorts of delicate and decorative "drama."

Jonson wrote more than thirty masque-texts, and endowed them with a lyric charm seldom equalled; but he felt in the end—as perhaps every masque author is certain to do—that his work was badly overshadowed by the showier elements of scenery, costuming, and dancing. After him John Milton wrote *Comus*, distinguished by flowery allegorical verse most amazingly bound up with sublime moral passion. And of a truth, a form of drama usually quite trivial or merely pretty is here elevated to the region of majestic poetry and immortal imagery. It is one of the superb tributes to Purity. If it suffers a little in stage-worthiness, seems none too deftly shaped to acting, we may recall that masque-texts are likely to be formless anyway—and forget the fault in delighted reading. As an example of how the masques were shaped to occasions, *Comus* was written for performance at Ludlow Castle, and was produced, in 1634, as part of a long series of festivities in honor of the appointment of the Earl of Bridgewater to the Lord-Presidency of Wales. The players were amateurs, including the three children of the Earl, while the staging was superintended by the composer who wrote the masque-music.

By this time the courts had quite gone mad over masques, and no "occasion" was complete without one. The more elaborate productions were lavish and wasteful almost beyond belief. And in connection with the "trimmings" of the productions, as the disgruntled Jonson might have put it, we come to that singular figure in English theatre history, Inigo Jones. Long ago, in the very earliest years of the seventeenth century, this eminent architect had started to experiment with "Italian style" stages and stage-setting. He travelled in Italy, learned the advantages of a curtained stage, and picked up knowledge of all the "effects" that were then delighting Italian audiences. He wrote out detailed descriptions of the Palladian stage at Vicenza, and he made drawings for similar perspective-vista and Roman-*skene* theatres. He introduced the proscenium-frame into England, and ushered in the approved "painty" scenery and allegorical-florid costuming. He is an important theatre-artist because he, more than any other, determined the direction of development of the English theatre after the extinguishment of the inn-yard type of playhouse in 1642. He more than any other established the proscenium-frame theatre and the picturized stage as a substitute for the Elizabethan acting-platform. A few features of that platform stage (most notably the apron-doorways) reappeared in the eighteenth century theatres; the rest went down under the popular demand for Italianate "scenery."

Even in Shakespeare's day there had been in London a roofed theatre, the Blackfriars, to which his professional company had resorted at times; but there is little evidence to tell us how far this departed from the Globe-theatre type, how close it may have approached toward masque-stage elaboration. "Regular" plays were often presented for the court, sometimes by the professional men's companies, oftener by the favorite boys' companies. Long since, it had been a custom to train grammar school students into acting troupes; and for two hundred years the choir boys had combined music and drama on occasion —there is a more or less vague relationship to the Boy-Bishop activities.

At any rate, in time the acting companies out of the schools and choirs became favorites. Plays were specially written for them, with special care put on the interpolated songs; and the Children of the Royal Chapel, and Paul's Boys, are mentioned again and again in the records of theatrical events of the period; and no less in the protests of the Puritans. In 1597 the master of the Chapel Children had been officially empowered to "take up" boys to fill his company, and to provide living accommodations for them; and he made the group into a professional troupe that appeared at the Blackfriars' Theatre, apparently with the approval of Elizabeth.

But in general we may think of the boy companies as playing at "special" functions, and particularly for court circles. They link up less with public entertainment than with the privately arranged "social" productions. (The Blackfriars, to be sure, was called a "private" the-

A masque setting by Inigo Jones, for a production in 1635 of *Florimène* in the Italian style [From *The Theatre of Tomorrow*, by Kenneth MacGowan.]

atre too, but more for the sake of evading the law against theatres in town than as a restriction against the general public; it was more "select" than the open-air playhouses, but not truly exclusive like the court ballroom productions.) The phenomenon of The Boys, indeed, belongs to that half of the late Elizabethan and the Jacobean theatre that we have found more interesting than the fast-declining public stage: the masque-making, the command performances in exotic settings, the ornamental theatre.

After the suppression of public plays by Parliament in 1642, there was a scattering of the professional actors (not unaccompanied by some historic plaints), and a long silence on the part of playwrights. Until the Restoration in 1660 there was practically no activity on the London stages—if indeed they were not all pulled down. Sir William Davenant alone had the temerity to force an opening for dramatic productions in the interim, and he succeeded only by pleading that he intended musical and not strictly dramatic offerings—that is, opera. Davenant had been poet, playwright, and theatre manager, and Royalist to boot, and had no reason to expect special favors at the hands of the governing Puritans. His were the first productions, nevertheless, to break the long silence. In 1656 at Rutland House he cautiously staged an "Entertainment, by Declamation and Musick, after the Manner of the Ancients." Immediately after, he put on the boards his *The Siege of Rhodes*—rather a play with music than an opera.

It was the masque tradition that led on to this event, rather than the tradition of the Elizabethan public theatre. And there is a notable separation of all succeeding theatrical activity from what had been known in the Shakespearean playhouse: not only a different type of stage and of scenery but a new sort of literary drama, generously influenced by the dramatists of France. Opera, to be sure, did have a fitful flight in England soon after this; but the next chapter in *that* story, after Italy, belongs rather to France, as we shall see shortly. Davenant's courageous experiments, moreover, have greater importance here as leading on to the next form of non-musical tragedy. For evidence, one may note how Dryden, the only great or near-great tragedy-writer in post-Elizabethan England, wrote of Davenant as the initiator of the Heroic Drama:

> For heroic plays . . . the first light we had on them, on the English theatre, was from the late Sir William Davenant. It being forbidden him in the rebellious times to act tragedies and comedies, because they contained some matter of scandal to those good people, who could more easily dispossess their lawful sovereign, than endure a wanton jest, he was forced to turn his thoughts another way, and to introduce the examples of moral virtue, writ in verse, and performed in recitative music. The original of this music, and of the scenes which adorned his work, he had from the Italian operas; but he heightened his characters, as I may probably imagine, from the example of Corneille and some French poets. . .

And no one should know more than Dryden about this same heroic drama; for no other name, save possibly that of Thomas Otway, who wrote *The Orphan* and *Venice Preserved*, and starved to death, needs to be remembered out of the history of this Restoration play-form.

If we approach the heroic *genre* with an eye to the continuity of the English tradition, we may find reason, by virtue of the seriousness of the times, to say that the irresponsible violence of the late Elizabethan tragedy-writers was here rendered *serious:* that here was a grave extravagance. But it takes no eye at all to see some operatic awkwardness and floridity in Dryden's rhetorical plays; and the influence of French classic drama is obvious in the greater formality in both structure and verse. Extraneously, too, there is plenty in Dryden's writings to prove devotion to the purists across the Channel. Tragedy lost all the Elizabethan rambling freedom; the tendency to mix comedy into tragedy came to an abrupt end; and blank verse went out in favor of the rhyming couplet. If acting had been artificial before, the actor now had just the stuff for rant, and just the characters for high strutting. The persons in the heroic tragedy were largely princes and conquerors and great ladies. The stories were of love and war. The virtues of the drama no longer lay in emotion and sympathy and adventure, but in neatness of versification, didactic purpose, heroic story, and display of rhetoric.

John Dryden's *The Conquest of Granada* is the type example of heroic drama. It is not without a greatness: in outline, in a certain mighty heedlessness of nature, and in gorgeous declamation. It achieved a bigness that swept it to popularity in its time; it might have continued to move audiences even down till today, were not the faults of rhymed speech as a medium for drama, and of operatic conception, bound to vitiate any play for other than artificial eras. In his Epilogue Dryden claimed that he wrote "to please an age more gallant than the last"; excusing earlier poets for being not so good, he saw his own play as reflecting a higher taste:

If love and honor now are higher raised,
'Tis not the poet, but the age is praised.
Wit's now arrived to a more high degree;
Our native language more refined and free.
Our ladies and our men now speak more wit
In conversation, than those poets writ.

If both language and taste were now more "refined" than ever before, morals were not. And the sophisticated audiences that welcomed the heroic tragedy demanded an equally unlifelike sort of comedy, with dry wit taking the place of dry rhetoric; and with that wit spiced out of town tattle and boudoir scandal. Before turning to the sparkling "Restoration comedy," however, one may recall, not without pleasure tinged by malice, that some contemporary playwrights saw through the pretensions of Drydenesque tragedy, and concocted a mock-heroic entitled *The Rehearsal*, which burlesqued all the noble "effects," and quite took the town. It was long attributed to the Duke of Buckingham, but is probably a collaboration from several hands. It well-nigh put an end to heroic tragedy in England. One should add that Dryden later turned to blank-verse drama, and frankly imitated Shakespeare. He also directly adapted some of the latter's plays. Considering how bad most alterations of Shakespeare are, Dryden's, while inferior to the originals, seem occasionally very good. And in *All for Love or The World Well Lost*, a reworking of the story of *Antony and Cleopatra*, he wrote, in more or less Elizabethan manner, a play that some critics still consider very great.

In approaching Restoration comedy, one does better to check one's moral sensibility, one's conscience, one's "taste," at the door. These brilliant plays are shocking, contrary to all later conceptions of what is "in good taste"—quite indefensibly unmoral in outlook and licentious in expression. If the playgoer cannot achieve a detached point-of-view, he had better stay away. And yet what brilliancy, what wit, what sustained style!

Half a century ago Brander Matthews wrote that "Congreve and Wycherley, Farquhar and Vanbrugh helped themselves to Molière's framework only to hang it about with dirty linen." And with hardly more mention than that, he dismissed the Restoration playwrights out of his history of drama. The world has so far "broadened," since then, that today Congreve's plays are staged, new editions appear, the Restoration dramatists are touted as veritable masters of comedy-writing. In this age of greater intellecual emancipation, of extended tolerance—and of cynicism—Congreve and Wycherley have come back into their own. The point is, perhaps, that they wrote for a very small "advanced" audience in their own time; and today a similar audience has come into existence. Those who belong to it will explain that it is composed of the only truly "civilized" spectators: the open-minded, the men of the world, the intellectually emancipated. The others will say that it is an over-sophisticated audience, to whom only the affected and the over-spiced can give delight. And, indeed, here is typically the drama for the few: graceful, witty, with extraordinary style and finish; but totally unnatural, losing its lustre the moment one tests it by the touchstone of human feeling.

The audience for which the Restoration comedy was written was the elegant and limited court "society." There were no theatre activities outside London—the Puritans could still control everything except the King's own circle—and only two playhouses in London. There the fops and beaux were wont to gather for entertainment, with their equally light-thinking and easy-living court-ladies and fashionable courtesans. There were scarcely any theatre-goers outside this circle of gallants and town wits and court hangers-on. For a debauched society, headed by a debauched king, the playwrights shaped their entertainments. Nothing could then be in worse taste than a show of human feeling, a suggestion of moral concern, an honest heartiness. Everything must have a hard surface glitter, the artifice of wit alone could continuously please, brilliancy and style and grace were the only virtues worth achieving.

There were more or less transitional figures, carrying on from Jonsonian comedy, and not wholly committed to the artificiality of the time of Charles II. Dryden wrote some in-between plays, and George Etherege harked back somewhat to Jonson and Fletcher; still his three comedies, *The Comical Revenge, or Love in a Tub*, and *She Would if She Could*, and *The Man of Mode, or Sir John Fopling*, sufficiently indicate in their titles the trend of playwriting. It was rather William Wycherley who established the smart dialogue and sparkling style for the period to follow: in *The Country Wife* and *The Plain Dealer*, coarse plays both but greatly amusing. After him came the truly typical group of dramatists, composed of William Congreve, Sir John Vanbrugh, and George Farquhar.

Of these, Congreve proved himself the possessor of the most sustained style, the readiest flow of wit. And in *The Way of the World* and *Love for Love* he wrote the most famous of English artificial comedies. In his affected pose of not caring about his plays, he is, again, the soul of his age. If morals are mentioned in his plays it is only because by their inversion a certain effect is gained; if life is reflected, it is only the life of the trivial-minded and licentious court society. No human being stalks through the artificial plots. And yet here are verbal repartee and witty dialogue unmatched. *Love for Love* comes nearer to being pure comedy; some of its characters are Scandal, Tattle, Foresight, Trapland, Mrs. Frail, and Miss Prue. But if the reader—our players no longer have the right artificiality to put these brittle pieces on the stage—if the reader will spend two hours over *The Way of the World*, he will have the genre at its best, and with almost a seriousness beyond the wit, and such spirited characterization as never else happened within the limits of pure artifice. Indeed, here Congreve stripped the Restoration comedy of half the grossness of its other practitioners; and he sharpened the sword-play of wit till the flash of it well-nigh blinds us to all other considerations. Two lines of the character Witwoud touch to the heart of the matter: "A wit shou'd no more be sincere, than a woman constant; one argues a decay

Nell Gwyn, a portrait probably by Sir Peter Lely. Her rise as actress and courtesan provided material for several plays, most notably *Sweet Nell of Old Drury*, by Paul Kester. From orange-seller in the theatre to girl actress, then leading lady at London's most important playhouse, Sweet Nell capped a sensational career by becoming a mistress of King Charles II. [From the painting in the National Portrait Gallery, London, by courtesy of the Bettmann Archive.]

of parts, as t'other of beauty." There one has a summary, almost: as regards truth, style, sincerity, epigrammatic dexterity, artifice, inversion, cynicism, skill.

The company that acted Congreve's comedies included, according to Colley Cibber, "thirteen actors standing all in equal light of excellence"; and though we moderns suspect that often an actor high-praised in his day would ill please us now, we may visualize Betterton's company as perfectly formed to show out the Congreve rapier-thrust of wit and parade of brilliancy. Perhaps the ladies of the stage—this is the first time we meet them in the story of the English theatre—were even better fitted than the men to give authentic ease and flippancy to the parts: they lived like the heroines and courtesans the comedies portrayed. Most famous for her acting was Mrs. Bracegirdle; though Nell Gwyn's name is writ the larger in history, partly for her adorable pertness, partly because the King took her under his protection, so that theatrical blood crossed with Royal.

The "King's Servants," one of the two companies in London just after the accession of Charles II, had been made privileged members of the Royal household, with the title "Gentlemen of the Chamber"; while the other troupe was known as "The Duke of York's Company" —ample indication of standing quite different from that suffered by the "rogues and vagabonds" of other days. The stage at this time was the Italian proscenium-frame affair and the masque-settings had found their way into the regular playhouses for good. Stage costuming was a strange mixture of conventions. Some characters must have romantic and plushy "historical" costumes, while in the same play others might appear in any stylish robes of the day or recent fashionable French dresses. This mixing of conventions and styles had been a curiosity of Elizabethan times, and is to last for almost a century yet.

In 1682, the two companies were merged, assuming the title "King's Company," and Drury Lane Theatre became its first home. In the engraving of the Duke's Theatre (or Dorset Garden Theatre) stage, the reader should not be misled into thinking this is a modern "box-set" scene. Back-cloth and flats (of which more later) were designed to give this effect when viewed from one point in the house, the Royal box, but never achieved the ideal from any other viewpoint. The fore-stage and boxes, too, are here cut off.

The drawing by Sir Christopher Wren, generally supposed to be a design for Drury Lane Theatre, sufficiently indicates how London at this time fell into line with continental practice in theatre design. Here are the raked stage, designed for perspective scenery, and the horse-shoe of hen-coop boxes, and the Renaissance pilasters and moldings; with only the apron before the curtain and the doors under the

Interior of the Duke's Theatre in Lincoln's Inn Fields, as shown in a print of 1809 based on an engraving of 1673—there captioned "The stage of the above theatre and its very elegant frontispiece"—indicating the appreciation in England of the Italian prosceniums then just introduced into the "regular" theatres. A scene in Elkana Settle's *The Empress of Morocco*.

314

stage boxes as heritage from the Elizabethan acting-platform. Indeed, in more ways than one the British stage had become internationalized. If the heroic tragedies had owed both to Italian opera and to the French school of Corneille, no less had Restoration comedy been influenced by Molière. And it had been the French example that led to the banishment of boys from the stage, and the appearance of actresses.

And oh, yes! there was a lady playwright, too—an authoress who is vividly, almost epochally, remembered. Mrs. Aphra Behn was one of the many near-great dramatists who made Restoration audiences

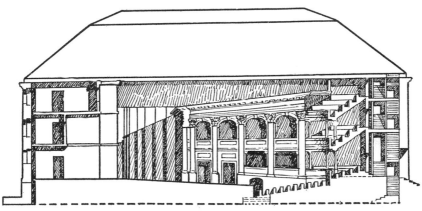

A theatre design by Christopher Wren, probably for the 1674 Drury Lane Theatre. Note the raked stage, wings, stage portals, the many boxes and the small pit with benches. [Redrawn after the original sketch now in the Library of All Souls College, Oxford.]

laugh; and this first woman among English drama-writers yielded nothing to the men in her racy treatment of scandalous themes. Her immodesties seem, in the light of today, no less than stupendous. (They gained for her, incidentally, the honor of burial with England's immortals in Westminster Abbey.)

But this sort of vicious pandering to the taste of King and nobles brought a reaction that completes the circle to the point at which the chapter started. In 1698 Jeremy Collier issued his *Short View of the Immorality and Profaneness of the English Stage*. This time it was no bigoted zealot speaking, no blindly-raging extremist. A man well-informed, somewhat humorous, even-tempered, simply showed up what he knew to be true about the depravity of the stage in his time. And the effect was immediate and far-reaching. Serious indecency was almost cut off; or at least the theatres developed no new artificial dramatists after Congreve, Farquhar, and Vanbrugh. The literary value of drama also declined; one can hardly count Colley Cibber important as a playwright, though he was an outstanding figure as actor-writer-manager—"an industrious poet and an honest man," someone has called him, in addition. Richard Steele wrote some plays that ushered in the sentimental note, the one note most foreign of all to the true Restoration writers; and Joseph Addison wrote a correct tragedy entitled *Cato* that enjoyed a vogue. But these pieces interest us today chiefly as indicating the extraordinary reaction to Restoration freedom. Collier was already triumphant within the first quarter of the eighteenth century. Dryden even publicly apologized for having dirtied his hands with indecent comedies.

Two formal stages of the Rederijker societies, at Ghent and Antwerp, in the mid-sixteenth century. [From *The English Drama in the Age of Shakespeare*, by Wilhelm Creizenach.]

TO FRANCE, and the last of the Renaissance stages, in a moment. First, we must pause to note that, in a brief story like this, the theatres of the minor countries suffer from a perhaps undeserved neglect. There is Denmark, where the theatre suddenly appeared at this very time, under the direction of that Holberg who is accounted one of the leading two writers of all Europe in his generation. His comedies are played to this day, not only in Scandinavia but in Germany and occasionally in even more distant lands. And then there is Holland, which had had a vigorous theatre in the days of Christian religious drama, and which felt the breath of Renaissance freedom and experiment as early as England. For the world historian, the Dutch theatre is particularly interesting by reason of some strangely Italian stages that appeared in the fifteen-hundreds and may have influenced the English; and for a curiously mixed playhouse that shows more kinds of influence, classic, mediæval, and local, than any other ever recorded. On this page and the page previous I reproduce illustrations which tell the story and will allow us to hasten across to France and the main show.

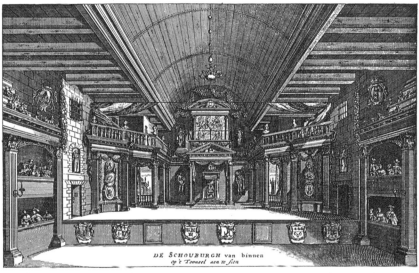

The strange stage of the Amsterdam *Schouburgh* in 1638, wherein one may see elements reminiscent of the medieval simultaneous stages, the Elizabethan platform with balcony, and the Italian vista stage. Note the curtain, and the gallery benches above the boxes. The auditorium was of the ballroom type, with flat floor and a double tier of boxes all round. [From a contemporary engraving by Nicolaes van Kampen, as reproduced in *Das Bühnenbild*, by Carl Niessen.]

CHAPTER
14

❦❦❦❦❦❦❦❦❦❦❦❦❦❦❦❦❦❦❦❦❦❦❦❦❦❦❦❦❦❦❦❦❦❦❦❦❦❦

Kings, Courtesans, and Dramatists of France

❦❦❦❦❦❦❦❦❦❦❦❦❦❦❦❦❦❦❦❦❦❦❦❦❦❦❦❦❦❦❦❦❦❦❦❦❦❦

PICTURE, to yourself, if you please, the Court of Louis XIV: the pageant of magnificence: the great King himself, Louis the Grand, The *Roi-soleil*—"*l'Etat, c'est moi*"; the vast palaces and gardens at Versailles and St. Cloud, the Louvre in Paris; the retinue of gentlemen-in-waiting and fine ladies, the pretty and accomplished courtesans, the dandies; the laces and frills, the love nests, the satin and silk clothes—like a perpetual masquerade; the fêtes, the fireworks, the ballets, the ceremonies; the circles of literary men and artists, aspiring to be courtiers too, just as the courtiers must dabble in the arts to be fashionable. Bring to focus the picture of this gay and elegant society, consistently artificial, overdecorated—overstuffed, the upholsterers might say—and you will have the key to the changes that came into the theatre in the seventeenth century. For courtliness is to be a characteristic of the stage art for two full centuries.

Soon after 1600 Paris becomes the centre and all of French life: France is thereafter to be milked to support this capital city. And the Court is to rule brilliantly all activities in Paris. The form of the playhouse and the methods of stage setting are to be determined by the needs and tastes of the royal family and favorites; even playwriting is to be controlled. The surface aspects of a fastidious and frivolous courtliness are to be imposed on the theatre, so effectively that they will hardly be questioned until well into the nineteenth century—and so glamorously that even in the early twentieth century we shall find

318

The *parade* or showing of the actors, before the theatre at the *Foire Saint-Laurent* in Paris, about 1750. The equivalent of the "teaser" or "come-on" (in American theatre slang), the *parades* put on by touring companies playing the fairs in France exploited natural freaks, remnant scenes from the expiring Commedia dell'Arte, *tableaux vivants*, or, as here, simply well-made ladies, as box-office bait. [Engraving from *La Foire Saint-Laurent*, by Arthur Heulhard, 1878.]

them hovering over the playhouse and hindering the attempt to create an art appropriate to the new machine-age.

At the beginning of the seventeenth century, France emerged from a period of chaos, wherein there had been little leisure for serious attention to the arts, no centralization of social or cultural life, not even an unchallenged political capital. Theatrical conditions were almost as crude and unformed as in the neighboring Germany; whereas the golden age of the Renaissaince had already come and almost gone in Italy, Spain, and England. France had lagged, knew only a rude native stage, or an occasional imported troupe from one of these more favored countries. Yet within sixty years France is to see its most glorious theatrical achievements, its most magnificent plays; is to become the most brilliant centre of the stage arts in all of Europe, is to be recognized as arbiter in matters dramatic over all the Western world. The glory of this accomplishment is to prove so dazzling, indeed, that there is nothing but imitation of it till the end of the eighteenth century; and then when Democracy brings a real challenge, the little democratic artists will be so under the spell that unconsciously they will imitate and perpetuate the very qualities imposed on the theatre by the kings—and, only too often, by the kings' courtesans. Indeed the whole bourgeois conception of art, up to a time perilously close to the present day and hour, has embraced something romantically different from ordinary life, romantically royal, decorated, befrilled, and plushy. Instead of art as an intensification of life, Democracy visioned it as an escape back into the soft days, as the privilege of a few, as a basking in the effulgence of an orientally wasteful diversion. The theatre most of all has suffered from the aristocratic incubus; and it is therefore somewhat important to know from the start this "courtliness" for the thing it is.

We may remember, if we wish, that it was the opulent Italian courts that brought in the ballroom theatre and pictorial settings, and that it was under their protection that the neo-classic drama developed, and that opera was invented. France picked up all these impulses, and the one great centralized Parisian Court gave new authority to classicism, stamped with approval the Italian playhouse and lavish Italian stage decoration, and imposed operatic elements on theatre art for, apparently, all time.

The legitimate theatre was affected by the French Court activity in two ways: The whole idea of a ruling class with powers and laws divinely guided was imposed on playwriting. And the outward glow of court life, including not a little of the element of tinsel-and-fine-clothes demanded by the courtesans, was thrown over the productions on the stage.

Two seventeenth-century paintings of outdoor platform stages. Above, *Charlatan sur une Place de Paris*, by Pierre Wouwermans. Below, a painting of the stage of Orvietan, by Gerrit-Adriaenaz Berckeyden.

In the matter of playwriting, the Italian rules were diligently codified and set forth as an inalterable basis for future composition of drama. The term "classic" was rigidly defined; thenceforward there was separation between the orthodox practitioners, within the rules, and reckless experimentors who would bring playwriting closer to life, or perhaps only let playwriting and life develop hand in hand. Academies were created whose function it was to endorse and honor those authors who conformed, and to resist all apostates; and special theatres were subventioned, made the official homes of classic drama, and often given monopolies on legitimate tragedy-and-comedy production.

This codifying of rules and granting of privileges had great effect on playwriting: for even while the dramatist was stirred by the brilliancy and the patronage of the courts to give his best substance, he found himself hampered by the arbitrary "laws" of composition. He generally, moreover, fancied the idea of being part of the aristocracy of the intellect, and thus akin to the aristocrats of the blood. Of course the one greatest genius of the period broke all the laws, was refused admittance to the Academy, and challenged the privileged acting company—but found a king who was discerning enough and broad enough to stand against his own court-made distinctions. Still, in general, the whole period is marked by the characteristic knuckling to authority; there is deference to rules, an artificial formality and reserve in playwriting, a lack of depth of feeling. Etiquette is more important than creation. The dramatist worked within the limits of an artificial decorum, a hollow elegance, in serious mood, or else descended to fashioning pretty trifles for the amusement of the court at garden parties, balls, and royal command performances, in the spirit of masquerade and pageantry.

The courtesan element crept more insidiously into the physical playhouse. An exuberance and delicacy of decoration, more fit to wrap a king's mistress in than for the fitting up of a theatre, came to be the accepted thing in playhouse ornamentation (though it only reached its apotheosis two hundred years later in the Paris Opera House and a hundred tinselly imitations); the auditorium became practically tier on tier of private boxes; and stage decoration became soft and luxurious. A lot of other playthings were added—as we shall see in another chapter. With all these concrete additions there came the more subtle one, the casting of a courtly "glow" over stage life. The gorgeous dressing extends to the performers, and elegant manners, and courtly vivaciousness. There is constant interchange between the few regular theatres and the ballroom stages, until finally the old platform stage is lost in the court theatre building, and production has become a privileged function by royal grace. Here the ancient Dionysian joy of the theatre gets mixed with some of the surface glamour and the petty intrigues of the less-royal hangers-on at court. But at any rate the brilliancy of the great kings is on the theatre.

In 1600 there is only one theatre in Paris: a rather rude affair known as the *Hôtel de Bourgogne*, modelled in part after the old outdoor Miracle stages, and retaining their arrangement of "station" settings. There is no permanent troupe of actors in the city. Playwriting activity is practically non-existent, though there is a body of old religious plays and farces, and a few literary men have written tragedies in imitation of the neo-classic Italians. The theatre itself exists only in the visits of strolling comedian troupes, particularly at the seasons of the fairs—though a quack may bring a company with him at other times of year, to act on his outdoor platforms. In England this is the very heart of the glorious Elizabethan flowering, when Shakespeare's *Romeo and Juliet* and *As You Like It* have been enlivening the London stage, and just when the poet is turning to *Hamlet* or *Othello* or *King Lear*. In Spain Lope de Vega is at the height of his brilliant power. The crest of the wave of creative activity that followed on the Renaissance is past in Italy; and indeed it is the infrequent visits of Italian acting companies that occasion the few bright entries in the dull theatrical annals of the times. Even on the *Hôtel de Bourgogne* stage as recently as 1599 a visiting Italian company has so shown up the crudeness of a native competing troupe that Paris is left again without any offerings. And as late as 1622 there will come a season when the city is without theatrical entertainment.

In the years between 1600 and 1622 there are to be frequent starts toward permanently settled theatrical activity, as we shall see. But the more interesting productions for long will be those of the strolling players. We may picture them setting up their temporary curtained stages in the grounds allotted to the *Foire St Laurent* and the *Foire St Germain*. These fairs are gala occasions, and even kings are known to frequent the gambling booths, the sales pavilions, the stage productions, and the strange side-shows. Sometimes an acting troupe has come here independently, bringing old farces or new, harlequinades or jugglery and tumbling. More likely the actors are part of the retinue of one of the great quacks of the period (who are much more important personages than any licensed doctors), and they give their plays as an adjunct to medicine-selling. Perhaps their exhibition is only of a vaudeville sort, with the emphasis on clowning, conjuring, and the showing of freaks; but again a complete farce is presented. Even so important a company as *I Gelosi* is known to have been brought into France by a quack.

The prints of the period show oftener than not the medicine-sellers and their bottles on the stage, along with the actors: as in this illustration of the platform of Tabarin in the *Place Dauphiné*. An audience of the time, the group of buyers, the great quack Mondor, Tabarin himself, and other performers and musicians, all these are shown, as well as the plain platform with a curtain back-drop. The more pretentious booth theatre of the Italian farceur-quack Orvietan is shown

Mondor and Tabarin on their stage in the Place Dauphiné, Paris, as etched by Abraham Bosse. [From *Les Rues du Vieux Paris*, by Victor Fournel.]

among nearby illustrations, along with a later street stage. His stand often was a feature at the Pont Neuf. The popular vogue of the outdoor productions is to persist long after the "serious" drama has become the plaything of courts, and after indoor stages in the Italian style have become the proper frame for both tragedy and comedy.

Even in 1600 the *Hôtel de Bourgogne* was a privileged theatre, though it had no actors and was a mere way-station for this and that travelling troupe. As early as 1402 Charles VI had granted the Brothers of the Passion permission to act holy Mystery Plays in Paris, and the seasonal performances had been highly esteemed for years. But when the Church, alarmed by the freedoms that had been brought into "religious" play production, at first withdrew approval, then actively fought against further performances, the privilege was modified. In 1541 the actors of the Brotherhood were officially termed "ignorant workmen," and it was charged that "in order to lengthen *The Acts of the Apostles* they have added several apocryphal things, and at the beginning and end of it have introduced loose farces and pantomimes, and have extended their play to the length of six or seven months, which led and leads to neglect of divine service, indifference in alms-giving and charity, adultery and incessant fornication, scandals, mockery and scorn." Moreover it was shown that during the plays "all preaching stopped," and even members of the clergy hurried through their offices to get to the performances. By 1548 the agitation against the Brotherhood had been so strong that the members were thenceforward restrained from presenting Mystery Plays, though their privilege to present profane drama, "decent and lawful," was continued and their monopoly on production in Paris and its suburbs officially endorsed. Protests continued, and in 1588 the King had been petitioned to do away with "a cesspool and House of Satan, named the *Hôtel de Bourgogne.*"

Now, however, in 1600, the Brothers of the Passion have given up acting—after all, the members are artisans and tradesmen, the theatre is becoming professionalized, and audiences are demanding something up to the standard set by the Spanish and Italian companies. But no one is allowed to present plays in Paris except under the *name* of the Brotherhood and to its profit. They determine to work their royal privilege for all it is worth, closing any performances outside their own house, and collecting tribute from every troupe that operates in it (though they can't put an end to the special dispensations to provincial companies to act in Paris at the fairs; and the court occasionally has its own command performances, by any company it likes). But the *Hôtel de Bourgogne* is the first "regular" theatre in Paris; and within a few years we find it let out to this and that courageous provincial company, to the Italians (including *I Gelosi* and the Andreinis); and finally, about 1610, to the first company that could claim anything like permanence in Paris. This troupe, headed by Valleran Lecomte, stayed in the house a dozen years, was known as "The King's Players," made a real place for itself in the community, and helped to develop a true dramatic literature. And after the cupidity of the Brotherhood drove the actors out of the theatre again, resulting in a playless season, and after a brief tenancy by a second company, known as the Prince of Orange's Players, Lecomte and his King's Players returned and settled down to a half-century occupancy.

In 1629 Paris is ready for a second, competing company; the Prince of Orange's Players establish themselves as permanent rivals to the royal troupe; and soon they open the second famous Parisian theatre, the Marais. And more notable, the rival group has turned up a new dramatic author, Pierre Corneille, whose first play, *Mélite*, is acted in 1629.

Playwriting has been almost as chaotic as stage conditions. Since the tradition of the old amateur farce-writing ran out in the preceding century, everybody has been influenced by the Italian comedies. There was, of course, no native French tradition in tragedy, and it is the Italian neo-classic form that has been reflowering in France. Shortly after 1550 the dramatist Stephen Jodelle, a disciple of Ronsard

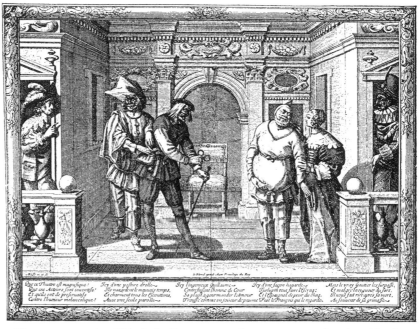

The stage at the *Hôtel de Bourgogne*, from an engraving by Abraham Bosse. The central figures in the scene are Turlupin, Gros-Guillaume, and Gautier-Garguille.

in the famous literary group called the "Pleiad," composed *Cléopatre Captive*, a Senecan tragedy, very rhetorical and trailing such classical remnants as ghost and chorus. Jodelle is called "the Father of French tragedy"; and he not only established the Italian neo-classic form as model, but introduced (though he did not use exclusively) the Alexandrine verse-measure, the six-foot line rhymed in couplets, which is to be the characteristic French dramatic medium for centuries thereafter. Among many imitators only one, Robert Garnier, rose to eminence: he wrote tragedies that are the least rhetorical and stilted up to the time of Corneille's appearance.

As in Italy, the group of early literary dramatists in France had only contempt for the current popular theatre, and there was little connection between the stage and tragedy-writing for a considerable period. The men-of-letters clung to the chorus, the rhetorical account of action instead of the thing itself, and similarly inappropriate and deadening dramatic heritages. They acted their own plays, in amateur groups. They stayed wholly aloof from the dramatic activities of the fairs and market-places.

But it was inevitable that the currents should flow together in time. Perhaps the pastoral and the romance, bearing in from Spain and Italy, brought a softening influence on the rigid tragedy. At any rate tragedies begin to appear in not unliterary form on the popular stage; and a new type that is neither comic nor tragic, strictly speaking, and that pleases a wide public with romantic-literary materials. There has had to be no radical change in comedy to reconcile it with slowly improving public taste; for there was no great gap between popular French farce and the Terentian comedy that was brought out of Italy by the literary comedy-writers. Indeed the popular stage long since had absorbed from visiting *Commedia dell'Arte* companies the characters and the masks of the *Dottore, Pantalone, Arlecchino* and the others; while distinguished authors were putting these very characters, and many "stock" situations into their comedy-texts. A good deal of the recorded comedy-writing, indeed, was merely a transcription of the late Italian Renaissance product, none of it very important to begin with.

The writer who came to Paris with the troupe that entered the *Hôtel de Bourgogne* in 1610, as The King's Players, was Alexandre Hardy, who "thanked Heaven that he knew the precepts of his art while preferring to follow the demands of his trade." No other notation is necessary to indicate his perfect fitness to bring together the literary and popular currents. He combined something of solid structure and poetic language out of the aloof literary product with the ease of story-telling out of chronicle-play and romance (particularly Spanish); and he knew how to point up a situation with speeches that would register tellingly in the delivery. It is said that he invented tragi-comedy. All the way along he seems to have been the joiner-together and the compromiser so needed at just this moment. His poetry as such—he finally adopted the Alexandrine verse—leaves something to be desired. Perhaps his greatest service was as model: for the actors he was a guide toward the literary (there were to be an exceptional number of actor-playwrights), and doubtless the poets let down the bars a little to join him as purveyor of plays to the royal troupe or their rivals at the Marais Theatre.

Those poets did not, however, stray outside the more sanctified rules of the drama as understood from the ancients. Nor did they give up declamation in favor of Hardy's free-flowing dramatic action. What they did was to accept the conventions of the current stage, drop out such obviously anachronistic elements as the chorus, and train the classic form a *little* closer to human motive and individual character. But still it was a stiff, artificial thing that emerged, and only redeemed—according to modern notions—by the nobility of the poetic investiture. The court element is strong upon it.

The physical stage to which the nobler poets came down, so to speak, was crude enough. We do not know exactly what were the architectural antecedents of the *Hôtel de Bourgogne*. But the other theatres in Paris were converted tennis-courts. When it seemed that the time had come to take the drama indoors, the producers had sought nothing else than a convenient "place for seeing," and the covered courts, with balconies and benches for spectators, were exactly that. The Prince of Orange's Players occupied three tennis-courts in succession, between the opening of *Mélite* in 1629 and 1634; the last being the Marais Tennis-Court that gave the troupe its name thenceforward. We may picture the auditorium as long, narrow, and almost bare, with balconies along the side walls, the benches placed on the main floor, facing a platform stage at the end. The sketch opposite indicates the somewhat cramped intimacy and the arrangement of the place. The *Hôtel de Bourgogne* was similarly long and narrow but the only portion about which there is undisputed evidence is the stage. This was modelled on the Mysery or Miracle platforms, whereon a neutral acting space was bordered at back and sides by representations or suggestions of the several localities in which the action was supposed to pass. A whole book of sketches for these composite settings has been preserved. It shows exactly how the stage "decorator" at the *Hôtel de Bourgogne* set about to provide "simultaneous settings" for each new play of Hardy or his fellow-dramatists —even up to Corneille.

At the Marais Theatre on an afternoon late in November 1636, Corneille's *Le Cid* was acted for the first time. The date is underlined in all histories, for the great era of French tragic drama is supposed to have been ushered in that day. Corneille's comedies had been popular, but no tragedy had yet come from his hand. If we had been present at this most noted of Paris premières, we would have seen something like this:

Within the dim candle-lit auditorium is an audience of the most mixed sort. Courtiers and dandies fill the balcony boxes, and on this special occasion have the best benches on the main floor; and close by them are litterateurs, officers, travellers, tradesmen, even down to the court pages, idlers, and adventurers—an element so unruly that

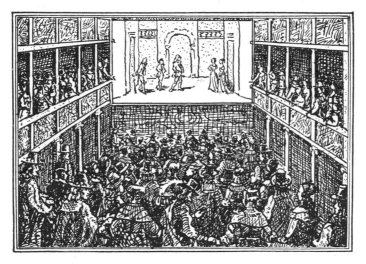

A tennis-court theatre, showing the simple "shelf for acting," in this case without the simultaneous scene. [Drawing by Warren D. Cheney after a contemporary sketch by F. Chauveau.]

A simultaneous setting at the *Hôtel de Bourgogne*, showing how the influence of the religious plays persisted on the secular stage. [Redrawn from the design by the stage artist Mahelot, preserved in a book of drawings in the *Bibliothèque Nationale*, Paris.]

the actors will be lucky to get through without disturbance or battle. This audience has been admitted by a brawny and heavily armed doorman, whose duty it is to exclude by violence all who refuse to buy tickets—all, that is, except the nobles, against whom a mere theatre proprietor or ticket-taker must not stand out. (Had not Battistino, the actor-proprietor who undertook to dispute with a courtier who refused to pay—had he not been openly murdered, and nothing ever done about it?) The stage is curtainless; on it are spread out the several "mansions" or "stations" indicating the locale of the action, each touching upon that central space where the actors will stand. Here are indicated a king's council-room, a woman's apartment, etc. There are practically no properties.

When the auditorium candles have been snuffed,[1] two actresses appear, richly apparelled. They break immediately into the verse-dialogue, strongly, sonorously; there is no pretense of nature here. Indeed the Confidante's second speech is thirty-six lines in length. But now the women have gone, the men enter—this one will be Mondory, chief of the troupe. These actors are violent fellows. Mondory's plan of attack is to startle the audience with a sudden explosion, pause, then wear it down by a series of lesser detonations. This is acting and no mistake. Of course, there have to be quieter passages. But the French verse runs swiftly, fluently. And the poet continually comes back to the rhetorical fireworks that Mondory so relishes.

The fable is a borrowed one, taken quite directly from a Spanish play of almost the same name. It revolves about the old favorite theme of the point of honor. Don Rodrigue, to avenge an insult to his own father, kills the father of Chimène, whom he loves. How shall the two lovers be brought together despite this barrier? We see Don Rodrigue torn between duty and love. Then we see Chimène fighting against her love, for a decent regard to convention, while her hero goes off to wondrous deeds in the wars. Well, we know how it will turn out; but what chance for high acting!

And indeed this performance takes the house. For days and weeks *Le Cid* is on every tongue. All Paris is buzzing with the sensation

---

[1] It may be that they were not snuffed. Some authorities believe that auditoriums remained fully lighted during the centuries of staging in candle-lit theatres, and possibly during most of the era of lighting by gas. In other words, carefully darkened audience-chambers arrived only with the realistic nineteenth-century drama and the marvels of electric lighting. Although candles were standard from the time of the Italian Renaissance, lamps, torches, and even "floating wicks" are known to have been utilized. Gas lighting of theatres was introduced in the opening years of the nineteenth century; electric lighting from about 1880 on.

of a new type of play, by the young *avocat* of Rouen, Pierre Corneille. The older established playwrights are furious. A great controversy is waged. Cardinal Richelieu throws the weight of his authority against the youthful dramatist—even orders the Academicians to turn thumbs down: it seems the three unities have not been observed. But the public and the Court take Corneille's side. The new French dramaturgy is established.

What is it that Corneille has brought to the French stage which has not existed before? Out of Spain he has caught a new hint of heroic dramatic situation, of largeness, of nobility. He has brought this under control, under French discipline. Instead of Spanish succes-

Pierre Corneille. [From an old print.]

sion of incident he has put a stirring human story into the heroic framework. It isn't human in the present-day personal sense, nor stirring except in a detached grandiose way, and no near neighbor to probability; but infinitely closer to the audience than the academic exercises of the earlier French classicists had been. And if rhetoric still remains, at least the verse—the rhymed Alexandrines, of course—is swift-flowing and at times majestic. It is the perfect verse-medium for the tirade-loving actors, for the formality-loving courtly audience. And the stripping of the dramatic story to one main conflict, without ramifications or sub-plots, to a climactic simplicity, sets up a model for future French tragedy.

Corneille goes on to other successes: *Cinna, Horace, Polyeucte.* He squirms a little under the necessity of confining his art within the limitations of the three unities and other Aristotelean "laws"; but perhaps he sees that what he brings by way of heroic framework and grandeur and concentration, when married to the older classicism, may result in a play-form for all French stages—perhaps for all tragedy-writing everywhere, for all time. He accepts the rules. Perhaps the discipline of bringing his action into one day and one place made him a greater dramatist; or perhaps he would have written more magnificent plays if left unhampered No one will ever know. But Corneille became the very type dramatist for that Academy which had tried at first to exclude him. Through him the French became the guardians and exponents of the Greek tradition.

What it was that French classicism thenceforward demanded of every "legitimate" dramatist in Europe may be summed up in a few brief rules: the unities of time, place and action must be observed; every play must be in five acts; every play must be in verse; all violent action must be accomplished offstage, must be merely recounted to the characters and the audience; no comic relief or sub-plot could be included; the themes must be lofty, and the characters noble.

Corneille fashioned dramas after this code; and his characters are indeed so lofty, and the verse so fine, that one goes to the *Comédie Française* to this day to enjoy the glitter and parade of them. It is only when one compares them with Shakespeare's more human creations that one discovers a well-nigh intolerable formality and bareness. For this French classic art is for a time and a place and an intellectual mood. It is a very great art within narrow limits, a dry art, an art that demands detachment from sentiment and personal emotion. Its excellencies are formal, to be intellectually relished and appreciated.

After Corneille came Racine, who made passion less intellectual, but further simplified and concentrated the play-form, accepted all the rules—and established indisputably the type-tragedy that Corneille

Jean Racine, greatest French poet-dramatist, who, with Pierre Corneille, established French classic tragedy as the supreme serious drama of Europe in the seventeenth century. His influence waned in the eighteenth century, but his *Phédre* and other tragedies survive as staples of the European repertory theatres today.

had somewhat fumblingly initiated. As a writer Racine was a meticulous craftsman; and he understood perfectly the shaping of action and dialogue to acting—to declamatory delivery. In the field of an art somewhat cold, never unbending, flawlessly literary, decorous, he still somehow managed to build dramas with tremendous climaxes, with superbly moving situations. *Phèdre* is the greatest "acting part" in the French language: that is, it gives the actor richest opportunity for scoring by a display of rhetorical passion.

With a few characters, and a plot simple but perfectly proportioned —nearly always chosen from orthodox Greek or Roman sources— Racine built majestically and surely. In one sense, his was a psychological method: he was more interested in showing forth what his characters suffered than what they did; but it was oceans apart from what the modern world understands by the term "psychologic drama."

It is unfortunate that the English language is incapable of translations preserving the values of the French verse; we are thereby incapacitated from judging fairly, will always feel a sense of fragmentary grandeur. In the original, one of Phèdre's many soliloquies runs thus:

> O toi, qui vois la honte où je suis descendue,
> Implacable Vénus, suis-je assez confondue?
> Tu ne saurois plus loin pousser ta cruauté.
> Ton triomphe est parfait; tous tes traits ont porté.
> Cruelle, si tu veux une gloire nouvelle,
> Attaque un ennemi qui te soit plus rebelle.
> Hippolyte te fuit; et bravant ton courrous,
> Jamais à tes autels n'a fléchi les genoux.
> Ton nom semble offenser ses superbes oreilles.
> Déesse, venge-toi: nos causes sont pareilles.
> Qu'il aime. . .

But in the English this proportioned verse, so perfectly fitted to the French recitative-acting, so swift-flowing, becomes, even at the hands of a generally satisfactory translator:

> PHAEDRA (*alone*)
> Venus implacable, who seest me shamed
> And sore confounded, have I not enough
> Been humbled? How can cruelty be stretch'd
> Farther? Thy shafts have all gone home, and thou
> Hast triumph'd. Would'st thou win a new renown?
> Attack an enemy more contumacious:
> Hippolytus neglects thee, braves thy wrath,
> Nor ever at thine altars bow'd the knee.

Thy name offends his proud, disdainful ears.
Our interests are alike: avenge thyself,
Force him to love. . .

Thus we are always at one remove from the drama that Racine wrote. We know the dignity and majesty of theme and story; but only imperfectly the rightness of the word-vehicle. Perhaps some day the miracle of an adequate transcription into English will come, not with the same values—of rhymed couplets—but with others, compensating by stirring poetry. Gilbert Murray has accomplished as much in his transcription from the Greek of the very play upon which Racine modelled *Phèdre*, the *Hippolytus* of Euripides.

Racine based others of his famous tragedies on the works of Euripides or the earlier Greeks, most notably *Iphigénie*, *La Thébaïde* and *Andromaque*; but at times he ranged further afield, to the Bible for the materials of *Esther* and *Athalie*, and to almost contemporary history for *Bajazet*; though he never strayed beyond themes that were great and noble and characters of a sufficient stature.

The dramas of Racine and Corneille are, of course, typically of the theatre, shaped for acting; but of a particular and rather limited theatre, that of a select and educated audience to whom the literary polish and an actor's virtuoso delivery weigh heavily. They belong

The ballroom stage in the palace of Cardinal Richelieu, with a setting for his play *Miramé*. [From a print reproduced in *l'Ancienne France: Le Théâtre et la Musique*.]

to the simple platform-for-acting theatre, and not to the lavishly pictorial stage that was even at this time being introduced. Richelieu already had his ballroom theatre by 1641, with a stage proscenium-framed, as here shown, and with all the improvements that could be imported from Italy by way of machinery and scenery—and by the way, the great Cardinal more than any other one man established French dramatic art firmly, by his encouragement and patronage, though he failed to touch greatness in his own efforts at playwriting. The King, too, had a theatre fitted up at the *Petit-Bourbon* palace, of the same Italian sort.

At a later time Racine's *Alexander the Great* was acted by rival companies on the two types of stage, that of the *Hôtel de Bourgogne*, and that at the *Palais Royal* (formerly Richelieu's palace), then given over to Molière's company. The audiences at both sorts of theatre, however, may be thought of as courtly.

In the literature of the French tragic stage there are no names beyond those of Corneille and Racine that are internationally important. Voltaire is sometimes added as a third figure in a triumvirate; but it was assuredly his battle for the unities that made him famous in theatrical annals, and not his plays. He believed, as did some of his contemporaries, that he had surpassed Racine; but even the French theatre has allowed his uninspired tragedies to sink into a probably permanent neglect. The clever and versatile Voltaire, nevertheless, dominated the theatre of his time as he dominated literature and thought. And he put down a definition of tragedy, or rather a statement of the tragedy-writer's duty, which deserves to be kept forward:

> To compact an illustrious and interesting event into the space of two or three hours; to make the characters appear only when they ought to come forth; never to leave the stage empty; to put together a plot as probable as it is attractive; to say nothing unnecessary; to instruct the mind and move the heart; to be always eloquent in verse and with the eloquence proper to each character represented; to speak one's tongue with the same purity as in the most chastened prose, without allowing the effort of rhyming to seem to hamper the thought; to permit no single line to be hard or obscure or declamatory;—these are the conditions which nowadays one insists upon in a tragedy.[2]

And be assured Voltaire did insist upon them. He became the very pope of the Theatre-realm. He had his bishops and his minor clergy

---

[2] Translation of Brander Matthews, in his *The Development of the Drama* (New York, 1906).

in France, in Italy, in Germany, even in England, as we have seen (though drama was "down" at the moment over most of Europe). Everywhere tragedy was made to bow to the French rules. For had not the French dramatists become the successors of the ancients—nay, had they not improved upon the Greeks? Certainly. At least, for those courtly times, for those stiff audiences, it was an improvement.

The dictator, nevertheless, being broad-minded, took a liking to the plays of Shakespeare—as one sure of his own civilization will take to an attractive barbarian—one of those diamonds in the rough. While chiding the dead bard for his forgetfulness of the rules, Voltaire found in him qualities to praise: even essayed some adaptations in which Shakespeare's worst faults were corrected. But he found in Racine's *Iphigénie* the "*chef d'œuvre* of the stage." And of course his own correct dramas were played and discussed wherever civilization had reached.

The crowning of Voltaire at the *Théâtre Français* at the sixth representation of his *Irène*, March 30, 1778. [Portion of an engraving by Gaucher after the design of Moreau le Jeune.]

But not to spend too long with one whose influence soon after waned (Lessing was born before Voltaire wrote his second play, and launched his attack on French Classicism long before Voltaire wrote his last), the reign of this dictator was long and adventurous and infinitely exciting. And after the little man had been exiled again and again—for his political and religious opinions that were far less orthodox than his playwriting practice—he was recalled to a triumph in the theatre. He went back to Paris in 1778, at the age of eighty-four, attended a performance of his tragedy *Irène* at the *Comédie Française*, and saw a portrait bust of himself crowned at one of the most brilliant assemblies in the history of the French stage. But we have now gone forward to a time long after the triumph of Molière and the glory that was French comedy.

There is, however, one matter of theatre custom which demands mention before Voltaire's name is dropped: for every later playwright, actor, and stage worker owes him a debt. By his persistence he drove spectators off the stage. You will remember how the dandies in Shakespeare's theatre had made themselves obnoxious by parading up on the platform beside the actors, how they detracted from the drama. In Paris, it is said that seats were first set upon the stage when Corneille's *Le Cid* scored its epochal success. The abuse grew until the actors had hardly more than a strip of playing space between two rows of benches as shown in the illustration here.

And the beaux and fops who claimed the privileged platform seats were no silent and attentive group; they strolled in and out when they pleased, made audible comments, took delight in showing superiority to the play, the players, and the audience. Voltaire is credited with driving them out permanently, with freeing the stage for acting. God bless him!

IN 1643 a company of amateur and semi-professional actors known as *Les Enfants de Famille* made the momentous decision that they would enter into competition with the "regular" theatre groups in Paris. They hired a tennis-court, obtained a noble patron, and announced productions of tragedy under the name "The Illustrious Theatre." The venture promptly, and apparently repeatedly, failed. The Illustrious ones were driven to touring the provinces. Among them was a young man of native wit and education above the average. His name was Jean Baptiste Poquelin, and he was the son of an upholsterer. For the purposes of the stage he took the name "M. de Molière." Perhaps he would not have made that name the greatest in the story of the French theatre if he had not so promptly failed when he first came to the stage. At any rate, we may well believe that he gained out of twelve years of "trouping" in the provinces two things that went into his equipment as first of the world's comedy-writers: a first-hand knowledge of the stage effects that infallibly amuse audiences; and a seasoning of philosophical humor and gentle wisdom, born out of struggle, companionship, intrigue, poverty, and checkered success.

A scene with spectators on the stage, at the theatre of the *Petits Comédiens*. [From Gravelot's engraving as reproduced in *Shakespeare in France under the Ancien Régime*, by J. J. Jusserand.]

Molière, the actor, returned with his company to Paris in 1658, and at this time he was already Molière the playwright, with a record of several farces or comedies tried out and found effective. If they were little more than adaptations from the *Commedia dell'Arte*, still there must have been a freshness about them. At the first Paris performance, before the King and the Court in the theatre at the *Petit-Bourbon*, it was not the tragedy but the farce after-piece that won approbation; so much so that the company was accorded the privilege of playing regularly at the royal theatre, alternating with the Italian Comedians. From that day to the end of his life, though he was compelled to fight through personal disappointments and intrigues arising out of professional jealousy, Molière marched forward to success after success, recognized as a chief figure in the theatre of France.

For one thing, those who valued restraint in acting above the old tragic declamation or comic buffoonery, began then to count him the best of actors, particularly for comedy. He was also a shrewd manager and director. And by 1659 he had written and presented *Les Précieuses Ridicules*, a brief satire on the groups of affected ladies who made pretence to a superior culture; and this witty take-off on the dilettanti, the *précieuses*, met with enormous success. (Indeed, the theatre immediately doubled its prices of admission.) The plot is negligible; the trick by which two servants play the substitute to their masters in wooing vain ladies is an old one; and the characters are hardly more than borrowings from the stock figures of the Italian Comedy. But Moliére put rich fun into the farcical trifle, a swift gaiety and a freshness of humor quite uncommon; *and* social point. *That* the comedy of France had not had before. Other minor pieces followed; and in 1661 Molière brought out the *École des Maris*, first of a long series of masterpieces in satiric comedy.

It is possible to trace back and discover the origin of many of the materials and qualities that had gone into Molière's "stock in trade." There was the old native French farce, the honest drollery of *Pierre Pathelin;* there was the imported Spanish play of piled-up incident and stressed intrigue; most of all, there were the improvised farces and the stock caricature-figures of the Italian *Commedia dell'Arte*. To these last Molière had gone directly for tutelage; he had competed with them for popular favor; since boyhood he had been laughing at their tricks and their genius. (Even in *Les Précieuses Ridicules*, Molière's fellow-players Jodelet, La Grange and Du Croisy appeared as characters bearing those names, a convention taken from the Italians.) Corneille, too, had written a forerunner of later comedy, *Le Menteur*, in which he had made over a Spanish original into a true comedy of character.

But here is the miracle of one man picking up all these borrowings and influences, and so transcending them that he creates a new form of art, reaches a height in comedy-writing that never after is touched by any dramatist of this or any other land. Just as Shakespeare borrowed material with a freedom quite amazing, and began writing in a style that he found ready-made to his hand, and yet transcended all his fellows in all ages in the range and richness of his achievement, so Molière in comedy imitated and took, but lived to create with an originality unequalled in the comic literature of the stage.

Shakespeare, to be sure, had written unmatched comedies in a limited field, in addition to his incomparable accomplishment in the realm of tragedy; or perhaps it is better to say that he had written the finest plays ever produced in a mixed form that is half comedy, half fantastic drama. It is usually termed, inexactly, "Romantic Comedy," and embraces, of course, the plays of the type of *Twelfth Night* and *As You Like It*. There is, too, the comedy-nearer-farce—*The Merry Wives of Windsor*. But in the sort of dry comedy that usually is considered to contain the very essence of the comic spirit, Molière is accounted supreme.

French and Italian farceurs of the Paris stage in the sixty years preceding 1670. Molière is at the extreme left. Besides Jodelet, Gros-Guillaume, Scaramouche, and other famous actors, still others are represented merely under the names of their masks. [From a painting in the collection of the *Comédie Française*.]

Demanding a certain seriousness in all drama that raises claim to importance, and setting aside the old crude test of happy or gloomy ending, we may usefully distinguish comedy (from tragedy) as a form of dramatic action which touches upon our sense of the laughable, rather than upon the emotions of pity and anguish. Comedy is the drama of laughter, be that laughter in the manner of sympathy or of ridicule. The usually applied test of the excellence of any given comedy is the extent to which it evokes "thoughtful laughter." The play that begets thoughtless laughter, by sudden improbabilities, by extravagant coincident, by physical by-play, we call farce.

True comedy arises rather out of character—usually the clash of foibles in character against common-sense truth; out of the vices and weaknesses of human nature held up to ridicule. If at the same time sympahy is aroused, the play borders on sentimental comedy—which may run off into tenderness and sweet vaporings quite cloyingly trivial and empty, without ever getting into farce or burlesque (wherein the laugh arises out of contrast between characters and the action in which they are placed). But what is generally accepted as essential comedy, "high" comedy, is the satiric sort, untinged with sympathetic appeal.

The French feel that they are the guardians of the true comic spirit. In discussing these matters, they claim that other nations vitiate comedy by tagging along sympathy and personal emotions. They, instead, place life on the rack and watch the result from an aloof viewpoint, without becoming entangled in an emotional or human reaction. We need not debate here whether a more human type of comedy is more enjoyable—whether it is "legitimate." We shall do better to grant to the French spectator a detachment which permits him to enjoy the pure wit of satiric comedy as we Anglo-Saxons cannot. He comes to the playhouse dispassionate, he leaves his personal emotions at home. And in the field of the detached comedy his Molière is supreme.

The distinction is a difficult one—for all drama is human—it is action by human beings before us, up there on the stage, that conditions the art. The theatre is trying out today the experiment of making the action very intimate, the character very personal, in realistic plays. But we read Molière with the feeling that here is a fine lofty reserve, a view of the foibles and follies of human beings that never descends into the mud or the easy sentimentalities of their personal lives. Somehow types are fixed, are held for our view, act their ridiculous bits, are gone. The characters are gracious and real, vigorous and socially true, but they never ask that we take them to our hearts. Let us grant that this detached comedy is "high" comedy.

Molière painted such a gallery of these social characters that only in Shakespeare may one find more figures that are universally used as touchstones. Molière quickly developed the serious critical note that he had added to the rich fun, the lively intrigue, of the older comedy. The social point that had distinguished *Les Précieuses Ridicules* became the distinguishing feature of his dramaturgy. The ridiculous conventions in life, the faults in the structure of society, the frailties of human nature, these became his targets. With good-natured humor, with barbed wit, he held up to view pretensions, absurdities, habits, religious superstitions. Beyond the playwright there came to exist the

Molière and his troupe playing before the King and Cardinal Mazarin. [A reconstruction of the scene by the nineteenth-century artist V. A. Poirson, in Moland's *Molière: Sa Vie et Ses Ouvrages*.]

343

philosopher, the moralist, the flayer of folly. And he brought his satiric gift to bear in searching out the weaknesses of *contemporary* society; in that, he brought drama one step closer to realism. No one had written so seriously before of the life at one's elbow. And Molière wrote with a marvellous finish, a superb grace, whether in prose or in rhymed couplets. The verse is not "poetic" in either the lyric or the florid sense; it is rather distinguished by ease, flow, and flexibility. His range of comedy—though the satirical comedy-of-manners is at the heart of his achievement—is extraordinarily wide; from farce through comedy of situation to comedy of character; and beyond that, excursions into tragi-comedy, ballet, and interlude.

From his very titles the world has taken by-words: *Le Bourgeois Gentilhomme*, *Les Femmes Savantes*, *Les Précieuses*. And from his characters we judge a man today as a Tartuffe or an Alceste. But rather it is the range of comic characters that is most notable: for here are the most memorable of hypocrites, humbugs, quacks, and snobs in all theatre literature. The ladies with pretensions are shown up in—to switch to the Englished titles—*The Affected Misses* and *The Learned Ladies*; the tradesman putting on airs, in *Le Bourgeois Gentilhomme*; the holy hypocrite in *Tartuffe*; the doctors in *Le Médecin Malgré Lui* and *l'Amour Médecin*; "the best society" in *Le Misanthrope*; the miser in *l'Avare*; and so on.

Tartuffe is an example of Molière at his best. The action passes in the house of Orgon, a French gentleman of assured position, with two grown children, who has taken a second wife, a charming and beautiful young woman (a part written by the author, as so often, to the measure of one of his actors, in this case his own wife who was hardly half his age). Orgon has taken up religion, and has brought into his house a pious impostor named Tartuffe. The young people, with the aid of an astute maid, are struggling to dislodge the hypocrite, while the credulous Orgon and his old mother fight back. Through two acts we see this situation explored, with special attention to the love affair of Orgon's daugher Mariane, which he breaks off in order to give her to Tartuffe.

But the impostor (he is known as such to the audience from the start) has other and more wicked plans: besides annexing Orgon's wealth, he will seduce his wife. He enters first in act three, and from that time his power seems to grow—the comedy is mixed with a sinister seriousness here. He immediately makes love to Elmire, Orgon's wife; and when the son exposes his duplicity to Orgon, the latter's only answer is to turn over to Tartuffe a deed to his property as a mark of confidence. Finally, to break through her husband's blindness, Elmire hides Orgon under the table and permits Tartuffe to continue his advances. And then when Orgon, convinced, faces Tartuffe and orders him from the house, the latter brazenly claims that the deed of gift has made the house his and that Orgon is rather the one to go. In the final act, when calamity seems to have come to completion, the dramatist solves the difficulty a bit mechanically, by having the King send in an officer to apprehend Tartuffe as a wanted criminal. The house is thus cleansed; and Mariane of course is restored to her rightful lover—while Orgon presumably will let pious phrases dupe him no more.

A bit of the scene when Tartuffe is making love to Elmire may serve to illustrate the surety of the characterization (quoted here in Curtis Hidden Page's translation):

TARTUFFE (*handling the lace yoke of Elmire's dress*)
Dear me, how wonderful in workmanship
This lace is! They do marvels nowadays;
Things of all kinds were never better made.

ELMIRE
Yes, very true. But let us come to business.
They say my husband means to break his word,
And marry Mariane to you. Is't so?

TARTUFFE
He did hint some such thing; but truly, madam,
That's not the happiness I'm yearning after;
I see elsewhere the sweet compelling charms
Of such a joy as fills my every wish.

ELMIRE
You mean you cannot love terrestrial things.

TARTUFFE
The heart within my bosom is not stone.

ELMIRE
I well believe your sighs all tend to Heaven,
And nothing here below can stay your thoughts.

TARTUFFE
Love for the beauty of eternal things
Cannot destroy our love for earthly beauty;
Our mortal senses well may be entranced
By perfect works that Heaven has fashioned here.
Its charms reflected shine in such as you,
And in yourself its rarest miracles; . . .

I could not look on you, the perfect creature,
Without admiring Nature's great Creator,
And feeling all my heart inflamed with love
For you, His fairest image of Himself.
At first I trembled lest this secret love
Might be the Evil Spirit's artful snare;
I even schooled my heart to flee your beauty,
Thinking it was a bar to my salvation.
But soon, enlightened, O all lovely one,
I saw how this my passion may be blameless,
How I can make it fit with modesty. . .

But one needs the full-length portrait to know why the play precipitated a years-long controversy in Paris. There were those, it seems, who read into the deceitful Tartuffe a symbol of the Church, or perhaps of one of the powerful Religious Societies, and for a time even the King who had been Molière's generous protector felt compelled to ban the play. It was five years later that *Tartuffe* was unreservedly given to the public.

Molière had fought through many another quarrel and intrigue—not least, a competitive war with the troupe at the *Hôtel de Bourgogne*. And he fought against unhappiness brought upon him by his young wife, against libellous accusations, against court cabals. Through it all he kept on with his management of the theatre, with his acting, with his writing of plays. But fifteen years after his return to Paris his health broke under the strain. Returning home after stumbling through the fourth performance of *Le Malade Imaginaire*, he went to bed and died within a few hours. The local priests refused the last rites of the Church and opposed burial in the parish cemetery. An appeal to the Archbishop of Paris, who happened to be a notorious waster, only resulted in a confirmation of the ban. Finally the King's intercession brought permission for interment, provided that there were no ceremonies or pomp; and this great man, beloved and gentle and generous, as Shakespeare and Sophocles had been, was sneaked into an obscure grave in the middle of the night. But his genius has lived on, until his fame is greater than that enjoyed by any other artist out of France. Even the French Academy discovered and honored him a hundred years later.

After him there came no other comedy writers of first magnitude. The only one who demands mention is Jean-François Regnard. His plays have survived, and have a liveliness and a heartiness; but he is Molière's imitator, by no means his companion.

Molière wrote often for the Court of Louis XIV: ballets, interludes, "improvisations." He was too busy with his theatre to join regularly in the activities of "society" (he had the stage in the *Palais Royal* after that in the *Petit-Bourbon*); or else he was temperamentally not fitted to live the decorative life of a courtier. He was of the court, but always strangely a stranger there. And yet there are records of his contributions to the fêtes and the ceremonies. And this weaker side of his art got mixed up with the frills and furbelows that the fops and courtesans were just then mixing into opera and ballet.

Le vray Portrait de Mr de Moliére en Habit de Sganarelle.

Molière in the character of Sganarelle.

More than any other dramatist, however, Molière held his serious comedies clear of the courtly influence. Neither the demand for scenic aggrandizement nor the threat of disbarment from the Academy if he defied the rules, led him to compromise in his comedy-writing. His plays demand no scenery, and no properties except for a table in *Tartuffe* and an occasional chair elsewhere; and he wrote them as seemed to him right, without regard to rule, genuine, hard, precise, with what characters he willed. He was of a court and a courtly age, yet above it; he shaped his art to a rude theatre as he first found it, yet transcended it with an art that fits all theatres. He was indeed greater than his time.

But aside from him, the limitations of those times settled down over all stages. The kings and courtesans and Academicians and dilettanti-artists with whom the chapter started are still ruling France. They are making the theatre courtly. They are building private theatres in palaces and country houses, and they are acting on those stages. Even the King himself has appeared in ballets. They have made a vogue of decorative "theatricals." Machine-effects, scenery, dance, all have been imported from Italy. Look at the nearby illustrations—especially the sketch below and the dozen following pictures—to see how the courtly glow has spread over the playhouses and the actors. Then turn to a new chapter, and the continuation of the story of operatic influences.

The French theatre as designed for the aristocracy. Note the very low orchestra floor which throws the best seats into the balcony. [Drawing by Warren D. Cheney after the water-color by Gabriel de St Aubin.]

CHAPTER
15

Opera, Picturing,
and Acting

THE MEAT of this chapter, I warn you, is in the pictures. For my purpose is to show how the trappings of drama came to glorification; and then to name the personalities that shone out in "the Age of Great Acting." There is little to record about the essential theatrical thing, the dramatic play, the rounded stage performance. After Molière, France hardly turns up a world-dramatist until 1830; and this is a dull age in the playhouses of Spain, Italy, and Germany. Ballet, opera, spectacle, great actors—these are the outstanding phenomena.

Ballet—which we may define as dramatic dance in a musical and scenic investiture—had been a favorite court pastime for nearly a century, at the time of Molière's death. In 1581 the French Court of Henry III had enjoyed the more or less Italian *Ballet Comique de la Royne* at the Château de Moutiers; and there is a record of the event in the picture which you will find back in the chapter on the Renaissance and the beginnings of scenery. After that, attempts at the founding of native opera alternated with importations of complete Italian operatic productions. But at last Louis XIV so enjoyed a musical-dramatic performance of a pastoral by the Abbé Pierre Perrin that he lent official encouragement; and in 1669 Perrin was granted a royal charter under which the *Académie de Musique* (the present-day Paris *Opéra*) was founded.

Meantime, however, there had risen to power at the court that Italian who was destined to write his name as first among the great

349

opera-producers of France: Jean Baptiste Lully. He had come away from Florence, as Lulli, when he was ten or twelve years old, had been either page or kitchen scullion in the service of the King's niece, had risen to be leader of *les vingt-quatre violons du Roi* and accepted court composer. By 1671 he had composed music for no fewer than thirty of the court ballets—including several by Molière—had acted in some of them alongside the King, and had wormed his way into the position of favorite, partly by very dubious devices. And so it is not surprising that in 1672, by conspiring with one of the King's mistresses, Mme de Montespan, he succeeded in wresting the *Académie de Musique* charter and privileges from Perrin. From then on Lully *was* French opera for fifteen years. And the ballet element was strong in operatic production ever after.

Italian opera, you will remember, had already escaped from the courts and had claimed public theatres of its own. But in France it remained at least a court-protected, if not a privately shown art, operating under an official monopoly. It is said that Lully limited his art to please the taste of Louis XIV, who disliked brilliant and over-melodic music; and we may allow that here a real French decorum restrained the operas from an exuberance that sometimes ran wild farther south. At any rate Lully preserved Italian grace, added some orchestral elements, and fitted the recitative perfectly to the French verses of his collaborator Quinault. He established the type-form of French opera. With his great knowledge of practical stage technique, gained out of his long experience in presenting ballets, he made opera stageworthy; and of course he made ballet numbers a fixture in every musical-dramatic production. (So if today you go to a performance, and wonder why they stop the play for that dance-divertissement, you may think back to this excitable French-Italian, who transformed the amateur diversion of the court ladies and gentlemen into a professional operatic interlude.) And aside from the shaping of the opera-structure and the tasteful improvements in the music as such, the court artists added to those extraneous scenic effects that have weighted down "grand" opera ever since.

Because the ballets had long been danced by the nobles and ladies, the costumes had been royal approximations of the dress of ancient kings, goddesses, shepherdesses, sorcerers, and such; with occasional excursions into contemporary exotic costume, Oriental, American, etc. In a contemporary engraving the Duke de Guise appears in amazingly elaborated "American" regalia; and that sort of glorification seems to have been common in all stage dress of the time. The progress of dancing in opera-ballets during the fifty years after Lully was conditioned by the reluctance of producers to give up the stiffly ornamental

Ballet costumes of Neptune and an African, by the decorator Martin.
[From *l'Ancienne France: Le Théâtre et la Musique.*]

Costumes for an eighteenth-century ballet. [After Gillot.]

and weighty garments inherited by the professional dancers from the court ladies. It was not until the time of the famous *danseuse* Camargo (about 1730–40) that a gradual stripping process ended by bringing the foundation of costuming down to tights; and twenty years more before Noverre fully "reformed" stage dancing. Even so the ballroom slippers persisted, along with many another artificiality, down to our own century and the revolution accomplished by Isadora Duncan.

Nor was the costuming on the legitimate stage less scrumptious than that on the operatic. Drama must not fall behind this new rival, in appointments, in appeal to the courtly eye. So one sees characters in quite ordinary plays remarkably upholstered in silks and satins and plush, with truly monstrous head-dresses, their heads bowed under helmets and plumes, their bodies trailing vast quantities of brocaded stuffs. The mode was not out of keeping with that of serious acting, which was slow-moving, stately, stilted. Or was the acting partly conditioned by this costuming?

Watteau, who himself designed for the stage in the early years of the eighteenth century, fixed, with his inimitable courtly touch, portraits of the actors of the *Théâtre Français* in all their finery, as illustrated here. The *Théâtre Français* was the new name given to the privileged royal acting troupe in 1680, when Louis XIV ordered the two existing companies, that at the *Hôtel de Bourgogne* and that of Molière (still carried on by his widow) to amalgamate. To the combined group he gave the sole right to present plays in the French language in Paris; though this did not work to the injury of either the Opéra producers or the ever-popular Italian Comedians. The date of the amalgamation of the two legitimate companies, 1680, is usually recorded as foundation-date of the present *Comédie Française*. (The terms *Théâtre Français* and *Comédie Française* are often used interchangeably, when the larger *institution* is in question.)

If the ballet costuming spread to the regular stage, that other plaything of court-artists, scenography, was equally exploited on both legitimate and operatic stages. The Italian perspective settings were adopted, and Italian influence determined the form of the French playhouse—though the Paris-Versailles Court added luxuriousness in decoration. The painted settings grew to an elaboration never surpassed (though they were made more natural and credible in later eras), and stage machinery for trick effects again gained in range and complexity. We may believe that some of the scenery was gorgeous, and compelling of admiration, however much we may deplore the spread of showy settings to the dramatic as well as the operatic stage; and we may grant, too, that the apparitions and the wire-riding and other trickery provided sensational moments.

Two paintings by Watteau, typical of the decorative French theatre of his time. Above, "L'Amour au Théâtre Français." Below, "Les Comédiens Français." [After engravings by C. N. Cochin and J. M. Liotard, reproduced in Dacier's *Le Musée de la Comédie Française*.]

The artist Giacomo Torelli produced at the theatre in the *Petit-Bourbon* Palace some of the most eleborate stage-pictures and effects of the times. He had come to Paris from Venice, it is said, because in the latter city he had staged some tricks so mystifying that spectators put on masks and tried to kill him, thinking he must be in league with the Devil. And he established a new standard of gorgeousness, as well as a new efficiency in rapid scene-changing. I am showing illustrations

Scene with elaborate machine effects of cloud-riding figures, moving ships, etc., in the opera *Les Noces de Thétis et Pelée*, Paris, 1689. [From *l'Ancienne France: Le Théâtre et la Musique.*]

to remind the reader that the proscenium-frame came from Italy along with scene-painting—a simple version at page 356, and a more elaborate one on page 358.

After Torelli, who left Paris in 1660, came another Italian, named Gaspare Vigarani, who fitted up a palace theatre for the King, wherein the scenic features so far outweighed all other considerations that the place was called *Salle des Machines*. On the stage there, any known effect could be staged; and the settings might aspire to rival even the marvellously piled-up creations of the Bibbienas. A little later Paris was to have that famous follower of the Bibbienas, Jean-Nicholas Servandoni. But also the French artists were learning to design in the new style.

In theatre architecture, the horse-shoe type of auditorium was being perfected: it was the logical accompaniment to the /\-shaped perspective scene, in a time when audiences wanted exclusive boxes rather than solid banks of seats. The opera house in the Château at Versailles, though built later than the time of Louis XIV that we have been exploring, is representative of the French variation of the Italian originals. The later opera theatre, familiar from many prints of the period, shows how the audience in a large theatre was disposed in relation to the stage; and also how perfectly the stage had become a picture—how far it had changed from that platform, that shelf for acting which had served up to the time of Corneille. In truth, all theatres had become opera houses. (See pictures on pages 358 and 440.)

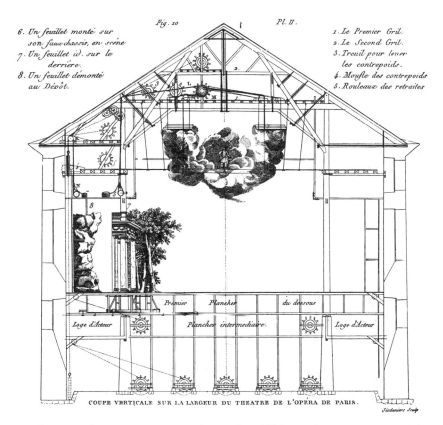

Diagram of a stage with machinery for shifting painted scenery and for staging cloud effects, apparitions, etc. [From Grobert's *De l'Exécution Dramatique*.]

THE ideal of theatre art as a synthetic form, in which no one element predominates—neither acting nor literary drama, and certainly not setting—has so far engaged the artists in the theatre in the twentieth century, that there is even a sentiment against discussing acting as a separate art. Certainly the greatest gain made in the playhouses within the last sixty years has been the new standard of ensemble production, the progress toward seeing the performance *as a whole*.

But in past times there were eras when story and poetry weighed heaviest, others when spectacle and trick-effects alone satisfied the audiences; and still others when a vigorous show of virtuoso acting was the *clou* of the stage art. To us today there seems no doubt that acting should be considered a *contributive* art—perhaps the central one of those grouped to make whole the stage production, but still a craft within an art rather than an independently important manifestation. Yet in a period covering the late seventeenth and most of the eighteenth century, acting was the most conspicuous element in the theatre's activity, and the only element about which a history of the playhouses of the times could be written. Dramatists of world significance are not

The King's ballroom theatre in the Petit-Bourbon Palace. The group of spectators includes Louis XIII, Anne of Austria, and Cardinal Richelieu. Note how the proscenium frame has been permanently introduced here, by the imported Italian artists. [From the painting in the Louvre.]

met with in France for a long time after Molière, nor in Spain after Calderon, nor in England after Dryden; and Germany won't bring forward any contribution till the star of Goethe and Schiller rises a century hence. The actors are left to carry on the story.

In France there has been a steady progression from the days when actors were amateurs or near-vagabonds to the brilliant time of the honored *Comédiens du Roi*. Richelieu particularly deserves remembrance for bettering the estate of the players. But when a princely actor like Molière represents the stage, it is natural that great honor be done to players. And it is in Molière's time that we meet the figure that comes earliest in the list of great French tragic actors. (Those who have played tragedy nobly seem better remembered than those who shone in comedy; though there is a general belief that comedy-playing is the more difficult art.)

Michel Baron rose to eminence by opposing to the old stilted and pompous playing a sort that measurably reduced the unnaturalness and woodenness. It was difficult, nay impossible, to escape artificiality when acting the rhymed-couplet plays. But where his predecessors (of whom Mondory had been the greatest) had declaimed the lines with sing-song regularity, emphasizing the rhyme, Baron broke the lines, and threw the words into a more natural rhythm, at the same time modulating his voice to natural emotions. He was the first great fighter in that progressive battle between convention and naturalness, which has continued down to our own day. His facial play was expressive beyond any known before his time; and he refused to be bound by the rules for gesture which had grown into a tradition. Once when criticized for his over-natural movements, he answered: "My comrades contend that even in bursts of passion I ought not to let my arms go above my head. But if passion carries them there, I shall let them go. Passion knows better than the rules." And that, indeed, was highly revolutionary in a time when there were laws about everything, and Academies and such to enforce them. Acting had become a recognized separate art, and courtiers, writers, and the *précieuses* went to the playhouse to see how so-and-so handled such-and-such a passage out of Corneille or Racine. And every effect and method had been tabulated.

Baron quite recognized that he had gained the peak in his art. "The world," he said, "has seen only two great actors: Roscius and myself. Every century has its Cæsar; two thousand years are necessary to produce a Baron." But when he had made himself the greatest figure in the French theatre, he suddenly retired, at the age of thirty-eight. Apparently he felt that the world of the stage was too small for a Baron. Conceit, of course, has never been lacking among players—I could name you a few even today!—but it is seldom that the superiority is so ingrained that an actor feels impelled thus to quit the stage.

After thirty years in private life, Baron returned to the boards; and he scored again almost as notably as before, and with further innovations. And it was he who handed on the torch to another generation of players.

In the historic year 1789 the upper-class theatres in France were fully in the Italian operatic current. This is the *Comédie Française*, in Paris at century's end—the building typically overdecorated, the "scenery" pictorial and sensational.

Among those who made their reputations in the older sort of acting, the frankly declamatory, the most famous were Mlle Champmeslé and Mlle Duclos. The former was particularly celebrated for the skilful use of her voice. "She shows so much art in the use of it," a contemporary wrote, "and she accommodates its modulations so well to nature, that her heart really seems to be full of the passion which is only in her mouth." And, indeed, *there* is a key to the fault in "majestic" acting; after all our praise of the effects, our thrill at the bigness and force of it, in the end it is remembered as only "in the mouth." If we would make out an excuse or a reason for the steady advance of "naturalness" since that day, we must study how the actors spoke increas-

ingly from the heart, from the emotional centre. The appeal to an
artificial taste, even the appeal to the intellect, may ride over on the
declamatory method; but the deeper emotional-spiritual message that
we believe today to be the essence of serious drama—*that* cannot be
carried on verbal rockets or mannered gesticulation. Mlle Duclos continued on with the recitative sort of thing, to even greater extremes
than her tutor, Mlle Champmeslé; and she gained fame with many,
though she lingered on into a time when the pompous style was pretty
well discredited—temporarily.

In the gallery of celebrated French actors of the time we might
linger before the portraits of the Quinaults. Best-known out of that
stage family was Quinault-Dufresne, who seems to have been the
"matinée idol" of the early eighteenth century. But it is rather Adrienne
Lecouvreur who soon commands all eyes. And she brings us back into
the full tide of the reforms instituted by Baron. She came to the stage
with a distaste for the bombast, intrigue, and pretense that were so
large a part of "artistic" life. When the most celebrated actresses were
mannered and stilted, she was simple and sincere (that is, within the limits
allowed by Alexandrine verse); where the accepted tragediennes were
fullsome and florid, she was slender and gentle and undecorative. She
added to her native sincerity and feeling the schooling of Michel
Baron; and she seemed to the spectators to "live" her part as no one
before her had done. As distinguished from the passion that was in the
mouth only, Adrienne Lecouvreur gained hers from the heart and the
soul. And in a very short time she became leading actress at the
Théâtre Français.

Her success offstage was hardly less brilliant than on, and her *salon*
became a meeting-place for the élite in the social-artistic life of Paris.
But unfortunately her semi-royal lover divided his attentions between
the humbly-born Adrienne and one who had been born a princess; and
when jealousies had been aroused, a plot to poison the great actress
was uncovered. One day in 1729 Lecouvreur took a theatrical revenge:
in playing *Phèdre* she stepped to the box where her rival was sitting,
and delivered full-face the lines about those who, resting secure while
committing crime, have learned to show an unblushing countenance.
The audience rose to this drama within a drama, and left no doubt
where *their* sympathies lay. But within the half-year the beloved
Adrienne was suddenly dead—of poison, everyone said, but nobody
dared seek out the poisoners.

Once more was repeated the old injustice: the greatest artist of her
era, though an honored favorite but yesterday, in death was borne
from her house at midnight, having been refused burial by the Church
and the law, and laid in a grave so obscure that no one has found it

Adrienne Lecouvreur as Cornélie in *The Death of Pompey* by Corneille, at the *Comédie Francaise*. In a time of stilted, declamatory acting, she introduced naturalness and quiet emotion. The soulful expression in the portrait here is attributable to her role: she is pressing to her bosom an urn holding the ashes of her murdered husband, Pompey the Great. A painting by Charles Coypel. [From Dacier's *Le Musée de la Comédie Française*.]

out even to this day. And yet the great Voltaire wrote of her as "this incomparable actress, who almost invented the art of speaking to the heart, and of showing feeling and truth where formerly had been shown little but artificiality and declamation."

Voltaire did much to aid the advancement of the theatre, outside the playwriting field. (You will remember that he freed the stage of spectators.) Perhaps his long residence in England had something to do with it, but certainly he saw through the worst mannerisms of French

Two productions with Harlequins, of the time when the Italian improvised farces were being turned into "Harlequinade" plays. [From old title pages.]

playing; and when acting seemed to be slipping back into the old pompousness, after Lecouvreur's death, he stimulated the *Comédie Française* players to further efforts after some sort of restraint. If he had a certain success with Mlle Dumesnil, who nevertheless overdid passionate nature at times, he failed to keep her co-star, Mlle Clairon, from being very rhetorically "sublime." Indeed, it was Clairon's self-consciousness and grandiloquence that carried on to the pre-Revolution theatre and made necessary Talma's new fight for restraint and naturalness. Unfortunately Mlle Dumesnil's weakness was such that toward the end "Bacchantes were the only ones she could play naturally"; and her influence waned.

Meantime, however, Voltaire had found a young actor named Lekain whom he could train after his own ideas. In the end Lekain became leading actor at the *Comédie Française*, could hold up his end of a grand scene with the florid Mlle Clairon, but withal tempered outlandish convention with an individual natural charm. And it was Lekain who handed on the torch to the young Talma, who, fifteen years later,

The Actors of the Comédie Italienne. In Paris, early eighteenth century. Painting by Nicolas Lancret, in the Louvre. [Archives Photographiques.]

is to make the fight for nature while France is in the throes of political revolution. But in the meanwhile the *Comédie Française* company is to suffer a sad relapse into "high" acting. With the passing of Lekain the "Era of Great Actors" in France is gone.

Generation after generation the Italian Comedians had been a fixture in Paris, and the fame, even the popularity, of their troupe had been more sustained than that of the French actors. In general their subsidies had been more generous. They had not always escaped persecution at the hands of their jealous rivals; and by 1697 the King was prevailed upon to withdraw their "privilege," and they left France. But twenty years later a new company was summoned to the capital, and continued till the Revolution to delight the Parisians with farce-comedies, and, in later days, operas.

In the time of Molière, the Italians claimed two actors whose names have gone down in the annals of the great: Scaramouche (Fiorilli) and Dominique. It was Fiorilli who broadened the Italian Scaramuccia part into the celebrated character that has gone down in history under the Scaramouche name. Others played Scaramouche after him, but his will always be the glory of the creation and of the supreme playing of the character. One of his biographers wrote: "We may say that every part of his body spoke, his feet, his hands, his head, and that the most insignificant of his gestures was studied." And Gherardi, who is remembered because he published a collection of the plays of the *Théâtre Italien*, speaks of "the incomparable Scaramouche, who was the adornment of the theatre, and a model to the most celebrated actors of his time . . . He made people nearly die with laughter for a quarter of an hour by a scene in which he expresses his fright without saying a single word. He touched more hearts merely by simple natural means than the ablest speakers by the beauties of the most persuasive rhetoric."

Dominique, who was really Giuseppe Domenico Biancolelli, greatly broadened the part of Harlequin, from the limits within which it had previously been played. Indeed, there is some reason to believe that he made the character more serious than the true *Commedia dell'Arte* troupes would have wished; the Italian company in Paris was being influenced by French surroundings. But he was enormously popular, and when he died in 1688, the theatre was closed for a month. And after him there was never again such an outstanding figure in the troupe. The King exiled the Italian players only nine years later, and the eighteenth century company never reached such heights.

The Italian comedians had served Paris exceedingly well, not only in purveying entertainment, but in their determining influence upon the genius of Molière.

Giuseppe Biancolelli, known in France as *Dominique*, in the role of the Doctor. [From a painting formerly in the Sambon collection.]

THOMAS BETTERTON'S company of actors, that so perfectly presented the artificial Restoration comedy in London, has already found mention; and the names of Mrs. Bracegirdle and of Nell Gwyn have been accorded all the space proper in a brief survey like this. In their time Betterton acted tragedies with Mrs. Barry, who perhaps should be the better remembered, since she helped to carry on the tradition that was to lead over to the later eighteenth century players.

Here again there is a fascinating gallery of portraits: Colley Cibber and his fellow actor-managers at Drury Lane, Booth and Wilks; Anne Oldfield, Kitty Clive, and Peg Woffington; James Quin and Charles Macklin. Of these, however, only the last-named can be said to have made progress toward the future—a future summed up in the person and personality of one man: David Garrick. In the Age of Great Acting, in England, all other names pale beside his.

Acting, indeed, was properly artifical in comedy, but pompously artificial in tragedy. The sonorous line, the strutting effect, these were the esteemed qualities, from Betterton to Quin. Then came little David Garrick, to prove that the natural thing was more pleasing, more stirring, than the most elegant declamation. Here was a man not too well-favored physically, who by sheer mobility and expressiveness moved spectators to a new understanding of Macbeth and Lear and Hamlet; who by a native brightness and vivacity put new spirit into comedy. And off the stage, Garrick was as well liked as on: he was amiable, intelligent, well-read, witty. Indeed, his success on the stage as actor was, if one may so express it, very little due to his being a born actor; to an undoubted natural gift for mimicry he brought influences out of wide learning, out of intelligent training, out of a broad purpose to meet life nobly. His first connection with the theatre was as dramatist, not player: his first dramatic effort was staged at Drury Lane Theatre in 1740.

In 1741 he acted at the Theatre in Goodman's Fields the part of Harlequin, incognito, as a substitute for the regular player; probably half as a lark, half as a test of his fitness for a profession to which his desires impelled him—though his respectable family sought to dissuade him. Only seven months later he appeared as Richard III, to an extraordinary popular success. And soon after, he gave over his wine business and turned all his energies to acting and playwriting. So great was his appeal that he leaped into first place in the theatrical world in England; within six years he was enabled to buy a two-thirds ownership of Drury Lane Theatre, building as well as business, and for thirty years reigned over the foremost London stage.

As player, Garrick brought actual revolution with him. Richard Cumberland wrote: "Old things were done away, and a new order at once brought forward, bright and luminous, and clearly destined to dispel the barbarisms of a tasteless age, too long superstitiously devoted to the illusions of imposing declamation." In short, by an intelligent reference to nature, Garrick avoided the grandiloquence, stiffness, and rant of the old school of acting. He turned the art into the channel known as "character acting." Just as true comedy can be tested by its rise out of the clash of character, rather than out of mere situation,

David Garrick between Comedy and Tragedy. Mezzotint by Corbutt after the painting by Sir Joshua Reynolds. The original title reads: "Strive not Tragedy nor Comedy to Engross a Garrick Who to Your Noblest Characters Does Equal Honour. *Reddere Personae scit Convenientia cuique.*" Typical of the sentimental and pompous painting of the period. (Garrick's dates were 1717 to 1779; Reynolds' 1723 to 1792.)

so genuine acting may be judged as having character-depth—and not merely the hollow shell of type-impersonation. Garrick brought mimicry into touch with life. Quin said, "If this young fellow is right, we are all wrong." He spoke more truly than he knew.

As manager and director Garrick created a new standard in many directions. He reduced the coarseness and grossness (there had already been progress from the time of Jeremy Collier's attack, but there was plenty of room for improvement still). He brought costuming and scenery more into line with the dictates of common sense; though here we may feel that the advance was but half-way out of the woods of showiness and artificiality. And he made for the theatre a sure place among the recognized arts of his day in England. Seldom else have actors enjoyed so much of equality and consideration in respectable society and among artists (though often before they had been accepted by none too virtuous court circles). And in choice of plays Garrick went back to the Elizabethans; he scored his own greatest success in Shakespearean parts, and he made productions of no fewer than twenty-four of Shakespeare's plays. The less said about the way he adapted these plays, the better. Let us grant that it was a step toward a more dignified and nobler stage that he should revive the great Elizabethan so fully, after the vogue of Restoration comedy and heroic tragedy.

In shaping his playing company Garrick let a natural fairness and breadth of view outweigh his own desire to shine as actor. He sacrificed much for ensemble, he introduced strict discipline, and before any other he foreshadowed that modern ideal which has determined the finest achievements of the acting art in this twentieth century. He created an acting machine. It was as a means to give this machine a fair road that he banished spectators from his stage.

The one-sidedness that is implied in the very term "Age of Great Actors" is thus somewhat belied by Garrick's conduct of his theatre. Even he cannot be exonerated of the charge of "writing up" the good acting parts in Shakespeare; but that dramatist suffered less then than in the hands of many a less gifted player-adapter in later times. And we may, with pleasure, mark Garrick as the one great "star" of the eighteenth century who did most to advance the theatre toward that ideal which has found such wide acceptance within our generation, the ideal of "the acting company" as against star-and-support.

But it would be unfair not to end the chapter on the note of his individual achievement as an actor; and since I have mentioned his tragic parts, I will choose an account, by a German traveller, G. C. Lichtenberg, of one of his comic characterizations:

> At first he wears his wig straight, and you see his round, full face. Afterwards when he comes home quite drunk, his face looks like the moon a few days before its last quarter, as nearly half of it is dimmed by his wig. The uncovered part is bloody and shining with sweat, yet most benevolent, so that it entirely compensates for the loss of the other half. The waistcoat is open from top to bottom; his stockings hang in wrinkles; the garters are loose and—very significantly—are not a pair. It is a wonder that Sir John has not put on shoes of different sex.

In this sad state he enters his wife's room, and to her anxious question what is the matter with him (and she has good reason enough for her question) he replies: "Sound as a roach, wife!" Yet he does not move away from the door-post, against which he leans as heavily as if he wanted to rub his back against it.

Then he becomes alternately brutal, drunkenly wise, and again, kindly, all amid the loud applause of the audience. In the scene where he goes to sleep he astonishes me. The way in which, with closed eyes, swimming head and pale face, he quarrelled with his wife, and mixing up his r's and his l's to a kind of inarticulate sound, now scolded, now babbled out scraps of moral sentences with which his own state contrasted most abominably; then the way in which he moved his lips, so that you were at a loss to say whether he was chewing or tasting or speaking—all this surpassed my expectations as much as anything else I have seen this remarkable man do. You should hear him pronounce "prerogative" in this part. It was not till after two or three efforts that he was capable of getting to the third syllable.

This illuminating bit is quoted from a German critic, and is the first indication we have had of dramatic interest or activity in that country since the era of the Miracles. But now, in the eighteenth century, Germany's day has come.

CHAPTER
16

❧❧❧❧❧❧❧❧❧❧❧❧❧❧❧❧❧❧❧❧❧❧❧❧❧❧❧❧❧❧❧❧❧❧❧❧❧❧❧

Sturm und Drang

❧❧❧❧❧❧❧❧❧❧❧❧❧❧❧❧❧❧❧❧❧❧❧❧❧❧❧❧❧❧❧❧❧❧❧❧❧❧❧

FOR an extraordinarily long period following the Renaissance, the theatres of Germany remained rude, clownish, and wholly unliterary. This was the country where the first surviving Christian plays had been written after the eclipse of the Roman theatre; and a country second to none in the vigor of its medieval religious drama. But from the late fifteenth to the mid-eighteenth century the theatre existed only in an incredibly crude form: the stages were outdoor booths or platforms, or at best a vacant hall; the dramas were sheerest farce or coarsened foreign plays, with added acrobatic turns and Hans-wurst or Pickle-herring characters; the acting was clownish or stilted, exaggerated and unstudied. The other theatres of Europe had experienced a period of this sort of thing, during the generations when the secular drama was refinding itself in Spain, England, and France. But nowhere else was the period so prolonged or so unrelieved by flashes of truer theatrical genius. Literally for centuries the cheapest theatre, the clown theatre, was all the theatre in Germany.

This crude popular stage is continuously vigorous, from medieval times on, manifoldly active, widespread over the German nations; but it is so poor in achievement that it leaves not a single play that is important to later times, and hardly a memory that is of more than local significance—up to 1750. Then, almost suddenly the cross-currents will be turned into one channel, the stream of German national drama will begin flowing strongly and irresistibly—the stream that is to wipe out French domination, and within a few decades to send German plays

369

and German influence into all the theatres of the Western world. But in these earlier times there is no literature of the stage—and much less any theory of the theatre. In short, a remnant of theatrical activity hangs on: the stage, with its ignorant and suspected actors and its coarse audiences, exists in a world wholly apart from that of the scholars, the literary men, the cultured, the ordinarily progressive.

Reasons enough for this condition are to be found in the broader history of the Germanic peoples before the eighteenth century. There is no national unity, no national consciousness, no centre of cultural or artistic life. The "society" of the times is itself uncentralized, even chaotic. A terrible war blights the land, kills out budding literary endeavor, makes established theatres an impossibility. When the many independent courts turn to amusement, it is seldom that of the stage—despite their aping of the French kings—except as a foreign troupe may be invited in for an isolated engagement. In the capital cities nearer to Italy—Munich or Vienna—an Italian opera-theatre may flourish for a time; but it remains an exotic.

In one sense foreign acting companies overran Germany more than any other country, as we shall see; but no one country's drama and actors formed a single coherent thread with which to tie together the theatrical events.

Religious drama in Mediæval Germany had been, toward the end, turned from its normal course to the uses of the Reformation. Not seldom it served for attack on the Catholic Church that had given it birth. Thus a play by Niklas Manuel, of the early sixteenth century, entitled *The Pope and His Priesthood*, showed the Pope parading in all his worldly splendor and display, accompanied by his court and his soldiers, while the simple Peter and Paul walked behind, speculating as to who this regal man might be.

But it may be said in general that the Miracles, which at first had admitted spectacular and farcical features as a concession to an ignorant public, ended by turning into popular farce-comedies. The German Shrovetide or Carnival-play is a perfect parallel to the transitional French farce of the late Middle Ages; with this one difference, that where the French playwrights concerned themselves largely with cuckold stories, the Germans found their materials more in the comic aspects of peasant coarsenesses. The sketches in either case, viewed in the light of modern taste, are degraded and offensive—with the exception of a few wherein the naïveté and shrewd humor outweigh the coarseness. Usually the Shrovetide play preserved, as a survival from its ancestor-Miracle, a tail-end justification, a few verses in which the author trusted that he hadn't offended too greatly against those moral principles that were his real concern. (In Germany as elsewhere in Europe the Jesuits

A stage as arranged in a church, for the Meistersingers. [Drawing after a reconstruction by Albert Köster.]

1 5 4 5 : HANS : SACHS : ALTER : 51 : IAR

371

combined elements out of the Miracles with others from the student-plays—of which, more in a moment—in a type of didactic play, in Latin, for cultivated audiences.)

From the Shrovetide plays, and from the activities of the Meister-singers—bands of amateur actor-singers who were then the favorite entertainers over a considerable section of Germany—the shoemaker-poet, Hans Sachs, of Nuremberg, drew nourishment for his unique art. His is the one important name in the sixteenth century German theatre. He wrote dialogues, based on the older religious plays, in which the action is admirably simplified and made palatable to the simple audiences of the time. Escaping most of the coarseness of the transitional farces and avoiding the sensationalism, the blood and thunder and violence, which were to distinguish the adaptations of the next century, he created a type of comedy that is the only true folk-play of his period. He spent little effort in either characterization or literary embroidery; nor was his type of play carried on recognizably by successors. But he made straightforward little verse plays, contrived with simple artfulness, getting fun out of recognizable types of people without malice or great exaggeration. He is something more than a picturesque humorist, but something less than an epochal figure, in the theatre of his time. He and his fellow-amateurs staged plays in the inn-yards, in convents or in churches. They were doubtless crude in their craftsmanship; but everything considered, play, stage, and acting, they were more notable as theatre artists than the native professional acting companies that were to carry the burden of the drama for a century and a half after them.

That phenomenon which we have noted several times since the Roman theatre faded out under the pressure of Christianity, the persistence of an active *student* theatre at the universities and schools, often affecting the professional drama, and in turn absorbing into itself such notable influences as Italian humanism and French classicism—that phenomenon we find again obscurely in the Germany of the Renaissance and Reformation periods. The universities have kept alive the interest in the classic authors, more especially Plautus and Terence. The students act in plays, sometimes as exercise in Latin, sometimes as seasonal festival. New special student-plays are written—first rewritten from old models, then more originally, finally with incidents from the lives of the students themselves and the townsmen about them.

The student productions are likely to be given with more finish, certainly with more care, and often with more elaborate settings and costumes, than the contemporary crafts or professional offerings. And certainly the large indoor assembly halls or the secluded open courts of the universities were more attractive settings than the platforms and

booths often utilized by itinerant actor-troupes. At Salzburg, where
the Italian influence flowed very early and very persistently (the town
is one of the most interesting meeting-grounds of medieval and rococo
in all Europe), there were very elaborately staged productions; and
this independent current flows throughout the time of the rule of *Hans
Wurst* on the German popular stage. Occasionally one hears of a leading actor-manager of a popular troupe who has come from undergrad-

Scenes from a student production on a market-place stage, 1574. [From
F. R. Lachmann's *Die Studenten des Christophorus Stymmelius*, by courtesy
of *Theatre Arts Monthly*.]

uate university experience to the professional stage; Johannes Velten
who managed the Electoral Saxon Comedians toward the end of the
seventeenth century was such a one. But in general the universities and
the regular stage are oceans apart, in aim, in tastes, in achievement.

What did serve to leaven the popular theatre, to stir into its heavy
bulk some new quickening, was the example of the invading troupes
of foreign players. Not that these visiting "artists" brought anything
pure and different, and stuck to it. Sooner or later, they all add *Hans
Wurst* to their casts of characters, even in tragedy. But they do bring
new plays, and doubtless at first new methods of acting and staging.
The most notable, though coming long after the Italian companies,

are "the English Comedians." There is record of a *Commedia dell'Arte* company visiting Linz and Vienna in 1568, and remaining six years, and the Bavarian court had seen examples even earlier. But the English arrived in the late sixteenth and early seventeenth centuries. These troupes from across the Channel brought a repertory of English plays, but they seem to have picked up on the way into Germany some trimmings not so obvious in London; for we are told that the productions were not only full of bloody incident and exciting intrigue but horrific and violent as drama seldom has been elsewhere, and that the vogue of "grotesque" acting in Holland, where the comedians had been, influenced their presentations. Some accounts have it that the players were at least in part students from the Dutch universities. At any rate, the English drama was introduced into Germany, and if it had little lasting effect on German playwriting endeavor then, it built well toward the time when eighteenth century Germans were to challenge French rule of the European theatre.

The visits continued over a long period, and in time the French companies are as much heard of as the Italian, English, and Dutch. To the remnants of drama from these countries, even adaptations, the Germans add elements that have become more or less their own, so that a later "native" play may easily be tagged as having the plot of *Hamlet* or *Romeo and Juliet* or *Tartuffe*. Soon after the classic period in France, one finds adaptations of Corneille, Racine, and Molière beside the plays out of Shakespeare and Italian comedies. Some of the troupes seem to have been well organized—they even attained to the dignity of official appointments to one petty court or another—but for the most part they were as second-rate and go-as-you-please, and as loose-living, as the cheaper *Commedia dell'Arte* companies in Italy. Some returned home soon or late, others doubtless stayed to become wholly Germanized—until no one knows how much of seventeenth century theatre activity is native, how much borrowed.

One thing is certain about the material, the story, and characters, in the plays: the level of dignity and truth was lowered for the groundling audiences. All plays apparently were presented with generous additions of acrobatic, juggling, dancing, and clown acts. Traditional comic characters, not to say buffoons, played their way through not only comedies but tragedies. These additions were quite in place when the piece was something handed down by the Italian comedians, but hardly added to the dignity of a Noah story from the Miracles, or an Iphigenia. In short, vaudeville, of a particularly cheap and coarse sort, was made out of every material, whether Italian comedy or opera, Shakespearean romance or French classic drama.

Scene from a German production of Terence's *The Eunuch*, with modified Italian street setting, late fifteenth century. [Illustration in the Dinckmut edition, Ulm, 1486.]

The visible symbol of the spirit and practice of these centuries is *Hans Wurst*, the "Jack Pudding," the debased Harlequin of the time. He may be, indeed, only an Italian Harlequin, brought lower by native coarseness. But there are no talented and famous actors associated with his name, as in Italy; in general, he is warred upon by those who would better the theatre, as the very impersonation of stage trickery, grossness, and obviousness. At his best he is an amusing buffoon, the typical blundering fool, sticking his nose into everything funnily, here fatter and more obtuse than elsewhere. The difference between him and those vigorously alive clowns of the better *Commedia dell'Arte* productions, which we admired so much if so vulgarly a few chapters back, is the difference between the intelligence behind those Italian parts and the coarseness of the German professional actor and groundling audience. The filling in of the scenarios of the Italian comedies was left to the actors, often quick-witted and inventive comedians, with the broad background of citizens of the world; the German dialogue was quite often partly improvised (because rehearsals were few), and the written text was as likely as not the work of a member of the company, after a foreign original—but this company was composed of near-outcasts, of half-educated show-people, acrobats, quacks, etc. Many troupes were hardly more than family groups; for one reason, if one were connected with actors, there would be little else by way of respectable occupation open.

Hans Wurst appeared, of course, in many variations, and it is impossible to disentangle his lineage entirely from that of the Dutch comic, Pickle-Herring. Not only is he mixed at times with Harlequin (or is it Pulchinello?), but there is a "female Harlequin" who borrowed some of his characteristics. For special sections he might take on the characteristic drolleries of a neighboring district: Vienna saw him for long as a caricature of the Tyrolean peasant. But he remains essentially Hans Wurst, dominating figure in the German theatre for two centuries.

Even when plays presumably more serious—*Hauptaktions*—are taking the place of mere interludes, farces, and turns, their titles are as likely as not to use Hans Wurst as bait to the potential audiences: *The World's Great Monster or The Life and Death of the Late Imperial General Wallenstein, Duke of Friedland, with Hans Wurst*. A typical comedy is announced as *A Schoolmaster Murdered by a Pickle-Herring, or the Bacon Thieves Nicely Taken In*.

In this time the producing stage was so far divorced from literature that the few men who became imbued with the idea of creating a German literary drama comparable to the Italian, English, Spanish, or French—and of course in the image of one of those types—remain

merely names in history, with no known body of drama to illumine
them: such are Andreas Gryphius, Jakob Ayer, Martin Opitz, and
Christian Weise. A more lasting fame was achieved by Daniel Caspar
von Lohenstein, but only because he stepped down somewhat, to meet
the taste of the times: he wrote some of the most violent and bloodiest
plays ever penned. Still, his reputation seems to have been of the
library rather than of the stage.

Hans Wurst (in black) on a roadside stage. [From a painting by an
unknown artist.]

And so we come to 1750. Acting is still ultra-exaggerated. A declamatory and bombastic delivery is considered a true sign of tragic
art, of the "sublime." Movements are stiff, over-deliberate in tragedy;
over-hurried and boisterous in comedy. If settings are anything more
elaborate than platform-curtains, they are meagre painted stuff, probably not more than three scenes for the entire repertoire of plays (you
will find them like that still in some stock theatres—particularly in
French municipal playhouses: "cottage," "palace," and "wood" settings). The theatre might be an open-air booth or rough curtained
platform, a town hall, or, on occasion, a ballroom in a castle. Companies by this time were wandering all over Germany and Austria,

not a few with court titles; and often they· carried their productions far outside of what we now know as those countries, to Scandinavia, to Russia, to Switzerland. But still there is no unity, no group purpose, no centralization.

Enter, a pretty girl. The time is 1727; the scene—badly enough painted, I daresay!—is this chaotic world of the theatre. Frederika Carolina Neuber, lovely of face, with a well-proportioned figure, comes onstage with that authority, that sense of combined capability-and-fairmindedness, which leads an audience to mark a character immediately as heroine. She is already an experienced actress; ten years ago she and the boy who was to be her husband ran away and joined a theatrical troupe—hardly any other shelter would be open to her after *two* elopements from her unhappy home. The husband is with her now, but he is rather a supernumerary in the drama of the awakening of a national spirit in the world of the theatre.

There are two villains in the piece. One is symbolic, obviously villainous, standing for all the cheapness and coarseness that are to be driven off the German stage, our old friend Hans Wurst. The other, as so often happens, appears first as hero, and is only found out as a sinister influence several acts later: a Prussian named Johann Christoph Gottsched, who has become literary dictator of Leipzig and aspires to organize and rule literature and the theatre throughout Germany. We see Carolina Neuber make an alliance with him, pledge with him to lift the stage from chaos to the heights.

Now anyone should have been able to see through Gottsched's pretensions: he is organizer above all, an ambitious, dictatorial sort of person, not at all a poet, and without real knowledge of the stage. Worst of all, he has capitulated to French classicism, and his idea of elevating the theatre is to bring it under the rule of the unities and the other laws fixed in Paris for the guidance of the world's dramatists. Still he has written books on rhetoric and poetics, is president of the Leipzig Poetic Society, and has already succeeded in making himself a sort of centre toward which flow all the channels of information about intellectual advancement throughout Germany. Carolina Neuber has recognized two things in her dreaming about establishing a new stage in Germany: first, Hans Wurst must be overthrown and cast into outer darkness, while acting is purged of the excesses that persist even in the *Hauptaktions;* and second, there must come somehow a union between the stage people and literary, or at least "cultured," circles. The Neubers have brought their company—yes, it is theirs now—to Leipzig, the intellectual centre of an awakening Germany, in this memorable year 1727. And the first act ends with our lovely Carolina and the

Costume studies by Jost Amman, a Swiss-German artist of the sixteenth century.

dictatorial Gottsched clasping hands in a pact which really is going to go far toward vitalizing theatrical life.

Years pass, and we see the Neubers with their "Royal Polish and Electoral Saxon Court Comedians" travelling over Germany in the difficult effort to lead the public from a love of *Hanswurstiades* and old-favorite *Hauptaktions* to appreciation of translated "sublime" French tragedies or comedies-in-verse. Gottsched has been true to his bargain in one way: he has supplied translations of the approved French classics, and he and his friends have written native plays in imitation of them.

There is something heroic about the determination with which Carolina Neuber undertakes and persists in the task of reforming a reluctant public; and something pathetic too, for there is no reason why the audiences should like this pompous, lifeless fare better than the clowneries that at least are amusing. About all we see as gain toward her central idea, in these first years, is the emergence of a new spirit in a group of actors—and beyond that, a spirit among literary men and students who now have been led to take a first-hand interest in the stage.

Out of that change in the spirit (and practice) of acting is to come Carolina Neuber's own tragedy: for beautiful and experienced as she may be, she is not one of the very great figures among actors, and after she lifts her company to a certain new standard, she is destined to see the world move on without her, to find her talents outgrown. Partly the inevitable actress' tragedy of a lost youth; partly the glorious flight of the human spirit beyond human capability. Her bravery persists for long; and perhaps it is bravery rather than common irritation that leads her to quarrel openly with her audiences in Hamburg— a thing theretofore unheard of—until the company's performances are officially cancelled. Certainly it is bravery that prompts her to refuse the dictator Gottsched's proffer of a new translation of Voltaire's *Alzire* (by his wife), because it is obviously inferior to the version already in her repertoire; though we see her antagonize the dictator thereby, see him become her enemy, an enemy discomfited but powerful enough to break her.

But first that other villain, Hans Wurst, is officially cast into outer darkness. Returning briefly to Leipzig, the Neubers put up a booth-stage—they have lost their old stage in the Butchers' Guild-hall to one of the hated Harlequin-companies—and there, with Gottsched's moral support, they put on a ceremony of the banishment of Hans Wurst (and all his Harlequin and other aliases). For a moment Carolina's star flames bright again, for the symbolic gesture stirs interest throughout Germany.

In the next act, however, Hans Wurst comes to life again. Hardly a year has passed when we see the Neubers' company itself presenting a play "with Hans Wurst." From which we know that things have gone so badly with our heroine that there is nothing to do but stoop to the old tricks. Indeed the world has ill treated the once beautiful, brave, and far-seeing Carolina. Hamburg has received her again, only to punish her spirited rebellion with a perpetual ban; she has lost the most valued members of her company; a tour in Russia has brought financial disaster. She pauses in Leipzig long enough to all-but-slay Gottsched, now her most hostile critic, by producing an act out of one of his plays exactly as he has clamored to have it produced, and by staging a satire she has composed portraying him as Censor. There follows change after change, an almost frantic effort to catch hold here, there, or anywhere. Debt, dissolution of troupe after troupe, official discourtesy, public indifference, finally abject poverty.

Her death-scene, in a little farmhouse near Dresden, affects us by the proud spirit she shows to the very end, and by the devotion and tenderness of all the other characters—no longer the actor-friends but those simple country people whom she has drawn to her in the final years of retirement and poverty. Perhaps she smiles a little, toward the end, to think that Gottsched too has come down, has been deposed from his pretentious position as arbiter of literature and stage—has even been ridiculed by the younger artists, writers, and actors. We hope that she knows that she, more than any other one person, has made possible the march of this new generation directly on to one of the world flowerings of dramatic art. With the cruelty of youth, the adherents of the new stage have found her "old-fashioned"; but perhaps some glimpse of the ultimate truth comforts her. She has accomplished the union of stage and literature, and she has given a new purpose to acting.

In a scene so incidental that it escaped our notice, in next to the last act, we might have remarked a young Leipzig student named Gotthold Ephraim Lessing, one of the intellectuals who were drawn into association with the troupe of the Neubers. Indeed the boy Lessing was hanging about for some two years—a pretty soubrette in the company had something to do with it—and he gleaned first-hand knowledge of stage methods without which he never could have become the world's second notable "theatre theorist" and Germany's first great dramatist. Carolina Neuber even staged an immature play of his, about his fellow-students; and of course from that time he began to neglect his theological studies and to shape his life toward the professional theatres.

Even the most superficial student of the stage knows by name the *Hamburgische Dramaturgie*, which is really little more than a series of dramatic criticisms, such as scores of critics write today after the important "openings" in the theatres of Paris, Berlin, or New York; but there must have been more than average meat in them, because scholars still read and refer to them—and besides they were the first serious "reviews" of play performances published in Germany. But immediately the many capital cities were full of imitations, and indeed of pirated editions of the *Dramaturgy* itself. Another impetus had been added to the stream started by Carolina Neuber.

The occasion of Lessing's *Dramaturgy* was the attempt to establish in Hamburg the first German National Theatre, during the years

A stage with wing settings, as seen at Strassburg in 1655. This is probably truer to the average effect achieved than are the usual idealized depictions, with wing edges suppressed. [From *Wiener Szenische Kunst*, by Joseph Gregor.]

1767–69. The company was doubtless the best yet brought together in Germany, including both Konrad Ekhof and Friedrich Ludwig Schröder, noted in history as the greatest two actors ever to grace the German-speaking stage; and the standard of play choice was high.

There was, however, grievous mismanagement and not a little intrigue among the players; and the attempt to set up a permanent national stage proved abortive. The event may be marked as significant, however, as the first effort toward an established theatre in a country where the institutional playhouses were destined to be Europe's finest in the nineteenth and early twentieth centuries. (But Vienna had had a "resident" theatre from 1712 on, and the famous *Burgtheater* traces its history back to 1741, although it became a "National" theatre only in 1776.) And there is that more tangible monument, the criticisms of the Hamburg theatre's "official critic" Lessing.

The publication of the *Hamburg Dramaturgy*, indeed, had not only local and national but international implications. For it was here that Lessing laid down the challenge to French Classicism. He has been called the first great critic after Aristotle—but that is perhaps crying down the Frenchmen a little. Nevertheless the German was broad enough to see world drama as a whole, he was the first outside England to set Shakespeare's name among the stage immortals; and he did more than any other to turn the attention of German dramatists away from the stiff French tragedies and toward the more human and freer English ones. He even had the audacity to prove that the Voltaire-Racine tradition wasn't "classic" at all—was, indeed, anti-Greek. He had no German masterpieces to offer as substitutes for the French which were being deposed; he kept on, however, "plugging Shakespeare," as our theatre people of today would put it. It wasn't long until Shakespearean production became a great national pastime in Germany, so that in the early decades of the twentieth century the real home of the great bard was to be in Central Europe—while English-speaking nations honored him chiefly in the reading, and only occasionally in production.

Lessing went further. Even while disclaiming any serious pretensions as dramatist—he had refused the post of official poet in the Hamburg venture, preferring that of paid critic—he proceeded to write some of the *humanest* dramas ever staged up to that time. He was, doubtless, following hints out of another and somewhat apostate Frenchman, Diderot, as well as impulses gained out of his study of the Elizabethan playwrights. His prettiest play, *Minna von Barnhelm*, is still acted endlessly on the German stage. It is a tender, rather serious, prose comedy, dealing with real characters. His tragedy, *Miss Sarah Sampson* approaches the later *bourgeois* type, is a play of ordinary life that avoids the false sublimity and courtly twaddle of the transplanted French mode; and *Emilia Galotti* treats regal characters with new honesty and reticence. None of these plays by Lessing can properly be enrolled among the works by the great immortals of the stage: they are a bit too slight for such company. But they are emi-

nently actable, and sympathy-provoking; and they mark Germany's
entry into dramatic literature.

Brander Matthews, who insisted vigorously that drama should always be studied with relation to contemporary conditions of representation, notes illuminatingly that Lessing is the first dramatist to
shape his plays so that changes of scene occur between acts; avoiding
breaking any act into scenes demanding different settings, and thus
avoiding the long waits, the disillusioning pauses, except after the

Among the occasional productions at the German courts, apart from any
connection with the popular stage, were operas in the Italian style. This is a
scene from *l'Erinto* at Munich as early as 1661, with perspective setting on a
proscenium-framed stage. [From *Geschichte der Münchner Oper*, by Max
Zenger.]

act-dénouements. By this time, of course, the Italian picture scenery
had come to dominate legitimate as well as opera stages, in Germany
as in the rest of Europe.

Sturm und Drang. The name is usually applied to the period
following Lessing, and covering the theatrical activities of a courageous
and zealous group of playwrights from which emerged the immortal

Goethe and Schiller. The words signify both unrest and excesses. It has seemed to me that one might carry the application farther back: the story of the German theatre has been stormy enough from the very start, and certainly this particular tempest has been brewing ever since those days when Germany was a meeting ground of the *Commedia dell'Arte* players, the English Comedians, and the correct French troupes; and the Neuber-Gottsched episode was something more than a gusty prelude. But it has seemed to many historians that just now, immediately after mid-century, Germany was quite suddenly alive with stirrings of young genius, with wild experiment, with painful travail—was caught in the storm and stress of a violent literary and dramatic rebirth.

The term *Sturm und Drang* is taken from the title of a play by a minor dramatist now all but forgotten by the rest of the world—Germany was simply teeming with playwrights intent on establishing the forms of German national drama. The storminess was evident not only in the general restless activity, not to say upheaval, but in the violence and extravagance within individual plays. There was the flood of horrors and licentiousness that often follows after a new-found freedom. But when the succeeding steadiness came, there were many solidly productive dramatists; and on the crest of the storm waters, Goethe and Schiller had been carried into the theatre.

In the matters beyond playwriting, in acting and staging and theatre architecture, there was similar activity and progress. Ekhof—since called "the Garrick of Germany"—had already set an example of unstilted, sincere acting, and the conventional declamatory and ranting method was losing its one-time popularity. More important, the wave of *purpose* among actors had strengthened; great numbers of them preferred the new plays and dignified company-effort, to the old *Hanswurstiades* and catch-as-catch-can trouping. Even at this time not a great deal can be claimed in regard to *thoroughly*-rehearsed productions—not a little of the old methods of careless improvisation (not the creative sort) persisted. And in more serious realms even a fairly natural and blunt tragedy would be played in stiff courtly costumes, in correctest Versailles fashion. But there are stirrings and promise of greater things. And Ekhof's successor, the young Schröder, is already on the scene.

Stage settings improve, too. That is, they tend toward operatic display: the new picture settings are well painted instead of badly painted. "Machine effects" have come in: plays are advertised "with metamorphoses, machines, and disguises." Here and there a really fine theatre is being erected. Already there are proscenium-frame stages like those of France and Italy; one of the earliest of those permanent

Johann Wolfgang von Goethe, 1749–1832. The history of the German drama through two centuries might be summed up in the phrase, "from Hans Wurst to Goethe." [From a contemporary engraving after the portrait by Pecht.]

Court Theatres, which are to become so distinctive a feature of German theatrical life, is built, at Gotha, in 1776. (It was here that Ekhof spent his last years, acting and directing.)

Out of the period—between Lessing and Goethe—a very few names of dramatists should be recorded. Friedrich Gottlieb Klopstock wrote a number of religious and patriotic plays. Christoph Martin Wieland wrote dramas that are no longer important; but his translations of Shakespeare give him a memorable position. Heinrich Wilhelm von Gerstenberg and Maximilian Klinger were nearer the *Sturm und Drang* culmination. But all these names, and all the works of these men, pale into insignificance in comparison with that Johann Wolfgang Goethe whose name remains even today the latest in the list of unquestioned world geniuses in the field of stage literature.

Of those six or eight "immortals" of the theatre, Goethe is least of all the typical theatre artist. He is greatest of all the writers who went into the theatre but became not of it; the mightiest literary figure who came to dominate but not to exist on the boards. Sophocles, Shakespeare, Molière had been stage people, with no other thought, life, or purpose; but Goethe, next in that noble line, walked apart, ever the lone poet.

Certainly here was one of the profoundest minds that ever came into the service of the theatre, in any capacity, and one of the noblest characters. Had Goethe given his life to writing for the stage, instead of making that one out of several interests—philosophy, politics, science, literature—he might have been accepted in all later times as on the very height with Sophocles and Shakespeare; as it is, there is always that reservation: his dramas are not shaped to actability, to exist primarily as *stage flow*. As related to the theatre, there is a sense of fragmentary grandeur about them. Dramatic conflict is interrupted by illuminating philosophic speculation and by compellingly beautiful verse; but these things are not immediately born out of an acted story.

He was for twenty-six years director of the Court Theatre in Weimar, and he thus had every opportunity to learn practical stage technique and to gauge the relationship between actors and audience. But still he remained somewhat detached, aloof. There is not the exact, the perfect rightness of the play *in the theatre*, as with Shakespeare or Molière, or even—to take lesser examples—with Lope de Vega or Lessing. The peculiar life of the stage, the "feel" of acting, the sheer stageworthiness, is not in his works. And yet, such magnificent fragments! For the first time since the Elizabethans, we feel that drama is again, in the wider implication, "of a certain magnitude."

He began, as might be expected, with a play only fumblingly dramatic, but with the marks of genius on it: originality, spirited emotion, daring freedom—and poetry. *Götz von Berlichingen* was, indeed, a final landmark in the way marked out by the *Sturm und Drang* progression. There could be no longer any doubt that the French domination was ended, that the classic rules were shattered, that the German national drama would follow a line drawn nearer to Shakespeare's practice than to that of the Corneille-Racine-Voltaire school—and with a native spirit and freshness added.

Other dramas followed, prose and poetic, similarly unequal in values; including a series of pastorals for his court. With a belated Renaissance interest in, and study of, the remains of antiquity, Goethe wrote an *Iphigenia* and a *Tasso*, but the formal limitations of his own conception of Neo-Classicism curbed what might have been the dramatic effectiveness of these plays. A minor domestic drama, *Clavigo*, is perhaps most effective of all in performance; and *Egmont* has extraordinarily dramatic scenes, but loosely held together in the play-framework. It is really only in the masterpiece *Faust* that Goethe exhibits the qualities that warrant naming him with the highest.

This tragedy was the fruit of almost a lifetime of thought and endeavor. The first conception preceded the finishing of Part II by more than a quarter-century. It is almost hopeless to attempt a summary or description of the work, for only the poetry, the profound philosophy, and the occasional intense feeling of it make up for a framework disproportioned, a tale undramatically slow. Goethe took the old legend of Faust, who sold his soul to the Devil, as a basis for the drama; and he set out to shape a tragedy that would have all of personal experience in it, his own and that of mankind.

The play (doubly inadequate word here!) begins with a "Theatre Prologue," where the manager, the poet, and the Merry Andrew of a booth theatre debate life, the stage, and audiences. A second Prologue, in Heaven, shows Mephistopheles wagering with the Lord that he can lead Faust astray—a portion of the drama that is sometimes considered blasphemous and unprintable. How closely Goethe molded it to the simplicity and naïveté of the mediæval religious plays becomes apparent in the closing lines:

> MEPHISTOPHELES (*alone*)
> I like, at times, to hear the Ancient's word,
> And have a care to be most civil:
> It's really kind of such a noble Lord
> So humanly to gossip with the Devil!

But in the first scene of the play proper, in a Gothic chamber, we find the serious motive of the drama set out, the erudite Faust pushing against all limitations in his intellectual curiosity, tempted to suicide but putting the poisoned goblet aside. From there the action moves on, never swiftly, but with the most varied embroidery: Faust out among the people, Faust in his study tempted by Mephistopheles, Faust making the pact, Faust deserting Knowledge and Theory for the pursuit of enjoyments; and so on to the story of the simple and innocent Margaret. From her first entry to her final tragic appearance in the dungeon with reason gone, her story is told in eighteen scenes or episodes, varied by minor flights and by that major one known as *Walpurgis Nacht*—seemingly interruptions to the human drama, and yet so right in a higher sense that the tragedy cannot be visualized without them.

To this Part I, Goethe added in later years a Part II which is in itself a full drama, but far more difficult to grasp, more obscure, without a primarily human story as basis. It is indeed a flight into the supernatural that has daunted all but the German theatre directors; and they as a rule have been content to overcome the very grave dramatic difficulties of Part I. It was G. H. Lewes who wrote of that, in his excellent *The Life and Works of Goethe*, as "this wondrous poem, the popularity of which is almost unexampled. It appeals to all minds with the irresistible fascination of an eternal problem. It has every element: wit, pathos, wisdom, farce, mystery, melody, reverence, doubt, magic, and irony; not a chord of the lyre is unstrung, not a fibre of the heart untouched." And, indeed, outside of the three Greek tragedy writers and Shakespeare, no dramatist has given the world a tragedy more sought out by serious readers the world over. I would like to quote here excerpts that might stand for the quality of the poem; but the design is so vast and the excursions so bewilderingly rich, that no chosen bits could be adequate—and it is a sad fact that the translations into English are hardly more than serviceable, bringing the larger drama vividly before us, but with grievous loss of poetic values.

The poet-dramatist who wrote this *Faust* appears, in later histories, like a giant among the Lilliputians of the Weimar court. There is a tragi-comedy there—you will find yourself both amused and moved if you will read through one of the biographies. The great dramatist, so aloof from the stage in a way, is yet, professionally, the head of a special sort of theatre; intimately connected at first with amateur theatricals, he is then the active director for twenty-six years of a company of second-rate professional actors. He is even author of a very detailed code of rules for acting. And he is seen, toward the end, at the mercy of his petty master, the Duke of Weimar, and of the Duke's mistress. Together they make Goethe's life miserable over a term of years, until finally by insisting on the production of a play

Homage to Schiller as he leaves the theatre in Leipzig after the première of his *Jungfrau von Orleans*, 1801. [After a drawing by Theobald von Oer, in *Illustrirte Zeitung*.]

in which a trained poodle is chief actor, they force his resignation from the directorship of the Court Theatre. It is a pleasure to add that while in the position Goethe enjoyed ten years of collaborative producing with Schiller, before that poet's premature death.

Johann Christoph Friedrich von Schiller (1759–1805) combined a lesser poetic gift with a far better grasp of stage technique. He wrote historic dramas that continue to stir us in performance to this day: *Maria Stuart* and *Wilhelm Tell*. And the romantic *Don Carlos* and a play of intrigue, *Cabal and Love*, remain among the most effective of sheer "theatre pieces." Far from being aloof from the stage, Schiller learned every value and every trick of production, so that modern *régisseurs* find his dramas perfect media for *tours-de-force* of staging. He had a way, indeed, of dressing something very like melodrama in fine poetic clothes.

His first play, written when he was twenty-two, and entitled *The Robbers*, wobbled between melodrama and passionate tragedy, all done up with the uncertainty of immature genius. But he was immediately accepted into the theatre for it (the Mannheim National Theatre made an "event" of the production), and he set to work to master his art from the stage point of view as well as from that of the literary man. He even had some idea of becoming an actor—an ambition he did well to give up. Gradually he brought his extravagance under some sort of control, and by the time of the first verse-tragedy, *Don Carlos*, he is marked as one of the great serious dramatists. He treats history with a great deal of freedom, being less reverent toward historical accuracy and toward what earlier had been considered good play-form than toward a certain unity of human-dramatic expressiveness. He did nothing to further that compacting of the play-structure, that tightening of technique, which is to mark so distinctively the playwriting of the nineteenth century; he is rather a late flowering of the impulse that gave Calderon and the lesser Elizabethans to the theatre, the more romantic, more sentimental, far-riding poet-dramatists of extravagant eras. His *Wallenstein*, sometimes considered his most impressive work, rides a bit outside the limits of ordinary theatre production, though its serious literary values and philosophic implications cannot be denied.

There was in Germany in the time of Goethe and Schiller a spirit of idealism, of glowing personal initiative, that led directly to the choice of subjects such as Joan of Arc (*Die Jungfrau von Orleans*) and William Tell. At Weimar, where Goethe and Schiller spent so much time together, there was developing a new nationalism, a devotion to liberty and humanism; there is a breath of that wind of Revolution that is so soon to fan destructive fires, overturn political institutions, and incidentally transform the theatre. One root of the new growth goes back to Rousseau, whose ideas had been subscribed to in Germany widely and passionately.

The one-time current toward naturalness and prose, on the other hand, was arrested. Times were too exciting, the storm-and-stress violence had been too great, the new idealism of young Germany was too strong, to permit immediate drifting of the theatre into that

A theatre in a market square in Brussels, as seen by the painter F. van der Meulen. [From the original in the Liechtenstein Gallery, Vienna.]

realism which will mark the nineteenth century. First there will be the so-called Romantic Period. And just preceding that is this flowering of the poetic, the high, drama under Goethe and Schiller—something far finer than mere Romanticism, and the very opposite of Realism—but again, with a freedom, vigor, and freshness unknown to the then accepted Classicism.

Among playwrights immediately after Schiller and Goethe, however, there is a lapse to a sentimentality that is in direct line toward Romanticism. The tearful domestic drama becomes a special favorite, though most of the popular authors alternate between that and imitations of the two German masters. "The Great Schröder"—the theatre's historians still call him that—wrote many plays now forgotten except

in name. Another actor-dramatist, Auguste Wilhelm Iffland, was likewise prolific, and made good his claim to a place among those who
wrote plays "for acting, not reading." They attained an extraordinary
popularity in the theatres of the time; but their vogue was as much
based on current taste and a passing emotionalism and as little on

Scene from a German domestic drama, on a wing-set stage.

eternal principles as are those plays of earlier and later actors, Garrick
and Pinero, or David Belasco and George M. Cohan.

But while Schröder and Iffland retain a place in history for their
acting and for their service in establishing institutional theatres in
Germany, August von Kotzebue has been a more or less permanent
victim of his fame as playwright. He was mistaken by critics of his
time as a genius of first water, and his plays were pirated throughout
the Western world. When the reaction came which showed up his
work as thinly disguised melodrama, he became suddenly the typical
bad example of playwriting, achieving a notoriety as great as his
fame had once been. He is the logical culmination of the bad en-
thusiasms of the storm-and-stress group, as Goethe and Schiller had
been of the better tendencies. He is the embodiment of the good

craftsman who mistakes sensational action for essential drama.

There are those who would treat the story of the German stage before Romanticism (and aside from the two outstanding literary figures) as a chapter in the story of "the Great Actors." Mantzius in his six-volume *History of Theatrical Art* covers this whole period in the volume devoted to "Great Actors of the Eighteenth Century"; and he portions the material under the three names, Ekhof, Schröder, and Iffland. Schröder's was perhaps a strong enough and a universal enough genius to support such head-line fame; the others were hardly world figures. Ekhof had brought in restraint and sincerity when those qualities were much needed; but he was quietly and humanly effective rather than commanding.

Schröder, however, had been not only the best German actor of his time but the dominating figure in the most formative period of the national stage, a recognized example to all other actors; and he had directed his companies with true command and insight. He carried on the fight for a national theatre from the point where the ill-fated venture in Hamburg (that had been made famous by Lessing) left it. It was in that same Hamburg that he directed a later theatre, over two periods totalling twenty years, with such success that this became the theatrical centre of Germany. He built a company ensemble as no one before him had done; he introduced Shakespeare *on the stage*—and thus the dramatists saw that what they had accepted in their reading as model was equally effective in the theatre; and he imparted a sort of grandeur to the acting profession. At the time of his retirement to a life of ease, at a comparatively early age, he had accomplished to the full those purposes which to the youthful Carolina Neuber had seemed like golden dreams. The stage of Germany had been "established," actors had become creative artists, and out of the union of stage and literature had flowered the works of Goethe and Schiller. This was no longer a Germany relishing *Hanswurstiades*, or grateful for a foreign company importing sometimes academically good, and more often very bad, dramatic art. It was a Germany enjoying the most prolific and most original theatre in the world, exporting plays to the rest of Europe; a Germany in which "the best minds" were excited about the stage, creating for it, finding inspiration and sustenance in it.

CHAPTER
17

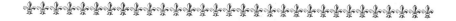

The Theatre and
the Birth of Democracy

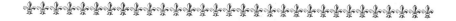

ALONG toward the end of the eighteenth century some large bonfires were lighted in Europe and America by men variously calling themselves patriots, rebels, sons of liberty, brothers, and— Democrats. As is usual in times of Revolution many good people actively disapproved, and the great mass of mankind merely looked on apathetically. But such was the burning sincerity and the intense energy of the rebel minority that soon one could see, by the light of the red glow in the sky, here a royal head popped off by a very bloody guillotine, and there the remnants of a Royalist army fleeing before a handful of lusty Republicans. And very soon democracy was an established fact, and all the kings of Europe were sitting up rubbing their eyes and wondering if that really could have happened to brother Louis of France (and more horrible, to his once beautiful Marie Antoinette), and whether those upstart American colonists had really whipped Cousin George's troops.

Since the days of the Renaissance and the birth of Humanism, when man reached out after knowledge and refused longer to let the Church do his thinking for him, there had been no overturn comparable to this one. Before the Renaissance the Catholic Church had ruled, by divine right. After the Renaissance, kings and queens ruled, also by divine right. After the American and French people threw out their kings, presumably the Democrats were going to rule, again by divine right. Whatever else had happened, clearly the spirit of man had found a new release. And since the theatre has to do first with the spirit, surely this must be a great moment for the stage, another Renaissance perhaps.

A revolution in ways of thinking, such as that which ushered in democracy, goes back to causes and events and abortive efforts through many generations earlier; and similarly, its full effects, and right judgment of its values, will not be evident until many generations later. Indeed, today, a century and a half after the event, we are likely to be so blinded by sheer superstition toward the institution of democracy

French stage costuming of the mid-eighteenth century—symbolic of the stage and theatre of the time.

that we hesitate to ask whether the freedom that was born and reborn in 1776 and 1789 did not bring with it disadvantages almost as great as the advantages. It would be a doughty one among us who would admit allegiance to any other political faith before democracy. There is, indeed, our common sense telling us that the spirit of man must be free, that the Divine Right of Kings is an illusion, and that only out of liberty of conscience and action can justice be born. But in the theatre particularly there is reason for dissent and wobbling. Not many years ago I heard an artist whom I consider one of the greatest in the theatre, protest after this fashion: "The old theatre is dead, the new theatre is not born. The stage is in the hands of tradesmen and upstarts. It all started with that damned French Revolution!"

The melancholy fact is that the birth of democracy neither ushered in a Renaissance of the arts of the stage, nor even served to carry on the impetus of the only fresh theatrical achievement of the period immediately preceding, the development of a poetic drama under the banner of Goethe and Schiller. It would be pleasant to record that immediately upon the coming of the spirit of democracy, the theatre burst into glorious activity, revived something of its old nobility, and became again the handmaid to man's reawakened spirit. As a matter of fact it entered into a decline, or else continued a decline which in most of Europe had been under way long since. For a full hundred years

A theatre at Rheims in 1785: a typical small theatre of the times. Note that part of the pit is still reserved for standees. [From Paris' *Le Théâtre à Reims.*]

there will not be a playwright of more than near-immortal fame; not until the Democrats who more or less rule Europe and America come under fire for their bourgeois morality and for their capitalistic exploitation. There will be no new giants or near-giants until Ibsen and Shaw. If the mantle of divinity was transferred from kings to the common people, it was a sort of divinity from which the Dionysian spirit was notably absent.

Immediately preceding the French Revolution the courts of France and Germany and Spain had kept up at least a tinselly show of theatrical activity; and in England and Italy there had been real flare-ups of playwriting genius, in Goldsmith and Sheridan, and in Goldoni and

Gozzi. In reviewing these pre-Democratic developments, before turning to the actual years of the Revolutions, we shall do well to note
certain relevant facts: that in this earlier time the theatre is still being
coddled at courts, aided with patronage which it may find necessary
beyond the support of popular audiences. And that drama has not yet
been brought down to common life, in the analytic and fact-finding
sense; it is still more theatrical, with a life of its own, than reportorial
and photographic. But that there are unmistakable signs that drama,
in a larger view, is marching on, if jerkily, to greater familiarity, to
closer identification with life; the old aloofness and remoteness are
giving way to a personal emotion growing out of nearness to ordinary
events of living.

SINCE Voltaire there has not existed a dominating figure in the theatre
of France. There has been the age of great acting, but now even that
is more a memory than a fact. The world has moved on; but French
officialdom and the French stage, with their characteristic indifference
to—nay, scorn of—all art that develops outside of French territory, go
on sleepily in the old worn paths. The Germans have demolished for
all time the superstitious "rules of playwriting"; but officially the laws
still hold in France. German and English players have put new life
and humanity into acting; but you would never guess it from anything
you might witness at the *Comédie Française*. Tragedy is still played
"with much convulsion and contortion." In the 1780s France is living
on the past, dying slowly.

The stage of the time does not fail to be characteristic and, as we
shall see presently, picturesque. There is the elegance persisting from
the great days of Louis XIV, a hollow elegance, perhaps, now that
there are no truly noble forms to fill out the gorgeous clothes; and the
salles are still the most beautifully decorated and the stages the best
equipped in Europe. There is too a tradition. It is tradition, indeed,
that has made the *Théâtre Français* the stereotyped, half-alive institution that it is. Without leadership from among its own personnel, it
submits tamely to capricious court rule. Courtiers, completely ignorant
of stage art, but appointed by the King, regulate every detail of the
running of France's official playhouse, not least of all the matter of
which ladies shall be elevated into the showy parts. Their only other
concern is the censoring of plays so that nothing derogatory to the
old régime shall be spoken from the stage. And there are no Racines
at court now.

There are individually picturesque figures crossing this strangely
dead-alive stage. Here is the actor Ducis discovering Shakespeare at
second-hand, falling in love with the plays of the Barbarian from

across the Channel, but rewriting them in accordance with the sacred classic unities, devitalizing them by banishing all violent action to off-stage, adding such conventional characters as the confidant, and beautifully decorating the texts with high poetry! Imagine *Hamlet* squeezed into one day's time and into one place; Polonius as the King's confidant, a new character inserted as confidante for Gertrude, and much

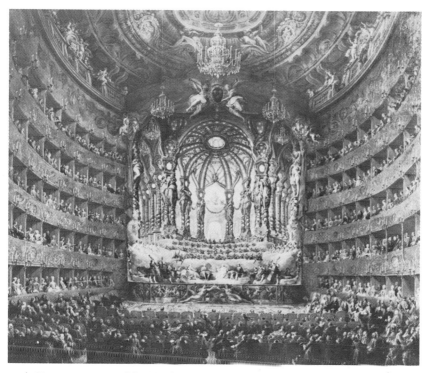

A Performance with Music: a painting by Giovanni Pannini, in the Louvre. Just as the Italian street scene and the *Commedia* companies became standard in France, so also the Italian operatic playhouse was accepted in the North. Here the scenery and the bizarre stage effects are notable in an overdecorated, operatic house—not yet identified as certainly Italian or French.

of the original action deleted and the events recounted by these four; and the Hamlet-Ophelia love interest played up—all in rhymed Alexandrines!

There was, of course, a succession of vivid courtesan-actresses (an official-ruled stage makes for that); but the strangely contrasting Mlle Raucourt was a better artist than any of them. She made a sensational success with her first appearance, as Dido, at the age of sixteen, and after the *Comédie Française* discharged her a few years later, for the fault, unforgivable in stage circles, of unexplained absence on a night of performance, her unrivalled ability soon led the company to recall her as a permanent member. Still it was her flaunted masculinity, and such extra-theatre affairs as beating up her landlord, serving prison terms, and continuous scandals in the rôle of *galant* that got chronicled the more vividly for later generations. In this period there was, too, the early acting of the great Talma—but he will appear where he better belongs, up in the thick of the French Revolution, and as Napoleon's favorite.

From among the crowd of futile but popular playwrights there stands out one figure by contrast—the only dramatist to be remembered out of the period, Beaumarchais. His pleasant and shrewd comedies, *The Barber of Seville* and *The Marriage of Figaro* are still played today. But their author is more famous for his independence of thought and action, in a time when wise people pretended blindness and authors as well as common folk buckled neatly to authority. Beaumarchais fought firmly and courageously against court censorship and against the powers that ruled in the official playhouse in Paris. He insisted upon an author's right to have a say about casting, thus crossing no end of favorites, as well as a number of powerful "protectors," and he even wrote out detailed "stage directions" for the productions of his plays, a proceeding theretofore unheard-of. In refusing to be cheated out of his royalties by the actor-group in the *Comédie Française*, he made a stand that ultimately led to those author-guilds that today guard the dramatist so effectively from pirating and exploitation.

But most apropos here, Beaumarchais contributed to the stage the only play that may be said to have forwarded, through its performances, the march toward democracy. The witty *Marriage of Figaro* is so full of references to a decadent nobility, and so patently a reflection of widely current but carefully suppressed bitterness, that Louis XVI personally ordered the play banned; and it took the tenacious dramatist five years to fight through the various censorship offices to a first performance. It was a sign of gradually changing times that he was able to win through, after an expression of royal displeasure. It was even more significant that this ironic comedy, painting boldly a feeble aristocracy in contrast with rising common folk, should be played at the official subventioned theatre of France, to crowded houses, through what was for those times a "long run." The opening at the *Théâtre Français* on April 27, 1784, was occasion for smashing in doors and near-rioting. The spirit was already abroad that would find climax in the storming of the Bastille and in considerable reflected violence within the walls of the national playhouse.

A private theatre as seen from the stage. [From an engraving by LeRoy after Binet.]

But in general the French stage of these years was tame, undisturbed by genius, content with the old acting and routine plays, servile or at least complacent under domination by an enfeebled but still ruling court. Its staging was as artificial as the old playwriting that decreed the longest way around as the prettiest way of expressing a sentiment; its costumes as puffed and ornate as its tragic poetry; its relation to full-blooded life as insecure as that of the affected court society. Its actors were as often as not ignorant in every department except that one so admirably but so disproportionately prized in French theatres: *diction.* In Paris at this time there were five regular theatres: the specially privileged and subsidized *Comédie Française,* with a company known as *Les comediens ordinaires du Roi,* an institution with a monopoly on "tragedy and comedy"; the Opera, known as the *Académie royale de musique;* the *Théâtre de l'Ambigu-Comique* and the *Théâtre Nicolet,* given up to farce, spectacle, and pantomime; and finally the *Théâtre Italien,* at times a real rival to the official theatre, but usually forced to a policy of music-plays. For many decades the artificial limitation of legitimate theatres, the court-decreed monopoly, had militated against new stage creativeness. When the Revolution puts an end to the monopoly, we shall see nearly half a hundred theatres in place of these five.

In France in the half-century before 1790, the important theatres are really less interesting than the unimportant, i.e., the amateur, ones. One might have seen, in these years, real theatres in king's palaces, miniature theatres in chateaus, stages in country houses, even in the town houses of society leaders. In Germany, the court theatres are already becoming the "standard" playhouses, fully professionalized, and there is real dramatic progress there, in the historic sense. In France they are toys, for the amusement of amateurs, and interesting only because kings and queens are concerned. Back in the days of Louis the Grand, as we have seen, the court had to do with the development of a national art. Under Louis XVI the private opera house at Versailles is used but fitfully, with productions brought out from Paris.

But in the Chateau at Versailles there is also the *Théâtre des Petites Apartements;* and out in the park, over toward the Trianons, is the private theatre which has been specially erected for Marie Antoinette. It is, indeed, a queen's plaything, *par excellence.* Today we damn quite heartily the decorators who strew our modern playhouses with faded and sterile copies of regal magnificence. But what could be more fitting in a queen's own personal theatre than this profusion of decoration, this jewel-box prettiness, this boudoir intimacy? One may note in the illustration many features common to the larger theatres of the epoch: It is designed on the usual horse-shoe plan, with three floors of seats.

Features not uncommon are the presence of the prompter's box, the comparative shallowness of the auditorium, and the very low orchestra floor designed to throw the best seats into the first balcony. (This balcony in Marie Antoinette's time was not so large as that shown in the drawing, and probably much more graceful in line; it was enlarged

Interior of the dainty but courtly theatre of Marie Antoinette at the Trianon, Versailles. [After a drawing by A. Benard in *La Comédie à la Cour*, by Adolphe Jullien.]

by the addition of the cross-boarded portion of the floor, with a consequent squaring of the railing, in 1836, under King Louis-Philippe, "to accommodate his large family.") The stage was equipped with every device that money could buy, and leading artists were drafted to design the settings. Marie Antoinette acted on the stage, when the whim took her, over a period of five years—though not so regularly as Mme de Pompadour in the less pretentious theatre in the Château.

The last performance under the Queen's "direction" occurred on the evening of August 19, 1785, when the shadow of revolution was already over the land. And as if it were not indiscreet enough for the court to flaunt its wasteful extravagance and its flippant pleasures in such a time, Marie Antoinette chose the comedy *The Barber of Seville* as a vehicle (playing Rosina herself), and invited Beaumarchais to the performance. The incident of the opening of *The Marriage of Figaro*

A famous actor-manager of a Court theatre. Queen Marie Antoinette of France, from the painting by Madame Vigée-Lebrun. Eventually she was guillotined.

at the *Comédie Française* had but just occurred, and the town was already agog over Beaumarchais' audacious criticism of the nobles and his defiance of the royal ban on the play; and yet here was the Queen inviting the author of that play to the performance of another of his comedies, at the palace where he would necessarily meet the King. One may ask whether it was bravado, or if there was, as some think, personal point in this gesture of an actress-queen conspicuously crossing her none-too-faithful King for the sake of a favored courtier. In any case, one may be sure the court theatricals had their bit of effect in stirring public hatred toward that day when the Democrats were to use the guillotine alike on this King and this Queen.

But if play-acting on the part of a Queen was odious to a portion of the French people, it might be indulged in by Royal Mistresses and courtiers with impunity and as a natural part of the interminable round of fêtes, balls, and entertainments at Versailles and the other palaces. And to at least one noble courtesan, theatricals proved a godsend. To put it bluntly, Mme de Pompadour had felt herself slipping as favorite of the pleasure-surfeited Louis XV. She must devise a new means of diverting him and showing herself to the best advantage. She could act, she could sing, according to historians, and she was very beautiful; all she needed was the proper stage. In one of the smaller galleries of the palace a tiny auditorium was arranged, and a lavishly equipped stage was appended. The nobles of the court responded to the call for a company of actors, and Mme de Pompadour became the most prominent and most applauded member of one of the most distinguished amateur companies the world has known. Her success was so great, her charm and ability so irresistible, that she not only won her King-lover completely, but established the private court theatre as a four years' attraction at Versailles.

We are fortunate in having a pretty drawing by Cochin of a production of *Acis and Galatea* in this theatre. It shows Mme de Pompadour on the stage as Galatea, and the Vicomte de Rohan as Acis; and one may discern the King and Queen and members of the court among the spectators, as well as every detail of the seating arrangement. It is worth while to pause and note the daintiness and intimacy of the auditorium, so appropriate to a theatre which was in reality a toy of a monarch's favorite. There is in this drawing, too, a graphic illustration of the seventeenth and eighteenth century drift toward picturized setting. A theatre building is necessarily architectural, and the stage is presumably a platform for acting. But here one sees the architecture lost out of one-half of the building, and the platform absolutely disguised. The painter's ideal has wholly prevailed, and the actors are (the modernists point out) ill-fitting figures in an easel picture.

The theatre of Madame de Pompadour in the palace at Versailles. [From the etching by Guilmet after Cochin's drawing.]

The court theatres were but one phase of the widespread amateur dramatic activity of this time. What the King and his circle did, the next stratum of society below must do, and so on down to the very fringe of the elect and near-elect. "A little theatre," wrote the Goncourts, "is set up in the city mansion, a great theatre is built in the château. All society dreams the theatre from one end of France to the other . . . The *grandes dames* cannot live without the theatre, without a stage to themselves." And yet the phenomenon has importance only socially. Occasionally amateurs are better than professionals, less stilted,

Drawing, after Cochin, of Madame de Pompadour and the Duc de Nivernois in *l'Oracle*. [By courtesy of *Theatre Arts Monthly*.]

more sincere, truer to the spirit—as we happily know today, when a "little" theatre movement has swept over two continents. But not for long does any stage but the professional demand attention when the theatre is being studied.

IN ENGLAND, during this period, audiences had been enjoying the late fruits of Garrick's epochal innovations, though the British theatre was already entering upon a decline. Acting, to be sure, was far advanced as compared with that to be seen in France; but when Garrick retired from management of Drury Lane in 1776, the greatest of English actors left the stage, and at the same time the London theatre lost the only director who had been able during his century to organize dramatic activity in a masterly fashion, to make the stage a dignified and worthy companion to the other arts.

Playwriting had been at a low ebb for a very long time; and what Garrick and his fellows had done to earlier texts—particularly those of Shakespeare—is enough to mark current taste as decadent if not inhuman. Tediously bad plays were being written, but worse was the almost unbelievable adaptation, nay, mutilation of earlier masterpieces, to make good "acting vehicles." Still the theatre had been raised to a position of respect, of wide public interest, and of widespread critical attention among men of letters. And a group of actors had achieved a dignified standing till then unknown in English society.

Here there was no wave of interest in amateur playhouses, and the Court, least of all, felt any devotion to the stage—at least, only the masculine side of the royal family felt it, and then only toward the feminine side of the theatre. The tradition of the actress-courtesan, indeed, persisted. The public expected a reigning actress to have a noble or fashionable lover, or perhaps one after another; and many a prince and duke enters here into the annals of the stage. The vivacious and popular soubrette Dorothy Jordan even achieved a somewhat matrimonial connection (ten children) with him who later became William IV; Elizabeth Farren, described by Horace Walpole as the most perfect of actresses, cut short her stage career to marry the Earl of Derby, when the fortunate death of his less esteemed first wife made possible her elevation to ladyship; the versatile Mrs. Robinson, after experience of "society," authorship, imprisonment, and acting, achieved two years of mistressing to the then Prince of Wales (later George IV) who ill rewarded her devotion. But these were not connections that in any sense wedded royalty to art. In fact, from this time on, British kings and queens were to go their separate untheatrical way (their allegiance and patronage were to be turned thenceforth to "sports"); and thus the theatre, even before the recognized birth of Democracy, had been wholly dependent upon "the people" for its maintenance. The shrewd Garrick had actually made a fortune out of Drury Lane, even while maintaining a high standard in production and as near a standard in play choice as the artificial and skeptic taste of the time would permit. But with his relinquishment of that theatre, there begins a record of ups-and-downs, of the struggle of the stage to establish itself as an independent economic institution, a record spotted with brief flare-ups of beauty and prosperity, but without sustained importance. During 190 years after, England had nothing approaching a "national" theatre, a condition to be remedied only in 1963.

The one burst of genius came in the three years preceding Garrick's retirement, and curiously enough, at a rival playhouse, Covent Garden Theatre. Oliver Goldsmith's *She Stoops to Conquer* was first produced in that one-time pantomime-house in March 1773, and Richard Brinsley Sheridan's *The Rivals* in January 1775. Thus appeared suddenly, in the deadest of times, England's only near-immortal dramatists of the eighteenth and nineteenth centuries.

Goldsmith is less indebted to the great comedy-writers of the past, and more a forerunner of nineteenth century dramaturgic developments, than is Sheridan. He brings a certain freshness and naturalness, comes nearer to an escape from the coldness of wit and the careful aloofness from life that had characterized the great Restoration playwrights—although one can hardly yet bring in the word "realism" when the characters act under names like Croaker, Hardcastle, and Lumpkin. And yet the homeliness of the opening lines of *She Stoops to Conquer* persists through the play, in spite of generous asides and many "Zounds!":

MRS. HARDCASTLE

I vow, Mr. Hardcastle, you're very particular. Is there a creature in the whole country but ourselves, that does not take a trip to town now and then, to rub off the dust a little? There's the two Miss Hoggs, and our neighbor Mrs. Grigsby, go to take a month's polishing every winter.

HARDCASTLE

Ay, and bring back vanity and affectation to last them the whole year. I wonder why London cannot keep its own fools at home! In my time, the follies of the town crept slowly among us, but now they travel faster than a stagecoach. . .

. . . I love every thing that's old: old friends, old times, old manners, old books, old wines; and I believe, Dorothy (*taking her hand*), you'll own I have been pretty fond of an old wife. . .

A snatch of dialogue between Marlow and Kate exhibits this fresh tenderness coupled with an old artificiality:

MARLOW (*aside*)

By heaven, she weeps. This is the first mark of tenderness I ever had from a modest woman, and it touches me. (*To her.*) Excuse me, my lovely girl, you are the only part of the family I leave with reluctance. But to be plain with you, the difference of our birth, fortune and education make an honorable connection impossible; and I can never harbor a thought of seducing simplicity that trusted in my honor, of bringing ruin upon one whose only fault was being too lovely.

MISS HARDCASTLE (*aside*)

Generous man! I now begin to admire him. (*To him.*) But I am sure
my family is as good as Miss Hardcastle's, and though I'm poor, that's
no great misfortune to a contented mind. . .

Goldsmith had previously written another comedy *The Good-
natured Man*, but it is less vivacious and less celebrated, and less honestly merry, than *She Stoops to Conquer*. The dramatist died the year
after the première of that success—when it had hardly begun its triumphant march across the stages of two continents.

Sheridan flamed brilliantly across the theatre sky, as dramatist and
producer, and then faded away in a dull haze of politics, "good living,"
and debt. For a brief few years he was the most spectacular figure in
the British theatre, not only as playwright but as producer; but then,
even though he nominally controlled Drury Lane for a score of years,
he progressively sank further from serious importance in either capacity. *The Rivals* and *The School for Scandal* remain on library
shelves, and in repertoire where repertory theatres still exist, to attest
his phenomenal gift as comedy-writer. Even schoolboys who have forgotten the titles of his plays remember Mrs. Malaprop, and Lydia Lan-
guish, and Sir Lucius O'Trigger, and Lady Sneerwell, Charles Surface,
Lady Teazle, and Sir Benjamin Backbite.

At twenty-four the gay blade Sheridan was already famous as the
author of *The Rivals*, was already a sought-after wit and society man,
and hero of a romantic elopement. At twenty-five he scored a second
sensational success with *The Duenna*, a play written for presentation
with music, which had a phenomenal run, and his fortune was so made
that he was able to buy a controlling interest in Drury Lane Theatre
from the retiring Garrick. At twenty-six we find him managing that
historic playhouse (with the aid of half a dozen members of his family), apparently initiating a new and glorious era in the London theatre; and bringing out, as the event of the season, his own *The School
for Scandal*, at a première of incomparable brilliancy. Walpole wrote,
"It seemed a marvelous resurrection of the stage."

Sheridan was no mere man-of-letters stepping into the theatre with
a script and some theories of staging. His father was an actor, not too
able or successful, but respected, and his mother a writer. He had
moved in circles where the stage was a living interest. He came
equipped also with—considering his years—a rich personal experience
of life. When he took over Drury Lane he fell heir to the best acting
company in England, and he knew how to value that asset. He knew
also the elegant world of playgoers whom his productions must please.

For a few years he gave London the very best possible dramatic fare within the limits of what was then considered theatre art. If a vacancy occurred in the ranks of his players, he shrewdly went out and obtained the best new talent in the country.

But it is a fact that Sheridan wrote only one additional play—*The Critic, or a Tragedy Rehearsed*—and there were no other living dram-

The School for Scandal at Drury Lane Theatre. The famous screen scene as performed with wing setting. The bookshelves, windows, and landscape are painted on the backcloth. [From *Shakespeare's Theatre*, by Ashley H. Thorndike.]

atists worthy the name. Shortly it became patent that with four plays Sheridan had burned out his playwriting genius, or ambition. Moreover, it soon developed that the theatre after all was only a secondary interest and avocation with him. Politics and the demands of social life —being a fashionable gentleman—were too exacting to leave time for the activities of authoring or producing. Management was left more and more to other hands. One night his theatre, which he had rebuilt to be the second largest in Europe, with a capacity of 3900 spectators, caught fire; but he refused to leave a debate in the House of Commons when told that the theatre was burning. That was in 1809, thirty-three years after he had taken over the directorship. With the conflagration ended his direct connection with the stage. His connection with it as an art had all but terminated twenty years earlier.

First, lack of direction had permitted disorganization and intrigue to creep into the once beautifully efficient company. Others than the director managed affairs, sometimes well, sometimes ill. As the theatre became more and more merely a "business proposition" to the now preoccupied director, his ambitions developed in the direction of greater size and display—looking only to wider popularity and increased receipts. Perhaps Sheridan's need for money and more money, to keep up his position of fashionable host and social leader, was at the root of the whole trouble. More and more he grasped at those adventitious "aids" to drama: spectacular scenery and interpolated sensational incident. The settings for some forgotten plays and an acting dog seem to have been equally talked about in the later days of his ownership of London's "first theatre." The time had passed when the retention of Sheridan could be urged on the grounds of art. It had been long since he entered the theatre except at night, and then he was able to see his actors only through an alcoholic haze; for he drank like a gentleman, as was the custom of important persons in his time.

But *The School for Scandal* is the most delightful comedy out of two whole centuries of British playwriting. It derives from Restoration models, but it brings a freshness and a later heartiness none the less. As an example of sustained "style," it is inferior to Congreve; but there are deeper qualities—without ever touching into the field of serious satire. We somehow take to ourselves these characters, feel personal sympathy with them, as we never did in Restoration days. And that is a sign that England, like Germany and France, is moving along toward the *human* comedy of a democratized theatre, a realistic time. The humor of *The School for Scandal* is so much of situation that no brief extract could convey the quality of it; and as a taste of Sheridan's witty characterization we may be content with these bits from the more obvious but celebrated Mrs. Malaprop in *The Rivals:*

Observe me, Sir Anthony. I would by no means wish a daughter of mine to be a progeny of learning; I don't think so much learning becomes a young woman: For instance, I would never let her meddle with Greek, or Hebrew, or Algebra, or simony, fluxions, or paradoxes, or such inflammatory branches of learning—neither would it be necessary for her to handle any of your mathematical, astronomical, diabolical instruments.—But, sir Anthony, I would send her, at nine years old, to a boarding-school, in order to learn a little ingenuity and artifice. Then, sir, she should have a supercilious knowledge in accounts;—and as she grew up, I would have her instructed in geometry, that she might know something of the contagious countries; but above all, Sir Anthony, she should be mistress of orthodoxy, that she might not mis-spell and mis-pronounce words so shamefully as girls usually do; and likewise that she might reprehend the true meaning of what she is saying. This, Sir Anthony, is what I would have a woman know; and I don't think there is a superstitious article in it. . .

. . . There, sir, an attack upon my language! what do you think of that? an aspersion upon my parts of speech! Was ever such a brute! Sure, if I reprehend anything in this world, it is the use of my oracular tongue, and a nice derangement of epitaphs!

Interior of the Little Theatre, Haymarket, London, in 1815. Note the proscenium doorway, boxes, and pit seats without backs.

Sheridan and Goldsmith, then, are alone memorable for anything bequeathed to later times. But there are several minor figures, in the period, with claims to passing mention for their picturesque qualities or great contemporary fame—and in the case of one actress a lasting celebrity. Among playwrights there were the two George Colmans, father and son, Thomas Holcroft, John O'Keefe, and Frederick Reynolds, all of them characterized by prolificness—the last named is said to have written a hundred plays. There is something a trifle ludicrous and infinitely pathetic about these writers who know their theatre of an era so perfectly that they succeed sensationally, become "all the rage," and then disappear utterly. In treating the stock characters bequeathed to them from older tragedy and comedy, this group even progressed toward the future. The comic characters begin to be more than butts: a bit of sympathy is aroused for them. The gruff old father is seen to have a heart of gold. The *ingénue*, the sweet innocent girl, bewitchingly childlike, starts on her conquest of the popular comedy stage. There is here a thrust toward "modern" character-writing, toward the conception of characters as rounded-out human beings; but the execution is vitiated by a rank sentimentalism.

Among actors, for a long time, there is even less breaking away from traditional type characterization, very little dipping deeper than a stereotyped stage conception of life. The period is an "elegant" one, wherein real feelings are properly concealed, and a hard brilliant surface presented to the world. A witty skepticism covers over all evils and all good feeling. Emotion and spirituality are alike out of fashion. How then should actors get down to anything like sincerity of feeling or deep purging emotion? Up to the time of the Kembles, the eccentric characters among actors are the more interesting: that "Gentleman" Smith who was thus named because he was so different from the general run of players, in being educated, elegant, dressy, rich, and married to a nobleman's daughter—*he* could bring authentic dandies to the stage; and sharp-tongued and capricious Mrs. Abington, who had certainly "lived a life-full" before she made such a success of Lady Teazle; and George Frederick Cooke, the typical actor who finds his inspiration in drink, rising briefly to mad heights of genius under its stimulation but wrecking his fitness for sustained acting, and wrecking many individual performances when the inspiration went to his legs rather than his creative centres. (He left for America after making London untenable for himself, and achieved a prodigious success even while wilfully insulting the provincials—and ended with the utterance of moral sentiments about the wickedness of drink.)

But Sarah Siddons was of stature beyond these, one of the truly great figures on the British stage; and her brother, John Philip Kemble, ruled nobly if less brilliantly at her side over a period of a quarter-century. As she was outside the superficially gay life of the fashionable world, being virtuous, dignified, even a bit cold, so she also rose above those difficulties, intrigues, and quarrels that honeycombed the stage realm. Only one failure marked her career: a too early début at Drury Lane Theatre after she had enjoyed great success in her father's company, as child-actor and then as leading lady (though not yet twenty). But a second Drury Lane début, in 1782, when she was twenty-seven years old, proved to be one of those occasions when a metropolitan public recognizes and hails a new and undisputed queen of the stage. From that triumphant night she reigned unrivalled and unassailed, from the eminence of first actress at Drury Lane or Covent Garden. The style of acting she brought in is described as "classic." It had little enough to do with the French classic playing then in vogue; it deviated in the direction of simplicity and restraint. It was still artificial, elevated, markedly "noble"—a reflection in part of her spirit and her outward stately appearance. But somewhere in her, too, there burned fire and imagination. And the dignified and stately impersonations, when shot

Sarah Siddons, England's leading actress during the late eighteenth and early nineteenth centuries. A portrait by Sir Joshua Reynolds, entitled *The Tragic Muse*.

through with this personal passion, aroused and thrilled audiences accustomed only to tamely or extravagantly conventional acting. She played the great Shakespearean heroines, achieving particular acclaim for her Lady Macbeth, as well as the more sentimental leading rôles in current "popular" drama.

John Philip Kemble was a perfect masculine counterpart of his sister—except that he lacked the imagination and fire. He accomplished all that is possible when noble appearance is linked with resolute devotion to lofty ideals, without great inspiration. His acting was elevated, stately, and elaborate; and he studied through to a certain sincerity—where his sister had intuitively achieved it. He had studied for the priesthood, and some critics pointed to the fact later as a reason for a certain heaviness and over-dignity in his acting. This temperamental deliberateness made him ever a reliable actor rather than a thrilling or inspired one. Still he and his sister ruled the London stage for two decades.

For fifteen years he was not only leading actor but stage manager at Drury Lane Theatre, under Sheridan's nominal directorship. It was he rather than his sister who made a point of the newness of their method of acting, who showed out Classicism as a thing of stateliness, austerity, and restraint. He staged a number of more or less Shakespearean plays in a manner that amazed and thrilled London, substituting for the old and poverty-stricken settings, or the French-Italian rococo ones, a sort supposed to be "true"—but with truth interpreted classicist-fashion, elaborated and made stately or grandiose. And from the Garrick era the tradition of "bettering" Shakespeare persisted; for Kemble and his prompter readapted *Coriolanus:* it was billed as "*Coriolanus, or The Roman Matron*, a tragedy altered from Shakespeare and Thomson."

Sarah Siddons and John Philip Kemble lived well into that next century which was to see destroyed all old standards in acting, playwriting, and staging. They are less transition figures than in themselves the summation of an era. If we count that there was here a period that can be called Classic—as different from the coming Romantic and Realistic —they are the outstanding representatives.

But if the forces for change that gave us our chapter-heading are little apparent in England (though a *measure* of democracy had come in that country long before the American and French Revolutions), there is one incident out of the Kembles' reign that betrays an underlying drift toward popular rule in the theatre. If you had gone to Covent Garden Theatre any evening between September 18 and December 15, 1809, you would have seen an extraordinary performance in the auditorium, not on the stage. In those three months Kemble's company acted its plays, to be sure, or perhaps pantomimed them; for every time a player opened his mouth to utter a speech, the spectators would begin shouting a rhythmic refrain: "O-P, O-P, O-P." And then the whole audience would get up and perform a "dance," stamping the floor or beating canes to the rhythmical shouts of "O-P, O-P," varied by cat-calls, hisses, ringing of bells, and other approved auditorium signs of protest. Through sixty-one performances, during the three-

A riot at the Covent Garden Theatre in 1762. [From an old print as reproduced in *The Stage Year Book*, 1927.]

month period, this counter-performance continued—not monotonously or uniformly, for there were interruptions in the nature of fist-fights, arrests, parades with banners bearing the "O-P" device, etc., but effectively so far as excluding the actors from attention was concerned.

"O-P" stood for "Old prices"; and the audiences of London were merely showing that they would brook no rise in admission prices at their then-favorite temple of dramatic art. Kemble and his associates had found the new methods of staging, and the immense new opera-house building, too costly to maintain at the old scale of admission, and they tacked six-pence or a shilling to the price of each seat. The house was sold out continuously for the next sixty-one performances; but from the time Kemble started to speak the Prologue on the opening night till the performance when he capitulated three months later, the actors' voices were drowned in a lasting wave of noisy protest. "Old prices! Old prices!" degenerated into the refrain "O-P, O-P, O-P."

The audience became organized, the O-P dance was invented, and attendance at the riots became a social affair.

By this means the audiences of London demonstrated that when royalty has withdrawn patronage from the theatre, thus tacitly turning the art over to the care of the masses, the people may express their will no less effectively and capriciously, if less curtly, than a purse-holding and law-making monarch. They proved that in one part of the theatre democracy had come with a vengeance.

WE HAVE seen that a spirit of liberty had grown up at Weimar, where Goethe and Schiller were associated at a Court Theatre that was significant out of all proportion to the importance of the company of actors there, or the Duchy that supported it. But the flame of Democracy really did not burn more than feebly in Germany either then or for long after; and we may think of the liberty in the air as a very vague and elusive ideal. In Goethe himself the theory and the practice clash most instructively. His devotion to liberty is unquestioned; no more sincere idealist ever lived. But there he was, serving, in his capacity as theatre director, a petty puffed-up duke, tyrant of a tiny principality, who for years allowed a frivolous and ambitious mistress to strike at the poet through humiliating "state" orders. (Just how petty this monarch was, the poodle-dog incident [page 391] finally proved.) And Goethe himself, despite his expressed ideas about freedom and equality, was a notable despot in his theatre. He ruled aloofly, severely; and he even extended the despotism from the stage part of the house to the auditorium. Clapping and hissing were alike prohibited.

It is recorded that hissers were arrested; and once a critic who really criticized a performance was banished from the dukedom. The rules for actors were pitilessly enforced. One actress who went away to an engagement in a Berlin theatre, in violation of the rule that the Weimar players should not appear elsewhere, was arrested upon her return and imprisoned in her own house for a week, with the further penalty of paying for the sentry who guarded her. Thus did love of liberty and parade of authority go hand in hand in Germany while actual democracy was being born elsewhere. The next period in Germany is to be called Romanticism; the Democratic era is skipped.

In Italy there has been a flare-up of playwriting genius, in a country too chaotic to claim a national theatre. In tragedy there is a real spirit of liberty embalmed in the more or less political dramas of Vittorio Alfieri. These are in the grand historical style, impassioned after the eighteenth century fashion, lofty in sentiment, but more suited to stir Latin peoples (when presented with Italian virtuoso acting) than to warm the hearts of more northern audiences. Still Alfieri is considered the greatest of Italian tragedy writers. The only other name in his century is that of Scipione Maffei, who wrote the famous *Merope*, and who linked up with the Voltaire school in France.

But Carlo Goldoni is more a world figure, in comedy-writing. He is still played both in and out of Italy. He was an accomplished technician, who wrote sixteen plays in one year, and at least one hundred

A Bavarian court theatre: the *Residenz-Theater* at Munich. All but destroyed during World War II, it was restored and reopened in 1958. [By courtesy of the German Information Service, New York.]

and fifty during his stage career. Displeased by the buffoonery and indecencies to which the *Commedia dell'Arte* had descended, and finding no models in the national literature (he could hardly turn back to Aretino and Machiavelli, when he had made a stand against licentiousness), he struck out along independent lines, and wrote of people and things about him. He was one of the bourgeois dramatists, and humanity "in the raw" interested him. His characters were so familiarly real, the language so near to everyday speech, that again we may mark a milestone in the steady march from ancient stateliness and high aloofness toward intimacy and realism. And this is the more remarkable in a country where comedy had been concerned with traditional type characters and largely compounded of stock situations and repeated scenes.

But Goldoni gave rise in his own country to opposition rather than a following. The romantic Italian nature loves neither realistic observation nor bourgeois pathos: there must be heroics in tragedy and boisterious display in comedy, and vivid characters. A critic, named Carlo Gozzi, challenged Goldoni's supremacy, and he ultimately drove the elder author to the more congenial France; and he discomfited Goldoni most by himself becoming playwright and the most esteemed figure in the Italian theatre. It is said that the two men met in a Venetian bookshop, and Gozzi, taunted by the other with the truth that it is easy to write caustically about a play but difficult to compose a good one, answered that he would undertake to compose within a few days a comedy that would please so light-minded an audience as this of Venice. And in an incredibly short time the Venetian playgoers were laughing over the humors of *The Three Oranges*, into which Gozzi had incidentally imbedded some telling satire on Goldoni's newly-invented types of drama, and not a little personal ridicule. And the audiences straightway flopped over to Gozzi's side and ever after remembered that he and not Goldoni represented the rather florid national genius.

Whether the anecdote is true or invented, it is certain that Gozzi was more in the line of logical development in Italy, where Democracy has seldom felt at home. He grasped much out of the *Commedia dell'-Arte* (which he rightly esteemed as a real and unique flowering of theatric art); and he added exotic elements out of his love for the Orient, and rich texture and extravagant incident. His was a vivid and highly decorated art, not at all like any given to the world since. But the intense theatricalism of it promises frequent revival; in adaptation if not in direct translation. (It was an adaptation that I enjoyed immensely, for its colorfulness and the heartiness of its humor, when I saw Gozzi's *Turandot* as presented hilariously by a troupe out of Soviet Russia, in —of all places!—the Paris *Odéon*.) Gozzi turned back the current which had started toward "freedom" in Italy. For a century and a half that country disappears from our story.

RETURNING to the scene of the true Revolution, become now terribly real in life, if only a tame evolution in the playhouse, we find Paris mobs storming the Bastille in 1789. There already have been plays on the stage expressing, more or less guardedly, revolutionary sentiments. With the first political violence there comes a wave of "appropriate" playwriting, the first impact of the deluge inevitable at any world crisis—but out of it not one drama survives as important. Wartime always stirs up deep currents of feeling, but the outward clash and fevered excitement are no congenial environment for art. Man's creative faculties, along with his spirituality and his sense of right and justice, atrophy in the red glare of continuous battle. And so we find that neither the immediate heroic contest nor the shift in world thought leads directly to theatre activity. There is participation in the revolution by playwrights and actors. The members of the *Comédie Française* are so partisan that the company is split and for a time production is paralyzed. The dramatists are so fiercely democratic that their only thought is to use the stage to further their side in the political struggle.

There is, however, a meritless political drama of 1789 that has achieved an extrinsic immortality. It was one of the earliest political pieces to come to performance, appearing on the boards of the *Théâtre Français* less than four months after the storming of the Bastille. *Charles IX*, a play by Marie-Joseph Chénier, dealing on conventional tragic lines with the massacre of St. Bartholomew's Eve, was presented by a reluctant company that still leaned to the Royalist side but had to bow to "the people's will." The drama happened to touch off, with the spark of righteous heroics, the tinder of patriotism in every spectator's breast. Night after night the audiences came, surcharged with feeling, and night after night their enthusiasm flamed high with every incident of aristocratic tyranny and each answering burst of democratic sentiment. Eye-witnesses reiterate that the house at every performance went wild with approval, with frantic revolutionary ardor, with self-enthusiasm. Readers of the play are equally at one in terming the text tedious, unexciting, and dramatically tame. But here the art of the piece—poetry, depth of feeling, characterization, acting—had nothing to do with the occasion. It was merely that representing a play in which a king ordered a massacre of his subjects was like waving a flag at a political meeting at just the psychological moment. An emotion wholly outside the theatrical content of the drama was precipitated. For this was the interim between the fall of the Bastille and the Red Terror of the guillotine; and a king still held court at his country palaces. Drama or anything else that stirred popular sentiment might precipitate a demonstration.

The performance of *Charles IX* brought to prominent notice for the first time a young actor named Talma, who was to become later almost the greatest of all French players; and it happened that this Talma was the one ardent revolutionary within the ranks of the still court-subventioned company. He had the title-rôle in the production—because an older actor side-stepped it on account of his Royalist sympathies—and he it was who became the specific *casus belli* when the majority of the company tried a test with the Democratic audience. These older *Sociétaires* of the *Comédie Française*, perhaps under pressure from their King and certainly sympathizing with him, decided that with the slightest slackening of public interest in the play, it would be quietly withdrawn from the repertory. The time came when the pretext of lack of support seemed likely to cover the withdrawal. Here we know not how far patriotism entered in, and how far an author's desire to see his play and his royalties continue, and a young actor's natural desire to prolong his appearance in a first big part; but the friends of Liberty bestirred themselves to protest. Finally, one night while another play was in progress, a gentleman arose in the orchestra and insisted point-blank that *Charles IX* be restored to the stage the following evening. When the actors tried to carry on the play, the audience set up the howl "*Charles IX, Charles IX.*" A canny actor stepped out of his part to explain that to restore the play would be impossible as two players accustomed to take sizeable parts were ill; at which Talma stepped out to remark that the more important one really wasn't so ill as that, and that doubtless the public would accept

Talma as Regulus in *A Carthage! A Carthage!* at the *Comédie Française*, and as Mahomet II in a play with Oriental setting. He stirred controversy because, in the Roman historical play, he appeared in a Roman toga instead of fashionable French clothes. [From prints of the period, by courtesy of the William Seymour Theatre Collection, Princeton University Library.]

an emergency substitute in the other rôle. To which the house agreed with great enthusiasm; and the very next evening Talma played *Charles IX* once more. There was a riot, but the piece was presented.

This did not, however, make for amicability and fraternity within the company. Feeling ran so high that Naudet, the actor who had put forward the sick-actors excuse, fought a duel with Talma. Then the Royalist *Sociétaires*—still the King's Comedians—read Talma out of the *Théâtre Français* organization.

It was not long before the debarred actor's loyal friends organized a "theatre party," and drowned out the lines from the stage with shouts of "Talma! Talma!" They allowed themselves to be tricked into waiting for an answer till the following evening, when they found themselves in conflict with an almost equal number of Royalist partisans. This time there was not even a pretense of acting a play. The elder actors took their stand, insisting that M. Talma would not reappear until the matter could be passed upon "by higher authority" (the theatre was still technically subject to rulings of Louis XVI's four First Gentlemen of the Bedchamber). Then Dugazon, a beloved old comedian, cast for that night's leading rôle, stepped forward, said that M. Talma was right, and that he was leaving the theatre until his young colleague should be reinstated. There was some disorder after, and breaking up of railings and benches, but the audience actually settled down to a one-sided debate about these actors and the national theatre.

When the decision from a higher authority came, it was from city officials and not the King, and it ordered the company to take back Talma and Dugazon into their ranks. There was some delay, however—perhaps the Royalists still thought the Court might venture to speak; and on the evening of September 26, 1790, "the people" smashed their way into the theatre, rioted and fought and shouted down the entrenched Conservative actors. Next day the theatre was formally closed. After two months the *Sociétaires* capitulated, at least to the extent of summoning Talma and Dugazon back.

But no truce could last now; leading actresses began to resign, alleging that the company could not maintain its dignity and integrity with "Reds" in its midst. The troubles on the stage were duplicated by others in the auditorium. The old *Comédie Française* was disrupted beyond hope of either peace or artistic production. The National Assembly passed a decree cancelling the monopoly held by the King's Comedians, opening the field to any and all playing companies alike—a step away from privilege and toward liberty indeed. So Talma and his few fellow Reds seceded from the state company and formed a rival troupe. There were eighteen additional theatres opened that year; and fifty before the century was out. Naturally the new company, in the

Théâtre de la rue de Richelieu, and the old in the *Théâtre Français,* became respectively Revolutionary and Royalist strongholds and propaganda-bureaus, picking plays frankly for political expediency. Talma's group brought on some badly adapted Shakespeare—but this was really no time to tack up the shield of art above one's portals.

The two theatres reeled through the troublous period that followed. When the time of the end of kings came, both houses grasped at patri-

The burning of the Paris *Opéra* in June, 1781, as seen from the *Palais Royal.* [After the painting by Hubert Robert in the Carnavalet Museum in Paris.]

otic titles—one must display some outward devotion to *Liberté, Egalité, Fraternité.* For a few weeks the houses were closed—the show of the terrible guillotine kept people occupied. But immediately the Bloody Month was over, everybody wanted the theatres opened again. The mad production was resumed.

The two rival companies were no longer on an equal footing; and the old *Sociétaires,* now calling their house the *Théâtre de la Nation,* foolishly widened the existing breach by retaining indiscreet political pieces in their repertory. Talma and his group played safe. Then the *Nation* group put on a play called *l'Ami des Lois* which roundly denounced the extreme element in the Commune, counselled a moderate course, and even caricatured certain popular radical leaders. Immediately the storm broke, inside and outside the theatre. Public sentiment was still enough divided so that it was a question of battle, not mere suppression. There were riots, even the training of cannon on the theatre; but curiously the partisans of the Commune were defeated: the house was closed but after a few days reopened. This was a last and belated stand of the King's Comedians. They were too frankly of the old privileged regime. In September 1793 the members of the company were arrested and cast into prison, all except one comedian who was away taking a cure, and who died of apoplexy when he heard the news. And there was ground for fear, for these actors were apparently fated to follow many less genuine reactionaries to the guillotine.

Ironically the indictments setting the dates for the appearance of the *Sociétaires* before the tribunal were signed by an actor who had been so bad in his art that he had never succeeded in getting into the *Comédie Française* or any other dignified company. But it was the ruse of another actor within the Commune councils that postponed the executions—until a day when the Terror was over and the popular thirst for blood slaked.

But it was no time for art in the theatre. Decree after decree was issued to force the drama arbitrarily into Democratic channels. Laughable prohibitions were introduced: no play containing any title of nobility could be produced—even the appellations *Monsieur* and *Madame* were forbidden to be spoken, as they implied distinctions! Many classics from the kingly age were banned, others altered; every play must breathe the new Democratic piety. There was even a movement to force every town in the country to open a theatre, in the now presumably empty church, "to educate the people, to make them forget the foolishness of the priests." Talma's company did plays quite as vapidly patriotic as those offered by rival troupes.

Standards were gone, chaos ensued. Till finally in 1799 old animosities were sufficiently forgotten for the two companies out of the old *Comédie Française* to reunite. They came together in the *rue de Richelieu* house, which has remained the *Théâtre Français* to this day. And soon Napoleon helped the re-established company to bring order out of chaos. He granted a subvention far more generous than any known under the kings, restored the monopoly on "classic" drama, signed that *Decree of Moscow* under which the *Comédie* is still administered, and showed marked personal interest in the group. He failed to turn up a tragic dramatist who would grace his court as Racine had graced that of Louis XIV, though he sought assiduously and encouraged every budding talent. But playwriting as an art was dead. The only genius of this period is Talma.

We see him go on to triumph after triumph, till he has transformed French acting and become the great ornament of the Paris theatre of the pre-Romantic era. It is somewhat by chance that he is more broadly equipped for progress than any of his fellows. His father was a valet, but, being ambitious, had crossed out of France into England to set up as a dentist. His son François Joseph was sent back to school in France for a time. Then while he worked as dentist's assistant in London the boy became a leader in the amateur stage productions of the French colony there; but more important, he developed a taste for Shakespeare and the free methods of playwriting, and an admiration for English (comparatively) restrained acting. When he gave up dentistry and went to the school of acting in Paris maintained by the *Comédie Française*, he already had a horror of French bombastics and of conventionally elegant French staging. He became the exponent of classic simplicity and truth, in the Kemble sense. One of his earliest exploits was to upset his elder colleagues by appearing as a Roman Tribune, in Voltaire's *Brutus*, in a true Roman costume, with arms and legs bare —a startling contrast to the beplumed, decorated, and padded costumes then in vogue.

But it was only after the passing of many years, and after the events of the Revolution, that this strikingly handsome and spirited actor was to accomplish anything like a reform of French acting. By natural right he became leader of the Paris stage. He was constantly pushing forward to new experiments in naturalness—though there was still a mighty gap between his sort and the intimate personal playing of to-day. But he put humanity into many an impersonation, where before the same characters had been portrayed with a stateliness, a desire for nobility above all, a stilted artifice that removed them effectively from the plane of life. Talma was under the handicap, much of the time, of having to speak Alexandrine verse, a prime hindrance to naturalness of emotion. Indeed, king that he is within his own time, we feel that had he come a little later in history he might have been the great leader of leaders on the French stage. As it is, he is a hampered king, progressing valiantly through difficulties. Had he found a dramatist with ideas akin to his own, or even a skilful translator of Shakespeare, he might have transformed, totally, French acting in his own time. Under the handicap, he stirred up bitterness and conflict, and marked out the way to the future.

In his individual acting, as exemplar of his theories of freedom and naturalness, he had recourse to gloomy, insane, and horrific rôles. He acted a long line of abnormally delirious or horrible parts; here if anywhere one might escape from the shackles of stilted verse, and indulge in real expressions of emotion. The crowd and the young

Romantics found the innovation exciting and praiseworthy. The critics were less convinced. Abbé Geoffroy summed up the indictment: "His triumph lies in the portrayal of passion worked up to delirium, to insanity. He is a chief and leader of the company of lovers of gloom, like Ducis . . . The gloomy *genre* is bad in itself, because plays of horror are not suited to French audiences; they should be

An early American "opera house" at New Orleans. A survival of aristocratic discrimination in the four boxes; otherwise the auditorium has turned very democratic. [From *Before the Foot-Lights and behind the Scenes*, by Olive Logan.]

left to the population of London. . . Talma hits upon extraordinary intonations, that produce a shudder of fear; but these happy hits are so infrequent and their effect so transitory, that he would do well to return again within the boundaries of art."

Within that fragment of contemporary criticism there is doubtless the key to the chief fault in Talma's acting: the excess that went with the newly gained freedom, the contrast between the stressed points and the constraint imposed by the pseudo-classic playwriting. But the quotation equally illustrates the obstacles in his way; by the slur at English drama (presumably at Shakespeare most of all, since a performance of *Othello* occasioned the review), and by the smug reference to "the boundaries of art." The guardians of the traditions handed down from the older theatre were bound to resent any excursion outside the "rules," and particularly any indulged in upon the *Comédie Française* stage. Talma on his part accepted the challenge, played the rôle of reformer consciously and gaily (though he went after this critic Geoffroy not seemingly but with a horsewhip), and set about corrupting as many of the young writers and actors as were not too awed by tradition to listen. He died in 1826, four years before Romanticism—that might have been the perfect medium for him— "came in."

WHILE democracy was thus gradually, and perhaps somewhat blightingly, making its way into the theatres of Europe, the United States, technically a republic since 1776, was developing a life of its own, independent of English activity. The art of the stage in such centres as Charleston, Philadelphia, New York, and Boston remained reflective of London's activity. There were notable variations from the customs and the fare of the mother country, as might be expected with so adventurous and lusty a child, including a great deal that is interesting to the searcher after the picturesque and the racy; but there is nothing in the story of the American theatre up to 1820 that can be considered of world importance.

The fight of the Puritans against all vicious pleasures had been waged with particular energy in the North, and the South had responded earlier to the eternal dramatic urge; but in a truly colonial way. Indeed, we may better think of the activities as being about as important as those in any other cultural dependency of England: the very vital but not greatly distinctive stage of Dublin offers a parallel. The Colonies and then the States built theatres, just rude halls at first, then in imitation of approved London models. Through most of the eighteenth century such primitive theatres as the one shown over-page served the travelling companies; but at the century's end several pretentious playhouses were erected, most notably, perhaps, the Park Theatre in New York, opened in 1798, and the Chestnut Street Theatre in Philadelphia, opened in 1794, which had an auditorium copied in detail from the Theatre Royal at Bath. By this time American audiences expected elaborate pictorial scenery, and an Italian educated in Paris, one Charles Ciceri, aided in bringing stage decoration into line with orthodox European practice. Plays were mostly imported from London, and the real events in the theatre were the visits of English companies or English stars. But within a quarter-century America is to have actors who will dispute supremacy with the visiting artists. Meanwhile democracy in government has had no notable effect upon playwriting, acting, or theatre design in the Western continents.

The Park Theatre in New York, as painted by John Searle in 1822 (the second house of the name). Charles Mathews and Miss Johnson on the stage; in the auditorium many of the most prominent New Yorkers of the day, of whom eighty are identifiable by means of an existing key. Note the proscenium portals as in the English theatres of the time. [By courtesy of the New York Historical Society, owners of the painting.]

CHAPTER

18

Romanticism:
The Theatre as Escape

ON THE long road of progress from the epic and highly conventional drama of the Greeks to the journalistic and familiar drama of the twentieth century, there have been recurrent efforts to gain full "freedom" for the dramatist, and to bring the stage closer to "life." The Romantic playwrights of the nineteenth century blazoned forth the epochal news that freedom had been won, nature encompassed, and the art of the theatre for the first time fully and richly realized. And indeed, some of their manifestoes announced the millennium as convincingly as any document in criticism. Victor Hugo's preface to *Cromwell*, 1827, is the battle-cry of the movement, and proves stirring even today in the reading. But their practice failed to afford more than an episode in the march toward Realism.

If we accept a broader and better definition of Romanticism, under which we may visualize the dramatist as far-riding in imagination, unhampered in shaping theatric action and in choice of characters, writing with constant reference to the deeper life of the human spirit, utilizing every resource of physical staging and acting, choosing prose or verse or silence, drenching the work in sensuous beauty, then we may say that this is another name for drama ennobled, made free and splendid, and rendered human; and Shakespeare is seen emerging as the supreme artist of Romanticism in the theatre.

But the commonly accepted understanding of Romanticism, as applying to the dramas of the French playwrights of 1830, narrows the definition until Shakespeare is squeezed outside: he is seen to be Romantic but with a foot over in the territory sometimes called Expressionistic; there is too much intensification of life and too much carelessness of outward nature, too much insight into human character and emotion and not enough observance of surface fact, to allow his sitting well with the French group. For while the 1830 men went far-riding after the thing we call "picturesque," they accepted a limita-

The intimate relationship of actors and audience on the English stage of about 1810, pictured by Cruikshank. [From *Theatre Arts Prints, Series IV.*]

tion to natural detail and plausible surface truth that curbed imagination, prevented character-depth, and crippled truly theatrical expressiveness. Not one of their plays lives importantly today, either on the stage or in the library. The secret of their failure lies in that they made Romanticism merely a stopping-place in the realm called Realism.

Now I know that these terms are quite often cited as opposites. But if we continue to call Hugo and Dumas and Bulwer-Lytton Romantic, we *must* recognize that realistic limitations are the cause of the failure of Romanticism; or at least a companion-cause to sentimentalism and bombast.

In the nineteenth century, art was an activity not passionately lived, not close to life; indeed the arts in general had receded into retreats, museums, and precious "circles." And a belief took shape that creating and appreciating art were not so much activities of living as *escapes* from life. The gallery of paintings, the concert, the theatre show, were occasional refuges from the drab business of existing. What was afforded to the eye or the ear, there, must be unfamiliar, exotic, dazzlingly brilliant. But the age being what it was, matter-of-fact, military-material, and disillusioned, observed fact must be respected: the dramatist going out to capture the picturesque must not violate what might happen on the thousandth chance, must stick to observed

Interior of the Sans Pareil Theatre in London, 1816. A novel arrangement for audiences; picture scenery glorified. [From a contemporary print.]

detail, must not go beyond what a man might dream for himself in a sentimental moment.

The spectator wanted to be taken out of his ordinary grey world into a more colorful realm—but one which he could believe in as real. Indeed, he wanted it real enough so that he could identify himself with the hero going out to adventure, cry with the heroine abused. So we see magnificence hampered, noble characters dragged down, imagination cramped, to compass sentimental probability. There are no Hamlets or Othellos or Portias here—impossibly implausible characters, intensifications of the human spirit, of the living in us that begets drama; there are, rather, a lot of figures heightened in colors but believable to us in our softer moments. And the action is what they do in contrived circumstances, picturesque but plausible circumstances like fights, betrayals, lovers' partings, heroic sacrifice, etc.

In France this Romanticism, shallow as it was, accomplished great things negatively. It swept away the enfeebled classic drama, still bound up in rules and limitations. To that extent it ushered in Freedom. It cleared the way to Nature.

The playwrights thus freed reached out for grandeur. They planned to paint humanity on a magnificent scale, limited by no arbitrary laws of time or place, by no rules that figures must be noble or situations heroic. They would portray the weak with the strong, the high with the low, and find new drama in the contrast. The beautiful would be placed beside the ugly, the sublime by the grotesque—yes, they particularly affected the grotesque. They would add a wealth of color, a welter of incident, a pageant of life.

A scene in *Les Pauvres de Paris*, as played at one of the many melodrama theatres in Paris. [From *Anciens Théâtres de Paris*.]

But when they sought characters both plausible and picturesque, Hugo and Dumas found themselves constrained to choose types like criminals, bastards, and outcasts for protagonists. Other non-classical heroes were too tame or too slight for the huge play design. To gain another sort of contrast, they pitted innocence against vice, purity against passion. Here they borrowed from the despised melodrama theatres of Paris. Beside the failing classic stages had grown up some very unclassic ones that asked nothing more than to hold unlettered audiences with unliterary "plays," contrived out of surprise, shock, machine-effects, and some characters as obvious as J-O-Jo. The action of these melodramas was, in the total absence of characterization, heightened to the last degree. Romanticism, with its freedom for all effects, would grasp this raw and exciting action in its catch-all of the colorful and picturesque.

The "language" and the verse of drama were heightened, too. The result was a gorgeous lyric investiture in the case of certain of Hugo's plays; but in general a riot of rhetoric and bombast and common speech. Nothing more truly shows out the faults of Romantic drama than its literary envelope. In that is the grandeur along with the hollowness: the magnificent reach and the empty hand.

The dramatists put in too much; even while they held back their imaginations with that new conception of what is natural. They spread their characters too far—even Shakespeare for all his flights of fancy and all his extravagant piling up of incidents and figures, had character-concentration. But unless you have read one of Hugo's or Dumas' dramas this week, you probably can't name a character in them. (When we have come to Dumas *fils*, and when Romantic melodrama has been crossed with the well-made play, you will remember *La Dame aux Camélias*; but that is post-Romantic.)

It was the shattering of the classic rules that was the greatest achievement of the French group. They showed up the barren, stilted, and insipid plays for what they were. And it was because they wrenched free from the academic limitations that they first were called Romantic. The word comes from the characteristic literature of the people who spoke the "Romance" languages, the vernacular as distinguished from Church or learned Latin; and as that literature had first taken form in tales of love and adventure, the mediæval "romances," this seemed a proper appellation for any anti-classic, closer-to-life, abundant drama. But the playwrights narrowed the term instead of widening it: made "romantic" mean something far away from life instead of a deepening of life, an escape instead of an intensified adventurous experience.

The gallery of important Romanticists is small. In connection with the earlier melodrama, the playwright Pixérécourt is usually chosen for mention. He was a skilful constructor and prolific. And those early melodramas did free the physical stage for larger effects and excursions (witness the pictures nearby).

Alfred de Vigny wrote some dramas that were in the copious new style, but weighted down with rhetoric. Victor Hugo was the giant of the movement, wrote its most telling manifestoes, produced in *Hernani* (1830) its most-fought-over play, and settled the operatic splendor of his genius over the Romantic *genre* for all time to come. As he had tremendous lyrical and theatrical gifts, so the drama rose in a blaze of glory; as his genius was corrupt, lacked sensibility and depth, so the Romantic play, when it fell back out of the spent fire of its rhetoric and pathos, was found to be thin, characterless. *Hernani, Ruy Blas*, and *Marion Delorme* are remembered today as hardly more than landmarks. After Hugo were Casimir Delavigne and Alexandre Dumas.

The latter rivalled Hugo in contemporary fame, but was less the type-figure of the Romantic revolutionary—and his copious and skilful plays have lapsed into a more all-blanketing silence.

Hugo defined Romanticism as "nothing else than liberalism in literature." The French literary stage before 1825 had been sadly in need of liberation. The melodramatists had already freed that theatre which was wholly divorced from literature. Hugo and Dumas made literature liberal by uniting it with the melodrama stage. They brought the legitimate stage down, not up, to freedom.

A LONG time before, in England, a playwright named George Lillo had written a play called *George Barnwell*, wherein "a London 'Prentice ruin'd is our theme." The event is marked as the first appearance of bourgeois domestic tragedy. Certainly a new familiarly human note was then ushered into the theatre. And some critics trace the Romanticism of Hugo back to this brief revolt against the aloofness and sublimity of earlier drama. Insofar as the Romanticists claimed freedom to set the low by the high, the 'prentice by the prince, the point is well taken. And it may serve to remind us that a form known as tragi-comedy had developed, and had had a fitful progress in both France and Germany. The French Diderot had taken Lillo as model, and had written some near-natural plays that might be considered a link, if a weak one, in the chain to the future; and Marivaux had added a similar note of tenderness in sentimental-real comedy. It was rather Lessing in Germany who made tearful comedy and bourgeois tragedy widely palatable. Hugo and Dumas, even if not in direct line, may have felt influence from all these.

In England, however, the Romantic Revival of 1830 or thereabouts was less a conscious revolt than in France; and the theatre adds the least glorious chapter to the story of a freeing impulse that flowered gorgeously in lyric poetry and at least profusely in fiction. (Unless we bolster the theatre's case by claiming Shelley on the evidence of *The Cenci*, and Byron as author of *Manfred* and a half dozen other dialogue poems; but these are only dramatic in literary form, not in stageworthiness.) The English Romantic drama, indeed, is strangely like a weak reflection of Dumas and Hugo. Barnwell has been abroad, and has come back with a magnificence mixed into his simple pathos, and with a great load of rhetoric.

Sheridan Knowles perhaps was the last of the stately tragedy-writers —the activity had been maintained even if the quality had not—rather than the first of the romantic playwrights. William Hazlitt, nevertheless, writing in the year when Knowles' first play came to the boards (1820), called the age "critical, didactic, paradoxical, romantic," and therefore not dramatic; and again he wrote of Knowles that he "has hardly read a poem or a play or seen anything of the world, but he hears the anxious beatings of his own heart, and makes others feel them by the force of sympathy." Here indeed is another step toward familiar drama. But Knowles' subjects were Virginius, William Tell, and Caius Gracchus; though *The Beggar's Daughter of Bethnal Green*

Staging in the Romantic era. A scene from *Les Deux Pigeons* at the *Théâtre du Palais-Royal*. Paris, 1838—an example of novelty-seeking in the settings of the time.

and *The Hunchback* tell in their titles that the author was fulfilling some of the lowly and grotesque aims of the Romanticists.

Bulwer-Lytton gave to the theatre two plays that are sometimes brought to the boards even today, and one, *The Lady of Lyons*, is quite regularly revived in the remoter provinces—wherever, indeed, weepsy audiences without too keen a sense of the ridiculous can be gathered. In this play is the very essence of nineteenth century Romanticism of the tenderer sort. When Pauline, the great Lady, has been told that she was tricked into the union with the lowly Claude Melnotte, and he, confessing fraud, has decided to return her to her parents, this scene occurs:

PAULINE (*to her parents*)

And you would have a wife enjoy luxury while a husband toils! Claude, take me; thou canst not give me wealth, titles, station—but thou canst give me a true heart. I will work for thee, tend thee, bear with thee, and never, never shall these lips reproach thee for the past.

COLONEL DAMAS

I'll be hanged if I am not going to blubber.

MELNOTTE

This is the heaviest blow of all! What a heart I have wronged! Do not fear me, sir; I am not all hardened—I will not rob her of a holier love than mine. Pauline!—angel of love and mercy!—your memory shall lead me back to virtue! The husband of a being so beautiful in her noble and sublime tenderness may be poor—may be low-born; . . . but he should be one who can look thee in the face without a blush, and to whom thy love does not bring remorse,—who can fold thee to his heart, and say,—"Here there is no deceit!"—I am not that man!

DAMAS (*aside to Melnotte*)

Thou art a noble fellow, notwithstanding; and wouldst make an excellent soldier. Serve in my regiment. I have had a letter from the Directory—our young general takes the command of the army in Italy, —I am to join him at Marseilles,—I will depart this day if thou wilt go with me.

MELNOTTE

It is the favor I would have asked thee, if I dared. Place me wherever a foe is most dreaded,—wherever France most needs a life. . . And thou!—thou! so wildly worshipped, so guiltily betrayed,—all is not yet lost!—for thy memory, at least, must be mine till death! If I live, the name of him thou hast once loved shall not rest dishonored; if I fall amidst the carnage and the roar of battle, my soul will fly back to thee, and love shall share with death my last sigh! . . .

The next act, two and a half years later, finds Melnotte returned from a glorious career at the wars; but the very day of his arrival is that upon which Pauline, to save her father from ruin, is giving herself to the wealthy villain Beauséant. Melnotte in disguise seeks an interview with Pauline to learn the truth, and she, unknowing, pours out her heart (ay, there's a situation that brings the tears!). But of course Melnotte tears up the iniquitous papers, himself saves the father from ruin, with money honorably taken as booty from the Italians, and presses Pauline to his heart. And there is a "moral" at the end:

MELNOTTE

Ah! the same love that tempts us into sin,
If it be true love, works out its redemption;
And he who seeks repentance for the Past
Should woo the Angel Virtue in the Future.

So far toward nature and no farther, the Romantic current had
carried the drama. And so far toward splendor. The French had given

An example of equestrian drama, at Astley's Amphitheatre, London, 1815,
wherein circus and theatre elements were combined. [From a contemporary
print.]

the form heroic outlines; and their plays were usually straight verse,
where *The Lady of Lyons* is mixed verse and prose. But the influence of melodrama is seen in Hugo and Lytton alike. Nor did this
point escape critics of their own time: the London *Times*, in reviewing the first performance of *The Lady of Lyons* in 1838, said: "The
characters are the overdrawn characters of melodrama. Claude, who in
a fit of ill-humor is persuaded to be an impostor, turns out to be a
prodigy of valor; Beauséant is one of those monsters not to be found in
nature, but only in the melodrama of twenty years ago; but is almost
equalled by the old gentleman, who, to avoid insolvency, would sacri-

fice his daughter to such a ruffian." And yet Lytton's was the most "literary" drama that found its way to the stage of that era. At lower strata one found unpretending melodrama, farce, and some strange special forms such as nautical drama and equestrian drama, and plays built around animal-acts. Here, as in France, the most lusty and the most inventive theatre of the time was that of the unimportant out-and-out melodrama.

Shakespeare, of course, was occasionally revived; indeed, up to seventy years ago the finest of his plays were kept in repertoire by all the great actors, in some sort of adaptation; it was only within the new century that London lost interest in them. But the Romantic Revival did not notably increase his vogue: the new definition of Romance was too limited to include him.

If we are pleased to call Edmund Kean the first great Romantic actor, then there *was* a revival; but Kean had made his phenomenal entry at Drury Lane back in 1814. In one direction he perfectly fulfilled the aims of the Romantics. Certainly he *heightened* acting in a way that shattered all traditions. Coleridge wrote that "to see Kean play is like reading Shakespeare by flashes of lightning." And he added natural effects to grandeur in the manner approved by the manifestoes; only he went deeper than the playwrights did, basing his impersonations on a conception of deep and informing character. He was brilliant, even dazzling, one of the true geniuses, beyond explanation, in the annals of acting. And yet his one fault was typically a failure of the Romantic school as a whole: when he came to a place where repose and serenity were necessary, his resources failed him. He must be always up on a height, always moving fast. He lived his life off the stage in the same way, violently, madly, excessively. If we grant that this is Romantic, then he was the greatest figure of the Romantic theatre. His Shylock and Othello and Richard III are the parts by which he is remembered, not anything out of contemporary authors.

Shelley wrote more of beauty into *The Cenci* than had been put into an English tragedy since Elizabethan times. The last words of Beatrice before she is led away to execution, the final lines of the play, are:

> . . . Here, Mother, tie
> My girdle for me, and bind up this hair
> In any simple knot; aye, that does well.
> And yours I see is coming down. How often
> Have we done this for one another; now
> We shall not do it any more. My Lord,
> We are quite ready. Well, 'tis very well.

But the simplicity and quietness and nobility of this sort of writing were not joined to adequate theatrical technique in the shaping of the action and the marshalling of the players. And so the finest so-called Romantic poets came not to the stage; only Romantic novelists like Lytton, who knew how to shake the last bit of tearfulness out of a pathetic situation.

The Italian Theatre in Paris (also known as the *Salle Ventadour*) in 1843. Opera-house architecture and picture scene carried into the Romantic era.

Byron himself wrote of *Manfred* as "a kind of poem in dialogue or drama . . . of a very wild, metaphysical, and inexplicable kind." And indeed, though there is the true Byronic magic in the lines, it is doubtful whether the "poem in dialogue" will ever be tamed to the stage. *Manfred*, *Marino Faliero*, *Sardanapalus*, and *Werner* were all acted at Drury Lane Theatre, and certain ones elsewhere; but they have not stood the test of time as theatre pieces. The actor William Charles Macready, next most important figure to Kean on the English stage of the early nineteenth century, was chiefly responsible for bringing Byron to the boards, and he played *Werner* over a period of twenty-one years. As late as 1887, *Werner* was acted in London, at a special matinée, with Henry Irving in the title part. But still, Byron belongs to the reading public—gloriously—and to the stage hardly at all.

The tradition of the literary drama persisted long after, in "plays" by Tennyson and Browning most notably; but stage conditions in

England did not invite poetic genius to an intimate collaboration. Incidentally, in the early decades of the century, the London theatres had been too large for any but broad effects; the licensing of only three theatres for "legitimate" drama had led the rebuilders of Drury Lane and Covent Garden to the fault of great spaces appropriate only to spectacular and violent or boisterous effects. The other theatres, of course, being denied the privilege of producing works likely to be considered competitive with those at the "patent" houses, fell back on farce and melodrama, variety and operetta. Melodramas were often produced as "musical plays" as a further disguise.

And by the way, the melodrama writers form a vivid gallery of skilled theatre craftsmen. Most of their works are permanently dead; but one still hears of the last and most famous of the line, Dion Boucicault, of his *Arrah-na-Pogue* and *The Colleen Bawn,* and of his outstanding comedy *London Assurance.* Still, comedy and "drama" alike, you may compare these with the last *great* English plays, with Sheridan or Jonson or Fletcher, and see how the coarseness and obviousness out of the debased melodramatic stage had vitiated them.

Out of the "lower" theatre, too, there came one actor whose name links the tradition of the *Commedia dell'Arte* with the story of the moving picture, the greatest name between Scaramouche and Charlie Chaplin: Joseph Grimaldi. Born of an Italian actor-father in London, Grimaldi became the supreme clown of his time. To the London pantomimes, those spectacular-sentimental shows so beloved by English audiences, so like a Harlequinade refined, prettified, and sugared for the children, he brought an authentic note of buffoonery. He invented "effects" and capitalized every outward resource and trick of the physical stage to the limit; but it was personal genius as actor and clown that made him a favorite in his time and an unforgettable tradition since. He was called "the Michelangelo of buffoonery."

In Germany so many of the ideals of the Romantic movement had earlier come to fruit in Goethe and Schiller—though without the bombastic fault—that there was no room for revolution in the Hugo-Dumas sense.

At the Court of Weimar at midnight on the eve of the new century, Goethe, Schiller, and a group of writer-friends drank a toast to the dawn of the new literature. Certainly in the plays of these two men a drama of spontaneity, of richness, of depth, was taking shape. But their work was incomparably finer than any accomplished by the French and English Romanticists: it refuses to be stuffed within the limits of the French definition of Romanticism. The work of the next group of German playwrights, however, is less significant than that of Hugo and Lytton. And so Romanticism in the German theatre hardly belongs to the chapter—just sort of fades from view.

Abstractly, we may feel that Romanticism is of the very fabric of Teutonic art. And practically we might adduce evidence in that the few significant German painters of the nineteenth century are of that persuasion, and the poets and novelists as well. But the stage bequeaths us no great names after Schiller, and not a notable one until the Realist Hauptmann.

A grand setting in the Bibbiena manner, by Giovanni Servandoni. Paris, mid-eighteenth century. [From *L'Envers du Théâtre*, by M. J. Moynet.]

The *theory* of a Romantic theatre, nevertheless, was discussed and analysed in Germany as nowhere else; and the activity led to one great good: Shakespeare was further acclimated to the German stage, and to this day he disputes with Goethe and Schiller the honor of being the most popular "national" dramatist. The outstanding figure in the period was not a playwright but a critic and translator, August Wilhelm von Schlegel. His book *On Dramatic Art and Literature* is still a standard reference work about the theatre. It helped to consolidate the gains of those who were freeing the stage from academicism.

Of the playwrights whom the German critics called Romantic, we may choose Heinrich von Kleist, Johann Ludwig Tieck and Zacharias

Werner for mention; but these were all before Hugo, and link less with later developments in the theatre. One might almost claim that the Romantic movement, in so far as it was effective in the German theatre, brought less of good than of evil—of chaos, almost. The one most important drama surviving out of the period is von Kleist's *Das Käthchen von Heilbronn*, which is more in the Shakespearean tradition than suggestive of the new aims of the French sort. Schlegel, in trans-

The elaborated perspective scene as carried into the late eighteenth century by a member of the Bibbiena family. [From Moynet.]

lating seventeen of Shakespeare's dramas into German verse, had more to do with turning the current of literary-theatric endeavor than had any German or French playwright of the times.

In Austria Franz Grillparzer was at just this period writing the finest dramas that came out of that country. He was an independent spirit rather than follower of a school. He took largely historical and legendary themes and developed them with his own conception of a new freedom and a new naturalness. He was too restrained, too delicate in touch, with a sort of belated Classicist fastidiousness, to link with the Romanticists. And he put more of permanent literary enrichment into stageworthy dramas; so that you will find two or three of his plays in the repertories of the Austrian and German state theatres even today.

In Germany as in England, an actor stands out as a more spectacular figure. Ludwig Devrient had those same qualities of violent ecstasy and wild vividness that characterized Edmund Kean. Mantzius has etched this portrait of the player of the time: "The German actor of the romantic type was a strange being, with long, wild hair, black if possible, framing a pale, emaciated face; deep, melancholy eyes under dark, contracted brows, and a bitter, sorrowful smile on his quivering lips; his form shrouded in a long Roman cloak, moving among his fellow men now with ostentatious, gloomy remoteness, now with hollow, rather scornful mirth." And of all these picturesque actors of Germany—the type has not entirely disappeared—Devrient was most strange, most extreme, most grotesque. He strained after Romantic effect in a way that resulted in the most remarkable testimonials to his genius, and at the same time some records of failure. He touched heights never touched before, and fairly dazzled audiences; but he could not compass a quiet effect, and to sustain such brilliancy for long was impossible. Like Kean, he got a good deal of his inspiration out of a bottle—always a treacherous friend for an actor, in the end.

France, too, had one of these Romantic alcoholic actors at about the same time. Frederick Lemaitre, however, neither drank so heavily nor rose to such giddy heights. He gained his first success in pantomimes and in the out-and-out melodramas of the *Boulevard du Crime*—the street of the popular theatres was called that because of the terrible murders, seductions, fires, and poisonings that occurred nightly on the stages there. He went on, however, to the plays of Victor Hugo and the other Romantic dramatists, and became the chief player of his period; though not such a revolutionary as Talma had been before him, nor so spectacular as Rachel and Bernhardt after him.

In a more specialized field, in Lemaitre's time, Deburau put his stamp permanently on an old character and created a tradition. As Pierrot in the French pantomime—a form that may be considered a bastard daughter of poetic drama by the *Commedia dell'Arte*—he charmed audiences and made over the character with a new dignity and depth. Not too deep, mind you, but deep enough for melancholy and a bit of wisdom. Indeed, it was Deburau who fixed Pierrot in the mold we all now visualize at mention of the name: sad, powdery, languishing, poetic. If you like your humor with a robustness and heartiness, you may think that this was a debasing of the Italian comedy type, a typical Romantic sentimentalization. Personally, I would agree with you. Nor was the sentimental-Pierrot vogue any more lasting than that of Hugo's and Dumas' plays. Deburau's son Charles and another tried to carry on the tradition at the theatre made famous by

Frederick Lemaitre as Georges Maurice in *La Dame de Saint-Tropez*.
[After a contemporary print.]

the father, the *Funambules*, but the impetus was too slight; the vogue had been due to one actor's appeal, not to the discovery of an important new slope in dramatic art.

OPERA is always artificial and is generally Romantic in the 1830 sense. Its history after Lully belongs by right to this chapter. In Italy the form developed in the direction determined by Scarlatti in the

late seventeenth and early eighteenth century: that is, it continued to grow in tunefulness, and with generous inclusion of the aria. Opera was an Italian art in origin, and always it flourished most abundantly in that country. But Lully's, as we have seen, was the next important name among composers, and he produced at the Court of France. Shortly afterward England had its creative flare-up, when Henry

Purcell produced, with the aid of girls at a boarding-school, *Dido and Æneas,* thus showing that he might have been a great opera composer if the taste of the times had not forced him to write incidental music instead. Later, England had its share of Italian, German, and French opera, but never again a significant composer. An isolated and unique sub-species was created and had a vogue, to be sure, in the "ballad-opera," as instanced in the still-enjoyed *Beggar's Opera,* arranged to a

In the late nineteenth century Honoré Daumier became history's most discerning theatre-satirist and pictorial recorder. The caption of the litho-graph opposite is: "Robert, be ashamed of yourself, or we go!"

libretto by Gay; and England later gave birth to the matchless musical fooling of Gilbert and Sullivan. But the English-speaking peoples are not operatic creators. (New York has long seen and heard the costliest and most resplendent opera in the world, but it is largely imported.)

The comic operas and operettas of Gilbert and Sullivan, though a phenomenon in English stage history, were the culmination of a century and a half of endeavor to capture the lighter pleasures of music in works less sedate than "grand" opera. Indeed, *opera buffa* first appeared as relief from the tediousness of the long Italian *opera seria;* the unserious *inter-mezzi*, originally presented between the acts of the serious pieces, were in the early eighteenth century put together to form the first light or comic operas. The Italian Pergolesi was the first master, and Italy long the home of the form, but later the French took over the genre and made of it their *Opéra Comique*. There the term was widened to include not only humorous pieces, or satiric, but any lightly romantic music-play. *Opera buffa* was, of course, a needed corrective to serious opera, and often it prospered by burlesquing the more ridiculous "effects" of the form that gave it birth.

Germany, though practically without "serious" theatres, had opera at a number of the petty capitals before 1700, together with some native composing. But Handel, the first great artist in the field, forsook Hamburg for Italy, and surpassed the Italians in their own sort of composition. The German Gluck also went South and eventually excelled. But he became convinced that Italian opera was really only a sort of concert "for which the drama furnished the pretext"; and in Vienna and Paris he set to work consciously to "reform" it. Under patronage of Marie Antoinette, he produced a series of works that broke most of the rules for composition that the Italians had elevated into a sacred international code, laws about the number and kind of arias to be included, the number of singers, etc.; and he brought opera closer to the estate of a musical-dramatic art, by fitting the music to the interpretation of dramatic situation, to the expressive words and the pathos of incident. The Italian composers, to satisfy the vanity of singers, had arranged everything for the best display of individual voices: theirs was "show" music. Gluck asked only that his music "second poetry." He waged a merry war with the Italians, and he won to the extent of lopping off miles and miles of excessive vocal ornament.

Mozart and Beethoven both brought individual gifts to the art: the one with a grace that was closer to the Italians, but expressed with original freshness and with humor (he found *opera buffa* an inspiration as well as *opera seria*); the other with a deeper musical expressiveness, but only in one none-too-facile opera, *Fidelio*. And Weber introduced some of those motives which Wagner was to employ so notably later: musical characterization, in the *leitmotiv*, and certain orchestral innovations. All three of these composers had borrowed

The San Carlo Opera House in Naples, as seen from the stage and from the auditorium. The horseshoe and hen-coop system persisting. [From Brogi photographs.]

elements from the old German *singspiel*, instead of following blindly after the models originally introduced from Italy.

The Italians themselves changed chiefly in making their melodious works less classical and more popular—some would say, more sugary. They made little progress toward harmonizing the musical and dramatic elements: to this day Italian opera belies the word "grand" by its shallowness and showiness. But there is no doubting the fact that Rossini, Donizetti, and Verdi made operatic music more widely palatable and popular. No one ever lightened or brightened dire tragedy more prettily than did Donizetti in *Lucia di Lammermoor;* and Verdi rounded tuneful tragedy into its most plausible and decorative form in *Rigoletto* and *La Traviata;* though more might be said in praise of his *Aïda* and *Il Trovatore.*

In France, at the same time, the German Meyerbeer (he changed the Jewish Jacob Meyer Beer to Giacomo Meyerbeer after studying in Italy) had travelled in the opposite direction, forsaking what the Germans called "Italian sing-song" for a grand manner that tended to the heavy and grandiose: he was Romantic in the true French sense, with the melodramatic-vulgar fault. After him came Gounod with that *Faust* which was perhaps the best example up to his time of the music-drama composed with an eye to dramatic fitness and larger effect, and not merely as a singing display.

Such was opera before Wagner. In two hundred and fifty years since Peri's historic *Euridice*, no one had been able really to produce a drama-in-music, or to overcome a certain ridiculous convention of the solo singer stepping out of the play at intervals to show off. Wagner at least was giant enough to try. And he not only made himself a great figure in operatic composition, but initiated epochal changes in the construction of the physical playhouse. He made German opera production the richest the world has known.

With a revolutionary idea that opera should have unity, continuity, and cumulative interest, Wagner wrote his own librettos and learned the technique of staging at first hand, while composing his music. In that, he foreshadowed a whole school of later thought, in and out of opera. Distrusting Classicism, but noting that the superb Greek drama grew out of Greek life and tradition, he sought out the legendary background of his own people for subject-matter, and found in Teutonic mythology the richly appropriate materials for his dramas. He believed that music must be fitted closer to the emotional content of the drama, must be an intensification of feeling, and he shaped a sort of music-structure designed with primary purpose to emphasize plot and word-sense. He avoided individual vocal numbers that would interrupt the action or break the emotional continuity, and freely used the *leitmotiv*, or guiding motive, which could be repeated to prepare the auditor for certain characters or incidents.

As a boy Wagner showed no such phenomenal talent as did, for instance, Mozart. Born in Leipzig in 1813, he was brought up with exceptional opportunity for absorbing the "feel" of the arts: for one thing, his stepfather was actor, playwright, and painter. The boy was a reader of fairy tales and of tragic drama, and at fifteen a devotee of music. Dresden gave first productions to his earliest operas, *Rienzi* and *The Flying Dutchman*. The latter, though not one of Wagner's greatest works, was so far ahead of its time, so different from anything then known, that it failed. But it was rather with the presentation of *Tannhäuser* in 1845, and the composition of *Lohengrin*, that the world of German music became divided over the revolutionary composer: one camp hostile to this formless, tuneless, chaotic work; the other wildly enthusiastic over the glorious freedom, emotional expressiveness, and rich harmony.

The hostile camp was the larger; the production of *Lohengrin* was delayed for years, and Wagner was made to feel the pinch of poverty and the pressure of court intrigue. He also fell afoul of the authorities for his political beliefs. In 1849 he fled to Paris, found only discouragement there, went on to Zurich, and remained an exile for twelve years. But in that time he worked on his highly national *Ring*, including *Das Rheingold*, *Die Walküre*, *Siegfried* and *Gotterdämmerung*, and wrote *Tristan und Isolde*, and a number of books. In 1861 the Paris Opera decided to risk a production of *Tannhäuser*, but the audiences refused a fair hearing, shouted down the performers, and the piece was withdrawn after the third performance. In that same year the news came that Wagner could re-enter Germany, and at the age of forty-eight he returned to his own country; but only to experience further torturing years of poverty and battle. He eventually found patronage from the King of Bavaria, however, and continued planning for not only a national music-drama but a national theatre.

In 1876 his dreams were realized, more or less ideally, in the building of the Festival Theatre at Bayreuth. The *Ring* was produced there twenty-eight years after he began work on it. And for seven years longer he lived, though still not freed from worries, composed *Parsifal* in his sixty-fifth year and died in his seventieth, in 1883. He had made a gallant fight, had lived through more of abuse, intrigue, and wilful misunderstanding than any other artist of his time; and after his death he became known as one of the greatest innovators and one of the outstanding geniuses of the world stage. Today his works are current in every world capital that claims any breadth of taste in opera.

Wagner's ideas about reform of staging did not include reform of

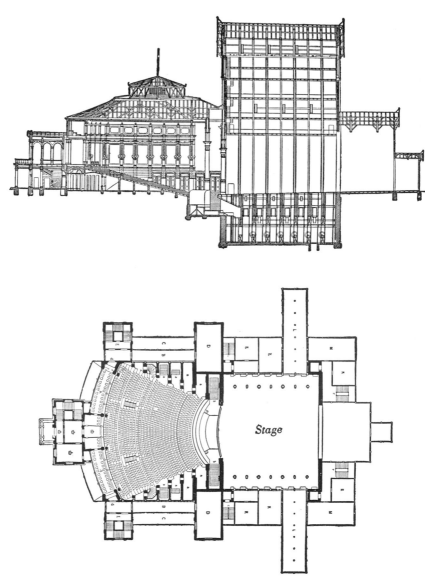

Section and plan of the Bayreuth *Festspielhaus*, showing the auditorium with a single wedge-shaped bank of seats: the beginning point of the modern revolt against the Italian-French type of theatre building. Designed by the architect Semper in collaboration with Wagner. [From Sachs' *Modern Opera Houses and Theatres*.]

the painted setting, and his stage at Bayreuth was designed for the equipment that had grown up around Italian-stage settings. But he did revolutionize the auditorium design. Elsewhere the houses had all been very slight variations of the horseshoe plan with tiers and tiers of boxes. At Bayreuth the seats are practically all on a sharply sloping single floor, as shown in the plan. And from that one house spread the influence that in fifty years transformed the theatres of Germany and America into places so democratic that practically every spectator could see the stage—whereas the older (and alas, some newer) opera houses had hundreds of seats good enough for the poorer public but little related to the place where the performers appeared.

The chapter opened with a reference to Shakespeare, who might have been a Romantic if the creators of that term had not narrowed its meaning by a realistic-sentimental limitation, if they had not made it inevitably suggestive of bombast and strut. The chapter ends with the achievement of this other giant, Wagner, who, in opera, did most of the revolutionary things that the Romanticists *hoped* to do. But he soared into a region too splendid, too extensive for labels. The auditor (in an opera house) experiences, to a certain degree, the true Dionysian ecstasy. It doesn't come often or sustainedly—the opera medium is still too imperfect for that—and maybe, after all, it is the music and not essentially theatre that *is* the magic. But again somehow there has been brought to the stage the beauty that immerses the spirit and stills the mind.

CHAPTER 19

❧❧❧

Well-Made Plays and Pretty Scenery: Victorianism

❧❧❧

WHEN Romanticism had won its victory at the *Théâtre Français* in 1830, there had been riots, battling, and shrill cries. *Hernani* had been the first of the "revolutionary" dramas to be accepted for presentation at France's official playhouse. The friends of Victor Hugo had aggravated the irritation felt among the entrenched Classicists, by appearing at the première in violet and scarlet waistcoats, pale green breeches and yellow shoes, under Rembrandt hats and flowing locks. They were Romantic outwardly as well as inwardly. The black-frocked conservatives bravely contested the field with these flamingly youthful and militant crusaders. Duels were fought, pamphlets were hurried through the presses, and the early performances were all but lost in the tumult of battle. But *Hernani* was a success. Classicism was thenceforward discredited, Romanticism supreme.

The next historic battle over a première at a Paris theatre was that in which *Tannhäuser* was literally howled down at the *Opéra*, in one of the most disgraceful episodes in the history of the stage. The judgment of the Parisians in both cases, in accepting Hugo and in rejecting Wagner, has been reversed by later generations.

But during all this period, from the 1830 victory to the 1861 disaster, a different sort of dramatist was working in Paris, without spectacular revolutionary notions or avowals, but in a way that moved worlds none the less. Indeed, Eugène Scribe went on to quiet success after quiet success, until his plays mounted up into hundreds, and eventually the stages of Europe and America were "sold" to his sort of playwriting as they had never been to Hugo's. The theatres of all lands capitulated completely to a vogue.

We have come now to the mid-nineteenth century. The era takes its name not from any French development, but from that half-German British Queen who typified plainness, Protestantism, and prudery as no other mighty monarch ever did. It is a time of unimaginative art, a time when extremes of any sort are avoided, the age of drabness. The power of kings is pretty well gone; those who really rule either are too weak to give direction to the age or else care not at all about the excitements of art and learning. Democracy is left to carry on without guidance. The English creative theater under Victorianism merely dries up. But in English civilization there are elements of shrewdness and materialism that make Scribe's type of play from France acceptable on the stages that remain.

For what Scribe was accomplishing, without spectacular manifestoes or scarlet breeches, between the years 1820 and 1850, was the creation of a play-frame so perfectly articulated, so facilely constructed, that any sort of sentimental stuff could be tacked on to it and made plausible. His was the supreme triumph of mechanics over dramatic content. Even while innocent of any of the larger virtues of the dramatist—he knew nothing of character drawing, and little of dramatic grip in the profound sense—he made hundreds of plays that pleased untold audiences. He mastered theatrical device, filled his pieces with obvious type figures, pathetic incidents, surprises, skilful ravellings and unravellings, clever sayings, happy endings, etc., etc., and developed a formula for theatrical effectiveness. He gave the Victorians what they wanted—a smooth article, a neat concoction. It was no time for genius or poetry or incisive characterization.

The French *pièce-bien-faite* is the perfect emotional tickler. Prettily fashioned, superficially brilliant, without literary or spiritual value, it came pat for an age timid about beauty, afraid of the mysterious thing called art. The emphasis on neat technique in the theatre had its parallel in the other arts, of course: in smoothed-down sculpture, highly varnished furniture, Landseer painting, the architecture of the Eclectics, etc. But nowhere else was the triumph of neat mechanics so complete as on the stage.

Not that the development had no beneficent effects in later times. It was Scribe's form on which Ibsen built his "social" drama; though Scribe would have wondered what such a term could mean. Drama was for amusement—what more? If one could take the uncertain old comedy-outlines, hammer them into a shape with just the right juxtaposition of laughter and tears, make them more intricate, put

The professional card of Charles Burke, a leading American actor of the mid-nineteenth century. In the unsettled conditions of the time, particularly as regards touring companies, actors were forced to advertise; here the actor is shown straight and in six roles. [From the *Autobiography* of Joseph Jefferson, who was a half-brother of Charles Burke.]

surprise and tenderness and sweetness into them—what more would an audience ask?

And so there grew up, beside the grandiloquent plays of the Romanticists, this type of smooth-gliding drama, not built with reference to any theories, or conviction of any sort—just out of the desire and intent to please. It is not surprising that no works of Eugène Scribe's have lasted. He wrote near half a thousand plays (aided by hack-assistants), he shaped the stage of an era, he is remembered as father of "the well-made-play"; but you probably never will see one of his dramas performed. There were, of course, those who guessed the shallowness of his work even in his own time, but they were no large part of the public. It is said that the poet Heine on his deathbed, when his breath was failing, was asked if he could hiss; and his answer was, "No, not even a play of Scribe's."

Scribe died in 1861, and in that very year Victorien Sardou made his first important stage successes. The tradition of the *pièce-bien-faite* was thus carried on without break. It is said that Sardou, in order to learn perfectly the technique of play-making, would read the first act of a Scribe piece, then write the other acts himself. And the mechanics of manufacture were so perfected that he picked up the knack in no time. Such was the lack of character in Scribe's plays that another could appropriate the technique without more than an exertion of cleverness. Sardou is written down as the *cleverest* playwright the French theatre has known.

Of course Sardou added some elements of his own. He even kept an eye out to the trend of national thought and fashion, and wrote topical or appropriate pieces. But his naturalness, if I may so put it, crystallized into a convention. He discovered how natural people like you and me would act if we acted invariably according to our sentimental longings. He developed a stage logic: he made up that romantic naturalness that leads us to say today that a thing is theatrically true but not psychologically true. His situations are too skilfully devised to be credible, his *ingénues* too sweet, his generalizations too sweeping. He carried the well-made-play a little of the way from mechanical-Scribe toward that branch of realism that we may term journalistic, for its facility and lack of depth.

His sort of clever shallow play interests us, of course, like a detective story or the average novel. But there is nothing of sincerity or deep feeling or beauty here—and the stage cannot subsist for long without those elements.

For fifty years the European and American stages largely *did*. Where the repertory theatres were strong, the classics persisted, most notably in Germany. But as for new work, everything was now imported from

Paris. In Germany there is not a memorable name out of the well-made-play period; all are adapters or imitators. Russia at this time developed a playwright who caught the knack of the Scribe thing perfectly, added a satiric slant, and turned out in *The Inspector-General* a comedy that has outlasted everything of Scribe and Sardou.

The Germans were already doing valuable experimental work as regards methods of staging, and were to evolve a new type of play-

The painter triumphant as designer of settings. The "platform" scene for *Hamlet:* a scant practicable terrace before a backcloth depicting grandly Elsinore Castle and the sea. [From *The Stage and Its Stars, Past and Present,* Philadelphia, 1887, by courtesy of the Theatre Collection, Free Library of Philadelphia.]

house, as we shall see. But their chief contribution to the perfection of the mechanical play-form was theoretical. Gustav Freytag published in 1863 his treatise called *Die Technik des Drama:* in translation, *The Technique of the Drama;* and well into the present century it was being used as text-book at the universities. It purported to show that great drama almost invariably exhibited a "plan" with well-marked parts: development, climax, and return. On analysis any play could be divided into exposition, first clash, rising action or complication, climax, falling action, dénouement or catastrophe, etc., etc. The system is an eminently useful one for critical analysis, and suggestive to the theatre worker. But, like Scribe's facility, it leaves out all those matters that in the final reckoning make art art.

The trick drama was as effective in one language as another: no local color, no complex characters, no troublesome poetry to translate; just some easily understood people in a series of cleverly manipulated situations. The theatre was therefore internationalized as never before. France dominated the commercial stages of Germany, England, the United States.

In England the adapters were legion. In farce there was John Maddison Morton, who made the perennial *Box and Cox* out of two French originals; James Robinson Planché was broader, refitting

The (old) Metropolitan Opera House in New York, 1883. The stage scene shows the apotheosis of Marguerite in Gounod's *Faust*. [From a newspaper illustration.]

Scribe's material and other French pickings into comedy, burlesque, and extravaganza as well. Thomas William Robertson began as adapter of the Scribe-Sardou sort of trifle, but either through an independent urge to observation or through the influence of Augier and Dumas the Younger, he took a step forward, in the direction of the "social" drama. *Society* and *Caste* are even mentioned sometimes as landmarks on the way to modern Realism. Anyway, London wanted the superficial thing more than seriously observed drama, and Robertson died disappointed and worn out at forty-two. Tom Taylor's unending adaptations were more popular, and the plays of that Wilkie Collins who gave utterance to the classic formula: "Make 'em laugh; make 'em weep; make 'em wait."

Aside from adaptations from the French, the story of the well-made-play in England is told almost wholly in the dramas of two men: Henry Arthur Jones and Arthur Pinero. Both came late enough to find their inspiration in Sardou rather than in Scribe. Each added his individual variations and touches. But in perspective they are seen as providing the culmination of the glorified-technical-facility movement on the English stage. They were the great playwrights of their period, but it was a period when the stage had alienated practically every important contemporary writer. They lifted the English drama out of the triviality and falsity of the French adaptations; but viewed today, their own plays are seen as deftly articulated stories rather than as stirring character-drama. In the argot of the stage, when performed today they creak.

Henry Arthur Jones wrote voluminously and often about the "modern" theatre, and he insisted particularly that the man of letters must become the stage craftsman, that drama must be more than mere popular amusement, and that there must be close connection between any living drama and the larger life and society in which the theatre exists. And yet his plays are defective in precisely the elements he insists upon: they possess no notable literary values, they are effective as entertainment but leave no after-thought either through deep characterization or by profound insight or philosophy, and they miss the social significance of, say, Ibsen and Shaw. They are admirably deft, they hold the spectator or the reader from moment to moment without the slightest letdown of interest, they flow oh! so smoothly. But suddenly one wonders what it's all worth. Why couldn't there be one genuine passion, one memorable character, one disturbing thought in the whole of this row of plays?

Read *The Liars*—it will be an entertaining hour—and you will have Jones at his best. You will see that he has advanced beyond Scribe and Sardou, whose plays you might easily find annoying. But note how the masterly structure builds up to the one big speech of Sir Christopher in Act IV. The play is perfectly capped. The French had learned well the value of those climactic speeches. Their term for them is *tirades*. Our meaning for the word is a little different; but believe me, by emphasis the actor made the "splendid" speech a "tirade" too. At the *Comédie Française* you will see an actor get set for this sort of scene, treat it like a thing apart from the drama, with beginning, climax, and end of its own—and then step out bowing to the applause. And the audience is trained to watch for these purple patches; is always ready to leave the drama to enjoy a virtuoso passage by the actor. The *tirade* is really a borrowing from opera technique—an operatic intrusion. And by the way, Scribe was almost as successful in the fields of

Behind the scenes during a play. Note the method of lashing the wing-pieces to the masts rising through the floor-grooves. [From Laumann's *La Machinerie au Théâtre*.]

operetta and grand opera as in farce-comedy, though he failed dismally as tragedy-writer.

But not to cry down Jones too easily, in this superior time when we have a satisfying social-intellectual drama behind us, and a stirring journalistic realistic drama with us, he presented an intelligent plot with masterly technique.

Arthur Wing Pinero spanned a greater range. From trivial adaptations and inventions in the seventies and increasingly serious studies in the eighties, he arrived in the nineties at a very telling sort of emotional play that verges on the true "social" drama. As deft as Jones in technique—you may prove it by reading the so-prettily absorbing *Sweet Lavender* and *The Gay Lord Quex*, or the perfectly articulated *His House in Order*—he added a certain character-depth and an intensity of feeling. One remembers Paula Tanqueray and Iris—not with the immortals of Æschylus and Shakespeare and Molière, but nevertheless theatrically and humanly. And beyond, if the plays creak a little, there is an emotional tension that helps us to get over the obtrusive mechanics.

It was in 1893 that Pinero composed *The Second Mrs. Tanqueray*, a play so advanced as compared with previous English playwriting that it is sometimes put down as the beginning-point of modern British drama. It followed Pinero's own formula for emotional-dramatic effectiveness. He once wrote: "Theatrical talent consists in the power of making your characters, not only tell a story by means of dialogue, but tell it in such skilfully-devised form and order as shall, within the limits of an ordinary theatrical representation, give rise to the greatest possible amount of that peculiar kind of emotional effect, the production of which is the one great function of the theatre." Here is Scribe's play-structure insisted upon, but not lightly, for amusement, to draw laughter and a tear, but for some deeper response, an "emotional effect." *The Second Mrs. Tanqueray* achieves that effect even while treating a "problem" somewhat memorably. It comes so close to being trenchant social observation, indeed, that we may leave discussion of its implications until a later chapter.

The truer Pinero may be found in *Iris*. Here is an emotional theme treated without wider social application. What is the theatre to which we go, to see *Iris* played? What is the intention of the dramatist, what the response of the spectator, what the special conditions of representation?

This is the true "emotional drama." We go to experience tragic stirrings, to be moved. The Scribe technique is reshaped to compass a story serious and pathetic. Thanks to the progress made by Sardou, Pinero is able to make his drama more compact than any since that of the Greeks. And like Greek tragedy, it is meant to wring our souls, to purge us. But as soon as the curtain is down we know that there is a great difference between this and the plays of Sophocles. Only in a certain directness and intensity is there likeness. Upon analysis we find two elements lacking: poetry and nobility of conception. Pinero has come down to prose; and we are now so close to the triumph of Realism that it is prose laboriously like everyday speech. And the characters are no longer lofty, the dramatic struggle no longer between gods and men. Rather the theme is, as so often since Pinero's time, human weakness, corruption of the spirit. The protagonist is a woman too frail for the struggle against material reality. Emotionally effective, yes; but tragic only if treated with profound insight and with high poetry. In the end *Iris* remains emotional drama, not purging tragedy "of a certain magnitude."

Covent Garden Theatre, London, about 1810. The English, like the French, built in the Italian opera-house tradition; but here the architectural decoration is comparatively restrained. [From a print of the period.]

We see the character Iris slipping down to ruin through her love of luxury. She finds the man she loves, but in a necessary period of waiting for him, gives in to a suitor who provides money for her ease and her whims; and when the true lover comes back to claim her, she loses both men. Such is the simple fable. It is plotted with masterly attention to cumulative effect, and with constant continuity of interest. We find, to be sure, the typical climactic speech in Act V, and the Scribe devices of letters, latchkeys and such aids to the facile unravelling of the knot. But the play *holds*, it grips the surface emotions, it clicks.

For this realistic-emotional drama there is a stage somewhat different from that of the early years of the century. The picture-frame proscenium remains, without the apron and the fore-doors. The acting space has mostly gone behind the curtain-line. And the interior settings are of the "box-set" sort—that is, with three surrounding walls instead of wings—though the exteriors are the same old half-painted, half-built pictures. The box-set interior affords more concentration of attention than the wing sort; the compact emotional drama therefore gains in a physical economy of interest. This is, indeed, a step toward the true naturalistic stage for the realistic plays of the Ibsenites, a step away from falsity and "spread" toward a sort of truth and concentration. The acting, too, is more natural, less conventional. Indeed, we may believe that in the perspective of the future the changes in Pinero's plays, like those in his stage, will be judged as not profoundly important, but as steps toward a later accomplishment of truth and dramatic intensity.

By way of utter contrast, to prove that the old artificial comedy goes on, revives whenever a man of genius takes it in hand, whether he has an eye to naturalness or not, we may pause a moment to consider Oscar Wilde. Within four years—exactly at the time of *The Second Mrs. Tanqueray*—Wilde wrote *Lady Windermere's Fan, A Woman of No Importance*, and *The Importance of Being Earnest*. These are distinctly "old" comedies, and not a little sentimental at times; but the sheer wit of them, the epigrammatic cleverness, disarms the audience. In production the plays go not quite so fluently today as they did in the nineties, but they are stageworthy enough for as frequent revivals as Goldsmith's and Sheridan's; and they mark Wilde as the only English comedy-writer of international importance between Sheridan and Shaw. They are ingenious—though without the obvious cleverness of the typical *pièce-bien-faite*—sparkling, and delightful. They have a permanent place in some lighter theatre than that of Pinero and his serious followers. In the field of poetic drama, Wilde was only half-successful in bringing his lyric gift into the service of the stage; though *Salomé* finds occasional production in several languages—is revived oftener, indeed, than any other English poetic play since Shakespeare's. (I find myself somewhat surprised at the statement, but can discover no evidence to the contrary. Stephen Phillips *promised* more, just after Wilde's time, but there is a literary burden on all his plays, and the first, *Paolo and Francesca*, remains his best—there is no growth toward stageworthiness. The plays of Yeats and Dunsany, also Anglo-Irish, may in time outweigh *Salomé* in popularity, in their special way.)

In the United States the nineteenth century theatre had developed after the pattern of the English: it was a reflection of Paris through London. The first notable American playwrights appeared during the *pièce-bien-faite* era. Bronson Howard was the earliest and perhaps most original: he produced immensely popular plays with a native flavor: *Saratoga* and *Shenandoah*. Clyde Fitch was more prolific, more facile, more extravagantly successful. We read his best plays today as we read those of Pinero and Jones, with mild interest and with admiration for the craftsmanship. None the less the works of Fitch seemed outmoded a quarter-century after they were written. And even Augustus Thomas, who lived to progress one step farther under the influence of the later Realists, never really freed himself from the formula of mechanical play-making. These three, Howard, Fitch, and Thomas kept the American stage supplied with "native" drama to leaven the mass of adaptations from Paris. But they also were America's sacrifice to the French tradition; they never escaped from the limitations of what is called throughout this chapter, somewhat damningly, the well-made-play. As a last word on the subject one may add that in the nineteenth century, Spain and Italy made their sacrifices on that altar too. Facility had become a god in all the theatres of the Western world.

BACK in the early and middle decades of the century, scenery had its "well-made" era. Despite the elaborateness, even the gorgeousness, of some of the older picture settings, there had been faults of construction, painting, and lighting that made the "scene" unnatural from all but one viewpoint in the auditorium (the king's box), and usually too "regular." The use of back-cloth and side-wings solely, in more or less regular rows, made the picture monotonous. With improvements in machinery, however, came "leg-drops," hinged wings, and other irregular pieces.

The two sketches of scenery from behind (reproduced on page 461 and at bottom of page 467), showing the backs of the wings, illustrate both the growing irregularity of shape in those pieces and the method of sliding them in parallel grooves; the one thing promoted variety in the edges, the other monotony in the main lines of the picture. By mid-century the tendency was strong to cut across the grooves with diagonal pieces, supported from the flies and with braces, and not merely by the standard in the groove. The drawing over-leaf tells graphically the story of the change from the conventional regularity of the wing-and-drop set toward the freely composed picture. Not *too* natural yet—but that will come. As in playwriting the new mechanics worked in the direction of Realism, but the Romantic current toward the grandiose was so strong that the chief result was a period of well-made display-scenery without either dramatic justification or the negative values of naturalness.

How far the mid-century scenographers went toward making the stage an exhibition-hall for their own talents, you may guess from the illustrations of French and English productions. The "trial of Hermione" scene from *The Winter's Tale* is an extreme example of the attempt to make the stage picture rival the worst excesses of the easel painters. Real actors and painted actors, real architecture and painted architecture, real shadows and painted shadows—*there* was a task, to make all those match. But nothing daunted the designers and producers who thought that by such displays they were advancing toward greater art in the theatre. The purple patches in the play-text and in the actor's delivery were no less to be added than the purple patches of the stage "decorator." These are, indeed, the *tirades*, the long *virtuoso* passages, in the history of scene-painting. A little later it was thought that archæological accuracy would justify such flights; but it seems never to have occurred (except to a very few radicals) that the whole structure of display scenery is out of place in connection with legitimate drama. Lately we have discovered the mischief played by showy settings on all stages except those given over frankly to spectacle or old-fashioned opera.

In Germany two or three artists—most notably Karl Immermann and Ludwig Tieck—were already experimenting in methods looking

The wing scene varied with oblique pieces. [From *Peintre-Décorateur de Théâtre*, by Gustave Coquiot.]

Nineteenth-century elaboration in scenery. Above, the "trial of Hermione" scene in *The Winter's Tale*, from a drawing by Louis Haghe, 1856. A classic example of the attempt—always futile—to shade real actors into painted crowds. Below, view of a wing setting from behind, in process of "building" during an entr'acte. [From *La Machinerie au Théâtre*, by E. M. Laumann.]

toward simplification of the scene and expediting the changes between scenes. They wanted to discover or revive stages upon which they could present Shakespeare without the wholesale cutting indulged in by most nineteenth century producers. In a vague way they foreshadowed the epochal changes to be ushered in by Gordon Craig and Adolphe Appia soon after 1900. But in their own time they were little more than voices crying in the wilderness of painted canvas and *papier-mâché* edifices.

Increasing Realism in the Romantic scene. A setting for *Tribut de Zamora* as played in Paris, by J. B. Lavastre. [From Pougin's *Dictionnaire du Théâtre*.]

The physical theatres remained operatic throughout the century, with a very few exceptions—most notable among them, Wagner's *Festspielhaus* at Bayreuth. Curiously, that house, built for a new conception of opera, failed to turn the current of practice so far as opera producers were concerned; but by 1890 it had convinced a few architects that Wagner was on the side of the future, and by 1900 the name of Semper was heard wherever "progressive" theatres (i.e., not on the Italian-French model) were being planned.

During the half-century before 1900 it was not unusual for American theatres to masquerade under names borrowed from more respectable cultural institutions. In New York a leading playhouse was known as "The American Museum;" its auditorium was advertised as "the lecture room of the American Museum." Out of deference to Puritan sensitive-

Modelled, in general, upon the theatres of London, the big-city play-houses in America tended to be vast in size. The Boston Theatre in 1855, with a typical large forestage and increasingly democratic seating plan. [From *Ballou's Pictorial Drawing-room Companion.*]

Drury Lane Theatre, London, during a performance in 1795. [A drawing by Edward Dayes, in the Henry E. Huntington Library and Art Gallery, San Marino, California.]

ness a theatre could not be called a theatre, in those times, any more than a leg could be called a leg. But "lecture-rooms" were fitted up with luxurious seats and fully equipped stages. The "Boston Museum" was one of the most famous of American theatres for decades. I am adding pictures of an earlier Drury Lane Theatre and of the Boston Theatre in 1855, indicating a change to somewhat smaller aprons, and illustrating the disappearance of the proscenium doorways. As to scenery, the Boston stage is quite evidently given over to the even-then old-fashioned wing setting; but on the Drury Lane stage the artist depicts a woods scene of a naturalistic sort—perhaps out of his own imagination, since in this picture he patently was most interested in the audience. In either theatre, actors must have spoken with extraordinary vocal power to reach spectators in the rear rows of seats.

A reason for the large theatres in London was the licensing system under which only two or three playhouses enjoyed "patents" for the production of legitimate drama. Thus with each rebuilding, Drury Lane and Covent Garden would be enlarged to accommodate as many additional patrons as possible. After Restoration days and the culmination of the Puritan boycott of the stage, two or three theatres sufficed for the London public that cared or dared to attend "shows." The drama had become a very special recreation, for the sophisticated and the fashionable. But by the early nineteenth century the populace had reawakened to an interest in the drama, and demanded more playhouses and more kinds of play. Theatres outside the law sprang up, and disguised their shows with music, magic acts, and trick-animal numbers, to avoid seeming competition with the licensed houses. Some of the strange things that happened in playwriting in this time might, perhaps, be explained by the desire *not* to produce drama like Shakespeare's or Sheridan's. It was in 1843 that the government passed a Theatre Regulation Act, and permitted an unlimited number of playhouses, under certain restrictions of censorship and building standards.

The large houses became all but useless when drama took its turn toward naturalness and compression in the latter half of the century. There was, of course, the corresponding change in acting. It had required grandiloquence and sweep to dominate in the vast spaces of the older theatres. Now the plays began to demand quietness, intimacy, intensity. And just at the right moment a new ally came to the actor who must make more of facial expression, of nuance of movement: electric light. As the playing-space shrank back into the box-set interior behind the curtain-line, electric lighting illuminated the player's face in a new and marvellous fashion. Given a house intimate enough, he was ready, when the playwright demanded, to interpret a character naturally, quietly, plausibly.

Since Kean and Devrient and Lemaitre, however, the world stage had seen some great actors whom we of today would call "of the old school." In Italy playing has always been grander, more impassioned, more fiery, than elsewhere—the national temperament is volatile and operatic. In the period of Romantic drama (and the quieter well-made-play sort of thing never quite conquered Italy as it did other lands), Tommaso Salvini and Adelaide Ristori blazed vivid trails across the

Tommaso Salvini, preëminent Italian actor of the nineteenth century. Powerful, even fiery, he gained an international reputation, especially in Shakespearean roles such as Othello and Lear. [William Seymour Theatre Collection, Princeton University Library.]

native stages; and then carried their spectacular art into the rest of Europe and to America. The tradition of their sort of acting long persisted, particularly in the playing of Giovanni Grasso—more rugged, but spirited and compelling. Still the one greatest modern player of Italy was Eleonora Duse, who belongs in spirit to the twentieth century: she made drama live nobly and intensely, without romantic elaboration, by the revelation of her own feeling. In her the simplicity of

Realism seemed to be illumined by a clear flame of personal expressiveness.

In France the great actors after Lemaitre were women rather than men; though Coquelin and Mounet-Sully will long be remembered for carrying on the traditions of "high" acting. The three women, however, Rachel, Réjane and Bernhardt, provided some of the most sensational passages in the annals of the Paris stage. Rachel and Bernhardt successively shook the foundations of the official *Théâtre Français*, the one by remaining a member of the company but as a star, the other by leaving the company because she was too brilliant. Rachel was a tragedienne born, with that unexplainable native flair for acting that is restrained by no rules of naturalness or probability. She was perfectly the *Phèdre* of Racine's drama, and specially born to the thrilling heroine-rôles of the strained Romantic plays. Sarah Bernhardt, a generation later, added the more naturally emotional rôles to the Romantic ones, but was in direct succession from the grand old figures. Her beautifully modulated voice remains almost as famous in history as her insistence upon the right to continue openly the tradition of the courtesan-actress, in a time when people accepted such irregularities only under cover. On and off the stage, personality made her a vivid figure, and her *tours-de-force* in acting gained for her the greatest international following of any actress of the nineteenth century. In view of the recent rise of the companies devoted to ensemble playing, it may be that Bernhardt's name will stand last on the list of erratic and brilliant geniuses of the stage; but it has already been a list full of surprises.

A few lines by W. Graham Robertson, a British painter, sum up the magic of the woman and the actress: "Was Sarah Bernhardt beautiful? Was she even passably good looking? I have not the slightest idea. Beauty with her was a garment which she could put on or off as she pleased. When she let it fall from her she was a small woman with very delicate features, thin lips, a small beautifully modeled nose, hooded eyes of gray-green shadowed by a fleece of red-gold hair, strong slender hands, and a manner full of nervous energy. But when she would appear beautiful, none of these details were to be perceived; her face became a lamp through which glowed pale light, her hair burned like an aureole, she grew tall and stately. It was transfiguration."

Up to the time of Edmund Kean, the great players on the American stage were visitors from London. Kean was first seen in New York in 1820, but his unexampled and tumultuous triumph ended in hardly less riotous failure. He was literally hissed back to England after needless

Sarah Bernhardt (at right) and Mrs. Patrick Campbell in Maeterlinck's
Pelleas and Melisande, 1904. Bernhardt several times played male roles, most
notably Pelleas and Rostand's *L'Aiglon*. [By courtesy of the William Seymour Theatre Collection, Princeton University Library.]

affronts to provincial audiences that had at first wildly acclaimed him. Only a few years later Edwin Forrest, first of the notable native-born stars, made his first success, at the famous Bowery Theatre in New York. He rose to first place in the world of the American stage, and even found in London appreciation for his Shakespearean interpretations. Unfortunately he was led into a controversy—probably his own touchiness and high spirits were to blame—with Macready, the ruling

Edwin Forrest, first native-born American actor to become an international star. His supporters incited the Astor Place riots in New York in 1849, during which twenty-two persons were killed, after an actors' quarrel.

English favorite; and it was the feud between factions supporting these rival actors that caused the fatal Astor Place Riot in New York in 1849. The partisans of Forrest resented the return of Macready to New York, when he was billed to play at the Astor Place Opera House; and they not only wrecked the performance from within the auditorium but attacked the theatre from without, as if it were a fort—a fort holding "autocratic English," the leaders told the mob. They even fought the police and then the militia, until twenty-two persons had been killed. Macready escaped back to London while Forrest went on to less dubious honors.

Edwin Booth as Hamlet. Painting by John Pope, in the Theatre Collection, Harvard University. [By courtesy of the Walter Hampden Memorial Library at the Players, New York.]

The American theatre from this time forward was alive with acting talent, and one might pause over many glamorous names. Here were the Booths, the Hacketts, the Wallacks, the Jeffersons, the Davenports, the Drews, and other actor-families. Here, among the women, were Charlotte Cushman, the first American-born actress to become a great star, the picturesque Adah Isaacs Menken, Mary Anderson, Helena Modjeska, Clara Morris, and that Ada Rehan who was for twenty years a star in the remarkable company managed by Augustin Daly. Daly himself is remembered as ablest of American producers of the nineteenth century. In his time, too, there was that strange genius—actor, director, designer, inventor—Steele MacKaye, whose mind leaped forward to many of the "reforms" and stage inventions of a later era.

But two figures may be given more space, the one as greatest of American actors, the other as great and distinctive of an American development: Edwin Booth and Joseph Jefferson. It is typical of the broad national interest in the stage that Booth first came to prominent notice in New York (when he unexpectedly filled his father's rôle in *Richard III*), but made his initial great success in California, and was thereafter idolized throughout the country. He had little of the unaccountable fire of Kean and Forrest, but his quieter art had a nobility that has become a tradition. Intellect and spiritual insight enabled him to score triumphs as Hamlet and in other Shakespearean parts. He progressed out of Romantic acting, and yet was of the elder school: a noble and dominating transitional figure. In New York during the sixties he once played Hamlet at one hundred consecutive performances. When he built his own theatre he plunged into the sort of elaborate scenic productions then in vogue in London, and due to the magnificence of the staging he went into bankruptcy. But later starring triumphs gave him position as representative of all that was finest in American theatre life in his time.

Joseph Jefferson—the third of that name—was a slighter figure, but equally beloved. He made himself master of a type of comedy rôle particularly palatable to American audiences. His acting was appreciated for the same reason that lay behind the success of playwrights who specialized in *The Old Homestead* sort of drama. Jefferson excelled in kindly character portraits. His greatest part was Rip Van Winkle, and he played it for decades to never-failing applause.

In England, after Kean and Macready, there was no figure of similar stature among the actors until Henry Irving's time. The Bancrofts formed a company at the Prince of Wales' Theatre, that did pioneer work in group-acting, and in the encouragement of the English playwrights who were trying to rescue the stage from French domination. But it was Irving who ushered in a new era. He is a great transitional figure, holding at once to the splendor of the past and foreshadowing great changes. His acting was less realistic, in the twentieth century sense, than personal and intellectual, and he usually played in old-fashioned Romantic pieces or in Shakespeare: he was not of a typically

Joseph Jefferson as Caleb Plummer, in *Dot*, an adaptation of Dickens' *The Cricket on the Hearth*. [From *The Autobiography of Joseph Jefferson*, 1889.]

new theatre either as actor or as chooser of plays. His famous scenic productions, moreover, must be set back into perspective as the culmination of the Victorian vogue for picturizing. He pictured more intelligently than any actor-producer before had done; but here was no breath of "modernism" as the term is understood today. What Irving accomplished, that entitles him to epochal fame, was the lifting of the English stage into a new importance, into an unexampled com-

Henry Irving, England's greatest actor-manager of the late nineteenth century, in the title role of *Becket*, 1892. [By courtesy of the Walter Hampden Memorial Library at the Players, New York.]

Three scenes from Henry Irving's production of *Dead Heart* at the Lyceum Theatre, London, 1889, showing the solidly realistic settings. In the middle sketch the central figures are Ellen Terry and Gordon Craig as Catherine Duval and Arthur de St. Valery. In the scene below the dominating figure is Henry Irving as Landry. [From illustrations in the souvenir programme.]

478

pleteness of achievement, and the raising of the actor's estate in the community above any level touched since Garrick's time. It is significant, indeed, of the long pull of the stage against Puritanic prejudice, that Irving was the first actor knighted at the English Court; and suggestive of the earnestness and sincerity of his efforts to create an institutional theatre, to bring his art to an eminence where it might justly be honored with the other arts. As actor he was richly satisfying without ever being spectacular. Perhaps most famous of his rôles were Hamlet and Shylock.

It was in 1878 that Irving took over management of the Lyceum Theatre in London; he had already tasted popular success there as an actor. He gave distinction to the term "actor-manager"—which later came into disrepute, when lesser actors used theatre-control for the exploitation of talents not worthy of stardom. In the first year of his management Irving invited in as "leading lady" the beautiful Ellen Terry, and there began one of the most famous and most successful artistic associations in the history of the stage. Ellen Terry played Ophelia and Portia within the first year—and became, deservedly, an idol of the English public. Several times the Lyceum company toured in America, where the noblest of England's actors and the loveliest of actresses found their triumphs repeated.

One is tempted to say that there is such a thing as well-made-acting, a sort of acting mechanically effective but lacking in depth and sincerity. Certainly one could list a number of tricks by which "effects" are achieved, and probably these were as rife in the mid-nineteenth century theatre as ever before. Irving and Booth, with their personal gifts and their intellectual approach, helped to kill that sort of trickery. If they did not go all the way toward the Realism of Stanislavsky and Moissi and the "ensemble" companies, at least they prepared the way for it.

The final quarter of the century saw an experiment in group acting and "artist-direction" that was to lead on fruitfully toward the innovations and successes to be scored by the Moscow Art Theatre and the twentieth-century German institutional theatres. At one of the minor German ducal courts, at Meiningen (now in Thuringia), the Duke of Saxe-Meiningen established a playhouse in which solo acting was played down, the more glaring absurdities were eliminated from "setting," and a new historical accuracy was achieved in staging. Chiefly it was the introduction of the group ideal in acting, and the consequent enlargement of the director's authority as artist, that has seemed historic to later commentators, particularly in view of the date 1874 when the "Meiningers" made their first sensationally different production of *Julius Cæsar*.

Ellen Terry. [By courtesy of the Walter Hampden Memorial
Library at the Players, New York.]

The Duke of Saxe-Meiningen had his own forerunners. Curiously enough his first inspiration seems to have descended from Edmund Kean, with also indebtedness to Schröder and to Wagner, and in a shadowy way to the Russians. His early successes were largely with productions of Shakespeare and Schiller, but he persisted with his innovations into the time of the "new" realistic playwrights, Ibsen, Tolstoy, and the others. By 1890 his company was well known in many parts of Europe, and if it had done no more than inspire Stanislavsky and his amateur actors in Moscow, it would have served toward an epochal change in the theatre art.

A setting for Ibsen's *The Pretenders:* drawing by the Duke of Saxe-Meiningen, about 1880. The Meiningen Players progressed toward twentieth-century modernism by introducing ensemble acting and a believable reality in settings. [From Grube's *Geschichte der Meininger.*]

CHAPTER 20

Realism:
Photography and Journalism
on the Stage

A ND so Realism arrived in the theatre. As we sit here in the darkened auditorium, expectant, we face not an apron stage, a platform to which some actors will come forth, to strut and to recite. Instead there is a curtain before us, dropped flat behind the footlights. All the acting space has gone behind it. The proscenium-frame is the only convention left.

As the curtain noiselessly rises, we see everything beyond just as it might be "in nature." This curtain is like the blinder the photographer used to draw out of his camera just before taking a view. Its withdrawal permits us to see a restricted bit of actuality—none the less actual for being viewed through a hole. The theorists say the producer has withdrawn not a blinder but the fourth wall of a room. We view everything beyond, within the remaining three walls, just as it would have been had the other wall remained. We, the audience, have not been allowed to disturb people at their business of living out dramatic lives. They will go on living their hates, their loves, their miseries, just as if we were not present. Not one of these actors will step out of the frame, not one incident will violate what might actually happen, next door, or down the street, or across the railroad tracks.

The stage picture has become a photograph. This is no longer a painter's counterfeit; this *is* the room.

The actors walk into it just as they do into those in their own homes. This is no pretense. It is the perfect illusion of reality. And the actors:

483

that one might be Mrs. Jones' own sister; and this girl reminds us of old widower Smith's red-headed daughter.

It doesn't take long for us to become absorbed in their actions: the playwright has provided some incidents as holding as the stories in the evening newspaper. The dialogue is interesting—and oh, so natural! We even cry a little. This scene is touching. What a curious thing life is, all mixed up in laughter and tears! But pshaw! after all this is only a theatre. And we go out after the show, into the street, and throw off the spell of the stage as easily as we throw down the evening paper.

Once in a great while, to be sure, one of these natural plays stirs us deeply—just as a bit of news will sometimes register so that we can't dismiss it for hours or days. It is generally something horrible that makes such a lasting impression—whether in the newspaper or the journalistic play. There is a difference between the response here and that to *The Trojan Women* or to *Hamlet*. There was the *glow* of the theatre in those days; now it's a downright disturbing emotional dislocation. After the shock there is no purging element—call it what you will, poetry, spiritual depth, beauty, Dionysian experience.

What is this Realism that has come into the theatre to make the "show" as natural as what passes in your own drawing-room, as common as the stories in the papers? It is an art creed. It puts forward the assertion that imitation is the first aim in art, that illusion is the purpose of play-producing. It implies that art must have to do with the familiar, the everyday, the natural, with the observed thing instead of the imagined thing.

You will remember that for centuries there had been a trend toward "naturalness," away from convention. The Romantic group were the first to let nature cramp them badly; but they escaped some of the consequences by flying into those regions where nature is wild, to unaccustomed corners and to picturesquely exotic climates and customs—though within known limits. The Realists scorned any such escape. They would find material in nature close by, in people (and places and situations) as familiar as your rector, your butcher, and your serving-maid.

What the Realistic playwrights usually did, to make these people interesting, was to pry down into those incidents and motives and passages in their lives that were hidden from the world. Mostly they were hidden because they had to do with weaknesses, disease, crimes, and abnormalities: and so nine-tenths of Realistic drama has criminal or pathological or sexual-physical aspects—and there is a superabundance of sensational or shocking revealment. On a hundredth chance a playwright paraded a hidden thing that somehow was tinged with nobility or heroic sacrifice or sweetness—and if he were master enough we went away with a breath of the old Dionysian ecstasy on us. But most Realism in the theatre left us excited but drab, stirred but feeling ignoble.

The fight for Realism on the stage was as protracted and as bitter as any other by which new "isms" had been brought into the theatre. And the Realists had hardly got full possession of the place before a new war was declared and they found themselves the defenders and not the attackers. A fearful lot of dust was kicked up, and so much of

Realism in setting in its final phase, impressively solid. An architectural scene for *Faust*, reasonably plotted for acting space, by Albert Roller.

it is still in the air that we shall have to know pretty carefully what Realism is, what its shortcomings are, if we are not to lose our way.

In the first place, we must grant that there are many kinds or degrees of Realism. The most extreme, in which observed fact is not only prominent but is emphasized, insisted upon—like the art of the painter who depicts every hair in a man's beard—we may dismiss as mere Naturalism. The true Realist looks down on the Naturalist just as you and I do; he says that art is selective: not just any bit of nature photographed exactly, but a special bit of nature, caught unawares, then the picture touched up a bit, and some unessentials eliminated. Still, the Realist adds, the main outlines and the background must not violate actuality.

Thus on the peep-hole stage—that is what the fourth-wall theory gives us in a glorified way—you may have a whole range of selective Realism, from the plain reportorial or slice-of-life sort, over near Naturalism, to the emotionally condensed sort over near Sentimentalism and Romanticism. But almost never does observed-life drama touch into lastingly significant art unless another element is added, in what we may term *intellectual-realistic* plays. And what the modern theatre achieved, of permanent value, between 1870 and 1920 was almost exclusively in this field where shrewd fact-observation is crossed with trenchant thought. The Realistic drama might be dismissed as a mere passing phase, had not some men of exceptional intellect lifted the photographic-familiar play to their own uses. Whether it is the deeply purposeful drama of Ibsen or the wittily intellectual drama of Shaw, it is Realistic drama first, but *drama of thought* second and more important.

We cannot here go into the æsthetics of Realism, cannot ask whether the play of familiar life does not, by working solely to accomplish an intensification of human emotion, inevitably wreck itself on the rock of "the pathetic fallacy." But from the exterior viewpoint, looking back at a half-century of accomplishment, we can make sure that only Realistic drama with this other thing added, with implications valuable in the fields of social thought and of intellectual stimulation, survived notably.

The theatre that housed the realistic-intellectual drama has been the least *theatrical* in history, a place used rather than a part of the essential means and material of the art, contributing definite values to the ensemble impression. The stage became a picture so like life that its first aim was to escape notice, glamour was suppressed for fear of disturbing the illusion of actuality, and acting became subservient. The extreme Naturalists, of course—David Belasco most conspicuously—developed stage settings with a *virtuoso* naturalness, with so exact likeness to actuality that they shouted for attention to the cleverness of the illusion. But later Realists guessed that selective imitation in the background picture was better for the play-illusion. On all counts the playwright became supreme. From 1890 to 1915, the stage belonged to the author as never before. Perhaps it was a reaction to the earlier divorce between literature and theatre. More likely the age of Realism kills inevitably the true theatrical appeal, implies transfer of the stage from the hands of artists to men of intellectual rather than emotional-æsthetic attainments.

By way of keeping a better perspective on Realism, before looking into the story of its triumphs in detail, we should remind ourselves that the rule of the Realists ended with World War I. Practically every

Above, a setting for Gluck's opera *Alceste*, by Karl Friedrich Schinkel. Below, a scene in *The Return of Peter Grimm*, as produced in New York by David Belasco, 1911. Realism in setting for its own sake, accomplished by multiplication of casual detail. This setting became a target for the revolutionaries of the time, who believed in emphasis upon the actor rather than the background—and above all else simplified their scene.

important dramatist of the movement was a pre-war figure: Ibsen, Strindberg, Tolstoy, Chekhov, Hauptmann, and Wedekind, of course; and Schnitzler, Brieux, Shaw, Barker, and Galsworthy substantially. And among the lesser men who wrote two or three notable plays in the *genre*—St. John Ervine, Stanley Houghton, St. John Hankin, Eugene Walter, Maxim Gorky—there is only infrequent orientation to the newer theatre, in which theatricalism, as crystallized in a new completeness of *production*, has become a prime consideration. Since 1920 the dramatist has no longer been the key figure in the theatre.

Alexandre Dumas *fils*, who was born in 1824, once wrote: "I realize that the prime requisites of a play are laughter, tears, passion, emotion, interest, curiosity; to leave life in the cloakroom; but I maintain that if, by means of all these ingredients, and without minimizing one of them, I can exercise some influence over society; if, instead of treating effects I can treat causes; if, for example, while I satirize and describe and dramatize adultery I can find means to force people to discuss the problem, and the law-maker to revise the law, I shall have done more than my part as a poet, I shall have done my duty as a man."[1] By grace of the attempt to put that theory into practice—though he and his collaborator Emile Augier failed to write "thesis-plays" that have survived —Dumas *fils* is sometimes credited with originating the realistic-social drama. Augier, to be sure, is remembered for his *Le Gendre de M. Poirier* and for other straight comedies; and Dumas for *La Dame aux Camélias*, a grand but somewhat cheap emotional play. But the consciously purposeful dramas of these two men failed to establish significantly the newly glimpsed society-conscious theatre.

And indeed, there is not one French playwright of the Realistic school who remains internationally important, of stature comparable to Ibsen and Chekhov and Shaw. Henri Bernstein fell heir to the overseas popularity of Sardou, but his plays were emotional-observation without the intellectual brilliancy or the true realistic truthfulness to detail. Much earlier Emile Zola had tried to bring the grand manner of Romanticism to the low-down subject matter that he discovered through his boasted devotion to Naturalism, but his plays are the least part of his literary achievement. Henri Becque instead is the first notable figure among the short-sighted Naturalists. After him a group of facile playwrights turned their realistic spotlights upon the old triangle situation, sometimes by way of comedy, sometimes for emotional-dramatic effect: Maurice Donnay, Georges de Porto-Riche and Henri Bataille. The term "psychologic drama" came freely into currency

---

[1] Quoted by Barrett H. Clark in *European Theories of the Drama* (New York, 1947).

with the emergence of their plays. Henri Lavedan and Alfred Capus ranged more widely for subject matter but are less in the direct Realistic succession. It is rather with Paul Hervieu and François de Curel that we return fully to the type of drama foreshadowed by Dumas *fils* and Augier: both are idea-dramatists; and only with Eugene Brieux do we arrive at the thesis-play triumphant. For Brieux is the moralist and the reformer consciously using the stage to set forth an indictment of society. Here the theatre has come to its most direct service as moral weapon; at the same time it has just about ceased to exist as an art in which theatricalism has a value of its own.

If it seems possible to omit further mention of all those other French playwrights, and of as many more who gave Paris its unending stream of triangle comedies, topical satires, and Sardou-like emotion-plays, without depth or stimulus, it is not possible so easily to pass by Brieux —because he marked the culmination of the movement toward a drama of social purpose. Not so graceful a writer as a half-dozen of the others, not a shrewd psychologist, not troubled by any canons of good taste, he still stirred audiences all over the world. He was the journalist-realist using the stage willy-nilly to force attention to social wrongs. In *La Robe Rouge* he showed tragedy growing out of that French judicial system which led the police to arrest *someone* for every murder or else be accused of inefficiency; an innocent man is sacrificed to the system, in order that a prosecutor may be promoted, with the final result that the wife of the accused kills the prosecutor. In *Maternité* he argued for birth control, and used the unpretty device of showing up society's injustice to the illegitimate child in contrast to the old-fashioned sentimental and often tragic encouragement of over-breeding. In *Les Avariés*, played in English as *Damaged Goods*, he exhibited a man afflicted with syphilis marrying, against his physician's advice, showed him contaminating others, and—not to dwell upon the really horrible details—ended with the physician pleading for enlightenment but refusing to aid the wife to divorce her tainted husband. Thus is the stage made to do for clinic and rostrum. It is a good sign that the vogue of Brieux has faded. We all went to see these plays in their time, and I think we considered them "advanced." Fortunately the theatre has since made headway in other and less noisome directions. For essentially the stage is more concerned with beauty than with morals. The theatre is the house of emotion, of passion, of ecstasy, rather than the house of correction.

During the reign of Realism in France only one theatre stood out sharp and clear from the background of increasingly commercialized playhouses; the *Théâtre Libre*. You will remember how Napoleon restored the privilege of monopoly to the *Théâtre Français* in Talma's time, after the "free" period of the Revolution; but in 1864 the field was again thrown open to all producers. Still production tended to become stereotyped, and a few people saw clearly that French play-writing was ingrowing and was becoming provincial. One of these was André Antoine, a clerk of the Gas Company. So he founded the *Théâtre Libre* in Paris in 1887, as a home for experiment, and to stage the plays that would not be seen otherwise. Realism was in the air, and

Scene in Ibsen's *The Wild Duck*, as produced by André Antoine at the *Théâtre Libre* in Paris, about 1880. First of the French theatres dedicated to naturalism, and one of the most influential "little theatres" of the modern movement. [From Darzen's *Le Théâtre Libre Illustré.*]

Antoine's "reforms" were limited to a Realistic programme. In the end he turned up no new playwright of permanent world importance. But he established the first of those amateur and semi-professional play-houses that have carried so much of the burden of experiment and progress toward a different theatre in the years since; and he introduced to Paris the giants out of the North, Ibsen, Strindberg, Tolstoy. After nine years the *Théâtre Libre* failed.

Henrik Ibsen was perhaps the greatest figure of the Realistic theatre and of the nineteenth century theatre. Today the world looks back at this little man with just the trace of a smile for his crusader's conceit and his personal pompousness and somewhat tight morality, but with sincere admiration for his achievement in lifting a limited form of stage art to its highest manifestation. He took the well-made-play structure and turned it to serious instead of trivial uses. He made the play-form taut and compact as it had not been before. He cut down the limits of the dramatic story, condensed, treated only the climactic or catastrophic action. He added a new meaning to the term "dramaturgic economy."

But most notably and most startlingly Ibsen achieved the purpose of Dumas *fils;* stimulated the spectator's mind, awakened his conscience. He made the drama social, revolutionary, topical. He diagnosed the ills of humankind, destroyed illusions, satirized conceit and provincialism and hypocrisy. His was a destructive work, in the social-intellectual view—perhaps Realism *used* can be nothing more. At any rate, he stirred the world even while affording audiences absorption in shrewd dramatic reports of contemporary living.

In his personal life economic pinch, social injustice, experience of theatre management, and long exile in broader countries than his own native Norway, helped to shape his course toward the writing of keen-edged social drama. His early plays were Romantic and poetic; of them only one, *Peer Gynt*, has survived with the later thesis-plays. It is un-Romantic, natural-as-your-hat, observed drama that is typical Ibsen-esque.

A woman, from being the petted and spoiled plaything of her husband, suddenly grows up to independence, and walks out of the house on her own: *A Doll's House*. A vague idealist, self-centered and ineffective, insists upon a code and brings specific tragedy and worse, mental inconclusion: *The Wild Duck*. A man grown above the expedient morality of a prosperous provincial town tries to correct evils for the sake of the people, but finds himself an outcast: *An Enemy of the People*. A woman has been persuaded by her pastor to return to her profligate and diseased husband, out of respect to the sacredness of the marriage vow; now their child, grown up, returns, and his hereditary disease and his hereditary philandering bring about a situation unendurably horrible—for audience as well as for the characters: *Ghosts*. Such are the ideas underlying Ibsen's work. He treats them humanly, with expert character-drawing; but it is the idea, not character-conception, that determines the situations, the plots.

Ibsen's plays had enormous influence outside the Scandinavian theatre. *A Doll's House*, first of the notable social dramas, was written in 1879, and others followed, at about two-year intervals, until 1899: including, besides those above-named, *Rosmersholm, Hedda Gabler, The Master Builder*, and others. As early as 1890 these had exerted an influence in Germany and in England. The tautly-constructed, natural-dialogue, thoughtful idea-play became the ideal of "advanced" playwrights. Realism had been raised to a new importance, socially if not theatrically.

Not to follow too tortuously the trail of "the new spirit" across the stages of Europe—always in thinking of these matters we should visualize certain less learned types of stage activity as going on endlessly, as a background, farce and melodrama and burlesque and vaudeville or "variety"—we may note these figures as giants or near-giants who walked importantly in the branchless groves of Thesis-Realism:

Björnstjerne Björnson, fellow-Norwegian to Ibsen, but less the born playwright, was characteristically a dramatist of social criticism; his best-known play, *A Gauntlet*, is a dramatic plea for the single standard in "sexual purity." August Strindberg was a greater figure, writing powerfully and often bitterly, of the foibles and miseries of mankind;

Henrik Ibsen, generally ranked as the world's greatest dramatist of the realistic era. [By courtesy of the Museum of the City of New York.]

The Father, of the longer plays, and *Creditors* and *Miss Julia* of the shorter, are perhaps the best known in translation, though all the theatres that wanted Realism in its most trenchant and distressing aspects have played Strindberg occasionally. Gerhart Hauptmann in Germany went beyond the Scandinavians in one respect: he dramatized not only individuals as type-figures out of society, but in *The Weavers* an entire

A scene in *Dead End* by Sidney Kingsley as designed and produced by Norman Bel Geddes in New York, 1935. A tour-de-force in realistic stage setting. [By courtesy of the Hoblitzelle Theatre Arts Library, University of Texas.]

social class; and beyond Realism he wrote several poetic-symbolic plays that have lived to survive many of the products of the other pre-war dramatists. Hermann Sudermann was only a Realist of the half-convinced Sardou type; his plays lack depth and truth, though he achieved in the nineties an international reputation beyond Hauptmann's—chiefly by the success of *Home* (*Magda*). Frank Wedekind caused a stir as great as those following the early productions of Ibsen's plays and the publication and rare showing of Brieux; he set out, sometimes mercilessly, sometimes bitterly, many of the subjects that people are most reticent about: most notably, perhaps, in *The Awakening of Spring*, a tragedy of adolescent awakening to love. In Austria, where German is the language of the stage, but the people and the art less Teutonic than Latin (with a bit of Oriental influence thrown in), Arthur Schnitzler was the master of Realism, and he carried the medium to a gracefulness unexampled before: his studies of transient love are superior to anything in the French, for truth combined with light sophistication.

At the other extreme are the Russians, utterly sincere, preoccupied with the miseries of the world, seeking to throw light into the dark spots of human characters and human haunts. They took audiences back toward Naturalism, they cut slices out of existence, showed out

"Built" realism, as practiced at the Moscow Art Theatre. A scene in Chekhov's *The Three Sisters*, 1901. Supposedly the sense of reality was heightened by glimpses into rooms beyond the one in which the action occurred.

life-as-it-distressingly-is. Maxim Gorky threw aside play structure entirely, and turned to picturing vividly his fellow-outcasts and sufferers —his was the great protest against dramatizing life "as they write of it in books." His plays achieve lifelikeness that is startling, in a performance such as the Moscow Art Theatre troupe could give, but a formlessness and a chaotic confusion far from essential theatre. Tolstoy was more a craftsman, but only half a one as compared with Ibsen or Scribe. Only the palpitating violence and emotion that he caught in his writing, the images hot from observed life, could outweigh the looseness of structure; but *The Living Corpse* and *The Power of Darkness* are still widely played. Leonid Andreyeff went deep into the portrayal of futile and miserable living, but rose to imaginative heights at other times. Anton Chekhov was the most individual of the Russians, and his apparently "natural" studies, carefully etched, come to life dramatically with understanding direction and skilful character-acting.

His art is one of delicacy, of nuances of feeling, of half-hidden spiritual values, and he has enjoyed a belated vogue after the heavier-handed Realists have begun to slip in popularity. Even today *The Cherry Orchard*, *The Three Sisters* and *Uncle Vanya* appear regularly in repertories all over the world.

The Russian theatre before the era of Realism had always followed fashions from abroad, without contributing with originality to the world's store of great plays; though often the theatres of Moscow and Petrograd were among the most brilliantly active in Europe. The ballet particularly had found patronage and encouragement there, and along with Realistic plays the country sent "Russian dancers" out to all the rest of the world. It was the Moscow Art Theatre, however, that was first to be recognized as a foremost experimental centre, and as home of a troupe unrivalled for ensemble acting. For a generation it was the best known, the most esteemed, playing company in the world—unless we want to dispute in favor of the amateurs of Ober-Ammergau. And its position, gained by its pushing of realistic acting over into a region of spiritual revelation, was maintained even in a later era when Russian directors were exploring every phase of unreal and frankly theatric acting and production.

Berlin had its *Freie Bühne*, after the pattern of the *Théâtre Libre*, in 1889, and here Otto Brahm became the arch-realist in staging. Settings and properties, like the plays, must be as familiar, as common, as your own kitchen, the office, the factory. Here came the beginning Hauptmann and Sudermann with their timidly or precipitately natural plays, and here Ibsen and Tolstoy were first introduced to Germany. Brahm taught Reinhardt, and the impetus ran out in the latter's famous *Deutsches Theater* in Berlin. After the Moscow Art Theatre, the *Deutsches* was the most famous playhouse of the early years of the twentieth century.

It was in 1891 that J. T. Grein established in London the Independent Theatre, in the image of the *Théâtre Libre* and the *Freie Bühne*. Ibsen (already a *casus belli* in England), Tolstoy and others of the Continental iconoclasts were exhibited, talked about, fought over. The established playwrights were influenced: two years later Pinero brought out his "thoughtful" play, *The Second Mrs. Tanqueray*; but most important, a new author turned to the stage, Bernard Shaw. His first play, *Widowers' Houses*, an exposé of respectable-shameful slum landlordism, was composed expressly for the Independent Theatre. In the following eleven years he failed to bring more than one successful play to the boards in London, although he began early to dress his obviously purposeful plots in abundantly witty dialogue. In 1904, after his dramas had gained an extraordinary success in printed form (the now-famous Prefaces are as entertaining and meaty as the acts that follow), a series of productions at the Court Theatre, under the Vedrenne-Barker management, established him as the leading figure of "the new movement" in England; and he never relinquishd his claim to that position. Indeed, his fame so grew that up to his death in 1950 there was none to dispute with him for the title of "the world's foremost living dramatist."

It was Shaw's destiny to lift the Realistic drama to its highest potentiality—by making it primarily and enjoyably intellectual drama. He is more "natural" than the average Realists: where others have to force nature at times, sentimentally or emotionally, to gain "effects," Shaw sails by on the wings of intellectual brilliancy. He more or less swallowed the well-made-play formula in its structural aspect; but he balked at the romantic and sentimental conventions that still clung to it—very obviously in Pinero and Jones, more covertly in Ibsen and Hauptmann. In his own words, he looked on "romance as the great heresy to be swept off from art and life."

As to his social purpose in the theatre, he wrote thus in his Preface to the *Pleasant Plays:* "I can no longer be satisfied with fictitious morals and fictitious good conduct, shedding fictitious glory on robbery, starvation, disease, crime, drink, war, cruelty, cupidity, and all the other commonplaces of civilization which drive men to the theatre to make foolish pretenses that such things are progress, science, morals, religion, patriotism, imperial supremacy, national greatness and all the other names the newspapers call them . . . To me the tragedy and the comedy of life lie in the consequences, sometimes terrible, sometimes ludicrous, of our persistent attempts to found our institutions on the ideals suggested to our imaginations by our half-satisfied passions, instead of on a genuinely scientific natural history."

And so Shaw raises the curtain on characters that act so naturally, with a scientific-intellectual honesty, alongside some romantically conventional ones, that the contrast becomes vividly dramatic and the world is vastly entertained. Military glory, medical infallibility, the righteous reform spirit, the masterful man, surface respectability— these and a dozen other pretenses and fictions serve as excuse for the brilliant display of his wit, his moral passion, his ability to strike to a basic human truth.

His realistic plays are not theatrical with the warm, human glow that has seemed in the past so characteristic of the stage art. Perhaps he would sweep away that side of the theatre as romantic and fictitious. To escape "stageness," he cast away much that made Sophocles and Shakespeare truly theatrical. To some, who see the sensuous element as legitimate in art, and who look for a deeper spiritual-emotional evocation as the characteristic excellence of the stage play, it seems clear that Shaw—in the final view—made the supreme success in a limited dramatic field, over toward the intellectual and away from the sensuous-theatrical. He eschewed theatre, but used the theatre compellingly, nay gorgeously.

Bernard Shaw, England's top-ranking dramatist of the first half of the twentieth century, and a world master of brilliant, intellectual realism. [William Seymour Theatre Collection, Princeton University Library.]

Certainly in the Realistic era, he gave us more to be glad for, more to entertain us intelligently, than any other writer: *Candida*, *The Devil's Disciple*, *You Never Can Tell*, *Man and Superman*, *Getting Married*, *Mrs. Warren's Profession*, *Arms and the Man*, *Androcles and the Lion*, *Heartbreak House*—the productions of these (on our American stages) afforded many of our most memorable evenings of playgoing, through two decades. In *Pygmalion* Shaw exhibited a deeper theatrical sense, and with the very fine *St. Joan* (1923) he attained a world-wide triumph. From then on his powers declined.

The impetus of the Ibsen battling and of the Independent Theatre spirit led to the founding of the Stage Society in London, that notable "tryout" organization established to present "uncommercial" drama, and to circumvent, for the sake of select audiences, the British official censor; and to the three-year stand of the Court Theatre in London. Under the Vedrenne-Barker management a thousand performances of "advanced" plays were given, of which seven hundred were Shaw. Other dramatists arose to the opportunity created by a broad and courageous policy. The Court Theatre brought to production plays by John Galsworthy, by St. John Hankin, and by the director of the en-

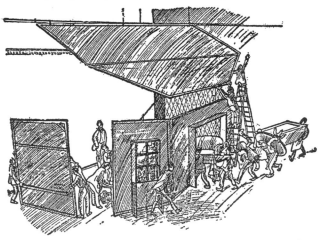

The simple act of letting down a ceiling, as shown here in a sketch by Ernst Stern, completed the box-set interior. This eliminated for scene designers a major problem that had existed for centuries: how to mask the machinery above the stage with "borders." From this time forward the natural room, with three walls, a ceiling, and doors and windows as wanted, was standard. [By courtesy of Oliver M. Sayler.].

terprise, Harley Granville-Barker; and three of the Greek tragedies so beautifully translated by Gilbert Murray. And at matinées in another house, John Masefield's *The Tragedy of Nan* was sponsored.

After Shaw, John Galsworthy enjoyed the widest vogue. His utterly serious and emotional thesis-plays are the best of their kind. Like Shaw, Galsworthy believed in using the stage to set out human follies, inconsistencies, injustice. He accomplished this vividly and often movingly, most notably in *The Silver Box, Strife, Justice, Loyalties*, and *Escape*. He gains in dramatic intensity by the consistency and sympathy of his character-drawing; but the idea is the thing that remains with the spectator after the last curtain.

Granville-Barker—actor and director as well as dramatist—composed some of the most sensitively conceived and delicately molded idea-plays in the language. He approaches Chekhov in the fineness and the quietness of his method. But his plays are seldom seen in production—perhaps await some less noisy theatre than that of the Realistic era. And indeed, in the reading of such a play as *The Secret Life*, one feels that there is groping at least toward a theatre where spiritual values can be set out more truly than now seems possible. In *The Madras House* the author earlier scored a success quite in the Shaw tradition, satirically, brilliantly.

Masefield in *The Tragedy of Nan* added a poetic touch to Realistic emotion-play. He almost gave promise of combining the new intensity with the old splendor—but nothing later came from his pen to fulfill the promise, if we read one into that notable play. J. M. Barrie dressed Realism in other trappings—those of sly humor, fantasy, and sentiment. His are the most palatable plays, for many audiences, that came out of the English theatre of the idea-play era. Lacking both the conviction and the brilliancy of Shaw's, and the burning sincerity of Galsworthy's, they have yet other qualities that are likely to give them as long life in the theatre. For no one can forget the ironics of *What Every Woman Knows* or *The Twelve-Pound Look*, or the tenderness —sometimes over-sentimental—of the less "thoughtful" pieces such as *Peter Pan* and *Dear Brutus*. There may be more of stageworthiness here than in clinical dramas.

It was during the later years of the Realistic era that the American theatre outgrew the estate of a dependency of the European stage, that it developed individuality and a self-sufficient life of its own. Long, long before, it had claimed outstanding genius in the figures of two or three star actors. But in playwriting for more than a century it had been dependent upon London, when it wasn't sending to Paris for its materials and models. Occasionally, to be sure, it had known triumphs in minor fields: the distinctive Indian dramas, Negro minstrelsy, the Harrigan and Hart farces, homely plays of the type of *The Old Homestead* and *Shore Acres,* and local melodrama. But in the well-made-play era, the first emerging literary dramatists had faithfully reflected European practice, and the bulk of plays were then still coming from overseas.

In the first decade of the new century, however, the abounding life of the country and a new will to amusement were reflected in a commercial stage intensely alive and sustained by native playwrights. This was the time of syndicate control and the killing off of all independent experiment and direction. But in turning out endless mechanical plays to the demand of the market, the American author came to an amazing skill. He made journalistic drama his own. The plays were often sentimental, crass, shallow, without purpose beyond amusement;

but the activity marked the lifting of another national theatre to independence of a vigorous if crude sort.

Against this background of continued grinding out of entertaining, even absorbing, realistic drama, occurred those phenomena which brought the American stage to the attention of the rest of the world: as home of such revolutionary and creative playwrights as Eugene O'Neill and Thornton Wilder; as a stage upon which the standard of scene design was as high (within the limits set by the choice of plays) as in any country; and as host-stage to numberless famous acting companies, including Stanislavsky's, Copeau's and Reinhardt's. Here incidentally the Naturalist mode in staging was given its most thorough trial, in the productions of David Belasco and his imitators—an experiment followed by the accomplishment of the best in selective-realistic mounting. But as in Paris, Berlin, Moscow, and London, the "insurgent" playhouses, the theatres revolting against the slick and shallow efficiency of the "regular" stage soon came to be more important, artistically, than the professional institution.

The story of the little and non-commercial theatres belongs to a later chapter: for one thing, they were established not more from the desire for a superior Realism than out of a devotion to some vague ideal of a later Expressionistic theatre. The insurgents had read Craig as well as Ibsen and Shaw. But it is proper to mention here the several playwrights who raised the standard of sincerity and truth above the elements to be detected in the plays of Clyde Fitch and Augustus Thomas. We might linger over the names of William Vaughn Moody and Eugene Walter. But it is rather with a younger generation that socialized Realism came into its American own: Edward Sheldon, Susan Glaspell, Sidney Howard, Maxwell Anderson, Philip Barry, Elmer Rice, Eugene O'Neill. It is difficult to draw a line between passing journalistic Realism and trenchant thesis-Realism on the American stage —the playwrights here seem to confuse their aims more than in other countries.

In the end the story of the Realistic dramatist in America comes down to O'Neill alone. He was played in many world capitals soon after his New York premières. True to the traditional manner of the making of Realistic playwrights—Chekhov, Hauptmann, Shaw, Galsworthy—he was a product of a minor insurgent stage, the Provincetown Playhouse. But from compelling Realism he went on to other fields—and there we shall meet him again.

A different sort of phenomenon on the American stage was to be seen in the plays of Charles Rann Kennedy, not of America originally but typical of developments there. In 1908–1910 his symbolic-realistic drama *The Servant in the House*, the best of its sort but not without

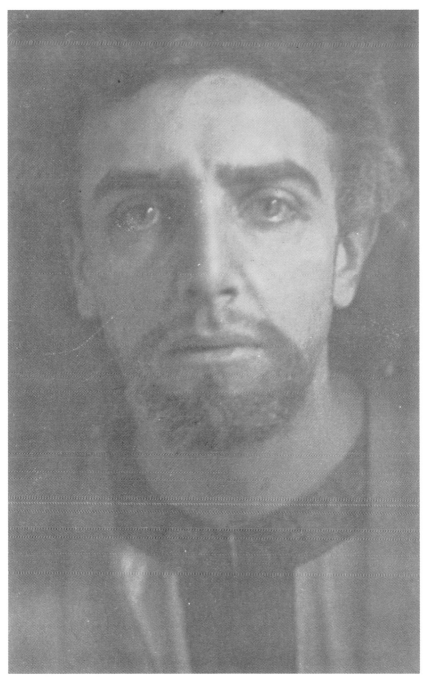

Walter Hampden as Manson in Charles Rann Kennedy's *The Servant in the House*, in Henry Miller's production, 1908. [By courtesy of the Walter Hampden Memorial Library at the Players, New York.]

sentimental moments, achieved a spectacular success in the regular theatres. Other plays followed, more realistic at times, literary-symbolic at others, and with an occasional tinge of what has since become known as Expressionism. The professional theatre was not ready for works so serious and so unusual. Kennedy and his wife, the gifted actress Edith Wynne Matthison, practically withdrew from contact with the "regular" stage. Stirred by the spirit that led to the founding of a thousand "irregular" stages in the same decade, they set about creating their own theatre; a company of three actors was formed, capable of playing on any platform in church, school, or playhouse, and thus economically independent. For it Kennedy wrote plays of greater poetic loveliness than any others written in America in those years, and highly enjoyable in performance for a "special" public, the public, say, that rates the Ober-Ammergau Passion Play above *Death of a Salesman*. The achievement of the tiny acting company, seldom seen in "regular" theatres, was symptomatic of the change that most truly represented theatre progress in America after 1925. That change will afford material for Chapters 22 and 23.

Realism ended, in America, with a stimulus to exploration of every phase of anti-Realism, at the hands of widely separated, self-sufficient acting groups and of playwrights not subservient to Broadway. Realism marches on, among the men of shorter vision, just as musical comedy and revue persist. But the people who have made history have been on some other quest, many in educational and community and "little" theatres.

Realism in art came pat to the life of the late nineteenth century and the early twentieth. In the age of scientific inquiry, in the age when social equality apparently was gained for great masses of men, in the age of the clearing away of superstition and pretense, art was brought down to the familiar, the analytical, the microscopic. This was also, we might note, the era when man went farthest toward self-destruction. It was natural that he should almost destroy the theatre.

And indeed, much as we may enjoy Ibsen and Shaw, they did go far toward destroying that theatre in which Euripides and Shakespeare and Sheridan were possible—or Scaramuccia or Grimaldi. The Realists completed the process of pushing back the theatre until it all but ceased to live as such. A picture of reality lived in a peep-show box instead. The truly theatrical elements were squeezed out. But those revolutionaries, building a thousand little theatres, out of some longing for theatrical expressiveness, and their playwrights who timidly started out to present a different sort of play—they are a sign of Realism's weakness, its limits, and (as an art creed) its passing.

CHAPTER
21

The Theatre and Its Swell Relations: The Other Arts

I T IS permissible to mark the convenient date 1900 as the turning-point into a new theatre. It is true that the parallel currents of the sentimental well-made play and of journalistic naturalism flowed on into the twentieth-century theatre. But if one judges by the "advanced" stages of the world, one recognizes that the new century has witnessed the beginnings of a different dramatic art: not unconnected with the Greek, the Elizabethan, the Oriental, but different in a very revolutionary way from nineteenth century Realism.

Now this new theatre art is as yet less a matter of performance than a world-wide formulation of a different theory, and an awakened consciousness. There is performance too, or the subject wouldn't be worth talking about; and the evidence of it will be material for the chapters after this one. But since the change in the spirit and aim of the world theatre is more evident than the practice, and since the understanding of the entire period after Realism is dependent upon a clear conception of all that change implies, it has seemed to me wise to break into the chronological continuity of my "story," and to set in here a chapter of undisguised theory.

I have no warrant from my fellow workers in the modern theatre to formulate a statement of the æsthetics of "the theatre art"—and I am only too conscious that no one has yet put down any such guide as I shall here attempt. But I have tried to see the "new theatre movement" broadly; and I have believed that I recognized elements in recent advance and experiment that linked stage progress with that in the other arts, in architecture, painting, and the dance particularly: in short, that "modern art" has already transformed certain stages and has engaged the minds of the most promising and most effective artists in the theatre of today. And so I shall proceed to explore the theory of "the theatre art" with constant reference to the recognized advance in "general" art.[1]

The theatre almost invariably has been looked down upon by the practitioners of the other arts, and by theorists and critics in particular. They all have made eyes at it, to be sure. The poet has seen here the very place to set forth his pretty verses the more movingly. The painter coveted the stage because he knew he could use it to the glory of picture-making—and for some centuries he did. The musician actually kidnapped drama at one time, married the jade to his own art and thus begat that strange interloper on the theatrical platform, Opera. The dancer, too, opining truly enough that drama was born of dance, has schemed to repossess the stage. And yet each of these artists, and all their apologists, have treated the theatre art itself as an inferior—if indeed they recognized it at all as a separate, self-sufficient art, and not merely a conglomeration.

It is easy to perceive reasons when one views not only the diverse people but the wide ranges of activity that actually are "theatre" in the larger sense, the complex nature of the materials of the art, the variable human element, the scattered manifestations. There is nothing clean-cut here, no neat rules, no lasting finished work. In a time when pigeon-holing was a passion with critics and with scholars, the theatre confusion was too puzzling. One might take ten examples of painting for study, and say, "These represent sixteenth century art at its best, and therefore the characteristics of that period are, etc., etc." It could be done with sculpture, with architecture, with poetry. Even with music, where a performer comes between the composer and the public; for a musical score comes infinitely nearer to fixing the values of the performance before an audience than does the written text of a

---

[1] In earlier editions of this book the chapter on theory carried no illustrations. In enlarging the volume it has seemed to me, considering the small number of plates formerly illustrating modern advances in stagecraft, that a series of pictures explanatory of the aims of Adolphe Appia, Gordon Craig, Robert Edmond Jones and other leaders of the reform scene movement might well begin here. Starting with two obvious examples of the old stagecraft—scenery in the one case tawdry and showy, in the other carefully naturalistic—a series of thirty pictures illustrates methods of simplifying the scene, rendering it suggestive and atmospheric rather than literal, and (most important) serving to restore the stage to the actor. Ten plates will be found in this chapter, the others scattered in the two chapters immediately following.

play. If you buy all the printed dramas of the Elizabethan or the Greek playwrights, and study them to your heart's content, you still won't know the theatre of the Elizabethan or the Greek age until you gain a vision of the complete performance and all that went to shape it: physical form of the theatre, architecture, color, light; actors, choruses, dancing; music; costumes, properties, settings, machinery; most of all, the flow of these things together, the underlying structure of emphasis, pause, interval, rhythm—the complexity brought into focus.

Not that nineteenth century scholars didn't try to explain theatre art wholly by the evidence of the plays on the library shelf. They had stage art almost stuffed into a pigeon-hole that was merely a department under "Literature"; and they dissected play texts and taught an exact formula of playwriting. They simply ignored those manifestations of theatre in which the written text is fairly incidental: dance-drama, the Professional (improvised) Comedy, pantomime, pageantry, etc. They were willing to write down acting as a minor reproducing art, and they allowed no creative value to directing, setting, and producing. They lost the very spirit of the theatre, as anyone must who fails to visualize the *flow* of the stage art, before an audience.

If this activity couldn't be squeezed in as a department of literature, on the obvious claims of a Sophocles, a Shakespeare, or a Molière, what else was there about the institution to align it with any of the recognized, the holy arts? Then in the nineteenth century, as the visual arts became more and more divorced from ordinary living—with painting and sculpture retreating into museums, and the artists getting themselves elected into academies and hierarchies—the theatre took the other road: with its degraded product it stayed by the people, in their accustomed amusement places, in tents and casinos and market-places. Such as it was—and almost never do the last shreds of glory depart from it, however incongruous—it was popular. Wherefore the high arts, the fine arts, came to look condescendingly on it. Under democracy, anything that so many people liked must be low.

There has been one disadvantage for the student in this escape of the theatre from canonization. While some of the best intellects of the late nineteenth century sought to disentangle the threads of art theory, and wrote volumes on the nature of the fine arts in general and of painting, sculpture, architecture, poetry, and music in particular (not *all* these volumes are more muddling than useful), no one has ever attempted seriously to write an exposition or explanation of the art of the theatre, that would clearly suggest what is the nature of the appeal that the stage performance makes to a spectator, or how the theatre artists put it into a play-production. Such a book, if not too narrowly nineteenth century in outlook, might help considerably those of us who work, very near-sightedly, in the theatre, might interest those who merely have felt the glamour of the stage, might make more intelligent the reviews by thousands of critics, the lectures before women's clubs and university classes and organized audiences. But there is scarcely an important learned work or a readable popular book on the theory of the stage.

A production at Niblo's Garden in New York, illustrating the final phase of realism in setting. The stale Victorian architecture, the regally decorated stage boxes, the plush curtain, and the elaborate half-built, half-painted "scene" belong to the era before the reforms initiated by Craig and Appia about 1900.

It seems to me that everyone must know something of this subject, if the twentieth century stage is to be understood as we understand, for instance, skyscraper architecture and the paintings of Cezanne; if we are to interest ourselves deeply in the noble as well as the vulgar theatre, in acting as well as drama, in those several arts that bridge over from the stage into painting and music and dancing and poetry. As I take the platform, I ask my readers not to become too alarmed: I have no intention of trying to expound the deeper principles of æsthetics. For one thing, nobody has ever really discovered them, at least not in such a simple way that they can be viewed briefly. But I would like to help my audience to look around at the chief uncovered turrets and towers of the subject, so that they won't think they are in the inner sanctums of appreciation when they are only enjoying some pretty scenery, or that they have exhausted the finer possibilities of drama when some character has "uttered a mouthful" that sums up their prejudices toward an aspect of life.

Perhaps I am only setting out to show my readers how to go *around* this subject, this edifice, picking up enough of the outstanding landmarks on the way to enable them to keep to the main road in the twentieth century theatre on the other side.

The confusion within the edifice alarms me too. Just as one puts his finger on the quality that seems the essential in art creation, on or off the stage, some new theorist, having looked from a different point of view, shows clearly that his predecessor has missed the main thing entirely, has excluded more than half the really creative work. And when you get a sight of these æstheticians fighting each other, it's a show in itself, with climax, suspense, surprise, bitterness, smart dialogue, and all!

But these few points I stand upon as guide in the pages that follow: I invite my readers to accept these fundamentals of *a* theory of art and of the stage until they can themselves set up a counter-edifice—or read Hegel and Ruskin and Croce and Freud and Bell, to say nothing of Aristotle, Voltaire, Lessing, Freytag, Meyerhold, Granville-Barker, Mitchell, and Young.

Art, in or out of the theatre, is an activity of human beings by which they create objects or "works" that are useful to other human beings in a special way. An artist, let us say, is interested in painting, and he sees in nature a landscape, a group of apples, or a cow that interests him in relation to painting, sees it differently from anyone else, with a special sort of painter's unity; and out of the characteristic materials of his art he creates something with a completeness of its own. This something, this picture, in which nature as seen by casual eyes or by the camera lens is distorted and has become secondary, is a new object in the world, and it is capable of satisfying a spiritual or emotional hunger in others—or if you prefer to isolate the experience, an *æsthetic* hunger. No other artist can make the same object, can create a thing with exactly the same appeal or satisfaction in it.

In these few lines one may note many of the outward characteristics of the work of art. It is "made," complete, unique, and useful in satisfying a special sort of craving. It is a product of perceptive experience on the artist's part and a source of æsthetic experience to the beholder.

Practically all investigators today isolate art from other fields of human activity with which it has at times been supposed to have a close connection: industry, the working out of moral systems, recreation, etc. Enjoy art as a special sort of experience in life, not to make you "better," or to remind you of this or that, or as a super-photograph. They also insist upon an understanding of the fundamental difference between art and nature, emphasizing the "made" character of art; for both works of art and scenes and objects out of nature may be beautiful, and a complex work like a presented play and a real court trial may alike be "moving"; the responses of the spectators at times being confusingly similar. Wherefore, say the theorists, let us

The forest scene in Wagner's *Parsifal*, as produced in Munich, about 1900. The naturalistic painter triumphant as stage designer.

get clear that the emotion felt over a view or a happening in life is different from the æsthetic experience; let us drop the word "beautiful" because it applies to both fields; let us remember that what nature supplies by way of subject matter is of only minor importance in art, what the artist creates or puts in of major importance; let us be mindful of the separate identity of the work of art, with qualities and merits of its own and a potential response for every intelligent and unspoiled spectator. Only thus, dear reader, will you be able to avoid mixing your art with other activities more personal but generally less noble.

It is particularly difficult not to use art as a tickler to your memory, or to start pleasant trains of thought, or as an inspirer of good deeds, or to divert you with anecdote, prettiness, and neat invention. We were all brought up to believe that those were its functions. We are just emerging from a period wherein art was thought of as anything except an activity valuable on its own account, a period of unexampled production of merely "diverting" works, of sentimental slush, of copying, of slick technique developed on its own account. Familiar landscapes, pretty girl heads, idealized nudes, kittens, the old homestead, the father of your country, parlor fiction, jingles, neo-classic epics, Renaissance public buildings and Neo-Gothic churches, happy-ending sentimental plays and slice-of-life drama—these are signs of art watered, sweetened, or perverted, of the timid imitative attitude, of awed transcription of natural loveliness or picturesqueness, of uncreative worship of "finish." It is a salutary call that aims to bring us back to art that is valued not for its usability or for transcribed values but on its own account, for an experience important in its own kind, a response that satisfies a separate human hunger.

Just as the artist is likely to be a different sort of fellow, careless of the conventions, wearing sombreros or corduroys in the most sacred places, and negligent of his hair, so he *sees* differently. Some critics assert that to paint or write a masterpiece, he must see things in an "ecstasy," must apprehend something, out of nature or life, in a flash. Personally I think that is hurrying the fellow more than is necessary; the important conception is as likely to come to him in a tranquillity or a travail, neither of which is necessarily ecstatic.

In any case, we may be sure that three elements enter into his creative process. He gets something out of nature, something different from what the rest of the world would observe in the same bit of actuality, with certain obtrusive details eliminated, no doubt, and possibly with the structural or characteristic essence standing forth with a fullness or completeness not clear to other eyes; then he shapes this subject, distorts it, arranges it, unifies it, to bring out the deeper thing he has apprehended, applies something out of his vision or his feeling for form or rhythm, brings its complex elements into focus; then, already having his "picture," he sets it out through the materials pertinent to his own art, paint or words or stone, in that other made picture which the world sees. He executes, within the limits of the means of his art, the work that becomes effective to other men.

Some writers minimize the later activity, the getting it into paint or the stage materials; they put more stress on the seeing, the conception, the visioning. But there is importance too in getting full expressive value out of the materials at his disposal; the richest values of the paint and color; the completest effectiveness of dialogue, movement, acting, lights, etc., in the stage art. In the theatre particularly, the creative handling of the rich and complex stage materials is imperative. Else the produced play fails of being *theatrical* and remains merely poetic, or a bit of mimicry, or reportorial.

The work of art thus created is a thing complete in itself, unified at the expense of seeming natural analysable truth, a fused production, indivisible, with a fulness of its own. And then only the smaller part has been said. For still the thing that used to be called "beauty" has escaped the definition. Recently that almost indefinable quality has been pinned down a little closer to comprehension, under the name "form." Clive Bell wrote a whole book to prove that "significant form" is the true earmark of visual art. And it is not impossible to identify,

A scene "before the house" for Maeterlinck's *The Blue Bird*, at the Moscow Art Theatre. Among the earliest types of revolt against naturalism was this story-book conventionalization. [From a painting by V. Egoroff.]

after experience, a fourth-dimensional quality in the paintings of, say El Greco and Cezanne, in the statues of Michelangelo and Henry Moore, in a work of Bach or Sappho or Shakespeare.

That is to say, a man, mystically inspired, if you prefer the term, or just seeing in a special way, adds to what he takes out of nature, and beyond certain elementary and understood elements of surface composition, of line, mass, color, etc., a "formal" quality, a quality born of his vision beyond the usual planes, of his feeling for perfect focus, of his realization of a world beyond the seen three-dimensional one, and of his understanding of the potentialities, the richness of his art materials. And this form in his work, this "expressive form," if you accept the handle most in vogue, appeals to an emotional receptiveness that is in every man to some degree, the true æsthetic or art-appreciating sense. If the beholder doesn't let subject matter or showy technique or personal prejudices get too obtrusively in the way, he will instinctively look for the fourth-dimensional quality, the thing that speaks to a deeper self. If he isn't too much concerned that the apples in Cezanne's painting are more bumpy than those on his own sideboard, he will discover in Cezanne's canvas a formal organization, a composition, that stirs him deeply. And Cezanne and all the other painters may be judged as of more or less account to the world according to the intensity, the richness of this half-identifiable quality in their work.

When Hamlet speaks:

Oh, what a rogue and peasant slave am I!

or

To be, or not to be,—that is the question:—
Whether 'tis nobler in the mind to suffer
The slings and arrows of outrageous fortune,
Or to take arms against a sea of troubles,
And by opposing end them?—To die, to sleep . . .

I repeat the lines to myself, speaking them first for the logic, for what they "say," and then for all the known excellencies of verse, the metre, the word sounds, the variations in measure, etc. Then I know that there is a quality beyond any of these, almost magic in its rarity and elusiveness, and this I call "form"—the expressive form of dramatic poetry. But, you object: it isn't necessarily *"form."* It's—well, just what makes the stuff poetry. There we have it: I am just trying to give a handle to the thing that is essentially the heart of painting, the thing that makes poetry poetic, or a played drama truly and richly theatric; because in a moment I think it will help us to understand certain things about the actors and the dramatists and the stage and the appeal to the audiences. In a sense, form is the sum of the unexplainable and unchartable elements that evoke æsthetic response in the beholder.

Now there has been a little comedy going on ever since Clive Bell took the centre of the stage to spread his thought about significant form being the essential thing. A lot of serious and otherwise dignified professors climbed right up on the platform and began to belabor him without mercy. "Nonsense!" and "Stuff!" they cried. And then when they were allowed to have *their* say, every one of them began to talk about some equally mysterious and equally undefinable quality in art that they called rhythmic order, or contrapuntal organization, or focus, or some other name that had no more apparent immediate meaning. When they had quite destroyed poor Mr. Bell's "form" structure, they simply went on squabbling among themselves over the shape the next structure was to take, and they ended by all but murdering one another. So the crowd is left with hardly more than the pleasant memory of Mr. Bell's try at an explanation.

But when we have rung down the curtain on the Professors' Comedy, won't we find it convenient to say simply that there is an unexplainable something about the work of art, which we can experience and almost point out, and that "form" is as good a name for it as any other? Of course, we shall slip occasionally, and speak of rhythm, of beauty, of the stage flow—but day in and day out, "form" is the handiest label.

With the introduction of the "horizon dome" bounding the stage at back—an improvement on the cyclorama-drop—the "space stage" was introduced. Wholly dark or lighted at will, it harbored many experiments in "the new stagecraft." This is a scene devised by Lee Simonson for the Theatre Guild's production of Lenormand's *The Failures*. [Photograph by Vandamm Studios.]

There are those who proclaim "There is no art of the theatre until it is brought to completion before an audience." I really couldn't say as to that. It seems to me a metaphysical question; and we are agreed that it would be useless to go deeply into matters of audience psychology, and particularly into crowd response. Still we must recognize quite simply that an audience at the theatre "gives" to the production as in no other art, joins the flow, helps thus to create. Beyond that, we may profitably inquire a bit into the nature of the response of an individual to *any* sort of art. It may help us to "see" the production on the stage more intelligently and enjoyably.

What little comedy there is here concerns the efforts of one group of combatants to tag the thing the spectator experiences as *emotion* of a peculiar sort. First thing we know, somebody has sent those fellows sprawling, and is pinning an entirely new label on bewildered Spectator. This time it is *pleasure*—"emotion" is far too indefinite a word to call it by. And quick as a flash someone over in the corner has picked off those pleasure fellows: pleasure is the result of the æsthetic emotion, not the thing itself. And what is the term these new comedians set up? You can *know* a work of art, that is all; it is all a special sort of knowing, unlike any other. "Go on," pipes up a voice way upstage, "it's more a matter of *feeling*."

Well, between you and me, they are never going to finish this comedy in time for us to get on to the main show. We might just as well choose the term we like best and get on to the next platform or turret. Personally I don't believe that knowing and feeling are terms definite enough to label that very true response that we have experienced before El Greco and Chinese sculpture and at a Bach festival; or in that hushed, glowing time when spirit speaks to spirit in the darkened theatre. I find myself drawn to those combatants who talked about emotion, who say that the greater the art, the greater the spectator's emotional response; and that the greatest works in the theatre are those pregnant with the deepest emotional appeal. *Only* I want it understood that I see emotion as embracing a very wide range, reaching over definitely into what mankind has tried to rope off as "spiritual." We can't go too deep, toward the soul or spirit, in seeking the true seat of æsthetic response.

What probably put emotion in bad repute, as a name for the spectator's response to art, is this: in the nineteenth century most people who called themselves art-lovers repressed their true emotions, and they took out their longings in enjoyment of sentimentality. They wanted art to compensate them for the barrenness of ordinary living. They asked that it be emotionalized in that part of the field at the far corner from what we have called spiritual, in that corner where emotion becomes personal, cushion-like, sweetened, and flabby. They wanted art to be a reminder of some vague ideal of a heaven-on-earth, wanted it to fit in with their sentimental dreams; they liked to identify themselves with a hero, to dream themselves the lovers. They asked that art create a field where they could enjoy a sweetened sort of life vicariously.

And the artists mostly accommodated them. That is why, for every dramatist who remembers logic, who is true to vision, there are a hundred happy-ending playwrights, aiming to satisfy the sentimental demand. Just as these hundred purveyors of slush are the most ephemeral of artists, so the public that asks for it is exhibiting the cheapest, the most watered form of emotional response.

A different angle on this response comes to view if we say that art in the nineteenth century was considered as an *escape*. Life as lived, the people argued, is hard, unimaginative, a sort of prison. Art must provide a means for periodic escape. It must devise another world into which tired and soul-hungry men may be taken at intervals, for recreation, renewment, relief from the strain of reality, from the tyranny of the commonplace. It must be as different from everyday life as possible, without ever distorting the outward appearance of nature, without disturbing prejudices or getting down to the terrible truths. This was the attitude that led to that sort of realistic Romanticism which had a fairy-tale sweetness without fantasy, a show of great deeds without spiritual conviction, a sweet false fiction of reality, wherein riches came easy and the current sort of virtue was rewarded. Flattering identity of the beholder with characters or with subject matter is a necessity in such art. The spectator intervenes his ego, his own case, between the artist and enjoyment. Subject matter becomes over-exploited; a theme must be proved—that life is pleasant.

There is the more recent Realism that affords a contrast to this Victorian school of art. It clings to the earthiest and least sentimental aspects of life as surfacely lived. It embraces the morbid and glorifies the wicked. The drama has been a favorite medium with these morbidizers. It has been made to show forth in merciless detail the seamiest side of life, proving that everything has a flaw, all action has base motive, every hero has his vices. There follow sewer realism, gloom, obscenity. Sex is dragged out and brought into an absurd importance, merely because before it had been hidden. Sordid living is portrayed as the natural end of the truly honest man. Disillusion, cynicism, "what is, is true"—what else can an intelligent person believe in?

This is a common reaction to the escape-into-sweetness sort of thing, to sentimental-compensation art. But don't you see, dear reader, that these Realists are perverting art in exactly the same way that the happy-ending ones did: they simply want to make art a glass through which spectators will peer into their cynical view of surface life, instead of a gateway to a tinsel paradise. The one sort intervenes the thesis that all life is unpleasant, while the other intervenes with "Life is all pleasant." While proving their cases, over-interested in their respective themes, they both have lost contact with the deeper bases of human living, with the nobler planes beyond the surface one.

I am likely to get excited just here. I want to climb up on the stage and shout: "Escape! Portrayal! Gloom! What have they to do with art? What but to prevent it? If we can't accept art as an activity important in itself, self-sufficient, with a value to the spectator in its own kind; if we don't find in it an intensification of living, not a gateway to some other sweetened or muddied fiction of life, it's not worth the powder to blow it to Limbo. It is a form of deeper living, a gathering into focus of the known and unknown finenesses of life. It is the human-divine made movingly expressive, throbbingly alive, an immersion to the spirit."

Two scenes from Max Reinhardt's production of *Hamlet*, in Germany, 1913. The space stage utilized with hardly more than a few "props" and cleverly lighted actors.

IN THE theatre—I am glad to be back in the cavernous auditorium, looking at an expectant stage—a whole troop of creators, of artists and workers, appear in place of the single sculptor or painter or poet of the simpler sister arts. And as for materials there is no end to them. Here we see dramatists, composers, designers, *régisseurs*, actors, electricians, carpenters, etc.; and they will use movement, gestures, words, music, silences, lights, platforms, screens, paintings, furnishings, costumes, etc. But beyond all these things and people contributory to the stage art, there is that quality "form." We won't explore now the dramatist's contribution or the actor's place in the conglomerate, but we must speak a little of the *régisseur*, because he is the typically twentieth century stage artist, and he has most to do with bringing the theatrical form into focus for the audience.

Looking at the stage before us—a better beginning point than the author's script or an actor's performance—let us visualize the created, unified production as a whole. What the theatre artists have "made" is this "play" that passes before our eyes, greater than a story, or the contributive poetry, or the pattern of movement, or the color and lights, or the revealing acting. Call it a procession of all these things, or rather a flow, since all the elements must be perfectly mingled, indivisibly fused. Implicit in that flow, beyond the appeal of any single element, is the form or rhythm, the typically theatric quality, out of which the spectator draws the theatric sustenance, the current to the spirit, the apprehension of things beyond the literal meaning and the surface seeable elements. And as color is to painting—one cannot think of significant form in the picture without a color implication—and as mass or a certain blockiness is to sculpture, so a fulness, a glow, a rich complexity unified in action, is of the essence of the stage art—is the very feel of it.

In certain types of theatre art the sensuous elements contributing to the flow, the sense-appealing attributes of the "form," are emphasized, doubly capitalized. The movement is then more musical, colorful, lilting in rhythm. The focus is brought about with the warmer, freer flowing elements rather than by the logical word, the calculated gesture, and the measured unfolding of plot. But even the less colorful and more literary play must be staged with continuous, unbroken, theatrical form. Otherwise it drags as theatre, remains literature acted. Stage people are not likely to analyse so closely, but they have their expressive terms for these things. A certain production, they say, had no pace, no go.

Surely if there is such a thing as a primarily intellectual art, it is at the far pole from this theatric one. In those minutes of wonder, those tranquil utterly unworldly times, when the mind is disarmed

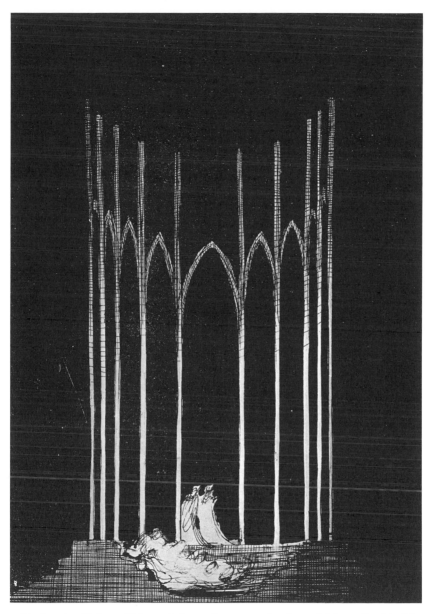

Design by Robert Edmond Jones for a production of Maeterlinck's *The Seven Princesses*. The atmosphere of a cathedral evoked on a darkened space stage. [By courtesy of *Theatre Arts Magazine*.]

and the soul immersed in drama, there is poised then the high moment of the glow, warmth, and richness of the theatre medium. It has been put down innumerable times that *action* is the essence of the dramatic art, that of the "materials" it is the one indispensable ingredient, the very *clou* of the stage production. Then the definition of action should be widened to include the sensuous flow, the unseen building toward the glowing moments. The wise director, of course, knows this; and he knows also that action in its commoner sense covers two important things in the presentation of the play: physical movement (the pattern of movement having become recently of enormous moment to the director-artist), and action in the sense of development of a story, plot movement, an unfolding of something to be understood.

Beginning with action, some people prefer to explain the whole theatre art in this way: There must be actors, obviously, to carry out the action. The actors must have a platform to lift them into visual eminence, and so there comes into the list of materials of the art the stage itself, with its shape, its lighting, its "looks"; and if the age be one that values ornament and intricate invention, a whole range of added values is created here, as "stage decoration." The dramatist then supplies an outline or scenario to serve as the backbone of the production, or perhaps he uses words as a chief means of revelation; and at times he sets these down with all the embroidered values of poetry. But now—and here we come to the chief contribution of the twentieth century to theatre theory—with all these people called in, and all these elements to be brought into unity, the playwright, the actors, the designer, the movement, the story words, the poetic values, and the decoration, we inevitably need another super-artist to get the production hatched: a new creator is necessary, to whip the others into co-operation and co-ordination, into proper subordinate and contributive places, the artist-director.

This *régisseur*, the re-creator of the whole, the man charged with making continuous and unbroken the flow, the combined evocation, is a comparatively new figure to the stage. In the past he has seldom been important enough to leave a name in history, unless he happened to be at the same time an outstanding actor; but recently several artist-directors have been more famous than actors or playwrights (excepting always that one lone figure, Bernard Shaw). In our own time, Gordon Craig and Max Reinhardt and Stanislavsky have become legendary. In a later chapter, on the rise of production as an art, the artist-director and his ways of widening the meaning of action will be fully treated. Now I want only the understanding that in some sense we have found new ways of looking at the materials of the theatre production, a new approach to the art; that at the same time there has been a shift of interest from the contributive artists of the stage to a central *régisseur*.

Let me take two examples, very different, of the way in which a director shapes a production to bring out primarily the form element. We go to a dance-drama, a production of the *Ballets Russes*. Our senses are caught up by the music, the dancing, the color, the "atmosphere," the silent story, the rhythm. The "form," become sensuous here, sweeps over us like an inundation. The director, M. Diaghileff, has vivified perhaps a threadbare fable theatrically, by co-ordinating and flowing the performance into one colorful stream.

The next evening we go to a production of a modern realistic play: let us say *John Ferguson*. It is not one of the sordid, purely journalistic things, but as bare, as limited in view, as dependent upon observed fact, as any piece from which you are likely to get a formal as well as a fictional reaction. The point is that, as directed by Augustin Duncan for the New York Theatre Guild, it emerges in a production that not only holds the audience as a novel on the same theme would, but at many points stills the literal mind and speaks directly to the spiritual consciousness, provides a true theatrical experience. The actors are so rightly chosen, are so trained into one perfectly balanced ensemble, that no "performance" stands out, the setting is forgotten or never noticed, the physical movement weaves a pattern so right that it is unseen, yet so proportioned and accented that every spectator is played upon subconsciously. In short, discounting the mere story-interest of the text, the director built a production, using every resource of the stage, which stirred us *theatrically*. The theatre *form* took possession of us as truly as in the case of the dance-drama.

RETURNING to our chapter title, the contributive arts have often enough tried to take over the stage. Literature especially has attempted periodically to capture the place. Writers who had hardly more than casually entered into the playhouse as spectators wrote literary dramas, and managers, or societies bent on "bettering" the theatre, arranged productions for them—most notably during the Renaissance and in the nineteenth century "closet drama" period in England. And when the classics had gone out of vogue, "reformers" tried reviving them, as examples of what true literature in the theatre had been. Since these last producers neglected all elements of production except securing good texts, their efforts remained in the field of literary endeavor—they showed something that might be absorbing in the library, and something that once had been gorgeous in the theatre, but a thing that remained dull in their performances because they failed to make it live *in stage terms*.

Three arrangements of a "unit" setting, in which certain parts remain standing throughout many scenes. One of the recent methods of expediting change of scenery. Drawing by Claude Bragdon for Walter Hampden's production of *Hamlet*. [By courtesy of *The Architectural Record*.]

About the time when I was a youth a whole generation was more or less soured on the classics of the theatre by just such corrupt producing. We decided that *Hamlet* and *King Lear* and *Romeo and Juliet* were reading plays far finer as poetry than as drama. But the greater importance now laid upon production as such, restores Shakespeare to his theatre place. His plays not only are supreme as poetry; they are figured, contrived for the stage as only the actor Shakespeare could contrive them. They are gloriously full of fat acting parts, of action, of patterned movement, of dramatic silences, of stage flow. They lend themselves perfectly to the shaping in stage form that distinguishes theatre art from dramatic literature. Marvellous as their word-beauty is, they have inherent in them every opportunity for the larger beauty of complete theatric performance. When Othello, before he stabs himself, says,

> Speak of me as I am; nothing extenuate,
> Nor set down aught in malice: then must you speak
> Of one that loved not wisely but too well;
> Of one not easily jealous, but, being wrought,
> Perplexed in the extreme; . . .

when he speaks thus, the pause in the action, as if to allow the mind a moment's comprehensive review of the whole drama up to that point, doubles the dramatic effect of his dying a moment later. Nor is "O Romeo, Romeo! wherefor art thou Romeo?" merely a pretty play of words: the entire tragedy is foreshadowed in the line.

There have been many times when conditions in the theatre were so depressing, so commercial, so false, that the authors in those periods were alienated, and talents that might have flourished in the field of playwriting were driven to fiction and other minor fields, to the everlasting impoverishment of the stage. Even authors as important as Dickens, Browning, and Stevenson seemed to knock at the theatre's doors in vain. But there was probably as much fault on one side as the other. It must be repeated that this is a jealous art like any other, demanding all a man's devotion or none. The people of the theatre naturally resent any attempt to make the stage a literary man's playground. If a writer fails to give his time to learning and understanding the essential conditions of staging, to bring clear his feeling for theatrical form, he will do better to stay away entirely. Where purely artificial conditions have obtained for long periods, as in stages over-centralized and commercialized like that of the late nineteenth and early twentieth centuries in New York, so that the writers met the barriers put up by the low intelligences controlling production, there is much to be said on the other side. But in general it may be said that the artist combining literary and theatric ability is welcomed. The point to remember is that the theatre as such is greater than any of its parts; that merely poetry in the theatre or music in the theatre or dance in the theatre is not theatrical.

Adolphe Appia, one of the two greatest reformers of scene design, pictured here before his setting for the forest scene in *Parsifal*. A painting by René Martin. [By courtesy of Mlle. Hélène Appia.]

PAINTING could hardly capture the stage as a whole; but for nearly three centuries painting imposed itself on the theatre as a supposedly important and inseparable part of the art. From the late sixteenhundreds up to 1890 no one ever thought of challenging the painted setting as an interloper and a nuisance. But then within no more than a few decades, progressive stages all over the Western world began to subordinate their "scenic artists," and what had practically always been a distraction for the audience, rather than an integral part of the theatre rhythm, has been eliminated. Color is left, richly, but in the light and in fabrics rather than in painted picture backgrounds. (When the picture changed from the painter's sort to a photographic sort, about 1900, in the hands of the Naturalists, it no more belonged integrally to the produced play, except to the slice-of-life sort.)

Painting came suddenly, seduced the theatre producers completely, reigned for nearly three hundred years, and now seems in process of dying out with Victorian completeness. Today the setting is flat, perspectiveless, simplified almost to bareness; surface reality no longer is pictured, but only faintly suggested, the "atmosphere" is caught in color and light. Progress today is all in the direction of space stages and honestly architectural stages. Painting on the stage seems to have gone into almost complete eclipse. The easel-picture as stage decoration has passed.

MUSIC more nearly belongs. The theatre, as a combined sight and sound art, relies on color pattern (if only in the lighting) for a considerable part of its glamorous appeal, and only less directly on sound: rhythm in speech, a balance of emphasized and subordinated sound played against stillnesses, and the more obvious borrowed musical accompaniment. There have been arguments against the alliance; but I can see no more valid reason for eliminating music from the theatre than for eliminating poetry. They both fit perfectly into the complexity, the created flow that is theatre—as the painted *picture* by its very nature never could.

The real objections to music in dramatic art can be found not in any separateness within the whole, but in certain questionable unions with acting and drama. Music is a respectable and respected contributive element in dance-drama and in certain forms is legitimate. But among its questionable if not downright disreputable offspring are opera and musical comedy.

Opera is still the most aristocratic, the most sought-after, the most fashionable among the arts—a sort of Episcopal Church among the art temples. But, my dear, you should hear what they whisper about its origin! Indeed, many a critic has said right out that it is a bastard art. We all of us go to hear and see it, for various reasons, social and otherwise. It may be the music of Wagner, or Flagstad, or a publicized new *décor*, or the dresses and the debutantes in the boxes; but did any of us ever see a perfect opera production, or even one that held together, in that sort of unity that we experience at a play, at a symphony concert, or in reading or hearing,

O Captain! My Captain! our fearful trip is done . . . ?

Opera is essentially a mixed, broken thing, with beautiful and compelling patches. Of musical comedy, except as it kidnaps a self-sufficient creative turn out of vaudeville, there is almost nothing to be said. It is sentimental sweet-ending comedy linked with sweet balladry, *very* pleasant in its picture-postcard way, but really significant theatre only for the tired and the jaded.

THE dance as an art enters creatively today into those stage productions that are primarily sensuous in appeal; but in ancient times it was an integral part in the production of tragedy. The pattern of the great Greek dramas made particular and important place for it—for

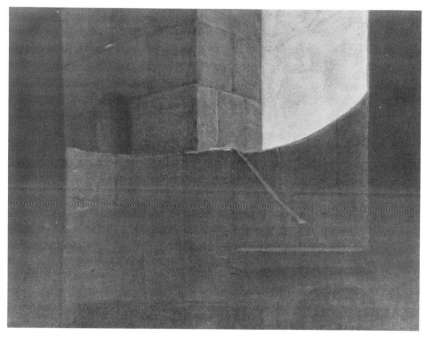

Adolphe Appia's design for Act II of *Parsifal:* the Castle of Klingsor.

relief from the emotional intensity, some say, for re-enforcement, others. At first in Greek tragedy it was the most important element, the truly Dionysian expression. Through opera it became debased, became an artificial interlude, cramped, stilted. From the more "regular" forms of play it disappeared altogether. In the current period of revaluation one dreamer after another finds it a place again in some coming form of serious drama. As a better understanding of "form" comes to dramatists, directors, dreamers, all the free rhythmic arts converge in again toward the playhouse, music, mobile color, dance. But as yet it would be mere speculation to say how the dance is to be utilized as an integral part of our day-in-and-day-out drama.

AS THE Western theatre, along with the other arts, is being shaken out of its pre-occupation with realism, its artists are impelled to examine the stages of other times, and especially those of Oriental countries where realism has never been known in our all-exclusive sense. The knowledge gained from such excursions is bearing strange fruit even in the proscenium-frame playhouse that is designed for narrowly picturing surface life. On the Miracle stages of the fourteenth and fifteenth centuries a character might be beheaded, and then, after a decent interval, rise, pick up his head and carry it offstage under his arm. In the Chinese theatre the property man is continuously on the stage, in view of the audience, erecting thrones or canopies, handing swords to the hero or hairpins to the ladies as wanted. In the one case the audience is living the drama so completely, so naïvely, that there is no incongruity in the dead actor walking off; in the other the spectator never really sees the property man consciously: this is a theatre and one gives one's self up to its story, to its flow of action. The natural things outside simply don't intrude. If the playwright and the actors and the scene-setter had made a pretense of truth to surface nature in the first place (as our playwrights and producers often do), the actor with his head under his arm would have been upsetting, the property man a continual intrusion into the picture. But these audiences were not fooled into thinking that they were seeing a slice of life. They were reminded by the very form of the stage that they were in theatres, they accepted the convention, what belonged rightly to the theatre might come before them at any moment or all moments.

Our theatre changes. There is no reason under the sun why anyone should think that the commercial theatre as it existed in the middle years of the twentieth century formed a final consummation of the art. On the contrary it may best be considered as a sick survival after the barren realistic era. Restricted in serviceableness, its stage gone into a box with a small curtained opening, given up to picturing the intimacies of private life, with a few survivals of the well-made-play-with-happy-ending, it exhibits all the symptoms of an art ready for a revolutionary overturn. The "conventions" of the mediæval and the Chinese stages may give us a clue to the direction that revolution is taking, and at the same time introduce our last point of theory.

The modernists say that the stage must become a medium for *presentative* as against *representative* production. For an age it has been merely representing life, in as near to natural surroundings as the scenic artists could provide. From now on the theatre will not pretend to show an imitation of life, will not aim above all else at creating an illusion of reality. The stage will be declared as stage (the realists tried to hide the platform, raising the curtain only to show out an actual place). Conventions, unnaturalnesses will be accepted and forgotten. Creative stage art will be presented as such, with emphasis on the formal qualities, the things that arise out of the nature of the theatre's materials and out of the artist's conception of action, flow, and show, out of sheer dramatic impact. The observed thing, the photographic recreation, will have less and less value. The spectator instead of being tricked into believing he is witness at a real series of events,

An early phase of anti-realism in stage setting was seen in the use of plain curtains as backing for the action. Particularly famous were Isadora Duncan's blue curtains. Here another American dancer, Ruth St. Denis, is shown with her troupe before a curtain drop with the slightest objective suggestion, as designed by Maxwell Armfield, about 1920.

will be made to feel that he is in the theatre, on a plane of imagination and spiritual emotion, above common life, theatrically exalted.

Some such statement must conclude any treatment of theories of stage art today. For we are in the confusion of the beginnings of a great overturn. Our day-by-day "commercial" theatres are still overwhelmingly realistic. But the experimenters and creators of the contemporary stage are busy with those anti-realistic and expressionistic thoughts, are trying one channel after another in the direction of a presentative stage art. They have even given us productions which we can hold to as definite examples of a glorious new theatre that is coming, at once in agreement with the great formal stages of the past and intensely expressive of the space-age living of today. They hold the key to our future.

I DON'T like to think of my readers, with five chapters still to go, as worn out, wearied with so much of theory and discussion. But the worst is over. I wanted—this book having been conceived as an *introduction* to the theatre, and for the younger generation of theatre-goers especially—to gain a viewpoint, to have as background something other than the conception out of the past, of art as an escape; wanted something besides the too easy inference that the art of the theatre is that of picturing reality on the stage. The casual reader who has been only a casual theatre-goer is likely still to read the story of the modern stage with the notion that what passes there can be judged by the closeness of its approach to actuality, by its faithful or faltering representation of existent life. He is likely to judge all theatres by the limited realistic one which is practically the only one he has known.

Above all, then, let us go forward to the later chapters freed from that realistic limitation, knowing the theatre to be the house of a deeper created reality, of intensified emotion, of an experience instinct with the feel of life but on a plane remote from commonplace living. When the herald or messenger of classic drama acted out movingly the approach of an army to the city gates, or recounted the exciting battle, we did not ask whether it would be better if the army were shown on the stage or the battle fought before our eyes; only whether he stood there before us as the intensification of the feeling of battle, whether our souls went out to him in communion. Let us not think that Mrs. Tanqueray is an improvement over Ophelia because she speaks a prose more like our own, or because she is first disclosed to us in a room that might be in a wing of our own house. In approaching the modern stage, let us not re-erect that mental barrier, the understood fourth wall; let us not insist upon the monotonous surface plane of life. For theatre is art, and photographic reality has precious little to do with it.

CHAPTER 22

The Theatre of the
Early Twentieth Century

THERE is a personal tragedy in the story of the Realist playwright. He had come to a theatre obviously sick, dying of too much sentimentality, too much mechanics, too much pretty scenery. The plays, he said, are so ridiculously artificial, the settings so faked, everything so sweetened, there is nothing living or lifelike about it; we must make it natural, and moving, like the drama of real life.

The Realist fought a good fight. He spent decades dislodging the entrenched well-made-play people. He had to justify himself not only with plays but with theory. He had to fight tooth and nail to gain entrance to the theatre at all. Realism became at once his battle-cry and his religion. With almost fanatical devotion, he slashed his way through to victory; he planted his banner at the very centre of the stage—a banner that raised the one word "Reality" as a first test of art.

Then, in the very flush of success he found that the theatre he had conquered, that he had thought to save, was dying anyway. After a lifetime of struggle, having lived for this one victory, having finally taken over the stages of the Western world, suddenly he saw the negativeness of his productions, the cramping limits of Realism as an art creed. While he had been fighting his glorious fight, pausing perhaps to enjoy his conquests, the world had moved by. Visionaries and prophets opened different vistas for art. Foundations for a new world theatre were laid in territory too distant from the realistic field for any bridge to carry over from the one to the other.

We may visualize the Realist-dramatist there on his battle-field, a bewildered victor. With a newspaperman's flair for what is dramatic in experience, he entered the clinic of life, he dissected, he analysed people down to the last bitter detail of motive, of feeling, of thought. He showed humanity the face of its own weakness, its passions, its selfishness, its follies.

Indeed, though Realism, the play of observed fact, of clinical examination, was treated in an earlier chapter, as if it were more a nineteenth than a twentieth century phenomenon, we must recognize here, as we cross 1900, that its story continues right up to the present, even past the middle years of the new century. The European and American commercial stages of today are crammed with it. Realistic plays automatically get themselves written, automatically turn up in performance. But to keep their hold, they seek yearly more and more sensational subject matter; they are driven to imbed shock and horror in their lines, to hold their audiences; they are even digging up hidden perversions to interest the nervous spectator—and there they parade in the name of art. The psycho-analysts found a good word for the phenomenon: "exhibitionism." That is the trouble with the present-day realistic stage: obsession with parading what is usually left buried or undisturbed, for the sake of parade—and money.

Meanwhile, outside the theatre, following the recognition that the realistic era was one of the most barren in art history, a wider revolution took place. In painting and sculpture, principles that had been held sacred for three centuries were unceremoniously scrapped, and a new seeking has, since 1910, changed completely the aspect of the galleries and the museums; a new architecture has appeared, after centuries of the rearranging of stealings out of old buildings. And although very few plays have been written to fill a new theatre, there have been prophets of a new art of the stage, and there has been exciting progress toward it in other departments than that of the playwright: revolutionary changes in stage form and stage settings, the rise of direction as a creative contributive art, a stripping away from playhouse architecture of the elements that used to be considered "theatrical," and shifts in methods of organization, looking to a squaring with social conditions under industrial capitalism—or whatever comes after. The fruits of these changes seem likely to outlast the plays of the realistic dramatists who flourished in the same era. As a matter of fact a very few Expressionist dramatists appeared soon after 1910.

THROUGH a period of three decades the physical playhouse has been purging itself. It has sloughed off elements of operatic display, elements out of seventeenth and eighteenth century palace ballrooms, elements out of general architectural-ornamental practice of the nineteenth century. The architecture of that time may be likened to the putting up of old-fashioned "scenery"; the architects were largely concerned with erecting fronts, having forgotten the basic elements of architectural "form." Uncreative themselves, they became busy with stylistic ornamentation as an end in itself, based on details out of past eras.

The Paris Opera House. [From *Paris in Old and Present Times*, by Philip Gilbert Hamerton.]

When they came to the designing of a theatre, their impulse toward decoration ran wild. Every playhouse must be a reminder of the apotheosis of French profuse taste, the Paris Opera. In the drawing of this building herewith, the reader may see just how little chance he would have to put his hand on any part of the façade and say "this is honest, sheer, built wall." Every inch was used for display, for the showing off of sculpture, for the hanging of stone wreaths or the support of fancy columns: it was showy, regal exposition architecture perpetuated in stone, opulent, fat, shallow. It may have been the masterpiece of typically French architecture, as so often claimed; but the disrespectful younger generation suggested that it need not for that reason become model for theatres the world over or for all time.

If you will look at the National Theatre in Prague, however, or in Sofia, or in Mexico City, or São Paulo, or in Buenos Aires, or in Madrid, or Vienna, or Oslo, or at the "leading" theatres in the dozen large French cities, you will find examples of this sort of design, overloaded, wasteful, falsely regal, dishonestly unarchitectural, without a vestige of the repose, the intimacy, and the simplicity that are appropriate to the showing of great drama—or even realistic drama.

Let us examine more closely "a little masterpiece" in this French style, as illustrated in the theater at Lille. It represents what the world was building for half a century before 1910. Presumably such a building should grow out of the needs of the thing it houses, or be appropriate to and suggestive of its function as a place for staging and seeing

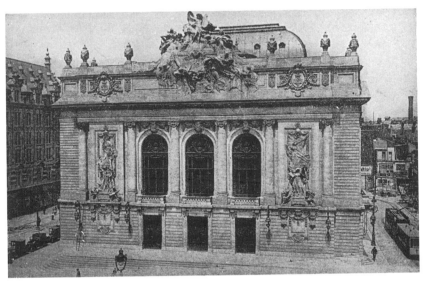

The Municipal Theatre at Lille, a survival of the courtly French type.

plays. Then why, the modernists asked, those urns along the roof? Why the flowering of the whole front in the pictorial-sculptural composition at the top centre—not even in cut-stone but in modelled-clay technique? Why the melodramatic sculptures in the panels below? Why the whole façade treated as a study in dead ornamentation—instead of an honest, well-proportioned wall with three doors and three windows knocked through? There is no answer except that this is usual nineteenth century theatre achitecture. It happens that the building was opened in 1922, but in a country that lives, more than any other, in the nineteenth century in matters of theatre construction and staging. It remains typical, not only in this façade, but in the over-dressed foyer (more urns), in the inevitable marble staircase of honor (more urns), in the crammed-full-of-ornament auditorium (more flowing sculptured figures, more strings of sausages, lyres, cartouches, wreaths, etc., etc.). Grandeur, regal red and gold, swank, display, display, display.

In contradistinction to this European model that was copied round
the world almost as unquestioningly as Paris modes in dress, there is a
type of commercial theatre that was popular in those years: better in
sight-lines, less conspicuously wasteful in either space or decoration,
logically theatrical in general plan, but equally nondescript and garish
in ornamentation. But beyond the examples of this "practical" com-

The Municipal Theatre at Jena, Germany, as reconstructed by Walter
Gropius and Adolph Meyer, about 1920. One of the earliest examples of
the transition from French-Italian courtly theatre architecture to simplest
modern.

promise type, a few typically machine-age playhouses then emerged,
as a promise for the future; or rather here and there a feature of the
new theatre has stood out, though usually in combination with old
stages or bits out of the old house. As for the honest wall with the
necessary openings pierced through, the exterior of the Jena State
Theatre is indication of the way the modernists are working; has been,
indeed, a widely discussed and widely illustrated "challenge." And all
over the world the little theatres are likely to be blessed with simple,
reposeful interiors.

In many countries are to be found, among the atrocious Hollywood-style "palaces," rare moving-picture houses that show a machine-like sheerness and flashing cleanliness, colorful and warmly lighted. And in Germany the moderately modern architects Max Littmann and Oskar Kaufmann, in legitimate houses, cleared out the ornamentation and established a new intimacy between auditorium and stage; and they created a sufficiently fresh decorative idiom. The Munich Art Theatre became known to revolutionaries everywhere and had extraordinary influence, after 1925.

IF NINETEENTH-century theatre architecture was metaphorically operatic, the stage setting of that time was literally so. Whether intended for opera, or grandly romantic play, or intimate drama, the "scenery" became, just before the realistic era, a thing of vast spaces, acres of painted canvas, spectacular vistas. The audience looked through the proscenium-frame into the stage box at a scene made up partly of rows of "wings" and partly of "set pieces" against a backcloth closing the vista. In general the painting in these picture settings was simply terrible, raw in color, muddy and crude, and the construction was flimsy. But the effects were grand.

The Realists who not only insisted on the importance of reality but composed imitative examples of the observed thing, with the detailed look of outward life, swept out the artificial and muddy operatic settings from one stage after another; meticulously real scenes, photographed from life, took their places. David Belasco, arguing from "the importance of the little thing," assembled thousands of little things out of life, in settings that touched the high spot in naturalness, and left the spectator agape at telephones, real doorframes, linotype machines, bars with real liquors, living flowers, complete restaurant interiors, thousand-cushioned love-nests, etc. But the actor was now lost, not in a vast painted picture, but in a veritable museum of ordinary surroundings, a complexity of real details. This was the naturalistic era—of photographic, not selective, realism. (See page 487.)

Then came the "decorators." They declared war on both the old artificial "scene painters" and the Naturalists. They had some vision of a cleared stage for a typical twentieth century drama—Gordon Craig had already startled the theatre world with what a leading American professor-critic termed "reckless and daring fiats," had foreshadowed the return to a stage cleared for acting. But they had only the realistic drama to practise on. And they simplified the scene so drastically, used pictorial composition so cunningly, warmed the stage so with color and controlled light, that they developed compromise settings far lovelier than the dramas played in them. They made a background that was realistic to the extent of indicating the scene described by the author; they never actually violated what the human eye might see in nature; but within that limitation they dressed the stage with all the appeal of line and mass composition, sensuous color—even style.

A scene in *Faust* as produced in 1913 by Max Reinhardt, with settings by Ernst Stern. Thus quickly the practical producers learned from the less practical Craig and Appia. The drawing here was made by Robert Edmond Jones at the production in Berlin. [From Kenneth Macgowan's *The Theatre of Tomorrow*, 1921.]

What is called in current theatre practice "stylization" is usually a sustained beauty of setting, a single, identifiable mode of design that runs through all the backgrounds of a play. The decorator some-times imposed it as a loveliness added; sometimes he worked well within the intent of the author and the plan of the *régisseur*, creating visually a *feeling* that was inherent throughout the production.

Often, indeed, in the theatre of 1920–1950, the playwright and the actor were less conspicuous, less talked about, than the scene designer. He extraordinarily widened the capabilities of the stage for a purely theatric—not painted—visual beauty. He afforded a succession of stage scenes so glowingly pretty, and in general so appropriate, that a new sensuous overtone was added to our mental visioning of the theatre's glamour. As the drama became more and more drab and photographic, the stage was made simpler, more reposeful, and compensatingly rich in color and soft light.

There was a time when the chief lighting problem of the theatre was how to get enough illumination. Candles, oil lamps, gas jets—they had their turns in history. But with the coming of the electric bulb not only was a practical problem solved but a new resource for beauty was added to the list of materials of theatric art. Electricity has been harnessed so that stage lighting can be controlled from a switchboard to the extent of flooding a scene or spotting one point in it, providing any desired color, and keeping a certain constant intensity or ranging it up or down to an unbearable glare or the barest hint of light. Banks of "dimmers," adjustable lenses on individual flood or spot lamps, and a bewildering array of border, strip, foot, and portable units serve to make the advanced theatre's equipment so flexible and so expressive that changes in lighting are imperceptible to the audience while every spectator's sensibilities are being played upon—even as by perfectly adapted offstage musical accompaniment.

Lighting has proved so serviceable a medium theatrically, indeed, that it has, on many stages, taken the place of "setting" in the old sense. A whole wing of the modernists has advocated the return to an architectural stage, practically without means of showing those individual places called for by the playwrights, but only one neutral scene to stand for all scenes, with changes of mood accomplished by lighting, with possibly bare *indications* of actual place in one or two introduced screens or pillars or "props." Thus the current toward simplification and conventionalization, after several decades, ends where the stage is no longer a picture box but becomes an abstract architectural thing, constantly but unnoticeably changing under projected light.

There were other methods developed in the search for a truly modernist mode of staging. Expressionist painting was dragged in for a while in an effort to provide modernist backgrounds for current plays, but proved merely an added source of amusement or distraction. Constructivism aided creatively toward the achievement of an architectural stage capable of a wide range of physical action, without changes of setting: it was a method of providing a perfectly engineered scene, the "practicables" of all the called-for settings nailed together in one composition, stripped of adventitious decorative elements, and set out on a bare stage without a curtain. Another group of experimenters have pushed as far as possible toward a "space stage"; they try to

Design by Adolphe Appia for Wagner's opera *Die Walküre*. The rock of the Valkyrs as designed plastically, for emphasis upon the actors and for atmospheric lighting. The scene below shows the action at the approach of Wotan. [From the portfolio, *Adolphe Appia*, Zurich, 1929.]

achieve a black void in which the actors are picked out by light. Most of the new methods have the immense advantage of doing away with the waits between acts which are inevitable when the old-fashioned picture-settings have to be changed in the course of the play.

Before the new dependence upon lighting, and the consequent drift toward space and architectural stages, many inventions were developed to speed up the bringing of the pictures successively before the audience; most notably the revolving or turn-table stage, on which half a dozen scenes could be set at once, ready to be brought before the proscenium opening (as shown graphically here in sketches by Ernst Stern); and the wagon-stages, which permitted one scene to be set up while the other was before the audience, ready to be slid into place as soon as the curtain was down. But these improvements merely made easier the manipulation of the old spectacular settings or the less ridiculous realistic ones. In a later phase it has seemed that both sorts, all the variations of the picture settings, are to be suppressed—unless in opera—in favor of space, architecture, and light creatively used.

With the passing of the detailed picture most of the heavy machinery of the nineteenth century theatre is disappearing, including possibly the immense scene loft that was so distinctive a feature of recent playhouse design. As an example of the heavily machined picture stage I am adding an "opened" view of the Prince Regent Theatre in Munich. It indicates the small size of the auditorium (seating 1106) in comparison with the vastness of the stage space. Note, please, the tininess of the human figure on the stage-floor in relation to the space above, note the scenery-storage room at the back, and the cellarful of machinery below and the two floors of machinery above the stage. The people who have been working toward a new twentieth century theatre, which will at least *begin* with simplicity, pointed out the artificial burden placed upon producing when the stage had become such a massive and complicated thing. Sweep it all out, they said. (But as late as 1965 the new Metropolitan Opera House at Lincoln Center in New York City was, inexplicably, burdened with all these machines, including revolving stage, wagon stages, etc.)

By way of contrast I have placed under this diagrammatic view a design by Adolphe Appia, an artist who profoundly affected the course of staging and the drift of latter-day theatre theory. The stage, he said, need be little different from the end of an ordinary room; with a few architectural elements like these, and perfect lighting control, the actor and the play can be better set out, and with more true visual beauty, than in the cavernous littered stage of the other sort of theatre.

Two men, Adolphe Appia and Gordon Craig (of whom more will be said in another chapter) inspired the early-century change of sentiment about stage setting. Both were more or less isolated from the busy producing theatres. But in the certainty that they were right, refusing to compromise their visions of new stages, they fought through misunderstanding, exile and loneliness; and by 1920 their names were on the lips of those thousands of "radicals" who were shaping the art theatres and little theatres. Others long ago took the ideas of these two pioneers, compromised with the realistic-minded people who controlled

Sketches of Max Reinhardt's revolving stage being set with a composite scene. Note the method of building the setting plastically, not as a painted representation of a place, and the small portion of the construction visible in each scene, through the proscenium as indicated at lower right. On such a stage changes of scene can be accomplished almost instantaneously, by rolling the turn-table part way round. [From drawings by Ernst Stern in *Reinhardt und Seine Bühne*, by Ernst Stern and Heinz Herald.]

Above, an opened view of the Prince Regent Theatre, Munich, showing the immensity of the stage and the elaborate machinery above and below. Here the auditorium has been simplified into a single curved bank of seats; but the stage is typical of the last and most extravagant phase of nineteenth-century picture staging. [Max Littmann, architect.] Below, by way of contrast, a simple design for a stage by Adolphe Appia. [From his *L'Œuvre d'Art Vivant*.]

the market-place theatres, and dressed realism in lovely and simple stage clothes, as we have seen. These compromising artists betrayed Craig and Appia in a sense, even while making the current "show" less offensively drab, less starkly analytical or intellectual or sensational. But the "decorators"—some of them being directors as well—included among their number those artists, in whatever country, who were most constructively working toward a new theatre. In America, above all were two visionaries of extraordinary ability, Robert Edmond Jones and Norman Bel Geddes. Jones was for thirty years the purveyor of the most faultlessly appropriate and the most sensitively beautiful settings known to our stages, while Geddes was a daring inventor and a flamingly imaginative designer. Beside them were Lee Simonson who beautifully mounted the plays of the Theatre Guild during its creative years; Joseph Urban, who came to New York from Europe with a talent for colorful Viennese design; and Claude Bragdon, Rollo Peters and Herman Rosse. Before 1935 the names of more youthful designers began to appear importantly: Jo Mielziner, Donald Oenslager, Boris Anisfeld, Mordecai Gorelik and Stewart Chaney. Out through the country, little theatre groups produced veritable miracles of lighting and staging, while in general lacking the plays worthy of such investiture.

THE rise of the "little theatres" was the most striking phenomenon in American art-life between 1910 and 1940; and there was a parallel development, though less out-standing, in every European country, even in Japan, South America, and other distant lands. In the United States the spirit had been at work many years earlier, but the first burst of activity came in 1914–15. Suddenly, it seemed, little theatres sprang up everywhere. Leaders quickly appeared, exhibitions of the new stage-craft were organized, a barrage of magazine articles was laid down, even publications devoted wholly to the "non-commercial" stage. The youngsters immediately drew the fire of the professionals too; the "Wizard of Broadway" deigned to notice them in an article calling them the Cubists, the degenerates, of the theatre art. But in many a season the insurgents offered the more interesting half of the stage fare served up in America, sometimes out through the country in their unpretentious local theatres, and, for a few years, in competition in the market-place playhouses on Broadway.

To understand the little theatres, why Maurice Browne fought through five years of Chicago's apathy and misunderstanding, to maintain the Chicago Little Theatre as a center of experiment, and in many cases, of beautiful staging; why Zona Gale and her group tried to carry

the Wisconsin spirit into playwriting and producing; why Aline Barns-
dall quixotically established the Los Angeles Little Theatre with three
directors in charge (a one-season stand that did permanent service in
bringing Norman Bel Geddes professionally into the theatre); why
the Provincetown group began that struggle for existence that ultimately brought America's first internationally famous dramatist to the
boards; why Stuart Walker toured with his unique "Portmanteau"
stage from Broadway to the Golden Gate: to understand these things
it is necessary to know the abuses that had existed in the domain of
American theatre *organization*. For the little theatre movement was
essentially a revolt. What the insurgents revolted against was a commercial domination of "amusements" such as no other country had
known, as pretty and powerful a trust as any that ever controlled steel
or oil or wool and made millions while competition was stifled.

The story of "the syndicate war" is overlong for a brief history like
ours. We can pause only a moment over the results. Between 1890 and
1910 astute businessmen found that by buying up a certain number of
physical playhouses they could obtain, by a combined method of jock-
eying, intimidation, and combination, control over the entire machinery and art of theatre production. By owning the theatres in certain
key cities they could make touring impossible to any but companies
playing on their terms; they could undersell rivals on occasion, then
later raise prices when competition had been killed; they could force
an isolated house owner to play one of their inferior shows on pain
of never being allowed another from the syndicate headquarters in
New York. They actually strangled independent production, swallow-
ing the smaller producing unit or driving it into bankruptcy or exile.
"Stars" who had secure publics were driven into capitulation; otherwise they found themselves without stages to act on—though there is
an epic chapter there in the fight for freedom waged by Francis Wil-
son, Mrs. Fiske, and a few other established favorites.

At any rate, the American theatre was soon prostrate under the
strangle-hold of a commercial "trust." As always, some advantages
accrued all round, in greater security of bookings, in centralized responsible control of circuiting, in certainty of profits; all round, that
is, except to the artist and to the public. Repertory producing disappeared: there was more profit in long runs. The actor was condemned
to months and years in one part, without opportunity to develop in
versatility, in richness, in breadth. Well-tried types of play were demanded of the playwright, or else the conventional French or English
plays were adapted by professional "doctors." The dramatist with new
ideas or vision found the doors of the theatre locked to him. The public saw no more classics, no more experimentally new plays; only what

businessmen in New York thought popularly sweet or thrilling enough to survive as "best sellers."

That is, of course, an overstatement of the case; but in general that is what the little theatres rebelled against. They wanted to put on the plays that nowhere came to the boards, the classics of other times, the Shaw and Ibsen and Strindberg that they thought were the classics of the new time. They wanted the native dramatist with un-French vision

The architectural stage of Jacques Copeau's *Théâtre du Vieux Colombier* in Paris, as arranged for a production of *The Brothers Karamazov*. [From a drawing by Robert Edmond Jones.]

to see his plays acted—otherwise he would keep on in-growing instead of becoming the Great American Playwright. They wanted to try out new ideas of staging, to challenge the old painted-perspective mode of setting—they had seen those strange designs of Gordon Craig's, had been spurred by his barbed writings about the old living-dead theatre and about new artist-directors. No matter that they opened their tiny theatres to merely amateur acting; had not the famous Moscow Art Theatre started as humbly, had not the Irish Players uncovered new virtues in an unprofessional simplicity? Had not the so-called "art theatres" of Europe started in literary-dramatic circles or salons or semi-professional studios? Even then the most interesting spot in Paris, dramatically, was the tiny *Théâtre du Vieux Colombier*.

The American little theatres multiplied until no one could count them. Some disappeared, but the total number continued to grow, up into the depression-ridden thirties. Through all those years, the little theatres, in whatever guise—local community companies, college and school theatres, and a few larger institutions that approached "art theatre" status—formed the most important group of producing organizations in America. Some never grew up but did pioneering work that served as example and encouragement to the idealists and struggling insurgents everywhere: the Chicago Little Theatre as directed by Maurice Browne, the Arts and Crafts Theatre at Detroit as directed by Sam Hume, the Neighborhood Playhouse in New York, the Provincetown Players, and many more. The larger gain was the founding of certain creative groups that *did* last, to provide the better part of the advanced dramatic fare offered to the American public between World War I and World War II. Outstanding were the Pasadena Playhouse, the Cleveland Playhouse, the Hedgerow Theatre at Rose Valley, Pennsylvania, and (in the earlier years) the Theatre Guild in New York.

For a time the insurgents and dreamers seemed destined to push their way onto Broadway and to present typical art-theatre fare among the commercially chosen offerings of the entrenched businessmen. Once in the season 1924–1925 there were being offered in New York thirteen plays produced by organizational theatres, nine of them in Broadway houses, including works by Ibsen, Shaw, Congreve, O'Neill, Molnar and Kennedy. These were staged by five of the organizations that then made New York a teeming center of experiment and of theatrical service to the community: the Neighborhood Playhouse, the Theatre Guild, the Actors' Theatre, the Stagers and the Provincetown Players. This was perhaps a record period in the fight of the "outside groups" against the powerful business-for-profits producers; and certainly after a very few years there began a melancholy decline for the idealists on Broadway, for the insurgent artists, for the groups that were working toward repertory status and permanent home theatres.

In meeting the competition of the progressive organizations, the businessmen of the theatre made certain improvements that can be counted lasting gains: an approach to ensemble acting, a phenomenal betterment in settings, a slightly bettered standard in choice of plays. But they effectively killed, in a very few years, the revived ideal of repertory companies, and they bought off key artists, especially playwrights and directors, from among the insurgents. It would be unfair not to add that a very few idealistic, if not inspired, producers had place among commercial theatre managers, and memorable productions of theirs paralleled the institutional theatre offerings. Above all there was Arthur Hopkins, who brought to New York a succession of fine plays not matched outside the institutional theatre groups, beautifully staged; and equally high-minded if less a genius as director, Winthrop Ames;

and later Brock Pemberton and Eddie Dowling. These were artist-directors who preferred to stay within the confines of the theatre-as-it-was.

DURING the late nineteenth and early twentieth centuries in Europe, the national and royal theatres continued under their old administrative form, enjoying generous royal or state patronage, until World War I. Many, after the war, simply switched over to the name State Theatre instead of Court Theatre. The people in place of the kings and princes provided subsidies. In Germany particularly the state authorities continued to count the stage one of the important activities of national cultural life. Ten years after the war's close the State Theatres in Berlin, Munich, Dresden, Darmstadt, Stuttgart and Frankfort were offering the greatest body of fairly progressive or advanced productions to be seen anywhere—though the stages in Soviet Russia were the scene of wilder and (to the specialist) more exciting experiment. The German theatres then attained a standard of public theatre service unknown at any time in most countries. In addition to the palpitatingly alive but often superficial realistic plays, they maintained extensive repertories of the greatest dramas out of the past, mounted with fullest understanding of the saner forms of modernism. In a following chapter we shall hear more of their contribution to the ensemble ideal of production.

France held to its system of playhouses under state or municipal subsidy, with resident repertory companies. In general these continued to live in the past, attempting to protect the old traditions, pretty musty now, against the assaults of progressives. The *Odéon*, to be sure, jumped half-understandingly at "modernism" in staging. About 1930 I saw there—for example—the resident company in a presentation of *The Blue Bird* in Gallicized Teutonic settings, distinctly Munichesque, with the too usual French mixture of old-fashioned declamatory and new-fashioned "natural" acting. At the *Comédie Française* in the same week I saw a pretty and spirited revival of a play of Molière, which turned out to be an excellent museum piece.

Between the two great wars the *Comédie* did its short-sighted best to preserve a great tradition. Nevertheless the record continued to be that of a theatre transparently under political control, riddled with intrigue, over-conservative in method, and generally mediocre in offerings. The company of seventy-odd actors (including thirty-two *sociétaires* or regular members, and a complement of *pensionnaires*, recruits and less seasoned members) operated under an administrator appointed by the Government and a managing committee of the *sociétaires*. The administrator and his superior, the Minister of Fine Arts, were not

A theatre transformed into a cathedral. A scene in *The Miracle* as produced in New York by Max Reinhardt in a "setting" devised by Norman Bel Geddes, 1924. [By courtesy of the Hoblitzelle Theatre Arts Library, University of Texas.]

wholly free from suspicion of wire-pulling, appointing of nieces and favorites as *sociétaires*, etc. The *Comédie* had long been distinctly a theatre in very old age—though idealists in younger countries could not but admire the national spirit that counted a theatre, as Napoleon III put it, "worthy of support, for it is part of the national glory."

Other countries of Europe had their similarly subsidized playhouses, varying in their sorts of excellency or unimportance. The repertory house remained a fixture in the chief capital cities. The Burg Theatre in Vienna (which had become a National Theatre in 1776) was for decades one of the most celebrated. Under inspired direction one or another of the repertory theatres in the less visited countries emerged into world notice in the period 1910–1930, as the National Theatre at Prague did after World War I, and the National Theatre at Stockholm almost as early. Plays from the theatres at Prague and Budapest became staples on the programs of the advanced and insurgent stages of America; especially memorable were Karel Capek's expressionist piece *R.U.R.*, and *The Insect Comedy* written by Karel and Josef Capek, at Prague.

The true repertory system had all but disappeared both in Great Britain and in the United States, with the rise of the actor-manager in London, and during the undisguised commercialization of the New York stage. After 1915 there had scarcely been a first rate company presenting plays in English according to the repertoire plan as known in Continental Europe. As a consequence German audiences were accustomed to see ten times as many productions of Shakespeare's plays as those in either English-speaking country. It is hardly too broad a statement that a whole generation in America grew up without more than a rare taste of the classics of the theatre.

In both England and America adherents of the system pointed out the great loss to theatre-goers in the passing of repertory. In no season could one be sure of seeing revivals of Shakespeare or the Greeks or even of Wilde or Shaw or Synge. One was at the mercy of commercial producers, accepting what they believed would be profitable in long-run competitive production. It became clear, moreover, that the repertory company is the only sort in which the actor gets continual and varied training; that only in groups playing together year after year, ensemble acting mellows as in the extraordinary performances of the Moscow Art Theatre.

In the professional American theatre Augustin Daly's famous company of the eighties and nineties had marked the last stand of the repertory idea. In the early twentieth century there were occasional experiments and attempts to restore repertory production. The New Theatre in New York in the years 1909–1911 seemed for a time destined for great things. But it proved unrelated to any segment of community life and it succumbed under the burden of monumentally wasteful building and over-luxurious, or over-expensive, staging. In the wave of revolution of the twenties the Neighborhood Playhouse pioneered with the idea in an underprivileged district of New York, but had to modify the repertory feature, and eventually closed. The Civic Repertory Theatre, managed by the talented and idealistic actress Eva Le Gallienne, gave New York its last season of repertory before mid-century, but shut its doors finally in 1933.

London had better luck in that the Old Vic company, distinctly an "outside" organization with a theatre on the unfashionable side of the river (until it was bombed in 1940), gave Shakespearean repertory performances continuously from 1914 on. By 1923 it had produced all the Bard's plays, under the direction of Lilian Baylis. Driven to touring during World War II, the company, numbering many of England's finest young actors, was to return to its old home early in the 1950s— but this forms an incident in a later time. What is significant in the history of the early twentieth century theatre is that one remnant of repertory thus survived, was considered revolutionary in its principles, and eventually reversed the order when it became (to the rest of the world, at least) England's one most interesting theatre.

The system of private ownership of leading theatres which has become standard in America, and to some extent in England, soon made inroads in Germany. All over the continent, indeed, commercially managed long-run companies increased in number as compared with the resident repertory houses. Max Reinhardt's name was long associated with four privately owned theatres in Germany and Austria, and there were a few other important independents. But in general the very fine work in Germany was done at the State and institutional theatres. The making practical of the ideas of Craig and Appia, and the rise of "production" as an art, were there advanced as nowhere else just after World War I. France was having a very unproductive quarter-century.

France, indeed, like America, was seeing its best productions in the very few little or insurgent theatres, grouped in Paris. The French provinces were already ill-served as regards anything but moving pictures. Even cities that once had boasted theatrical glories of their own had become way-stations for second-rate acting companies traveling with skimpy antiquated scenery. These were generally booked into the old municipal theatres. The impulse of a generation earlier, when Paris had known the challenge of the *Théâtre Libre*, a pioneer among little theatres, had pretty well run out. The spirit had passed on to Germany where the *Freie Bühne* had been established in 1890, then to England and to America. The first World War and the following depression had sapped the French progressive theatre of much of its energy.

Nevertheless, Jacques Copeau carried on at the *Théâtre du Vieux Colombier* in Paris in the most fruitful experiment recorded in the conscious struggle against the realistic theatre. He formed a company not fully professional at first, but one that gradually took its place as superior to all others in France for ensemble acting. He built a repertory that included every sort of contrast to the realistic fare of the commercial houses, specializing at first in Molière and Shakespeare, but adding a variety of poetic, symbolic and expressionistic plays—adding too the untried works of new playwrights. During World War I he came as good-will ambassador to New York and produced through two seasons at the Garrick Theatre. Returned to Paris he wrote the most glorious chapter in the history of France's revolutionary theatre.

In England the insurgent theatres came and went, after the initial wave of courageous experiment had brought Ibsen and Shaw to the boards. Gordon Craig's ideas were wholly overlooked, and the first impetus to anti-realistic experiment and especially to stylized staging was brought over from Germany. Harley Granville-Barker pioneered as producer of a series of Shakespeare's plays, and being actor, playwright and producer, was well-fitted to achieve the ideals of ensemble presentation. Alongside the Old Vic, sometimes termed England's real National Theatre (in the absence of a nationally supported, subsidized playhouse), repertory companies were established in Manchester and Liverpool, serving their communities with types of play not provided by touring companies, at low cost and with generally high standards of acting. Repertory "seasons" were numerous, at big theatres as well as little, and sometimes these made stands through several years. The most persistently idealistic venture was perhaps that of the Birmingham Repertory Theatre, founded in 1913 by Barry Jackson. In London the Gate Theatre and the Everyman Theatre (the latter in suburban Hampstead) gained international notice in the twenties, both being organized more nearly on the lines of the American insurgent groups. In England, it should be added, "repertory theatre" does not always mean a playhouse offering several plays in any given week; but only a company permanently banded together, resisting the allurement of inordinate long runs, and holding a number of productions in reserve, ready for immediate presentation.

State or official subsidy continued to be unknown to the British theatres as to the American during the early decades of the century. But subsidies from private sources were common. Some of the bravest chapters in the story of the revolt against commercial domination have told of an alliance of progressive artists with interested "patrons." John

Masefield once asked, "What greater glory can a man have than to build that which will be the home of knowledge, beauty and mirth for centuries to come?" But the gifts to the American stage have been in the nature of temporary subsidy rather than permanent endowment.

The Neighborhood Playhouse in New York was handsomely endowed for experimental producing over a period of ten years, by Irene and Alice Lewisohn, and in that time served fruitfully for its audiences and as an experimental center for artists. The Provincetown Players did epic work while enjoying driblets of contributions from widely

Jacques Copeau, straight. The greatest theorist and one of the most creative producers in the modern French theatre.

scattered sources. The Actors' Theatre, doing things on a bigger scale, with star-studded casts and in a Broadway house, found (and lost) nearly a quarter million dollars of patrons' money. Such superlative productions as *The Wild Duck* and *Candida* under the direction of Dudley Digges and the all-star presentations of *Hedda Gabler, She Stoops to Conquer* and other "non-commercial" plays scarcely justified so great a pouring-in of money—unless indeed the experiment taught the wisdom of building slowly and unspectacularly, from humble foundations.

In New York, during the years here under review—roughly 1910–1930—the Theatre Guild was the outstanding insurgent organization, and most important historically. Organized in 1919, by a group of artists experienced in several pre-war little theatres, it had the luck to obtain subsidy to the extent of free rental of its first home, and to make a notable financial success of its second production, St. John Ervine's *John Ferguson*. It early lost, through dissension, its first directors, Augustin Duncan and Rollo Peters, and immediately gave up the repertory ideal. Thereafter it operated as a producing group owned by a board of directors, including actors, playwrights and an enlightened stage designer, with a financial cushion in a subscription audience.

From 1920 to 1930 it presented the most distinguished list of original plays and revivals offered in New York (from 1925 in its own beautifully appointed theatre, financed by investors from its subscription audience). Few New Yorkers fail to remember the pleasure, and sometimes the shock, of seeing *From Morn to Midnight, Liliom, The Brothers Karamazov, The Adding Machine, Strange Interlude* (a nine-act piece presented in two sessions with a dinner recess between), *Heartbreak House*, and many another "unusual" play. The Guild, so-called because some of its organizers had been interested in Guild Socialism, in those years gave up a good many of its advanced ideas, including that of a permanently banded-together acting company. It called in many of the best contemporary American players, and relied upon visiting artist-directors for many of its outstanding productions. The end of its artistic pre-eminence was in sight in 1930, when the younger and bolder actors who had been organized as a dependent Theatre Guild Studio were cast loose, to found the Group Theatre. The Guild itself was to go on as a diminishingly important entity in the experimental theatre field, to take a better-than-average place among commercial producing firms.

Those who believed that the artist-owned theatre is likely to render better service to audiences than the businessman-owned theatre were heartened in 1924–1926 when three outstanding figures in the modern movement formed a partnership to produce in New York. Operating first at the tiny Provincetown Playhouse, then in the larger Greenwich Village Theatre, Robert Edmond Jones, Eugene O'Neill and Kenneth Macgowan offered programs even more advanced than the current ones of the Theatre Guild, and with special emphasis on experimental pieces by native playwrights. Imported plays ranged from Congreve's *Love for Love* to Strindberg's *The Spook Sonata;* but the memorable landmarks were the first offerings of O'Neill's *Desire under the Elms* and *The Great God Brown*. Few organizations since 1926 have come so near to demonstrating what a real "art theatre" in New York might mean.

Outside New York the institutional theatre—the only sort that can re-establish repertory, break the stranglehold of commercialism, and foster experiment—made history in a larger way. Only a few type organizations, of the many that were founded in the key years 1910–1920, were destined to survive into the 1950s. But the Pasadena Community Playhouse (founded in 1917) and the Cleveland Playhouse were as near permanent, perhaps, as can be expected in a world given to change, and during a half-century notably unkind to cultural institutions. Under a courageous director, Gilmor Brown, the theatre at Pasadena served its community more of the fine plays of the past and more experimental plays of the present—including difficult pieces never attempted elsewhere, such as O'Neill's *Lazarus Laughs*—than any other American theatre, or perhaps any English-language theatre. A single half-year, for instance, saw on its boards *The Merry Wives of Windsor, Major Barbara, Hedda Gabler* and Capek's *The Makropoulos Secret;* another, *The Great God Brown, Pygmalion* and *Cæsar and Cleopatra*.

The Cleveland Playhouse, growing up from an amateur little theatre established in 1916 to the estate of a community theatre opening its own near-ideal building in 1926, and offering a modified repertory program, prospered under the guidance of Frederic McConnell. True to the ideal of continual experiment, the directors at Cleveland built a fully equipped laboratory theatre under the same roof with the larger community playhouse. As in the British "repertory" system, a proportion of new productions were held ready for revival.

In America the only repertory house continuously operating on the European system—several plays reappearing each week—was the Hedgerow Theatre at Rose Valley, Pennsylvania, where memorable pioneering work, and constant theatre service to a suburban community, were accomplished under the direction of Jasper Deeter. Other progressive local institutions that built toward the art-theatre ideal and made outstanding names for themselves were the Dallas Little Theatre, the Arts and Crafts Theatre at Detroit, the Santa Barbara Community Theatre

Two designs for scenes in Shakespeare's *King Lear*, by Norman Bel Geddes. The production planned as primitive, with a hint of the massive architecture of Stonehenge.

(too early lost to the moving picture interests), the Goodman Memorial Theatre in Chicago and *Le Petit Théâtre du Vieux Carré* in New Orleans.

The little and art theatres that became renowned in this period were hardly more numerous than the university and school theatres. Suddenly, about 1915, the campuses came alive with new producing projects, a new progressive spirit. Old dramatic clubs, accustomed to present an occasional academically-interesting revival, under a "coach" and in horribly antiquated "scenery," discovered the ideals of the new stagecraft and the repertory of the "free stages" of Europe. Harvard University had seen some pioneer productions earlier, and Professor George Pierce Baker had for some years been offering there a famous course in playwriting.

A certain crystallization came in 1925 when Professor Baker was called to Yale University to head a new post-graduate school of playwriting and production, housed, together with the old Yale Dramatic Association, in a then modern building containing a complete theatre, workshops and classrooms, library, collections, etc. As long ago as 1913 the Carnegie Institute of Technology in Pittsburgh had installed a complete theatre for its Department of Drama; and many another educational institution, usually under pressure of student demand, converted a building to theatre uses during the following decade. The University of Iowa opened in 1936 the theatre that was then the nearest ideal combined community playhouse and experimental theatre-arts plant in the Americas, under direction of E. C. Mabie. In 1939 the University of Wisconsin was to build an outstandingly fine theatre.

To future historians of the theatre it may seem curious that developments outside the main run of professional producing should have taken on more significance than the typical Broadway offerings during the first third of the new century; but there can be no doubt that the novel phenomenon of the period was the rise of the "outside" theatres, their introduction of new ideals of stagecraft, along with a fresh and literate taste in play choice. Important too was the provision of educational facilities for playwright, actor, stage designer and artist-producer, at a time when repertory and other frameworks for apprenticeship were disappearing from the theatres controlled by businessmen-managers.

In Europe there developed one further type of dissident or radical theatre. In view of the drift of the whole continent toward socialism, a drift historic but not widely marked in the arts at the time, it is important to note that in Germany a true "democratic" theatre had developed before World War I. During the twenties and well into the thirties there was a people's theatre of a unique sort in Berlin. The

Volksbühne was no little or sidestreet theatre; was, indeed, housed in a monumental stone building of its own, complete with every latest invention in stage machinery and audience comfort. It was owned by its audiences, had been paid for by a fractional addition to the cost of each subscription ticket in its pioneering days. Attendance at the notably fine productions, which would have been outstanding in any land, cost the owner-spectator about one-tenth of the cost of a theatre ticket in England or America of the time.

The plays were either classics (from all languages) or modern. Naturally ones with a socialistic tinge, say of Hauptmann or Toller, were specially favored. The acting standard was high and the staging uniformly "advanced" and frequently as unusual and striking as the Russian innovations of the same period. It was at the *Volksbühne* that Toller's *Masse-Mensch* was presented in a stirring production that became internationally famous. This theatre was one of the earliest to fall victim to the intolerance of the Nazi regime; but it may be remembered as the first notable forerunner, outside Russia, of the socialistic, labor-front stages which were to become a phenomenon in many countries before World War II.

A *régisseur* who was too revolutionary even for the *Volksbühne*, Erwin Piscator, was eased out of the organization, and established his own radical stage, devoted to politically slanted plays; he was driven out of Germany by the Nazis, spent the years of World War II in New York, and then returned to West Germany. It was he who taught and abetted Bertolt Brecht, who was to be the foremost *avant-garde* leader in Europe after the war. But Brecht's story belongs to a later chapter.

OF INDIVIDUAL acting in the early twentieth century there is little to record that is of historic importance. Despite the spread of the star system under commercial nurturing, no new stars arose in America to take places beside the meteoric Forrest, the great Booth, the beloved Jefferson.

Graceful acting, charming acting, radiantly appealing personalities, these we had. John Drew was a gentleman-actor of the old school who never failed to please us thoroughly, to hold us sympathetically, gaining his steady command by never trying to rise to heights. The Drew-Barrymore nobility lived on in the playing of the ever-beautiful Ethel Barrymore, and in the too-occasional appearances of John Barrymore, who might fairly be put down as first American actor of the period, remembered especially for his Hamlet. Maude Adams is tenderly recollected for her irresistible personal appeal, especially in *Peter Pan*. Mrs.

John Barrymore, straight. The most widely acclaimed American actor during the opening years of the century, he was especially known for his playing of Hamlet, 1921. [By courtesy of Kean Archives, Philadelphia.]

Fiske, E. H. Sothern, Julia Marlowe, George Arliss, Otis Skinner—these were leaders, but not giants and prophets. Nor were those who became the idols of the later twenties and early thirties, Jane Cowl, Laurette Taylor, Madge Kennedy, Walter Hampden, any too firmly seated in the theatre-as-organized. All of these favorites suffered the loss of years of their professional life, between calls from the managers.

A younger generation, youthful, charming, promising a new fire, were then coming to maturity: Helen Hayes, Clare Eames, Blanche Yurka, Pauline Lord, Katharine Cornell, Eva LeGallienne, Lynn Fontanne and Alfred Lunt. But on the American-speaking stage since 1900 there have been no towering figures to dominate in the old sense. Eva LeGallienne found aristic security for a few years while acting, memorably, at her own Civic Repertory Theatre. Walter Hampden took place as the most enlightened, indeed the noblest, of the actors of the period, by an extension of the actor-manager system, having, between 1925 and 1930, presented plays of his own choice at his own theatre. His impersonations in *Cyrano de Bergerac*, *Richelieu*, and *The Merchant of Venice* were outstanding, and his Hamlet was one of the most sensitive and satisfying seen in America. But like many others—this being one of the most disquieting circumstances of the time—Hampden's appearances became less and less frequent from the mid-thirties on.

In London there was even less of star playing: for a long time not a figure widely known outside England after Irving died and Ellen Terry retired. Nevertheless some spectators guessed that a few of the younger men would push on to pre-eminence and a sort of idolization, most notably John Gielgud—again one of the great Hamlets of the new century—and Laurence Olivier. Of the women of the time Sybil Thorndike and Edith Evans had devoted followers and never failed to please in the classic and superior modern plays which they especially favored. Both began their careers in the outside or special theatres, and both were associated at various times with the Old Vic and other repertory companies.

In German theatres solo acting had come to be frowned upon somewhat earlier, and the ensemble ideal was generally accepted. Distinguished actors were numerous in the companies of the subventioned State theatres, and in such other "special" theatres as the *Volksbühne* and Reinhardt's *Deutsches Theater* in Berlin. Alexander Moissi emerged and was as near being a world-recognized star as any living. Great as Moissi was, however, it was Max Reinhardt, his director, who became the more famous of the two. In Germany especially, at this time, production as an art was eclipsing acting.

In France the Guitrys had their adherents, and one recalls easily a showy actress or two; but assuredly there came no successor to Sarah Bernhardt, or even a rival to the reputation of Coquelin. The one-time amateurs of Copeau's company at the *Vieux Colombier* were the most satisfying and most moving actors of the period, including Copeau himself, Suzanne Bing, Louis Jouvet and Charles Dullin. In Russia,

A setting for Shakespeare's *Twelfth Night* as designed by Norman Wilkinson for Granville-Barker's production in London, 1912. Typical of the moderate modernism of the English stage designers. [By courtesy of the Daily Mail Studios, London.]

ensemble acting had already reached a peak during the realistic era, in the performances of the Moscow Art Theatre, and there was some talk of Kachaloff as a player without peer. But there were a half-dozen actors in the one company as beloved and perhaps as accomplished; and after all, it *was* the ensemble that was the marvelous thing. It may indeed be true that the ensemble ideal, which came in substantially with the twentieth century revolt against one-sidedness in theatre art, had ended virtuoso acting, in the old sense, for good and all. At any rate, right up to mid-century, audiences will show preference for complete rounded-out performance over an exhibition by one outstanding player.

(The story in the field of moving pictures is different, of course, possibly because of less critical audiences. All can agree that Charlie Chaplin in early century took rank as the most celebrated, and perhaps the most individually creative, actor of his time. He carried on the tradition of the great clown-comedians, and added his distinctive variation to what had gone before. By grace of the picture medium, through which acting is photographically transmitted to the ends of the earth, he has probably pleased more people than any other performer in history. But the story of the films will come later.)

One interesting development in connection with acting was the formation of the so-called "actor's union" in the United States, the Actor's Equity Association, and its rise to power in the realm of the commercial theatre. Players had banded together in the past—we met an actors' guild, the Artists of Dionysus, when we explored the Greek theatre—but only in the twentieth century has the actor been able, by group effort, to remedy the conditions under which he works, economic, moral and physical. The organization was enabled, partly by a "strike" that developed stirring incidents, to gain for the players fair standing before the law, decent dressing rooms and stage conditions, and a position of equality in the community. Never since Greek times has the professional actor enjoyed so much respect and consideration as is his lot today. That he had to grasp at trades-union methods need not detract from his glamour, since thereby he gained rights needful to him as self-respecting man and creative artist.

OUR picture of the early twentieth century theatre would be incomplete without a glimpse of such playwrights as the Irish Yeats, the Belgian Maeterlinck, the German Expressionists, and the American O'Neill (on one side of his talent). Realistic drama, forming the main stream, has been sufficiently treated in a preceding chapter, but minor counter-currents and streamlets have flowed in a manner to warrant at least brief mention. At times they seemed to flow so strongly that they gave promise of developing into a major new-century drama.

If anyone had the patience to assemble a list of all the plays produced in English-speaking theatres from 1910 to 1930, say, the section covering the work of that greatest of all dramatic geniuses, William Shakespeare, would be very small indeed. For while lip service continued, those who controlled the English and American theatres simply had not conviction and interest enough to stage the great poet-dramatist's works. (One had to travel to Germany, or Vienna or Stockholm, to see any large number of Shakespearean plays presented in any one season. They were always in repertory there, and new productions at the various resident theatres were regular occurrences.) But at times a poetic current came to the surface. The Irish school had a vogue, even in production. Just when William Butler Yeats was writing his plays, a happy combination of circumstances brought into existence the Abbey Theatre group in Dublin, generally known as the Irish Players. They not only had a taste for the frail poetic dramas of Yeats, but added a talent for beautiful speech as such; these virtues, combined with a natural simplicity of acting, brought a refreshing note to the larger British theatre.

The Irish Players, moreover, found in J. M. Synge a dramatist who took fairly realistic material and treated it in language that extraordinarily captures the poetic values of Irish-English speech. Within their limited field the plays of Synge are as full-flavored and distinctive and poignant as any in the whole range of theatre literature. He touched Realism with fresh verbal beauty, irony and salty satire. He even satirized his own countrymen; and one of the amusing sights in the modern theatre occurred when the Abbey Theatre company brought *The Playboy of the Western World* to America, and transplanted Irishmen rioted in efforts to prevent performances. Along with Yeats and Synge, Lady Gregory achieved fame as one of the pioneer writers for the Abbey stage. Her short comedies of peasant character are notably deft, comic and pithy.

The flowering of Realism in the theatres of the rest of the world influenced the Abbey group, and the Yeatsian note of poetic imagination was heard less and less. The Abbey players discovered other playwrights. But they lost, by rejecting his first play, the most gifted of later Irish playwrights, Sean O'Casey. He wrote (at first) realistic studies of the seamiest side of Dublin tenement life, imbedded scenes of delicious comedy and patches of starkest and genuine tragedy, but depended most upon depiction of observed detail and transcription of rich native speech. As his mastery grew, he became the foremost Irish dramatist of his era, a favorite in the theatres of many countries.

In France the Romantic current flowed along feebly up to the time of World War I, all but submerged in the flood of triangle studies of which French audiences never tire, but calling attention to its persistence by an occasional new play of Edmond Rostand or Maurice Maeterlinck. Rostand sometimes broke through to spectacular success: *Cyrano de Bergerac* with Constant Coquelin in the title rôle, and *L'Aiglon* with Sarah Bernhardt. But in the end he must be judged a good stage craftsman seduced by the beauties of a poetic-romantic literature that is no longer vitally alive. Maeterlinck was even more definitely of the school that makes art an escape from life. *The Blue Bird* is a symbolic, other-worldly fable-play, rather too heavily sweetened for normal consumption, and generally hung with too much tinsel in the producing. Only in a rare play like *Pelléas and Mélisande* did Maeterlinck rise out of a rather forced romanticizing into the field of true poetic tragedy—and the theatre between-wars was hardly in a mood to welcome anything so gentle, slow-moving, and, yes, literary. Nevertheless, several of the French-Belgian mystic's early plays seem likely to survive into later repertories.

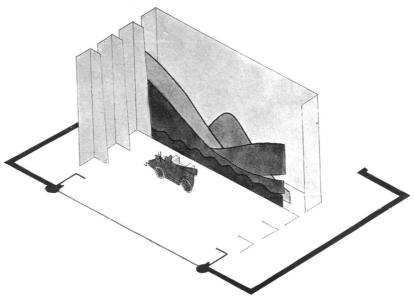

Louis Jouvet, when he produced *Knock* by Jules Romains at the *Comédie des Champs-Elysées* in 1923, arrived at a sort of stage setting that he called "non-pictorial"—being rather "space diagrammed for acting." [From a drawing made by Jouvet for Cheney's *Stage Decoration*.]

Hauptmann, not the crusading Hauptmann of *The Weavers*, but a more yearning and poetic creator, wrote a memorable symbolic-romantic play in *The Sunken Bell*, and a more touchingly human "dream play" in *Hannele*. All of these became staples in other countries, and *Hannele* was a landmark on the way to Expressionism. The only other German "poetic" playwright of the period, Hugo von Hofsmannsthal, did over some older legend-plays, chiefly Greek, in what seemed at the time the modern spirit; but the charm of their neo-classicism has in general faded—though several of his plays recast from old masterpieces served Max Reinhardt for memorable productions, as in the case of *Jedermann*.

Eleonora Duse, considered by many the most appealing and satisfying of twentieth-century actresses. [William Seymour Theatre Collection, Princeton University Library.]

August Strindberg of Sweden, but most widely played in Germany, progressed, like Hauptmann, from success in the realistic or naturalistic metier to success in a new sort of drama, close to Expressionism. Indeed, *A Dream Play* is sometimes cited as the first outstanding example of that genre, and certainly it has been endlessly staged by the experimental and special theatres. The Hungarian Ferenc Molnar, who departed occasionally from his gracefully sophisticated realism, brought out *Liliom* (first produced in 1909), a play compounded of reality and fantasy, and perfectly suited to the needs of the consciously revolutionary producing groups. The Theatre Guild staged it memorably in 1921.

Of the out-and-out poets contributing to the stage at this time the fiery Gabriele D'Annunzio created the greatest stir and certainly wrote the most theatrical and lurid plays. *La Gioconda* (made internationally famous by the acting of Eleonora Duse) and *The Daughter of Forio* eventually were judged to represent a revival of a violent sort of romanticism rather than a contribution to a new theatre of poetic expression. Of English poets, John Masefield wrote a single drama, *The Tragedy of Nan*, that found wide currency in the little and repertory theatres.

Of Americans, Percy Mackaye was outstanding, and contributed in *The Scarecrow* a conventionally poetic drama that proved effective in production; but he became better known for his masques, presented outside both the "regular" theatres and the art theatres. The widely loved Edna St. Vincent Millay, although at one time an actor at the Provincetown Playhouse, wrote only a very few plays, and of these only the one-act *Aria da Capo* has reappeared in later repertories. Alfred Kreymborg for many years toured alone with his dramatic sketches and wrote delightfully distinctive if slight free-verse plays for the little theatres. Lord Dunsany, Irish but not of the Abbey Theatre group, became the best-known of all authors producing poetic and fantastic short plays. His success on little theatre and art theatre stages was enormous, but his work never really got into the commercial theatre.

The truth is that not one of these poets or plays diverted big-theatre audiences for more than a moment from preoccupation with realistic drama, with musical comedy, with, increasingly, the very unpoetic "pictures." Nor did the poetic counter-current to realism provide any preponderant part of the programs at the insurgent theatres. A few plays of the time, of Hauptmann, who goes back to the eighteen-nineties, of Maeterlinck, whose *Pelléas and Mélisande* was as early as 1892 and *The Blue Bird* as late as 1908, of Yeats, whose finest work may be dated from the founding of the Abbey Theatre in 1904, seem likely to reclaim place in repertory theatres.

The Expressionist playwrights—of a little later date, and especially active in the years just following World War I—caused a greater stir. They were more revolutionary in aim, and more violently destructive of traditional ideals, than the Romanticists or the Symbolists or other groups that had set out consciously to challenge Realism.

A design for Shakespeare's *Macbeth*, by Robert Edmond Jones, for Arthur Hopkins' New York production, 1921. Expressionistic symbols and vague distortions on a space stage.

Expressionism, in the larger art sense, means expression of the artist's emotion rather than the depiction of the object exciting it; means emphasis on "form" rather than on observed fact, escape from the limitation of what can be seen with the eye; means intensification, not portrayal of life; means presentative as against representative production, with consequent shift of emphasis (in the theatre) to creative use of the characteristic means of the stage art, to movement, color, lighting, acting, as well as words and their "meaning"; means usually the violation of actuality, the distorted piling-up of emotionally effective incident.

The Expressionist (no working artist admits the name, of course) aims to get back to a place where the vast imaginative conception, the direct appeal to the soul, the gorgeously rich sensuous impression—all impossible to Realism—can be compassed on the stage; having regained the freedom, he will use it not as in Greece or in Elizabethan London, but to project in terms of the new intensity of modern life.

Several playwrights emerged whose intentions were obviously Expressionistic, most notably the Germans Ernst Toller and Georg Kaiser, whose plays were seen on the American stage, and the native experimenter, John Howard Lawson. But it is apropos to note that Gordon Craig—who would be the last artist in the world to bow unprotesting under the label Expressionist—did more than all the playwrights to bring a sane Expressionism into the theatre: by his leadership in the fight against Realism, by his clearing out from the stage the old picturing paraphernalia, by his insistence upon the use of the stage itself, the actors, the movement, the lights, the color, as a creative medium, by his sweep of imagination that transcended all sense of surface actuality, by his ideal of "a noble artificiality" as against that of naturalness, by his fathering of those hundreds of artist-directors who were making over the stage from a photographic peep-show box to a theatrically articulate medium.

The most famous early example of Expressionist playwriting was Kaiser's *From Morn to Midnight*, a hurried, kaleidoscopic study of contemporary life. It was immensely effective, in production, as a theatric-emotional experience, whether viewed in Max Reinhardt's German showing or the adaptation presented by the Theatre Guild in New York in 1922. Th latter event influenced many an American writer, producer, and director. The old play form, that had become progressively more smoothly articulated, more natural, more tightly journalistic—dealing always with the personal, the individual story or problem—was seen to be possibly less effective than the unfolding of emotional scenes in successive flashes, with staccato dialogue, against settings evocative or imaginative, in an acted fable symbolizing or illustrating mass experience. Unreality was here re-enthroned in the theatre. *From Morn to Midnight* is far from being a masterpiece of playwriting, and Kaiser was not a profound observer of human life; but the *method* he brought in was historic.

A more notable play was Ernst Toller's *Masse-Mensch* (translated as *Man and the Masses*), and this was presented in what must assuredly rank as one of the most vivid and moving productions in modern times, at the *Volksbühne* in Berlin in 1922. Scenery had largely disappeared and figures, single, dramatically grouped or in swaying crowds, were picked out by light against a black void. The theme was violently proclaimed in the opening scene, and episode followed episode with shotgun explosiveness—but varied with realistic bits set against wildest fantasy. The story was that of a woman who leads workingmen to rebel against their condition of near-slavery, succeeds, then tries to halt the mass of men short of violent anti-social destructiveness, but, ironically, is executed as their leader. The implications of personal

Two scenes from *Masse-Mensch* by Ernst Toller, at the *Volksbühne*,
Berlin, 1921, as designed by Hans Strohbach and directed by Jurgen Fehling.
The space stage utilized expressionistically, with effective mass action.

tragedy are great, but Toller's emphasis was all on the mass rather than the individual, on collective feeling and group emotion. It was in connection with plays such as this that the *sprechchor* or speaking choir took effective place on the stages of Germany's revolutionary theatres, and became a commonplace of workingmen's dramatic sketches at socialistic and communistic meetings.

Expressionism became almost immediately an international movement, but Expressionist playwrights of the stature of Toller and Kaiser were few. Most important was Karel Capek of Czecho-Slovakia, whose *R.U.R.* (standing for Rossum's Universal Robots, manufactured machine-men who get out of hand, then begin to acquire the more idealistic human traits) was endlessly played by progressive producing groups, with a combined melodramatic-thoughtful effectiveness. In America John Howard Lawson wrote the exciting industrial play *Processional*, and Elmer Rice forsook his more accustomed realistic metier to contribute *The Adding Machine*, an Expressionistic drama of the typical wage-slave. It has been a favorite of "advanced" stages all over the world since it was written in 1923. A little later Sean O'Casey went on from what may be called scrambled Realism to occasional use of Expressionistic heedlessness and distortion.

Italy's foremost dramatist of modern times, Luigi Pirandello, is commonly listed with the Expressionists, perhaps only for lack of a more convenient category, because of the way in which he tangled up reality in his plays. He is comparable with the Cubist painters who shift the planes of the "actual" to rearrange them in a more revealing pattern; only his planes are the mask which each man thinks of as himself and those realer selves which ordinarily lie hidden. Or else he plays with several levels of consciousnss. This is anti-Realistic, but it grew out of Realism illuminated through an understanding of Freudian psychology. It is a return part way from the Expressionist's obsession with mass forces to concern with the personal.

America's one internationally known playwright of 1925–1935, Eugene O'Neill, was significant for his achievement in lifting American drama out of a purely provincial or reflective activity (as viewed from Europe); and as the foremost English-writing dramatist who made Expressionism a broadly successful mode. American plays, to be sure, could then be seen in the theatres of Moscow, Vienna, Berlin, Rome and London but these were generally the cheaper pieces with obvious appeal, melodramatic crook-plays, slangy and racy comedies, journalistic but picturesque emotional dramas—which merely meant that the centre of routine commercial playwriting in English shifted for a time from London to New York, that our vulgar theatre was then perhaps the livest in the world. But O'Neill was a phenomenon because everywhere he attracted the attention of those who were watching for the dramatist original enough and able enough to challenge convention.

He was a Realist first, with a keen selective sense and sometimes an uncanny knack for the revealing unpleasant word, and perhaps he did not transcend Realism in any great way; but in *The Emperor Jones*, *The Hairy Ape*, and *Lazarus Laughs* he threw off the chains of imitativeness and widened the expressiveness of our stage. He did this with

Eugene O'Neill, a portrait from his younger years when he was an insurgent with the Provincetown Players. [William Seymour Theatre Collection, Princeton University Library.]

violence and speed and piled-up emotion rather than with serenity and depth; he broke over the old rigidities of well-made-play dramaturgy, without suggesting a new play-structure with positive virtues, utilizing a form still jerky and unfinished; but he moved audiences, with a new thrill, a fresh revelation, with theatrical directness.

The more "standard" dramatists of the period, those who mold or follow the popular taste as understood by the commercial managers, without creating values likely to outlast the generation, continued to feed the West End theatres of London and the Broadway theatres of New York with plays of sentimental Realism, plays often topically pat, as *What Price Glory?* and *Journey's End*, or nostalgically affecting or cynically smart. In these years "the Road" increasingly lost importance; though a few conscientious actors or actor-managers—Katharine Cornell, Walter Hampden—took their New York companies on tour intact, while other producers sent out occasional "second" companies. The best plays, aside from the classics as offered by Hampden, were as a rule those by Maxwell Anderson, Robert Sherwood, Sidney Howard and Philip Barry. Just as Eugene O'Neill and Elmer Rice, more especially noted for their Expressionistic contribution, should be added to the list of effective Realists, so in reverse Maxwell Anderson may be stressed as bridging over into poetic drama, for his serious effort to bring the lasting poetic element to the treatment of modern life. But it was more especially the tendencies noted in the Expressionistic drama that were to lead on to the important phenomena of 1930–1950: particularly to the imaginative plays of Thornton Wilder, and to a brief burst of activity in socially conscious if not baited and barbed mass-drama, slanted toward the proletariat.

HISTORICALLY, with regard to the theatre as an art, the early twentieth century had been an excitingly changeable time. Although not a single superlatively great actor had appeared, or a superlatively great dramatist—Shaw, if one wished to classify him so, must be counted the last figure of the School of Ibsen of the 1890s—an epochal shift had occurred in the social organization of the theatre. The commercial stage had come to a peak of prosperity, then had entered upon a long decline. The institutional theatres had enjoyed a period of revival, the state, little and art theatres taking to themselves the major interest of international students of the theatre arts. Moreover, a mode of play-writing wholly new in the history of the Western theatre, challenging Realism, had found adherents among producers in all lands; and (subject of the next chapter) a new conception had developed as to the aim of stage production, a new ideal of an integrated flow of the sometime divided arts of acting, plot unfoldment, setting, lighting, movement.

A setting for Wedekind's *Franziska*, at the Raimund Theatre, Vienna. Anti-decorative constructivism, utilized for varied and effective acting levels. [By courtesy of the Willinger Studios.]

CHAPTER

23

The Rise of Production
as an Art

W HEN the wave of revolt against domination of the stage
by the playwrights broke over the theatre, when the first
protests were made against confining theatre history to what could be
discovered in printed play texts—shortly after 1900, that was—the insurgents had been vague about what figure should take the place of the
dramatist in the chief position. Not the actor, surely; since the decay
of the *Commedia dell'Arte* only an isolated creative actor had lifted
his head here or there in any generation. The player of the day was
uncreative, interpretative, content in a co-ordinate rôle (except the actor-manager who formed a company, hired or bought a theatre and
met current competition on its own commercial grounds, exploiting
himself in made-to-measure star plays).

The literary people, who had been the outstanding artists of the
Realistic era, raised the cry that the dramatists were going to be butch-
ered to afford a decorators' holiday. The alarm in that direction came
about logically, because the chief of the attackers, the first prophet of
the new theatre, Gordon Craig, was designer as well as actor and director; he had made some very beautiful pictures of stages and scenes
so different from the 1890 product that he was considered half-mad—
even a shade more than that—in spite of his being the son of that
wholly lovely and universally respected idol of the nineteenth century
British stage, Ellen Terry.

Here is what Gordon Craig wrote in his first book, in 1905:

> The art of the theatre is neither acting nor the play, it is not scene
> nor dance, but it consists of all the elements of which these things are
> composed: action, which is the very spirit of acting; words, which are
> the body of the play; line and color, which are the very heart of the
> scene; rhythm, which is the very essence of dance . . . One is no more
> important than the other, no more than one color is more important
> to a painter than another, or one note more important than another
> to a musician. . . .
>
> If you were for once to see an actual piece of theatrical art, you
> would never again tolerate what is today being thrust upon you in place
> of theatrical art. The reason why you are not given a work of art on
> the stage is not because the public does not want it, not because there
> are not excellent craftsmen in the theatre who could prepare it for
> you, but because the theatre lacks the artist—the artist of the theatre,
> mind you, not the painter, poet, musician.

A model by Gordon Craig for a stage scene utilizing only an arrangement of screens. [From Craig's *Towards a New Theatre*.]

And later he wrote: "Let me repeat again that it is not only the
writer whose work is useless in the theatre. It is the musician's work
which is useless there, and it is the painter's work which is useless there.
All three are utterly useless. Let them keep to their preserves, let them
keep to their kingdoms, and let those of the theatre return to theirs."
And, listing the scores of workers in the theatre, and the several voices
of authority, he added:

"Seven directors instead of one and nine opinions instead of one.

"Now, then, it is impossible for a work of art ever to be produced where more than one brain is permitted to direct; and if works of art are not seen in the Theatre this one reason is a sufficient one, though there are plenty more."

In other words, put out the literary man, and if any other one-sided artist tries to climb into first place, put *him* back where he belongs too; unless one among these artists can prove his mastery of *all* the materials of the stage art—in which case he may be called the master of the theatre. To him only should the place be entrusted.

No master arose who was playwright, music-composer, scene-designer and director-of-actors, all rolled into one. The ideal is difficult to obtain in a world where a genius in any single line is born once in hundreds of years, and where specialization is the rule. But Craig's insistence shifted emphasis from all other theatre figures to that of the man charged with placing the play on the stage. Like as not he had been called stage-manager before, or he had been the theatre owner and primarily a business man. But now he got to be a specialist, a *régisseur*, with extraordinarily increased powers.

Where settings had been ordered in blindly from an unrelated scenic studio before, the new artist-director imparted his conception to, and worked with, a sympathetic designer, or created his own scenes. Where actors before had enjoyed broad license to develop personal idiosyncrasies, they now could do so only within the limits set by the artist-director's conception of the total production. Almost for the first time the art of the theatre was being seen as a whole, with someone experiencing a complete vision of the *total* performance before rehearsals started.

In twenty years the artist-director progressed from being a hireling of the manager, a slave of the leading actress, a mere assistant, to the point of being the key figure in the modern theatre. *Production* became the important thing, as distinct from the play values alone, or *virtuoso* acting, or spectacle. The *régisseur*, the master of the production, since 1915, has been recognized as the most creative artist in the theatre.

We don't know much about the figure in ages past, of course. We suspect that his unifying work was seldom done at all. But soon there were three or four examples of him that were better known than any living actor, and better advertised than any living dramatist—again, except Bernard Shaw.

The development of artist-directors stimulated interest in the search for "form" as an attribute of stage art. The revelation of form is possible only through the unified stage production, the complete use of stage materials, the bringing of all the elements into focus—and that is the work of this artist-director of artists. The flow, the continuity, the sensuous undercurrent, the spiritual overtones—these are his cares.

His methods are all but unexplainable: his way of employing not only the tangible materials, actors, lights, dialogue, movement, and setting, but proportion, stress, pace, contrast, interval, variety, etc. But one may visualize him as he brings the work to the stage, after years of planning, perhaps, and then through weeks and months of rehearsal; getting it first to come to focus in his own mind's eye, then

Design by Gordon Craig for *Electra*, 1905.

setting out to obtain the right actors and to rig the right stage environment; in rehearsal slowing the pace here, hastening it there, struggling to bring so-and-so to the peak of his performance—and the center of attention—at the right moment; building up the sound sequence through one stretch, playing a silence against it at the end; flowing color over

Design by Gordon Craig for Hamlet, *Act I, Scene 5*. "I am thy father's spirit." Published in 1907, this simple design, although it seemed revolutionary then, is perfectly in keeping with the best practice more than sixty years later.

the performance, then letting the stage go grey; clearing out everything for the moment when the dramatist, suddenly turned inspired poet, has provided lines too pregnant for any assisting elements. Working thus, with seen and unseen materials, the *régisseur* develops that flow of theatricality, that continuous, unbroken appeal, that consti-

The same scene in Edwin Booth's production of *Hamlet* in the 1860's, placed opposite Craig's design for purposes of contrast. The nineteenth-century setting illustrates the realism, the stress upon historical place, and the dwarfing of the actor, against which the moderns were rebelling. [By courtesy of the Walter Hampden Memorial Library at the Players, New York.]

tutes the stage "form." And it is this element that distinguishes the "new" stage from that of the past.

Max Reinhardt was the most famous early practitioner. He became known over all the Western world as the most sensational of *virtuoso* directors, the great popularizer of the new stagecraft. He was once a minor actor; then a producer who believed in Realism. He actually planned two productions with Gordon Craig, but the latter eventually withdrew. Timidly he took leaf after leaf from the book that was being written by Craig, Appia, and other "impractical" dreamers; he adapted some surface aspects of their designs to practical producing. He trained up a group of first-class poster-artists to provide simple, colorful, and striking settings. He took over more and more power as director, and assumed an alarming freedom in the "treatment" of plays. Sometimes he buried a finely dramatic Greek or Shakespearean text under smothering spectacle or shout and gesture; again he developed irresistible drive in the performance of plays that had been unsuspected of any such effectiveness.

At times he over-dressed and over-circused the drama; at others he created *theatre* where ordinary direction would have left only deadness on the stage. He exploited cheap stuff like *The Miracle* by genuinely theatricalizing the one or two fine scenes, and glossing the rest over with stressed movement, crowds, stirring music, colored lights. In such world-known events as the Salzburg Festivals he mixed the questionably spectacular things with those in which he showed his true genius: classics recreated, with all the elements of theatrical appeal brought into one flow, one finely dramatic evocation. He was the unchallenged master of mass effects on the stage, the effective marshalling of armies of actors.

In his best quiet works he was as near a master of creative and contributive direction as existed. He was the more important as example, having taken his work from Germany and Austria to the rest of Europe, to England, to America. For reasons unconnected with the theatre art, because he was Jewish and could not stand against Nazi persecution, he ended his days in Hollywood, where he failed to duplicate in the moving pictures his spectacular successes of the legitimate stage.

Other German artist-directors achieved a creative theatricality in their productions, not quite so spectacularly but with a thoroughness that made them world-influences. At the State Theatre in Berlin, Leopold Jessner gave "stylization" a new breadth of meaning. In his productions one felt the same style permeating not only the settings but the acting, the movement, all the seen and heard elements. He cleared his stage almost to bare walls, and raised platforms and steps the better to show the actor out; indeed *Jessnertreppen*—Jessner's steps—became as well-known to students of stagecraft as Gordon Craig's screens or the Constructivist stages that the Russians were just then developing. In his placing and guiding of actors on his stepped platforms Jessner opened the way to realization of new values in movement as such. His designer, Emil Pirchan, shared praise for the achievement, for making even the barest stage seem warm, colorful, and contributive, and for playing the lights cunningly as a constant silent aid to the acting.

Drawing by Robert Edmond Jones of a scene in *Othello* as designed by Emil Pirchan, for Leopold Jessner's production at the State Theatre, Berlin, 1922. A minimal construction on a space stage, with the producer's famous *Jessnertreppen*. [By courtesy of Robert Edmond Jones.]

At another theatre in Berlin, the *Volksbühne*, Jurgen Fehling was presenting classics and "workingmen's plays" with a vividness and animation that marked him as one of the foremost of artist-directors. As a means of heightening the ensemble effect and putting first emphasis upon the actor, he threw out stage decoration as generally known and opened up small or vast areas of playing space, picking out the actors with light. His was perhaps the first internationally important demonstration of production on the "space stage," as a method of avoiding the distractions of scenery that Craig had so eloquently condemned; his, too, the earliest sustained big-theatre demonstration of the beauty and dramatic effectiveness of stage lighting in the Appia tradition.

Nevertheless, Fehling's historic place transcends that of a mere experimenter in stagecraft. As artist-director he was second to none in his way of *imagining* a play, in complete unity of performance, then presenting it with full control of all the elements of production. Before his acting company was liquidated by the Nazis, for being democratic, his productions such as *Masse-Mensch* became known around the world.

The German system of repertory gave exceptional opportunity for development of the *régisseur*, and there were a dozen of the type scattered in state theatres and art theatres throughout the land. Even opera, which always had suffered through the inherent difficulty of correlation of acting and music, came in for directional "treatment"; and such productions as those at the Prince Regent Theatre in Munich left the hearers with a sense of unity not before known to opera-goers. But the most typical achievement, in the history of production as an art, was that of Reinhardt, Jessner and Fehling. To these names must be added that of Erwin Piscator, if only because he became the extremist of the movement. At his own theatre in Berlin, politically more leftist than the *Volksbühne*, he whipped his productions into unified, exciting and unforgettable "versions" of the author's texts; but his insistence upon Communism in and out of his plays, and his ruthless "adapting" of texts, brought serious condemnation along with excited praise. A later period in America found him practically excluded from production in the commercial theatres; but as late as mid-century he was demonstrating his methods at a laboratory or work-shop theatre in New York. Happily he was able to return to Germany—unlike Brecht, to *West* Germany—for a further term of creative and sometimes wild experiment.

The Russian stage during the twenties and early thirties, before the party line was so insisted upon by bureaucrats, was the most revolutionary, and the most fruitfully experimental, in the Western world; and the chief figures were the artist-directors. Vsevolod Meyerhold, Eugene Vachtangoff and Alexander Tairoff were daring *régisseurs* who tried out new ways of organizing theatres, new relationships between audience and player, new sorts of music-drama, new acrobatic acting, bare stages, Constructivist settings (all the needed "practicables" nailed into one composition), new extremes of rewriting the classics.

As a background to all this wise and unwise experiment there was the achievement of the Moscow Art Theatre, the first world-famous exemplar of artist-direction and inspired ensemble production. The earliest achievement of the sometime amateur troupe had been in the field of illusional Realism, under the direction of Constantin Stanislavsky, who was internationally known as a creative *régisseur* even before Reinhardt. But the theatre which Stanislavsky directed from 1898, in conjunction with Vladimir Nemirovich-Danchenko, staged experimental productions as far afield from Realism as Shakespeare's *Hamlet* and Maeterlinck's *The Blue Bird* (the *Hamlet* with the assistance of Gordon Craig). Some of the younger actors were then fired with ideas of creative direction and of non-realistic presentation that led them to secede from the Art Theatre company.

Meyerhold was at once the most brilliant and the wildest of the rebels against Realistic methods, and he is remembered as the most influential of the artist-directors who transformed the Russian theatre after the Revolution of 1917. He had already scored limited successes in presenting the plays of the Symbolists, in establishing a new rapport of actors and audience, and in imposing a sustained sense of stylization upon each production. Given a theatre of his own by the

A costume design by Gordon Craig for his production of *Acis and Galatea*, London, 1902.

Bolshevik government, he went on to score success upon success, usually with plays which he personally made over, in performances rendered vivid by his imagination, in settings that always negated naturalism. These settings became finally three-dimensional Constructivist concoctions, whose complexities of platforms, steps, runways, bridges, ramps, etc., gave fullest opportunity to capitalize upon theatrical movement. Eventually, as happens to extreme individualists in the arts under a political dictatorship, Meyerhold was discharged from

A constructivist setting for Meyerhold's production of *Le Cocu Imaginaire*, Moscow, 1922. The structure was designed by L. Popova, who advocated "anti-decorative" settings but sometimes arrived at a distinctive machine-age decorativeness.

his post as not serving the best interests of the State. Actually he was sent to Siberia—or worse.

Vachtangoff was equally a student of Stanislavsky, and indeed directed at first a "Studio" of the Moscow Art Theatre. After the Revolution this became an independent playhouse and the scene of a succession of brilliant productions of rewritten classics and new plays, each remade into a theatrically stylized entity. *Turandot* was here given in an unforgettably lush and brilliant interpretation. In the very year of its presentation, 1922, Vachtangoff died, but the theatre subsidized by the Soviet Government in his name carried on his experimental and vital work.

The third of the outstanding artist-directors of the extreme Modernist group, Alexander Tairoff, had established a small personal theatre in Moscow at the beginning of World War I; but he got his chance to experiment widely and freely only under Soviet subsidization. He treated plays cavalierly, according to his own idea of synthetic and stylized production, and eventually he made the Kamerny Theatre one of the best known in the modern world.

There were other artist-directors of extraordinary talent in the Russia of 1917–1935; and, however one may dislike or distrust the Soviet nation, one can hardly deny that for nearly two decades it fostered the most exciting and fruitful series of experiments toward a twentieth-century art of production. The Western visitor found among the offerings in Leningrad and Moscow—and in many a distant capital —certain disturbing and frightening things, such as the blasphemous yet subtly effective anti-religious plays, and dramas turned from their purpose of evoking a purely theatrical emotion, in order to bolster a political theory and teach a Communistic lesson.

In the thirties it became apparent that no new playwrights of the stature of Tolstoy, Chekhov and Gorki had been developed under Communism, nor any as effective as the French, the British and the American of the same period. An even stronger hand was being held over the theatres by the policy-makers of the Kremlin, and before the mid-thirties the decline in Russian theatrical leadership had been noted in the West. At least one entire acting company escaped the country. The Habima Jewish Theatre, which had been encouraged under the more liberal cultural policies of Lenin's time, and which gained international fame with its rich production of *The Dybbuk* under Vachtangoff's direction, settled eventually in Israel. It was given a playhouse at Tel-Aviv and was accorded the name "Habimah: the National Theatre of Palestine." (In 1970 the company reopened in a building worthy of the National Theatre label.)

In France it was the sometime amateur Jacques Copeau who became the nation's first internationally known artist-director; and indeed he had, as writer and actor, and one might add, philosopher, an equipment uniquely fitted to render him the imaginative, all-seeing, all-directing *régisseur*. His theatre, the *Vieux Colombier* in Paris, has been sufficiently characterized in the preceding chapter. The only other international figure was Copeau's sometime lieutenant at the *Vieux Colombier*, Louis Jouvet, versatile actor, canny designer, and a director with a flair for virtuoso comedy effects. He was especially fortunate in his presentations of Molière, whose plays his company transported to the unoccupied countries of Europe when the Germans held Paris, and to Egypt and the South American capitals. His last visit to North

Louis Jouvet in Jean Giraudoux's *Ondine*, at the *Théâtre Athenée*, Paris, 1939. [By courtesy of the French Cultural Services, New York.]

Gordon Craig. The most gifted and most influential theorist and designer in the early twentieth-century theatre.

America was in 1951, when Montreal and New York saw a spirited and theatrically stylized production of *The School for Wives*, on a stage typically pared down to a platform for acting, yet with slight settings that somehow imparted a suggestion of richness and warmth (this time from designs by the famous Modern painter Christian Bérard). It was a performance that could be described only as typical Jouvet.

He died in that same year, 1951, in Paris, in his theatre. He had become France's foremost producer of superior plays, ranging from the classics of Molière to the newly poetic dramas of Jean Giraudoux and Paul Claudel. He was also the most beloved actor in France, and, to his intimates, one of the noblest characters. His position as leader of the progressive artist-producers in France was taken by Jean-Louis Barrault, who staged many revolutionary types of play independently, and then went on to modernize one of the national theatres in Paris, the Odéon, from 1959 on.

Paris in the thirties was accustomed to speak of the leaders of the modern theatre movement as "the Big Four," indicating that in addition to Jouvet there were three *régisseurs* who had gained national reputations as innovators and purveyors of stylized productions. They were Charles Dullin, also a graduate from Copeau's acting company, Georges Pitoeff, originally a Russian of Georgian descent, and Gaston Baty. It was they who brought to bear upon the rather static tradition of French playwriting the impact of the authors of the international art-theatre movement: Pirandello, Shaw, O'Neill, and even the mid-European Expressionist dramatists. Making their mark with these new offerings, together with the classics highly stylized, in various types of anti-Realistic presentations, the Four were eventually invited to produce at the National Theatres; to their influence can be credited the dissipation of the mustiness and the pedantry that had long given the *Comédie Française* reputation as one of the world's most conservative, and backward, theatres.

Gordon Craig became in those years the outstanding inspirational figure of the modern theatre; so much so that his early practical work as actor and as artist-director was all but forgotten. Lacking a theatre of his own, he made occasional trips to collaborate with other *régisseurs*, most notably to aid Stanislavsky's production of *Hamlet* at the Moscow Art Theatre as early as 1912, and to serve as *ober-régisseur* at a production of *The Pretenders* at the Royal Theatre in Copenhagen as late as 1926. Through Jacques Copeau who once planned a school of the theatre art with him, through Stanislavsky, and through a dozen others who visited him in exile and came away imaginatively inspired, Craig exerted an immeasurable influence upon production as an art. Only one

Two scenes from an imaginative production of Dante's *Divine Comedy* as designed by Norman Bel Geddes, 1921. A specially built stage planned as a stepped hillside with a crater in centre and plinths at the back, for movement of masses of actors in settings changed by lighting.

other Englishman might be mentioned as an artist-director renowned outside his own country: Harley Granville-Barker. His debt to Craig came less direct than through knowledge of the productions of Reinhardt and Stanislavsky. In the same period performances at the Old Vic often took on the virtues associated with art-theatre production—ensemble acting, harmoniously inconspicuous sets, and a flow of all the theatrical elements—but no single figure was outstanding as *régisseur*.

In America the value of creative directing was fully recognized, but the country developed *régisseurs* of national rather than international fame. Outstanding was Augustin Duncan, who did more than any other to make realistic plays live as unified emotional experiences for the audiences, with extraordinary character values. (With a resident company and continuous opportunity for production he might have given America an acting-machine second only to that of Stanislavsky and Nemirovitch-Dantchenko in Moscow). Arthur Hopkins, most notable artist among the Broadway producers, accepted the principle of one directing mind but deplored *virtuoso* directing, tried to discover creative actors, and left to them as much latitude as is consistent with unified total effect. It was he who, with Robert Edmond Jones, startled New York with an Expressionist mounting of *Macbeth* in 1921; and he achieved solid and notable productions of *The Poor Little Rich Girl, The Devil's Garden, The Jest, Redemption (The Living Dead Man), Hamlet,* with John Barrymore in the title role, *Richard III* and *Anna Christie.* More than any other American director he developed an individual and valuable theory of production—by a method termed "unconscious projection." Similarly Eddie Dowling, operating as actor and director on Broadway, gave himself over to "special" productions of the sort more common at the art theatres, and by some alchemy peculiar to his own genius endowed play after play with memorable spiritual values. In retrospect William Saroyan's *The Time of Your Life,* Philip Barry's *Here Come the Clowns* and Tennessee Williams' *The Glass Menagerie* afford examples of the several elements of theatre art brought into a quiet flow and made theatrically intelligible in a way that warms the heart years afterward.

More famous internationally, but for productions planned and not got onto the stage rather than for his occasional Broadway offering, was Norman Bel Geddes. His most famous published work, a project for the presentation of Dante's *Divine Comedy,* on a specially built "pit" stage, with masses of actors marshalled for theatrical effect, with controlled lights (and shadows) doing much of the service once assigned to "scenery," is still dramatically moving as one turns the pages of drawings. Next to Craig, Geddes had the most profound influence upon the budding American directors and producers—who, coming to the actual theatre, found no opportunity to stage projects so superbly imaginative, so theatrical. Geddes' *King Lear*, like his *Divine Comedy*, remained in the project stage; but his daring and imaginative setting for the production of *The Miracle* by Max Reinhardt in New York in 1924, gave the public some inkling of the impact those projects might

Costume design by Leon Bakst for the *Ballets Russes:* Echo in the ballet *Narcisse*, 1911.

have upon audiences if realized in terms of acting, lighting, movement and rhythmic words and sound. (See page 545.)

The principle of artist-direction was early accepted by the little theatres. Indeed many of the notable groups were organized by creative directors and touched importance only by virtue of that fact. Maurice Browne of the Chicago Little Theatre, Frederic McConnell of the Cleveland Playhouse, Oliver Hinsdell at the Dallas Little Theatre, and Sam Hume and Irving Pichel, first in the Middle West and later in California, literally "made" their respective theatres in the image of their own visions. Nearer the professional type, the Goodman Memorial Theatre in Chicago, from planning of the building through the productions of the pioneer seasons, was stamped with the personality and ideals of Thomas Wood Stevens; and the Pasadena Community Playhouse grew out of the work and thought—social thought as well as theatric—of Gilmor Brown. The absolute creativeness of these artists, all designers, in the large sense, as well as directors, collectively surpassed that of the playwrights or actors of the same period.

IF "FORM" is the ultimate consideration, if a welding together, under visionary direction, is the matter we are studying, then we may best call to witness the so-called *dance-drama*, for in that a "flow," a complete theatrical evocation, is most identifiable. Between 1905 and 1925 this type of theatre production was carried to new heights of freedom, of purity, of gorgeousness, particularly in the practice of the *Ballets Russes*. There are those who feel that a new art was created; but it was really the old art of the ballet, recreated under a new lavishness of painted scenery, a new freedom of the dance as revolutionized especially by Isadora Duncan, and the opportunities uncovered in electric stage lighting—all directed into a fresh unity.

This art of danced drama did not rival the spoken drama in its many forms; it involved no revolution of the whole stage art. It simply came as a well-nigh perfect thing of its own kind, filling one niche completely, satisfyingly. Or, changing the metaphor, it filled one corner of the theatre's field: the corner which is farthest from literature and psychologic and intellectual drama, the corner closest to free use of color, sound, and movement.

There was a *fin de siècle* theory, propounded as a reaction against too much literary, anecdotal and photographic activity, to the effect that the nearer any art touched toward the estate of music, the purer, the more "artistic" that art became. A distinction was drawn between the more æsthetic and the less æsthetic arts, between the less and the more logical or imitational. In the division of the stage art, the territory including dance-drama was "æsthetic drama," as against the other extreme, "the drama of thought." One approached the state of music in that it used largely abstract means; the other depended chiefly upon words, used logically. A serious composer would not think of directly imitating the sound of a waterfall, or a battle, or the neighing of a horse; the artists of the new ballet would depend as little as possible upon the natural world around them, and not at all upon spoken or sung words. They would use line and color abstractly rather than illustratively, sound tonally, and movement as pure dance, so far as possible. No logic, no tied story to be untied, no legend except as a skeleton, as an excuse for dancing: thus the intellect of the spectator would be stilled, only his senses left alert.

Picture to yourself the darkened interior of a theatre; the richly ornamented theatre, warmly colored, is particularly in keeping here. In the glamorous half-light, the music has prepared you. When the curtain is drawn a sea of color overwhelms you. Mountains of swelling scenery rise up into the very skies, hugely patterned curtains are half caught up, hang down, lie in folds across the floor; gay rugs, tapestries, bizarrely ornamented arches; vermilion, orange, madder, peacock blues, sea-green, purples, gold, silver—an impossible mixture of colors, but you find yourself gratefully drowned in it. The music goes on, lost to your consciousness at first, but reasserting itself, swelling with the color in that drowning of your senses. Then a dancing figure floats in, one or more, perhaps dozens, seemingly hundreds, myriads. Dancing, movement, rhythm, ever-changing line, pattern; all completely lost in the music, the picture. A perfect synthesis of sound, color, and movement, sheerly theatrical.

Costume designs by Bakst for the *Ballets Russes*. [From redrawings in *Play Production in America*, by Arthur Edwin Krows.]

A drama is played—it doesn't much matter what: one has been filled with a lasting pleasure, a pervading current of feeling, a glow. One only asks that the rhythm of music, lights, setting, dancing figures, continue until the curtain's fall.

One has been intoxicated; but it is an intoxication that vaguely lasts, that is pleasant in memory. One's senses have been bathed. A sort of sensuous ecstasy has taken possession. This is not the response one has felt after Greek tragedy. There one was purged by experience, taken beyond the world, left with a deeper ecstasy that clarified. Here one is of the world, knows it as lush, sensuously soft and infinitely pleasurable. The thing that the Russian ballet gives me, as against Greek drama, is the thing that Gauguin gives me, as against the profounder rhythms of Cezanne or El Greco. It is decorative drama, with little story to be followed or dialogue to be listened for; it is a sheer surface delight.

The legends are as likely as not to be Oriental. *Scheherazade* at base is an unrefined tale of Arabian Nights monarchs, harems, intrigues, passion. It is full of eroticism and violence that are hardly noticed; these elements are lost in the total sensuous design. Other legends are less turgid, less wildly passionate: they are picked, one imagines, more for their setting than for the story. The whole show may be stylized, dancing included, from feeling for a color, or a place, or a musical phrase.

It was Leon Bakst who created the most sumptuous of the *Ballets Russes* backgrounds and costumes. No modernist simplification of the setting for him! He took the old muddy painted scenery, sifted the mud out, poured in buckets of raw color, and created stage pictures of more prodigious proportions, vaster spaces, and more overwhelming colorfulness than any ever invented before. His fellow Russians, Benois, Roerich, Golovine, and Anisfeld were hardly less lavish and brilliant. Whether Bakst (and his is still the most celebrated name out of the *Ballets Russes* history) actually became artist-director, one does not know. The most famous company was known as Diaghileff's *Ballets Russes*, and presumably Sergei Diaghileff was *régisseur* or at least *ober-régisseur*.

The true *Ballets Russes*, in this sense, as something lush, orientally colorful, and overwhelming, went through many modifications in the twenties and thirties. New dancers appeared to fill the places of Nijinski, Pavlova, Karsavina and Fokine, seemingly incomparable artists all of whom were in the company that came from the Imperial Palace theatre at St. Petersburg to Paris in 1909, a company that took Western audiences by storm. New materials were found by the choreographers far from the typically exotic fairy-tale themes seen in the *Prince Igor* suite and *Petrouchka*. The Diaghileff company split and split again, so that several claimants to the *"Original Ballets Russes"* title enlivened the international scene; and eventually something very like the *Ballets Russes* product, though seldom so magnificently colorful, could be seen in the performances on tour of the Swedish Ballet or the Sadler's Wells Ballet or companies organized by one or another French or Russian or American *entrepreneur*.

A scene in *Lysistrata* as produced by the Moscow Art Theatre Musical Studio. A decorative constructivist erection on a curtainless stage, designed by Isaac Rabinovich. On a revolving platform, the construction showed a different face for each new scene. [Photograph by courtesy of Morris Gest.]

A new hybrid form of dance-drama was developed especially by the Germans and the Americans when the full force of the pioneering of Isadora Duncan and Ruth St. Denis met the impulse from Russia; and eventually Germany sent out to the world a notable character-dance variant in the Jooss Ballet, as well as the "purer" dance *divertissements* of Mary Wigman; while in America Martha Graham brought imagination and originality to the creation of dance-dramas approaching the abstract. Certainly there has been a renaissance of the dance art since world-audiences first saw the miracle of Isadora Duncan as dancer, the miracle of utter surrender of masses of spectators to the spell of the dancing of one woman, to music, on a stage hung simply with blue curtains; and in this renaissance there has been no element more surprising than the variety of it. Against the colorful, decorative, lulling quality of *Petrouchka* one may place Kurt Jooss' *The Green Table*, which was a brilliant satire on international political conferences—and one has dance-drama at almost unimaginable extremes. Or beside the memory of the overwhelming Bakst-Diaghileff *Scheherazade* place for contrast one of Martha Graham's starkly modern but wholly moving dance programs, and you have the measure of a vast creative pattern. All these impulses and end-results are now part of history; but happily all were destined to be as alive as ever as the theatre entered into the second half of the century. Curiously the older ballet forms, against which Diaghileff and Fokine had revolted before the first World War, have been brilliantly fostered, since 1920, by the Soviet Government, in their Czarist theatre in Leningrad.

The literary-minded critics, fearing for the dramatists, long continued to deplore "the craze for glorified production." Not so much disturbed by the competition of the dance-drama as apprehensive of the revamping, even emasculation, of texts at the hands of dictatorial art-directors, they opposed (in England especially) the "excesses" of a Gordon Craig or a Max Reinhardt. Nevertheless what happened in the history of the theatre in the twenties and the thirties is most illuminated in light of directors' imagination. Even in the field where written drama, word-for-word dialogue, is the basic theatrical ingredient, the influence of the artist-director and of the ensemble ideal was revolutionary. The most taut realistic plays, thirty years after the burst of activity in the art theatres, were being staged with a unity of emotional effect, a sustained theatrical flow, gained from the example of those artists who were exploring the paths leading away from Realism.

Each mention of this sort of seeming anomaly leads us back to the Moscow Art Theatre, which in its early years had been particularly concerned with realistic presentation, and had developed its perfection of ensemble acting in that mode as notably as in interpretations of Shakespeare or Maeterlinck. There are play texts so realistic or so thought-provoking that they seem to defeat the artist-director before his company is assembled. The very term "thesis play" implies predominance of an element untheatric and unglamorous. And those slice-of-life plays that are intended to afford the audience a glimpse of living in the raw, they *cannot* be treated with other than imitative technique. But the better part of Realism, as say Ibsen and Chekhov, can be brought to something approaching a distinctive theatrical entity at the hands of an artist-director using his materials orchestrally. I have already mentioned the memorable production of *John Ferguson* as creatively shaped by Augustin Duncan. I felt something of the same living theatrical intensity in Ibsen's *The Wild Duck* as directed for the Actor's Theatre by Dudley Digges, in O'Neill's *Anna Christie* as directed by Arthur Hopkins, in certain productions of the Irish

Players. But all of us experienced the quality, the fullness, most notably in the performances of the Moscow Art Theatre company (which, by the way, the Soviet authorities suffered to carry on free of serious interference).

It has been said that the directors of this troupe "treated" a play text to so complete a realization of the author's intention that they came

Constantin Stanislavsky, leading spirit of the Moscow Art Theatre, as Prince Ivan Shuisky in Alexei Tolstoy's *Tsar Fyodor Ivanovitch*. [By courtesy of the Walter Hampden Memorial Library at the Players, New York.]

out at a sort of reality beyond surface life; at a *spiritualized* Realism. There is a point at which a Realism apparently true to the smaller observed facts of life plunges suddenly to planes of revealment and heartbreak; and the Art Theatre actors were adept at carrying the spectator along facilely, and suddenly bringing him to a sort of illumination, to understanding. The plays in which they accomplished this, under Constantin Stanislavsky's direction, were not the journalistic Realism of the Broadway and West-End best-seller playwrights, but the serener, constantly repressed Realism of Chekhov, or an immense canvas of contrasting characters such as the dramatization of Dostoievsky's *The Brothers Karamazoff*. Perhaps this is not Realism essentially, for Realism's sake, but in the one case a realistic mask which is suddenly lowered to reveal a spiritual or a theatrical truth, and in the other a character display theatricalized far beyond naturalness.

At any rate, the point here is that the artist-*régisseur* Stanislavsky, by virtue of his ability as visionary and practical director, brought into being a playing company more notable than any other in modern recorded history, for the perfect ensemble impression conveyed to the audience. In plays like *The Blue Bird* and *Hamlet* it helped to crystallize the thing called Stylization, which artist-directors were working for everywhere in connection with revivals. It showed that new plays, even realistic ones, could be submitted to a creative *régisseur* and to actors with precision of presentation, and gain unaccustomed values in the revealment of nuances and colorings. I say *even* because it seems to me clear after these many years of the increasing importance of production as a craft, that such marvelous treatment of Ibsen and Chekhov was an exceptional thing, possibly not on the main road to the future: that the rediscovery of theatrical values served to turn a new generation of dramatists and directors to what is anti-realistic and Expressionistic.

So far as the American theatre was concerned we arrive at the truth that nothing in the lists of Realism was so rewarding and memorable as rare plays like *The Green Pastures*, produced in 1930, or *Our Town*, seen first in 1938, which at every turn negated what is natural. *The Green Pastures* was understandingly dramatized by Marc Connelly from Roark Bradford's anecdotal retelling of Bible stories, as transformed in the Negro imagination. It restored to the stage, in a performance combining reverence and humor, a long-lost quality of ritualistic grandeur. In beautifully evocative settings by Robert Edmond Jones, and with moving choral accompaniment, the play came through to the spectator as symphonic and spiritually impressive.

In *Our Town* Thornton Wilder offered a touching little fable of life in a New England village, presenting his characters as individuals with universal implications, illustrating, always theatrically, the life-path of representative Man. His insistence that there should be not only no scenery but no settings, just a bare stage, was no more a declaration of anti-Realistic faith than his placing of the final act in a cemetery that is also strangely Heaven. The play, which could hardly have found a producer thirty years earlier, was soon playing in "advanced" theatres around the world. It might be taken as the type achievement of the 1910–1940 period. An old magic had come into the playhouse again, and some of the responsibility for it might well be credited back to the artist with whom the chapter opened, Gordon Craig, and to the "impossible idealists" whom he had inspired.

Scene from the original production of *Our Town* by Thornton Wilder, New York, 1938. With Frank Craven, Martha Scott and John Craven. [By courtesy of the Museum of the City of New York.]

CHAPTER
24

Machine-Age Developments: Moving Pictures, Radio, Television

SIXTY years is a short span in the perspective of art's history. But as regards the theatre, the *quantitative* expansion of certain minor and mechanically reproduced sorts of "play" has been, since the early years of the twentieth century, phenomenal. Theatre is with us as never before; yet it is theatre lacking the integrity, and the intense and intimate appeal, of what was, until shortly after 1900, the whole theatre—and now is accorded a divided place as "the legitimate theatre."

The legitimate commercial theatre exists as always, though both quantitatively and qualitatively it has suffered a sad decline since the great days of the twenties and early thirties: quantitatively especially in the United States; qualitatively especially in the Soviet Union and other areas where creativeness was choked off if it did not follow a political line. The little and special theatres continued to prosper. But if one could consult such a picture-map of the theatres of the world as was suggested in Chapter I, the legitimate houses, big and little, would appear amazingly outnumbered by something called "picture theatres."

Less than sixty years ago all the public theatres owned stages on which living actors appeared. But at mid-century there could be counted some 85,000 theatres in which no actor in person had ever acted. These were, indeed, theatres for showing pictures of acting.

They depart in curious ways from the norm as we have seen it develop down the ages. This playhouse actually *has* no stage, only a curtain at the end of the auditorium. It offers not the old two-hours of entertainment; indeed, as often as not its play or pair of plays goes on continuously, with no distinction between matinée and evening performance; and—can you imagine it?—patrons drift in and out casually, recking little the time of "first curtain."

Moving pictures are a tremendous thing in many ways. The potentialities of cinema art are, creatively, vast, and we all have witnessed photo-plays that moved us profoundly and left us with the sense of having experienced a dramatic story continuously entertaining, and, though oh! so rarely, spiritually purging. Against each of these rare creative offerings we have had to chalk up so many hundreds of trivial, false and puerile cinematic plays that millions of us have all but despaired of the art; and we have stayed away from the theatres so persistently that in the nineteen-sixties the biggest thing about Hollywood has been its retrenchment program.

Nevertheless the moving-picture theatre continues to overshadow its legitimate prototype. It is incomparably more popular: cheapness in both senses has something to do with that. It claims the largest (and most blatant) playhouses in the world, and those farthest-flung from the centers of dramatic enterprise; and the legend over the portal or the billboard may read cinema or *lichtspiel* or whatever is the Chinese or Afghanistan or Kaffir equivalent of "picture house." Moreover, as a further obscuring factor, in scanning our once simple map of the world's theatres, there is a sort of playhouse art that has been extended into untold millions of homes: first as radio, a sort of blind stage art because the actors are only heard, not seen; then as television, which brings a fair equivalent of picture-drama into one's living-room —and this may be the most tremendous change of all.

In this book I have tried to show the major developments of the theatre art in relation to major changes in human civilization: the flowering of the drama in Greece; its degradation under the materialism of Rome; the reverent plays in the Church, then decline, in the Dark Ages and the Middle Ages; a reflowering in the Renaissance period, climaxed in Elizabethan England; the slow coming of democracy and the overthrow of kings, with theatre descending to the familiar, the common, the photographic, and poetry and imagination whipped off the stage in the name of Realism.

Some of us had thought, in the twenties, that a renaissance might be in the making. Noting especially that a new style in architecture had pushed up into view, grown organically out of modern needs and visions, the first truly new style in six centuries, and that the arts of painting and sculpture had, within a generation, undergone a revolution that destroyed standards and codes held sacred three hundred years, changing entirely the complexion of exhibits in art galleries and museums—noting these revolutionary accomplishments in sister arts, and similar ones in the near-theatrical art of the dance, we pictured to ourselves a revolutionary overturn and advance in the theatre. Certainly we got as far as exploration of many of the roads of anti-Realism, and our playwrights provided notable examples of poetic and Expressionistic drama, truly revolutionary and finely theatrical. There

A scene from *The Golem*, a German film based on the Jewish folk tale, in a setting devised by the architect Hans Poelzig. Typical of the vast spaces and the armies of actors possible only to the moving-picture theatre.

was, around 1930, a ferment, a state of flux, of which the little and art theatres were the conspicuous sign and the result.

But the legitimate theatre, the commercial theatre, is cumbrous, slow to change, expensively weighted. It responds but sluggishly to the stimulus of new thinking and new creative vision. And under the burden of businessman-ownership of the physical theatres and their equipment, the revolution in the theatre art, as compared with those others, was halted, postponed. As to plays, Realism was still king on Broadway, while the old game of entertaining tired businessmen and tourists with farce, burlesque and musical comedy continued as always. Under these conditions, in the midst of a generation-long decline of the legitimate drama, and legitimate acting, it is fair to ask whether the picture-theatre and its radio and television variants do not best represent the theatre in the age of commerce and invention.

Now truly this is a mechanical extension of the old stage art. It could have been invented in no other era than ours. It could have spread its net of entertainment over the world only after the modern, the almost contemporary, development of speeded-up communication and travel. But there are those who will point out that this alone does not make it the best, the essential, part of the theatre. The theatre of the living actor remains the heart of the art. No one who has ever felt the lure of the personally acted drama in an intimate theatre can be fooled for more than a few moments at a time into forgetting that picture-drama is a *photograph* of action, not the action itself. One enjoys it, of course, but as one enjoys well-taken photographs of sculpture. Seeing the sculpture itself would be the incomparably realer experience.

This disability, that it is shown always at one remove from the living thing, will be on the moving picture and television so long as they aim at those effects that have belonged, historically, to the stage drama. There are, of course, potentialities of the picture medium that open up realms of enjoyment impossible to the stage of the living actor; but these have been too little explored and capitalized upon—though the "documentaries" that began seriously with Robert Flaherty's *Nanook of the North* and *Moana* and flowered especially in the works of the Russian Eisenstein, and the experiments in abstract design that reached a magnificent climax in the Creation sequences of Walt Disney's *Fantasia* have shown us a characteristic cinematic beauty. However, before going back to trace in a few paragraphs the history of the picture-medium, let us pause a moment over the changes in the field of machinery in the legitimate theatre.

On the historic stage we have seen this machinery progressively developed from Roman times to the heyday of revolving and wagon stages in the early twentieth century. Has the staging paraphernalia arrived at new complexity and glory in the speeded-up machine age, has it become a super-stage-machine, with a further extension of its amazing powers to speed production and surprise audiences? Well frankly, that stage machinery has been all but scrapped. The entire intricate edifice of engines, wagons, turntables, rockers, gridirons, etc., etc., has been discarded by many progressive designers and producers. Not entirely, but so substantially that the outstanding paradox of the machine-age legitimate theatre is that machinery has been swept

Utter simplification of the scene for concentration of interest upon the actors, in a Broadway realistic play. Setting by Robert Edmond Jones for the examination scene in *The Devil's Garden*, as produced by Arthur Hopkins in New York about 1918.

out. The secret is, of course, that the machine accomplishments never were theatric in the deeper creative sense: they were an intrusion, with their startling "effects," or else an aid to picture-making. They belonged typically to the realistic age, to the scientific-thought age. They were used to perpetuate dying types of drama. Artists of the new age will let them return to the stage warily if at all.

But electricity for lighting brought new and perfectly assimilated wonders into the art of staging. The craft of acting and a medium involving movement require adequate illumination—and did not have it for centuries, from the time when shows went indoors to, roughly, 1900. Now the artist-director has at his command a range of lighting expressive of every nuance of dramatic feeling, in color, intensity, design. This indeed is a matter of machine-age precision, an attribute of stage art never before possible. And in the larger view, here is an element quite truly contributing to, furthering, the glamour, the glow, of essential theatre. In the average production today the acted drama is unfolded to an unnoticed accompaniment of color-light that reenforces the dramatic and spiritual values while warming the production with a sensuous glow, a flush. The name likely to be best remembered in history in connection with the twentieth century advance in lighting is that of Adolph Linnebach, a German designer of settings who made practical many of the effects visioned by Appia and Craig.

IN 1889, in New Jersey, workers in the laboratories of Thomas A. Edison completed a practical machine for exhibiting moving pictures. One person could look into a box and see events pass photographically. In that "kinetoscope" many principles and inventions were involved for which individual credit might fairly be divided among a halfdozen experimenters who had worked in New York and London as well as in remote places in California and in Eastern Europe. But it was Edison's inventiveness that brought into existence a machine that showed photographed action automatically—even as much as 13 seconds of it. Other mileposts on the way to the present-day super-film were passed: films fifty feet in length; films thrown on a screen, outside the box (or was the box enlarged and the spectator taken into it?); and then a 2000-foot film "reporting" the Ober-Ammergau Passion Play. French and British inventors were especially successful in standardizing projection equipment and "shooting" documentary scenes.

It is generally considered that the first "screen drama" was *The Great Train Robbery* presented under the Edison trade-mark in New York in 1903. From then on "the art of the motion picture" grew steadily toward bigness, toward self-reliance, toward elaboration. What had been a photographic toy was thenceforward one of the arts of the theatre, with dramatists, actors, playhouses—and unfortunately speculator-owners who knew art only in its most vulgar forms.

The growth of the picture-drama has been attended with stirring rise-from-obscurity incidents. The change to the contemporary "picture palaces" out of the abandoned barroom nickelodeons is of itself a considerable step-up for an art so young. More than twenty thousand theatres for pictures alone, in the United States—and among them more examples of "the largest theatre in the world" than any country ever claimed before. Studios that have grown from what the word originally meant to vast plants with multiple stages and unbelievable property rooms and zoos and whatnot. And Hollywood from being a favorably known minor suburb has become the most famous stage production centre in the world, and the most cursed city. It has its marvels, its Babylons built and destroyed, its armies of beautiful girls, its monumental "turnover," its collection of native and foreign leading artists. It also has furnished more thousands of miles of drivel, of fatuous, trivial and puerile entertainment than any other amusement centre in history.

Startling, too, in relation to any known form of theatre in the past, are the attendance figures. Let us be conservative. Let us say that this week not more than 250,000,000 people attend moving-pictures. Still that is a considerable figure. A year's attendance goes a bit beyond the point where ciphers have any meaning for us. All the spectators at all the Greek dramas ever played, in the theatres of Greece and her colonies, and of the later Roman Empire, over a period of eight centuries, probably numbered fewer than the attendants at the world's 86,000 picture houses last week. The next Hollywood super-film will play to more people in its first year after release than *Hamlet* has in three and a half centuries. To accomplish this the pictures have had to proceed like an industry. No wonder the picture people have made claims about the fourth largest industry (or is it the third?) and talk loosely about enormous social influences, etc.

In the modern world great industries live and grow by competition for the patronage of the masses. An art turned industry brings down its appeal to attract the uncritical, the uneducated, the unwary. The moving-picture people, in being so overwhelmingly successful at the box-office sacrificed many of the qualities that make for mature appeal. They cheapened the general run of their product to attract childish and mediocre intelligences (despite many marginal films of which we shall take notice in a moment).

Certainly they created in a new sense a democratic theatre, provided dramatic entertainment as a staple experience for millions who never or very seldom would have got into theatres of the living actor. That they betrayed these new democratic audiences, with a slick, superficial product, is a commonplace of criticism. As to the enormous social influence they claimed, it has generally been negative, even harmful: by and large Hollywood drama has set up a false ideal, of materialistic attainment, of easy living, of night-club indulgence, of un-Christian love of the heroics of war and crime and unearned success.

This is history; it was continuing history in the late nineteen-sixties. And as moving pictures continue their competitive struggle with television for popular favor, their owner-producers seem to see no other way than to render more spectacular and more salable their girl-and-music shows, their crime plays, their "Westerns"—the latter a distinctive product of the American studios, and the most wholesome of the lot (and enormously popular among the Chinese, and for that matter the French and the Germans and the Italians, as well as in Keokuk and Kalamazoo); though all but a fraction are melodramatic, pseudo-heroic and puerile, strictly in the Nick Carter literary tradition. When

Moving pictures opened up a new world of "effects" for the scene designer. While remaining essentially realistic, the artist could build ideal settings for processional and mass scenes, romantically picturesque but architecturally solid. The sketches here were made by Klaus Richter for the Ernst Lubitsch production in Germany of *Carnival in Toledo*. The picture well composed, the acting space cleverly framed.

Hollywood attempts to be serious, too, there is often an unwhole-some superficiality, a slick effectiveness that is reflected out of cheap fiction.

Nevertheless, the record of an art is eventually written in terms of the outstanding "masterpieces"; and there have been enough films approaching that category to warrant a brief review. The early pro-ducers, after the prize-fight-reporting stage was past, and when multi-reel pictures became possible (about 1910), saw the film medium only as a means of duplicating stage plays, with some additional advantages in the direction of realism, in more extensive backgrounds, in lifelike presentation of character-emotion (closeups, fadeouts, etc.). What they could not copy from nature and silent actors in photographs, they presented in sub-titles, in wording flashed on the screen between photo-sequences.

At first the producers of slap-stick comedy were most successful; they shrewdly grasped at one potentiality impossible to the legitimate stage, the chase—and the old Mack Sennett farcical skits are as genuine as anything out of the pioneer period. We remember best, perhaps, the early Chaplin Essanay "shorts," which included their share of slap-stick, and often the chase in which the hero outdistanced and humbled the cops, because Chaplin brought comedy a little over toward the thoughtful side. At any rate the greatest comedian of the twentieth century there began his career—though once he had been a minor figure in turns at music-halls (vaudeville houses) in his native London. He appeared in his first film, with Sennett, in 1914, and in 1915 had progressed to featured player in two-reelers. By 1916 he was inter-nationally famous and was recipient of a fantastically large salary.

In Hollywood, which at this time was outdistancing all eastern or foreign centres of production, the more serious impulses were climaxed in 1914 in the showing of *The Birth of a Nation*, an epic drama of the Civil War, directed by D. W. Griffith. It was perhaps the first photoplay with sweep and grandeur; though Adolph Zukor's *Quo Vadis* antedated it by a year, and was no doubt the truer begin-ning of the spectacular melodramas that were to appear as "historic recreations" through later years: *Ben Hur, The Ten Commandments, Samson and Delilah*, and on down to *David and Bathsheba* and a new again-enlarged *Quo Vadis*—all skillfully and grandly combining re-ligious themes with sex appeal, in stories unfolded in blown-up settings, gorgeous costumes and processional scenes with thousands of "extras." One director boasted that his spectacles had played to more than three billion spectators, to a box-office take of $362,000,000. Assuredly the-atre had become Big Business.

The adaptation of successful stage plays continued, however, the staple of Hollywood—a village that had grown up into the undisputed centre of the motion-picture industry during World War I, when the producing studios of France, Germany, England and Italy were closed or limited to slight activity. Commercially, America was to maintain its leadership in the between-wars period. The adaptation of popular magazine stories and of best-seller novels followed; and some of the foremost authors of the era were taken to Hollywood, generally with little effect upon the quality of the film turnout, since the entrenched studio writers, who "knew film technique" and "knew what the public wants," had the final say.

Technically, new milestones were passed, as specialized theatres were built, and the number of reels shown went up to five, then seven or eight. Color was added, in a few passages at first, then to the whole film, and by 1918 color films were well established as a "feature." By 1930 all the big spectacles and many musical comedies were being projected in full color. In 1928 the sound track was synchronized with the film track, and as soon as the then 20,000 picture theatres of America could be equipped for the "talkies," the silent movie lapsed into historical obsolescence.

If no great actors were developed in the early days (aside from Charlie Chaplin), there was no dearth of popular favorites who enjoyed enormous box-office draw. These were mostly lovable people who largely played themselves, with no sure hold upon histrionic ability. Perhaps they are important because they were known and loved internationally, by more millions of spectators than any actor had ever dreamed of in the past. Mary Pickford, William S. Hart, Tom Mix, Douglas Fairbanks and Rudolph Valentino are names that stir nostalgic memories for all who followed the pictures between 1914 and 1925. A more serious note was struck by a group largely imported from European countries, and oftener seen in dramas making pretense to literary or social values: Pola Negri, Greta Garbo, Emil Jannings, Erich von Stroheim, Gloria Swanson, Marlene Dietrich; and to this list may be added Lillian Gish and Fredric March among native-born favorites. Certain individualists—eccentrics, if you will—touched us by sheer theatrical genius: most notably W. C. Fields and Mae West.

Among film plays certainly masterpieces were few, and continued to be up to the nineteen-sixties. The stories, the texts, even when taken from the dramas or novels of top-ranking authors, Tolstoy or Dickens or O'Neill, or more likely the current best-seller writers, Steinbeck or Hilton or Cronin, were generally so emasculated in the process of "adaptation" by the industry's hack writers, that integrity, individuality and flavor were lost. The memorable productions were those in which a passable script was rendered alive by a beloved actor's performance—with a further vividness and meaning added occasionally by inspired directing. Thus one remembers most easily the series of not very important plays rendered enjoyable by the ingratiating James Stewart, from *Mr. Smith Goes to Washington* to *Harvey;* Gary Cooper, whose successes were as "serious" as *For Whom the Bell Tolls* and *Sergeant York* and as light as *Ball of Fire;* or *Ninotchka*, made striking by the brilliant Greta Garbo; or the many performances illuminated by the acting of the ever-charming Ronald Colman or the ever-lovely Claudette Colbert; or the more solid and varied acting of Fredric March, who consistently sought sound vehicles, as did Leslie Howard, as does, more recently, Gregory Peck.

A specially happy field for historical pictures was found in the biographical film, which became popular in the thirties. A long series of absorbing life stories appeared, from *The Story of Louis Pasteur* (1936) and *The Life of Emile Zola*, made striking and sympathetic by the performances of Paul Muni, through *Abe Lincoln in Illinois*, with a noble performance by Raymond Massey, to Orson Welles' slightly veiled impersonation of a then-living celebrity in *Citizen Kane*.

If it has to be noted that many of the first line of actors in Hollywood were not natives of the United States—Colman, Massey and Muni in addition to those mentioned in a paragraph above, and later the brightest stars among our actresses, Ingrid Bergman and Vivien Leigh— it should be recorded too that waves of foreign films, though never competing commercially with the American product, again and again proved the greater artistry of foreign directors and actors. In the twenties we had hardly adjusted ourselves to the truth that the Germans were producing films which for artistic soundness and rich characterization were superior to the home product when Russia sent us a series of incomparably moving films. Cinema history was made by *Variety, The Cabinet of Dr. Caligari* and *Metropolis. Dr. Caligari* constituted the one most successful demonstration of Expressionistic technique in setting and directing a picture play. *Variety* showed how far the Germans had progressed in giving depth to Realism, and with *The Last Laugh* (made by the director F. W. Murnau and the actor Emil Jannings), took to the rest of the world a theretofore unrealized technique of virtuoso camera-shooting, with marvellously revealing sequences of detailed imaging.

The Russians produced the no less vivid and startling *Potemkin*, the story of the mutiny of a warship's crew under the Czarist regime, with unforgettable mass scenes, directed by Sergei Eisenstein. A series of later Eisenstein films, generally treating of the Bolshevik revolution

Two scenes from the German film *The Cabinet of Dr. Caligari*, most famous example of the use of pictorial expressionism to further the mood of a dramatic production.

of 1917 or its historical background, though semi-documentary, seemed to foreign audiences no less brilliant; and certainly they were emotionally moving and socially compelling in a way then unknown to Western pictures.

After World War II, with the resumption of imports from Europe, other films arrived to strengthen the hands of critics of the mass-produced, synthetic Hollywood product. France gave us some delightful, simply effective picture-plays, as in *The Baker's Wife* and *The Well-Digger's Daughter*, as well as experiments in modernist techniques. Italy sent over *The Bicycle Thief*, *The Open City*, *To Live in Peace*, and other bits of naturalism so honestly and unpretentiously filmed that they went straight to our hearts. And as recently the British studios have shown a knack for turning out heart-warming story-book films such as *Love on the Dole* and *Passport to Pimlico*, together with the more serious *Odd Man Out*, *In Which We Serve*, and Olivier's *Henry V*.

American events in the later years, say after 1935, could be counted rather by the large, if not pretentious and colossal things: *The Grapes of Wrath*; *Gone with the Wind* (a record-breaker in length, in the 100,000,000 people played to, in profits, and in its long runs—more than fours year, for instance, in London); *The Ox-Bow Incident*; *The Song of Bernadette*; and *The Treasure of Sierra Madre*. Of quieter and possibly more sincere films the public responded memorably to *Our Town* and *Good Bye, Mr. Chips* (the original version, not the inferior one released in 1970). These all, of course, represented film adaptations of already popular novels or stage plays. The dramas thought up by Hollywood's kept writers were still generally superficial and false, where not sensational and bathetic. One picture play of the period stood out for its honesty, dramatic validity and tense emotion, *The Informer*, a story of Ireland in the days of the Rebellion, as directed by John Ford.

Far from all these in intention, method and result was the collective work of the designer Walt Disney. Setting aside his original animated cartoons, through which a handful of characters became familiar to international audiences, and one, Mickey Mouse, a favorite (with children) hardly less renowned than Cinderella, Alice and Br'er Rabbit, one may say that Disney's long films such as *Bambi*, *Snow White* and *Pinocchio* afforded a form of dramatic entertainment not before known. Ingratiating, pretty, and with occasional brief flashes of brilliant artistry, these nevertheless dropped to frequent levels of calendar-art sentimentality and candy-like sweetness of design.

But in *Fantasia* Disney accomplished, in long stretches of abstract or near-abstract composition, the finest original achievement in a medium that lends itself peculiarly to the free manipulation of light and color. In the Creation scenes of *Fantasia* rhythmic visual design was utilized for its own sake, beautifully and movingly. Call it pattern or form or merely continuous movement (which is the first condition of cinema) wrought into a dramatic sequence, it had a quality that made for imaginative enjoyment. It was a lone product in a field in

Charles Chaplin, first immortal actor of the screen age, and, in theatre history, possibly the one actor seen by the greatest number of spectators.

which moving-picture artists might have scored some of their most characteristic triumphs. Perhaps because it occurred to Disney and his associates that without the human actor (or his drawn image) they could not sustain any sort of story-line, they set their superb abstract compositions between some ordinary actual scenes and immature cartoon sequences.

In any case this was one peak of moving-picture achievement during the first fifty years of the medium. A contrasting one, over where the actor still stands supreme, had been attained long before by Charlie Chaplin, who as actor and clown overshadowed all his contemporaries

on the legitimate stage, making the old art of pantomime live again
in a variant both personal to him and unique to the medium. In pictures such as *City Lights, The Gold Rush* and *The Kid* he proved
himself a great artist of the theatre, creative, individual and authentic.

It must be added—we are violating chronology here—that the centers
of experiment and of artistic production shifted so that, in the nineteen
sixties especially, the most talked-about films were produced in European studios. Hollywood ceased to make headline news—except for
such a colossal failure as *Myra Breckinridge*, a multi-million-dollar
film that was termed by more than one critic "a disgrace to the human
race." Something like an international cult grew up. The names most
frequently cited were not those of actors but of creative directors:
especially Jean Renoir, Ingmar Bergman, Roberto Rossellini, Michelangelo Antonioni, Jean-Luc Godard, François Truffaut, Federico Fel-
lini, and Luis Buñuel.

THE miracle of Radio, of the broadcasting of news, music and drama
from central studios to millions of listeners, developed especially in
the years 1919–1925, against a background of invention in wireless
telegraphy and wireless telephony. So many receiving sets had been
sold in America in 1922 and 1923 that in the latter year more than 600
broadcasting stations were sending programs over the air waves. Interference among wave lengths then led the Government to step in and
regulate "channels"; though in all other respects the new medium was
left unhindered, to develop through private, that is, commercial enterprise. This free system was to persist and lead to the advertiser-
dominated radio industry of later years. European countries, reserving
the broadcasting privilege to government agencies, found it necessary
in 1925–26 to unscramble and allot channels internationally, forming
a regulative union with headquarters in Switzerland. Slow but inevitable
spread of radio broadcasting to every civilized part of the world followed.

The miracle of radio was recognized by theatre artists as offering
a fantastic enlargement of their art. And indeed—beyond the one great
limitation that sound alone must carry the play—the possibilities were
startling. Yet a generation later a disillusioned historian could only report that there was no exciting story of a characteristic extension of
theatre art through radio. The primary service of the medium to the
public had been in the direct dissemination of news, an incalculable
boon; in broadcasting of music; and in providing a new form of parlor
entertainment in quiz-shows and patter shows. After nearly fifty years
it is clear that the controlling powers developed no variation of theatre

art especially fitting to radio, and turned up not a single significant actor not already known in legitimate production or moving pictures. Radio as theatre art was still, in 1950, near the infantile stage. Certainly between 1935 and 1950 no dramatic program in America was looked forward to weekly, with anticipation of certain enjoyment, as were the superb symphony programs (often conducted by a Toscanini or a Stokowski) or the quiz show *Information Please*.

The two types of play in which radio script-writers pioneered, serial or strip dramas played in installments daily for months or even years, and crime plays, both led in the direction of the corruption of public taste. The special broadcasts by the few organizations pretending to standards of artistry too often were popular recent moving-picture "successes" further watered down; or capsule versions of older Broadway plays or of classics. There have been memorable exceptions to the rule of mediocre adaptation, as we shall see—but in general the rule holds.

Two circumstances led to the degraded place of the theatre art in radio. First (in the United States and some other countries), the medium was taken over by the advertisers, and they have proceeded with the usual businessman's assumption that the lower the artistic appeal the more numerous will be the audience. Second, the time limitation upon the producer, the rigid time-table by which hours or half-hours are allotted to the play, forced a system of cutting and adaptation which has generally proved fatal to drama-integrity. For a news event the time-table could be swept away. All can remember the sense of the importance of our radios to us, the immediacy of the appeal and the magnificent coverage, on the day, say, of President Kennedy's death, or when Pearl Harbor was attacked. Time limitations were scrapped; but no radio *play* is ever important enough for the succeeding program to be postponed for an instant. The British and those other peoples who avoided the incubus of advertising, fared better in this matter; programs could be fitted around play performances with some elasticity. And indeed, British audiences have heard better drama, and generally better played, than have American. There is regular programming of Shakespeare's plays, and frequent offerings of the Greek classics, Shaw, Chekhov, Ibsen and other historically approved dramatists. Nevertheless, in Britain as in America, the foremost contemporary authors have generally shunned radio as a field for original writing.

By way of balancing this dismal record, it must be said that American audiences, if they are willing to overlook the insistent advertising, have been able to enjoy regularly many of the foremost comics of the time (mostly graduates from the vaudeville stage); and that occasionally a beloved actress of the living theatre has put on the air a moving version of a classic or an absorbing contemporary drama: say, Eva LeGallienne or Ethel Barrymore or Helen Hayes. Among men, Leslie Howard and Fredric March and Ronald Colman have repeatedly become our beloved companions for a space.

Perhaps the nearest to a radio personality was (and still is, too infrequently) Orson Welles, who had some genius for packing emotion into the speaking voice, and a canny eye for tense situation that would carry by sound alone. Difficult as it is for anyone to remember masterpieces of radio-theatre, we somehow remember the impact of Welles' characterizations. It was in line with types of play previously associated with his name, especially in the Federal Theatre Project of 1936–37, that there came a development seeming to point the way to an original radio variation of historic drama, projected over the air waves with theatric effectiveness and not a little poetic beauty. A writer-director, Norman Corwin, produced a series of what might be termed semi-documentary plays or socially-conscious *revues*, climaxed when Paul Robeson first sang *Ballad for Americans*. At about the same time (1937) the poet Archibald MacLeish contributed what has been generally considered the outstanding play written especially for radio, *The Fall of the City*, compellingly presented with Orson Welles and Burgess Meredith in the cast.

Corwin had used effectively the technique of the *sprechchor* or speaking choir, which had earlier made vivid the socially-conscious dramas of the working-men's acting groups in Germany, and MacLeish had employed a particularly telling sort of recitative verse, two elements suited essentially to the radio medium. But ten years later there was little drama on the air waves that showed the influence of this original and promising expansion of the radio medium. Day after day the housewife could listen to a succession of those sentimental, fatuous story serials, dealt out in homeopathic portions, which some sociologists count the most eloquent sign of the failure of American education and of deterioration of the national mind. Known as "soap opera," the serial household plays comprised, indeed, a new way of serving audiences with dialogue-stories spoken by actors; but no new form was ever so promptly degraded, for purposes having no connection with art. Night after night the citizen, and his children, could tune in on an imposing series of crime plays—murder having become the prime obsession of national networks and of local stations, the one dramatic subject most trusted by advertising executives to attract huge listener-response. An incredible amount of brutality, and instruction in innumerable methods of murder, were thus brought into our homes daily.

For many years this sort of instruction continued and grew, against a background of general neglect of the enormous educational potentialities of the radio. By 1950 a wave of protest from educators and religious organizations broke over the broadcasting studios; and this, with the dislocation of many programs due to the competition of television, seemed to be leading to new openings for educational use of the medium. As for those who fostered religious drama on the air,

Mary Pickford, most famous of the early film actresses, familiarly known as "America's sweetheart." [By courtesy of the Bettmann Archive, New York.]

they had enjoyed one of the exceptional praiseworthy successes. Tabloid Biblical plays, rather elementary but reverent and generally effective, broadcast on Sundays under the title *The Greatest Story Ever Told,* a similar Jewish series titled *The Eternal Light,* and less consistently mature, weekly evening broadcasts by the Family Theatre, were generally praised. The British Broadcasting Corporation, with its more enlightened policy of reserving one air-channel continuously for offerings on a higher level of appeal—serious music, lectures, serious plays—had already gained wide response when it broadcast a twelve-part radio dramatization of the life of Christ by Dorothy L. Sayers, under the title *The Man Born to be King.*

TELEVISION, between 1945 and 1950, restored the lost visual element to the theatre of the air waves. The box in one's living room was enlarged, with a moving-picture screen in miniature built in to afford a complete audio-visual appeal. One saw only photographs of actors still, but the eyes of the radio listener were restored to him: listener-viewer now. Where radio theatre had depended upon the spoken word alone (somewhat aided by sound effects), here was the whole equipment of the talking-picture theatre delivered to the consumer at home. Such was the third miracle of machine-age invention as brought to bear upon the theatre art.

The record of television, except for a few basic facts of origin and first development, does not yet belong to history, and so not to this book. Both as an industry and as an art, television was still, in recent seasons, in a state of flux. The actors and the plays were being taken largely from Hollywood, and top vaudeville turns from radio. Of "live" drama, originated for telecasting, crime plays were in the ascendancy, followed by Westerns and other juveniles and serials addressed to women. As fillers, in order to keep the stream of drama flowing, old film plays were being resurrected from dead storage, to be relayed over the television channels. Many smaller producing units in Hollywood were being reorganized to make pictures solely for television consumption.

In France, one of the three countries already provided with considerable telecasting and receiving equipment, the overwhelming part of available programs consisted of relayed films. England was somewhat better off, though to suggest that anything like a distinctive and important form of theatre art was developing would be hazardous. Early television, like early cinema, was most successful everywhere in conveying news, especially sports events, and interviews and discussion; to which may be added quiz games and opportunity programs taken over from radio. Its only claim to originality, and this on the edge of theatre, was a sort of variety show of music and comedy turns, held together loosely by a raconteur or patter-artist. The progress of regular drama at this time can be judged by a report from Los Angeles that viewers could witness in any week eighty to ninety murders over their television sets, in crime plays.

What is really impressive historically is that television should have been invented at all, that within a few years the apparatus has been perfected by which, shortly, any play or opera produced anywhere can be channeled to a screen in each man's home. There every viewer may have an easy chair, at just the right distance from the screen, and no crackers of peanuts and rattlers of popcorn bags within earshot.

During the year 1950 in America alone more than seven million receiving sets were manufactured and there was already the prospect that in time the medium would be as widely diffused over the world as radio. In 1951 Americans owned more than 100,000,000 radio sets, as against possibly 14,000,000 television receivers. There were nearly 3,000 broadcasting stations as compared with about 100 telecasting stations. For technical reasons telecasting had been limited to the more populous parts of the country. But who can doubt that through this miracle of diffusion, drama of a sort will be conveyed to the ends of the earth, multiplied to an extent that no theatre-lover could have foreseen or dreamed possible fifty years earlier? And as a new art of poetic drama has been proved possible for radio, though only barely tested, so there may be unpredictable changes for television, in playwriting, acting and forms of staging.

Of course it will be, in the originating theatre, the eternal art of presenting action by the medium of living players. I, for one, believe that that art will go on forever—at least beyond any developments we can now foresee. If the legitimate drama has been hurt or curtailed during the period of the rise of cinema, radio and television, it seems to me that the cupidity of producers, wanting to make ever more money by exploiting the obvious and popular at the expense of the finely creative play, has had more to do with it than has the competition of the photographic and radio mediums. Other sorts of competition will come, but there will always be audiences to gather where the actor personally is, where the spectator is in the presence of the stage action.

There is talk of the "actorless" theatre and many are the guesses at new forms of machine-made drama wherein no player appears—merely moving shapes or symbolized forces or whatnot. But they hardly belong to a book that is, after all, primarily a history of what has been done in the world playhouse. The story of the wooden actor, of puppets, might more properly have a place; but it is a story so long, so different, that it would need a volume in itself. The impersonality, the obedience, of the marionette actor, the different appeal of the manipulated figures—these are matters that set the subject aside from the record of the regular theatre. Suffice it to say that through most of the centuries during which the theatre of personal acting has existed, a puppet theatre has lived also, if not always in the West then in the East; and that in the second third of the twentieth century the marionette, after a period of degradation, has been enjoying something of a revival in Europe and America.

CHAPTER
25

❧❧❧❧❧❧❧❧❧❧❧❧❧❧❧❧❧❧❧❧❧❧❧❧❧❧❧❧❧❧❧❧❧❧❧❧

The Theatre in Decline; War, Commercialism, and Other Evils: 1930–1950

❧❧❧❧❧❧❧❧❧❧❧❧❧❧❧❧❧❧❧❧❧❧❧❧❧❧❧❧❧❧❧❧❧❧❧❧

THE SAD truth is that an institution glorious in the larger historical view entered, in the early thirties, into a decline. The era was one of small promise if judged by the number of great dramatists emerging or by innovations in the field of acting. As against the devastating evils of the period—war, economic depression, a cramping commercialism—the gains might seem to be slight. They were, however, in advances new to the theatre and possibly of large portent for some not completely imaged future.

Especially novel were the workingmen's theatres, some further explorations in anti-realism, and a theoretical thing called the Theatre of Commitment—in which could be found auguries of the mid-century Theatre of Absurdity. The giant animating figure of the two decades was Bertolt Brecht, who from his Berlin theatre fought stormy battles with Hitler and his Nazis, fled to America, lived futile years in Hollywood, but survived to establish Europe's single most influential revolutionary theatre. We shall meet him at the end of the chapter.

But first let us examine those evils, and especially their effect upon the American commercial theatre. (We are here setting aside the startling visions opened by the medium of television, and the generally unfulfilled hopes for a stirring drama in the radio medium. We are returning to the traditional art of the living actor performing before group audiences—with a glance now and then toward "the pictures.")

In 1930, in the United States, the Great Depression was taking a costly toll of show business. The decline was to continue through the

1930's and the 1940's. The most significant statistic of the time is this: in New York, the only substantial producing center of commercial plays, there were seventy-five theatres showing legitimate plays in 1930; in 1950 only thirty-two had survived. The number of significant productions had shrunk even more markedly. Of the lost theatres, some had been taken over by the movies, a few became home bases for the television octopuses, others had been demolished in the march of building "progress."

By 1932 the moving picture industry was shaken by bankruptcies, following a reported forty percent loss in public attendance; and that other industry, the "trust" that controlled booking of commercial plays in most of the country's legitimate theatres, lost a number of houses temporarily—but eventually tightened its hold on both Broadway and the road. This resulted in a further swing to the lighter forms of musical entertainment, whether operetta, musical comedy or the hybrid revue.

The musicals became, in New York and other large cities, more popular than the play of spoken words; and indeed the successes of *Oklahoma*, *South Pacific*, and *The King and I* were fabulous. These marked the emergence of Richard Rodgers and Oscar Hammerstein II as a composer-librettist team not surpassed since the days of Gilbert and Sullivan.

The Depression of the early thirties brought the end of a minor sort of legitimate drama: variety or vaudeville. For generations vaudeville houses had brightened the theatrical scene in every large American city, offering a melange that included short plays or dramatic sketches (everything from Sarah Bernhardt to melodramatic or farcical one-acters); monologues, dance acts (from aesthetic dance to the trickiest hoofers), acrobatic turns, the best of magic; simulated nude posing, always in motionless, statue-like compositions, made respectable by the wearing of tights; natural freaks; and singers (from stars lured briefly from opera through all types of "popular" singers to eccentrics). For generations vaudeville had been the theatre for a large segment of the national audience; a clean, highly entertaining if somewhat fragmented form of theatre. The comparable phenomenon in England, the "music hall," succumbed more slowly, but was only a shadow of its old self. Incidentally, the following years were to see the gradual decline of that famous British type of production known as the Christmas Pantomime: a seasonal offering composed of fairy story, music and dance, masquerading in one season as Cinderella, in another as Mother Goose, or as glorification of any nursery or fairy-tale character.

Another casualty of the times was burlesque, a less innocent minor type of entertainment. It was generally a two-attraction affair, with comedy turns and strip-tease alternating. (A strip-tease artist is a girl performer who by stages removes most of her clothes.) In the United States, burlesque had its own theatres, numbering perhaps half a hundred in the twenties, and of course its own devoted male audiences.

Realism as it persisted toward mid-century. Arthur Kennedy and Lois Wheeler in a scene from Arthur Miller's *All My Sons*, in the original New York production, 1947. The setting is an exact replica of somebody's suburban back porch. [By courtesy of the Museum of the City of New York.]

But the comedy grew broader and broader, and the girls took off more and more. The many raids on the houses by the police and moral authorities served to kill burlesque, with an assist from general Depression conditions. The genre, when transported from its center in New York to London, never caught on in a big way. In the thirties the British theatre still had its all-powerful censor, the Lord Chamberlain, who could grant or withhold licenses to theatres and producing organizations; he could prohibit performance of any play, act, scene or line which he considered damaging, libelous or morally questionable.

In New York the 1930's saw the influx of new plays changed in two ways, first and already noted, a swing to musical comedy as the most popular offering—and indeed, even the British critics cited this as a dramatic form in which the Americans excelled, with continuous importing of examples to London theatres; and second, a turning back to the realistic (or naturalistic) play. The impetus of the art theatres of the twenties had all but subsided. The "smash hits" were likely to be of the nature of two plays by a new playwright, Lillian Hellman: *The Children's Hour*, an effective exploration of the disaster caused by a child's charge of Lesbianism against two teachers, and *The Little Foxes*, a holding but depressing study of decadence in a Southern family; or (a little later) Arthur Miller's *All My Sons*, a contrived but insistently naturalistic tragedy of "common" people. Since the following chapter will treat largely of a theatre presenting formless plays, absurdly inconclusive, often insistently irrational, it is well to note that Lillian Hellman and Arthur Miller were writing dramas each with a well-marked story line, with more than a little dependence upon the principles of the well-made play. Their dramatic material and their mental allegiance were, perhaps, more on the negative or mean side than had been the case with their immediate predecessors, and this may be considered a step toward the sordidness-for-its-own-sake plays of the sixties.

As a matter of fact, the "standard" dramatists of the early decades of the century were still writing in the 1930's; among memorable successes were Sidney Howard's *Yellow Jack* (1934), Maxwell Anderson's *Winterset* (1935), and Philip Barry's *Here Come the Clowns* (1938). Elmer Rice, however, failed to match with any new production the success of his realistic masterpiece *Street Scene*, which had come in 1929. (It had received that year's Pulitzer Prize.) Eugene O'Neill, whose ambitious and serious work, *Mourning Becomes Electra*, had been seen in 1931, was represented in 1933 by his most conventional realistic play, *Ah, Wilderness!*, a delightfully nostalgic and entertaining comedy.

During the drift back to standard realism and to musical comedy (of an elevated sort) there came a quite extraordinary counter-current of poetic, fantastic and spiritually incisive dramas. But the American development was part of an international movement, and the record of it may best be read after a few words about another great evil.

World War II (1939–1945) was the most destructive war of all time. Wars had slowed the development of the theatre art many times in the

A scene in Sophocles' *Oedipus the King* in a carefully stylized German production. [By courtesy of the German Information Center, New York.]

past, but the introduction of bombing of unprotected cities now resulted in unprecedented damage to the arts. In parts of Europe, with the decimation or erasure of cities and the displacement of populations, creative theatre was all but wiped out; although there were striking instances of communities remaining true to their acting companies even under bomb fire, and of companies organized to entertain the fighters in improvised underground shelters. Many of the ranking stage stars visited the various fronts, and the emotional pleasure of homesick soldiers at merely seeing these beautiful people—for actors, or in this case especially actresses, are just that—was incalculable.

In the thirties and forties certain favorable international trends continued. As to stagecraft, and specifically "decoration," everywhere scenery had become scene. That is, the *régisseur* and designer began by considering the demands of acting space (and acting levels), then created suggestive, and generally very simple, backgrounds. In like manner, the whole problem of staging continued to be in the hands of artist-directors; the impetus that had begun theoretically with Gordon Craig, and practically with the Meiningen Players, the Moscow Art Theatre, and Reinhardt, Jessner and Fehling, continued. The artist-director had become a fixture. While Russia fell back from its position as the world's foremost experimental laboratory of staging, this did not mean retrogression to old methods of mounting and directing. (Party control of government meant bureaucratic interference in the matter of plays chosen for production, with a consequent decline in the quality and scope of playwriting; but in general the staging was left to the artists.)

No new directors, however, of any nationality, were widely heard of in the war or immediate post-war years, as Reinhardt and Jessner, or Meyerhold and Vachtangoff, had been in the old days. But if virtuoso figures were lacking, it was no less true that the presence of the artist-director was taken for granted, wherever any claim was made to thorough staging. Theatres proudly announced "a Margaret Webster production" or "directed by Elia Kazan"—to mention but two of the most talented artists then in the field.

When, back in the twenties, the idealists had suppressed painted scenery of the sort that "got a hand" regardless of its relation to unfoldment of the action, they also had banned the star actor who stood out from his "support" like a rocket cutting across a faintly lighted sky. The ideal of ensemble acting then introduced was never relinquished, and it was taken for granted that each acting company would have balance and each performance smoothness and integration. Star billing was usual still. We all went on occasion to enjoy the performance of a John Gielgud or a Vivien Leigh, of a Walter Hampden or a Judith Anderson; but we found it shocking if the star's performance was not cushioned in a smoothly flowing ensemble, without noticeable "holes" in the supporting company. Playgoers whose recollection goes back no further than the twenties would hardly credit the prevalence of "ham" acting and sheer amateurism in the companies of ranking stars only a generation earlier.

The acceptance, in both Europe and America, of the ensemble ideal, and of the shaping of the production into one style, one flow, toward which every element of stagecraft contributes, had been the primary historic gain of the era: the most memorable fact about theatre art as it changed between 1900 and 1930. Among the stars who came to prominence after 1930, great as they were, there was not one to rival the giants of other times: in France no new Bernhardt, in England no rival to Henry Irving and Ellen Terry, in America no Booth or Forrest

or Jefferson. The meteoric actor had disappeared. In some few backward areas the ensemble ideal seemed still to be honored only theoretically. Many French provincial cities were especially badly served; and
in the United States, where an elaborate system of "summer theatres"
had developed, these seasonal houses reverted in general to an uneven
if not style-less standard—visiting players from among Broadway's featured actors being inserted into local casts with no more than a week's

Katharine Cornell in Clemence Dane's *A Bill of Divorcement*, New York,
1921. [Abbé photograph, by courtesy of the Museum of the City of New
York.]

rehearsal given to each play. Vacation audiences, however, proved
tolerant, and summer companies prospered.

In America, despite the decline of meteoric figures, glamorous acting
continued at a high level. A stage graced with such players as Helen
Hayes, Katharine Cornell, Lynn Fontanne, Tallulah Bankhead, Katharine Hepburn and Cornelia Otis Skinner could hardly be less than exciting. If these were the routine "attractions" on the Broadway stage,
there were four others, who practiced their magic in a different way:
they were devoted primarily to the classic drama and to superior mod-

ern plays. Judith Anderson, especially in the too neglected field of Shakespeare and the Greeks, Blanche Yurka, who played Ophelia to John Barrymore's Hamlet and later starred notably in Ibsen's *The Wild Duck*, Eva LeGallienne, whose devotion and brilliancy gave distinction to her Civic Repertory Theatre in New York (until 1933), and Uta Hagen, in a shorter but very distinguished career: these gave evidence that, were institutional theatres, repertory theatres, properly subsidized theatres established in America, the acting would be brilliant and adequate.

Actors, as distinguished from the reigning actresses of the time, formed no such brilliant galaxy. Rather, the favorites were substantially gifted and individual in appeal. Best-loved, perhaps, were Leslie Howard, Dudley Digges and Raymond Massey. Nearest to the earlier-day idol type was Alfred Lunt. In sharp contrast—very masculine, even specializing in "tough" roles—were James Cagney and John Garfield. Probably Maurice Evans (British-born) did most to bring back the classics to the American commercial stage. If all of these gifted men, except Lunt and Evans, deserted to Hollywood, in time, it was a sign of the decline in the American legitimate theatre that has been the unfortunate subject of this chapter so far. A poll of public familiarity with names of celebrities, taken by *Variety* magazine in 1931, showed film stars in first place, gangsters second, athletes third; legitimate actors were then in seventh place.

IN ENGLAND the institutional and repertory theatres gained after the war, partly because for the first time the Government supported the theatre art financially; and the acting companies were surpassing (except in the musicals) those of the American theatre. Actors of the stature of Laurence Olivier and John Gielgud were then undertaking the work of the *régisseur*, both carrying on from experience with the Old Vic and other repertory companies, and they and their less celebrated fellow-directors were establishing a remarkably high standard of ensemble casting and smooth-flowing performance. The theatre in England, moreover, had turned noticeably to a more serious taste in play choice. By 1951, it could be said that the nation's classics were becoming popular, with Shakespeare and Shaw rating as best-sellers. The English were by way of catching up with the pre-war German producers and German audiences in devotion to Shakespeare's plays.

Even more significant, perhaps, was a revival of interest in contemporary poetic drama. The realistic play had persisted, was still central in the play lists of the countries relying upon a competitive commercial theatre. It could not fail to appear also in the repertories of state theatres; and especially in the propagandist theatres of Russia and in all areas where Communist influence penetrated. There have not been lacking, for a century past, playwrights prepared to explore, in common men's prose, the emotional situations and the newsworthy incidents of everyday life. Journalistic realism flourished especially, after 1940, in war plays and political plays. But there was too a renewed effort, among playwrights, to restore those elements of imaginative approach, poetic expression and grandeur of thought that transcend Realism. This eventually came to the proportions of an international trend.

Taking the term "poetic drama" in a broad interpretation, as not limited to plays in verse, including rather the several sorts of imaginative writing earlier illustrated by the Hauptmann of *Hannele* and the Toller of *Masse-Mensch* alongside the actual poetry of a Yeats or a d'Annunzio, we find a well-marked revival in the poetic field.

England and Ireland especially contributed plays that went on to success in other countries; but it was French audiences that saw the new anti-realistic drama in its fullest expression. A few of the younger French playwrights were writing plays to which had been restored grandeur of conception and philosophic depth. Jean Anouilh became more than the foremost French dramatist of the time when his plays began to be produced in other than the French cities of Europe, and finally in New York. A writer with a profound tragic sense, but finding tragedy less in violence than in emotional and spiritual situations comprehended quietly and serenely, he recast several of the Greek dramas in modern terms. His *Eurydice, Antigone* and *Medea*, all written after 1940, are peopled with characters out of contemporary society, but the protagonists bear the ancient names and act out plots recognizably familiar and tragic. The difficulty, perhaps impossibility, of finding happiness in earthly life is a recurrent theme, and Fate hardly less an unseen motivating character.

Anouilh progressed from fantasy and wry comedy in his early plays to this sort of philosophically significant drama. A considerable group of contemporary French dramatists joined him in the exploration of non-realistic ways of playwriting, though none was so consistent in development or so highly successful. *The Madwoman of Chaillot*, the last play written by Jean Giraudoux, was an outstanding example of the fantastic-philosophical *genre*. Produced by Louis Jouvet in Paris in 1945, it was seen in New York in a satisfying adaptation in 1948. It was not unlike a civilized and witty improvement upon the sort of Expressionist drama initiated by Georg Kaiser in *From Morn to Midnight*.

From the half-dozen other names that a French playgoer might cite, one may choose Jean-Paul Sartre as an international figure. Although the philosophical idea he fathered achieved wide popularity after the war, his plays showed him to be far less profound, less tragic in the true sense, than Anouilh. Adept in utilizing non-realistic devices, he yet stayed closer to the earth, and to the brutish, even to the dirty, side of humanity. Avowedly attempting to apply the formula of Greek tragedy to the life of today, he seems generally to have mistaken violence, cruelty and pitiable degradation for the high transgressions and noble atonements of classical drama. He became especially well known in America in 1948 when *The Respectful Prostitute* enjoyed a long run in New York. A typically paradoxical and bitter play, and not very deep, it had a factitious interest for Americans since it dealt with a threatened lynching in a Southern state.

In England there was in the forties a drift toward actual verse dialogue. There were, of course, those poets who occasionally wrote a play, as there long had been—in Byron, Browning, Stephen Phillips, Masefield—but Christopher Fry proved to be primarily a dramatist using poetry as his natural and felicitous medium. His *The Lady's Not for Burning* was a commercial theatre hit in New York as well as in London, and in 1951 his impressive religious play *A Sleep of Prisoners* was staged in a church in New York, with a professional British cast. Alongside these successes there was that of *The Cocktail Party* by T. S. Eliot, the expatriate American who was a leader in the modern poetry movement in Britain. A verse-play with a modern theme, dealing obliquely with psychiatry, it afforded one of the most satisfying experiences offered in the Broadway theatres of 1950–51.

Fifteen years earlier Eliot had scored with a play more impressive in theme and perhaps richer in poetic investiture, *Murder in the Cathedral*, a drama dealing with the assassination of Thomas à Becket. A success in England, in original production, it was beautifully staged in America by the Federal Theatre of the Works Progress Administration, and has appeared often on little theatre and community theatre programs since. W. H. Auden and Christopher Isherwood joined in the poetic-drama revival, and attempted to use an Expressionistic looseness and distortion in the service of political satire; but their *The Dog beneath the Skin; or Where Is Francis?*, proved to have limited dramatic impact in production.

Without being essentially a poet Sean O'Casey continued to write with such a gift of fantasy, and so rich a sense of language that he too helped forward the poetic revival in the theatre. If he is better termed an Expressionist with a profound tragic sense and an ear for rhythms of speech, he is perhaps not far from the category into which history will place Anouilh and Eliot. As for the Americans, of the actual poets one may in passing bow with sincere respect to the veterans

John Gielgud and Judith Anderson in *Hamlet*, New York, 1937. In the early twentieth century Gielgud was widely hailed as the most appealing, and the most poetic, interpreter of the Hamlet role. [Photograph by Alfredo Valente, by courtesy of the Museum of the City of New York.]

Maxwell Anderson and Percy Mackaye; but it is clear that the real event of the era in the theatre of poetry was the bringing of the tragedies of Robinson Jeffers to the stage. Most notable was the production of *Medea* in his adaptation in New York in 1947, with Judith Anderson giving a magnificent performance in the title rôle.

The borderline plays, fantastic or imaginative and otherworldly but not in verse, had come to the commercial theatre more generously back in the twenties and thirties. In one season, 1929–30, New York audiences had seen in addition to *The Green Pastures*, a group of moving dramas with spiritual overtones: *Berkeley Square* by John Balderston, *Hotel Universe* by Philip Barry and *Death Takes a Holiday*, from the Italian of Alberto Casella. If in no season thereafter did so many otherworldly pieces appear, the genre was illustrated now and then; delightfully so in the plays of Paul Vincent Carroll (again an Irishman) such as *Shadow and Substance*, a study of an uneducated girl who sees visions, and the reactions of a conventional Churchman and a "liberal" to her faith, and *The White Steed;* and again in *Father Malachy's Miracle*, dramatized by Brian Doherty from a novel by Bruce Marshall. On the lightly and sentimentally fantastic side, there was Paul Osborn's *On Borrowed Time*, a success in the late thirties, and in 1944 *Harvey*, by Mary Chase, was staged. This delightfully different play, in which the main character was an invisible rabbit, was a heart-warming fantasy. Incidentally it won a Pulitzer Prize and played on Broadway through more than 1700 performances.

The two American dramatists in the near-poetic group who were to go on most frequently to fame in the international theatre were Thornton Wilder and Tennessee Williams. In 1945 Williams' *The Glass Menagerie* was rendered memorable in a production beautifully acted by Laurette Taylor, Eddie Dowling and Julie Haydon. It marked the return to the stage of the incomparably gifted Laurette after years of absence. The next play by Williams, an even greater commercial success, lost the tenderly fantastic note and proved, rather, a searching and compelling study of a girl's decline out of make-believe romance into madness: *A Streetcar Named Desire*. The most notable event of the forties, however, was the production of a second play, following the well-beloved *Our Town*, by Thornton Wilder. In *The Skin of Our Teeth*, which had only a limited success in New York, Wilder took the whole history of man, past and future, for theme; and if the play puzzled casual audiences, it had its exciting moments and profound implications. That it went on to greater success in the Central European theatres than in America was a sign, perhaps, that audiences nurtured in a richly continuing theatre tradition are better equipped to enjoy philosophically canny drama than those brought up chiefly on movies, musical comedy, and television.

Scene design for Maxwell Anderson's *Winterset*, by Jo Mielziner, New York, 1935. [Photograph by Peter A. Juley & Son.]

It was in Germany especially that *The Skin of Our Teeth* was put into the repertories of the surviving theatres, to the astonishment of Americans who had missed the significance of the play at home. It should be recorded of Germany that the theatre there, at first ruthlessly and brutally censored by the Hitler regime but otherwise supported, suffered grievously toward the end of World War II. Nevertheless many companies continued to act, often in half-ruined houses or on improvised stages. And as soon as the war ended, in the midst of crippling poverty and want, often literally in the midst of debris, the acting companies were organized and audiences were found. And repertories blossomed again, with the classics revived, and new plays drawn from progressive channels in all countries.

It is to Germany that we must turn for first light on the one remaining international development to be recorded as important in the 1930–1950 period, the labor stage. It will be remembered that the *Volksbühne* in Berlin had been in the early thirties a unique co-operative or socialistic theatre, housed in a monumental building owned by its workingman-audiences. It became famous for the vivid plays staged there by Jurgen Fehling, such as Toller's *Masse-Mensch*, Hauptmann's *The Weavers* and other works heavily charged with social message. At other levels the members of the left-wing parties, socialistic or communistic, were seeing a wide range of "socially conscious" plays. These might be at little or experimental theatres, such as Piscator's. Again there were acting groups with no higher purpose than agitation for the workers' revolution, presenting plays or dramatic sketches before mass meetings. Their plays were very elementary, but anyone who saw them, in the bitter days of the Nazi-Communist struggle, will attest to their stirring appeal, their living dramatic impact. Some of the most effective sketches were offered by companies made up of a few actors and vast choruses.

It was here that the *sprechchor*, or speaking-choir technique was most tellingly developed. A typical sketch might bring out a protagonist from among the men, to say that the revolution has failed, followed by the men's chorus; then the protagonist of the women to agree, followed by the chorus of women; finally a child comes forward to harangue the massed actors, pleading that for the sake of the children of the world the fight must be continued; the children's chorus joins in the appeal—and suddenly everyone is joyously ready to carry on. So simple a "plot," as presented in the exciting, staccato *sprechchor* technique in Berlin in the early 1930s impressed many a foreigner as being overwhelmingly dramatic. That these left-wing acting groups had connection with the flourishing experimental theatres and the travelling *Agitprop* brigades in Russia cannot be doubted, nor can the purpose of the movement: revolution.

If the Nazis put a sudden end to the activity, to liberalism as well as to the extremism of Communists, in Germany, it was nevertheless evident that the worker's theatre had taken hold all over Europe. What came to be known as *Agitprop* groups could be widely found, most especially in countries where conditions were oppressive for la-

The mid-century theatres saw continuation of experiment in stagecraft. In the setting for a performance of Ibsen's *Peer Gynt* in Germany there was an unusual combination of constructivist elements and a stylized pictorial background. [By courtesy of the German Information Center, New York.]

bor: in Austria-Hungary, Belgium, France, even in Scandinavia. The labor-stage movement represented the first great flowering of a frankly propagandist theatre since the era of the Jesuit plays, in the time when the Miracle plays had gone out and secular professional drama had not yet come in.

In England the activity of proletarian acting groups was less evident. It is probable that the mild socialism of Shaw, a fully professional dramatist, did more than the extreme revolutionary groups to undermine old political parties and wreck old social superstitions, thus speeding labor's political triumph. But like any other of the socialized nations, Britain can look back on a network of workingmen's amateur theatres. The history of the movement is more striking in the United States, where conventions of delegates from socially-conscious producing groups were held in the mid-thirties, a magazine was published, and brilliant new playwrights were discovered.

The earliest American groups, some of them organized by immigrants, in the image of workingmen's theatres in their own countries, and playing as often as not in their native languages, dated back to 1929 and 1930. For a few years the European pattern was reflected in the names: *Agitprop* Groups, Shock Troupes, the Blue Blouses, Rebel Players, etc. But before long the name most frequently heard was Workers' Theatre, with such common variations as Workers' Laboratory Theatre (Chicago), Jewish Workers' Theatre (New York) and so on. There was shortly a League of Workers' Theatres, with member groups from coast to coast.

While the productions of these amateur companies were often moving and never less than sincere, and socially symptomatic, the phenomenon would not have been so widely noticed (or have furnished material for history) had not the New York groups staged in 1934 and 1935 several plays that challenged the professional productions on Broadway, for emotional and dramatic impact, for social significance. *Peace on Earth*, a fighting anti-war play by George Sklar and Albert Maltz, was staged eloquently by the Theatre Union, which had taken over the building of Eva LeGallienne's Civic Repertory Theatre. What the play lacked in "finish" it compensated for in the drive of its message and its sledge-hammer theatricalism. Next came *Stevedore*, by Paul Peters and George Sklar, equally imperfect as a drama, but exciting and absorbing, and perhaps of some social importance as bringing the problem of discrimination against the Negro to a public stage for the first time. When the Group Theatre (mainly secessionists from the Theatre Guild) produced *Waiting for Lefty* and *Awake and Sing* by Clifford Odets, full recognition of the labor play and socially-conscious groups of players was achieved, even among "uptown" critics. A climax came when another new playwright, Irwin Shaw, was introduced, with perhaps the most vivid and stirring play of the series, *Bury the Dead*. Here were new and flaming talents in the service of the theatre—and in a segment as removed from routine Broadway ground as had been the art theatres and little theatres of a decade earlier.

If the workers' theatres were less heard of a few years later, the Depression had something to do with it; and also the fact that some of their playwrights went on to other fields, even to Hollywood. The Federal Theatre of the WPA drew upon the left-wing ranks as well as those of the Broadway professional actors and technicians. And indeed, it was largely the intellectuals once leagued with the proletarian leaders who shaped the policies and the productions of the Federal Theatre. They helped make the WPA productions the outstanding phenomenon of the American stage in the years 1936–39. Never since has there been a period when so much of exciting dramatic fare has been offered; and the service to the country was the greater in that cities from coast to coast had their WPA acting companies.

The unemployed actors and other stage workers came into the theatre by the back door of relief, but they justified themselves by presenting a repertory of plays unparalleled in variety, vigor and brilliancy. There is nothing in the record to challenge such novel and stirring productions as the all-Negro *Macbeth* and *The Swing Mikado* or the unforgettable "editions" of The Living Newspaper, especially *Triple-A Plowed Under* and *One-Third of a Nation*. The Living Newspaper productions, in a technique originated by Federal Theatre workers but not wholly unlike productions in the advanced experimental theatres of Russia, were starkly dramatic, abruptly thought-provoking—and, of course, being commentaries on burning social questions, controversial. At the other extreme, people who long had dreamed of establishing a poetic theatre were given their opportunity. It was they who staged the impressive production of *Murder in the Cathedral*. And indeed, among most of the Federal Theatre groups the standard of play choice was of the highest, with revivals ranging from the Greeks and Shakespeare to Shaw and O'Neill; yet unknown authors often found here their first opportunity to see their works on the stage. The Federal Theatre project was ably directed by Hallie Flanagan, who recruited a remarkable producing staff, especially in New York, where at one extreme the master dramatist Elmer Rice was in charge, but with such deputies and advisers as the poet-playwright Alfred Kreymborg and the imaginative actor-director Orson Welles.

Brilliant as the production record of Federal Theatre was, and successful as it had been in solving the unemployment problem while serving the community—it had nine thousand employees at one time—it was cut off by the government in the summer of 1939, when a few Congressmen became afraid of what they considered the subversive tendency of certain of its productions. Thus ended the one conspicuous example of state subsidy of the theatre art in the United States.

One remnant remained. The Project had initiated the historical-poetic pageant-like play *The Lost Colony* by Paul Green, which is still given every summer on Roanoke Island, North Carolina. In the forties similar seasonal pageant plays were established, in permanent outdoor theatres, at various historical sites, often with community or state assistance. Paul Green continued to be the leader in this movement, most importantly as author of *The Common Glory* at Williamsburg, and of *Faith of Our Fathers* at Washington. But perhaps the most vivid, and certainly the most novel, poetic-historical production in the Americas is *The City of the Gods*, staged among the pre-Columbian pyramids at Teotihuacan outside Mexico City. The play, without seen actors, is a uniquely beautiful unfolding of dramatic story in spoken words, color and lights—especially lights. There are both Mexican and English versions.

The most heartening instance of a government subsidizing progressive producing groups was seen in England, a land where the state and Court had consistently stood apart from the theatre through good eras and bad. In 1940 a Council for the Encouragement of Music and the Arts had been organized by a philanthropic institution, acting with government aid, to provide music and drama to displaced or evacuated populations. At the war's end the organization was renamed the Arts Council of Great Britain, and proceeded, wholly on government funds, to provide the necessary margin to many a repertory project struggling to return to full community service; as well as administering certain companies and theatres of its own. It helped in the reorganization and expansion of the Old Vic company, and the Sadler's Wells Ballet.

The Arts Council might well claim most of the credit for the rise in standards so noticeable on London stages between 1945 and 1950, an advance involving revivals of the classics, appearance of a wider range of serious new plays, and improved stagecraft. Incidentally it should be mentioned that the Shakespeare Memorial Theatre at Stratford-on-Avon, after years and years when its productions had seemed to most visitors mediocre and dull, had, by 1951, been caught up in the wave of betterment, and was offering, under adequate direction, festival plays worthy of the theatre's name. A National Theatre for London, for which funds had been in hand at the time of the Shakespearean tercentenary celebrations in 1916, had failed of building due to the outbreak of World War I; and then, when the project seemed again on the point of materializing, in 1939, was again delayed, by World War II. In the following decade, however, foundations were laid for the National Theatre of Great Britain, which was destined to become a reality in the 1960's.

In America there was but one striking attempt, after the demise of the Federal Theatre, to provide stage fare of the sort known through the art-theatre groups in the twenties. In New York Orson Welles founded the Mercury Theatre and startled audiences with a highly original and socially-conscious production of *Julius Cæsar*, among other items; but after two seasons went over to radio. The Mercury Theatre marked the last stand of the institutional playhouse and the *virtuoso* artist-director on Broadway, until the Off-Broadway theatres, from about 1950, began to send occasional productions to the commercial houses.

A theatre in the round designed by Norman Bel Geddes as early as 1922. A type of theatre that became popular in the 1950's.

A happy compromise of theatre in the round with the old proscenium stage was the "thrust stage" widely introduced in Germany and Russia between 1920 and 1950. Here the jutting stage, with audience on three sides, is shown in a scene in Max Reinhardt's production of *Danton* at the *Grosses Schauspielhaus* in Berlin, 1922. [From a drawing by Ernst Stern.]

Toward 1950 there was a flurry of interest over a new type of staging: production in the round. In summer tent theatres, in hotel ballrooms, even in professional little theatres, stages were abolished and actors appeared in the centre of a bowl-like room, with spectators all around. There was a new vividness, a new actuality in the staging of certain types of play in this arena-type playhouse; but the wiser producers recognized that the main way to the future was likely to be discovered in a modification of the platform-stage theatre, preserving at least an implied separation of audience from actors, and an opportunity for all spectators to see the actors' faces. The arena theatre, as a matter of fact, was not new. At the Penthouse Theatre in Seattle, Glenn Hughes had been presenting productions in the round for many years, and many little theatres experimented in "arenas." In Dallas an artist-director well known in New York, Margo Jones, had utilized the method brilliantly. Long before the American experiments Max Reinhardt had occasionally marshalled his actors out on an arena floor, but with the audience extending around only three-fourths of the circle. This resulted in the "thrust stage" which was to become popular in the following two decades.

If a historian elects to record these "special" developments and events —the labor stage, the latest gains in state subsidy, the variant stages, and the poetic or imaginative phases of playwriting—in place of the season-by-season march of firmly established types of play, and the long-run hits and the favorite actors in them, it is because in the long run history is the chronicle of successive innovations, and the story of the recurrence of imaginative and deeply philosophical elements. This historian is interested and intrigued by many a routine "commercial" play, by the smash hits of the veteran realists, by sentimental comedy and emotional problem-play; indeed finds pleasure in a large part of the current product. But the larger fact, in America, is the twenty-year-long decline in the number of plays produced on Broadway, and especially the continued decline in the quality of those offered.

By the way, it *should* be recorded that one routine comedy, a delightful one, *Life with Father*, as dramatized by Howard Lindsay and Russel Crouse from the book by Clarence Day, reached the amazing total of 3224 consecutive performances in New York alone. (While a record long-run, it is topped, of course, by such an old favorite as *Uncle Tom's Cabin* in non-consecutive showings.) There is seldom a time when one cannot find a similarly "good" legitimate play to spend an evening with in New York. Nevertheless, I note that in 1951 the finest of all non-musical offerings was a revival from the old art-theatre days, Shaw's *Saint Joan*. It was acted with real inspiration in the title part, by Uta Hagen, and the production had been put together with understanding; but there was sufficient unevenness in the playing to remind us of a sad truth: there were no longer enough actors skilled in poetic diction and imaginative interpretation to cast such a play superlatively. Versatile acting, inspired acting, poetic acting, had declined sadly in the realistic era.

Since the routine American playwrights have been less than fully reported in this chapter, it should be added that, in addition to those especially mentioned—Thornton Wilder, Tennessee Williams, Marc Connelly, Lillian Hellman, Arthur Miller—there were other gifted writers who contributed richly to audience entertainment. On the serious side, Sidney Kingsley wrote *Men in White*, a play about doctors (a Pulitzer Prize winner), and *Dead End*, a sociological drama that was appropriately and grandly staged by Norman Bel Geddes. John Patrick scored with an ingratiating comedy, *The Hasty Heart*, in 1943, although his most famous and most imaginative play, *The Teahouse of the August Moon*, based on a novel by Vern Sneider, was not seen until 1953. Doubtless history will reserve a footnote for two "workhorses" of Broadway, George S. Kaufman and George Abbott. They were seldom known as full-length dramatists. As co-authors, however, often teamed with minor stage people or with non-theatre celebrities, they put over innumerable "hits." As rewrite men, as play doctors, they were supreme theatre craftsmen.

As if to mark the close of an era, the end of a half-century, a remarkable play opened in New York in 1949. *The Death of a Salesman* by Arthur Miller seemed to sum up the main tendencies of the preceding twenty years, even while it foreshadowed movements to follow in the fifties. The play was in substance a realistic record of the downward progress, toward suicide, of a mindless drummer, faced with the failure of his dream of being well-liked by business associates and family. Weighted in dialogue with vulgarisms of speech—considered "advanced" at this time—it touched nevertheless into real tragedy and philosophic stimulus. In form the realistic story was modified by recourse to expressionistic cutbacks and distortions. The generally sordid atmosphere of the play and its implications of futility and the emptiness of life marked a step toward the vacuous realism of Beckett, Ionesco and the other "Absurdists" of the following decade. Miller's play was not only a popular success in the commercial theatre; it went on to endless production in stock and summer theatres and at the universities. But it is notable that the playwright patterned his story in the well-made-play tradition, with preparation, development, climax, etc.

The foremost revolutionary figure of the period 1930 to 1950, Bertolt Brecht, had little effect upon the theatre of Europe and the

Americas before mid-century. But then his theories and his productions were to achieve a fame approaching those of a Craig or a Stanislavsky. One of his early projects—not in the main line of his development as a theatre artist—was enormously successful; it was he who rewrote John Gay's *The Beggar's Opera* and with Kurt Weill as composer, launched *Die Dreigroschenoper*, or, as it is known in English-speaking countries, *The Three Penny Opera*. Its picturesque cast of

Design by Jo Mielziner for Arthur Miller's *The Death of a Salesman*. A multiple set with changes of scene controlled by lighting. [Photograph by Peter Juley & Son.]

thieves, prostitutes and beggars, its inversions of bourgeois conventions, its spoofing of the heroics of grand opera, and its music gave delight to audiences in advanced theatres everywhere. Brecht was drawn to the *Beggar's Opera* because his sympathies lay with the rejected and the proletarian; he was a born rebel.

His next step was toward contemporary Marxism and Communism, and he strove to use his theatre effectively in those causes. In his productions—he was playwright, poet, producer, actor—he sought thenceforward to *change* the playgoer. He declared against the old theatre, with its plays that left audiences emotionally moved, amused, fascinated, satisfied. He wanted the playgoer to leave the theatre with the desire to help—toward Communism.

His personal life became a part of the history of the times. The National Socialists were coming to power in Germany. He caricatured Hitler and made ironic fun of the goose-stepping Nazis, and savagely satirized their pretensions to racial superiority. Defiant to the end, he nevertheless abandoned his theatre in Berlin and fled from Germany in 1933. His immediate wanderings took him to Czecho-Slovakia, Austria, Switzerland, France, and Denmark. As the Nazi armies approached, he went on to Sweden, then Finland. Everywhere a few theatre people knew the innovations of Brecht; but he failed to re-establish his production work, except occasionally and mostly in workingmen's theatres. From Finland he pushed on via Vladivostok to California. He spent years in Hollywood, almost fruitlessly, doing hack work and planning; though a happy association with Charles Laughton resulted from that actor's desire to stage his play *Galileo*. The production, delayed until 1947, was a failure from Brecht's point of view; Laughton had tamed Galileo. Even the New York critics, when the production was imported from the West Coast, condemned it. Brecht meantime was hauled before the notorious House Committee on Un-American Activities, where again he touched on history: Richard M. Nixon was one of the trial committee members. Not author of any treasonable poems or scenarios, and not a member of the Community party, Brecht went unpunished (though ten other playwrights or scenarists were imprisoned for a year, for refusal to testify).

Quickly he left America for Switzerland. There he found happiness for a time because he was accepted as one of the foremost geniuses of the modern theatre, especially at the Zurich *Schauspielhaus*. Late in 1948 he and his wife, Helene Weigel, the great Viennese-born actress who had been his co-worker through more than twenty years, were permitted to return to their beloved Berlin. Immediately the East German government gave Brecht the Berlin *Stadttheater*, and the foundations of the famous *Berliner Ensemble* were laid. In 1954, Brecht's old theatre in Berlin was rebuilt and became a center of experiment and the home of the *Ensemble*. Among advanced groups this came to be called the most accomplished acting company in Europe.

Brecht revived his old plays and wrote new ones. He adapted ancient plays, especially from the Greeks, although from Shakespeare to Hauptmann he found classics that he felt needed "sharpening up." (Usually his changes were to emphasize tyranny and oppression, or to forecast the workingman's world.) His theories of theatrical art are spelled out in words—he was a lifelong dialectician and controversialist—but are not readily understandable. His early differentiation of his as "Epic" theatre, as against all the types of theatre before him, and especially as contrasted with the bourgeois Ibsen theatre, was widely noted but scarcely of historical importance. Epic theatre was to be the ideal theatre of the new collectivist world, stimulating the playgoer to thought and action, over and above his involvement emotionally. Brecht was rebelling against not only the mass of "narcotic" drama from which he had to choose as actor and director of a theatre; he disliked the museum-like atmosphere prevailing in leading repertory houses. As a committed Communist he wanted to make all play production active in the Cause.

If "Epic" failed as a descriptive term, the critics and leftist workers found plenty to write and talk about under the rubric "The Theatre of Commitment"; though some preferred the more descriptive names:

Bertolt Brecht, founder of the "Theatre of Commitment" and foremost creative force in the experiment and turmoil of the mid-century theatre. [By courtesy of the German Information Center, New York.]

"Theatre of Social Action" or "Theatre of Social Conviction"

Out of the turmoil aroused by Brecht's plays and his manifestoes came the "Theatre of Alienation," and this foreshadowed the most striking movements of the fifties and the sixties, beginning with the "Theatre of the Absurd." The playgoer, Brecht had said, was not to be lulled and left satisfied as in the older theatre. He must be brought

Hanne Hiob as Johanna in Bertold Brecht's *St. Joan of the Stockyards*, as produced by the *Deutsches Schauspielhaus*, Hamburg, 1959. In most Brecht productions there was careful avoidance of aesthetic values or "decoration" in the settings. [By courtesy of the German Information Center, New York.]

alive for action. To this end each drama, even each scene in a drama, was to be vitalized, must be made potent beyond mere pleasing of the individual. The actor, the scene designer, the composer of the music, even inserted film sequences, must contribute to the "alienation" of the playgoer. Purists appeared to point out that the "Theatre of Aliena-tion"—the name accepted widely in the English-speaking world—should have been called the "Theatre of Estrangement," because Brecht's Ger-man word had been mistranslated.

In any case, Brecht's plays and Brecht's theories re-animated left-wing theatre art, as mid-century approached, as had no other catalytic force. When Brecht died in 1956 his plays were the most popular, in numbers, after the German classics and Shakespeare, even in West Germany; and Brechtian was a way of production in advanced theatres in England, the Americas, and as far away as Japan. In 1950—our breaking-point between chapters—Brecht's ideas, like time-bombs, had been planted on stages all the way from the home of the *Berliner Ensemble* to the farthest-west campuses of America. He had taken from Craig, from Stanislavsky and from Piscator, among the pioneers of the "modern" theatre, just as he had taken unashamedly from Sophocles and Shakespeare; and he was more talked about in mid-century, than any one of them.

The Broadway theatre was practically untouched by the left-wing movements of the time. In the twenties the Art Theatre movement had exerted beneficial influence on the establishment theatres—that is, the commercial theatres—as seen especially in the gains of ensemble acting and simplified, atmospheric scenic investiture. But if the reader remembers the statistic with which this chapter opened, the fact that the count of commercial houses in New York shrank from seventy-five in 1930 to thirty-two in 1950, he has an indication of the decline of the marketplace theatre. The quality of play choice and production, except in the musicals, had suffered an equally melancholy decline. A number of the old-time stars were to be seen, and an occasional play by a new dramatist, or even a fine drama according to the older standards, might be sandwiched between the increasingly light or sensational offerings; but Broadway had become wholly unrepresentative of what the American theatre-lover might be expected to want. At this time the theatre syndicates—landlord owners of New York theatres and dictators of national booking—were in almost complete control. Their choice of plays was determined by one of the most ignorant and unrepresentative audiences known to the theatre world. A great segment of lovers of serious drama had long since been excluded from the Broadway playhouses by prohibitive ticket prices. The rich in purse do not necessarily make bad audiences; but in New York the playgoers had become largely tourists seeking diversion, businessmen entertaining out-of-town buyers, sensation-seekers, "expense account" spenders. The producers, become profit-seekers above all, and these artificial audiences, not only degraded the New York theatres, but determined what plays would go on the road, that is, tour the rest of the United States.

But one credit might be added for 1950: the plays were comparatively "clean." In comparison with the list of 1970, when an incredible number of New York theatres will have been sold out to dealers in pornography, the mid-century offerings were morally acceptable.

CHAPTER
26

Absurdity and Defilement,
with Bright Interludes—
1950–1970

THE bright, shining thing that is the theatre entered into the second half of the twentieth century in an atmosphere beclouding and confusing. The following twenty years were to be, more often than not, dark and dismaying, in what was offered as drama on the stage, in the world from which came the audiences. On stage and off, futility and shock became watchwords. The infections of cynicism and uncleanliness were to be spread, even by some who were touted as world-leading playwrights, by some of the theatre's leading directors.

The film theatres no less than the legitimate were to experience an unprecedented pull toward the degraded and the degenerate. But, in the midst of decline, there were bright spots or interludes. Let us begin with two hopeful happenings and in two unlikely places, London and New York.

The English theatre in the few years just before 1950 had shown signs of new life, as recorded a few pages back; especially in activities supported by the Arts Council of Great Britain. Repertory companies had been encouraged. The classics, especially Shakespeare, came to a new importance. Plans for a National Theatre, advocated actively from the time of David Garrick, and especially in the period of Henry Irving's leadership more than a century later, were revived. In 1960 the acting company at the Shakespeare Memorial Theatre in Stratford-

Laurence Olivier, possibly England's most distinguished actor at mid-century, recently appointed director of the National Theatre of Great Britain. [By courtesy of the J. Arthur Rank Organization, New York.]

on-Avon was given the title Royal Shakespeare Company. It was in effect *a* National Theatre, with a second home in London, at the Aldwych Theatre. Then, in the early 1960's, personnel mostly from the Old Vic company but with reinforcements from a provincial repertory company which Sir Laurence Olivier had fostered, became The National Theatre. Temporarily the Old Vic building served as a home.

Appropriately the National Theatre opened (with a performance of *Hamlet*) on the four hundredth birthday of William Shakespeare, in 1963. Laurence Olivier was its director. Its success since that date has been phenomenal. Naturally the classics formed the basic plays of the repertory; *Hamlet* with Peter O'Toole and *Othello* with Olivier were especially praised by the critics. But more unexpected applause followed productions of plays by little known writers—even those of followers of Brecht, or of Beckett, the leader of the Absurdists.

London was not alone in enjoying the benefits of government subsidization of acting companies. Resident companies flourished in a number of provincial cities.

In the sixties, actors of the highest rank abounded in England. If the giant figures did not quite come up to the measure of Henry Irving, nevertheless this could be counted a golden age. In no other country were so many actors known as internationally important figures; never before had so many been recognized by their government and on the official honors lists. John Gielgud, Laurence Olivier, Ralph Richardson, Alec Guinness, Michael Redgrave, Anthony Quayle and Paul Scofield were stars known beyond the English borders—and five of these had been knighted. (In 1970 Sir Laurence Olivier was further elevated when he was named by Queen Elizabeth a baron; he was thus the first actor to become a member of the House of Lords.)

The star actresses of the time were fewer, although Vivien Leigh, until her death in 1967, was extraordinarily accomplished: beautiful, versatile, brilliant. Her reputation was international. Margaret Leighton was hardly less admired. Of older actresses, Dame Edith Evans was most beloved and most honored.

It is notable that practically all the actors and actresses named had been members, in their formative years, of the Old Vic Theatre company. Repertory had paved the way for this (minor) renaissance of the theatre art in England. The British repertory companies, incidentally, were generous in visits to other lands, to the Commonwealth countries as far away as Australia and New Zealand, but also to France and the Americas.

In becoming thus one of the brightest spots in the theatrical world, in a difficult time (the country was "on austerity" and the arts not too well nourished), London felt influences from many directions. A stream of new vitality flowed from those countries where revolutionary forces were most active. The *Berliner Ensemble* visited London in 1956, the year of Brecht's death; and Brechtian ideas of play choice, of the needfulness to rewrite or "sharpen up" ancient plays, and of dynamic staging, were not lost on British actors and directors. Even earlier *Waiting for Godot* by Samuel Beckett, considered by many historians the key play of the era, and certainly the type play of the

Vivien Leigh, most famous English actress in the two decades preceding her death in 1967. [By courtesy of the Museum of the City of New York.]

Theatre of the Absurd, had been staged in London. In 1960 *Rhinoceros* by Eugene Ionesco, another Absurdist playwright, was produced in London within three months of its opening in Paris; Laurence Olivier and Joan Plowwright were in the cast. It was the Royal Shakespeare Company itself that presented in London *Marat/Sade*, the wildest, most creatively acted play of the decade. The production was brought to New York the same season.

Of the native dramatists of this exciting time in England's theatre, there is less to be said. In the other arts as in that of the theatre there was much talk about the Kitchen Sink School and of the Angry Young Men. But there were no new playwrights of the stature of Shaw, or even of Sean O'Casey (Irish to the core, but resident in England for more than thirty years, until his death in 1964). The outstanding follower of the school of the Absurdists was Harold Pinter, whose plays dutifully remained in the atmosphere of futility characterizing the school, but less brilliantly than Beckett's or Ionesco's.

As a postscript to the paragraph about writers, it should be added that, on the "light" side, the two decades saw the final triumphs of a commercial playwright—actor, director and composer, too—who epit-

Scene in *Who's Afraid of Virginia Woolf?* in the original production, New York, 1962. The actors are Uta Hagen, Arthur Hill, and George Grizzard. [By courtesy of the Museum of the City of New York.]

omized the old-time concept of the successful theatre-artist: Noel Coward. Through forty-five years, from the date of his first successes as comedy-writer and deviser of musical revues, he pleased a vast public. He was supreme as a leader in "show business," author of some of the cleverest realistic comedies of the era—and a genius in the craft of self-advertising. His career was at various points linked with one of the loveliest actresses of the time: Gertrude Lawrence. She was equally attractive as comedienne and as musical comedy star—an incandescent and magnetic figure direct in the line from Isabella Andreini and Nell Gwyn.

The commercial theatre in America knew little of the creative forces that had thus transformed England's professional theatre. The decade after the mid-century mark brought a number of exciting productions, more often involving the plays of foreign dramatists—Shaw, Anouilh, Christopher Fry, O'Casey—than American; though Tennessee Williams, Arthur Miller, and Thornton Wilder, who had provided unforgettable and world-honored dramatic scripts in the forties, were still writing, their later plays seemed less important. Of the new playwrights, only Edward Albee scored in a big way. His *Who's Afraid of Virginia Woolf?* was clever, absorbing, controversial. On the lighter side there was Neil Simon, author of deft, thoughtless and unfailingly entertaining comedies. He was destined in the sixties to produce nine commercially successful plays—a record for successive "hits." At one time four of his comedies were running concurrently in Broadway houses. The events of the period, however, were likely to be in the nature of classics or revolutionary modern plays brought to New York by foreign repertory companies: Louis Jouvet's in 1950, Jean-Louis Barrault's in 1952, and then the venerable *Comédie Française;* and, especially in the 1960's, National Theatre groups from London, Stockholm, Athens, and repertory companies from the German cities, from Moscow, even from Israel and Japan—not forgetting the even more famous *Folies Bergère.*

Of American plays perhaps the most remarkable was *Long Day's Journey into Night,* by Eugene O'Neill, for which he was posthumously awarded a third Pulitzer Prize. This tragic, dramatic story of his own family—his father and mother, he and his brother were the only characters—was a sort of key to the bitterness that so often had entered into his playwriting. He had known neglect and lack of love, and the autobiographical record became a black classic of the world theatre, intriguing theatre directors and fascinating audiences. It was written, often in tears, when O'Neill was entering that phase of his life when a degenerative disease had made even the effort of writing all but impossible for him. The mood of the play was right for the time in which it was finally produced, in 1955 in Stockholm, in 1956 in Germany and in New York.

It was not in the commercial theatre, however, that history was made in New York in the years following 1950, but in the founding of revolutionary companies which later became known as the Off-Broadway theatre. The impetus of the art theatre movement of the twenties and thirties had been largely lost. There were no groups producing with the idealism that had made notable the Provincetown Players, the Neighborhood Playhouse, the Actors' Theatre, the Group Theatre, and, a little later, Eva LeGallienne's Civic Repertory Theatre. The one persisting group from that golden era, the Theatre Guild, had gradually been driven into the commercial ranks.

Orson Welles and his Mercury Theatre had marked the last stand of the revolutionaries on Broadway, in 1937. If a start had been made

Scene from Eugene O'Neill's *Long Day's Journey into Night*, in the first New York production, 1956. The actors in the foreground are Florence Eldridge and Frederic March; behind them, Bradford Dillman and Jason Robards. [By courtesy of the Walter Hampden Memorial Library at the Players, New York.]

now and then, in the following years, to provide stages free of the restrictive costs of producing which had driven experiment from the commercial houses, there were no lasting projects until about 1950. In that year the Circle-in-the-Square, an arena theatre, was opened—well off Broadway. Between 1950 and 1955 a dozen new revolutionary groups came into active production work; including the controversial Living Theatre, opening in 1951, and driven out of New York in 1963, and the Theatre de Lys. In the sixties the Off-Broadway theatres had become so set in a pattern—and in some cases so obviously trial theatres for Broadway—that the more radical experimenters invented a new name: Off-Off-Broadway. The merely Off-Broadway groups had caught up with Brecht ¡and the Absurdists, and indeed the plays of Brecht, Beckett, Ionesco and their fellows had become staple offerings; the more radical groups were variously moving toward the Theatre of Shock and the Theatre of Audience Participation, if not, indeed, non-theatre, as in Happenings and total improvisations.

By the season 1956–57 the more serious drama critics were covering outstanding off-Broadway openings almost as routinely as they covered regular Broadway offerings. If they often found the productions less than inspiringly acted, they encountered superior plays and a general atmosphere of fresh theatrical life and intelligence. In the New York district a generous portion of the creative directing was to be seen at the non-commercial houses; and increasingly the most sensitive professional actors, under privilege from the Actors Equity Association to accept less than the fixed minimum commercial salaries, went out to join the semi-professional groups. Thus some of the most illuminating acting of the period was to be seen at the Theatre de Lys, the Circle-in-the-Square and similar playhouses. Most off-Broadway acting companies had to be content with housing in attics, church basements, converted stores, or such little theatres, surviving from the activity of the twenties, as the Provincetown Playhouse and the Cherry Lane Theatre.

One group, however, opened (in 1953) in a full-size house: the Phoenix Theatre. It was, as distances are measured in New York, very far off Broadway; but its casts were fully professional (at lowered salaries) and its direction of the best. The acting group, under T. Edward Hambleton and Norris Houghton, was built around the idea of presenting unusual plays, not likely to be hazarded by the commercial producers. A long-time Phoenix aim was the establishment of a true repertory theatre in New York.

For many years the Phoenix directors had to hold the repertory feature in abeyance; once they extended a long run through a full season. In the sixties they provided New York with its most distinguished series of productions, including classics from Shakespeare, Goldsmith and Sheridan to Ibsen, Shaw, Tolstoy and O'Casey. An alliance with the Association of Producing Artists helped to maintain the Phoenix productions at the highest levels of staging. But the company, failing to receive sufficient subsidy, found itself in 1970 still less than a true repertory institution.

A sadder story was that of the Vivian Beaumont Repertory Theatre, in New York's Lincoln Center for the Performing Arts. The two sister theatres at the Center, a new Metropolitan Opera House (costing forty-two million dollars) and a State Theatre for musical shows and ballet, had been designed on nineteenth-century, court-theatre models. The Beaumont Theatre, however, was designed on modern lines, with due regard to twentieth-century innovations in staging. A company was developed under two artist-directors, Robert Whitehead and Elia Kazan, and a fairly successful season followed, with Molière, O'Neill and Arthur Miller plays featured. But the administrative head at Lincoln Center, not believing in repertory, all but wrecked the project by trying to appoint a "sensible"—that is, a commercial—business manager over the artist-directors. The company was shattered, the directors lost.

A new company was assembled, with about one-third of the actors from the old company retained. Two directors from San Francisco, who had been experimentally successful in staging plays at their Actors Workshop there, Herbert Blau and Jules Irving, were commissioned to re-form the company. They brought fourteen of their actors from the Coast with them, and then filled out with as many new faces. Although there were some sterling actors in the company, the consensus among critics has been that the productions after 1965 lacked the sort of distinction theatregoers expect from an experienced and dedicated repertory institution. Despite some exceptional and sometimes revolutionary productions, there has not been inspired ensemble acting. And the Vivian Beaumont Repertory Theatre in 1970 carries the word "repertory" only in its name, not in its method of play presentation. It is hardly more, after six years of experimenting, than a glorified stock company. The account of a near-failure would not be worth telling in a history if the pattern had not been that of practically every attempt in the United States to develop repertory theatres serving communities as do those of Russia, Germany, France—and at last, England. Culturally America just had not caught up with the standards of the Old World.

History may record that outside New York the foundations were somewhat more stable. The project most successful, as the community and visiting critics judged it, was the Minnesota Theatre Company at Minneapolis, known also as the Tyrone Guthrie Theatre. The organizers were fortunate in bringing Guthrie, a distinguished British actor and director—once director of the Old Vic repertory company—from London to organize their producing company and to direct in the early years. For a group necessarily immature at first, and given to experimental treatment of the classics, the Tyrone Guthrie players served their community well in the years 1963–1970; although they are hardly to be compared with the European national theatres.

Other cities served (sometimes briefly) by repertory companies were Chicago, San Francisco and Milwaukee. An accomplished group that appropriated the name National Repertory Theatre aspired to take plays in repertory fashion to a chain of cities, and at times to the campuses of the universities. In some communities encouraging efforts were made to develop non-commercial but fully professional compa-

Experiments in stagecraft continued through the 1960's, especially in Germany. This scene from a production of Goethe's *Iphigenia in Tauris*, in Darmstadt, is based on a spiral design by Ruodi Barth, borrowed from the then-current Op Art painters. [By courtesy of the German Information Center, New York.]

nies—often revolutionary in play choice and in methods of staging— which would later blossom into full repertory institutions. Some such ideal must have been in the mind of Margo Jones when the Dallas Little Theatre graduated from amateur to professional status in the fifties. The Arena Theatre in Washington, D.C., the Mark Taper Forum in Los Angeles, and the American Conservatory Theatre in Chicago, then San Francisco, did pioneer work in advanced production; in general they looked to establishment of a dedicated theatre identity rather than mere presentation of individually exciting plays. But still, as the season 1969–1970 closed, there was no true national repertory theatre in the United States.

In Canada the picture was better. A seasonal theatre, a summer Festival theatre, flourished at Stratford, Ontario. The Stratford Shakespearean Festival, organized in 1953 under the direction of Tyrone Guthrie (with strength drawn from both the Old Vic of London and the Shakespeare Theatre of another Stratford) built up its acting company and its repertory until, in the sixties, it was hailed as one of the foremost institutional theatres in America: a company with a tradition and a long, unbroken record of service.

The Off-Broadway theatres in New York seldom aspired to repertory status. They were established rather as experimental centers, as protests against a commercial theatre in which production costs prohibited the tryouts so important to young playwrights. They were part of a vast network of experimental theatres—mostly little—that had developed over the country, with especially fine theatre buildings on the university campuses. In New York by 1960 the number of Off-Broadway houses was about forty. During the following decade the number was slightly increased; but exact listing had become impossible because restaurants, barrooms or "clubs" were offering "shows" not always to be classified as drama. Insofar as new ideas were developing in America, Off-Broadway was the prime breeding area; though sometimes a play by a foreign innovator, perhaps a Brecht or a Beckett, made a success in London and then was brought to Broadway. Nevertheless, the absurd, the shocking, the incredible was most often seen on the experimental stages.

THE Theatre of the Absurd not only summed up the negative philosophies of its time—or the abandonment of philosophy—it was a natural culmination of the succession of pessimistic and irrational tendencies in theatre experiment between 1920 and 1950. The despair of O'Neill, the insistent irreligion, even atheism, of Sartre and the other existentialist playwrights, the willful irrationality of the Dadaists and Surrealists (more pronounced in the other arts than on the stage), the alienation aims of Brecht: all these led toward a theatre that would demonstrate the futility of living and the impotence of man.

The most picturesque, but undramatic, Absurdist play was *Waiting for Godot*, or *En Attendant Godot* in the original French. It was produced in 1952 in Paris, and ran there nearly a year. Its author was Samuel Beckett, an Irish writer who had become an expatriate, writing his plays and novels in the French language. It was played in many European theatres; Beckett's own translation was seen in London in 1955. A Broadway production in that year was not a success (that is, not a success on Broadway's terms, at excessive production costs, excessive seat prices, and for New York audiences). But when the play was released for other than the commercial circuit, its popularity ran like wildfire through the university and other progressive theatre centers, not only in America but wherever the modern spirit had touched producing groups. It was widely hailed as the representative play of the era.

Waiting for Godot is played by two tramps, two drifters, who have met "at a country road. Evening." This is the whole description of the

Scene in *Waiting for Godot* in the first production, at the *Théâtre de Babylone*, Paris, 1953. The purposely scant setting is by S. Garstein. [By courtesy of the French Cultural Services, New York.]

scene—spare like everything else in the play. Two additional tramps drift in, and once a boy appears to say that Godot will not arrive tonight, but will come tomorrow night. There is no action, but a steady stream of talk, recollection, bickering, surmise. The first line of dialogue is "Nothing to be done." The first of the two acts ends with this dialogue:

Estragon: Well shall we go?
Vladimir: Yes, let's go.
   They do not move. Curtain.

The end of the second act is exactly the same except that Vladimir asks the question and Estragon answers. The final curtain goes down on the two men waiting. Doing nothing is the theme, sum and substance of the play. There are many passages wherein the futility of action and the emptiness of life are spoken of. It all points up the absurdity of living. A few critics pointed out that Beckett's intention may have been less than completely negative: although Godot does not arrive during the play, the protagonists are still waiting, and so the playwright ends on a note of hope. But hope is about the last of the virtues instilled by the Absurdist dramatists.

Thus we come in the mid-twentieth century to plays from which *story* has been excluded. Through the ages an *action* has been the primary component of drama. In earlier pages representative plays have been briefly outlined, from the moving tragedy of *Oedipus the King* to the sad story of Iris, in the age of emotional realism, and the hurried newsreel effectiveness of the Expressionistic *Masse-Mensch*. If we think of the medieval religious drama as instructional and naive, its substance nevertheless was the stories of Jesus, of Mary, of Adam and Eve, and especially of the saints. The Absurdists brought us to non-story, non-action for its own sake. They were especially partial to the non-hero.

In a second play of Beckett's, *Krapp's Last Tape,* there is but one actor and his "speeches" are hardly more than murmurings about a tape recording of an earlier episode in his life, when he had been an author, and vaguely in love. His comments are those of a resigned, defeated, but not always bitter man: a failure, beyond help, and probably destined not to hear any further recordings. In a second "static" play, *Happy Days*, an old man and his wife are literally stuck in the mire of their past life, or (in some productions) in trash cans. When the curtain goes up the figures are seen only from the waist up. The symbolism is deliberate: this couple has passed a footless, meaningless life without foundations in reality. Before the end, they have slipped until only their heads and shoulders can be seen. The gist of the play is in its humor, and perhaps pity is intended. The woman is an incurable optimist, pointing out repeatedly that every catastrophe or annoyance heralds a blissful event. She clings to all the clichés, sentimental justifications and illusive daydreams that have (in the Absurdist view) served her in place of reality during her lifetime. A bag beside her holds all her possessions: mirror, comb, etc., but also a revolver.

That Beckett's plays were of the texture of the times is scarcely to be doubted. He mirrored, perhaps hastened, the era of disillusion, violence and faithlessness of the world's young people, whose actions have shattered great universities, cast serious doubt on the wisdom or capability of the world's rulers—and rendered the theatre as often as not a house of hopelessness, filthiness, and aimless escape. The universality of Samuel Beckett's acceptance was signalized in 1969 when he was awarded the Nobel Prize for literature, the first dramatist so honored since O'Neill.

Among the other playwrights of the school who appeared between 1950 and 1970 were the French Genêt, the Rumanian Ionesco, writing in French, and the English Pinter. Before these, and recognized as a prophet of their kind of theatre art, there had appeared another Frenchman, Antonin Artaud. He had been an actor, a poet and a director, but he was unsuccessful in bringing his revolutionary ideas into actual production. He called for a return to pure theatre and especially the abandonment of words as the main instrument in forwarding dramatic action. Words describe; gesture or motion more surely conveys meaning and feeling. But Artaud was unable, beyond one production in 1935, to attempt demonstration of his theories. He died in 1948, in destitution, defeated and pronounced insane. However he wrote a book, *The Theatre and Its Double*, which went onto the shelf with the revolutionary works of Craig, Appia, Stanislavsky and Copeau. He called his visioned theatre the Theatre of Cruelty. Everything active is cruel, he said. As the theatre becomes non-wordy, it becomes more cruel.

It was Eugene Ionesco who, beginning in 1950, wrote plays that most vividly combined Artaud's bias toward the non-literary drama with the philosophies of the Existentialists and the Absurdists. Labelled an "anti-play," *The Bald Soprano* dispenses with "development" in the old well-made-play sense; and the dialogue has meaning not in what the words say but rather as sound. Rationality has been overthrown; the speeches often border on gibberish. A sample stage direction is "Mr. Martin kisses or does not kiss Mrs. Smith."

Ionesco's *The Chairs* opened in London in a notable production in 1957. The curtain went up on two empty chairs. The theme of the play is emptiness, or as the playwright put it, nothingness. An Old Man and an Old Woman recount their empty, meaningless lives in talk, describing many invisible characters, for whom they keep bringing onto the stage chairs that remain empty. The audience must be made to realize that a meaningless existence is all that can be expected in this absurd world.

A brighter bit of Ionesco's invention was *Rhinoceros*, a play that was a success in Paris, in London and in New York in 1960 and 1961. Some critics thought the playwright had compromised his Absurdist ideas: there was almost a story-line in the unfolding of a man's efforts to hold to his identity as a man when those around him were turning into rhinoceroses. But along the way were included the inanities, the trivialities, the ironic nothingnesses that stud all Absurdist "plots." The play seems to end inconclusively: the protagonist, who refuses to conform, has not yet become a rhinoceros. But in an agonizingly long final speech, during which he watches himself in a mirror, he reveals his increasing ugliness; he is so ugly a monster that he cannot be a rhinoceros. Rhinoceroses have become beautiful creatures. Their sounds, which have been like an evil choral accompaniment during

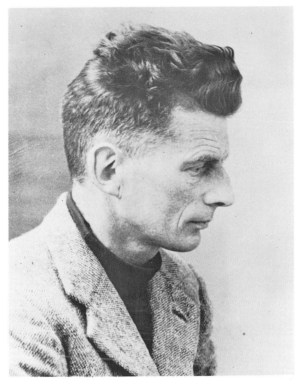

Samuel Beckett, Irish dramatist who writes his plays in French. Most creative playwright of the Theatre of the Absurd. [By courtesy of the French Cultural Services, New York.]

the play, have become melodious and charming. His failure in not having become one of them is the final irony.

The Theatre of the Absurd, though at first a substantially French development, became the most popular advanced type of theatre internationally within the decade of the fifties. It seems that the English are as without purpose in life as the French; at least the deprived classes and the lower middle classes are as ignorant of reality. Their lives afford the material for Harold Pinter's plays. The emptiness is less marked than in Beckett's works, and there is little of Ionesco's twisting of word-values. In fact, Pinter might pass for a typical naturalistic playwright following the world-wide downward trend in choice of subject-matter, except that the theme always seems to be failure; the characters are failures. There is effective comedy along the way, but the end is likely to be nightmarish. In this the English dramatist may link with the French Genêt rather than with the more familiar Absurdists.

In 1956 Jean Genêt's most famous play, *The Balcony*, was presented in London, not for the general public but for a small subscription audience. England's theatres were then under control of an official censor. But in the following years it was produced all over Europe and the Americas, as a staple of the emancipated theatre. The setting is a brothel, one of the best, to which come all the best people—rulers, judges, labor leaders, police—to have their disguises removed, their pretensions ridiculed. Genêt is the great leveler. He levels every character to the plane he knows, the lowest. An orphan, brought up in asylums and reformatories, a jailbird and a drifter, he yet had a genius for writing, and he wrote of the world he knew, a world peopled by criminals, prostitutes, homosexuals. Journalistic, somewhat imaginative, he was Absurdist to the extent that his plays ridiculed all the images of respectability, morality and distinction assumed by man. He made his mark especially in the sixties, when the content of literature, and particularly of drama, touched bottom, concerning itself with the defeated, the tortured, the dissolute.

The flow of thin Absurdist plays as "the new thing" in the world theatre was at least temporarily deflected when in 1964 *Marat/Sade* was produced in Germany, and in an English version in the same year. A German playwright, Peter Weiss (living in Sweden), here widened the theatre art to encompass a play within a play, to embroider a drama of older type with so much of accompanying comment, characterization and sideshow, that pure theatre triumphed over routine story-unfoldment. The inner play was the often dramatized story of the assassination of the revolutionary leader Marat by the gentle-born Charlotte Corday. The added theatricalism is explained by the full title: *The Persecution and Assassination of Jean-Paul Marat as performed by the inmates of the Asylum of Charenton under the direction of the Marquis de Sade.*

Peter Weiss had learned a great deal from Brecht, who had originally been nurtured upon Expressionism. Weiss had the inspiration to bring together the old Marat story, that of the accomplished but generally denounced Marquis de Sade, and the horde of lunatics and social outcasts resident at Charenton. Lunacy has its comic side, and it is a revealer of character. The incessant interruption of the inner story, by a large cast, permitted a great deal of clever characterization at the edges of the play, so to speak. The result, as the piece was staged by the Royal Shakespeare Company, under the creative direction of Peter Brook, in London and New York, was a theatrical circus, entertaining always, startling at times, puzzling if an observer sought an over-all

Scene in Rolf Hochhuth's *The Deputy*, in the production in Berlin, 1963, under the direction of Erwin Piscator. Günther Tabor is shown as Riccardo and Richard Häussler as the Nazi "doctor" in the controversial final scene at Auschwitz. [By courtesy of the German Information Center, New York.]

meaning. That it heralded a new modern form in the theatre would be hazardous to say, but certainly it introduced a richness of dramatic ingredients, a full panoply of theatrical effects, which had been absent from stage production ever since the clinical realists and the Absurdists took over.

Doubtless there were some observers in every audience at *Marat/Sade* who were shocked and sickened at certain episodes and at occasional lapses to gutter language. But the play had largeness and joy in acting. Joy had been generally lacking in the plays of Beckett and Pinter.

Marat/Sade signalled the arrival of the most notable group of post-Absurdist dramatists known to the theatres of the sixties: the Germans. In addition to Peter Weiss there were at least three internationally recognized figures, Rolf Hochhuth, Heinar Kipphardt, and Günther Grass. In general these dramatic authors may be said to have gone back to the play with story, and to have been politically minded— if not propagandist. The name of the Swiss playwright Friedrich Dürrenmatt should be added, as a creative member of the group.

Rolf Hochhuth made his first outstanding success when the veteran revolutionary Erwin Piscator, having returned to Germany from his years of exile in the United States, staged *Der Stellvertreter*. Produced in London as *The Deputy* in 1964, it became the subject of endless controversy. In effect the play asked why Pope Pius XII did not direct Germany's Catholics to oppose Adolf Hitler's persecution of the Jews and thus prevent the horrors of Auschwitz and Buchenwald. A hardly less controversial play by Hochhuth was *The Soldier*, a similar documentary composition that asks what justification can there be for the wartime aërial bombing of defenseless cities. The protagonist is Winston Churchill, who is taken to pieces and discredited systematically and ruthlessly. In Churchill's country the play was promptly banned, but elsewhere—because it fitted nicely into the world-wide propaganda of the pacifists—it was produced amid cheers and bitter protest.

A play about an equally controversial subject, by Kipphardt, was *In the Case of J. Robert Oppenheimer*, produced in Germany and Switzerland in 1964, and in the United States later. Because it touched upon the subject of the military use of the atom bomb, although the drama is more immediately concerned with the shameful treatment of Oppenheimer by a governmental commission in Washington, the production was another sign that the public, and especially the German public, had not lost interest in the play of ideas.

The other German dramatist (and novelist) of the sixties who contributed to the flow of politically oriented plays over the stages of the Western world was Günther Grass. Again, as in *The Deputy* and *The*

Soldier, the theme is the (assumed) failure of a central character to live up to the highest concepts of humanitarian service. In this case the protagonist is the theatre revolutionary Bertolt Brecht, who is but thinly disguised as "the Boss." It was Grass' belief that when a minor revolt of workers took place in East Germany in 1953, it failed only because it lacked a leader, that Brecht should have been its leader, and

Scene in the first production of Heinar Kipphardt's *The Case of J. Robert Oppenheimer* at the *Berlin Freie Volksbühne* under the direction of Erwin Piscator, 1964. Superlatively cast, with Dieter Borsche in the title role, the play served to establish the "Theatre of Fact" as a successor to the "Theatre of the Absurd." [By courtesy of the German Information Center, New York.]

that he compromised because he wanted to please the government (which had subsidized his theatre). The play—the title has been translated into English as *The Plebeians Rehearse the Uprising*—was produced with some remarkable Brechtian effects in West Berlin in 1969; an equally brilliant staging was that of the Royal Shakespeare Company in London in 1970.

In these several modern German plays—except in some respects, the one about Oppenheimer—there were signs of a reversal from the presentation of spare, quiet scripts emphasizing the emptiness of life. The pieces by Weiss and Grass marked return to theatricalism in the fullest sense. Whether it is the lunatics of Charenton, acting sometimes as individuals, sometimes as choral groups, muttering and wailing, or again pushing in to interrupt the Marat story, or the Plebeians of Berlin, driven by the Soviet tanks, breaking in on a Brecht rehearsal, the many secondary characters add drama, and not unimportantly, richness of thought and deadly conviction. This sort of play belonging obviously, or at any rate politically, to the Theatre of Commitment (as we met it in Brecht's time), belongs also to the Theatre of Fact, as one of the concerned playwrights named it. These are plays reaching far out into documentation.

IT WAS in the late sixties that the university campuses were struck by insurrection and turmoil, in the United States and in France especially, but hardly less so in Japan and Mexico and Spain. The visual arts had known revolution since the first decade of the century: painting and sculpture from then until the sixties took forms that would not have been recognized as serious art by nineteenth-century "authorities." The theatre is rightly a part of the cultural picture, and cannot be considered apart from the educational establishment and from the other arts. It thus was appropriate that in the late sixties the most radical theatre change of all was proposed—and demonstrated. The actors and directors of a few European and American producing groups decided that the immemorial separation of performers from audience must be abolished. Actor and observer must be one. Thus a final break with the old-fashioned theatre was accomplished. The result was the Theatre of Involvement. Even rebel students and abstract painters could not ask for a more drastic change from the past.

In the Theatre of Involvement there is no longer a dividing line between actor and spectator. The theatregoer buys his ticket as of old, but instead of lingering in an auditorium he is brought on-stage, to act with the (other) actors. Sometimes he is invited to go through a ritual such as taking off some (or all) of his street clothes, or reading an outline of the action of which he will be a part, or perhaps he is simply asked to carry, symbolically, a lighted candle—these devices serving to cancel out the abyss that has traditionally existed between stage and auditorium.

The genius of the Involvement movement was Jerzy Grotowski, director of the Polish Laboratory Theatre, who brought his extraordinary plays to New York in 1969. Immediately productions featuring audience participation were reported from Los Angeles, from New York's Off-Broadway houses, from the European centers of experiment. Some were serious attempts to add a new dimension to enjoyment of the theatre art; and indeed there were eminent critics who testified to achieving a mood of exaltation at a Grotowski performance. They were drawn into an experience through the intensity of the actors' passion and the closeness of contact. "Touch" was a new and compelling factor. The mood and the contact were at times less innocent.

That the Theatre of Involvement could not mark out a main direction for the art soon became evident, because the audience participants seldom numbered more than twenty or thirty. There were, of course, indignant critics who asked why it was necessary to mention the theatre at all. One could as well be an actor in a demonstration, an orgy, or a get-together that ends up a social evening with song and dance. But Grotowski and his accomplished ensemble of actors seemed destined to go on to exceptional achievement.

The story of the revolutionary leaders and cults, from the Theatre of Commitment to the Theatre of Involvement, was as necessary to our present purposes, in a brief history of the theatre art, as would be a chronicle of the twentieth century "isms" if we were dealing with painting and sculpture. Nevertheless, the most lasting and the most widely accepted of the theatre movements, Absurdism, though obviously relevant to the times and the state of the world, was based on a negative philosophy and a pinched view of humanity. It was important as a reaction from the shallowly bright comedies of the days of the ten-twenty-thirty stock companies and circuits, not forgetting some of the later well-made-play fare on Broadway. And there is food for thought in the claim of the Absurdists that all life *is* grist for the dramatist; that the lowest, the most dismal and disillusioning facets of living should be brought to attention in dramatic form. Nevertheless, this in the end was recognized as a negative and divisive force in the modern theatre, and a force totally unable by its nature to spell out a future for the art.

The reader should remember that while the "isms" come and go, each demanding attention, that other theatre—the theatre of the Establishment, if you wish—continues to pour forth the traditional forms of entertainment. And if you happen to live in a theatrically fortunate country such as Germany, your hunger for drama can be appeased as easily and with as rich fare as in olden days. Where state repertory theatres do not exist, there are acting companies subsidized by the cities. In West Germany more than one hundred and fifty subsidized repertory theatres continued to offer classic and modern productions. (Germany's basic classics are Schiller, Goethe and Shakespeare. The moderns offered are as likely as not Thornton Wilder and Tennessee Williams.) The acting companies are of a standard unknown where the repertory system does not prevail; emphasis is on the total effect rather than the brilliant playing of stars.

Naturally some repertory houses tended to be old-fashioned in choice of plays and in acting methods, according to the abilities of the director, sometimes because of interference by the civic authorities, and to a certain extent according to the intellectual and artistic tastes of the audiences. The point is that in German-speaking countries— Austria and part of Switzerland are to be included—the repertory theatres, the commercially administered theatres, and a wide range of workingmen's theatres and experimental stages, were combined in a richly rewarding service to the playgoer.

The system which results in this sort of service, because countries or local communities consider the theatre as worthy of public financial support as the symphony orchestra or the public library, is still flourishing in many countries of Europe. At this chapter's beginning the story was told of England's new national theatres. In Russia the two decades since 1950 have seen no lessening of services to audiences— thirty-six repertory companies in Moscow alone—and the variety of fare and the brilliance of performance is probably unsurpassed anywhere. The Russian system is different, of course, in that all theatres are state-owned; and it must be added, in sadness, that in the one matter of censorship the Soviet theatre has been backward: certain political themes are forbidden. This circumstance may explain why the half-century of Russian Communism has failed to bring forth one dramatist of the stature of Tolstoy, Dostoievski, Chekhov and Gorky.

The theatres in other Communist countries flourished as did the Russian. Sometimes, as in Poland, extraordinary progress was made in sharpening the staging in accordance with the latest techniques, and in showing the newest plays from both Russia and the West. In Czecho-Slovakia and Jugoslavia some little progress was made in liberalizing the ban against politically divergent plays, within the excellent theatre service normal to these countries.

In Finland the number of acting companies to which the government contributed subsidies rose to more than thirty. The Finnish National Theatre was at the center of an extraordinary attempt to make the classics, recent foreign plays, and especially plays by native writers available to audiences of all classes.

In the picture of current theatre activity, the Irish playhouses, so long counted among the most interesting in the world, had come upon comparatively poor times. Long ago, when William Butler Yeats and Lady Gregory had created a new poetic theatre, which was also a glorified folk theatre, and trained the Abbey Theatre Company into an organization famous in all lands, there were Irish actors and Irish playwrights among the most famous. But by an ironic twist of fortune, when Sean O'Casey submitted his first play to the Abbey Theatre directors, it was rejected. Outside Ireland he was to become the most honored Irish dramatist, but he left his native land never to return. The Abbey company nevertheless was so successful that it was designated the Irish National Theatre. Because it became in some respects conservative, and very much involved with the nationalist (Gaelic)

Jean-Louis Barrault and Jean deSailly in a modern adaptation of Ben Jonson's *Volpone*, in a French production. [Photograph by Daniel Frasnay, by courtesy of the French Cultural Services, New York.]

movement, it stimulated a new generation of revolutionaries to found an opposition playhouse and company. The Gate Theatre, also in Dublin, in its turn did yeoman's service not only in encouraging native playwrights but in producing plays from France, England and America. In the early sixties the impetus passed on to other groups and the Gate company faded from sight. A new incursion of commercialism brought down the standards in Dublin's playhouses (except the Abbey), but the "outside" theatres increased in number and afforded new reason for faith in the future.

In Ireland a second theatre, beyond the English-speaking theatre for which the great Irish dramatists—Yeats, Synge, O'Casey—wrote, had been active especially in the decades before mid-century. The government even subsidized a company of Gaelic players. But the language group had produced no dramatist or play heard beyond Irish borders. In the United States a second theatre came into prominence especially in the sixties. The Negro theatre up to that time had been integrated into the white man's theatre. The record had been creditable enough for the black actors, and occasionally for a black playwright—but on the terms of the white theatre as traditionally organized, and in forms attractive to white audiences.

For a century there had been featured black shows. Most popular, and indeed a staple American theatrical product, exported to England and France at times, was the Negro minstrel show. This full-evening entertainment cleverly combined badinage between an interlocutor (generally white) and members of a Negro company deployed in a semi-circle on the stage, the "end men" delivering the most telling lines, varied with song, dance and vaudeville turns, sometimes farcical, sometimes melodramatic. The minstrel show form had been worked out by whites—Negro companies were not permitted in theatres until after the Civil War—and the materials were taken from what the authors considered the comicalities and the picturesque customs of Negro life.

Down the years there were other attempts to bring the blacks into the establishment theatre, and some effort to provide black theatre, especially at the black colleges. In the time of the art theatre movement, and a concurrent liberal attitude toward civil rights, there were notable Negro triumphs in the white theatres, most memorably Paul Green's *In Abraham's Bosom*, the Pulitzer Prize play of 1926; *Porgy*, by DuBose and Dorothy Hayward, staged by the Theatre Guild in 1927, and in adaptation as a folk-opera entitled *Porgy and Bess* in 1935; and the monumentally successful *The Green Pastures* by Marc Connelly, dramatized from Roark Bradford's stories of Bible incidents purportedly as a Negro preacher imagined them. The performance of Richard Harrison as "De Lawd" in *The Green Pastures* has been a legendary memory among both blacks and whites. About the same time Paul Robeson took high rank among actors, especially with his performance as Othello. The Federal Theatre of the Works Progress Administration organized Negro acting companies in several cities, and the *Black Macbeth* and the *Swing Mikado* became famous examples of the Negro spirited style of acting.

But in the sixties a new attitude of disgust for all attempts at racial integration in the theatre swept through the centers where civil rights were a living issue; and in the late years of the decade there appeared black playwrights who contributed the most forceful and certainly the most frightening plays then being produced on the American continent. Sometimes crude as drama—incomplete, seldom rounded out in story line, given to stock characterization rather than portraiture in depth, as any graduate from a drama class could have pointed out—they nevertheless blazed through some marginal white theatres with searing effect. LeRoi Jones was the first and most gifted Negro writer to find outlets for his angry, brutal and purposely offensive plays, as early as 1964 and 1965. In the worst of them he advocated violence, armed rebellion and the ultimate triumph of Black Power. In others he treated with undisguised hostility and scorn white characters in confrontation with black. He was joined by other playwrights, equally indignant, forthright and—to most audiences—jarring. In any case, this was the most original and theatrical playwriting of the mid-century in America. It was "theatre of commitment" with a vengeance. In a country hardly more than beginning to settle the staggering problems of a mixed black-white population, it seemed certain to remain one of the liveliest segments of stage production.

THE period 1950-1970 saw further growth of the progressive theatres at the universities. The greater institutions, which had offered courses in dramatic literature through a half-century, gradually established experimental theatres. Some of these had specialized in playwriting—Harvard University, then Yale, in the twenties, and the University of North Carolina—and some had gone on to a full curriculum of writing, acting and staging. The advance since the mid-century was largely in bringing professional actors to the campuses, to acting companies still composed largely or partly of recent graduates but sufficiently professional to escape the mistrusted amateur rating. The theatre artists turned out by these schools ended usually as teachers and directors in the expanding group of theatre arts departments at lesser universities and colleges; but some graduates went on to service, even stardom, in the still declining Broadway establishment or in the revolutionary groups Off-Broadway.

The development of the university theatres, and the resultant flow of trained and dedicated workers into professional channels, were generally considered the most hopeful steps toward an eventual "comeback" of the American stage, out of utter commercialism and disregard for the institution as an art, to a decent and permanent status comparable to that enjoyed by the collective theatre of England or Germany or Russia.

In 1969 the Yale School of Drama—the undergraduate theatre kept the old-fashioned name—opened a second theatre, transformed from an abandoned church, with a program staged by the professional "Yale Repertory Theatre Company." In the several theatres and studios main-

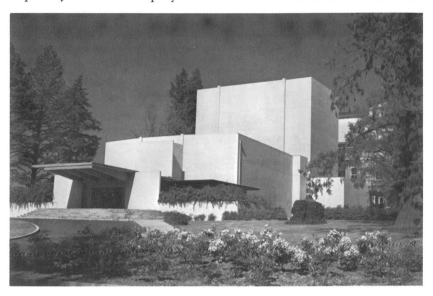

The American university theatres, architecturally, have been in the fore-front of modern design. From Eugene and Berkeley on the West coast to Cambridge and Philadelphia on the East, the new buildings have been cleancut, functional and attractive. This is the theatre at the University of Oregon at Eugene, seating 401 spectators. Designed in 1950 by the architects Annand and Kennedy, with Horace W. Robinson as consultant.

tained by the University's theatre department more than fifty produc-tions were offered in one season. The community at large as well as the students profited.

A different sort of advance was registered by the Department of Theatre Arts at the University of California at Los Angeles. Estab-lished at a school close to Hollywood, it undertook from the start, in 1945, to train workers in the techniques of moving pictures as well as legitimate theatre. In the period 1950 to 1970 it graduated workers who were successful in a wide range of teaching, as well as a horde of young experimenters and creative artists.

WHEN Gordon Craig was leader of the *avant-garde* in the modern theatre—this was a little after the time of Ibsen, rather bridging the time from Brieux and O'Neill to Genêt—he fought the realists as the most insidious enemy of serious dramatic art. He wrote:

> The modern Realistic Theatre, forgetful of all the Laws of Art, set out to reflect the times. It reflects a small particle of the times, it drags back a curtain and exposes to our view an agitated caricature of Man and his Life, a figure gross in its attitude and hideous to look upon. . . . Photographic and Phonographic Realism injure the minds of the people. They thrust upon them a grotesque and inaccurate representation of the outward and visible life—with the divine essence—the spirit —the beauty of life left out. . . . This modern Realistic Theatre pays no heed to the Masters, even if it be aware of the existence of their works. . . .
> With the Freedom of the theatre—free to select what it shall show— comes new hope. Only by its freedom can its health be restored.

As we approach the close of this record of triumphs and crises in the theatre art, I quote gratefully these lines from Gordon Craig, because they may remind us of a truth recently forgotten in many progressive theatres: *freedom* is the lasting element; for the playwright, the actor, the artist-director, there is freedom to select what will be shown on the stage.

The present chapter has been concerned mostly with that last refuge of the realists, the Theatre of the Absurd and some closely related naturalistic cults. Craig had the perfect words for the depressing mood of the Absurdists:

"The gloomy expressions, the shuffling movements—the dark and closed-in scenes—the spasmodic exclamations of the actors—the strange muffled atmosphere—all these things lend themselves to form one sinister impression."

So much of this is true of Beckett's theatre or Ionesco's theatre that one might well term theirs the Sinister Theatre. Others have named it the Theatre of Anarchism or the Theatre of Nihilism, and this better suggests its philosophy of the emptiness and futility of human life. In the generation before Beckett's there had been signs, among the greatest of the Realist playwrights, of a recognition that journalistic realism, or naturalism, was on a perilous course, toward pettiness, anarchism and a bitter cynicism. Eugene O'Neill, after his successes in the realistic field, had turned to study of the classics, having tired of what he termed the "shallowness" of modern life and theatre; and thus came to his monumental work, *Mourning Becomes Electra*. Anouilh reached back in the same way for classic structure and for contact with universality in shaping his plays. And even Bertolt Brecht, for all his concern with the immediate moment, took a great part of his playwriting materials from history, preserving structure while reshaping meaning and detail.

THE final phenomenon that must be recorded in any report upon the theatre of the nineteen-sixties is a decline into scarcely believable depths of pornographic exhibitionism and lewdness, accompanied by a general bias toward anti-religion, if not blasphemy. All that Tertullian had warned about, in A.D. 198, theatres being in his view the very houses of dissoluteness, immodesty and blasphemy, and all that the Puritans of England had deplored thirteen centuries later, picturing the playhouses as schools teaching how to play the harlot, to allure to whoredom and to speak filthily: all this was to disgrace the theatres of Europe and America in the mid-twentieth century.

The wave of pornographic exhibitionism swept over many countries of the Western world, and some in the Orient, engulfing most of the arts—literature, painting, and the theatre both of the living actor and the picture screen. An incredible number of theatres in New York, for instance, by 1970 were offering so-called sex-interest shows, perhaps not to the extent that this might be called the most immoral stage display in history; one has always the theatre of the declining Roman Empire as the most shocking example. But—on Broadway and off—any playgoer could choose from an assortment of "dramas" in which the ultimate sex act was played, actually in the movie versions, "simulated" in the living-actor versions. As if this desecration were not enough, these realists contrived that audiences could witness all the perversions invented during man's sensual history. If your taste were centered less on nudity and straight sex than on serious drama, you could choose plays in which the troubles of homosexuals and especially Lesbians were explored. There were musicals with generous interludes played in the nude or semi-nude. In numberless shows the language of the ghetto gutter was habitually or occasionally heard. The realism of the foul-mouthed follows close on the realism of fornication. There were even theatres advertising "adult" shows with all-male casts: these being houses catering frankly to homosexuals.

In 1969 an entertainment entitled *Oh! Calcutta!* opened in New York. In his script Kenneth Tynan, an English writer, put together erotically poetic, bawdy and extremely dirty one-act plays, by a dozen playwrights, in a melange that made history and started endless controversy. The limits of permissiveness were again pushed outward. The peephole or voyeurist intentions of the producers were underlined when tickets in the first and second rows were priced at twenty-five dollars each. The show was still prospering a year after opening, and was advertised as "the hottest show in town." A rival pornographic entertainment, which had the alluring title *The Dirtiest Show in Town,* also used the line "hottest show in town," because a critic had so described it. Such was competition among headline attractions in New York City in 1970.

Oh! Calcutta! made history in a new sense. There had long been a tradition of underground theatre, in small, unadvertised channels, and it was known that entertainers for stag parties (at national conven-

The theatres at the universities as early as the 1920s were training grounds for designers of the new stagecraft. This is the "idol" scene for Eugene O'Neill's *The Emperor Jones,* as designed by Donald Oenslager for the Yale University Theatre, 1931.

tions, usually, or at other away-from-home affairs) could be found, for nude appeal or dirty-story appeal. But *Oh! Calcutta!* was probably the first full-length, intentionally shocking show—insistently filthy in language, exploring various types of fornication, featuring mass scenes of mixed male and female nudity—to be brought into an American public theatre with Broadway-size company of actors and dancers, open and extensive advertising, critical acclaim in leading newspapers, and all the decorative aids, in lighting and setting, that modern staging can provide. (The costuming was negligible.) The point is that the big theatre, the public theatre was invaded by avowed pornographers for the first time, successfully, profitably, and without hindrance from censors or police. And of course this sort of theatre of exposure was widely copied in lesser houses. The music halls of Paris had long been famous for skits that often were suggestive but satirically; and their scenes of nudity could be reasonably explained as artistic and even beautiful. The English-American product, as described above, wholly lacked the taste and sense of style maintained by the French. In *Oh! Calcutta!* improvisation by the actors was encouraged by the authors and directors, so that action and words and degree of nude exposure and gesture changed from performance to performance; and the printed text varied again.

In the preceding season Off-Broadway had made history with *Hair*, advertised as "the American Tribal-Love Rock Musical," a revue speeded-up, inescapably loud, and spontaneous beyond all earlier musicals. That it achieved a new "style" was noted by many critics, an impetuous, pressed-to-the-limit style dictated especially by the rock music. Most fully reported by the news media was a mass orgy scene, mainly in the nude. The show became a success in cities as far away as Los Angeles, London, Paris and Tokyo—and, of course, Copenhagen. Designed to shock rather than lull the audiences into attention, *Hair* was not basically a pornographic show in the *Oh! Calcutta!* sense. To look at the favorable aspects of it, it was new in dramatic form, youthful and energetic (where the other breathed tired corruption). From the young and sometimes brilliant devisers, if occasionally corrupt too, there might come elements helpful in shaping a more normal, not yet envisaged theatre art. Whereas *Hair* was, in the hasty view, compounded of loudness, speed, ridicule (and a sprinkling of indecencies), on the road directly away from the quiet development and slowly attained emotional exaltation of most traditional serious drama, nevertheless it was the theatre's response to life as understood by a great many young people of the time, by a generation often loud, violent and mannerless. Whether the existence of audiences for such a "play" was due to the false education afforded the young in the television age, or due to the blundering of schools and universities the world over, and to the lunacies perpetuated by war-making rulers, is a question that only future historians can pretend to decide. It is sufficient here to chronicle that such a show (as well as many imitators) appeared and was widely hailed as introducing new elements into the theatre art.

As to the nudity in such shows, it was possible to look on this too as on the side of the future, and of progress. The Western nations had come a long way on stage and off since Isadora Duncan courageously started her campaign against ballet costumes, corsets, and all-enveloping bathing-suits fifty years ago. The theatre was doing its part in destroying the ridiculous self-consciousness, even shame, felt by respectable educated people at any glimpse of the nude body. The theatre—in still rare cases—was showing that nudity, *when* kept free of debauchery, can be beautiful, in theatrical terms.

If shows such as *Oh! Calcutta!* have been the sensations of the seasons with which I am closing my history, they are not too important in the perspective one gains in knowing the theatre art through the ages. But they are yet to be reckoned with as intruders, where once the New York stage knew Shakespeare and Shaw, where the season's sensation was a play with John Barrymore or Laurette Taylor or Judith Anderson. It is only fair to remind the reader that even now—I am writing in 1970—there are many "wholesome" shows, including a number of the musicals, a few comedy-dramas (including, in the absence of ranking playwrights, more revivals of comedy successes than ever before: successes such as *The Front Page, Our Town,* and *Three Men on a Horse*); and Off-Broadway, sincere little anti-war plays, Brechtian bits, and the like.

Also on the credit side, especially in some backward sections of the country, in New York and the mountainous areas of certain states, there were efforts, hardly more than semi-professional, to provide theatre fare for audiences that had not before seen living actors.

Nevertheless it is true that the cynics, the atheists and the lechers have recently been in control of a considerable segment of theatreland. They have exploited, as the ultimate realists, the last materials, the last forbidden subjects, open to the dramatist. Under widely flaunted banners proclaiming a new permissiveness and the death of morality, the evil-minded have teamed with the commercial producer to fill numberless theatres with depressing images of the human condition, with shameless enactments of what they conceive love to be.

This, we all know, is not the normal theatre. The offerings of the Absurdists and the commercial pornographers together afford but the narrowest, the most distorted view of life. Their plays mark only degradation, despair and sensuality. Theirs is an image of man stripped of his noblest attributes. At its worst this is the theatre wallowing in dirt.

The theatre does not die. The world and society change, and the theatre changes with it. This has been a phase—doubly shameless in stricken New York, but evident in cities from San Francisco to Zagreb, even to Tokyo. But only a phase.

The virtues of faith and love and dedication are not extinguished. Religion cannot be destroyed, although some religions may fairly be attacked, reformed and possibly weakened. Even the zeal and urge of our younger artists may be basically religious. Though often outraged in recent civilian life, common decency and the tacit prohibition against blasphemy should be basic to our art.

Let us remember those eloquent words about the Freedom of the Theatre quoted a few pages back: "The Theatre is free to select what it will show." The theatre is free to go on to new splendors, is in itself an incomparable vehicle for the expression of thought, imagination, vision. There is not one reason in the world why a Sophocles, a Shakespeare, a Molière cannot again be born, to speak in accents of our time, with the old lure, the old joyousness.

Humanity wakes from one epoch, from one horizon to another. After every decline into the commonplace, the gross and the commercial, idealism reasserts itself. I hope that a consideration of the theatre's history in its entirety has afforded you the faith to believe, with me, in the inevitability of its return to health, full beauty, and a creativeness brought forth by the life of our times.

A lithograph by Honoré Daumier, entitled *The Theatre in August*. An observation by the great nineteenth-century painter and cartoonist about the summer doldrums known to theatres everywhere.

Selected Bibliography

Selected Bibliography

BY ARTHUR B. HOPPER, JR.

This bibliography was designed with the lay reader and student in mind. It represents a selected list of standard references for the major periods covered in the text. It does not include play anthologies, biographies, or works dealing with specific artists (except in cases where the theories of an individual reflect a major movement).

GENERAL

In this section are listed reference works which are general histories of the theatre, its drama, stagecraft, and criticism.

Altman, George et al. *Theatre Pictorial; A History of World Theatre as Recorded in Drawings, Paintings, Engravings, and Photographs*. Berkeley, 1953.
   The story of the development of the theatre as told in pictures. Certainly one of the best sources for illustrative material available under one cover.
Brockett, Oscar. *History of the Theatre*. Boston, 1968.
   One of the most recent and thorough histories in print. Scholarly, objective, and readable, it covers Oriental and Western theatre from the beginnings to the present. It contains an excellent bibliography.
Cheney, Sheldon. *Stage Decoration*. New York, 1928.
   Through brief essays and a wealth of illustrations, the art of stage decoration is traced from its origins to the twentieth century. An excellent summary of theatrical styles.

677

Clark, Barrett H. (ed.). *European Theories of the Drama.* Newly revised by Henry Popkin. New York, 1965.

An anthology of critical writings from Aristotle to Bentley. The best single source for original theoretical documents of twenty-five hundred years of theory and criticism. A must for all students.

Duerr, Edwin. *The Length and Depth of Acting.* New York, 1962.

The only history of acting which traces the evolution of its style from Aristophanes to Brecht. Enjoyable reading for anyone interested in theatre.

Freedley, George and Reeves, John A. *A History of the Theatre.* 3rd Newly Revised Edition, with a Supplementary Section by George Freedley and a Group of Eminent Scholars and Critics. New York, 1968.

The writing is unimaginative, but the illustrations and the extensively detailed text provide an abundance of information. The supplementary section adds reviews of the progress of the theatre art through the period 1940–1967 in about thirty countries of the Western world. These reviews, by a score of authors, vary from routine to excellent. The combined bibliographies, original and supplementary, are extremely valuable, although at times difficult to decipher.

Gascoigne, Bamber. *World Theatre.* Boston, 1968.

This is an interesting history of theatre illustrations, containing over three hundred plates covering the theatre from its beginnings to the Modern period. In the text itself, Mr. Gascoigne has analyzed what, in his opinion, the pictures reveal about the theatre. A unique and worthwhile volume.

Gassner, John. *Masters of the Drama,* 3rd ed. New York, 1954.

A valuable companion to students, this is an interestingly written survey of the development of drama covering all major dramatists from Aeschylus to Saroyan.

Hartnoll, Phyllis. *A Concise History of the Theatre.* London, 1968.

The best brief history, readable, authoritative and up-to-date. Most attractively, even glamorously, illustrated (262 illustrations, many in color). With a very brief bibliography.

Hartnoll, Phyllis (ed.). *The Oxford Companion to the Theatre.* 2d ed. London, 1957.

A thorough encyclopedia of the theatre covering all phases of the art as well as personalities and playhouses.

Hewitt, Barnard H. *Theatre U.S.A. 1665 to 1957.* New York, 1959.

An historical survey of theatre in America with many citations of primary accounts. Not always accurate, it nevertheless is of much value for the amount of information included.

Kernodle, George R. *From Art to Theatre.* Chicago, 1944.

An analytical history of the development of scenic background from the Greeks to the seventeenth century. Well illustrated.

Mantzius, Karl. *A History of Theatrical Art in Ancient and Modern Times.* 6 vols. London, 1903–1921.

A monumental work that is interesting in the reading and in places very informative, but often inaccurate. Must be read cautiously.

Nagler, Alois M. *Sources of Theatrical History.* New York, 1952.

Here in one volume are over three hundred primary documents which reflect the evolution of the theatre from its origins to the present.

Nicoll, Allardyce. *World Drama: From Aeschylus to Anouilh.* London, 1949.

———. *The Development of the Theatre.* 5th ed. London, 1966.

Any book by Mr. Nicoll is a valuable source of information, and these two are among his best. With scholarship and style he has traced the development of drama and theatre from their origins to modern times. They are books for the specialist as well as the student.

Southern, Richard. *Seven Ages of Theatre.* New York, 1961.

A short and popular history of the theatre viewed not in terms of chronology, but in various phases: the costumed plays, great religious festivals, the rise of professional players, the organized stage, the roofed playhouse with scenery, illusion and anti-illusion.

Stuart, Donald C. *The Development of Dramatic Art.* New York, 1928.

Not just a survey of drama, but a survey of drama that has contributed to the development of the forms of drama. The general reader as well as the student will find this a helpful guide and source. It contains an excellent bibliography.

Wimsatt, William and Brooks, Cleanth. *Literary Criticism: A Short History.* New York, 1957.

A brief introductory source tracing the history of criticism past and present; written with wit as well as scholarship.

THE BEGINNINGS

Brown, Ivor. *The First Players: The Origin of Drama.* New York, 1928.

A brief and informal essay on pre-classical acting and drama.

Gaster, Theodor. *Thespis: Ritual, Myth and Drama in the Ancient Near East.* New York, 1950.

Here is a valuable source to both the student of theatre and religion which traces the evolution of ritual and myth into theatre.

Havemyer, Loomis. *The Drama of Savage Peoples.* New Haven, 1916.

A very readable summary of primitive drama and dance.

Ridgeway, William. *The Drama and Dramatic Dances of Non-European Races.* Cambridge, 1915.

An important study for the advanced student, but not recommended for the casual reader.

THE CLASSICAL THEATRE
(Greek and Roman)

Allen, James T. *Stage Antiquities of the Greeks and Romans and Their Influence*. New York, 1927.
A concise survey of all that is known of the Greek and Roman theatres, written for the general public by a respected scholar.

Arnott, Peter. *Greek Scenic Conventions in the Fifth Century, B.C.* Oxford, 1962.
Professor Arnott is the best of the modern Greek scholars and writes with much clarity and understanding. In this work he covers, with the exception of costumes, all aspects of production.

Arnott, Peter. *An Introduction to the Greek Theatre*. Bloomington, Ind., 1959.
Better than any other single book, this introductory survey includes most that the student needs to know to enjoy the classical Greek theatre.

Beare, William. *The Roman Stage: A Short History of Latin Drama in the Time of the Republic*. 2d ed. London, 1955.
The standard work on the Roman stage; devoted essentially to drama, but draws summary conclusions about the theatre as a whole.

Bieber, Margarete. *The History of the Greek and Roman Theatre*. 2d ed. Princeton, N.J., 1961.
A general history containing questionable conclusions drawn from the most inclusive collection of pictorial information of the period available.

Duckworth, George. *The Nature of Roman Comedy*. Princeton, N.J., 1952.
The most informative book dealing with the subject; invaluable to both the theatre and literature student.

Flickinger, Roy C. *The Greek Theatre and its Drama*. London, 1914.
Still one of the most highly regarded books on the subject. It traces thoroughly, yet cautiously, the origin and development of all theatrical elements.

Harsh, Phillip Whaley. *A Handbook of Classical Drama*. Stanford, Calif., 1944.
A most interesting, informative and indispensable survey of every extant Greek and Roman drama.

Kitto, H. D. F. *Greek Tragedy*. rev. ed. New York, 1950.
Of all who have written on Greek tragedy, no one is more highly regarded than Kitto and this is his most valuable book.

Nicoll, Allardyce. *Masks, Mimes and Miracles*. New York, 1931.
An extremely well documented and illustrated encyclopedia of the popular, non-literary theatre from before Aristophanes to the *commedia dell'arte* in the seventeenth century.

Picard-Cambridge, A. W. *The Theatre of Dionysus in Athens*. Oxford, 1946.

A survey of the physical theatre by one of the most respected of Greek scholars. Most of the book is devoted to proving there was no raised stage in the fifth century.

Webster, T. B. L. *Greek Theatre Production*. London, 1956.

This book is of interest not only because of its survey of all aspects of production, but because it treats theatrical activity outside of Athens, a thing most studies do not cover.

THE MEDIEVAL THEATRE

Chambers, E. K. *The Medieval Stage*. 2 vols. Oxford, 1903.

For years this was the standard work on the period, and is still the only introductory survey for the general reader, but the serious student should check more recent scholarly authorities.

Hardison, O. B. *Christian Rite and Christian Drama in the Middle Ages: Essays in the Origin and Early History of Modern Drama*. Baltimore, 1965.

A very thorough study of a limited form of medieval drama: church drama as performed at Mass. For the advanced student.

Wickham, Glynne. *Early English Stages, 1300–1660*. 2 vols. New York, 1959–1962.

A scholarly study of a variety of theatrical forms which contributed to the development of the Elizabethan theatre.

Young, Karl. *The Drama of the Medieval Church*. 2 vols. Oxford, 1933.

A very detailed and authoritative study that is better for the advanced student than the general reader.

THE ORIENTAL THEATRE

Arlington, L. C. *The Chinese Drama from the Earliest Times Until Today*. Shanghai, 1930.

An informative and well illustrated survey, excellent for the producer of oriental drama.

Gargi, Balwant. *Theatre in India*. New York, 1962.

A wealth of information on traditional and modern theatre in India. Useful to any one interested in the subject.

Kincaid, Zoe. *Kabuki: The Popular Stage of Japan*. London, 1925.

Still the best book in English on the subject; thorough and readable.

THE RENAISSANCE THEATRE
(Italy, England, Spain)

Adams, John C. *The Globe Playhouse: Its Design and Equipment.* 2d ed. New York, 1961.

For years the standard work and still perhaps the most acceptable treatment of Shakespeare's theatre. As an alternative to the theories set forth in this book, one should read other sources as well, particularly Hodges' *The Globe Restored.* (See below.)

Adams, Joseph Q. *Shakespearean Playhouses: A History of English Theatres from the Beginnings to the Restoration.* Boston, 1917.

A thorough study of all known London theatres and the acting companies that played in the period covered.

Baldwin, T. W. *The Organization and Personnel of the Shakespearean Company.* Princeton, N.J., 1927.

A very interesting study of a limited subject. Although it deals only with Shakespeare's company it throws light on the total organizational structure of Elizabethan theatre.

Campbell, Lily Bess. *Scenes and Machines on the English Stage During the Renaissance.* Cambridge, 1923.

This thorough and scholarly work traces the development of stage scenery not only in England but in Italy, showing the influence one country had upon the other.

Chambers, E. K. *The Elizabethan Stage,* 4 vols. London, 1923.

Another long-time standard work that is now under question by more recent scholars, but is still of value to the general reader.

Duchartre, Pierre L. *The Italian Comedy: The Improvisations, Scenarios, Lives, Attributes, Portraits and Masks of the Illustrious Characters of the Commedia dell'Arte.* Tr. by R. T. Weaver. London, 1929.

A very detailed, yet readable, history of the *commedia dell'arte,* its beginnings, growth and influence. A beautifully illustrated book.

Hewitt, Barnard (ed.). *The Renaissance Stage: Documents of Serlio, Sabbattini, and Furttenbach.* Coral Gables, Fla., 1958.

Mr. Hewitt has done the student of Renaissance a great service by putting under one cover the original treatises of the three men who did the most to shape the physical theatre of the Italian Renaissance.

Hodges, C. W. *The Globe Restored.* London, 1953.

A book looked upon most favorably by recent scholars. It introduces a new concept of the physical nature of Shakespeare's stage.

Joseph, Bertram. *Elizabethan Acting.* London, 1951.

At present the only book which attempts to propose an acting style for the period.

Kennard, Joseph. *The Italian Theatre.* 2 vols. New York, 1932.

A thorough history of the Italian theatre from its inception to the early twentieth century. Of value to the history, literature and theatre student.

Nagler, A. M. *Shakespeare's Stage.* New Haven, Conn., 1958.

The most reliable brief introduction to Shakespeare's drama and stage.

Parrott, Thomas and Ball, Robert H. *A Short View of Elizabethan Drama.* New York, 1958.

An invaluable companion to the reader of Elizabethan drama; includes a brief discussion of all the major playwrights—their lives, development, and work.

Rennert, Hugo A. *The Spanish Stage in the Time of Lope de Vega.* New York, 1909.

For many years the only thorough treatment of Spanish theatre. It is for the general reader as well as the serious student.

Shergold, N. D. *A History of the Spanish Stage from the Medieval Times until the End of the Seventeenth Century.* Oxford, 1967.

The most recent and authoritative work on the Golden Age of the Spanish Theatre; however, the general reader may find this scholarly work far too detailed.

Smith, Winifred, *The Commedia dell'Arte.* New York, 1912.

A factual and theoretical survey of the form from its inception to the present. Interesting because it views the influence of the *commedia* in many countries.

Symonds, John A. *The Renaissance in Italy.* 7 vols. London, 1909–1937.

This monumental storehouse of information is a readable history of an age, not just an art. There is an excellent condensed version by Alfred Pearson entitled *A Short History of the Renaissance in Italy.*

Wickham, Glynne. *Early English Stages.* 2 vols. (see Medieval Theatre).

THE SEVENTEENTH CENTURY
France and England

Bentley, Gerald E. *The Jacobean and Caroline Stage.* 5 vols. Oxford, 1941–1956.

The most detailed study of the period; a history of companies, actors, playwrights, and plays. Invaluable to the serious student.

Hotson, Leslie. *The Commonwealth and Restoration Stage.* Cambridge, Mass., 1928.

Mr. Hotson is not only a thorough scholar but a readable author who has here collected a wealth of documentary evidence, providing excellent material supplementary to a general history.

Joseph, Bertram. *The Tragic Actor.* New York, 1959.

An excellent survey of the techniques and careers of the great English actors of the Seventeenth and Eighteenth centuries.

Jourdain, Eleanor F. *An Introduction to the French Classical Drama*. Oxford, 1912.

A brief survey of the major influences upon and developments in French playwriting of the seventeenth century.

Lancaster, H. C. *A History of French Dramatic Literature in the Seventeenth Century*. 5 vols. Baltimore, 1929–1942.

This is the first reference source for both general reader and specialist, the unchallenged work on the subject.

Nicoll, Allardyce. *History of English Drama 1660–1900*. 6 vols. London, 1955–1959.

Another of Mr. Nicoll's outstanding contributions to theatre history, this has been for years the standard reference for English dramatic history of the period covered.

Odell, G. C. D. *Shakespeare from Betterton to Irving*. 2 vols. New York, 1920.

Interesting, informative, invaluable is this chronicle of the evolution of Shakespearean productions on the English stage. More than its title implies, it is an excellent history of the theatre and of scene design.

Summers, Montague. *The Restoration Theatre*. London, 1934.

One of the most readable histories ever written of any period. Essential to the theatre student and invaluable to the producer of Restoration drama.

Thaler, Alwin. *Shakespeare to Sheridan*. Cambridge, Mass., 1922.

This is not a thorough history, but a most readable story of the English stage covering almost two hundred years.

Turnell, Martin. *The Classical Movement: Studies in Corneille, Moliere, and Racine*. New York, 1948.

By combining literary criticism with historical and biographical backgrounds, this study relates the achievements of France's three great playwrights to the literature, philosophy and life of the age.

Wiley, W. L. *The Early Public Theatre in France*. Cambridge, Mass., 1960.

The only book in English which deals with the theatre of France as it developed from church drama to neo-classical drama. An interesting and readable story.

Wright, Charles Henry Conrad. *French Classicism*. Cambridge, Mass., 1920.

Despite its brevity, this outline of principles and practices of French Classicism goes beyond the basic contributors to the lesser known writers as well as the political and social environment of the movement.

THE EIGHTEENTH CENTURY
England, France, Germany, and Russia

Bernbaum, Ernest. *The Drama of Sensibility; a Sketch of the History of Sentimental Comedy and Domestic Tragedy*. Cambridge, Mass., 1915.

Covering a period that attracts few students, this is an interesting survey of the drama of England in the eighteenth century.

Bruford, Walter H. *Theatre, Drama, and Audiences in Goethe's Germany.* London, 1957.

This standard work brings together in a most interesting way a wide variety of subjects relating to the German theatre: the times, the artists, the plays.

Hawkins, Frederick. *The French Stage in the Eighteenth Century.* 2 vols. London, 1888. Reprinted 1968.

Hawkins combines scholarship and good writing to make this the standard history of the period.

Krutch, Joseph Wood. *Comedy and Conscience After the Restoration.* New York, rev. ed. 1949.

As the author admits in a second preface this is not a perfectly accurate book, but no work has yet replaced it that the reader will find more interesting.

Lancaster, Henry Carrington Conrad. *French Tragedy in the Reign of Louis XVI and the Early Years of the French Revolution, 1774-1792.* Baltimore, 1933.

———. *French Tragedy in the Time of Louis XV and Voltaire, 1715-1774.* Baltimore, 1950.

These two works are companion studies to Mr. Lancaster's study of the seventeenth century. They concentrate on the major writers of the period, and do not serve the function of a complete history.

Lynch, James J. *Box, Pit, and Gallery; Stage and Society in Johnson's London.* Berkeley, 1953.

Under one cover, Mr. Lynch has dealt with a wide variety of subjects related to the theatre of the second half of the eighteenth century. Excellent for the general reader.

Nicholson, Watson. *The Struggle for a Free Stage in London.* 1906, republished Bloomington, Ind., 1966.

A very interesting survey of what is perhaps the most significant aspect of theatrical development in the eighteenth century, the legal problems which theatre had to overcome.

Nicoll, Allardyce. (See 17th century)

Odell, G. C. D. (See 17th century)

Pascal, Roy. *The German Sturm und Drang.* Manchester, 1953.

More than an excellent study of an influential theatrical movement, this well-written study reveals much about Germany of the period.

Varneke, B. V. *History of the Russian Theatre: Seventeenth through the Nineteenth Century.* Tr. by Boris Brasol, New York, 1851.

This is the basic work, written with enthusiasm and scholarship, making it a very interesting history.

NINETEENTH CENTURY

George, A. J. *The Development of French Romanticism.* Syracuse, New
     York, 1955.
     A brief and liberal view of a complex literary movement. The emphasis
is upon Romanticism as a result of the Industrial Revolution.
Melcher, Edith. *Stage Realism in France Between Diderot and Antoine.*
     Bryn Mawr, Penn., 1928.
     A clear and precise study of activities in France which contributed to
the development of "realism" late in the century.
Odell. G. C. D. (See 17th century.)
Rowell, George. *The Victorian Theatre,* London, 1956.
     A brief but informative survey for the general reader. Excellent bibliog-
raphy for further reading.
Vardac, A. N. *Stage to Screen: Theatrical Method from Garrick to
     Griffith.* Cambridge, Mass., 1949.
     A survey for the general reader of stage theory and practice of the nine-
teenth and early twentieth centuries.
Wagner, Richard. *Opera and Drama.* Tr. by Edwin Evans. London, 1913.
     An excellent translation of Wagner's influential theoretical treatise on the
total art of the theatre.
Walzel, Oskar F. *German Romanticism.* New York, 1932.
     Not as readable as one might wish, nevertheless this is one of the better
comprehensive and scholarly studies of Romantic theory and practice.
Watson, Ernest B. W. *Sheridan to Robertson; A Study of the 19th Century
     Stage.* Cambridge, 1926.
     A scholarly and well-written compilation of most that is known of the
English theatre of the 19th century. Especially good in tracing the development of realism.

TWENTIETH CENTURY

(There are many fine books published each year dealing with the twentieth
century theatre. Due to the brevity of this bibliography, obviously many
excellent books have been omitted.)

Artaud, Antonin. *The Theatre and Its Double.* Tr. by Mary C. Richards.
     New York, 1958.
     Brief in its scope, but expansive in its influence, this little book represents
the credo of one of the most significant avant-garde artists of this century.
No lover of contemporary theatre should overlook it.

Bentley, Eric. *The Playwright as Thinker: A Study of Drama in Modern Times*. New York, 1946.

Thought-provoking and controversial, this is still one of the better studies of major dramatists of the late nineteenth and early twentieth century drama.

———. *In Search of Theatre*. New York, 1953.

Bentley is here again dogmatic, but presents a collection of interesting essays on the modern theatre, its dramatists, directors, designers, and actors.

Brecht, Bertolt. *Brecht on Theatre*. Tr. by John Willett. New York, 1964.

An excellent translation of theories and methods as set forth by one of the most influential artists of the twentieth century. Although at times confusing, the total work is very enlightening.

Brustein, Robert. *The Theatre of Revolt*. New York, 1964.

Although this work discusses only eight modern dramatists, it is one of the best of the many books of dramatic criticism that have appeared in recent years.

Cole, Toby. (ed.). *Playwrights on Playwriting: The Meaning and Making of Modern Drama from Ibsen to Ionesco*. New York, 1961.

A very stimulating collection of essays on the development of drama by the major playwrights of the Modern period.

Corrigan, Robert W. *Theatre in the Twentieth Century*. New York, 1963.

Divided into three sections, The Playwright, The Artist, and The Critic, this is a superb anthology of essays discussing the complexities of the modern theatre. Of value to all interested in the theatre.

Craig, Edward Gordon. *On the Art of the Theatre*. 2d ed. Boston, 1924.

One of the most controversial theorists of the modern theatre, Craig first introduced his ideas to the general reading public in this work.

Downer, Alan S. *Fifty Years of the American Drama 1900–1950*. New York, 1951.

A simple survey of the evolution of dramatic art in the first half of the century. Not as critical as other such studies, but a simple analysis that will prove informative to the general reader.

Esslin, Martin. *The Theatre of the Absurd*. 2d ed. New York, 1967.

The first and still the best historical and analytical study of the movement. As clear an analysis as one can find on a very complex subject.

Freedley, George and Clark, Barrett H. *History of Modern Drama*. New York, 1947.

Perhaps the most thorough survey of its kind, this work covers most of the dramatists who have made a significant contribution to the modern drama of the western world.

Gassner, John. *Directions in Modern Theatre and Drama*. New York, 1965.
———. *Form and Idea in the Modern Theatre*. New York, 1956.
———. *The Theatre in Our Times: A Survey of the Men, Materials and Movements in the American Theatre*. New York, 1954.

———. *Theatre at the Crossroads: Plays and Playwrights of the Mid-Century American Stage.* New York, 1960.

No one has written more about the modern theatre than Professor Gassner. His works are filled with valuable information and written in a most readable style.

Gorelik, Mordecai. *New Theatres for Old.* New York, 1940.

If not the best organized book, it is certainly one of the most penetrating studies of theatrical style written. Extremely valuable in tracing the evolution of modern stage practice. Generously illustrated.

Houghton, Norris. *Moscow Rehearsals, an Account of Methods of Production in the Soviet Theatre.* New York, 1936.

———. *Return Engagement: A Postscript to "Moscow Rehearsals."* New York, 1960.

In these two books may be found the best accounts of the modern Russian theatre by a man who fully understands his subject.

Macgowan, Kenneth and Jones, Robert E. *Continental Stagecraft.* New York, 1922.

An account of the theatrical changes that were occurring in Europe in the 1920's that helps the contemporary reader with an understanding of theatrical styles.

Novick, Julius. *Beyond Broadway.* New York, 1968.

An excellent survey of the regional professional theatres in America, which reveals much about the expansion of theatre in this country.

Price, Julia. *The Off-Broadway Theatre.* New York, 1962.

The only history of off-Broadway which, although taken up largely with brief plot summaries, introduces the reader generally to the total production process.

Stanislavsky, Konstantin. *An Actor Prepares.* Tr. E. Hapgood. New York, 1936.

———. *Building a Character.* Tr. E. Hapgood. New York, 1949.

———. *Creating A Role.* Tr. Elizabeth R. Hapgood. New York, 1961.

These are the three major sources in which this great actor/teacher sets forth his theories and methods. A must for any student interested in acting.

Index

Index

Note: Illustrations are indexed in this general list together with topics and names in the text. Pages for illustrations are distinguished by being set in italic numerals. When names of plays, authors, or artists appear in the illustration captions, the numerals likewise are italicized.